HOLT MATHEMATICS

Holt, Rinehart and Winston, Publishers
New York · Toronto · London · Sydney

Eugene D. Nichols
Distinguished Professor of Mathematics
Education and Lecturer
Mathematics Department
Florida State University
Tallahassee, Florida

Paul A. Anderson
Elementary School Teacher
Clark County School District
Las Vegas, Nevada

Leslie A. Dwight
Former Head of the Department
and Professor of Mathematics
Southeastern Oklahoma State University
Durant, Oklahoma

Frances Flournoy
Professor of Elementary Education
University of Texas
Austin, Texas

Joella Hardeman-Gipson
Professor and Program Director
College of Education
Wayne State University
Detroit, Michigan

Sylvia A. Hoffman
Resource Consultant in Mathematics
Illinois Office of Education
State of Illinois

Robert Kalin
Professor, Mathematics Education Program
Florida State University
Tallahassee, Florida

John Schluep
Professor of Mathematics
State University College
Oswego, New York

Leonard Simon
Former Assistant Director
Planning and Curriculum
New York City Board of Education
New York, New York

Cover Art by Gil Cohen. See page 458 for art and photo credits.

ISBN: 0-03-050541-0

3 4 5 6 7 8 9 032 9 8 7 6 5

TABLE OF CONTENTS

EVERY CHAPTER HAS

Maintenance: Keeping Fits/Basic Fact Checks/Basic Skills Checks
Review and Testing: Mid-Chapter Reviews/Chapter Reviews/Chapter Tests
Enrichment: Special Topics/Find Outs!/Activities

1 UNDERSTANDING AND USING NUMBERS 1–19

• **1** Making and Using Reports • **2** Reading and Writing Numbers • **4** Rounding Numbers • **8** Problem-Solving Skills • **10** Divisibility • **12** Factors • **14** Sequences • **16** Problem-Solving Application

2 WHOLE-NUMBER COMPUTATION 20–53

• **20** Finding the Sums of Consecutive Numbers • **22** Race Time • **23** Mental Addition • **24** Addition • **26** Subtraction • **28** Estimating Sums and Differences • **31** Race Time • **32** Problem-Solving Skills • **34** Multiplying BY 1- AND 2-DIGIT NUMBERS • **36** BY LARGER NUMBERS • **38** Dividing BY A 1-DIGIT NUMBER • **40** BY LARGER NUMBERS • **42** Division Shortcut • **44** Shortcuts for Multiplying and Dividing Multiples of 10, 100, and 1,000 • **46** Estimating Products and Quotients • **48** Properties • **50** Problem-Solving Application

3 EQUATIONS 54–77

• **54** Cover-up Technique • **56** Inverse Operations • **58** Addition and Subtraction Properties • **60** Solving Equations • **64** Multiplication and Division Properties • **66** More Equations • **68** Problem-Solving Skills • **70** Using Two-Equation Properties • **72** Solving Inequalities • **74** Problem-Solving Application

4 DECIMALS 78–99

• **78** Reading and Writing Decimals • **80** Place Value • **82** Comparing and Ordering Decimals • **84** Rounding Decimals • **88** Problem-Solving Skills • **90** Powers of Ten • **92** Scientific Notation • **94** Computing with Scientific Notation • **96** Problem-Solving Application

5 DECIMAL COMPUTATION 100–127

• **100** Computing with Money • **102** Adding Decimals • **104** Subtracting Decimals • **106** Estimating Sums and Differences • **110** Multiplying Decimals BY WHOLE NUMBERS • **112** BY DECIMALS • **114** Problem-Solving Skills • **116** Dividing Decimals BY WHOLE NUMBERS • **118** BY DECIMALS • **120** Rounding Quotients • **121** Estimating Products and Quotients • **122** Solving Equations • **124** Problem-Solving Application

6 MEASUREMENT 128–155

• **128** Metric Challenge • **130** Metric Measures of Length • **132** Changing Between Metric Measures of Length • **134** Precision and Greatest Possible Error • **136** Adding and Subtracting Lengths • **138** Problem-Solving Skills • **140** Significant Digits • **142** Metric Measures OF MASS • **144** OF CAPACITY • **146** Customary System of LENGTH • **148** WEIGHT AND CAPACITY • **149** Celsius Temperature • **150** Time Zones • **152** Problem-Solving Application

7 FRACTIONS 156–189

• **156** Greatest Common Factor • **158** Least Common Multiple • **160** Equivalent Fractions • **162** Simplifying Fractions • **164** Comparing Fractions • **166** Mixed Numbers • **168** Adding Fractions • **170** Adding Mixed Numbers • **173** Subtracting Fractions • **174** Subtracting Mixed Numbers • **176** Problem-Solving Skills • **178** Multiplying Fractions • **180** Multiplying Mixed Numbers • **184** Changing Fractions to Decimals • **185** Problem-Solving Application

8 GEOMETRY 190–223

• **190** Geometric Figures • **192** Angles • **194** Classifying Angles and Triangles • **196** Constructing and Bisecting Angles • **198** Polygons • **200** Angles of a Polygon • **202** Perimeter • **206** Problem-Solving Skills • **208** Circle: Radius, Diameter, and Circumference • **210** Complementary and Supplementary Angles • **212** Parallel Lines • **214** Perpendicular Lines • **216** Constructing Parallel Lines • **218** Problem-Solving Application

9 PROBLEM SOLVING 224–247

• **224** Order of Operations • **226** Open Expressions • **228** Writing Equations for SENTENCES • **230** WORD PROBLEMS • **232** Problem-Solving Skills • **234** Reasoning • **236** Distance Formula • **239** Ratio • **240** Proportion • **242** Lever Formula • **244** Problem-Solving Application

10 PERCENT 248–275

• **248** Meaning of Percent • **250** Fractions and Percent • **252** Decimals and Percents • **254** Finding a Percent of a Number • **256** Finding Percents • **258** Finding the Number • **262** Problem-Solving Skills • **264** Discounts and Sale Price • **266** Interest Formula • **268** Compound Interest • **270** Percent Change • **272** Problem-Solving Application

11 INTEGERS 276–303

• **276** Reading and Comparing Integers • **278** Opposites and Absolute Value • **280** Adding Integers with the Same Sign • **282** Adding Positive and Negative Integers • **284** Subtracting Integers • **286** Using Absolute Value to Add Integers • **288** Problem-Solving Skills • **290** Multiplying Integers • **292** Properties • **294** Dividing Integers • **296** Equations • **298** Negative Exponents and Decimals • **299** Expanded Numerals with Exponents • **300** Problem-Solving Application

12 REAL NUMBERS 304–331

• **304** Reading and Comparing Rational Numbers • **306** Rational Numbers and Decimals • **308** Adding Rational Numbers • **310** Subtracting Rational Numbers • **312** Multiplying and Dividing Rational Numbers • **314** Irrational Numbers • **316** Problem-Solving Skills • **318** Repeating Decimals • **319** Squares of Numbers • **320** Square Roots • **322** Square Root Table • **324** Pythagorean Theorem • **326** Real Number Line • **328** Problem-Solving Application

13 USING GEOMETRY 332–369

• **332** Congruent Triangles • **334** Constructing Congruent Triangles • **336** Similar Triangles • **338** Scale Drawings • **340** Trigonometric Ratios • **342** Area of Rectangles, Squares, and Trapezoids • **344** Area in the Metric System • **346** Area of a Circle • **348** Problem-Solving Skills • **350** Area in the Customary System • **352** Surface Area • **354** Volume in the Metric System • **356** Volume of Prisms and Cylinders • **358** Relating Metric Measures • **360** Volumes of Cones and Pyramids • **362** Volume in the Customary System • **364** Problem-Solving Application

14 GRAPHING, PROBABILITY, AND STATISTICS 370–401

• **370** Graphing on a Number Line • **372** Finding and Graphing Ordered Pairs • **374** Graphing Integer Pairs for Equations • **376** Graphing Equations with Two Variables • **378** Graphing Inequalities • **381** Symmetry and Coordinates • **382** Problem-Solving Skills • **384** Interpreting Data • **386** Graphing Data • **388** Frequency Tables and Histograms • **390** Circle Graphs • **392** Probability • **394** Sample Space • **396** Compound Probability • **398** Problem-Solving Application

Extra Practice 403–426
Table of Measure 427
Glossary and Symbol List 428–433
Index 434–442
Answers 443–458

Making and Using Reports

Ms. Barnard is an employee of the Hillesport Road and Highway Department. She did a study of the traffic control at the intersection of Gilbert Street and Route A.

TRAFFIC SURVEY OF GILBERT STREET AND ROUTE A

Day (9:00 am–3:00 pm)	*Number of Automobiles*			
	Drive Through	*Turn Right*	*Turn Left*	*Total*
Monday	72	43	6	121
Tuesday	96	29	4	
Wednesday	86	32	5	
Thursday	99	91	18	
Friday	96	38	7	
Total	449			

1. What is the total number of cars recorded which drove through the intersection during the 5 days?

2. What is the total number of cars recorded which turned right at the intersection?

3. What is the total number of cars recorded which turned left at the intersection?

4. What was the total number of cars recorded on Gilbert Street on Monday?

5. Find the daily totals of the number of cars on Gilbert Street for the rest of the week.

6. On what day did Ms. Barnard record the greatest number of cars on Gilbert Street?

7. On what day did Ms. Barnard record the fewest number of cars on Gilbert Street?

8. What was the total number of cars on Gilbert Street for the week?

CHAPTER 1
UNDERSTANDING AND USING NUMBERS

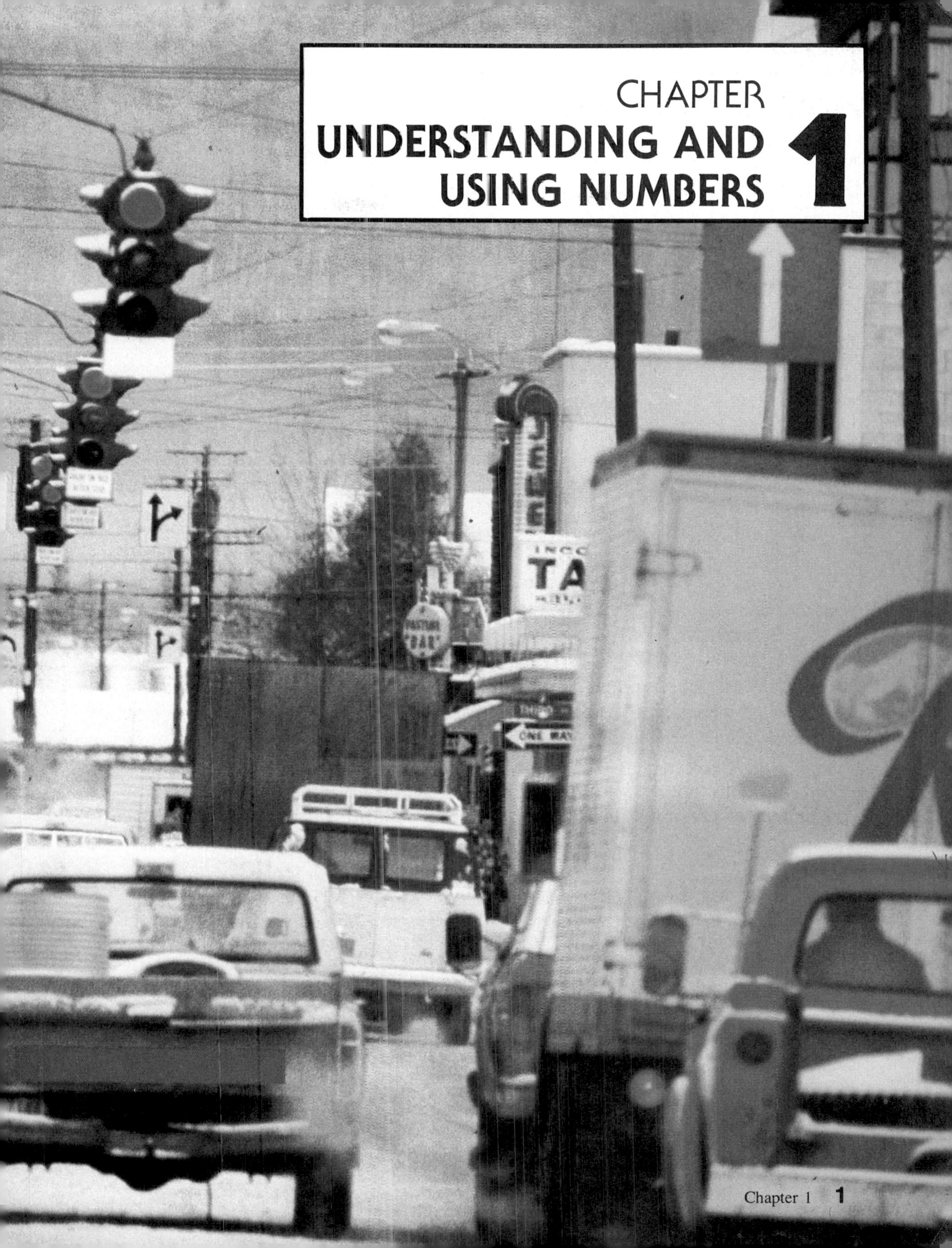

Reading and Writing Number Names

Los Angeles International Airport is one of the busiest airports in the world. One year, the number of people using the airport was 23,716,028. To read a number, think of the period names.

Period Names →	Trillions	Billions	Millions	Thousands	Ones
Place Value Names →	Hundred Trillions Ten Trillions Trillions	Hundred Billions Ten Billions Billions	Hundred Millions Ten Millions Millions	Hundred Thousands Ten Thousands Thousands	Hundreds Tens Ones
Standard Numeral →			2 3,	7 1 6,	0 2 8

Word Name:

Twenty-three million, seven hundred sixteen thousand, twenty-eight

A. Read the numbers.

1. 87,964 **2.** 564,192 **3.** 314,016,912 **4.** 974,184,312,147

B. Write standard numerals.

5. 23 thousand

6. 4 million, 167 thousand

7. Six million, seven hundred thousand, four hundred twenty-five

8. Forty-five billion, six hundred million, twenty-four thousand

C. List in order from the least to the greatest.

9. 81341070 81341700 81341007 82373710

D. Write standard numerals.

Examples $\frac{1}{2}$ thousand = 500 $6\frac{1}{2}$ thousand = 6,500

10. $14\frac{1}{2}$ thousand **11.** $\frac{1}{2}$ million **12.** $23\frac{1}{2}$ million **13.** $\frac{1}{2}$ billion

Practice

Write standard numerals.

1. 742 thousand
2. 60 million
3. 724 billion

4. 386 trillion, 519 million
5. 32 billion
6. 688 trillion

7. Thirty-three million, six hundred fifteen thousand, forty

8. Seven billion, two hundred million, five hundred thousand

9. Sixty trillion, five million, seven hundred three

10. Ninety trillion, thirty million, sixty-four

List in order from the least to the greatest.

11. Invoice numbers:

81341678	96213419
81439201	81432901
82493719	96203419

12. Identification numbers:

205608339	205607999
204703712	205315629
204715111	205017832

Write standard numerals.

13. $11\frac{1}{2}$ million
14. $123\frac{1}{2}$ trillion
15. $46\frac{1}{2}$ billion
★ **16.** 17.4 million

Solve.

17. If you spend three hundred dollars a day for forty years, you would spend four million, three hundred eighty-three thousand dollars. Write this amount as a standard numeral.

★ **18.** One year, the airport in Montreal had about $6\frac{3}{4}$ million passengers. Write the number of passengers as a standard numeral.

Rounding Whole Numbers

TODAY'S ATTENDANCE: 74,759

Round today's attendance to the nearest thousand and to the nearest ten thousand.

Round to	*Number*	*Think*	*Write*
nearest thousand	74,759	7 **4**,7 5 9 ↑ The digit to the right is 5 or greater.	74,759 $\doteq$ 75,000 ↑ is approximately equal to
nearest ten thousand	74,759	**7** 4,7 5 9 ↑ The digit to the right is less than 5.	74,759 $\doteq$ 70,000

Today's attendance rounded to the nearest thousand is 75,000 and rounded to the nearest ten thousand is 70,000.

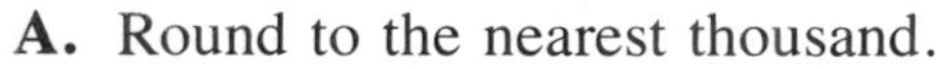

A. Round to the nearest thousand.

1. 6,489 **2.** 37,916 **3.** 530,549 **4.** 1,789,769

B. Round to the nearest ten thousand.

5. 54,320 **6.** 628,374 **7.** 2,635,000 **8.** 6,995,004

C. Round to the nearest hundred thousand.

9. 498,372 **10.** 752,135 **11.** 5,841,000 **12.** 555,555,555

D. Round to the nearest million.

13. 8,641,024 **14.** 34,952,000 **15.** 488,888,062

Practice

Here are the seating capacities in some famous stadiums.

Wrigley Field: 37,741
Candlestick Park: 58,000
Three Rivers Stadium: 50,230
San Diego: 48,460
Metropolitan Stadium: 45,719
Municipal Stadium: 76,713

Round the seating capacities to the nearest thousand.

1. Wrigley Field **2.** San Diego **3.** Candlestick Park

4. Metropolitan **5.** Three Rivers **6.** Municipal

Round the seating capacities to the nearest ten thousand.

7. Wrigley Field **8.** San Diego **9.** Candlestick Park

10. Metropolitan **11.** Three Rivers **12.** Municipal

Round to the nearest hundred thousand.

13. 613,716 **14.** 893,423 **15.** 450,000 **16.** 965,708

17. 7,517,214 **18.** 2,684,916 **19.** 21,750,000

20. 609,253,899 **21.** 802,409,999 **22.** 5,234,569,000

Round to the nearest million.

23. 2,316,419 **24.** 5,623,900 **25.** 6,500,193

26. 26,319,814 **27.** 419,624,000 **28.** 374,815,000

29. 609,253,899 **30.** 802,409,999 **31.** 5,234,569,000

★ **32.** How many whole numbers when rounded to the nearest thousand round to 6,000?

Mid-Chapter Review

Write standard numerals. *(2)*

1. Six billion, three hundred million, ten thousand, forty-five

2. Four trillion, nineteen thousand, two hundred six

Round. *(4)*

3. 3,714,016 to the nearest hundred thousand

4. 47,481,456 to the nearest million

5. 99,586,423 to the nearest ten thousand

6. 72,500 to the nearest thousand

FIND OUT!

Brainteaser

Choose the box that completes the sequence.

1. 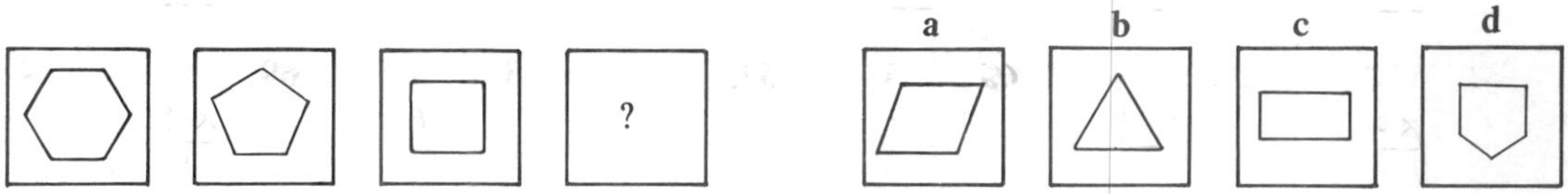 ?　a　b　c　d

2. 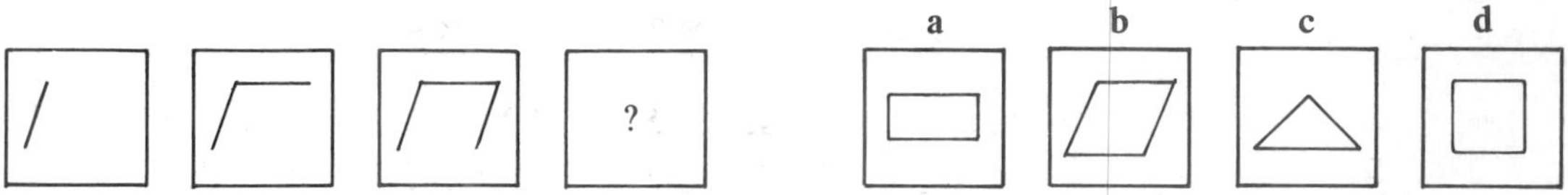 ?　a　b　c　d

3. 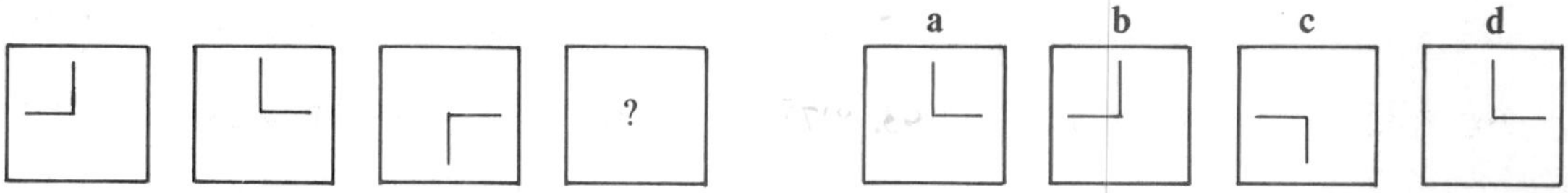 ?　a　b　c　d

4. 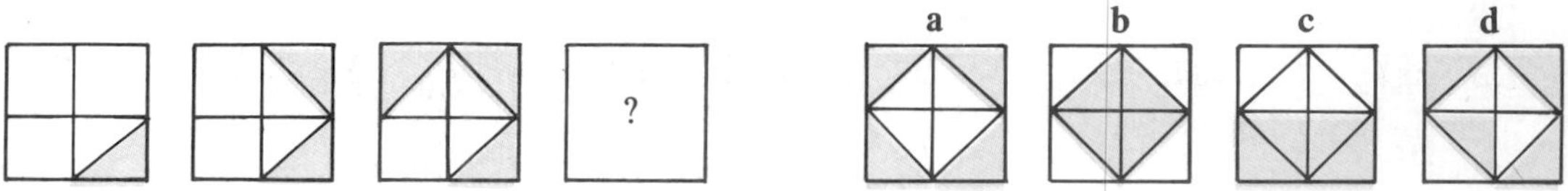 ?　a　b　c　d

Basic Facts Review

1. 7 + 5	**2.** 6 + 6	**3.** 5 + 6	**4.** 1 + 9	**5.** 8 + 8	**6.** 5 + 9	**7.** 8 + 5
8. 6 + 7	**9.** 7 + 7	**10.** 8 + 4	**11.** 9 + 4	**12.** 9 + 6	**13.** 8 + 7	**14.** 9 + 7
15. 5 + 7	**16.** 6 + 5	**17.** 9 + 3	**18.** 3 + 7	**19.** 9 + 9	**20.** 5 + 8	**21.** 8 + 6
22. 7 + 8	**23.** 6 + 9	**24.** 8 + 9	**25.** 4 + 7	**26.** 7 + 6	**27.** 9 + 5	**28.** 9 + 8
29. 17 − 9	**30.** 15 − 8	**31.** 16 − 8	**32.** 15 − 9	**33.** 11 − 9	**34.** 13 − 4	**35.** 12 − 6
36. 18 − 9	**37.** 14 − 7	**38.** 11 − 8	**39.** 12 − 9	**40.** 12 − 7	**41.** 13 − 8	**42.** 15 − 7
43. 12 − 4	**44.** 11 − 7	**45.** 14 − 6	**46.** 12 − 8	**47.** 11 − 3	**48.** 10 − 5	**49.** 13 − 6
50. 11 − 6	**51.** 15 − 6	**52.** 14 − 5	**53.** 13 − 9	**54.** 12 − 5	**55.** 17 − 8	**56.** 16 − 9
57. 8 × 6	**58.** 9 × 4	**59.** 7 × 5	**60.** 9 × 8	**61.** 4 × 7	**62.** 8 × 4	**63.** 3 × 8
64. 7 × 4	**65.** 6 × 8	**66.** 9 × 6	**67.** 9 × 9	**68.** 7 × 6	**69.** 6 × 4	**70.** 9 × 7
71. 5 × 5	**72.** 3 × 9	**73.** 6 × 6	**74.** 7 × 8	**75.** 8 × 9	**76.** 5 × 7	**77.** 4 × 9
78. 9 × 5	**79.** 8 × 7	**80.** 7 × 9	**81.** 5 × 8	**82.** 6 × 7	**83.** 8 × 8	**84.** 6 × 9

85. $8\overline{)64}$	**86.** $7\overline{)63}$	**87.** $6\overline{)24}$	**88.** $7\overline{)35}$	**89.** $6\overline{)54}$	**90.** $4\overline{)36}$
91. $8\overline{)40}$	**92.** $6\overline{)36}$	**93.** $8\overline{)72}$	**94.** $5\overline{)40}$	**95.** $4\overline{)28}$	**96.** $6\overline{)30}$
97. $9\overline{)81}$	**98.** $7\overline{)42}$	**99.** $6\overline{)48}$	**100.** $8\overline{)56}$	**101.** $7\overline{)49}$	**102.** $9\overline{)45}$
103. $7\overline{)56}$	**104.** $9\overline{)54}$	**105.** $5\overline{)25}$	**106.** $8\overline{)48}$	**107.** $5\overline{)35}$	**108.** $9\overline{)72}$

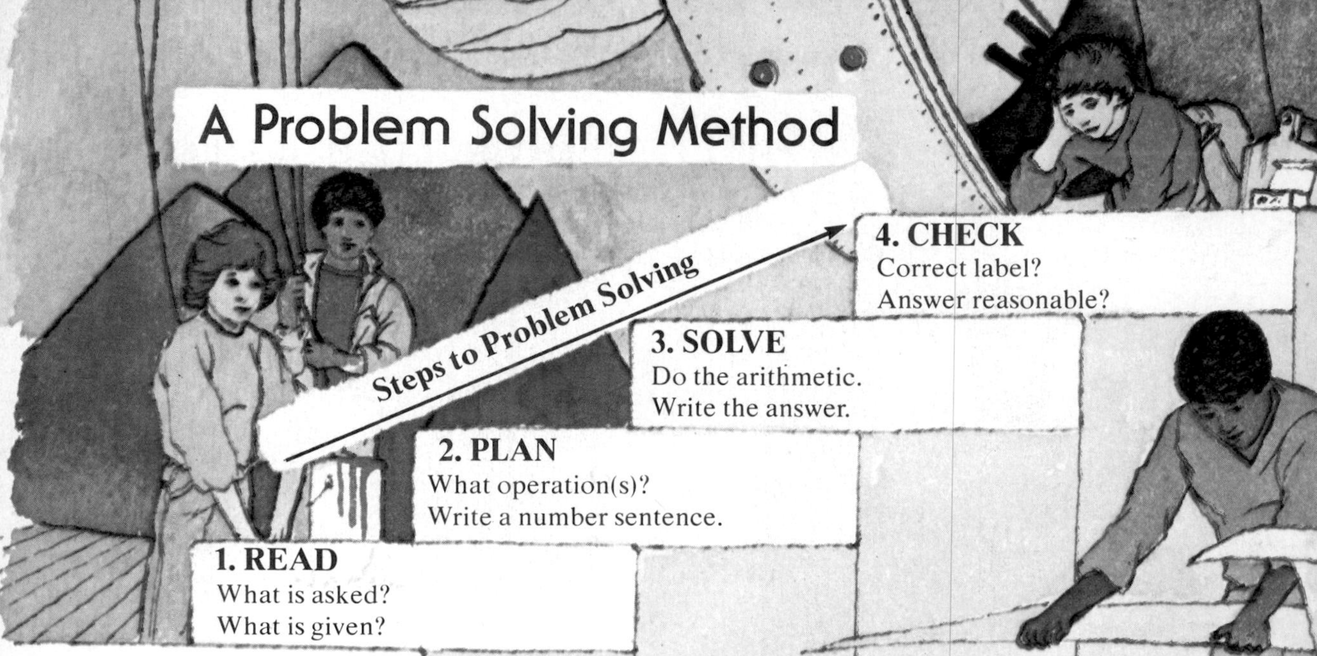

A Problem Solving Method
Steps to Problem Solving
1. READ
What is asked?
What is given?
2. PLAN
What operation(s)?
Write a number sentence.
3. SOLVE
Do the arithmetic.
Write the answer.
4. CHECK
Correct label?
Answer reasonable?

A. The drama school is giving a play. The scenery was prepared by 12 actors. Each actor worked 16 hours on the scenery. How many hours were worked in all to prepare the scenery?

Step 1 READ the problem.

1. What is asked? **2.** What is given?

Step 2 PLAN what to do.

3. What operation will you use?

4. Write a number sentence.

Step 3 SOLVE the problem.

5. $\begin{array}{r} 16 \\ \times\ 12 \\ \hline \end{array}$

Step 4 CHECK your answer. Reread the problem.

6. How many actors prepared the scenery?

7. How many hours did each actor work?

8. How many hours were worked in all?

9. Does it check?

B. Solve. Use the 4 problem-solving steps.

10. On Friday night 336 people attended the play. The auditorium has 24 seats in each row. How many rows did the 336 people fill?

Practice

Solve. Use the 4 problem-solving steps.

1. The script for the play was 36 pages, printed on one side. There were 24 copies of the script. How many sheets of paper were used to print the scripts?

2. Adult tickets cost $3.00 and children tickets cost $2.00 for the show. One night, 75 adult tickets and 112 children tickets were sold. How much money was collected at the ticket office that night?

3. The actors wrote the play in writing class. They used 20 periods of 45 minutes each to write the play. How many hours of class were used to write the play?

4. After the play refreshments were served. Cookies were sold for 35¢ per package and orange juice was 25¢ a container. Find the cost of 3 packages of cookies and 3 containers of orange juice.

5. The total cost of the costumes, scenery, tickets, and other items came to $100. A professional play recently cost $180,000. How many times as expensive was the professional play?

6. A special performance of the play was given for charity. Each ticket cost $5. The total amount collected was $1,000. How many people attended the performance?

Divisibility

There are 45 players in Mr. Kullen's basketball league. He wants to form teams with an equal number of players on each team. If each team has 5 players, will every player be on a team?

Since $45 \div 5 = 9$ *with no remainder,* 45 is *divisible* by 5. So, every player will be on a team.

▶ A number is divisible by a second number if the remainder is zero.

A. Tell whether the first number is divisible by the second number.

1. 15; 5 **2.** 17; 3 **3.** 20; 10 **4.** 600; 1

▶ A number is divisible by:
2 if the last digit is 0, 2, 4, 6, or 8.
5 if the last digit is 0 or 5.
10 if the last digit is 0.

B. Which numbers are divisible by 2? By 5? By 10?

5. 30 **6.** 62 **7.** 35 **8.** 40 **9.** 174
10. 285 **11.** 308 **12.** 400 **13.** 718 **14.** 68,405

▶ A number is divisible by:
3 if the sum of the digits is divisible by 3.
9 if the sum of the digits is divisible by 9.

C. Which numbers are divisible by 3? By 9?

15. 61 **16.** 93 **17.** 159 **18.** 207 **19.** 387
20. 427 **21.** 594 **22.** 675 **23.** 1,014 **24.** 7,614

▶ A number is divisible by 6 if it is divisible by both 2 and 3.

D. Which numbers are divisible by 6?

25. 36 **26.** 142 **27.** 908 **28.** 3,246 **29.** 8,490

Practice

Which numbers are divisible by 2?

1. 60 **2.** 455 **3.** 640 **4.** 935 **5.** 1,156

6. 1,400 **7.** 1,605 **8.** 12,015 **9.** 29,950 **10.** 46,662

Which numbers are divisible by 5?

11. 75 **12.** 501 **13.** 352 **14.** 680 **15.** 205

16. 315 **17.** 1,202 **18.** 5 **19.** 1 **20.** 5,435

Which numbers are divisible by 10?

21. 545 **22.** 6,455 **23.** 110 **24.** 17,320 **25.** 424

26. 4,000 **27.** 735 **28.** 820 **29.** 308 **30.** 10,005

Which numbers are divisible by 3?

31. 721 **32.** 903 **33.** 1,409 **34.** 5,013 **35.** 88,267

36. 683 **37.** 201 **38.** 1,333 **39.** 11,004 **40.** 771

Which numbers are divisible by 9?

41. 623 **42.** 409 **43.** 54,000 **44.** 818 **45.** 1,215

46. 3,000 **47.** 30,303 **48.** 991 **49.** 720 **50.** 1,116

Which numbers are divisible by 6?

51. 127 **52.** 309 **53.** 9,041 **54.** 5,013 **55.** 66,226

56. 72 **57.** 103 **58.** 192 **59.** 450 **60.** 518

Solve.

61. There are 89 baseball players. Each team has 9 players. Will every player be on a team?

★ **62.** Give a rule for testing whether a number is divisible by 4.

Factors

What are all the factors of 24?

Product	=	factor	×	factor
24	=	1	×	24
24	=	2	×	12
24	=	3	×	8
24	=	4	×	6

The factors of 24 are 1, 2, 3, 4, 6, 8, 12, and 24. Notice that 24 is divisible by each of these numbers.

A. List all the factors of each number.

1. 12 **2.** 20 **3.** 18 **4.** 23 **5.** 36

B. Study this table.

Number	*Factors*	*Number of Factors*
1	1	1
2	1, 2	2
3	1, 3	2
4	1, 2, 4	3
5	1, 5	2
6	1, 2, 3, 6	4
7	1, 7	2

A number that has exactly 2 different factors is called a **prime number.**

A number that has more than 2 factors is called a **composite number.**

The number 1 is neither prime nor composite.

6. Which numbers in the table are prime numbers?

7. Which numbers in the table are composite numbers?

C. Which numbers are prime numbers?

8. 15 **9.** 19 **10.** 21 **11.** 33 **12.** 47 **13.** 89

D. Which numbers are composite numbers?

14. 16 **15.** 11 **16.** 24 **17.** 37 **18.** 14 **19.** 111

Practice

List all the factors of each number.

1. 5	**2.** 19	**3.** 31	**4.** 6	**5.** 14
6. 27	**7.** 28	**8.** 32	**9.** 81	**10.** 30
11. 40	**12.** 48	**13.** 56	**14.** 60	**15.** 100

Tell whether each number is a prime number or a composite number.

16. 7	**17.** 11	**18.** 21	**19.** 23	**20.** 1
21. 32	**22.** 55	**23.** 36	**24.** 4	**25.** 9
26. 70	**27.** 21	**28.** 31	**29.** 85	**30.** 51

★ **31.** The number 5 is a prime number. Is there another multiple of 5 which is also a prime number?

32. Copy and complete this chart through 100.

1 ② ③ 4 ⑤ 6 ⑦ 8 9 10

⑪ 12 13 14

Cross out 1. Beginning with 4, cross out all the numbers divisible by 2, by 3, by 5, and by 7. Circle all the remaining numbers. These numbers are the prime numbers less than 100. List them.

FIND OUT!
Calculator Activity

Look at these numbers.

123,123 is divisible by 7, 11, and 13.
963,963 is divisible by 7, 11, and 13.
345,345 is divisible by 7, 11, and 13.

1. Give 5 more numbers divisible by 7, 11, and 13.

2. What is the smallest number that is divisible by 7, 11, and 13?

Sequences

A **sequence** is a group of numbers given in a specified order, according to some rule. . . . means and so on

Sequence: 5, 8, 11, 14, . . .
(add 3, add 3, add 3)

Rule: Add 3 to each number to get the next number in the sequence.
The next 3 numbers in the sequence are 17, 20, and 23.

A. Find the rule for the sequence.

1. 1, 4, 7, 10, 13, . . .

2. 1, 3, 9, 27, . . .

B. Find the number which fits the sequence.

Example Sequence: 1, 2, 4, 8, ___?___, 32
Rule: Multiply each number by 2 to get the next number in the sequence.
The number 16 fits the sequence.

3. 3, 9, 27, 81, ___?___

4. 95, 85, 75, ___?___, 55

C. The rule for a sequence can follow a pattern. Find the next 3 numbers in the sequence.

Example Sequence: 1, 3, 6, 10, . . .
(add 2, add 3, add 4)

Rule: Add 2 to the first number, add 3 to the next number, add 4 to the third number, and so on.
The next 3 numbers are 15, 21, and 28.

5. 1, 3, 6, 10, 15, . . .

6. 2, 2, 4, 12, 48, . . .

D. Sometimes a sequence has 2 rules. Find the next 3 numbers in the sequence.

Example Sequence: 4, 5, 7, 8, 10, . . .
(add 1, add 2, add 1, add 2)

Rule: Add 1 to the first number, add 2 to the next number, add 1 to the next number, and so on.
The next 3 numbers are 11, 13, and 14.

7. 5, 10, 11, 16, 17, . . .

8. 2, 4, 5, 10, 11, . . .

Practice

Find the rule for the sequence.

1. 2, 7, 12, 17, 22, . . .

2. 3, 9, 15, 21, 27, . . .

3. 3, 6, 9, 12, . . .

4. 1, 4, 16, 64, . . .

Find the number which fits the sequence.

5. 2, 12, 22, 32, __?__

6. 41, 39, 37, __?__, 33

7. 0, 4, 8, 12, __?__

8. 48, 24, 12, 6, __?__

9. 5, 7, 11, 17, __?__

10. 0, 3, 7, __?__, 18

11. 1, 1, 2, 6, 24, __?__

12. 100, 98, 94, 88, 80, __?__

13. 6, 7, 5, 6, 4, __?__

14. 1, 3, 6, 8, 16, __?__

15. 1, 2, 6, 7, 21, __?__

16. 10, 20, 15, 25, 20, __?__

Find the next 3 numbers in the sequence.

17. 2, 4, 4, 8, 8, . . .

18. 10, 20, 25, 35, 40, . . .

19. 100, 98, 98, 96, 96, . . .

20. 89, 80, 71, 62, 53, . . .

★ Find the numbers which fit the sequence.

21. 60, __?__, __?__, 42, 36

22. 5, __?__, __?__, 24, 25

FIND OUT!
Brainteaser

This grouping of numbers is called Pascal's Triangle.
Discover the pattern and find rows 6 and 7 of Pascal's Triangle.

row 1 ⟶ 1
row 2 ⟶ 1 1
row 3 ⟶ 1 2 1
row 4 ⟶ 1 3 3 1
row 5 ⟶ 1 4 6 4 1

Problem Solving: Reading a Train Table

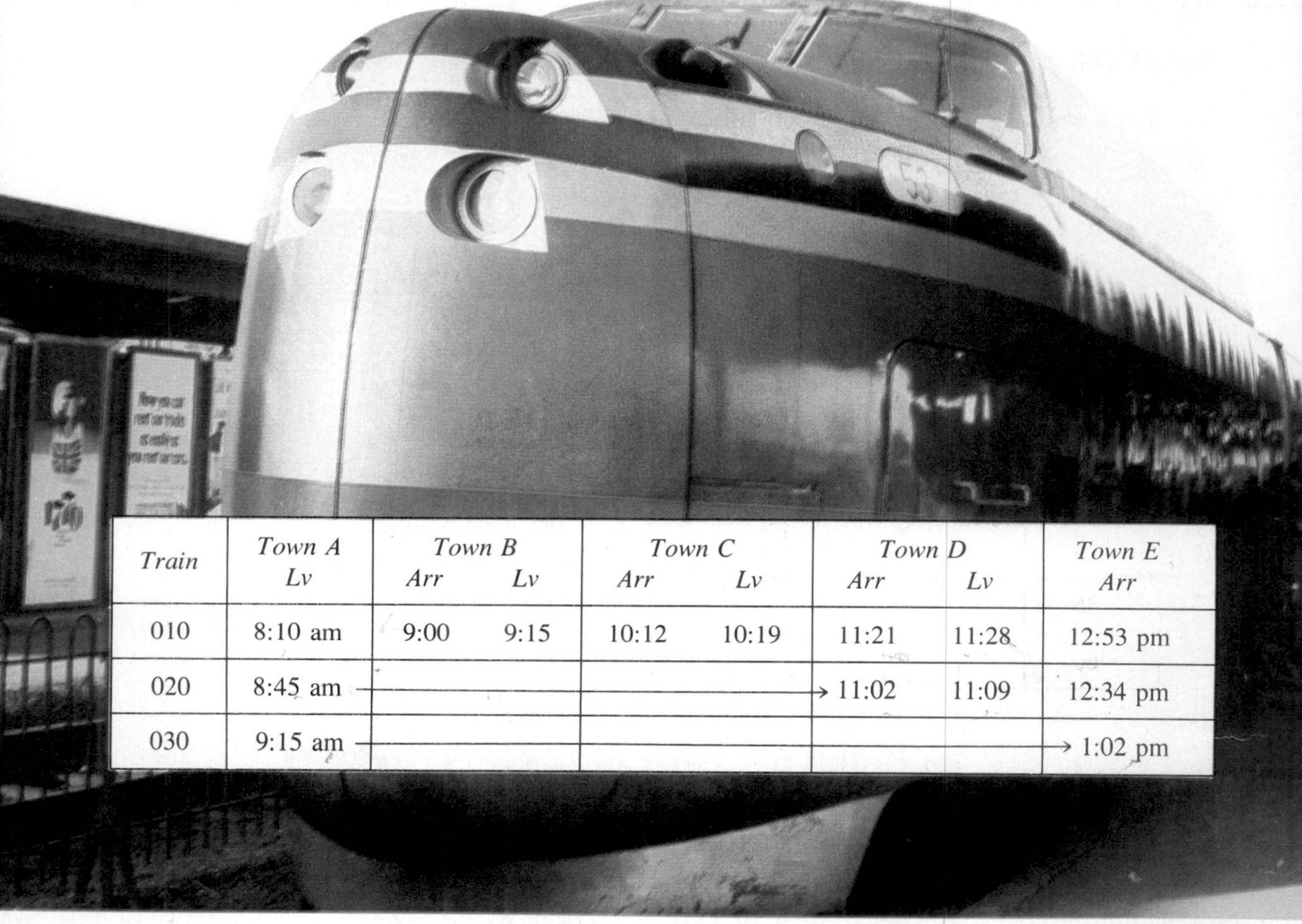

Train	Town A Lv	Town B Arr	Town B Lv	Town C Arr	Town C Lv	Town D Arr	Town D Lv	Town E Arr
010	8:10 am	9:00	9:15	10:12	10:19	11:21	11:28	12:53 pm
020	8:45 am					11:02	11:09	12:34 pm
030	9:15 am							1:02 pm

1. How long does it take train 010 to go from Town A to Town D? [HINT: Look at the Arr column under Town D.]

2. At what towns does train 020 stop?

3. How long does it take train 010 to go from Town B to Town E?

4. How long does it take train 020 to go from Town D to Town E?

5. Ms. Parker takes Train 020 from Town A to Town D once a month. How long does the ride take?

6. How much longer does it take train 010 than Train 020 to go from Town A to Town D?

7. Mr. Parker lives in Town A and goes to Town E bi-monthly on business. He takes the express train 030. How long does the ride take?

8. How much riding time is saved by taking the express train 030 from Town A to Town E than taking the local train 010?

Chapter Review

Write standard numerals. *(2)*

1. Three billion, five hundred million, eight thousand, fifty

2. Six hundred five trillion, twenty-two thousand, six

Round. *(4)*

3. 7,536,917 to the nearest million

4. 406,211 to the nearest thousand

Complete. *(10)*

	Number	*Divisible by* 2	3	5	6	9	10
5.	100	✓	?	?	?	?	?
6.	16	?	?	?	?	?	?
7.	36	?	?	?	?	?	?
8.	60	?	?	?	?	?	?
9.	81	?	?	?	?	?	?
10.	95	?	?	?	?	?	?

List all the factors of each number. *(12)*

11. 15 **12.** 26 **13.** 41 **14.** 64 **15.** 8

Tell whether each number is a prime number or composite number. *(12)*

16. 5 **17.** 30 **18.** 13 **19.** 19 **20.** 49

Find the next 3 numbers in each sequence. *(14)*

21. 3, 13, 10, 20, 17, . . . **22.** 3, 5, 9, 15, 23, . . . **23.** 62, 58, 54, 50, 46, . . .

Solve.

24. *(8)* There are 12 actors in a sewing class. Each worked for 6 periods of 30 minutes to make costumes for the play. How many hours did they work in all?

25. *(16)* A train left Town A at 10:32 am and arrived in Town B at 12:15 pm that day. How long did the trip take?

Chapter Test

Write standard numerals. *(2)*

1. Two billion, six hundred million, twenty

2. Three hundred four trillion, seven hundred fourteen million

Round. *(4)*

3. 4,817,900 to the nearest hundred thousand

4. 47,004 to the nearest ten thousand

Complete. *(10)*

	Number	*Divisible by*					
		2	*3*	*5*	*6*	*9*	*10*
5.	300	✓	?	?	?	?	?
6.	12	?	?	?	?	?	?
7.	42	?	?	?	?	?	?
8.	45	?	?	?	?	?	?
9.	72	?	?	?	?	?	?
10.	500	?	?	?	?	?	?

List all the factors of each number. *(12)*

11. 16 **12.** 24 **13.** 7 **14.** 33 **15.** 40

Tell whether each number is a prime number or composite number. *(12)*

16. 3 **17.** 20 **18.** 7 **19.** 87 **20.** 100

Find the next 3 numbers in each sequence. *(14)*

21. 4, 14, 24, 34, 44, . . . **22.** 4, 6, 10, 16, 24, . . . **23.** 41, 37, 33, 29, 25, . . .

Solve.

24. *(8)* There are 10 actors in an art class. Each worked for 4 periods of 30 minutes to make posters advertising the play. How many hours did they work in all?

25. *(16)* A train left Middletown at 9:47 am and arrived in Centreville at 1:11 pm that day. How long did the trip take?

Basic Skills Check

1. Add.

$$\begin{array}{r} 53{,}169 \\ 7{,}842 \\ 67{,}358 \\ +\ 9{,}014 \\ \hline \end{array}$$

A 136,383　B 137,383

C 137,833　D 138,383

2. Estimate the sum.

943 + 862

E 1,700　F 1,800

G 1,900　H 2,000

3. Subtract.

$$\begin{array}{r} 564{,}348 \\ -\ 272{,}140 \\ \hline \end{array}$$

A 292,288　B 292,280

C 292,208　D 292,200

4. Estimate the difference.

8,543 − 2,601

E 5,000　F 6,000

G 7,000　H 12,000

5. Multiply.

$$\begin{array}{r} 7{,}604 \\ \times\ 17 \\ \hline \end{array}$$

A 129,468　B 129,268

C 125,268　D 60,832

6. Multiply.

$$\begin{array}{r} 564 \\ \times\ 703 \\ \hline \end{array}$$

E 396,492　F 395,492

G 394,592　H 41,172

7. Estimate the product.

36 × 81

A 3,200　B 2,400

C 240　D none of the above

8. Divide.

$6\overline{)43{,}164}$

E 7,094　F 7,184

G 7,189　H 7,194

9. Divide.

$34\overline{)2{,}584}$

A 760　B 706

C 85　D 76

10. Divide.

462 ÷ 42

E 111　F 101

G 11　H 10r2

11. Add.

$$\begin{array}{r} 3.016 \\ 24.512 \\ 6.79 \\ +\ 17.2 \\ \hline \end{array}$$

A 51.518　B 51.428

C 51.418　D 51.4

12. Add.

$$\begin{array}{r} \$42.21 \\ 60.39 \\ 35.65 \\ +\ 17.88 \\ \hline \end{array}$$

E \$160.23　F \$156.13

G \$148.24　H \$146.03

13. Subtract.

$$\begin{array}{r} 83.05 \\ -\ 7.647 \\ \hline \end{array}$$

A 90.697　B 75.417

C 75.403　D 75.303

14. Subtract.

$$\begin{array}{r} \$421.65 \\ -\ 96.21 \\ \hline \end{array}$$

E \$425.64　F \$402.75

G \$350.68　H \$325.44

15. Multiply.

$$\begin{array}{r} 1.346 \\ \times\ 8 \\ \hline \end{array}$$

A 1.0768　B 10.668

C 10.768　D 1,076.8

Finding Sums by Multiplying

How many boxes are used in this arrangement?

1, 2, 3, 4, 5, . . . are consecutive numbers. The sum of consecutive numbers can be found by multiplying.

$$\begin{array}{r} 1 \\ 2 \\ 3 \\ 4 \\ \textcircled{5} \\ 6 \\ 7 \\ 8 \\ +\ 9 \\ \hline 45 \end{array} \qquad \textcircled{5} \times 9 = 45$$

Sum = middle number × number of numbers.

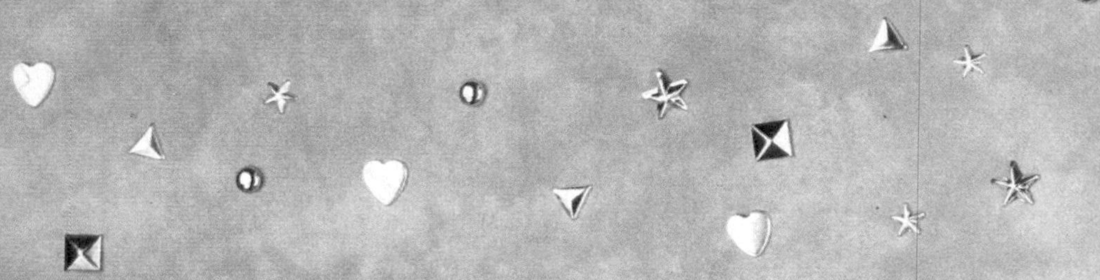

A. Find the sums using multiplication. Check by adding.

1.
$$\begin{array}{r} 2 \\ \textcircled{3} \\ +\ 4 \\ \hline \end{array}$$

2.
$$\begin{array}{r} 3 \\ 4 \\ \textcircled{5} \\ 6 \\ +\ 7 \\ \hline \end{array}$$

B. The same rule is used for finding the sum of consecutive even numbers. Find these sums using multiplication. Check by adding.

3.
$$\begin{array}{r} 2 \\ \textcircled{4} \\ +\ 6 \\ \hline \end{array}$$

4.
$$\begin{array}{r} 4 \\ 6 \\ \textcircled{8} \\ 10 \\ +\ 12 \\ \hline \end{array}$$

CHAPTER 2
WHOLE NUMBER COMPUTATION

C. The rule for sums of consecutive odd numbers is the same as the rule for sums of consecutive even numbers.
Find the sums using multiplication. Check by adding.

5.
3
5
(7)
9
+ 11

6.
9
11
13
(15)
17
19
+ 21

Practice

Find the sums using multiplication. Check by adding.

1. 4, 5, 6, 7, + 8

2. 2, 4, 6, 8, + 10

3. 3, 5, 7, 9, + 11

4. 1, 2, 3, 4, 5, 6, + 7

5. 2, 4, 6, 8, 10, 12, + 14

Find the sum of each sequence using multiplication. Check by adding.
[HINT: Try the rules you already know.]

6. 3, 7, 11

7. 1, 4, 7, 10, 13

8. 4, 6, 8, 10, 12, 14, 16, 18

See how fast you can add without making errors.

1. 8 + 7	**2.** 8 + 3	**3.** 6 + 8	**4.** 9 + 6	**5.** 9 + 3
6. 7 + 5	**7.** 0 + 9	**8.** 4 + 8	**9.** 8 + 5	**10.** 8 + 6
11. 8 + 8	**12.** 7 + 8	**13.** 7 + 6	**14.** 3 + 8	**15.** 7 + 9
16. 6 + 5	**17.** 7 + 7	**18.** 6 + 4	**19.** 9 + 8	**20.** 9 + 2
21. 3 + 7	**22.** 6 + 9	**23.** 8 + 2	**24.** 5 + 5	**25.** 7 + 4
26. 1 + 9	**27.** 5 + 4	**28.** 5 + 7	**29.** 6 + 6	**30.** 9 + 7
31. 8 + 4	**32.** 3 + 5	**33.** 9 + 1	**34.** 0 + 8	**35.** 9 + 5
36. 8 + 9	**37.** 5 + 8	**38.** 4 + 6	**39.** 5 + 6	**40.** 9 + 4
41. 4 + 5	**42.** 2 + 8	**43.** 6 + 7	**44.** 7 + 3	**45.** 9 + 9
46. 6 + 3	**47.** 5 + 9	**48.** 4 + 7	**49.** 3 + 9	**50.** 4 + 9

See how fast you can subtract without making errors.

1. 15 − 7	**2.** 9 − 6	**3.** 13 − 4	**4.** 8 − 2	**5.** 11 − 4
6. 14 − 9	**7.** 15 − 8	**8.** 7 − 6	**9.** 6 − 4	**10.** 17 − 9
11. 13 − 9	**12.** 16 − 9	**13.** 15 − 9	**14.** 14 − 8	**15.** 12 − 7
16. 7 − 5	**17.** 9 − 8	**18.** 8 − 3	**19.** 15 − 6	**20.** 11 − 3
21. 11 − 9	**22.** 9 − 7	**23.** 6 − 6	**24.** 13 − 7	**25.** 12 − 4
26. 12 − 9	**27.** 12 − 6	**28.** 11 − 8	**29.** 8 − 7	**30.** 10 − 2
31. 13 − 6	**32.** 10 − 5	**33.** 11 − 7	**34.** 11 − 5	**35.** 10 − 6
36. 8 − 6	**37.** 14 − 5	**38.** 7 − 0	**39.** 9 − 5	**40.** 17 − 8
41. 6 − 3	**42.** 7 − 3	**43.** 12 − 8	**44.** 10 − 4	**45.** 12 − 3
46. 9 − 3	**47.** 13 − 5	**48.** 16 − 7	**49.** 11 − 6	**50.** 12 − 5
51. 16 − 8	**52.** 8 − 5	**53.** 9 − 9	**54.** 14 − 7	**55.** 18 − 9
56. 7 − 4	**57.** 14 − 6	**58.** 8 − 4	**59.** 13 − 8	**60.** 10 − 3

Mental Addition

Mr. Becket, a bookkeeper, uses this method to add mentally. This is how he adds 23 + 34 + 21 + 68. He starts with the first number and says 23. Then he continues, 23 plus 4 is 27 and 27 plus 30 is 57. Here is the entire example.

			He says to himself:
	23		23
	↓	23 + 4	27
3 ←	4	27 + 30	57
	↘	57 + 1	58
2 ←	1	58 + 20	78
	↘	78 + 8	86
6 ←	8	86 + 60	146

The sum is 146.

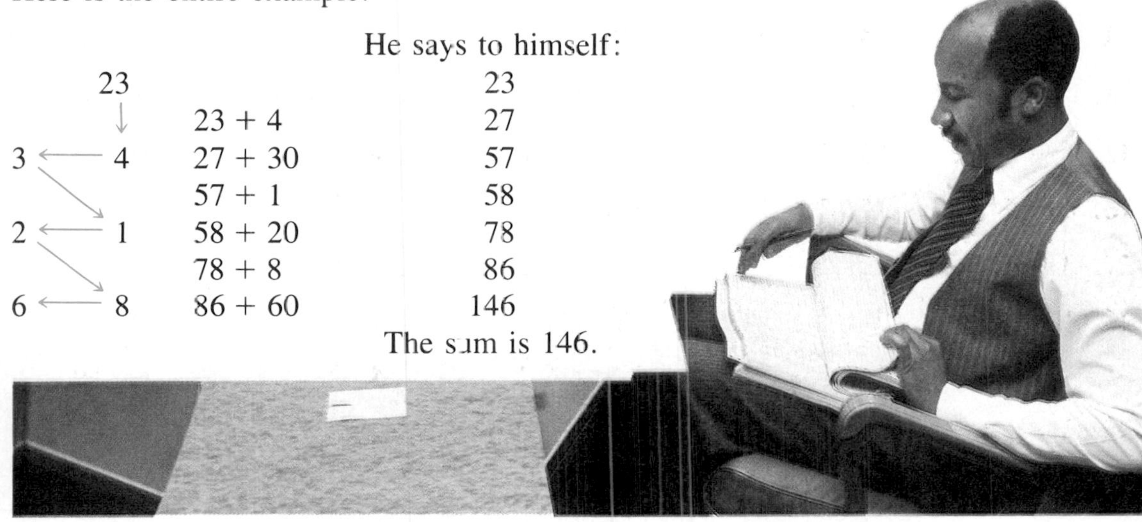

A. Add mentally.

1. 34 + 22 + 11

2. 25 + 14 + 34

3. 31 + 42 + 64 + 92

4. 27 + 34 + 86 + 75

5. 52 + 40 + 37 + 68

B. In horizontal form, Mr. Becket adds the tens first, then the ones.

23 + 34 + 21 + 68

He thinks: 23 53 57 77 78 138 146 The sum is 146.

(23 + 30) (53 + 4) (57 + 20) (77 + 1) (78 + 60) (138 + 8)

Add mentally. Write only the answers.

6. 43 + 22 + 31

7. 36 + 25 + 17

8. 43 + 52 + 67

9. 14 + 93 + 68 + 50

10. 54 + 77 + 68 + 31

11. 63 + 51 + 38 + 49

Adding Whole Numbers

Marcia is on the class bowling team. Her scores for 3 games were 129, 136, and 132. What was her total score?

	Step 1 ADD ONES	Step 2 ADD TENS	Step 3 ADD HUNDREDS
	1	1	1
129	129	129	129
136	136	136	136
+ 132	+ 132	+ 132	+ 132
	7	97	397
	17 ones = 1 ten and 7 ones		

Marcia's total score was 397.

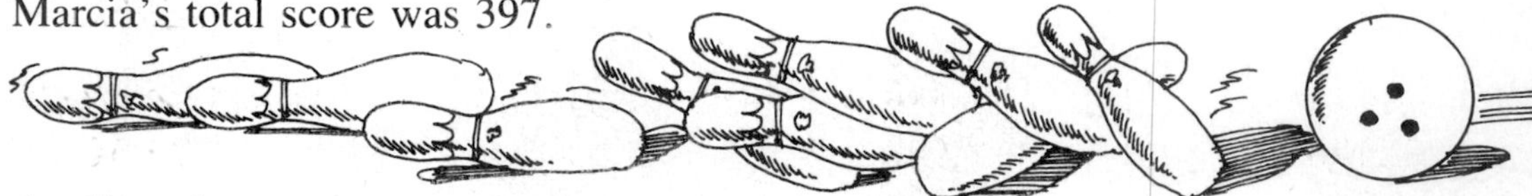

A. Complete.

1. 321 + 131 = ___2

2. 1,536 + 2,107 = ___43 (carry 1)

3. 368 + 429 + 148 = ___5 (carry 2)

4. \$ 23.37 + 36.84 + 12.93 = ___4 (carry 1)

5. 55,821 + 9,839 + 67,092 = ___2 (carry 1)

B. To add numbers in horizontal form, write them in vertical form and add.

Example Add 1,243 + 13,286 + 9,259.

```
 1  11
  1,243
 13,286
+ 9,259
 23,788
```

Add.

6. 352 + 1,586 + 982

7. \$123.56 + \$59.07 + \$368.92

C. Add.

8. 5,624 + 9,736

9. \$ 163.46 + 89.49

10. 31,684 + 3,714 + 23,932

11. \$ 1,784,819 + 68,720 + 718,619

12. 6,007 + 9,486 + 701 + 650

13. 5,986 + 10,665 + 4,586 + 65,002

Practice

Add.

1. 844 + 35

2. 1,600 + 2,200

3. 4,634 + 1,358

4. 5,201 + 865

5. 44,360 + 22,646

6. $364.58 + 288.01

7. 34,624 + 9,193

8. 567,896 + 65,417

9. 1,421; 2,121; + 1,215

10. $3,356; 4,107; + 225

11. 3,384; 4,462; 5,734; + 6,618

12. 36,582; 4,621; 59,007; + 3,982

13. 4,613; 2,176; 6,345; 2,186; + 1,794

14. 35,416; 8,902; 41,284; 32,369; + 8,416

15. $634,019; 284,678; 72,516; 832,743; + 62,713

16. $ 490,674; 7,785,109; 4,456,213; 489,113; + 5,340,113

17. 234 + 511 + 1,724

18. $98.72 + $4.61 + $30.01

19. 23,304 + 546 + 4,279 + 9,806

20. 4,987 + 9,801 + 406 + 586

Solve.

21. The 5 members of the Lions bowling team scored 172, 195, 156, 127, and 169 in 1 game. What was their game total?

★ 22. The sum of 7 addends is 137. 6 is added to each addend. What is the new sum?

★ 23. Four numbers are added. The sum of the first and second numbers is 13; the sum of the second and third numbers is 12; and the sum of the third and fourth numbers is 14. What is the sum of the 4 numbers?

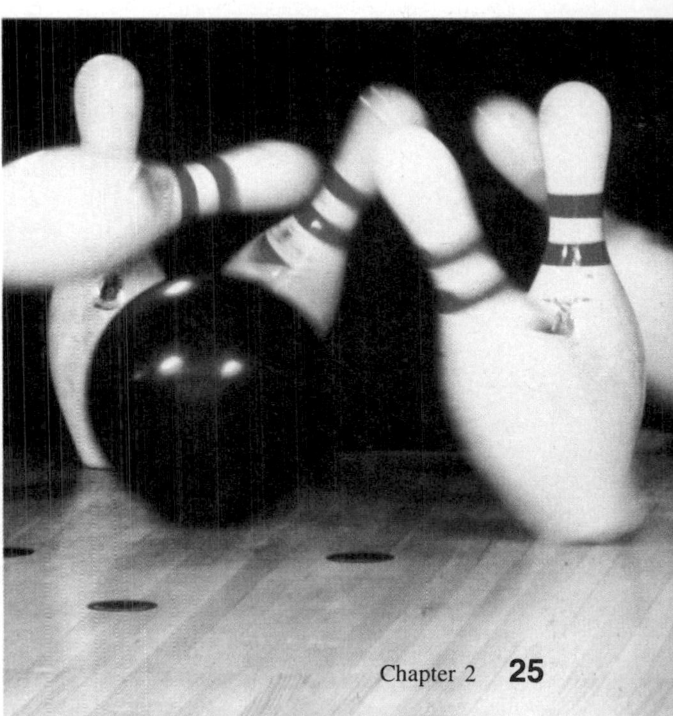

Subtracting Whole Numbers

There are 590 garbage cans along the city sanitation route. So far, 375 cans have been cleared. How many garbage cans remain to be cleared?

	Step 1	Step 2	Step 3
	RENAME TENS SUBTRACT ONES	SUBTRACT TENS	SUBTRACT HUNDREDS
	8 10	8 10	8 10
590	5 9 0	5 9 0	5 9 0
− 375	− 3 7 5	− 3 7 5	− 3 7 5
	5	1 5	2 1 5
	9 tens and 0 ones = 8 tens and 10 ones		

A. Subtract.

1. 780 − 264	**2.** 7,936 − 2,562	**3.** 89,837 − 64,018	**4.** $ 653,682 − 42,565

B. Sometimes you have to rename more than once to subtract.

Example		
		12 6 2 14
	734	7 3 4
	− 258	− 2 5 8
		4 7 6

Subtract.

5. 634 − 279	**6.** 4,316 − 2,087	**7.** 56,342 − 24,738	**8.** $ 841,356 − 12,467

C. Subtraction with zeros should present no problem.

Example		
		5 9 9 10
	6,000	6,0 0 0
	− 3,756	− 3,7 5 6
		2,2 4 4

Subtract.

9. 800 − 437	**10.** 3,000 − 1,594	**11.** 6,002 − 4,138	**12.** 50,000 − 3,759

Practice

Subtract.

1. 7,687 − 4,194	**2.** 4,732 − 3,691	**3.** 74,824 − 61,290	**4.** 621,987 − 500,239
5. 8,436 − 6,147	**6.** 8,936 − 6,247	**7.** 34,836 − 13,159	**8.** 521,987 − 436,123
9. 5,204 − 1,328	**10.** 3,241 − 986	**11.** 73,405 − 14,376	**12.** 89,361 − 4,475
13. $764,716 − 240,939	**14.** $743,168 − 15,274	**15.** $34,853 − 10,261	**16.** $85,163 − 63,548
17. 500 − 324	**18.** 700 − 239	**19.** 6,000 − 3,451	**20.** 4,000 − 2,981
21. 6,004 − 3,213	**22.** 7,005 − 6,178	**23.** 50,000 − 27,616	**24.** 60,000 − 25,750

25. 800 − 247 **26.** 9,000 − 3,416 **27.** 10,053 − 2,594

28. 648,316 − 26,129 **29.** 2,816,347 − 954,819

Solve.

30. A sanitation person makes $336 a week. Another makes $325 a week. What is the difference in their salaries?

★**31.** The difference of 2 numbers is 12. The smaller number is 95. What is the other number?

★**32.** The difference of 2 numbers is 192. The greater number is 400. What is the other number?

Estimating Sums and Differences

The Yellow Bus Company had 672 passengers in one week. The second week, it had 548 passengers. The third week it had 450 passengers. Estimate how many passengers it had in all.

Estimate the sum by rounding each addend.

ACTUAL		ESTIMATE
672	→	700
548	→	500
+ 450	→	+ 500
		1,700

There were about 1,700 passengers.

A. Estimate the sums.

Examples

361 is about 360
+ 23 is about + 20
380

15,842 is about 15,800
+ 756 is about + 800
16,600

1. 864 + 239	**2.** 1,207 + 6,641	**3.** 473 + 91	**4.** 7,111 + 326	**5.** 71,850 + 532

B. Estimate the differences.

Examples

4,949 is about 5,000
− 1,216 is about − 1,000
4,000

2,736 is about 2,700
− 287 is about − 300
2,400

6. 514 − 149	**7.** 8,279 − 4,630	**8.** 658 − 96	**9.** 3,339 − 602	**10.** 14,996 − 550

C. Estimate the sums.

11. 459 + 361 + 747	**12.** 4,516 + 8,290 + 927	**13.** 6,745 + 828 + 394	**14.** 64,078 + 3,953 + 17,224	**15.** 8,027 + 64 + 153 + 3,815

Estimate the sums.

1. 625 + 283

2. 371 + 59

3. 464 + 37

4. 3,219 + 6,540

5. 7,982 + 1,486

6. 5,195 + 644

7. 2,348 + 623

8. 4,591 + 74

9. 8,263 + 54

10. 14,889 + 63,241

11. 72,687 + 19,045

12. 53,622 + 8,829

13. 88,409 + 7,613

14. 41,720 + 231

15. $49,643 + 586

16. 456 + 713 + 949

17. 2,765 + 820 + 3,495

18. 907 + 5,634 + 723

19. 13,486 + 4,842 + 29,072

20. 3,268 + 40 + 312 + 652

Estimate the differences.

21. 748 − 394

22. 660 − 287

23. 882 − 25

24. 509 − 42

25. 5,072 − 2,458

26. 6,646 − 3,718

27. 8,643 − 399

28. 5,391 − 247

29. 8,416 − 99

30. 7,930 − 76

31. 36,212 − 14,084

32. 48,605 − 37,121

33. 45,116 − 4,470

34. 72,084 − 6,195

35. $24,192 − 901

36. 16,792 − 839

37. 52,817 − 13,680

38. 8,159 − 276

39. 7,518 − 7,485

★ **40.** 379,800 − 25,466

Solve.

41. A bus was driven 19,416 km one year, 24,961 km the second year, and 35,000 km the third year. Estimate the total distance driven.

42. One bus driver earned $9,345 and a second driver earned $4,745. Estimate how much more the first driver earned.

Mid-Chapter Review

Add. *(24)*

1.	**2.**	**3.**	**4.**	**5.**
2,346	\$73,694	639	1,053	\$13,867
+ 497	+ 2,867	258	975	29,045
		+ 384	+ 2,482	+ 6,690

Subtract. *(26)*

6.	**7.**	**8.**	**9.**	**10.**
897	\$6,734	9,000	42,000	371,279
− 645	− 2,456	− 2,463	− 8,751	− 286,485

Estimate the sums. *(28)*

11.	**12.**	**13.**	**14.**	**15.**
6,438	36,416	\$7,615	37,619	57
+ 7,126	+ 9,319	+ 82	4,823	391
			+ 23,914	+ 8,056

Estimate the differences. *(28)*

16.	**17.**	**18.**	**19.**	**20.**
8,341	7,016	40,041	5,218	\$16,962
− 2,942	− 914	− 9,562	− 76	− 703

FIND OUT!

Brainteaser

Which 2 shapes are mirror images?

1. a  b  c  d  e 

2. a b  c 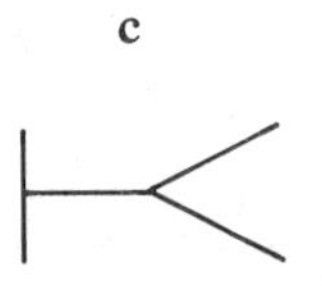 d  e 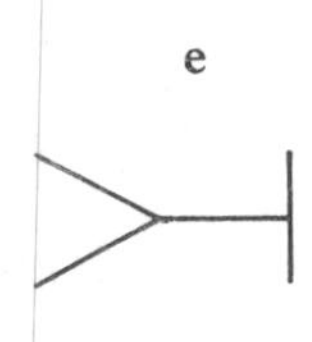

See how fast you can multiply without making errors.

1. 3×7 **2.** 6×4 **3.** 4×8 **4.** 6×7 **5.** 2×7

6. 8×6 **7.** 5×4 **8.** 9×7 **9.** 3×9 **10.** 2×8

11. 7×9 **12.** 3×8 **13.** 4×5 **14.** 5×5 **15.** 1×6

16. 3×6 **17.** 6×6 **18.** 4×9 **19.** 3×3 **20.** 9×5

21. 8×4 **22.** 3×5 **23.** 7×8 **24.** 8×9 **25.** 2×9

26. 9×8 **27.** 7×7 **28.** 4×7 **29.** 9×6 **30.** 6×5

31. 5×3 **32.** 8×7 **33.** 7×3 **34.** 5×7 **35.** 1×9

36. 7×4 **37.** 6×3 **38.** 7×6 **39.** 5×8 **40.** 8×5

41. 4×4 **42.** 8×8 **43.** 4×6 **44.** 9×3 **45.** 2×6

46. 8×3 **47.** 7×5 **48.** 9×4 **49.** 9×9 **50.** 1×8

51. 6×8 **52.** 5×6 **53.** 6×9 **54.** 5×9 **55.** 2×5

See how fast you can divide without making errors.

1. $27 \div 9$ **2.** $30 \div 6$ **3.** $30 \div 5$ **4.** $24 \div 8$ **5.** $18 \div 9$

6. $21 \div 7$ **7.** $20 \div 4$ **8.** $32 \div 8$ **9.** $18 \div 3$ **10.** $8 \div 4$

11. $35 \div 5$ **12.** $36 \div 9$ **13.** $36 \div 6$ **14.** $15 \div 5$ **15.** $14 \div 7$

16. $40 \div 8$ **17.** $24 \div 3$ **18.** $28 \div 7$ **19.** $21 \div 3$ **20.** $72 \div 8$

21. $24 \div 4$ **22.** $24 \div 6$ **23.** $45 \div 9$ **24.** $40 \div 5$ **25.** $15 \div 3$

26. $42 \div 6$ **27.** $48 \div 8$ **28.** $25 \div 5$ **29.** $36 \div 4$ **30.** $63 \div 7$

31. $18 \div 6$ **32.** $27 \div 3$ **33.** $35 \div 7$ **34.** $54 \div 9$ **35.** $12 \div 3$

36. $20 \div 5$ **37.** $63 \div 9$ **38.** $45 \div 5$ **39.** $12 \div 4$ **40.** $16 \div 8$

41. $42 \div 7$ **42.** $16 \div 4$ **43.** $56 \div 8$ **44.** $48 \div 6$ **45.** $12 \div 6$

46. $54 \div 6$ **47.** $28 \div 4$ **48.** $72 \div 9$ **49.** $49 \div 7$ **50.** $9 \div 3$

51. $81 \div 9$ **52.** $32 \div 4$ **53.** $10 \div 5$ **54.** $64 \div 8$ **55.** $56 \div 7$

Problem Solving

How much was saved by buying during the sale?

Diagrams may help solve problems.

Original price	
Sale price	Savings

$$\begin{array}{r} \$\,670 \\ -\ 538 \\ \hline \$\,132 \end{array}$$

A. Solve. Use the diagram.

1. Miss Greenberg bought a fishing boat on sale for $379. She saved $120.99. What was the original price of the boat?

2. Jane walked east from the campsite for 315 m. Olga walked west from the campsite for 405 m. How far apart were they?

3. Juan cut a board that measured 500 cm into 2 pieces. The smaller piece measured 150 cm. What was the length of the larger piece?

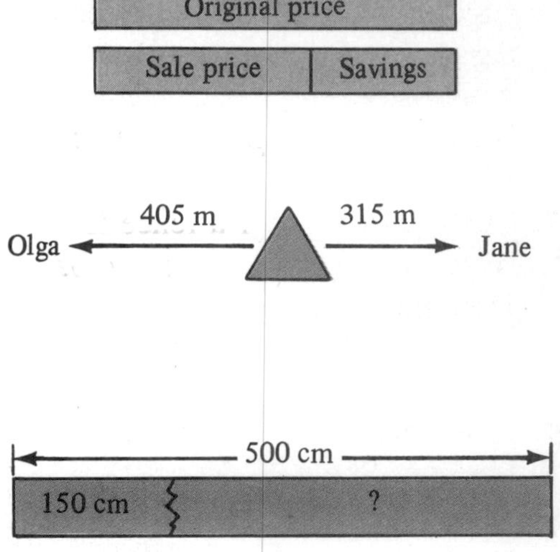

B. Draw a diagram for each problem. Solve.

4. Steve pitched his tent 5 km due north of the ranger station. Dave pitched his tent 8 km due north of the ranger station. How far is Steve's tent from Dave's tent?

5. Mrs. Donaldsen is putting up 3 shelves in the living room. Each shelf is 5 cm thick. She wants 50 cm between each shelf. What will the distance be from the bottom of the bottom shelf to the top of the top shelf?

Practice

Draw a diagram for each problem. Solve.

1. Ms. Sterling bought a car stereo on sale for $188. The original price of the stereo was $375. How much did Ms. Sterling save by buying the stereo on sale?

2. Mr. Lietzke bought a television set on sale for $628.50. He saved $130.90 of the original price. What was the original price of the television set?

3. Paul and Linda drove toward each other from towns 26 mi apart. When they met, Paul had driven 17 mi. How far had Linda driven?

4. Frances cut a 45-cm board into two pieces. The shorter piece is 21 cm long. How long is the longer piece?

5. Pedro built a 60-cm shelf. He painted 35 cm on the left side of the shelf to indicate that he would store tools there. How long is the unpainted part of the shelf?

6. In Fred's room, there are 2 shelves on one wall. The first is 3 ft off the floor, the second is 3 ft above that. This last shelf is 2 ft from the ceiling. How high is the room?

7. The total length of a fence is 50 m. All but 14 m needs repair. How much fence needs repair?

8. The area of a vegetable garden is 108 m^2. Tomatoes and broccoli are planted in 65 m^2. How much space is left for cabbage?

9. Jane bought 300 cm of seam binding. She used 40 cm on a vest and 110 cm on a skirt. How much seam binding is left?

10. Joe used 175 mL of milk in a bowl of cereal and 250 mL to make a milk shake. How much milk did he use?

Multiplying

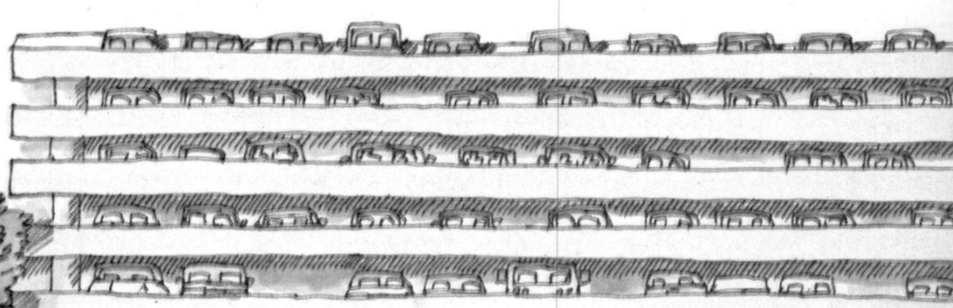

A parking lot has 7 levels. There are 246 parking spaces on each level. How many cars can be parked in the parking lot?

	Step 1 MULTIPLY ONES	Step 2 MULTIPLY TENS	Step 3 MULTIPLY HUNDREDS
$\begin{array}{r} 246 \\ \times\ 7 \\ \hline \end{array}$	$\begin{array}{r} {\scriptstyle 4}\ \ \\ 246 \\ \times\ 7 \\ \hline 2 \end{array}$	$\begin{array}{r} {\scriptstyle 3\ 4}\ \ \\ 246 \\ \times\ 7 \\ \hline 22 \end{array}$	$\begin{array}{r} {\scriptstyle 3\ 4}\ \ \\ 246 \\ \times\ 7 \\ \hline 1{,}722 \end{array}$

So, 1,722 cars can be parked in the parking lot.

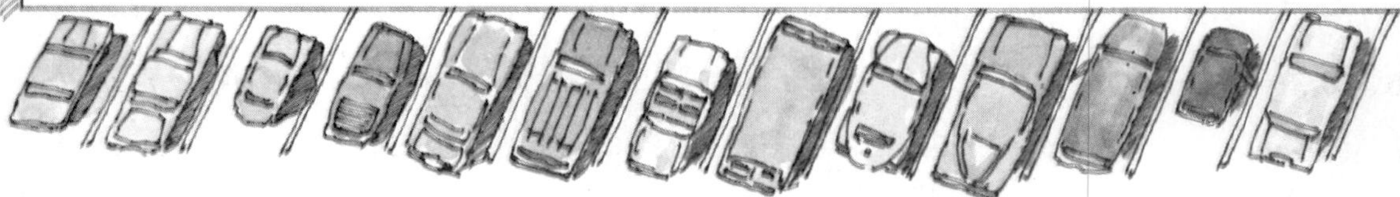

A. Multiply.

1. $\begin{array}{r} 234 \\ \times\ 8 \\ \hline \end{array}$ **2.** $\begin{array}{r} 1{,}312 \\ \times\ 7 \\ \hline \end{array}$ **3.** $\begin{array}{r} 2{,}106 \\ \times\ 5 \\ \hline \end{array}$ **4.** $\begin{array}{r} 14{,}081 \\ \times\ 8 \\ \hline \end{array}$ **5.** $\begin{array}{r} \$569.25 \\ \times\ 3 \\ \hline \end{array}$

B. Complete.

6. Step 1 MULTIPLY BY ONES	**7.** Step 2 MULTIPLY BY TENS	**8.** Step 3 ADD
$\begin{array}{r} 36 \\ \times\ 24 \\ \hline \end{array}$	$\begin{array}{r} 36 \\ \times\ 24 \\ \hline 144 \end{array}$	$\begin{array}{r} 36 \\ \times\ 24 \\ \hline 144 \\ 720 \\ \hline \end{array}$ ← The zero may be left off.

C. Multiply.

9. $\begin{array}{r} 47 \\ \times\ 35 \\ \hline \end{array}$ **10.** $\begin{array}{r} 673 \\ \times\ 46 \\ \hline \end{array}$ **11.** $\begin{array}{r} 5{,}708 \\ \times\ 72 \\ \hline \end{array}$ **12.** $\begin{array}{r} 32{,}411 \\ \times\ 18 \\ \hline \end{array}$ **13.** $\begin{array}{r} \$394.85 \\ \times\ 29 \\ \hline \end{array}$

Practice

Multiply.

1. 42 × 2
2. 236 × 2
3. 107 × 8
4. 247 × 9
5. 364 × 7

6. 2,316 × 4
7. 3,215 × 6
8. 1,432 × 2
9. 56,822 × 4
10. \$214.61 × 5

11. 22 × 34
12. 39 × 12
13. 46 × 37
14. 213 × 32
15. 324 × 16

16. 418 × 28
17. 672 × 53
18. 748 × 29
19. 6,133 × 24
20. \$75.06 × 48

21. 6,834 × 76
22. 4,527 × 36
23. 97,543 × 88
24. 13,116 × 54
25. \$358.96 × 21

26. 8 × 4,605
27. 92 × 27
★**28.** 54 × 8 × 61 × 7

Solve.

29. A survey showed that 256 cars used a parking lot each day. How many cars would use the parking lot in 5 days?

30. The cost of cleaning and lighting a parking lot in Suntown is \$2,436 a month. What is the cost for 12 months?

Multiplying Larger Numbers

A space shuttle makes 125 trips a month. The space shuttle has 257 seats on it. How many people can travel on the space shuttle each month?

Step 1	Step 2	Step 3	Step 4
MULTIPLY BY ONES	MULTIPLY BY TENS	MULTIPLY BY HUNDREDS	ADD
257 × 125 1285	257 × 125 1285 514	257 × 125 1285 514 257	257 × 125 1 285 5 14 25 7 32,125

So, 32,125 people can travel on the space shuttle each month.

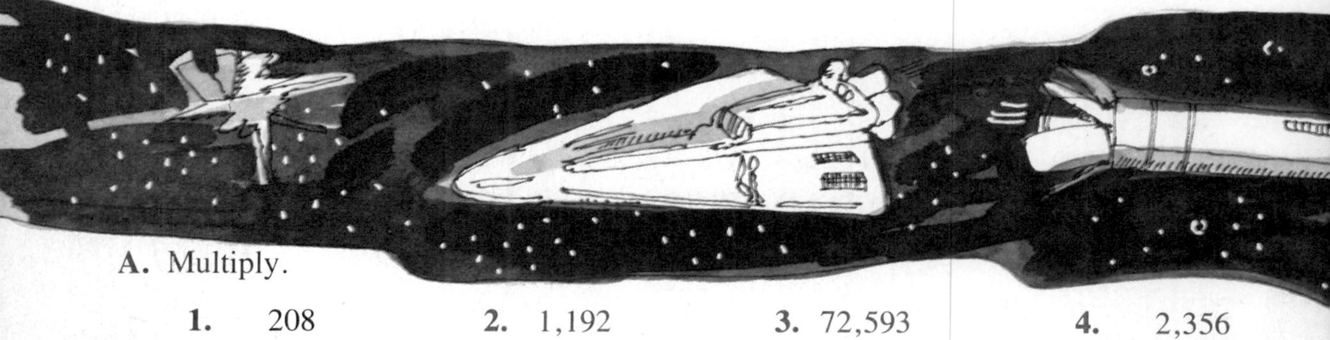

A. Multiply.

1. 208 × 764

2. 1,192 × 835

3. 72,593 × 219

4. 2,356 × 3,426

5. 1,583 × 19,037

6. 4,176 × 61,243

B. Be careful of the zeros.

Examples

238 × 604 952 14280 ⟵ 0 × 238 = 0 143,752	2,601 × 460 156060 ⟵ 0 × 2,601 = 0 10404 1,196,460

Multiply.

7. 416 × 408

8. 2,609 × 380

9. 5,275 × 1,004

10. 7,230 × 8,050

Practice

Multiply.

1. $\begin{array}{r} 234 \\ \times\ 311 \\ \hline \end{array}$

2. $\begin{array}{r} 642 \\ \times\ 236 \\ \hline \end{array}$

3. $\begin{array}{r} 705 \\ \times\ 782 \\ \hline \end{array}$

4. $\begin{array}{r} 318 \\ \times\ 945 \\ \hline \end{array}$

5. $\begin{array}{r} 4{,}630 \\ \times\ 324 \\ \hline \end{array}$

6. $\begin{array}{r} 5{,}724 \\ \times\ 678 \\ \hline \end{array}$

7. $\begin{array}{r} 7{,}834 \\ \times\ 349 \\ \hline \end{array}$

8. $\begin{array}{r} 9{,}076 \\ \times\ 414 \\ \hline \end{array}$

9. $\begin{array}{r} 16{,}854 \\ \times\ 521 \\ \hline \end{array}$

10. $\begin{array}{r} 2{,}508 \\ \times\ 1{,}366 \\ \hline \end{array}$

11. $\begin{array}{r} 6{,}815 \\ \times\ 2{,}437 \\ \hline \end{array}$

12. $\begin{array}{r} 32{,}184 \\ \times\ 5{,}183 \\ \hline \end{array}$

13. $\begin{array}{r} 236 \\ \times\ 806 \\ \hline \end{array}$

14. $\begin{array}{r} 1{,}342 \\ \times\ 280 \\ \hline \end{array}$

15. $\begin{array}{r} 9{,}612 \\ \times\ 5{,}001 \\ \hline \end{array}$

16. $\begin{array}{r} 3{,}152 \\ \times\ 3{,}010 \\ \hline \end{array}$

17. 656 × 2,034

18. 1,830 × 5,926

19. 4,030 × 7,085

★ 20. 90,009 × 34,341

Solve.

21. A trip on a space shuttle costs $836. There are 197 passengers on the shuttle. How much money will the space shuttle company take in?

22. There are 109 names on each waiting list for a trip on a space shuttle. There are 2,001 waiting lists. How many names are on the waiting lists in all?

Dividing by a 1-Digit Number

Disco Music Store ordered 456 records. Records are packaged 6 to a box. How many boxes of records did Disco Music receive?

Step 1
ESTIMATE.
How many 6's in 4? None
How many 6's in 45? Try 7.

$$6\overline{)\,45\ 6}\quad\text{quotient: }7$$

Step 2
MULTIPLY.

$$\begin{array}{r} 7\\ 6\overline{)456}\\ \underline{42} \end{array}$$

Step 3
SUBTRACT. The estimate is correct. 42 is less than 45. Bring down the 6.

$$\begin{array}{r} 7\\ 6\overline{)456}\\ \underline{42}\downarrow\\ 36 \end{array}$$

Step 4
Repeat the steps.

$$\begin{array}{r} 76\\ 6\overline{)456}\\ \underline{42}\\ 36\\ \underline{36}\\ 0 \end{array}$$

A. Complete.

1. $3\overline{)429}$ (quotient begun: 1)
2. $2\overline{)\$948}$ (quotient begun: \$4)
3. $5\overline{)745}$ (quotient begun: 1)
4. $2\overline{)816}$ (quotient begun: 4)
5. $6\overline{)192}$ (quotient begun: 3)
6. $4\overline{)\$344}$ (quotient begun: \$ 8)
7. $7\overline{)2,408}$ (quotient begun: 3)
8. $8\overline{)3,456}$ (quotient begun: 4)

B. Divide.

9. $4\overline{)3,224}$	**10.** $6\overline{)2,418}$	**11.** $3\overline{)5,121}$	**12.** $8\overline{)9,624}$
13. $3\overline{)164}$	**14.** $5\overline{)816}$	**15.** $4\overline{)314}$	**16.** $8\overline{)3,165}$
17. $4\overline{)848}$	**18.** $2\overline{)\$864}$	**19.** $3\overline{)9,969}$	**20.** $2\overline{)4,068}$
21. $3\overline{)951}$	**22.** $8\overline{)7,616}$	**23.** $6\overline{)4,874}$	**24.** $7\overline{)21,141}$

Practice

Divide.

1. $2\overline{)48}$
2. $3\overline{)96}$
3. $4\overline{)84}$
4. $3\overline{)76}$
5. $3\overline{)82}$
6. $6\overline{)89}$
7. $4\overline{)38}$
8. $6\overline{)59}$
9. $7\overline{)80}$
10. $2\overline{)420}$
11. $3\overline{)963}$
12. $4\overline{)884}$
13. $4\overline{)248}$
14. $3\overline{)159}$
15. $7\overline{)497}$
16. $6\overline{)846}$
17. $3\overline{)516}$
18. $4\overline{)\$568}$
19. $3\overline{)\$744}$
20. $6\overline{)852}$
21. $4\overline{)725}$
22. $3\overline{)609}$
23. $4\overline{)412}$
24. $5\overline{)105}$
25. $2\overline{)6,846}$
26. $3\overline{)\$9,936}$
27. $4\overline{)8,480}$
28. $3\overline{)8,196}$
29. $4\overline{)9,220}$
30. $4\overline{)3,284}$
31. $3\overline{)7,526}$
32. $4\overline{)9,704}$
33. $7\overline{)\$9,401}$
34. $6\overline{)\$6,006}$
35. $4\overline{)4,008}$
36. $3\overline{)1,509}$
37. $8\overline{)4,040}$
38. $7\overline{)6,314}$
39. $9\overline{)8,127}$
40. $4\overline{)31,284}$
41. $6\overline{)29,642}$
42. $7\overline{)12,346}$
43. $6\overline{)18,366}$
44. $5\overline{)25,250}$
45. $8\overline{)64,320}$
46. $9\overline{)732,402}$
47. $7\overline{)493,647}$

Solve.

★ **48.** 4,644 cassettes are to be packed in boxes of 3 each. Then the boxes are packed in cartons of 9 each. How many cartons will be filled?

Dividing by Larger Numbers

715 paperback books are placed in 31 boxes. Each box has the same number of books. How many books are in each box?

Step 1 Estimate.
How many 3 1's in 7 1?
Think: How many 3's in 7? Try 2.

Step 2 Multiply.

Step 3 Subtract. The estimate is correct. Bring down the 5.

Step 4 Repeat the steps.

```
    23 r 2
31)715
   62↓
    95
    93
     2
```

There are 23 books in each box. There are 2 books left over.

A. Divide.

1. 36)864 **2.** 63)3,404 **3.** 52)$12,168 **4.** 312)13,416

B. Sometimes the first estimate is too large.

Example

Step 1 Estimate.
How many 3 4's in 6 2?
Think: how many 3's in 6? Try 2.

```
     2
34)628
   68
   ↑
   └── Too large
```

Step 2 Multiply.

Step 3 Subtract. The estimate is not correct. Try 1.
The new estimate is correct. Bring down the 8.

Step 4 Repeat the steps. Complete.

```
    18 r 16
34)628
   34
   288
   272
    16
```

Divide.

5. 49)8,869 **6.** 37)9,472 **7.** 29)1,830 **8.** 38)64,214

9. 321)15,087 **10.** 716)499,052 **11.** 643)93,175

Practice

Divide.

1. $24\overline{)72}$ **2.** $23\overline{)69}$ **3.** $37\overline{)74}$ **4.** $17\overline{)87}$ **5.** $44\overline{)98}$

6. $63\overline{)378}$ **7.** $21\overline{)168}$ **8.** $43\overline{)349}$ **9.** $54\overline{)268}$ **10.** $82\overline{)616}$

11. $26\overline{)780}$ **12.** $37\overline{)740}$ **13.** $23\overline{)690}$ **14.** $45\overline{)459}$ **15.** $19\overline{)576}$

16. $41\overline{)902}$ **17.** $33\overline{)\$858}$ **18.** $36\overline{)475}$ **19.** $16\overline{)388}$ **20.** $27\overline{)820}$

21. $28\overline{)196}$ **22.** $27\overline{)162}$ **23.** $39\overline{)\$273}$ **24.** $49\overline{)353}$ **25.** $74\overline{)508}$

26. $29\overline{)762}$ **27.** $17\overline{)394}$ **28.** $27\overline{)675}$ **29.** $31\overline{)296}$ **30.** $63\overline{)450}$

31. $31\overline{)\$6,262}$ **32.** $24\overline{)4,872}$ **33.** $34\overline{)6,868}$ **34.** $75\overline{)8,625}$

35. $43\overline{)5,117}$ **36.** $21\overline{)9,093}$ **37.** $34\overline{)7,316}$ **38.** $52\overline{)9,407}$

39. $56\overline{)\$2,296}$ **40.** $68\overline{)1,656}$ **41.** $79\overline{)2,607}$ **42.** $48\overline{)3,009}$

43. $47\overline{)52,781}$ **44.** $67\overline{)54,605}$ **45.** $38\overline{)22,867}$ **46.** $87\overline{)436,200}$

47. $231\overline{)5,544}$ **48.** $313\overline{)7,180}$ **49.** $421\overline{)15,156}$

50. $428\overline{)52,644}$ **51.** $712\overline{)242,080}$ **52.** $541\overline{)124,971}$

Solve.

53. 24 cases of pencils cost \$2,352. What was the cost of each case?

54. 24 cartons of paper cost a printer \$672. What is the cost of a carton of paper?

A Shortcut in Division

Here is a short form you can use when the divisor is less than 10.

		Short Form
Step 1	$\begin{array}{r} 3 \\ 6\overline{)192} \\ \underline{18} \\ 1 \end{array}$	$\begin{array}{r} 3 \\ 6\overline{)19^{1}2} \end{array}$
Step 2	$\begin{array}{r} 32 \\ 6\overline{)192} \\ \underline{18} \\ 12 \\ \underline{12} \\ 0 \end{array}$	$\begin{array}{r} 3\ 2 \\ 6\overline{)19^{1}2} \end{array}$

Practice

Divide. Use the short form.

1. $4\overline{)172}$ **2.** $6\overline{)384}$ **3.** $3\overline{)6,468}$ **4.** $9\overline{)4,338}$

5. $7\overline{)6,412}$ **6.** $8\overline{)42,319}$ **7.** $5\overline{)36,510}$ **8.** $7\overline{)342,612}$

9. $2\overline{)189}$ **10.** $3\overline{)4,526}$ **11.** $5\overline{)26,729}$ **12.** $6\overline{)723,601}$

13. $7\overline{)42,079}$ **14.** $8\overline{)561,602}$ **15.** $9\overline{)3,600,453}$

FIND OUT!

Brainteaser

How many blocks are in the pile?

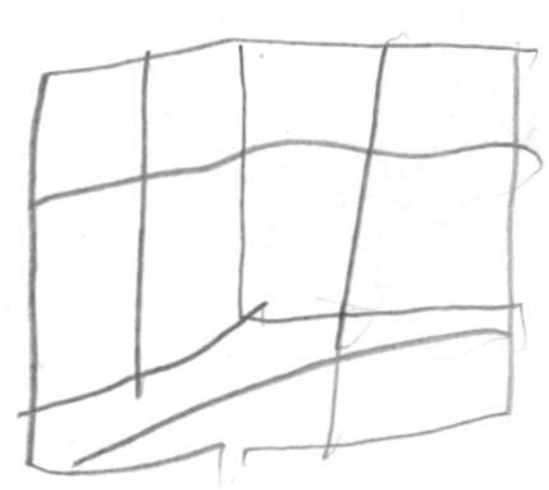

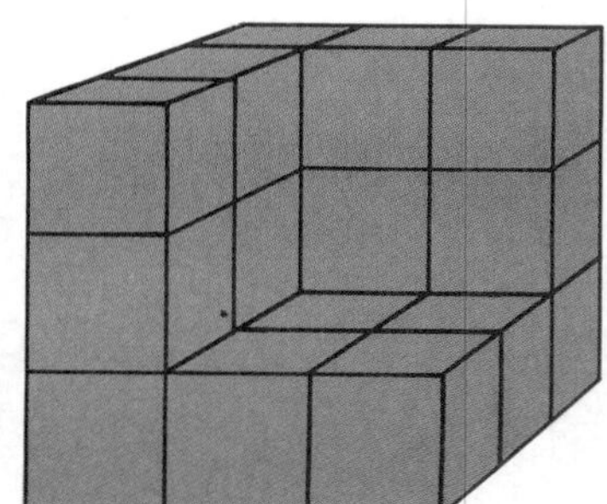

Keeping Fit

Write word names.

1. 849,027 **2.** 5,361,004 **3.** 8,090,207,104

Write standard numerals.

4. 942 billion, 671 thousand

5. 27 trillion, 86 million

6. Seventy trillion, three billion, six hundred two thousand

7. Eighty-nine billion, four hundred twelve million, eighteen

Round.

8. 549,020 to the nearest thousand

9. 7,624,109 to the nearest ten thousand

10. 8,473,001 to the nearest hundred thousand

11. 625,501,784 to the nearest million

Complete.

	Number	*Divisible by* 2	3	5	6	9	10
12.	300	✓	?	?	?	?	?
13.	150	?	?	?	?	?	?
14.	62	?	?	?	?	?	?
15.	24	?	?	?	?	?	?
16.	72	?	?	?	?	?	?

List all the factors of each number.

17. 22 **18.** 40 **19.** 200 **20.** 65 **21.** 72

Tell whether each number is a prime or a composite number.

22. 61 **23.** 42 **24.** 19 **25.** 2 **26.** 106

Find the next 3 numbers in each sequence.

27. 1, 5, 9, 13, . . . **28.** 11, 13, 16, 20, . . . **29.** 3, 6, 12, 24, . . .

Zeros in Multiplying and Dividing

$4 \times 60 = 240$ $\qquad$ $40 \times 60 = 2{,}400$ $\qquad$ $40 \times 600 = 24{,}000$

60 ←	1 zero	60 ←	1 zero	600 ←	2 zeros
× 4 ←	+ 0 zeros	× 40 ←	+ 1 zero	× 40 ←	+ 1 zero
240 ←	1 zero	2,400 ←	2 zeros	24,000 ←	3 zeros

A. Multiply.

1. 80 × 3 $\qquad$ **2.** 50 × 7 $\qquad$ **3.** 30 × 20 $\qquad$ **4.** 50 × 90

5. 800 × 40 $\qquad$ **6.** 900 × 80 $\qquad$ **7.** 600 × 700 $\qquad$ **8.** 500 × 300

9. 4,000 × 80 $\qquad$ **10.** 4,000 × 800 $\qquad$ **11.** 4,000 × 8,000 $\qquad$ **12.** 50,000 × 900

13. 80 × 40 $\qquad$ **14.** 600 × 30 $\qquad$ **15.** 700 × 400 $\qquad$ **16.** 7,000 × 400

B. Divide.

Example $\quad 30\overline{)600}$ = 20 $\quad$ 2 zeros − 1 zero = 1 zero

17. $40\overline{)160}$ $\qquad$ **18.** $60\overline{)360}$ $\qquad$ **19.** $70\overline{)140}$ $\qquad$ **20.** $80\overline{)640}$

21. $40\overline{)1{,}600}$ $\qquad$ **22.** $80\overline{)3{,}200}$ $\qquad$ **23.** $60\overline{)3{,}600}$ $\qquad$ **24.** $70\overline{)4{,}200}$

25. $400\overline{)8{,}000}$ $\qquad$ **26.** $800\overline{)24{,}000}$ $\qquad$ **27.** $700\overline{)210{,}000}$

Practice

Multiply.

1. 70 × 3
2. 40 × 7
3. 60 × 4
4. 90 × 2
5. 50 × 8
6. 30 × 20
7. 50 × 90
8. 40 × 10
9. 60 × 30
10. 70 × 40
11. 800 × 40
12. 900 × 80
13. 500 × 10
14. 300 × 20
15. 200 × 90
16. 600 × 700
17. 500 × 300
18. 400 × 700
19. 800 × 400
20. 700 × 700
21. 4,000 × 8
22. 4,000 × 80
23. 4,000 × 800
24. 4,000 × 8,000
25. 50,000 × 7
26. 50,000 × 70
27. 50,000 × 700
28. 50,000 × 7,000
29. 80 × 40
30. 600 × 30
31. 300 × 300
32. 20 × 7,000
33. 400 × 700
34. 7,000 × 400
35. 70,000 × 40
36. 800 × 40

Divide.

37. 40)160
38. 60)360
39. 20)140
40. 50)500
41. 70)140
42. 80)640
43. 30)180
44. 90)180
45. 4)1,200
46. 40)1,200
47. 40)12,000
48. 30)2,400
49. 60)3,600
50. 70)4,200
51. 50)4,500
52. 30)3,000
53. 400)16,000
54. 200)8,000
55. 400)160,000
56. 700)35,000
57. 800)24,000
58. 600)24,000
59. 300)30,000
60. 900)45,000
61. 43,000 ÷ 10
62. 43,000 ÷ 100
63. 43,000 ÷ 1,000
64. 7,000 ÷ 10

Estimating Products and Quotients

A case of juice contains 24 cartons. A truck is loaded with 275 cases. About how many cartons of juice are on the truck?

Estimate by rounding each factor.

$$\begin{array}{rlr} 275 & \text{is about} & 300 \\ \times\ 24 & \text{is about} & \times\ 20 \\ \hline & & 6{,}000 \end{array}$$

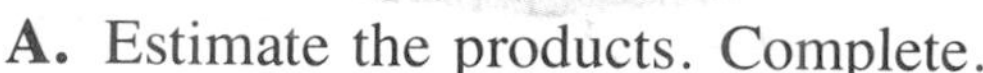

A. Estimate the products. Complete.

1. $\begin{array}{r} 64 \\ \times\ 31 \\ \hline \end{array} \longrightarrow \begin{array}{r} 60 \\ \times\ 30 \\ \hline \end{array}$ **2.** $\begin{array}{r} \$58 \\ \times\ 24 \\ \hline \end{array} \longrightarrow \begin{array}{r} \$60 \\ \times\ 20 \\ \hline \end{array}$

3. $\begin{array}{r} 653 \\ \times\ 56 \\ \hline \end{array} \longrightarrow \begin{array}{r} 700 \\ \times\ 60 \\ \hline \end{array}$ **4.** $\begin{array}{r} 4{,}830 \\ \times\ 750 \\ \hline \end{array} \longrightarrow \begin{array}{r} 5{,}000 \\ \times\ 800 \\ \hline \end{array}$

B. Estimate the products.

5. $\begin{array}{r} 78 \\ \times\ 51 \\ \hline \end{array}$ **6.** $\begin{array}{r} \$364 \\ \times\ 79 \\ \hline \end{array}$ **7.** $\begin{array}{r} 4{,}389 \\ \times\ 72 \\ \hline \end{array}$ **8.** $\begin{array}{r} \$6{,}431 \\ \times\ 893 \\ \hline \end{array}$

C. Estimate quotients by rounding both the divisor and dividend.

Examples $18\overline{)562}$ → $20\overline{)600}$ with quotient 30 ← Estimate

$27\overline{)68}$ → $30\overline{)70}$ with quotient 2 ← Estimate

Estimate the quotients. Complete.

9. $24\overline{)62} \longrightarrow 20\overline{)60}$ **10.** $37\overline{)\$821} \longrightarrow 40\overline{)800}$

11. $71\overline{)5{,}623} \longrightarrow 70\overline{)6{,}000}$ **12.** $253\overline{)71{,}684} \longrightarrow 300\overline{)70{,}000}$

D. Estimate the quotients.

13. $36\overline{)75}$ **14.** $63\overline{)420}$ **15.** $34\overline{)8{,}745}$ **16.** $125\overline{)65{,}120}$

Practice

Estimate the products.

1. 28×31
2. $\$36 \times 59$
3. 54×37
4. 21×45
5. 763×52
6. 681×86
7. 837×34
8. 450×126
9. 453×780
10. 786×431
11. $4{,}321 \times 67$
12. $6{,}512 \times 74$
13. $7{,}099 \times 35$
14. $8{,}312 \times 410$
15. $6{,}394 \times 513$
16. 43×46
17. 491×21
18. 803×194
19. $3{,}102 \times 55$
20. $7{,}732 \times 187$

Estimate the quotients.

21. $24\overline{)79}$
22. $36\overline{)\$78}$
23. $32\overline{)85}$
24. $48\overline{)502}$
25. $42\overline{)\$793}$
26. $25\overline{)912}$
27. $36\overline{)892}$
28. $91\overline{)873}$
29. $26\overline{)5{,}910}$
30. $12\overline{)\$6{,}341}$
31. $37\overline{)2{,}134}$
32. $58\overline{)66{,}178}$
33. $321\overline{)76{,}430}$
34. $478\overline{)21{,}316}$
35. $651\overline{)31{,}416}$

Solve.

36. Some cans of soup are packed 48 to a box. Estimate the number of boxes needed to pack 25,418 cans of soup.

37. A box of doughnuts contains 12 doughnuts. A truck is loaded with 346 boxes of doughnuts. Estimate the number of doughnuts on the truck.

★ 38. Baseballs are packed 20 to a box. There are 362 dozen baseballs to be packed. Estimate the number of boxes needed.

Properties of Operations

Addition Properties	*For all numbers a, b, and c*	*Examples*
Commutative	$a + b = b + a$	$6 + 8 = 8 + 6$
Associative	$(a + b) + c = a + (b + c)$	$(2 + 4) + 7 = 2 + (4 + 7)$
Property of Zero	$a + 0 = a$ $0 + a = a$	$3 + 0 = 3$ $0 + 9 = 9$

Multiplication Properties	*For all numbers a, b, and c*	*Examples*
Commutative	$a \cdot b = b \cdot a$	$7 \times 3 = 3 \times 7$
Associative	$(a \cdot b) \cdot c = a \cdot (b \cdot c)$	$(2 \times 3) \times 4 = 2 \times (3 \times 4)$
Distributive Property of Multiplication over Addition	$a \cdot (b + c) = a \cdot b + a \cdot c$	$2 \times (3 + 4) = (2 \times 3) + (2 \times 4)$
Property of Zero	$a \cdot 0 = 0$ $0 \cdot a = 0$	$4 \times 0 = 0$ $0 \times 8 = 0$
Property of One	$a \cdot 1 = a$ $1 \cdot a = a$	$5 \times 1 = 5$ $1 \times 6 = 6$

A. Name the property used.

1. $8 + (2 + 3) = (8 + 2) + 3$

2. $14 \times 0 = 0$

3. $4 \times (20 + 3) = (4 \times 20) + (4 \times 3)$

4. $45 + 27 = 27 + 45$

5. $7 \times 10 = 10 \times 7$

6. $3 \times (2 \times 4) = (3 \times 2) \times 4$

7. $0 + 23 = 23$

8. $1 \times 35 = 35$

B. Solve. Use the properties.

9. $3 + n = 7 + 3$

10. $8 \times (9 \times 2) = (n \times 9) \times 2$

11. $n \cdot 9 = 0$

12. $8 \cdot 3 = 3 \cdot n$

13. $3 \times (6 + 4) = (3 \times 6) + (3 \times n)$

14. $n + 0 = 42$

15. $31 \cdot n = 31$

16. $(2 + n) + 6 = 2 + (5 + 6)$

Practice

Name the property used.

1. $21 \times (40 + 6) = (21 \times 40) + (21 \times 6)$
2. $57 \times 1 = 57$
3. $151 \times 23 = 23 \times 151$
4. $81 + (90 + 2) = (81 + 90) + 2$
5. $0 + 19 = 19$
6. $56 \times (71 \times 38) = (56 \times 71) \times 38$
7. $16 + 32 = 32 + 16$
8. $0 \times 75 = 0$
9. ★ $3 + (17 + 4) = (17 + 4) + 3$
10. ★ $32 \times (80 \times 91) = 32 \times (91 \times 80)$

Solve. Use the properties.

11. $4 + n = 5 + 4$
12. $(5 + 6) + n = 5 + (6 + 8)$
13. $26 \cdot n = 0$
14. $9 \times (n + 6) = (9 \times 4) + (9 \times 6)$
15. $6 \cdot n = 3 \cdot 6$
16. $1 \cdot n = 18$
17. $3 \times (4 \times 9) = (3 \times n) \times 9$
18. ★ $(6 \times 23) + (7 \times 23) = n \times 23$

FIND OUT!
Calculator Activity

Study this pattern.

$1^2 = 1$

$2^2 = 1 + 2 + 1$

$3^2 = 1 + 2 + 3 + 2 + 1$

$4^2 = 1 + 2 + 3 + 4 + 3 + 2 + 1$

$5^2 = 1 + 2 + 3 + 4 + 5 + 4 + 3 + 2 + 1$

1. Check each equation above.
2. Continue the pattern for 6^2.
3. Check your answer on a calculator.
4. Continue the pattern for 7^2, 8^2, and 9^2. Check.

Problem Solving

Solve.

1. A few years ago, there were 708 commercial television stations. That same year there were 253 educational television stations. How many more commercial than educational stations existed that year? [HINT: Subtract.]

2. Northern Appliances was selling model number 1063 television for $469 and $33 tax and $10 delivery charge. Bob's Appliances was selling it for $500 and $35 tax with no delivery charge. Which is the better buy?

3. One year, $2,785,000 was spent on network advertising. In the same year, S2,125,000 was spent on spot advertising and $1,665,000 was spent on local advertising. What was the total number of dollars spent on television advertising?

4. A recent survey reported that 51,230,000 homes have at least one color television set and 18,370,000 other homes have black and white sets. How many more homes have color television sets?

5. Coral dish detergent had 4 thirty-second commercials aired one day. If it cost the company $55,000 a minute for television time, how much did the company spend to air the 4 commercials?

★ 6. A student survey reported that 7 out of every 10 eighth graders at Madison School watch television in the evening. There are 350 eighth graders. Estimate how many watch television in the evening.

Chapter Review

Add. *(24)*

1. 5,317 + 7,879

2. 81,756 + 7,975

3. 314,437 835,274 + 96,014

Subtract. *(26)*

4. 8,135 − 5,916

5. 37,156 − 8,529

6. 30,000 − 17,494

Estimate the sums. *(28)*

7. 1,661 + 1,857

8. 6,437 + 745

9. 7,801 528 + 4,039

Estimate the differences. *(28)*

10. 4,197 − 2,213

11. 64,201 − 3,198

12. 11,689 − 711

Multiply. *(34, 36)*

13. 6,517 × 6

14. $736 × 58

15. 6,286 × 408

Divide. *(38, 40)*

16. 4)848

17. 23)115

18. 43)$13,588

Estimate the products and quotients. *(46)*

19. 517 × 66

20. 7,721 × 18

21. 8,178 × 328

22. 63)6,245

23. 62)18,301

Solve. *(32, 50)*

24. Les bought 2 pieces of lumber each 12 ft long and 1 piece 8 ft long. What was the total length of the 3 pieces?

25. There are 725 commercial television stations and 258 educational television stations. How many television stations are there in all?

Chapter Test

Add *(24)*

1. $\begin{array}{r} 4{,}378 \\ +\ 7{,}516 \\ \hline \end{array}$

2. $\begin{array}{r} 91{,}568 \\ +\ \ 9{,}625 \\ \hline \end{array}$

3. $\begin{array}{r} 23{,}823 \\ 714{,}278 \\ +\ \ \ 8{,}925 \\ \hline \end{array}$

Subtract. *(26)*

4. $\begin{array}{r} 8{,}462 \\ -\ 1{,}839 \\ \hline \end{array}$

5. $\begin{array}{r} 16{,}343 \\ -\ \ 7{,}619 \\ \hline \end{array}$

6. $\begin{array}{r} 40{,}000 \\ -\ 16{,}257 \\ \hline \end{array}$

Estimate the sums. *(28)*

7. $\begin{array}{r} 8{,}418 \\ +\ 4{,}765 \\ \hline \end{array}$

8. $\begin{array}{r} 51{,}003 \\ +\ \ 7{,}114 \\ \hline \end{array}$

9. $\begin{array}{r} 17{,}813 \\ 28{,}902 \\ +\ \ 4{,}158 \\ \hline \end{array}$

Estimate the differences. *(28)*

10. $\begin{array}{r} 56{,}713 \\ -\ 42{,}834 \\ \hline \end{array}$

11. $\begin{array}{r} 19{,}621 \\ -\ \ 8{,}577 \\ \hline \end{array}$

12. $\begin{array}{r} 68{,}001 \\ -\ \ \ \ 982 \\ \hline \end{array}$

Multiply. *(34, 36)*

13. $\begin{array}{r} 6{,}417 \\ \times\ 7 \\ \hline \end{array}$

14. $\begin{array}{r} \$589 \\ \times\ 24 \\ \hline \end{array}$

15. $\begin{array}{r} 4{,}845 \\ \times\ 307 \\ \hline \end{array}$

Divide. *(38, 40)*

16. $3\overline{)969}$

17. $21\overline{)147}$

18. $62\overline{)21{,}204}$

Estimate the products and quotients. *(46)*

19. $\begin{array}{r} 634 \\ \times\ 17 \\ \hline \end{array}$

20. $\begin{array}{r} 345 \\ \times\ 836 \\ \hline \end{array}$

21. $\begin{array}{r} 3{,}734 \\ \times\ 529 \\ \hline \end{array}$

22. $32\overline{)5{,}861}$

23. $59\overline{)17{,}500}$

Solve. *(32, 50)*

24. Charlotte drove 75 km in the morning and 116 km in the afternoon. How far did she drive in all?

25. A survey showed that 39,320,000 homes have only 1 television set and 31,880,000 homes have 2 or more sets. How many homes have television sets?

Basic Skills Check

1. Ms. Barbiero bought a television set for $399.50, a refrigerator for $289.99, and a stove for $249.49. What was the total cost?

A $839.89 B $938.88

C $938.89 D $938.98

2. Milton is on a diet. He lost 7 lb the first month, 8 lb the second month, gained 5 lb the third month, and lost 12 lb the fourth month. What was his net loss for the 4 months?

E 32 lb F 27 lb

G 22 lb H 8 lb

3. What is the sales tax on $0.49?

Price	*Sales Tax*
$0.30 to $0.42	3¢
$0.43 to $0.54	4¢
$0.55 to $0.67	5¢

A 3¢ B 4¢

C 5¢ D 49¢

4. John's pay envelope contained 6 twenties, 3 tens, 1 five, 4 ones, 1 quarter, 2 dimes, and 4 pennies. How much money did he receive?

E $164.49 F $159. 49

G $159.39 H $158.49

5. Brenda is 5 years older than Ryan. Ryan is 12 years old. How old is Brenda?

A 25 B 17

C 20 D 7

6. According to the thermometer, what is the temperature?

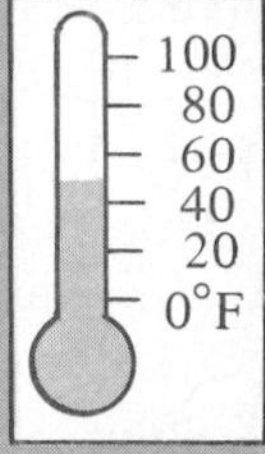

E 30°F F 40°F

G 50°F H 60°F

7. The Aurelios left their house at 8:35 am and returned home at 1:15 pm. How long were they gone?

A 3 hours, 40 minutes

B 4 hours, 40 minutes

C 5 hours, 40 minutes

D 7 hours, 20 minutes

8. According to the scale, what is the mass of the tomato?

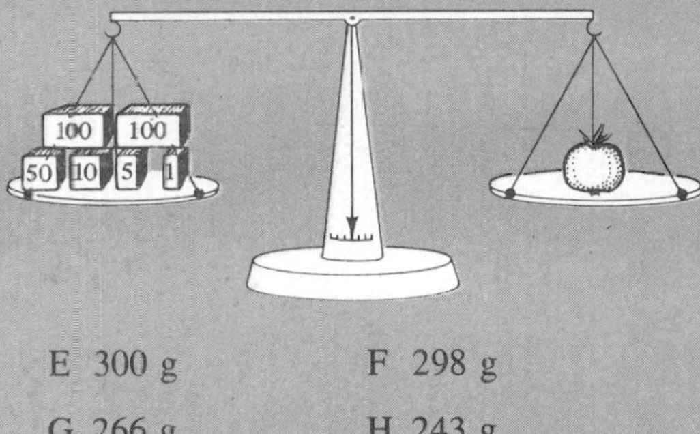

E 300 g F 298 g

G 266 g H 243 g

9. Sheila earns $896 a month. Estimate her salary for a year.

A $8,000 B $9,000

C $80,000 D $90,000

The Cover-Up Technique

Solve $x + 20 = 45$.
Cover up the variable, x. $x + 20 = 45$
Think: What number plus 20 is equal to 45?
Write: $25 + 20 = 45$
So, $x = 25$

The solution of the equation is 25.

A. Solve. Use the cover-up technique.

Example $x - 3 = 4$
Cover up the variable, x.
Think: What number minus 3 is equal to 4?
Write: $7 - 3 = 4$
So, $x = 7$

1. $x + 15 = 30$ **2.** $x + 100 = 250$ **3.** $x - 2 = 7$

B. $2x$ means $2 \cdot x$.

Solve $2x = 20$.
Think: 2 times what number is 20?
$2 \cdot 10 = 20$
So, $x = 10$

$\frac{x}{3}$ means $x \div 3$.

Solve $\frac{x}{3} = 6$.
Think: What number divided by 3 is 6?
$18 \div 3 = 6$
So, $x = 18$

Solve. Use the cover-up technique.

4. $3x = 12$ **5.** $\frac{x}{5} = 3$ **6.** $\frac{x}{4} = 4$

CHAPTER 3
EQUATIONS

C. Sometimes you use the cover-up technique twice.

$2x + 3 = 17$
$\blacksquare + 3 = 17$
$14 + 3 = 17$
So, $2x = 14$
$2 \cdot \blacksquare = 14$
$2 \cdot 7 = 14$
$x = 7$

Check

$2x + 3$	17
$2 \cdot 7 + 3$	17
$14 + 3$	

So, 7 is the solution.

Solve and check.

7. $3x + 4 = 19$ **8.** $5x - 2 = 13$ **9.** $\frac{x}{2} + 3 = 5$

Practice

Solve and check.

1. $x + 9 = 14$ **2.** $x + 18 = 31$ **3.** $x - 4 = 11$

4. $7x = 42$ **5.** $30x = 240$ **6.** $\frac{x}{2} = 9$

7. $\frac{x}{3} = 4$ **8.** $2x + 4 = 12$ **9.** $3x - 1 = 14$

10. A patchwork quilt has 64 squares. There are 8 rows. How many squares are in each row? [HINT: $8 \cdot x = 64$]

Doing and Undoing

Think of a number. *Add* 2. From the sum *subtract* 2. What is the result?

Suppose you thought of 8:

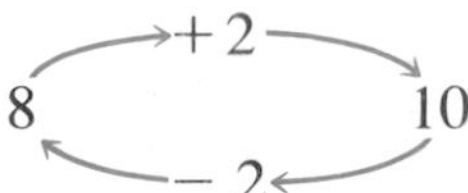

⑧ + 2 − 2 = ⑧

Adding and subtracting the same number undo each other.

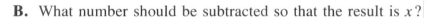

A. Start with any number. Represent the number by x.

1. Add 5. What is the result?

2. Subtract 5 from $x + 5$. What is the result?

3. Complete. $x + 5 - 5 =$ __?__

B. What number should be subtracted so that the result is x?

4. $x + 7$ **5.** $x + 4$ **6.** $x + \frac{3}{4}$ **7.** $x + 0.4$

C. Start with x.

8. Subtract 3. What is the result?

9. Add 3 to $x - 3$. What is the result?

10. Complete. $x - 3 + 3 =$ __?__

D. What number should be added so that the result is x?

11. $x - 2$ **12.** $x - 9$ **13.** $x - \frac{1}{2}$ **14.** $x - 0.4$

E. Multiplying and dividing undo each other.

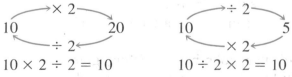

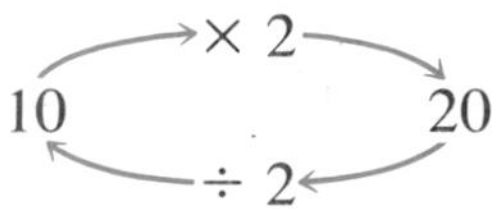

$10 \times 2 \div 2 = 10$

÷ 2
10 5
× 2

$10 \div 2 \times 2 = 10$

Tell what to do so that the result is x.

15. $3x$ **16.** $4x$ **17.** $\frac{x}{2}$ **18.** $\frac{x}{5}$

Practice

Tell what to do so that the result is x.

1. $x + 9$ **2.** $x + 12$ **3.** $x + 23$ **4.** $x + 1$

5. $x + \frac{1}{4}$ **6.** $x + \frac{5}{8}$ **7.** $x + 0.7$ **8.** $x + 0.06$

9. $x - 7$ **10.** $x - 8$ **11.** $x - 12$ **12.** $x - 14$

13. $x - \frac{1}{4}$ **14.** $x - \frac{2}{3}$ **15.** $x - 0.3$ **16.** $x - 0.016$

17. $2x$ **18.** $5x$ **19.** $8x$ **20.** $10x$

21. $6x$ **22.** $0.9x$ **23.** $0.15x$ **24.** $0.20x$

25. $\frac{x}{3}$ **26.** $\frac{x}{4}$ **27.** $\frac{x}{6}$ **28.** $\frac{x}{7}$

29. $\frac{x}{0.2}$ **30.** $\frac{x}{0.09}$ **31.** $\frac{x}{1.2}$ **32.** $\frac{x}{1.5}$

33. $x + 8$ **34.** $x - 2$ **35.** $\frac{x}{8}$ **36.** $7x$

37. $x + 0.2$ **38.** $x - 0.07$ **39.** $\frac{x}{0.8}$ **40.** $0.3x$

41. $x + \frac{7}{8}$ **42.** $x - \frac{3}{4}$ ★**43.** $\frac{3}{10}x$ ★**44.** $\frac{2}{3}x$

FIND OUT!
Brainteasers

1. There are some books on a shelf. All are mathematics books except for two. All are story books except for two. All are science books except for two. How many books are on the shelf?

2. Helene has 8 more baseball cards than John has. If Helene gives John 6 baseball cards, John will have how many more baseball cards than Helene?

Equivalent Equations

	Equation	Solution
	$x = 7$	
Adding 1 to both sides ⟶	$x + 1 = 8$	7
Adding 2 to both sides ⟶	$x + 2 = 9$	7
Adding 3 to both sides ⟶	$x + 3 = 10$	7

These equations are equivalent equations. They have the same solution.

▶ Adding the same number to both sides of an equation does not change the solution. This is called the *addition property for equations*.

A. Which equations are equivalent?

1. $x = 2$; $x + 3 = 2 + 3$; $x + 1 = 2$

2. $y = 3$; $y + 4 = 7$; $y + 5 = 9$

B. Write 2 equivalent equations. Use the addition property for equations.

3. $x = 7$ **4.** $b = 12$ **5.** $c = 4$ **6.** $d = 24$

Look at these equivalent equations.

	Equation	Solution
	$x + 3 = 12$	9
Subtracting 1 from both sides ⟶	$x + 2 = 11$	9
Subtracting 2 from both sides ⟶	$x + 1 = 10$	9
Subtracting 3 from both sides ⟶	$x = 9$	9

▶ Subtracting the same number from both sides of an equation does not change the solution. This is called the *subtraction property for equations*.

C. Write 2 equivalent equations. Use the subtraction property for equations.

7. $x + 7 = 12$ **8.** $d + 8 = 14$ **9.** $n + 4 = 15$ **10.** $r + 6 = 10$

D. Which are pairs of equivalent equations?

11. $r - 2 = 13 - 2$; $r = 13$ **12.** $z + 7 = 10$; $z + 7 + 7 = 10 - 7$

Practice

Write 2 equivalent equations. Use the addition property for equations.

1. $x = 3$ **2.** $x = 4$ **3.** $x = 7$ **4.** $x = 13$

Write 2 equivalent equations. Use the subtraction property for equations.

5. $x + 6 = 11$ **6.** $x + 7 = 15$ **7.** $x + 12 = 20$ **8.** $x + 14 = 30$

Which are pairs of equivalent equations?

9. $x + 1 = 5 + 1$; $x = 6$

10. $x + 8 = 2 + 8$; $x + 2 = 8$

11. $n + 2 = 18 + 2$; $n = 18$

12. $x - 1 = 19 - 1$; $x = 18$

13. $z = 14$; $z + 1 = 14 + 1$

14. $t + 1 = 8$; $t + 1 - 1 = 9 - 1$

15. $f + 4 = 7$; $f = 11$

16. $e - 9 = 22$; $e = 31$

17. $x + 3 - 3 = 9 - 3$; $x = 4$

18. $n - 8 + 8 = 11 + 8$; $n = 19$

★ **19.** $7 + y - 3 = 9$; $y = 12$

★ **20.** $4 + y + 3 = 13$; $y = 6$

★ **21.** $15 = 6 + d - 9$; $d = 9$

★ **22.** $11 - 8 = 8 - p$; $p = 5$

FIND OUT!

Calculator Activity

A special symbol is used for the product of consecutive numbers. The following examples illustrate this new symbol.

$1! = 1$ Read 1! as 1 factorial.

$2! = 1 \times 2$, or 2 Read 2! as 2 factorial.

$3! = 1 \times 2 \times 3$, or 6 Read 3! as 3 factorial.

Use a calculator to compute each.

1. 6! **2.** 7! **3.** 8! **4.** 9! **5.** 10! **6.** 11!

Solving Equations

Solve $x + 7 = 11$. Check your answer.

To get x alone, subtract 7 from both sides of the equation.

$$x + 7 = 11$$
$$x + 7 - 7 = 11 - 7$$
$$x = 4$$

Check

$x + 7$	11
$4 + 7$	11
11	

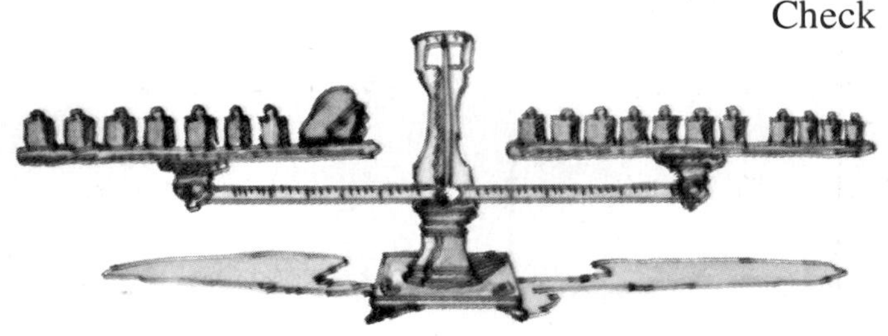

A. What should be subtracted from both sides of the equation to get x alone?

1. $x + 4 = 7$ **2.** $x + 5 = 12$ **3.** $x + 8 = 15$

B. Solve and check.

4. $x + 4 = 7$ **5.** $x + 5 = 12$ **6.** $x + 8 = 15$

C. What should be added to both sides of the equation to get x alone?

7. $x - 4 = 7$ **8.** $x - 5 = 12$ **9.** $x - 8 = 15$

D. Solve and check.

Example $x - 4 = 12$

$$x - 4 = 12$$
$$x - 4 + 4 = 12 + 4$$
$$x = 16$$

Check

$x - 4$	12
$16 - 4$	12
12	

10. $x - 4 = 7$ **11.** $x - 5 = 12$ **12.** $x - 8 = 15$

E. Solve and check.

13. $b + 9 = 14$ **14.** $13 + n = 22$ **15.** $45 = t + 29$

16. $m - 6 = 8$ **17.** $s - 32 = 14$ **18.** $28 = y - 11$

Practice

Solve and check.

1. $x + 3 = 8$

2. $n + 7 = 10$

3. $t + 5 = 12$

4. $z + 13 = 37$

5. $f + 18 = 45$

6. $e + 23 = 35$

7. $9 = x + 1$

8. $8 = c + 4$

9. $7 = b + 5$

10. $12 = d + 3$

11. $37 = x + 19$

12. $45 = r + 29$

13. $x + 17 = 123$

14. $y + 256 = 572$

15. $t + 173 = 426$

16. $323 = n + 58$

17. $199 = z + 47$

18. $387 = b + 241$

19. $a - 7 = 9$

20. $b - 14 = 17$

21. $d - 3 = 10$

22. $c - 21 = 45$

23. $x - 17 = 52$

24. $z - 25 = 41$

25. $37 = r - 17$

26. $39 = n - 10$

27. $12 = t - 7$

28. $8 = a - 5$

29. $12 = e - 9$

30. $14 = f - 3$

31. $b - 524 = 71$

32. $t - 36 = 649$

33. $1 = z - 417$

34. $112 = x - 42$

35. $413 = y - 58$

36. $x - 97 = 180$

37. $n + 12 = 48$

38. $r - 75 = 82$

39. $t + 24 = 87$

40. $f - 21 = 18$

41. $273 = b + 148$

42. $a - 73 = 572$

43. $c - 1 = 9$

44. $x + 3 = 16$

45. $5 + z = 27$

46. $b + 426 = 811$

★ **47.** $12 + f + 6 = 20$

★ **48.** $253 = 17 + z - 10$

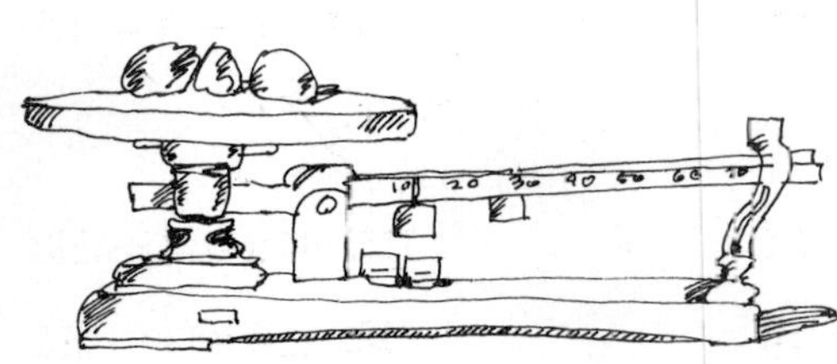

Keeping Fit

Add.

1. $\begin{array}{r} 543 \\ +\ 652 \\ \hline \end{array}$

2. $\begin{array}{r} 439 \\ +\ 168 \\ \hline \end{array}$

3. $\begin{array}{r} 4{,}511 \\ +\ 2{,}689 \\ \hline \end{array}$

4. $\begin{array}{r} 7{,}315 \\ +\ \ 856 \\ \hline \end{array}$

5. $\begin{array}{r} 36{,}618 \\ +\ 27{,}179 \\ \hline \end{array}$

6. $\begin{array}{r} 41{,}017 \\ +\ \ 9{,}043 \\ \hline \end{array}$

7. $\begin{array}{r} 8{,}036 \\ 1{,}920 \\ +\ 3{,}479 \\ \hline \end{array}$

8. $\begin{array}{r} 12{,}579 \\ 3{,}008 \\ 73{,}861 \\ +\ \ 420 \\ \hline \end{array}$

9. $\begin{array}{r} 868{,}413 \\ 93{,}016 \\ 234{,}526 \\ +\ 68{,}234 \\ \hline \end{array}$

10. $\begin{array}{r} 3{,}416{,}812 \\ 9{,}236{,}014 \\ 167{,}312 \\ 43{,}091 \\ +\ 9{,}234{,}185 \\ \hline \end{array}$

Subtract.

11. $\begin{array}{r} 927 \\ -\ 342 \\ \hline \end{array}$

12. $\begin{array}{r} 3{,}519 \\ -\ 1{,}736 \\ \hline \end{array}$

13. $\begin{array}{r} 8{,}634 \\ -\ \ 557 \\ \hline \end{array}$

14. $\begin{array}{r} 63{,}295 \\ -\ 48{,}039 \\ \hline \end{array}$

15. $\begin{array}{r} 78{,}134 \\ -\ \ 9{,}256 \\ \hline \end{array}$

16. $\begin{array}{r} 427{,}631 \\ -\ 275{,}988 \\ \hline \end{array}$

17. $\begin{array}{r} 541{,}397 \\ -\ \ 95{,}438 \\ \hline \end{array}$

18. $\begin{array}{r} 9{,}831{,}245 \\ -\ \ 760{,}098 \\ \hline \end{array}$

19. $\begin{array}{r} 6{,}000 \\ -\ 4{,}508 \\ \hline \end{array}$

20. $\begin{array}{r} 37{,}000 \\ -\ 18{,}124 \\ \hline \end{array}$

21. $\begin{array}{r} 29{,}003 \\ -\ \ 8{,}754 \\ \hline \end{array}$

22. $\begin{array}{r} 316{,}004 \\ -\ \ 94{,}625 \\ \hline \end{array}$

Multiply.

23. $\begin{array}{r} 3{,}248 \\ \times\ 8 \\ \hline \end{array}$

24. $\begin{array}{r} 516 \\ \times\ 23 \\ \hline \end{array}$

25. $\begin{array}{r} 3{,}481 \\ \times\ 68 \\ \hline \end{array}$

26. $\begin{array}{r} 15{,}088 \\ \times\ 41 \\ \hline \end{array}$

27. $\begin{array}{r} 912 \\ \times\ 296 \\ \hline \end{array}$

28. $\begin{array}{r} 4{,}168 \\ \times\ 257 \\ \hline \end{array}$

29. $\begin{array}{r} 20{,}461 \\ \times\ 318 \\ \hline \end{array}$

30. $\begin{array}{r} 7{,}239 \\ \times\ 1{,}451 \\ \hline \end{array}$

31. $\begin{array}{r} 647 \\ \times\ 30 \\ \hline \end{array}$

32. $\begin{array}{r} 821 \\ \times\ 509 \\ \hline \end{array}$

33. $\begin{array}{r} 2{,}417 \\ \times\ 408 \\ \hline \end{array}$

34. $\begin{array}{r} 1{,}560 \\ \times\ 7{,}003 \\ \hline \end{array}$

Divide.

35. $2\overline{)868}$

36. $7\overline{)147}$

37. $8\overline{)336}$

38. $6\overline{)424}$

39. $9\overline{)3{,}319}$

40. $6\overline{)31{,}416}$

41. $15\overline{)495}$

42. $23\overline{)138}$

43. $37\overline{)727}$

44. $63\overline{)9{,}054}$

45. $41\overline{)17{,}356}$

46. $23\overline{)93{,}840}$

47. $156\overline{)312}$

48. $238\overline{)4{,}998}$

49. $852\overline{)7{,}668}$

50. $311\overline{)41{,}026}$

51. $526\overline{)15{,}387}$

52. $792\overline{)946{,}305}$

53. $407\overline{)235{,}517}$

54. $127\overline{)508{,}254}$

Mid-Chapter Review

Which are pairs of equivalent equations? *(58)*

1. $x + 4 = 7 + 4;\ x = 28$

2. $x - 9 = 10 - 9;\ x = 1$

3. $5 + 2 = x + 2;\ x = 5$

4. $10 - 3 = x - 3;\ x = 7$

Solve and check. *(60)*

5. $x + 2 = 11$

6. $x + 4 = 16$

7. $x + 3 = 12$

8. $x + 41 = 70$

9. $x + 108 = 213$

10. $356 = x + 40$

11. $x - 3 = 7$

12. $x - 1 = 19$

13. $x - 11 = 20$

14. $x - 52 = 107$

15. $x - 39 = 21$

16. $129 = x - 57$

17. $x + 6 = 15$

18. $8 = b + 3$

19. $c - 3 = 4$

20. $249 = z - 128$

21. $b + 19 = 41$

22. $12 = n + 5$

23. $x - 19 = 34$

24. $212 = t - 15$

25. $13 = r + 7$

FIND OUT!
Brainteaser

Fill in the empty cells so that the sum of each row, each column, and along each diagonal is 65. Use each number from 1 to 25 only once.

17	24	1	8	15
23	5			16
4		13		
10	12	19		
	18			9

Equivalent Equations for Multiplication

	Equation	*Solution*
	$x = 5$	5
Multiplying both sides by 2 $\longrightarrow$	$2x = 10$	5
Multiplying both sides by 3 $\longrightarrow$	$3x = 15$	5
Multiplying both sides by 4 $\longrightarrow$	$4x = 20$	5

▶ Multiplying both sides of an equation by the same non-zero number does not change the solution. This is called the *multiplication property for equations.*

A. Which equations are equivalent?

1. $x = 2$; $3 \cdot x = 3 \cdot 2$; $5x = 15$

2. $n = 3$; $4 \cdot n = 12$; $2 \cdot n = 6$

B. Write 2 equivalent equations. Use the multiplication property for equations.

3. $x = 4$ **4.** $x = 6$ **5.** $x = 8$ **6.** $x = 0.7$

Look at these equivalent equations.

	Equation	*Solution*
	$4x = 16$	4
Dividing both sides by 2 $\longrightarrow$	$\frac{4x}{2} = \frac{16}{2}$ or $2x = 8$	4
Dividing both sides by 4 $\longrightarrow$	$\frac{4x}{4} = \frac{16}{4}$ or $x = 4$	4

▶ Dividing both sides of an equation by the same non-zero number does not change the solution. This is called the *division property for equations.*

C. Write 2 equivalent equations. Use the division property for equations.

7. $4x = 8$ **8.** $6x = 30$ **9.** $8x = 24$ **10.** $9x = 18$

D. Which are pairs of equivalent equations?

11. $x = 7$; $3 \cdot x = 3 \cdot 7$ **12.** $\frac{x}{2} = 4$; $x = 8$

Practice

Which equations are equivalent?

1. $a = 2$; $3 \cdot a = 3 \cdot 2$; $3a = 6$; $3a = 9$

2. $x = 4$; $3x = 12$; $4x = 16$; $2 \cdot x = 2 \cdot 4$

3. $z = 6$; $\frac{z}{2} = 8$; $\frac{z}{2} = \frac{6}{2}$; $z = 4$

4. $c = 9$; $\frac{c}{3} = \frac{9}{3}$; $\frac{c}{3} = 27$; $\frac{c}{2} = 16$

Write 2 equivalent equations. Use the multiplication property for equations.

5. $n = 6$
6. $r = 8$
7. $x = 3$
8. $z = 12$

Write 2 equivalent equations. Use the division property for equations.

9. $2b = 10$
10. $8d = 32$
11. $4n = 12$
12. $15r = 30$

Which are pairs of equivalent equations?

13. $2z = 2 \cdot 8$; $z = 16$

14. $3x = 15$; $x = 3$

15. $\frac{n}{4} = 20$; $n = 5$

16. $\frac{t}{6} = 7$; $t = 42$

17. $6x = 42$; $x = 7$

18. $\frac{x}{3} = 6$; $x = 2$

★ 19. $\frac{3x}{4} = 9$; $x = 3$

★ 20. $\frac{2x}{3} = 8$; $x = 12$

FIND OUT!

Brainteasers

1. The sum of 2 numbers is 70. Their difference is 18. What are the numbers?

2. The product of 2 numbers is 36. Their sum is 15. What are the numbers?

More Solving Equations

Solve $2x = 18$. Check your answer.

To get x alone, divide both sides of the equation by 2.

$$2x = 18$$
$$\frac{2x}{2} = \frac{18}{2}$$
$$x = 9$$

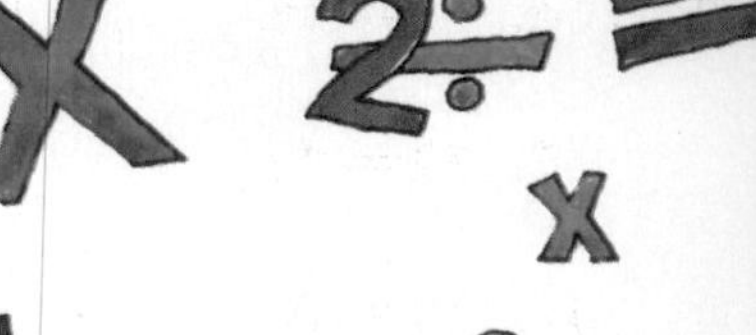

Check

$2x$	18
$2 \cdot 9$	18
18	

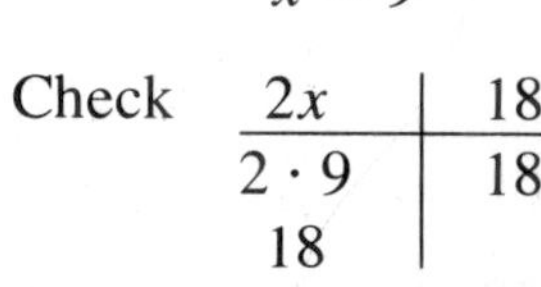

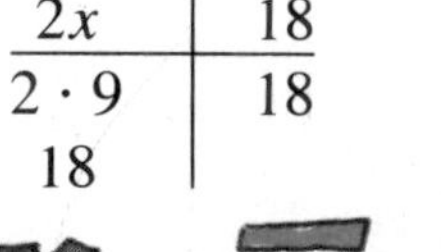

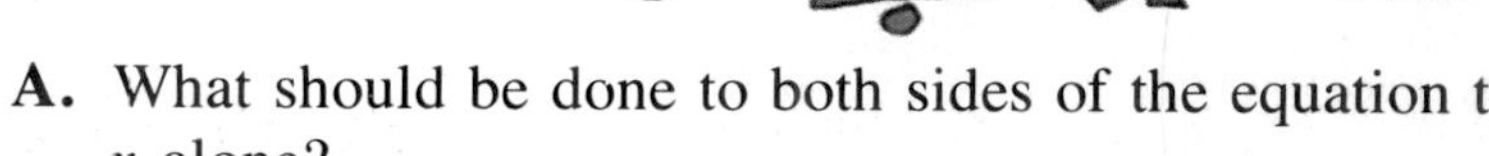

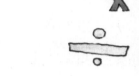

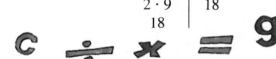

A. What should be done to both sides of the equation to get x alone?

1. $3x = 48$ **2.** $24 = \frac{x}{3}$ **3.** $12x = 156$

B. Solve $\frac{x}{4} = 10$.

4. What should be done to both sides of the equation to get x alone?

5. Complete $\frac{x}{4} \cdot$ __?__ $= 10 \cdot$ __?__

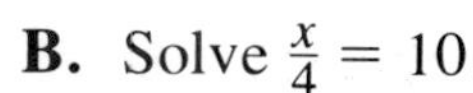

6. Simplify $\frac{x}{4} \cdot 4 = 10 \cdot 4$. What equivalent equation do you get?

7. What is the solution of $\frac{x}{4} = 10$?

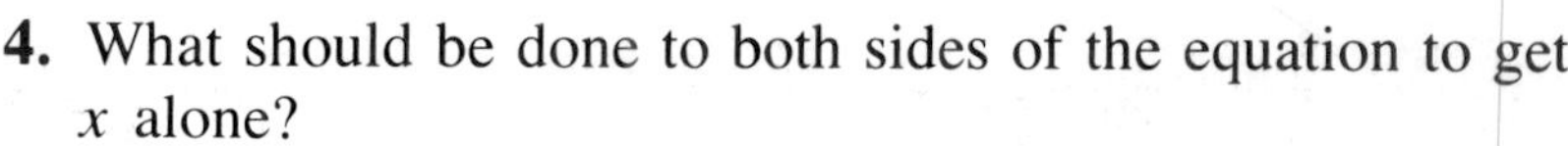

C. Solve.

8. $3x = 48$ **9.** $24 = \frac{x}{3}$ **10.** $12x = 156$ **11.** $\frac{x}{2} = 17$

D. Solve and check.

Example

$$\frac{x}{2} = 16$$
$$2 \cdot \frac{x}{2} = 16 \cdot 2$$
$$x = 32$$

Check

$\frac{x}{2}$	16
$\frac{32}{2}$	16
16	

12. $\frac{x}{4} = 7$ **13.** $5x = 35$ **14.** $14x = 84$ **15.** $24 = \frac{x}{13}$

Practice

Solve and check.

1. $2x = 8$
2. $3y = 15$
3. $4z = 32$
4. $5r = 45$
5. $7n = 42$
6. $8a = 64$
7. $32 = 4c$
8. $16 = 2d$
9. $42 = 6k$
10. $18 = 3t$
11. $35 = 7z$
12. $72 = 9r$
13. $3n = 126$
14. $4t = 196$
15. $17t = 102$
16. $360 = 4a$
17. $483 = 7b$
18. $396 = 18c$
19. $\frac{d}{2} = 3$
20. $\frac{t}{4} = 1$
21. $\frac{r}{3} = 6$
22. $7 = \frac{s}{3}$
23. $9 = \frac{k}{5}$
24. $17 = \frac{r}{4}$
25. $15 = \frac{d}{5}$
26. $\frac{n}{3} = 71$
27. $\frac{t}{4} = 29$
28. $\frac{z}{3} = 7$
29. $\frac{x}{4} = 9$
30. $\frac{d}{7} = 8$
31. $27 = \frac{c}{9}$
32. $301 = \frac{e}{4}$
33. $809 = \frac{a}{3}$
34. $\frac{x}{21} = 48$
35. $\frac{r}{83} = 526$
36. $\frac{n}{129} = 26$
37. $2t = 106$
38. $\frac{b}{15} = 6$
39. $5 = \frac{c}{7}$
40. $8x = 104$
41. ★ $\frac{3}{5}x = 15$
42. ★ $\frac{5}{6}x = 30$

Problem Solving: Broken-Line Graphs

Broken-line graphs are usually used to show a trend or to make comparisons.

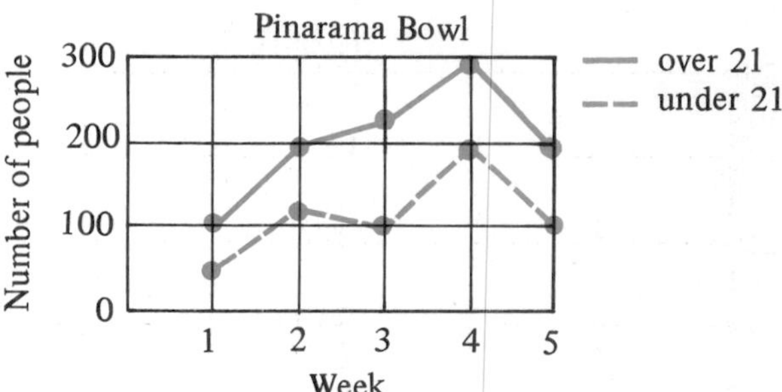

A. Look at the broken-line graph above.

1. How many people over 21 used the bowling alley during the third week?
2. How many people under 21 used the bowling alley during the third week?
3. How many more people over 21 than under 21 used the bowling alley during the third week?
4. In general, do more people over 21 or under 21 use the bowling alley?
5. What is the general trend of people over 21 using the bowling alley? Is it up or down?

B. Look at the broken-line graph at the right. Sometimes 2 broken-line graphs may intersect.

6. How much were the record sales for the fourth week?
7. During which weeks were the record sales greater than the tape sales?
8. About how much more was taken in from the sale of records than from the sale of tapes during the second week?
9. What can you say about the trend in tape sales?

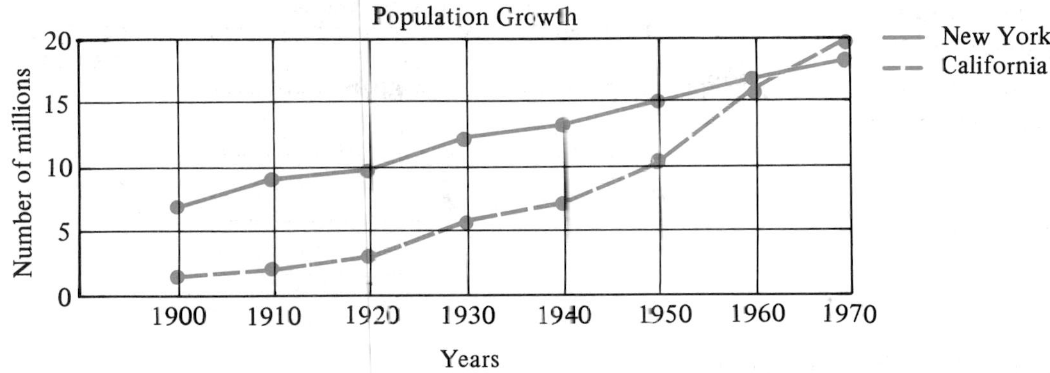

Answer the questions about the broken-line graph above.

1. The population growths of which two states are shown?
2. What was the approximate population of New York State in 1950?
3. What was the approximate population of California in 1950?
4. How much greater was the population of New York State than California in 1950?
5. What is the trend of population growth for New York State?
6. What is the trend of population growth for California?
7. Which state is increasing in population more quickly?

Answer the questions about the broken-line graph at the right.

8. What was Amy's score on the second test?
9. What was the class average on the fifth test?
10. How do Amy's test scores compare with the class average?
11. What is the trend for Amy's scores?

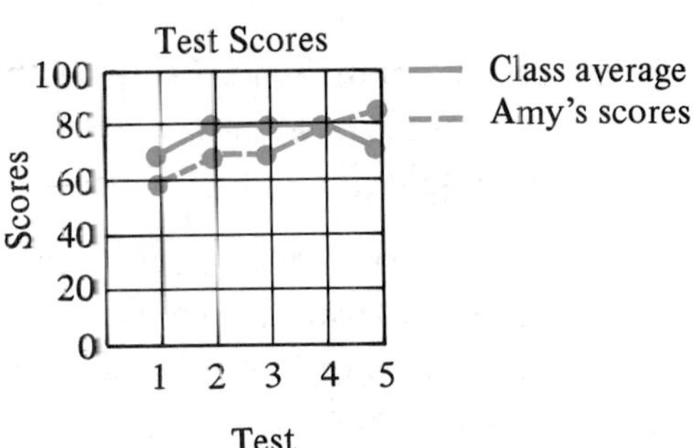

Using Two Equation Properties

Sometimes it is necessary to use 2 equation properties to solve an equation.

Solve $2x + 3 = 13$. Check your answer.

Think: Get $2x$ alone by subtracting 3 from both sides. To get x alone, divide both sides of the equation by 2.

$$2x + 3 = 13$$
$$2x + 3 - 3 = 13 - 3$$
$$2x = 10$$
$$\frac{2x}{2} = \frac{10}{2}$$
$$x = 5$$

Check

$2x + 3$	13
$2 \cdot 5 + 3$	13
$10 + 3$	
13	

The solution of $2x + 3 = 13$ is 5.

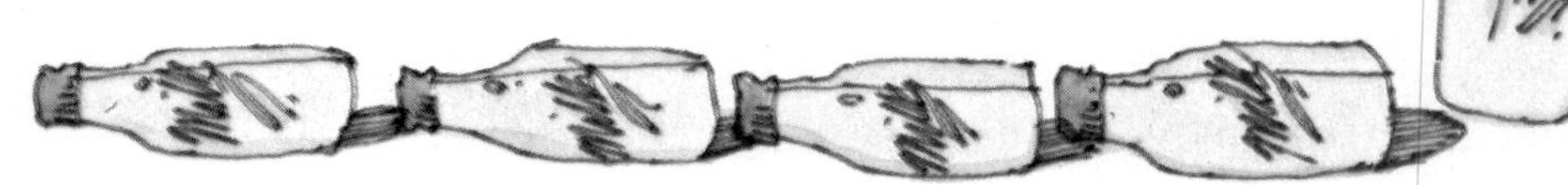

A. Solve $\frac{n}{2} - 4 = 7$. Check.

1. What should be done to get $\frac{n}{2}$ alone?
2. Complete. $\frac{n}{2} - 4 + \underline{\ ?\ } = 7 + \underline{\ ?\ }$
3. Simplify $\frac{n}{2} - 4 + 4 = 7 + 4$. What equivalent equation do you get?
4. Write an equivalent equation with n alone.
5. What is the solution of $\frac{n}{2} - 4 = 7$?
6. Check the solution in $\frac{n}{2} - 4 = 7$.

B. Solve and check.

7. $3a + 7 = 25$
8. $36 = 2b - 10$
9. $4c + 12 = 52$
10. $6 = \frac{d}{2} - 2$
11. $\frac{e}{4} + 3 = 19$
12. $\frac{f}{6} - 2 = 5$

Solve and check.

1. $3x + 4 = 19$
2. $4c + 7 = 31$
3. $7 = 3r + 1$
4. $2z + 19 = 51$
5. $3t - 18 = 57$
6. $9 = 2n + 1$
7. $59 = 3f + 8$
8. $62 = 8b + 6$
9. $421 = 10c + 11$
10. $3x - 1 = 8$
11. $4e - 7 = 21$
12. $8 = 3w - 16$
13. $7x - 21 = 35$
14. $9x - 27 = 72$
15. $18 = 2x - 20$
16. $21 = 2z - 9$
17. $43 = 8n - 13$
18. $500 = 9r - 103$
19. $\frac{x}{2} + 3 = 6$
20. $\frac{c}{4} + 7 = 10$
21. $\frac{e}{5} + 5 = 13$
22. $\frac{n}{5} + 7 = 12$
23. $\frac{z}{4} + 6 = 8$
24. $\frac{n}{8} + 1 = 4$
25. $\frac{m}{11} + 15 = 17$
26. $\frac{f}{9} + 18 = 25$
27. $15 = \frac{c}{11} + 8$
28. $\frac{z}{7} - 1 = 6$
29. $\frac{x}{3} - 2 = 3$
30. $\frac{r}{2} - 5 = 8$
31. $\frac{t}{5} - 7 = 2$
32. $\frac{n}{8} - 3 = 4$
33. $\frac{v}{50} - 32 = 20$
34. $\frac{w}{2} - 8 = 15$
35. $11 = \frac{z}{9} - 5$
36. $120 = \frac{t}{16} - 4$
37. $\frac{f}{2} + 3 = 12$
38. $5x - 3 = 12$
39. $8t + 1 = 17$
40. $40 = 3r - 2$
41. $100 = \frac{z}{7} - 85$
42. $4n + 5 = 29$
43. $\frac{x}{6} + 5 = 23$
44. $22x - 16 = 50$
45. $4x + 12 = 76$

★ 46. $\frac{2x}{3} = 6$

★ 47. $17 + x - 2 = 20$

★ 48. $\frac{3}{4}x + 1 = 4$

★ Solve.

49. Bruce filled 12 boxes with the same number of bottles and had 3 bottles left over. He started out with 135 bottles. How many bottles were placed in each box?

50. Janet cut a piece of wood into 2 equal pieces for book shelves. She cut 50 cm from one of the two pieces. It was then 150 cm long. How long was the original piece?

Solving Inequalities

Solve $x + 1 < 7$. Replacements for x: 0, 1, 2, . . . , 10.

To help solve an inequality, solve the related equation.

$x + 1 < 7 \longleftarrow$ related equation $\longrightarrow x + 1 = 7$

$$x + 1 - 1 = 7 - 1$$
$$x = 6$$

Try 6 in $x + 1 < 7$: $6 + 1 < 7$. False. So 6 is not a solution.
Try a number less than 6 in $x + 1 < 7$: $5 + 1 < 7$. True.
So, each number less than 6 is a solution.
Try a number greater than 6 in $x + 1 < 7$: $7 + 1 < 7$. False.
So, no number greater than 6 is a solution.
The solutions of the inequality $x + 1 < 7$ are 0, 1, 2, 3, 4, and 5.

A. Solve $x - 4 > 3$. Replacements for x: 0, 1, 2, . . . , 10

1. Write the equation related to $x - 4 > 3$.

2. Solve $x - 4 = 3$.

3. Try a number greater than 7 in $x - 4 > 3$. Is the statement true?

4. Try a number less than 7 in $x - 4 > 3$. Is the statement true?

5. Give the solutions of $x - 4 > 3$.

B. Solve $2x > 8$. Replacements for x: 0, 1, 2, . . . , 10

6. Write the equation related to $2x > 8$.

7. Solve $2x = 8$.

8. Try a number less than 4 in $2x > 8$. Is the statement true?

9. Try a number greater than 4 in $2x > 8$. Is the statement true?

10. Give the solutions of $2x > 8$.

C. Solve. Replacements: 0, 1, 2, . . . , 10

11. $n + 1 > 3$ **12.** $2t < 6$ **13.** $2r - 1 > 7$

Practice

Solve. Replacements: 0, 1, 2, . . ., 10

1. $a + 2 < 9$ **2.** $d + 1 > 8$ **3.** $t + 3 < 9$

4. $x + 4 > 6$ **5.** $y + 1 < 3$ **6.** $z + 2 > 6$

7. $n - 1 < 3$ **8.** $w - 2 < 5$ **9.** $r - 7 > 1$

10. $c - 4 > 1$ **11.** $d - 8 > 1$ **12.** $x - 1 < 5$

13. $3y < 9$ **14.** $3x > 12$ **15.** $2n < 20$

16. $3x + 1 > 19$ **17.** $6b + 7 < 31$ **18.** $9c + 18 < 36$

19. $x - 4 < 2$ **20.** $6r - 4 < 8$ **21.** $y + 4 < 10$

22. $2t - 1 < 9$ **23.** $3x < 9$ **24.** $4n - 8 < 24$

★ **25.** $\frac{r}{2} > 2$ ★ **26.** $\frac{x}{3} + 1 > 3$ ★ **27.** $\frac{n}{2} - 1 < 5$

★ **28.** $3t + 1 > 31$ ★ **29.** $4x - 2 < 2$ ★ **30.** $5x < 1$

FIND OUT!

Brainteaser

In each drawing, which line segment appears longer? Use a ruler to check what you believe you see.

1.

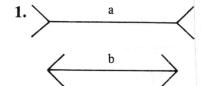

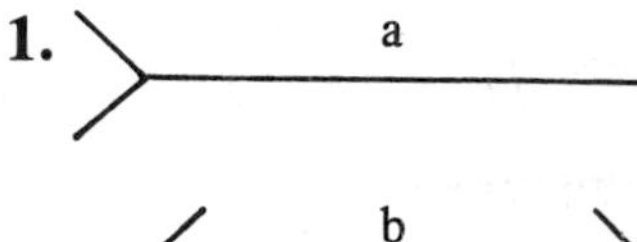

2.

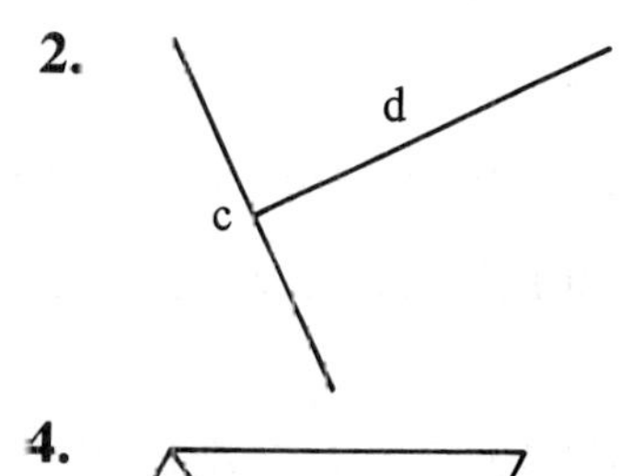

3.

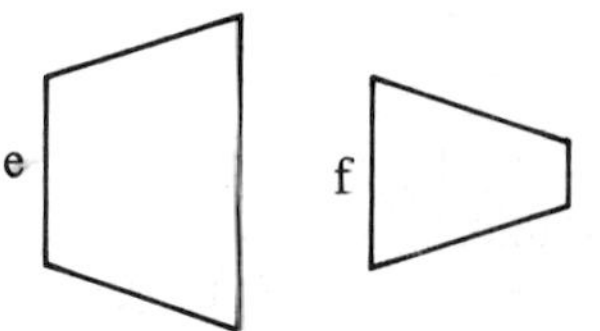

4.

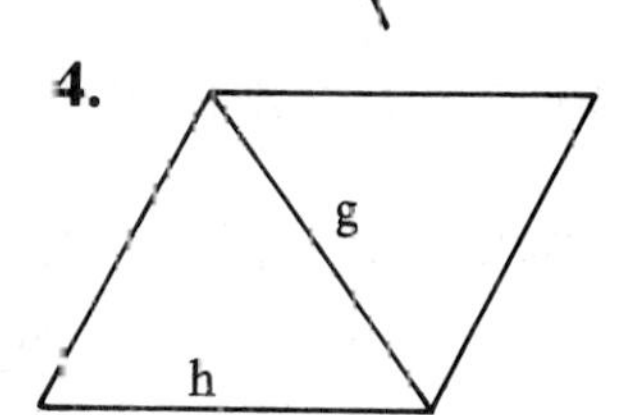

Problem Solving: Reading a Telephone Bill

	State-Local Tax		Federal Tax		Charges Excluding Tax	
Regular Monthly Charge	0	75	0	32	10	76
Local Usage	1	14	0	49	16	27
Toll Charges	0	66	0	46	15	27
Total Excluding Taxes					42	30
Taxes	2	55	1	27	3	82
Total of current charges					46	12

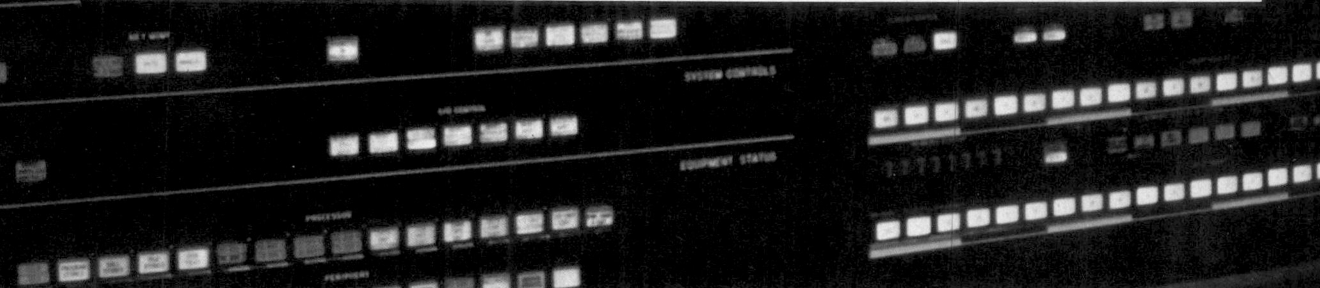

Solve.

1. What is the regular monthly charge excluding taxes?
2. How much is the total tax on the regular monthly charge?
3. How much more was the state and local taxes than the federal taxes on the local usage calls?
4. What would the total bill have been if there were no toll charges?
5. What would the total bill have been if there were no local calls?
6. What was the total cost of the local usage and toll calls?
7. During the month, 10 toll calls were made. About how much was the average cost per toll call including taxes?
8. The cost of local usage calls is divided among day and evening calls. If $11.23 was charged for 39 day calls, how much was charged for the evening calls?

Chapter Review

Which are pairs of equivalent equations? (58, 64)

1. $x + 2 = 6 + 2$; $x = 2$

2. $x - 3 = 6 - 3$; $x = 6$

3. $2x = 22$; $x = 11$

4. $\frac{x}{5} = 10$; $x = 2$

Solve and check.

5. $x + 7 = 18$ (60)

6. $x + 21 = 43$ (60)

7. $z + 16 = 54$ (60)

8. $c - 3 = 8$ (60)

9. $t - 24 = 37$ (60)

10. $x - 75 = 97$ (60)

11. $42 = b + 3$ (60)

12. $49 = z - 7$ (60)

13. $456 = n - 108$ (60)

14. $4x = 24$ (66)

15. $8n = 72$ (66)

16. $3z = 27$ (66)

17. $\frac{x}{3} = 4$ (66)

18. $\frac{t}{5} = 206$ (66)

19. $\frac{e}{7} = 9$ (66)

20. $603 = 9c$ (66)

21. $21 = \frac{t}{2}$ (66)

22. $64 = 8y$ (66)

23. $2x + 5 = 11$ (70)

24. $3n - 7 = 11$ (70)

25. $31 = 6t + 7$ (70)

26. $\frac{r}{4} + 12 = 36$ (70)

27. $\frac{e}{5} + 15 = 85$ (70)

28. $6 = \frac{n}{2} - 4$ (70)

29. $\frac{x}{4} - 2 = 10$ (70)

30. $\frac{n}{6} + 4 = 22$ (70)

31. $54 = \frac{n}{2} - 8$ (70)

Use the graph to answer Exercise 32. (68)

32. In which game did Robin and Darrin score the same number of points?

Basketball

Points: 0, 5, 10, 15, 20

Game: 1, 2, 3, 4, 5

— Robin
- - Darrin

Solve. (74)

33. The Browns made 4 toll calls, which cost $8.60 in all. What was the average cost of each toll call?

Chapter Test

Which are pairs of equivalent equations? *(58, 64)*

1. $x + 3 = 7 + 3; x = 7$

2. $x + 4 = 12; x = 16$

3. $7x = 21; x = 3$

4. $\frac{x}{2} = 4; x = 8$

Solve and check.

5. $x + 5 = 13$ *(60)*

6. $x + 65 = 461$ *(60)*

7. $z + 14 = 65$ *(60)*

8. $x - 9 = 21$ *(60)*

9. $c - 15 = 85$ *(60)*

10. $e - 86 = 159$ *(60)*

11. $16 = z + 5$ *(60)*

12. $48 = n - 36$ *(60)*

13. $647 = b + 86$ *(60)*

14. $4x = 32$ *(66)*

15. $9z = 225$ *(66)*

16. $2n = 96$ *(66)*

17. $\frac{x}{4} = 7$ *(66)*

18. $\frac{n}{12} = 8$ *(66)*

19. $\frac{r}{3} = 24$ *(66)*

20. $18 = 6z$ *(66)*

21. $10 = \frac{r}{5}$ *(66)*

22. $14 = 2t$ *(66)*

23. $2t + 7 = 19$ *(70)*

24. $3z - 4 = 11$ *(70)*

25. $30 = 6t + 6$ *(70)*

26. $\frac{x}{4} - 3 = 7$ *(70)*

27. $\frac{r}{2} + 4 = 10$ *(70)*

28. $10 = \frac{n}{4} + 7$ *(70)*

29. $\frac{z}{3} - 4 = 16$ *(70)*

30. $\frac{s}{7} + 3 = 4$ *(70)*

31. $25 = \frac{n}{3} + 16$ *(70)*

Use the graph to answer Exercise 32. *(68)*

32. How many more runs did Randy score than Terry in the fourth game?

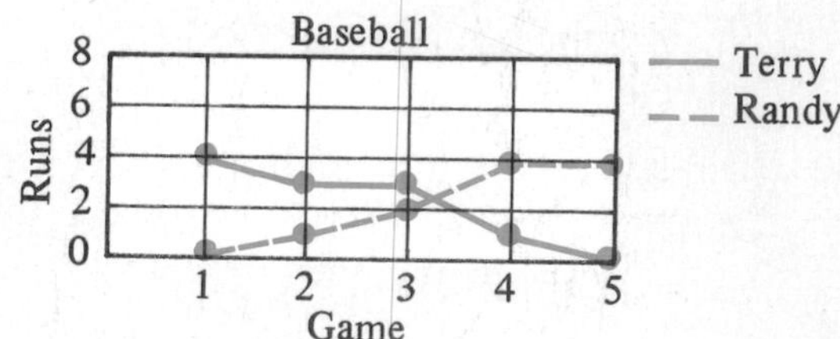

Solve. *(74)*

33. Elyse's phone bill for 1 month was $16.38 excluding taxes. The tax came to $1.57. What was the total bill?

Basic Skills Check

1. What is the value of the underlined digit in 9,26$\underline{7}$,341?

A	B	C	D
7	700	7,000	70,000

2. Which shows three million, seven?

E	F	G	H
3,000,700	3,000,007	3,700	3,007

3. What is 741,683 rounded to the nearest hundred thousand?

A	B	C	D
742,000	741,700	740,000	700,000

4. Which is the smallest number?

E	F	G	H
790,832	791,382	790,382	1,790,382

5. What is the value of the underlined digit in 3.41$\underline{9}$?

A	B	C	D
9	0.9	0.09	0.009

6. Which is the standard numeral for $(1 \times 1) + (4 \times 0.1) + (1 \times 0.01) + (3 \times 0.001)$?

E	F	G	H
1.00413	1.0413	1.413	14.13

7. Round 21.73 to the nearest whole number.

A	B	C	D
2,170	217	22	21

8. Which is the smallest number?

E	F	G	H
1.314	2	1.32	1.316

9. Give $\frac{8}{12}$ in simplest form.

A	B	C	D
$\frac{4}{6}$	$\frac{2}{3}$	$\frac{8}{12}$	$\frac{3}{4}$

10. Which number does not have the same value as $\frac{13}{4}$?

E	F	G	H
$3\frac{1}{4}$	$\frac{26}{8}$	$3\frac{3}{12}$	$3\frac{6}{8}$

11. Which is the greatest number?

A	B	C	D
$\frac{23}{50}$	$\frac{9}{20}$	$\frac{11}{25}$	$\frac{3}{10}$

12. What part of the rectangle is shaded?

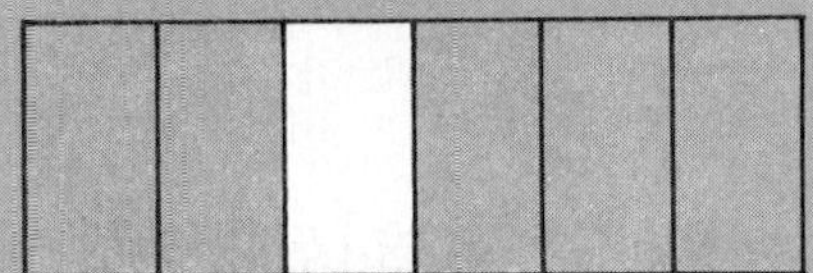

E	F	G	H
$\frac{1}{2}$	$\frac{3}{4}$	$\frac{5}{6}$	$\frac{7}{8}$

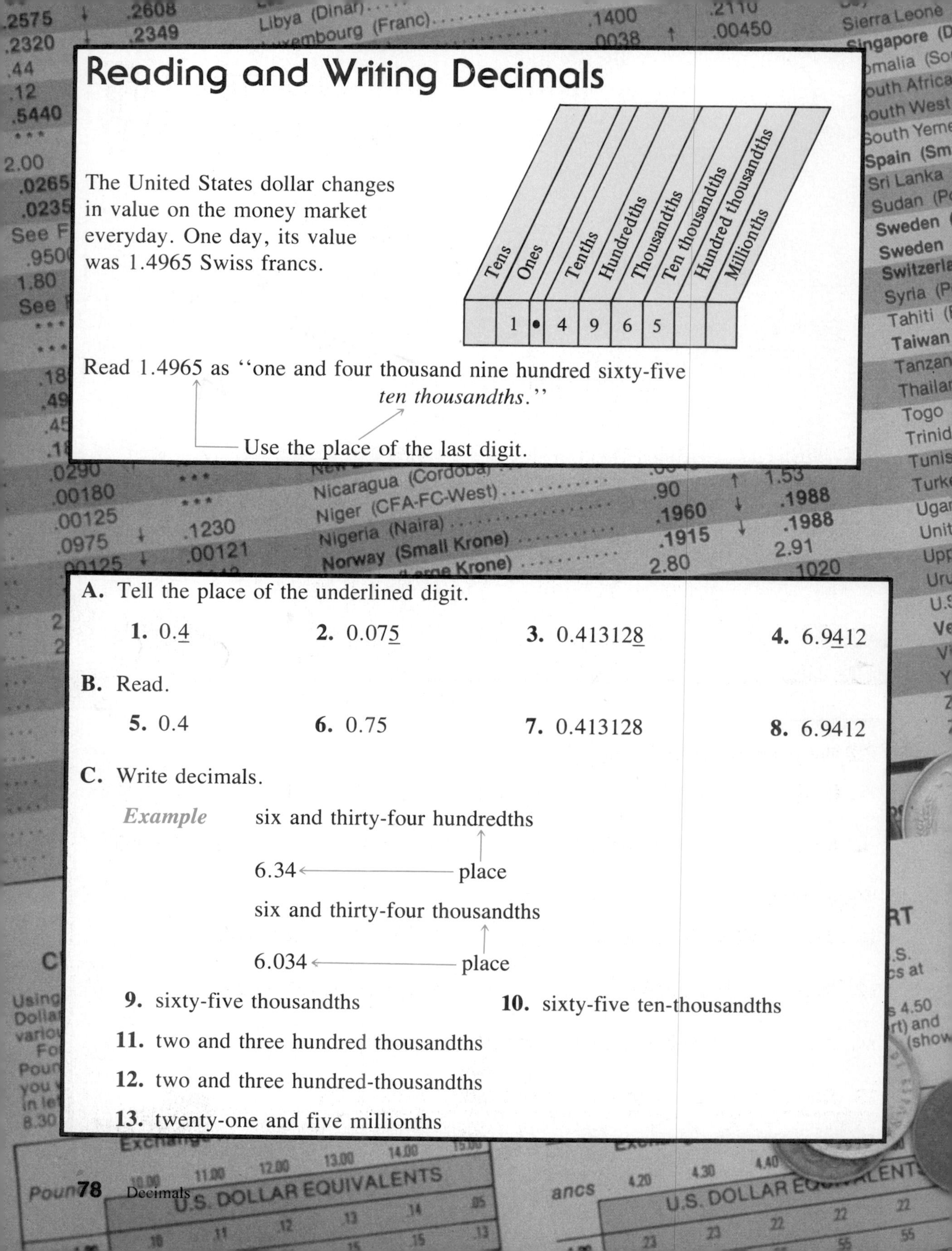

Reading and Writing Decimals

The United States dollar changes in value on the money market everyday. One day, its value was 1.4965 Swiss francs.

Read 1.4965 as "one and four thousand nine hundred sixty-five *ten thousandths.*"

Use the place of the last digit.

A. Tell the place of the underlined digit.

1. $0.\underline{4}$ **2.** $0.07\underline{5}$ **3.** $0.41312\underline{8}$ **4.** $6.9\underline{4}12$

B. Read.

5. 0.4 **6.** 0.75 **7.** 0.413128 **8.** 6.9412

C. Write decimals.

Example six and thirty-four hundredths

6.34 ← place

six and thirty-four thousandths

6.034 ← place

9. sixty-five thousandths **10.** sixty-five ten-thousandths

11. two and three hundred thousandths

12. two and three hundred-thousandths

13. twenty-one and five millionths

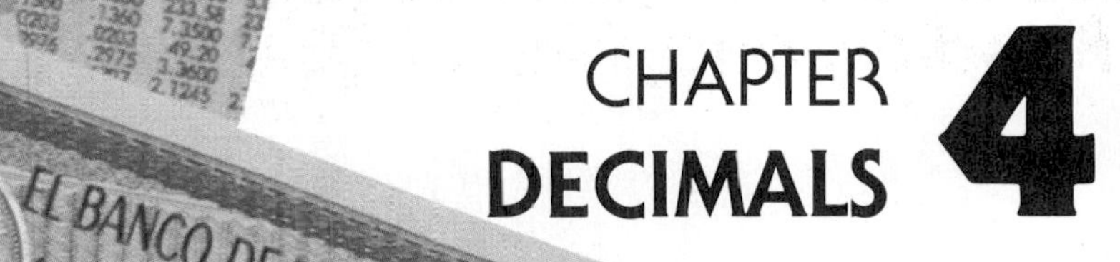

CHAPTER 4
DECIMALS

Practice

Tell the place of the underlined digit.

1. $0.0\underline{6}$
2. $3.\underline{6}$
3. $0.08\underline{1}$
4. $0.1\underline{3}1$
5. $0.3\underline{4}16$
6. $0.0000\underline{3}$
7. $0.00\underline{0}30$
8. $24.34161\underline{2}$
9. $28.00000\underline{1}$

Write decimals.

10. three hundred thousandths
11. three hundred-thousandths
12. forty-nine thousandths
13. ten and seven tenths
14. thirty-six and eight hundred twenty-two thousandths
15. fifty-nine and six thousand eleven hundred-thousandths

Place Value

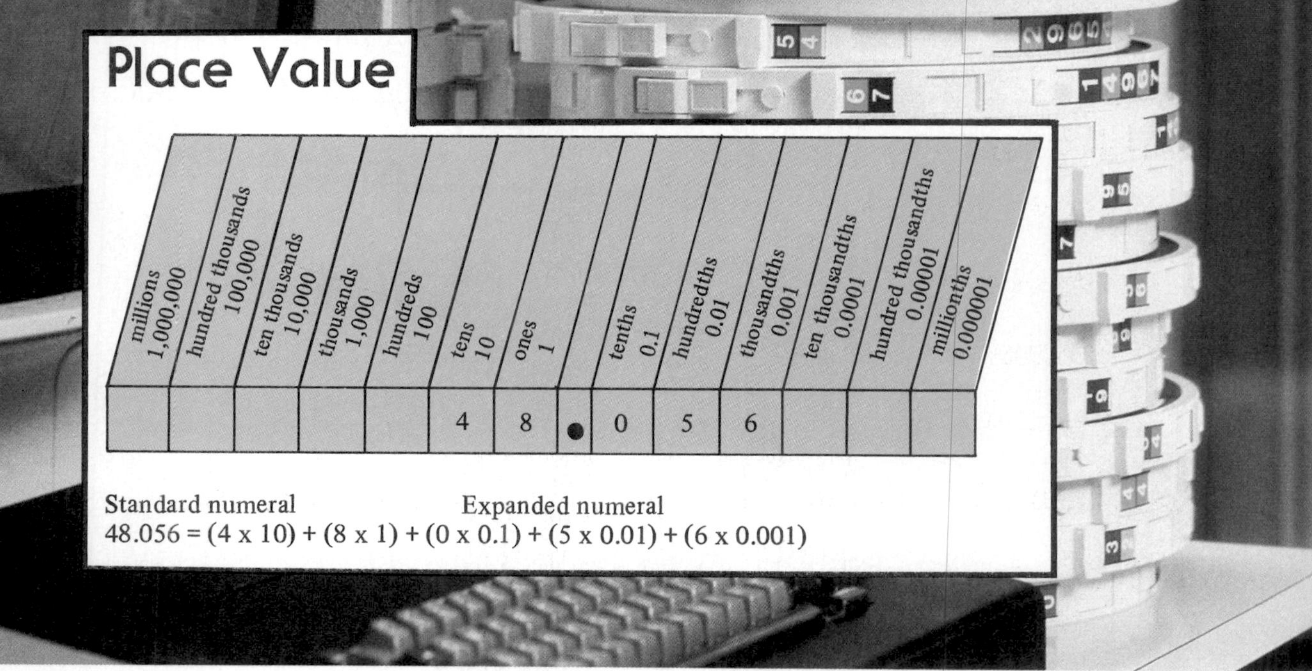

millions 1,000,000
hundred thousands 100,000
ten thousands 10,000
thousands 1,000
hundreds 100
tens 10
ones 1
tenths 0.1
hundredths 0.01
thousandths 0.001
ten thousandths 0.0001
hundred thousandths 0.00001
millionths 0.000001
4 8 • 0 5 6

Standard numeral Expanded numeral
48.056 = (4 x 10) + (8 x 1) + (0 x 0.1) + (5 x 0.01) + (6 x 0.001)

A. Write standard numerals.

Example (0 × 0.1) + (4 × 0.01) + (7 × 0.001) = 0.047

1. (9 × 100) + (6 × 10) + (0 × 1)

2. (9 × 0.1) + (0 × 0.01) + (4 × 0.001) + (6 × 0.0001) + (8 × 0.00001)

3. (2 × 10) + (0 × 1) + (5 × 0.1) + (2 × 0.01)

B. Use 134.5276 to complete each sentence.

4. The digit 3 has the value 3 × __?__ or 30.

5. The digit 5 has the value 5 × __?__ or 0.5.

6. The digit 2 has the value 2 × __?__ or __?__.

7. The digit 7 has the value 7 × __?__ or __?__.

C. What is the value of the underlined digit?

8. $0.\underline{3}$ **9.** $5.4\underline{7}$ **10.** $37.56\underline{9}$ **11.** $175.004\underline{3}$

12. $25.00516\underline{7}$ **13.** $1\underline{2}5.36$ **14.** $9\underline{8},762.4$ **15.** $2\underline{7}3,460$

D. Write expanded numerals.

16. 3,876 **17.** 143,762 **18.** 0.241 **19.** 0.78602

Practice

Write standard numerals.

1. $(5 \times 1{,}000) + (3 \times 100) + (4 \times 10) + (8 \times 1)$

2. $(0 \times 0.1) + (2 \times 0.01) + (0 \times 0.001) + (9 \times 0.0001)$

3. $(8 \times 10{,}000) + (3 \times 1{,}000) + (8 \times 100) + (0 \times 10) + (9 \times 1)$

4. $(7 \times 10) + (5 \times 1) + (4 \times 0.1) + (0 \times 0.01) + (7 \times 0.001)$

5. $(9 \times 100) + (6 \times 10) + (3 \times 1) + (5 \times 0.1) + (0 \times 0.01) + (4 \times 0.001)$

What is the value of the underlined digit?

6. $0.\underline{8}$	**7.** $0.2\underline{4}$	**8.** $10{,}67\underline{5}$	**9.** $1\underline{7}{,}634$	**10.** $73{,}543.2\underline{1}$
11. $34{,}\underline{7}28$	**12.** $5\underline{8}{,}916$	**13.** $\underline{3}9{,}816.25$	**14.** $\underline{8}16{,}312.72$	**15.** $34.000\underline{7}$
16. $0.12\underline{4}$	**17.** $0.2\underline{2}22$	**18.** $3.131\underline{3}$	**19.** $4.0000\underline{9}$	**20.** $0.0016\underline{7}$

Write expanded numerals.

21. 3,346 **22.** 725,798 **23.** 21.1576 **24.** 3.01608

FIND OUT!

Calculator Activity

Study the pattern. Complete and check with a calculator.

$$1 \times 8 + 1 = 9$$

$$12 \times 8 + 2 = 98$$

$$123 \times 8 + 3 = 987$$

$$1{,}234 \times 8 + 4 = \underline{\ ?\ }$$

$$12{,}345 \times 8 + 5 = \underline{\ ?\ }$$

$$123{,}456 \times 8 + 6 = \underline{\ ?\ }$$

$$1{,}234{,}567 \times 8 + 7 = \underline{\ ?\ }$$

$$12{,}345{,}678 \times 8 + 8 = \underline{\ ?\ }$$

Comparing Decimals

Miss Simon lives 0.3 km from her office, while Mr. Leonard lives 0.36 km from his office. Who lives farther from the office? Compare 0.3 and 0.36.

	tenths	hundredths	
0.3	0.3	0	3 tenths 0 hundredths
0.36	0.3	6	3 tenths 6 hundredths

0.3 = 0.30 and 0.30 is less than 0.36, or 0.36 is greater than 0.3

0.30 < 0.36 or 0.36 > 0.3

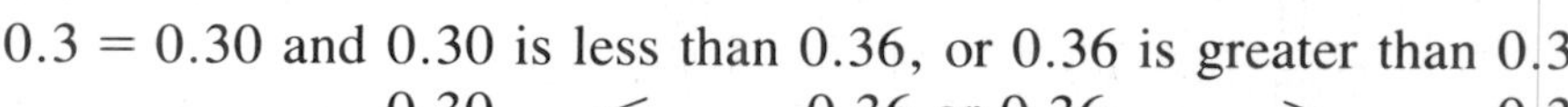

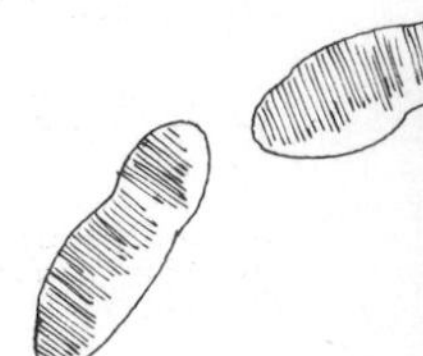

So, Mr. Leonard lives farther from the office.

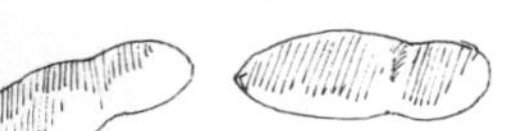

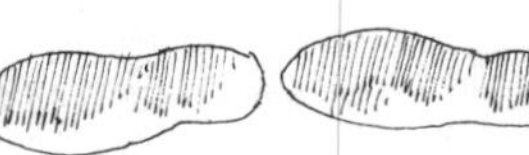

A. Change to hundredths.

1. 0.7 **2.** 0.6 **3.** 0.1 **4.** 3.0 **5.** 8.1

B. Change to thousandths.

6. 0.5 **7.** 0.8 **8.** 0.32 **9.** 3.0 **10.** 4

C. Compare. Use >, <, and =.

11. 0.9 ≡ 0.6 **12.** 0.07 ≡ 0.61 **13.** 1.350 ≡ 1.298 **14.** 0.9 ≡ 0.900

D. Change to hundredths and compare. Use >, <, and =.

15. 0.8 ≡ 0.04 **16.** 0.4 ≡ 0.39 **17.** 0.03 ≡ 0.3 **18.** 4.24 ≡ 4.3

E. Compare. Use >, <, and =.

19. 0.3 ≡ 0.139 **20.** 2.1 ≡ 2.009 **21.** 0.716 ≡ 0.85134 **22.** 0.64 ≡ 0.640

F. List in order from the greatest to the least.

Example 0.07, 0.516, 0.0031
Rewrite: 0.0700, 0.5160, 0.0031
Then compare: 0.516 > 0.07 > 0.0031

23. 0.06, 0.134, 0.9 **24.** 0.0037, 0.037, 0.37

25. 0.07, 0.201, 0.13 **26.** 0.104, 0.03006, 0.4

Practice

Compare. Use >, <, and =.

1. 0.4 ▒ 0.6 **2.** 0.1 ▒ 0.7 **3.** 0.7 ▒ 0.3 **4.** 0.007 ▒ 0.300

5. 0.07 ▒ 0.04 **6.** 0.09 ▒ 0.004 **7.** 1.34 ▒ 1.56 **8.** 0.004 ▒ 0.400

9. 0.6 ▒ 0.60 **10.** 0.04 ▒ 0.10 **11.** 2.3 ▒ 2.229 **12.** 5.06 ▒ 5.6

13. 0.9 ▒ 0.09 **14.** 0.7 ▒ 0.70 **15.** 1.5 ▒ 1.37 **16.** 0.2 ▒ 1.02

17. 0.6 ▒ 0.140 **18.** 0.3 ▒ 0.400 **19.** 0.6 ▒ 0.590 **20.** 0.04 ▒ 0.400

21. 0.06 ▒ 0.500 **22.** 0.01 ▒ 0.009 **23.** 0.56 ▒ 0.59 **24.** 5.2 ▒ 5.090

25. 3.01 ▒ 3.010001 **26.** 27.02020 ▒ 27.2020 **27.** 0.09 ▒ 0.090000

List in order from the greatest to the least.

28. 0.014, 0.0436, 0.14 **29.** 0.0049, 0.049, 0.000049

30. 0.1, 0.09, 0.009 **31.** 0.064, 0.0064, 0.00064

32. 0.04, 0.04444, 0.044 **33.** 0.025, 2.5, 0.0025

★ **34.** 3.66 . . . shows that the 6's continue indefinitely in the decimal. Which is greater, 3.6666 or 3.66 . . . ?

Solve.

35. One shirt costs $15.90 and another costs $15.09. Which costs more?

36. On Friday, the dollar closed at 1.4965 Swiss francs. On Monday, it closed at 1.49560 Swiss francs. On which day did it close higher?

ding Decimals

s chart shows how to round decimals.

Round to	*Number*	*Think*	*Write*
nearest thousandth	0.0036	0.0036 ↑ The ten thousandths digit is 5 or greater.	0.0036 ≐ 0.004
nearest hundredth	4.2931	4.2931 ↑ The thousandths digit is less than 5.	4.2931 ≐ 4.29
nearest tenth	3.647	3.647 ↑ The hundredths digit is less than 5.	3.647 ≐ 3.6
nearest whole number	7.506	7.506 ↑ The tenths digit is 5 or greater.	7.506 ≐ 8

A. Round to the nearest thousandth.

1. 0.4352 **2.** 0.7419 **3.** 2.31450 **4.** 3.006219

5. 0.1694 **6.** 0.1695 **7.** 6.09904 **8.** 3.000219

B. Round to the nearest hundredth.

9. 0.049 **10.** 0.054 **11.** 0.005 **12.** 0.6138

13. 6.4183 **14.** 7.0061 **15.** 8.997 **16.** 3.002

C. Round to the nearest tenth.

17. 9.68 **18.** 0.31 **19.** 1.0516 **20.** 3.449

21. 2.506 **22.** 6.92 **23.** 2.90 **24.** 3.95

D. Round to the nearest whole number.

25. 6.007 **26.** 7.3214 **27.** 2.63 **28.** 7.09

29. 0.516 **30.** 0.432 **31.** 0.9 **32.** 0.499

Practice

Round to the nearest thousandth.

1. 1.5638 **2.** 2.3409 **3.** 0.4554 **4.** 6.0015

5. 8.0140 **6.** 8.0193 **7.** 7.0095 **8.** 8.9996

Round to the nearest hundredth.

9. 5.164 **10.** 0.307 **11.** 6.009 **12.** 7.095

13. 4.3641 **14.** 8.70253 **15.** 9.695 **16.** 4.997

Round to the nearest tenth.

17. 0.78 **18.** 3.64 **19.** 6.893 **20.** 6.031

21. 2.7163 **22.** 3.57631 **23.** 4.953 **24.** 6.0493

Round to the nearest whole number.

25. 0.8 **26.** 0.3 **27.** 3.64 **28.** 8.09

29. 5.934 **30.** 18.349 **31.** 14.382 **32.** 19.641

Complete.

		Round to the nearest			
	Number	*thousandth*	*hundredth*	*tenth*	*whole number*
33.	4.3165				
34.	0.7209				
35.	4.3652				
36.	2.0706				
37.	3.1495				

Solve.

38. A mechanic found the diameter of a pipe to be 1.7675 in. Round this to the nearest hundredth.

39. The mass of a steel bar is calculated to be 13.9680 kg. Round this to the nearest tenth.

Keeping Fit

Solve.

1. $x + 7 = 13$
2. $x + 18 = 36$
3. $x - 5 = 9$
4. $x - 23 = 37$
5. $3 \cdot x = 27$
6. $4 \cdot x = 96$
7. $\frac{x}{2} = 4$
8. $\frac{x}{4} = 17$
9. $2x + 6 = 22$
10. $3x + 19 = 34$
11. $4x - 8 = 4$
12. $5x - 37 = 38$

Add.

13. 27 + 532 + 96
14. 2,153 + 705 + 6,927 + 458

15. 436 + 819 + 747 + 864 + 934

$$\begin{array}{r} 436 \\ 819 \\ 747 \\ 864 \\ +\ 934 \\ \hline \end{array}$$

16.
$$\begin{array}{r} 53{,}716 \\ 8{,}734 \\ 29{,}046 \\ 38{,}654 \\ +\ 68{,}019 \\ \hline \end{array}$$

17.
$$\begin{array}{r} 233{,}146 \\ 416{,}897 \\ 783{,}426 \\ 825{,}713 \\ +\ 624{,}316 \\ \hline \end{array}$$

18.
$$\begin{array}{r} \$\,43{,}617 \\ 7{,}816 \\ 35{,}706 \\ 19{,}816 \\ +\ \ 7{,}613 \\ \hline \end{array}$$

Subtract.

19.
$$\begin{array}{r} 4{,}369 \\ -\ 2{,}058 \\ \hline \end{array}$$

20.
$$\begin{array}{r} 38{,}619 \\ -\ 14{,}709 \\ \hline \end{array}$$

21.
$$\begin{array}{r} 345{,}678 \\ -\ 182{,}569 \\ \hline \end{array}$$

22.
$$\begin{array}{r} 234{,}700 \\ -\ \ 78{,}296 \\ \hline \end{array}$$

Multiply.

23. $\begin{array}{r} 428 \\ \times\ 9 \\ \hline \end{array}$
24. $\begin{array}{r} 8{,}063 \\ \times\ 8 \\ \hline \end{array}$
25. $\begin{array}{r} 24 \\ \times\ 31 \\ \hline \end{array}$
26. $\begin{array}{r} 36 \\ \times\ 15 \\ \hline \end{array}$
27. $\begin{array}{r} 40 \\ \times\ 25 \\ \hline \end{array}$
28. $\begin{array}{r} 93 \\ \times\ 30 \\ \hline \end{array}$
29. $\begin{array}{r} 613 \\ \times\ 43 \\ \hline \end{array}$
30. $\begin{array}{r} 438 \\ \times\ 64 \\ \hline \end{array}$
31. $\begin{array}{r} 7{,}450 \\ \times\ 36 \\ \hline \end{array}$
32. $\begin{array}{r} 657 \\ \times\ 90 \\ \hline \end{array}$
33. $\begin{array}{r} 134 \\ \times\ 165 \\ \hline \end{array}$
34. $\begin{array}{r} 43{,}167 \\ \times\ 803 \\ \hline \end{array}$

Divide.

35. $7\overline{)2{,}149}$
36. $8\overline{)8{,}328}$
37. $6\overline{)42{,}315}$
38. $21\overline{)672}$
39. $32\overline{)768}$
40. $43\overline{)5{,}762}$
41. $37\overline{)16{,}872}$
42. $49\overline{)83{,}146}$

Mid-Chapter Review

Write decimals. *(78)*

1. Thirty-one and six hundred four thousandths

2. Seventeen and four hundred thousand eight hundred millionths

What is the value of the underlined digit? *(80)*

3. $7.\underline{4}$ **4.** $0.65\underline{1}$ **5.** $2\underline{3}.08$ **6.** $1\underline{9},564$

Compare. Use >, <, or = . *(82)*

7. 0.7 ≡ 0.9 **8.** 0.6 ≡ 0.60 **9.** 0.59 ≡ 0.6

Round. *(84)*

10. 2.1385 to the nearest thousandth

11. 4.834 to the nearest tenth

12. 1.361 to the nearest hundredth

13. 24.824 to the nearest whole number

14. 0.14 to the nearest whole number

15. 5.0672 to the nearest hundredth

FIND OUT!
Brainteaser

Ann and Judy each have 30 birthday cards. Ann wants to sell her cards at 2 for 5¢. Judy wants to sell her cards at 3 for 5¢. How much would they receive in all?

If they combine their cards and sell them at 5 for 10¢, would they receive the same total income? Check your guess.

Problem Solving: Equations

Millie works in a store which sells lumber, paint, and other items to fix up homes. Each section of a wood fence costs \$11.99. Which equation should Millie use to find the cost of 8 sections?

$8 \cdot c = 11.99$ $\qquad$ $c = 8 \times 11.99$ $\qquad$ $c - 8 = 11.99$

PLAN In the equation $8 \cdot c = 11.99$, the total cost is 11.99.

In the equation $c = 8 \times 11.99$, the total cost is c.

In the equation $c - 8 = 11.99$, the number of sections is subtracted from the total cost.

SOLVE The correct equation is $c = 8 \times 11.99$ since each section costs 11.99 and Millie wants to find the cost of 8 sections.

A. Select the equation to solve the problem.

1. The regular price of an entrance door with 6 panels is \$159.99. During a sale the door sells for \$149.50. How much is saved by buying the door during the sale?

a. $s = 6 \times 159.99$ $\qquad$ **b.** $s = 6 \times 149.50$

c. $s = 159.99 - 149.50$ $\qquad$ **d.** $s - 149.50 = 159.99$

Practice

Select the equation to solve the problems.

1. Panels for suspended ceilings are $1.12 each. What is the cost of 15 of these panels?

   a. $15 \cdot c = 1.12$ **b.** $1.12 \div 15 = c$

   c. $c \div 15 = 1.12$ **d.** $15 \times 1.12 = c$

2. Fiberglass insulation costs $28.80 for 1 wall. A thinner insulation costs $16.00. How much more is the thicker insulation?

   a. $28.80 - 16.00 = c$ **b.** $28.80 + 16.00 = c$

   c. $c - 16.00 = 28.80$ **d.** $28.80 \div 16.00 = c$

3. Two folding doors for a closet cost $19.99. What is the cost of 6 folding doors?

   a. $2 \cdot c = 19.99$ **b.** $3 \times 19.99 = c$

   c. $16 \times 19.99 = c$ **d.** $19.99 \div 3 = c$

4. Two rolls of tape cost $2.75. What is the cost of a dozen rolls of tape?

   a. $12 \times 2.75 = c$ **b.** $2.75 \div 6 = c$

   c. $2.75 - 12 = c$ **d.** $6 \times 2.75 = c$

5. During a sale a person buying a can of paint for $8.90 received a second can of paint free. What is the average cost of each can of paint?

   a. $8.90 \times 8.90 = 2 \cdot c$ **b.** $2 \times 8.90 = c$

   c. $8.90 \div 2 = c$ **d.** $8.90 + 8.90 = c$

6. Sixteen lengths of lumber, marked $4.90 a length, were sold on sale at a reduction of $0.50 a length. How much did the lumber cost at the sale?

   a. $16 \times 4.90 = c$ **b.** $12 \times 5.40 = c$

   c. $16 \times 4.40 = c$ **d.** $4.90 \div 0.50 = c$

Powers of Ten

Look at the table.

Number (Standard Form)	Exponential notation 10 as factor	(base^{exponent})
1	no factor of 10	10^0 0 factors of 10
10	10	10^1 1 factor of 10
100	10×10	10^2 2 factors of 10
1,000	$10 \times 10 \times 10$	10^3 3 factors of 10
10,000	$10 \times 10 \times 10 \times 10$	10^4 4 factors of 10
100,000	$10 \times 10 \times 10 \times 10 \times 10$	10^5 5 factors of 10

Use a shortcut to write 1,000,000 in exponential form.

$1{,}000{,}000 = 10^6$

Count 6 zeros.

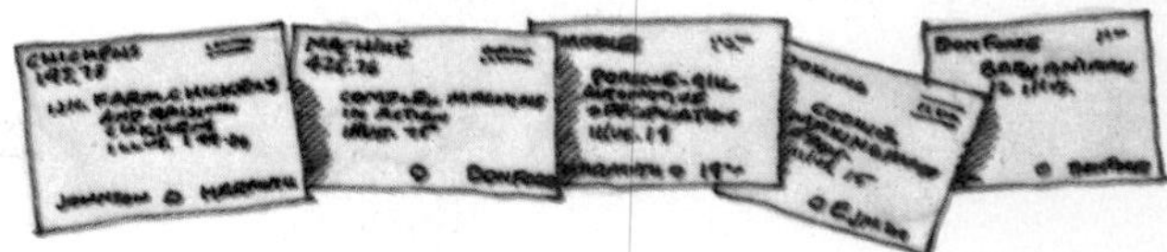

A. Write in exponential notation.

1. 10,000,000 **2.** 1,000,000,000 **3.** $10 \times 10 \times 10 \times 10 \times 10 \times 10 \times 10 \times 10$

B. Multiply in exponential notation.

Example $10^2 \cdot 10^3 = (10 \times 10) \times (10 \times 10 \times 10) = 10^5$

There are 5 factors of 10.

Shortcut: $10^2 \cdot 10^3 = 10^{2+3} = 10^5$

▶ To multiply powers of 10, *add* the exponents.

4. $10^2 \cdot 10^4$ **5.** $10^3 \cdot 10^3$ **6.** $10^2 \cdot 10^5$ **7.** $10^1 \cdot 10^4$

C. Divide in exponential notation.

Example $10^3 \div 10^2 = (10 \times 10 \times 10) \div (10 \times 10) = 10$

Shortcut: $10^3 \div 10^2 = 10^{3-2} = 10^1$, or 10 or $\frac{10^3}{10^2} = 10^{3-2} = 10^1$, or 10

▶ To divide powers of 10, *subtract* the exponents.

8. $10^5 \div 10^2$ **9.** $10^6 \div 10^4$ **10.** $10^7 \div 10^3$ **11.** $10^9 \div 10^4$

12. $\frac{10^7}{10^2}$ **13.** $\frac{10^8}{10^7}$ **14.** $\frac{10^{11}}{10^3}$ **15.** $\frac{10^{12}}{10^5}$ **16.** $\frac{10^4}{10^4}$

Practice

Write in exponential notation.

1. 10,000,000,000 **2.** 100,000,000,000 **3.** 1,000,000,000,000

4. 10×10 **5.** $10 \times 10 \times 10 \times 10$ **6.** $10 \times 10 \times 10 \times 10 \times 10 \times 10 \times 10$

Multiply.

7. $10^2 \cdot 10^3$ **8.** $10^2 \cdot 10^1$ **9.** $10^3 \cdot 10^4$ **10.** $10^7 \cdot 10^5$

11. $10^1 \cdot 10^3$ **12.** $10^4 \cdot 10^3$ **13.** $10^4 \cdot 10^4$ **14.** $10^0 \cdot 10^6$

15. $10^3 \cdot 10^8$ **16.** $10^3 \cdot 10^7$ **17.** $10^2 \cdot 10^8$ **18.** $10^8 \cdot 10^4$

Divide.

19. $10^4 \div 10^1$ **20.** $10^5 \div 10^4$ **21.** $10^7 \div 10^4$ **22.** $10^{12} \div 10^3$

23. $10^9 \div 10^1$ **24.** $10^8 \div 10^6$ **25.** $10^9 \div 10^3$ **26.** $10^{12} \div 10^6$

27. $\frac{10^{16}}{10^9}$ **28.** $\frac{10^7}{10^4}$ **29.** $\frac{10^3}{10^2}$ **30.** $\frac{10^5}{10^5}$ **31.** $\frac{10^9}{10^3}$

32. $\frac{10^5}{10^5}$ **33.** $\frac{10^9}{10^6}$ **34.** $\frac{10^8}{10^4}$ **35.** $\frac{10^7}{10^1}$ **36.** $\frac{10^7}{10^3}$

★ Multiply or divide.

37. $10^4 \cdot 10^5 \cdot 10^2$ **38.** $\frac{10^7 \cdot 10^3}{10^4}$ **39.** $10^x \div 10^2$ **40.** $10 \cdot 10^a$

Solve. Use exponential notation.

41. There are 1,000 library cards in a box. How many library cards are in 1,000 boxes?

42. Library cards are packed 1,000 cards to a box. How many boxes are needed for 10,000,000 cards?

43. How many \$100 bills make \$1,000,000?

44. There are 1,000,000 boxes in each of 100 warehouses. How many boxes are there in all?

Scientific Notation

Mercury is the planet closest to the sun. It is about 60,000,000 km from the sun. Scientists use scientific notation to name such large numbers.

Standard Numeral	Scientific Notation
60,000,000	6×10^7

Number from 1 to 10 (6) — Power of 10 (7)

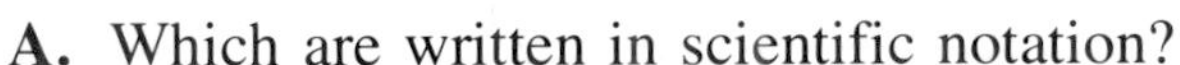

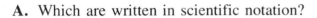

A. Which are written in scientific notation?

1. 3×10^6 **2.** 14×10^2 **3.** 3×2 **4.** 9×10^{12} **5.** 4.7×10^6

B. Write in scientific notation.

6. 500 **7.** 40,000 **8.** 600,000 **9.** 7,000,000 **10.** 80,000,000

> Write 360 in scientific notation.
> Think: 360 is between 300 and 400.
>
> $300 = 3 \times 10^2$
>
> $360 = 3.6 \times 10^2$ (3.6: Number from 1 to 10; 2: Power of 10)
>
> $400 = 4 \times 10^2$
>
> Shortcut: $360 = 3.6 \times 10^2$ ← Move the decimal point 2 places to the left.
>
> Need a number from 1 to 10

C. Write in scientific notation.

11. 7,400 **12.** 860,000

13. 3,800,000 **14.** 461,000,000,000

D. Write the standard numeral for 1.2×10^4.

The exponent is 4. Move the decimal point 4 places to right.

$1.2 \times 10^4 = 1.2000$

$= 12,000$

Write standard numerals.

15. 3.1×10^4 **16.** 6.2×10^6 **17.** 6×10^8 **18.** 7.31×10^9

Practice

Write in scientific notation.

1. 300 **2.** 6,000 **3.** 40,000 **4.** 800,000 **5.** 700,000,000

6. 240 **7.** 6,700 **8.** 31,000 **9.** 564,000 **10.** 3,120,000

11. 8,300,000 **12.** 16,000,000 **13.** 27,800,000

14. 6,400,000,000 **15.** 28,000,000,000,000 **16.** 716,000,000,000

Write standard numerals.

17. 3×10^3 **18.** 4×10^6 **19.** 6.1×10^3 **20.** 9.3×10^6

21. 3.12×10^3 **22.** 2.16×10^5 **23.** 3.49×10^6 **24.** 8.56×10^{10}

25. 7.62×10^{11} **26.** 7.216×10^4 **27.** 3.472×10^9 **28.** 4.1968×10^{12}

Write the numbers in scientific notation.

29. The earth is about 150,000,000 km from the sun.

30. Light travels about 6,000,000,000,000 mi in 1 year.

FIND OUT!
Brainteasers

Choose the letter of the correct answer.

1. If $A < 0.8$ and $0.8 < B$, then

a. $A = B$ **b.** $A < B$

c. $B < A$ **d.** $B = A$

2. If $X < Z$ and $Y > Z$, then

a. $Y < X$ **b.** $X = Y$

c. $X < Y$ **d.** $X > Z$

Computing with Scientific Notation

Light travels 5,870,000,000,000 mi in a year. How far does it travel in 1,000,000 years?
Write each number in scientific notation. Then multiply.
$(5.87 \times 10^{12}) \times (1 \times 10^6) = 5.87 \times 1 \times 10^{12} \times 10^6 = 5.87 \times 10^{18}$
Light travels 5.87×10^{18} mi in 1,000,000 years.

A. Multiply. Use scientific notation.

1. 93,000,000 × 1,000,000

2. 42,700,000,000 × 1,000,000

B. Multiply 30,000,000,000 × 20,000.

$$(3 \times 10^{10}) \times (2 \times 10^4) = 3 \times 2 \times 10^{10} \times 10^4 = 6 \times 10^{14}$$

Multiply. Write the answer in scientific notation.

3. 30,000,000,000 × 2,000,000

4. 3,000,000 × 3,000,000,000

5. 400,000 × 200,000,000

6. 2,000,000,000 × 20,000,000

C. Sometimes the answer must be rewritten to be in scientific notation.

$$6{,}000{,}000 \times 4{,}000{,}000 = (6 \times 10^6) \times (4 \times 10^6)$$

Think: 24 is not between 1 and 10. $= 24 \times 10^{12}$
Write 24 in scientific notation. $= 2.4 \times 10^1 \times 10^{12}$
$= 2.4 \times 10^{13}$

Multiply. Write the answer in scientific notation.

7. 400,000 × 70,000

8. 6,000,000 × 30,000,000

9. 70,000,000 × 300,000

10. 200,000,000,000 × 80,000,000

D. Divide 9,000,000,000 by 3,000,000.

$$\frac{9{,}000{,}000{,}000}{3{,}000{,}000} = \frac{9 \times 10^9}{3 \times 10^6} = 3 \times 10^3$$

Divide. Write the answer in scientific notation.

11. $\frac{4{,}000{,}000{,}000{,}000}{2{,}000{,}000}$

12. $\frac{36{,}000{,}000{,}000{,}000}{10{,}000{,}000{,}000}$

Practice

Multiply. Write the answer in scientific notation.

1. 3,000,000 × 100,000

2. 61,000,000 × 10,000,000

3. 4,000,000 × 20,000

4. 3,000,000 × 3,000,000

5. 20,000 × 6,000,000

6. 400,000 × 40,000,000

7. 200,000,000 × 600,000

8. 70,000,000 × 400,000,000

Divide. Write the answer in scientific notation.

9. $\frac{8,000,000,000}{2,000,000}$

10. $\frac{6,000,000,000,000}{3,000,000}$

11. $\frac{5,000,000,000,000}{1,000,000,000}$

12. $\frac{5,100,000,000,000,000}{1,000,000,000}$

13. $\frac{40,000,000,000}{200,000}$

14. $\frac{600,000,000,000,000,000,000}{2,000}$

15. $\frac{9,000,000}{3,000}$

16. $\frac{500,000,000}{50,000}$

Solve.

17. The earth is a space ship. It travels about 960,000,000 km a year. How far has it traveled in 4,000,000,000 years?

18. At times Neptune is about 2,700,000,000 mi from the earth and Mercury is about 135,000,000 mi from the earth. About how many times as far from the earth is Neptune than Mercury?

Problem Solving: Better Buy

1. At Tannenbaum's Gift Shop, 2 coffee mugs sell for $1.79. At Grand Gifts, 3 coffee mugs sell for $2.65. Which is the better buy? [HINT: Find the cost of 1 coffee mug at each store.]

2. A store advertised 2 pens for $1.35 and a package of 3 of the same pens for $1.90. Which is the better buy?

3. A package of 6 coasters is marked $1.44 and a package of 8 of the same coasters is marked $1.76. Which is the better buy?

4. A box of 4 drinking glasses is marked $1.80 and a box of 6 of the same drinking glasses is marked $2.50. Which is the better buy?

5. A 12-pack of small pads is $1.09 and an 8-pack of the same small pads is $0.89. Which is the better buy?

6. At Santiago Gift Shop, picture frames are marked 2/$1.67 (2 for $1.67). At Superior Gifts, the same picture frames are marked 3/$2.20. Which is the better buy?

7. A package of 6 place mats is marked $8.00 and a package of 8 place mats is marked $10.00. Which is the better buy?

Chapter Review

Write decimals. (78)

1. Four hundred twenty-five millionths

2. Sixty-two thousandths

What is the value of the underlined digit (80)

3. $40.\underline{6}$

4. $1.7\underline{9}1$

5. $5.\underline{3}27$

6. $280.51\underline{1}$

Compare. Use $>$, $<$, and $=$. (82)

7. 0.73 ≡ 0.730

8. 0.29 ≡ 0.3

9. 0.1 ≡ 0.009

Round. (84)

10. 4.329 to the nearest tenth

11. 2.359 to the nearest hundredth

12. 3.10459 to the nearest thousandth

13. 5.6214 to the nearest whole number

Write in exponential notation. (90)

14. 10,000

15. 10,000,000

Multiply or divide. (90)

16. $10^5 \cdot 10^3$

17. $10^4 \cdot 10^6$

18. $10^8 \div 10^8$

19. $\frac{10^7}{10^3}$

Write in scientific notation. (92)

20. 8,000,000

21. 4,900

Write standard numerals. (92)

22. 4×10^5

23. 3.7×10^6

Select the equation to solve the problem.

24. Ellen bought roof shingles for $5.99 a bundle. How much did she
(88) pay for 24 bundles?

a. $24 \cdot c = 5.99$

b. $c \div 24 = 5.99$

c. $5.99 \div 24 = c$

d. $24 \times 5.99 = c$

Solve.

25. Abner's Grocery is selling 4 cans of Colonel corn for $1.19.
(96) Westland Supermarket is selling 3 cans of Colonel corn for $0.95. Which is the better buy?

Chapter Test

Write decimals. *(78)*

1. Eighty-six millionths

2. Thirty-two hundred-thousandths

What is the value of the underlined digit? *(80)*

3. $7.\underline{8}2$ **4.** $1.3\underline{0}6$ **5.** $16.54\underline{3}$ **6.** $428.9\underline{7}$

Compare. Use $>$, $<$, and $=$. *(82)*

7. 0.3 ≣ 0.7 **8.** 0.61 ≣ 0.610 **9.** 0.09 ≣ 0.1

Round. *(84)*

10. 3.148 to the nearest tenth

11. 2.158 to the nearest hundredth

12. 4.1487 to the nearest thousandth

13. 34.512 to the nearest whole number

Write in exponential notation. *(90)*

14. 1,000,000

15. 100,000,000

Multiply or divide. *(90)*

16. $10^4 \cdot 10^2$ **17.** $10^5 \cdot 10^7$ **18.** $10^6 \div 10^1$ **19.** $\frac{10^7}{10^7}$

Write in scientific notation. *(92)*

20. 600,000

21. 2,300,000

Write standard numerals. *(92)*

22. 3×10^4

23. 4.1×10^6

Select the equation to solve the problem.

24. Ira paid $16.50 for 12 ceiling panels and $32.95 for 4 cans of
(88) paint. How much did he spend?

a. $c = 16.50 + 32.95$ **b.** $c = 32.95 - 16.50$

c. $c = 12 \times 16.50 + 32.95$ **d.** $c = 16.50 + 4 \times 32.95$

Solve.

25. R&L Auto Store sells a package of 6 spark plugs for $5.34 and a
(96) package of 8 spark plugs for $7.04. Which is the better buy?

Basic Skills Check

1. A radio that sells for $68.50 is on sale for $49.95. How much is saved by buying it on sale?

   A $118.45 B $18.65
   C $18.55 D $18.45

2. Henry works 35 hours a week. He earns $3.75 an hour. What does he earn each week?

   E $1,312.50 F $132.25
   G $131.25 H $130.25

3. Sam had $439.48 in his checking account. He made deposits of $120.14 and $96.50. What is his new balance?

   A $656.12 B $656.02
   C $222.84 D $210.64

4. The temperature is $^{-}5$°F outside. Which of the following temperatures is colder?

   E 15°F F 10°F
   G $^{-}4$°F H $^{-}10$°F

5. A roast was put in the oven at 4:15 pm. It takes $2\frac{1}{2}$ hours to cook. At what time will it be ready?

   A 6:16 pm B 6:30 pm
   C 6:45 pm D 7:45 pm

6. Ms. Jones ordered living room furniture October 2 and received it October 14. How long did she wait for her furniture?

   E 12 days F 14 days
   G 31 days H 377 days

7. Which unit would you use to tell the mass of an orange?

   A mg B g
   C kg D ton

8. Henry bowled five games and had scores of 145, 182, 175, 162, and 156. What was his average?

   E 175 F 168
   G 164 H 162

9. What is the perimeter of the right triangle?

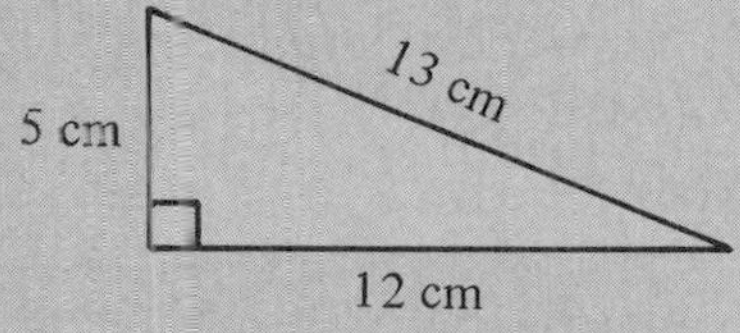

   A 780 cm B 60 cm
   C 30 cm D 25 cm

Getting Paid in Cash

The counselors at Park Summer Day Camp get paid in cash.

	Park Summer Day Camp Counselors								
	Week of July 19	*Currency Breakdown*							
Name	*Take-Home Pay*	*Bills*			*Coins*				
		$10	*$5*	*$1*	*50¢*	*25¢*	*10¢*	*5¢*	*1¢*
Maria	$ 89.35	8	1	4	0	1	1	0	0
Mark	91.26								
Harold	47.79								
Olga	86.84								
Total	$315.24								

A. Answer the questions from the chart.

1. What was Maria's take-home pay?

2. What bills did Maria receive?

3. What is the total value of the bills Maria received?

4. What coins did Maria receive?

5. What is the total value of the coins Maria received?

B. Complete the chart.

6. Find the total number of each bill needed.

7. Find the total number of each coin needed.

8. Check the total values of the bills and coins against the total take-home pay of $315.24. Are they the same amount?

CHAPTER 5
DECIMAL COMPUTATION

Practice

Complete the chart.

	H. and R. Supermarket									
		Week of September 5	*Currency Breakdown*							
	Name	*Take-Home Pay*	*Bills*			*Coins*				
			$10	*$5*	*$1*	*50¢*	*25¢*	*10¢*	*5¢*	*1¢*
	M. Villas	$ 93.46	9	0	3	0	1	2	0	1
1.	T. Schoenberg	87.89								
2.	M. Jackson	94.62								
3.	R. Glinka	137.64								
4.	A. Artuso	28.32								
5.	L. Font	78.04								
6.	Total	$519.97								

7. Check the total values of the bills and coins against the total take-home pay of $519.97.

Adding Decimals

A team of 4 eighth grade students ran in a relay race. Their times were 12.4 seconds, 11.9 seconds, 11.8 seconds, and 12.1 seconds. What was their total time for the relay race?

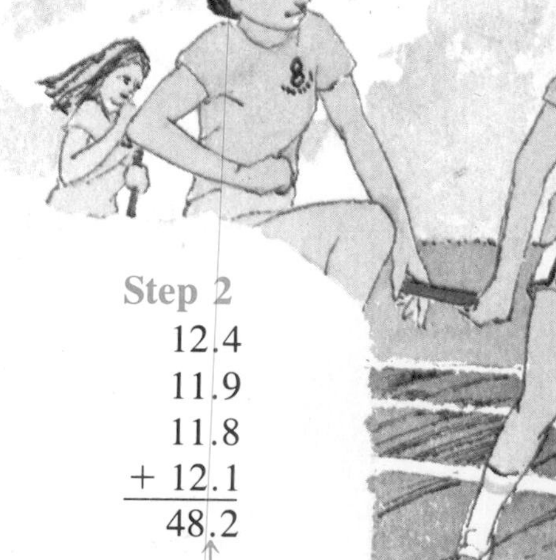

```
                     Step 1                          Step 2
  12.4                12.4                            12.4
  11.9                11.9                            11.9
  11.8                11.8                            11.8
+ 12.1              + 12.1                          + 12.1
                      48 2                            48.2
                                                        ↑
          Add as with whole numbers.     Line up the decimal points.
```

A. Add.

```
1.   0.3      2.   2.10     3.   1.432     4.   13.7194
     0.2           3.41          0.416          24.8236
     0.6           2.14          4.921           6.9139
   + 0.7         + 4.20        + 2.161       +   2.6004
```

B. Add.

Example 12 + 3.4 + 7.29

```
    12.    —— or, change to hundredths ——→   12.00
     3.4   ——————————————————————————→        3.40
 +   7.29                                  +  7.29
    22.69                                    22.69
     ↑                                        ↑
     └———— Line up the decimal points. ————┘
```

5. 4 + 2.7 + 6.008 **6.** 0.9 + 0.406 + 0.25 **7.** 1.1 + 6 + 3.006 + 0.91

C. Add.

```
8.  $ 6.41     9.  $ 17.36    10.  $ 0.31    11.  $ 719.34
      8.23            8.19           0.42            82.96
      9.46           14.23           0.93           135.87
    + 9.24         + 36.19         + 0.88       +     8.24
```

Add.

1. $\begin{array}{r} 2.4 \\ +\ 4.3 \\ \hline \end{array}$

2. $\begin{array}{r} 6.04 \\ +\ 3.32 \\ \hline \end{array}$

3. $\begin{array}{r} 41.74 \\ +\ 38.23 \\ \hline \end{array}$

4. $\begin{array}{r} 31.238 \\ +\ 41.750 \\ \hline \end{array}$

5. $\begin{array}{r} 0.96 \\ +\ 0.8 \\ \hline \end{array}$

6. $\begin{array}{r} 2.8 \\ +\ 3.49 \\ \hline \end{array}$

7. $\begin{array}{r} 34.065 \\ +\ \ 5.09 \\ \hline \end{array}$

8. $\begin{array}{r} 7.638 \\ +\ 9.84 \\ \hline \end{array}$

9. $\begin{array}{r} 0.6 \\ 0.7 \\ +\ 0.4 \\ \hline \end{array}$

10. $\begin{array}{r} 0.09 \\ 0.04 \\ +\ 0.08 \\ \hline \end{array}$

11. $\begin{array}{r} 0.348 \\ 0.253 \\ +\ 0.617 \\ \hline \end{array}$

12. $\begin{array}{r} 0.5367 \\ 0.7204 \\ +\ 0.1689 \\ \hline \end{array}$

13. $\begin{array}{r} 7.5 \\ 8.3 \\ +\ 5.6 \\ \hline \end{array}$

14. $\begin{array}{r} 17.3 \\ 24.8 \\ +\ \ 3.9 \\ \hline \end{array}$

15. $\begin{array}{r} 8.03 \\ 4.17 \\ +\ 5.23 \\ \hline \end{array}$

16. $\begin{array}{r} 12.05 \\ 13.78 \\ +\ 24.86 \\ \hline \end{array}$

17. $\begin{array}{r} 6.4163 \\ 7.3187 \\ 5.4128 \\ +\ 0.3517 \\ \hline \end{array}$

18. $\begin{array}{r} 24.3168 \\ 19.8904 \\ 7.7146 \\ +\ \ 0.8238 \\ \hline \end{array}$

19. $\begin{array}{r} 0.53016 \\ 0.71023 \\ 0.68424 \\ +\ 0.78346 \\ \hline \end{array}$

20. $\begin{array}{r} 3.10967 \\ 412.23687 \\ 8.40816 \\ +\ \ \ 3.27912 \\ \hline \end{array}$

21. 2.3 + 4.6

22. 7.04 + 6.39

23. 8.913 + 4.167

24. 3 + 1.4 + 0.56

25. 0.5 + 0.046 + 0.23

26. 12 + 3.5 + 0.069

27. $\begin{array}{r} \$\,0.64 \\ 0.79 \\ 0.64 \\ +\ 0.98 \\ \hline \end{array}$

28. $\begin{array}{r} \$\,3.41 \\ 0.89 \\ 2.63 \\ +\ 7.84 \\ \hline \end{array}$

29. $\begin{array}{r} \$\,36.40 \\ 8.68 \\ 29.37 \\ +\ 16.79 \\ \hline \end{array}$

30. $\begin{array}{r} \$\,513.49 \\ 89.84 \\ 614.23 \\ +\ \ 83.45 \\ \hline \end{array}$

★ 31. 19 + 0.753 + 1.69 + 3.2 + 5.0006

★ 32. 0.10569 + 25.6 + 3.992 + 104

Solve.

33. In a 400-m relay race, the times for the team members were 13.7, 12.9, 13.4 and 12.9 seconds. What was the total time for the team?

34. In three 100-m swimming races, a swimmer had times of 55.65, 55.49, and 56.02 seconds. What was the swimmer's total time for the 3 races?

Subtracting Decimals

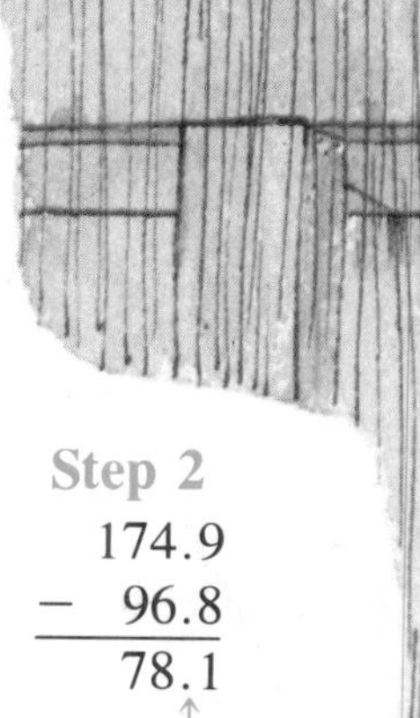

The heaviest rainfall in the United States was 96.8 cm in Florida. Hawaii has an average yearly rainfall of 174.9 cm. What is the difference in these rainfalls?

$$\begin{array}{r} 174.9 \\ -\ \ 96.8 \\ \hline \end{array}$$

Step 1

$$\begin{array}{r} 174.9 \\ -\ \ 96.8 \\ \hline 78\ 1 \end{array}$$

Subtract as with whole numbers.

Step 2

$$\begin{array}{r} 174.9 \\ -\ \ 96.8 \\ \hline 78.1 \end{array}$$

Line up the decimal points.

A. Subtract.

1. $\begin{array}{r} 0.34 \\ -\ 0.17 \\ \hline \end{array}$ **2.** $\begin{array}{r} 0.356 \\ -\ 0.170 \\ \hline \end{array}$ **3.** $\begin{array}{r} 3.4 \\ -\ 2.7 \\ \hline \end{array}$ **4.** $\begin{array}{r} 4.362 \\ -\ 2.574 \\ \hline \end{array}$ **5.** $\begin{array}{r} 9.3468 \\ -\ 3.1939 \\ \hline \end{array}$

B. Subtract.

Example 6.8 − 3.57

$\begin{array}{r} 6.8 \\ -\ 3.57 \\ \hline \end{array}$ —— Change to hundredths ——→ $\begin{array}{r} 6.80 \\ -\ 3.57 \\ \hline 3.23 \end{array}$

Line up the decimal points.

6. 0.4 − 0.07 **7.** 0.09 − 0.006 **8.** 0.59 − 0.412 **9.** 6.3 − 4.09

C. Decimals can be subtracted from whole numbers.

Example 7 − 2.4 $\begin{array}{r} 7. \\ -\ 2.4 \\ \hline \end{array}$ —— Change to tenths ——→ $\begin{array}{r} 7.0 \\ -\ 2.4 \\ \hline 4.6 \end{array}$

Subtract.

10. 6 − 3.1 **11.** 8 − 0.7 **12.** 58 − 3.47 **13.** 96 − 3.419

D. Subtract.

14. $\begin{array}{r} \$8.14 \\ -\ 2.23 \\ \hline \end{array}$ **15.** $\begin{array}{r} \$9.00 \\ -\ 6.14 \\ \hline \end{array}$ **16.** $\begin{array}{r} \$18.34 \\ -\ \ 7.30 \\ \hline \end{array}$ **17.** $\begin{array}{r} \$40.83 \\ -\ \ 6.14 \\ \hline \end{array}$ **18.** $\begin{array}{r} \$356.23 \\ -\ 218.49 \\ \hline \end{array}$

Subtract.

1. 36.8 − 24.4	2. 526.8 − 115.6	3. 3.7 − 1.9	4. 241.6 − 234.7
5. 24.29 − 13.36	6. 41.68 − 24.08	7. 34.74 − 19.85	8. 124.04 − 12.39
9. 0.008 − 0.004	10. 0.063 − 0.042	11. 0.746 − 0.213	12. 8.348 − 2.126
13. 0.621 − 0.424	14. 0.831 − 0.249	15. 8.340 − 1.621	16. 9.356 − 8.650
17. 0.0009 − 0.0004	18. 0.0063 − 0.0017	19. 0.0341 − 0.0169	20. 0.4516 − 0.2370
21. 2.0034 − 1.0104	22. 6.3412 − 4.1502	23. 7.3623 − 4.0428	24. 9.7164 − 2.3589
25. 0.8 − 0.3	26. 0.7 − 0.5	27. 0.07 − 0.03	28. 0.09 − 0.06
29. 0.008 − 0.006	30. 0.016 − 0.008	31. 0.934 − 0.824	32. 0.8136 − 0.4128
33. 0.6 − 0.24	34. 0.9 − 0.35	35. 0.07 − 0.008	36. 0.09 − 0.013
37. 0.46 − 0.234	38. 7.4 − 2.36	39. 8.9 − 2.47	40. 3.1 − 2.091
41. 6 − 0.4	42. 5 − 0.23	43. 8 − 1.16	44. 6 − 2.345
45. \$7.12 − 2.59	46. \$8.00 − 7.23	47. \$40.72 − 8.14	48. \$752.24 − 268.19

Solve.

49. One year Atlanta had 166 cm of rain. Jacksonville had 121.4 cm. How much more rain did Atlanta have?

50. One year Washington, D.C., had 128.3 cm of rain. San Juan had 130.2 cm. How much more rain did San Juan have?

Estimating Sums and Differences

Mario's 2 packed valises have masses of 9.3 kg and 6.5 kg. Estimate their sum and their difference to the nearest whole number.

Estimate by rounding.

Sum		Difference	
9.3 =	9	9.3 =	9
+ 6.5 =	+ 7	− 6.5 =	− 7
	16		2

↑ Estimates ↑

A. Estimate to the nearest whole number.

1. $\begin{array}{r} 4.683 \\ +\ 0.71 \\ \hline \end{array}$

2. $\begin{array}{r} 7.823 \\ 6.41 \\ +\ 0.862 \\ \hline \end{array}$

3. $\begin{array}{r} 5.86 \\ -\ 3.456 \\ \hline \end{array}$

4. $\begin{array}{r} 6.7234 \\ -\ 3.5138 \\ \hline \end{array}$

B. Estimate to the nearest tenth.

Examples

Sum		Difference	
3.623 =	3.6	4.86 =	4.9
0.29 =	0.3	− 1.374 =	− 1.4
+ 5.386 =	+ 5.4		3.5
	9.3		

↑ Estimates ↑

5. $\begin{array}{r} 0.3 \\ 0.26 \\ +\ 0.852 \\ \hline \end{array}$

6. $\begin{array}{r} 7.428 \\ 6.37 \\ 0.843 \\ +\ 1.609 \\ \hline \end{array}$

7. $\begin{array}{r} 0.89 \\ -\ 0.243 \\ \hline \end{array}$

8. $\begin{array}{r} 4.8417 \\ -\ 2.3689 \\ \hline \end{array}$

C. Estimate to the nearest dollar.

9. $\begin{array}{r} \$8.23 \\ 7.56 \\ 6.23 \\ +\ 8.95 \\ \hline \end{array}$

10. $\begin{array}{r} \$7.78 \\ 2.50 \\ 3.50 \\ 8.49 \\ +\ 6.38 \\ \hline \end{array}$

11. $\begin{array}{r} \$7.47 \\ -\ 2.89 \\ \hline \end{array}$

12. $\begin{array}{r} \$16.57 \\ -\ \ 3.58 \\ \hline \end{array}$

Practice

Estimate to the nearest whole number.

1. $0.89 + 2.083$

2. $6.724 + 2.58 + 0.923$

3. $8.316 + 2.492 + 3.542$

4. $6.4139 + 2.8238 + 3.2500$

5. $8.3 - 0.78$

6. $4.9 - 0.87$

7. $6.87 - 2.23$

8. $8.7234 - 2.6009$

Estimate to the nearest tenth.

9. $0.67 + 0.72$

10. $0.835 + 0.27 + 0.85$

11. $7.3 + 0.65 + 0.912 + 1.45$

12. $6.412 + 2.375 + 3.46 + 8.9$

13. $0.92 - 0.45$

14. $0.68 - 0.2$

15. $12.34 - 8.45$

16. $6.319 - 2.4834$

Estimate to the nearest dollar.

17. $\$7.56 + 8.23 + 6.54$

18. $\$6.47 + 8.37 + 9.52 + 6.89$

19. $\$7.37 - 2.54$

20. $\$24.88 - 9.48$

FIND OUT!

Brainteaser

Nine chickens look alike, but one is heavier than the others. How can you find the heavier chicken with just two weighings on a balance scale? You do not need to know the actual weights.

Keeping Fit

Add.

1. $\begin{array}{r} 16{,}814 \\ 29{,}312 \\ 8{,}768 \\ +\ 43{,}178 \\ \hline \end{array}$

2. $\begin{array}{r} 716{,}412 \\ 89{,}374 \\ 421{,}821 \\ +\ 86{,}764 \\ \hline \end{array}$

3. $\begin{array}{r} 1{,}693{,}704 \\ 286{,}803 \\ 4{,}416{,}214 \\ +\ 8{,}934{,}800 \\ \hline \end{array}$

4. $\begin{array}{r} \$71{,}604 \\ 86{,}416 \\ 9{,}789 \\ +\ 11{,}689 \\ \hline \end{array}$

Subtract.

5. $\begin{array}{r} 41{,}306 \\ -\ 29{,}800 \\ \hline \end{array}$

6. $\begin{array}{r} 23{,}518 \\ -\ 8{,}916 \\ \hline \end{array}$

7. $\begin{array}{r} 412{,}316 \\ -\ 89{,}427 \\ \hline \end{array}$

8. $\begin{array}{r} \$9.00 \\ -\ 4.87 \\ \hline \end{array}$

Multiply.

9. $\begin{array}{r} 4{,}136 \\ \times\ 7 \\ \hline \end{array}$

10. $\begin{array}{r} 4{,}789 \\ \times\ 28 \\ \hline \end{array}$

11. $\begin{array}{r} 3{,}418 \\ \times\ 204 \\ \hline \end{array}$

12. $\begin{array}{r} 5{,}689 \\ \times\ 860 \\ \hline \end{array}$

Divide.

13. $7\overline{)147}$

14. $8\overline{)65{,}624}$

15. $9\overline{)64{,}483}$

16. $38\overline{)61{,}236}$

Compare. Use >, <, or =.

17. 0.3 ≣ 0.19

18. 0.005 ≣ 0.04

19. 1.6 ≣ 0.28

20. 0.02 ≣ 0.2

21. 0.04 ≣ 0.040

22. 0.61 ≣ 0.6

Round.

23. 23.062 to the nearest tenth

24. 1.631 to the nearest hundredth

25. 3.782 to the nearest whole number

26. 0.02753 to the nearest thousandth

Write in exponential notation.

27. 10,000

28. 100

29. 100,000

30. 1,000,000

Write standard numerals.

31. 3.5×10^4

32. 6×10^7

33. 5.2×10^5

Write in scientific notation.

34. 800

35. 2,500

36. 90,000

37. 640,000,000

Mid-Chapter Review

Add. *(102)*

1. $\begin{array}{r} 8.6 \\ 7.4 \\ 6.5 \\ +\ 8.2 \\ \hline \end{array}$

2. $3 + 2.1 + 0.056$

3. $17 + 0.158 + 5.3$

Subtract. *(104)*

4. $\begin{array}{r} 8.4 \\ -\ 3.6 \\ \hline \end{array}$

5. $0.08 - 0.03$

6. $7 - 1.4$

Estimate to the nearest whole number. *(106)*

7. $\begin{array}{r} 6.734 \\ 2.04 \\ +\ 4.351 \\ \hline \end{array}$

8. $\begin{array}{r} 8.4 \\ 9.3 \\ +\ 6.4 \\ \hline \end{array}$

9. $\begin{array}{r} 7.3 \\ -\ 0.78 \\ \hline \end{array}$

10. $\begin{array}{r} 6.3419 \\ -\ 2.8124 \\ \hline \end{array}$

Estimate to the nearest tenth. *(106)*

11. $\begin{array}{r} 0.7 \\ 0.63 \\ +\ 0.41 \\ \hline \end{array}$

12. $\begin{array}{r} 0.841 \\ 0.27 \\ +\ 0.753 \\ \hline \end{array}$

13. $\begin{array}{r} 0.83 \\ -\ 0.64 \\ \hline \end{array}$

14. $\begin{array}{r} 17.56 \\ -\ 9.28 \\ \hline \end{array}$

FIND OUT!

Brainteasers

Choose the number that belongs in the blank in the sequence.

1. 2.3, 3.4, 4.5, __?__, 6.7, 7.8

a. 5.5 **b.** 6.5 **c.** 5.6 **d.** 6.0

2. 2, 8, 18, __?__, 50, 72, 98

a. 24 **b.** 72 **c.** 28 **d.** 32

3. Assume that this statement is true.
If the road is covered with ice, it is slippery.
Which of the following **must** be true also?
a. If the road is slippery, it is covered with ice.
b. If the road is not covered with ice, it is not slippery.
c. If the road is not slippery, it is not covered with ice.
d. If the road is not covered with ice, it is slippery.

Multiplying Whole Numbers and Decimals

The thickness of a metal part for a machine is 1.2 cm. How high is a stack of 4 parts?

$$\begin{array}{r} 1.2 \\ \times\, 4 \\ \hline \end{array} \quad \text{THINK} \quad \begin{array}{r} 1.2 \\ 1.2 \\ 1.2 \\ +\, 1.2 \\ \hline 4.8 \end{array} \quad \text{or}$$

Step 1

$$\begin{array}{r} 1.2 \\ \times\, 4 \\ \hline 4\;8 \end{array}$$

Multiply as with whole numbers.

Step 2

$$\begin{array}{r} 1.2 \\ \times\, 4 \\ \hline 4.8 \end{array}$$

1.2 ← one decimal place

4.8 ← one decimal place

Determine where to place the decimal point.

So, a stack of 4 parts is 4.8 cm high.

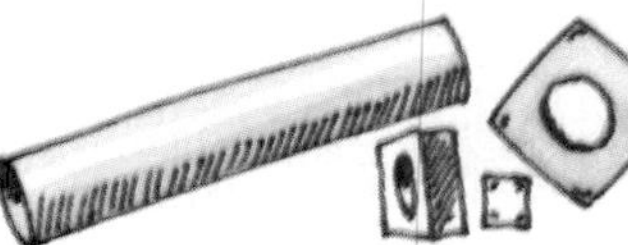

A. Multiply.

1. 3×0.2
2. $\begin{array}{r} 0.4 \\ \times\, 7 \\ \hline \end{array}$
3. $\begin{array}{r} 3.2 \\ \times\, 4 \\ \hline \end{array}$
4. $\begin{array}{r} 0.52 \\ \times\, 9 \\ \hline \end{array}$
5. $\begin{array}{r} 0.13 \\ \times\, 12 \\ \hline \end{array}$

Here is a shortcut for multiplying by powers of 10.

$$\begin{array}{r} 0.243 \\ \times\, 10 \\ \hline 2.430 \end{array} \qquad \begin{array}{r} 0.243 \\ \times\, 100 \\ \hline 24.300 \end{array} \qquad \begin{array}{r} 0.243 \\ \times\, 1{,}000 \\ \hline 243.000 \end{array}$$

$10 \times 0.243 = 2.43$ To multiply by 10, "move" the decimal point 1 place to the right.

$100 \times 0.243 = 24.3$ To multiply by 100, "move" the decimal point 2 places to the right.

$1{,}000 \times 0.243 = 243$ To multiply by 1,000, "move" the decimal point 3 places to the right.

B. Multiply by "moving" the decimal point.

6. 10×1.386
7. 100×1.386
8. $1{,}000 \times 1.386$
9. 100×2.34

C. Sometimes you need to insert zeros when you multiply by powers of 10.

Examples

100×0.6

$100 \times 0.60 = 60$

$1{,}000 \times 0.6$

$1{,}000 \times 0.600 = 600$

Multiply by "moving" the decimal point.

10. 100×0.9
11. $1{,}000 \times 0.9$
12. $1{,}000 \times 0.08$
13. $1{,}000 \times 3.1$

Practice

Multiply.

1. 2×0.4
2. 3×0.3
3. 6×0.1
4. 8×0.2
5. 0.7×4
6. 0.5×3
7. 0.9×6
8. 0.8×7
9. 3.2×3
10. 8.1×4
11. 9.3×5
12. 6.7×8
13. 24.3×6
14. 37.2×9
15. 124.3×53
16. 246.8×47
17. 3×0.03
18. 4×0.08
19. 5×0.05
20. 3×0.12
21. 0.06×2
22. 0.09×8
23. 0.14×3
24. 0.35×7
25. 2.31×2
26. 6.14×4
27. 3.04×37
28. 2.36×58
29. 4×0.002
30. 6×0.008
31. 3×0.012
32. 4×0.023
33. 0.007×6
34. 0.012×7
35. 0.123×48
36. 2.2376×75
37. 2.3×44
38. 3.14×26
39. 4.013×17
40. 6.2341×57
41. 10×0.63
42. 100×9.34
43. 100×0.8
44. $1,000 \times 2.75$

Solve.

45. A round bar of steel is 12.06 kg. What is the mass of 8 of these round bars of steel?

46. Metal sheets are each 0.98 in. thick. How high is a stack of 32 of these sheets?

Multiplying Decimals

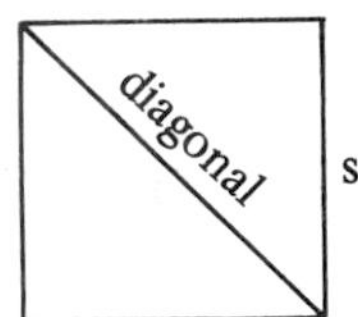

In a square, a side is approximately 0.7 times the length of a diagonal. How long is a side if a diagonal is 5.4 cm?

$$\begin{array}{r} 5.4 \\ \times\ 0.7 \\ \hline 3.78 \end{array}$$

- 5.4 ← 1 decimal place
- × 0.7 ← + 1 decimal place
- 3.78 ← 2 decimal places

The number of decimal places in a product is the *sum* of the number of decimal places in the numbers multiplied.

A. Multiply.

Example

$$\begin{array}{r} 4.24 \\ \times\ 1.3 \\ \hline 1\ 272 \\ 4\ 24\ \ \\ \hline 5.512 \end{array}$$

- 4.24 ← 2 decimal places
- × 1.3 ← + 1 decimal place
- 5.512 ← 3 decimal places

Multiply.

1. 0.6×0.8

2. 2.34×0.4

3. 6.213×0.7

4. 1.23×0.34

Sometimes it is necessary to insert zeros.

$$\begin{array}{r} 0.64 \\ \times\ 0.007 \\ \hline \end{array} \qquad \begin{array}{r} 0.64 \\ \times\ 0.007 \\ \hline 448 \end{array} \qquad \begin{array}{r} 0.64 \\ \times\ 0.007 \\ \hline 0.00448 \end{array}$$

Multiply as with whole numbers.

Place the decimal point. You need to insert 2 zeros.

THINK 2 decimal places + 3 decimal places = 5 decimal places

B. Multiply.

5. 0.4×0.003

6. 1.36×0.007

7. 0.004×0.002

8. 2.003×0.008

9. 1.34×0.9

10. 7.64×0.23

11. 1.007×0.6

12. 3.412×0.013

Practice

Multiply.

1. $0.2 \times .04$
2. 0.6×0.4
3. 0.04×0.3
4. 0.1×0.01
5. 0.7×0.4
6. 0.1×0.1
7. 1.8×0.2
8. 34.1×0.6
9. 0.02×0.3
10. 0.08×0.4
11. 0.24×0.8
12. 1.34×0.4
13. 0.306×0.2
14. 1.412×0.8
15. 0.34×0.21
16. 0.34×0.36
17. 0.236×0.04
18. 0.156×0.34
19. 0.862×0.23
20. 2.3464×0.94
21. 0.2×0.003
22. 0.47×0.002
23. 0.007×0.003
24. 0.04×0.01
25. 3.46×0.003
26. 2.403×0.008
27. 16.47×1.36
28. 8.341×0.204
29. 0.5×0.7
30. 0.03×0.04
31. 0.6×0.04
32. 0.53×0.02

Solve.

33. The diagonal of a square is about 1.4 times the length of a side. How long is the diagonal of a square whose side is 8.3 cm? Round to the nearest whole number.

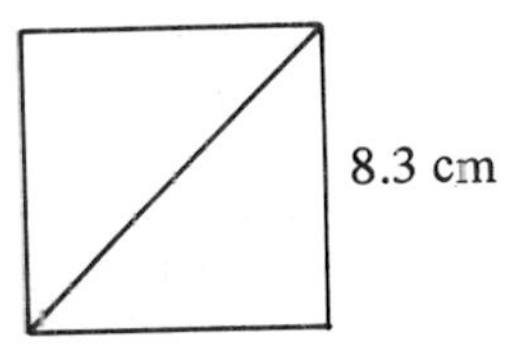

34. A 1-m long steel bar has a mass of 0.78 kg. What is the mass of a steel bar which is 3.64 m long? Round the answer to the nearest tenth.

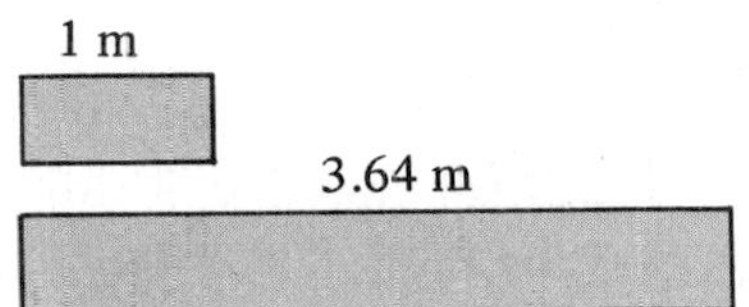

Problem Solving

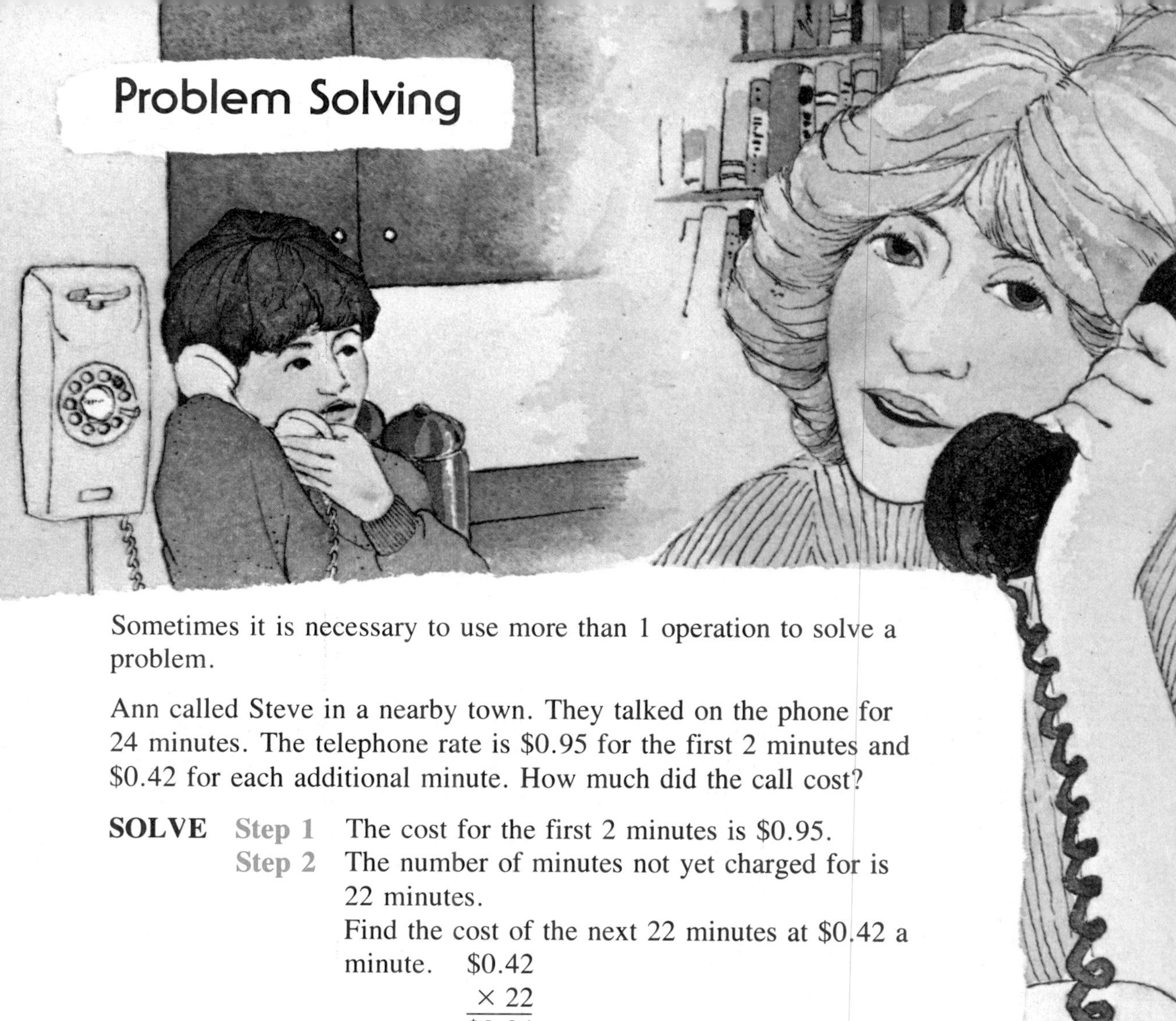

Sometimes it is necessary to use more than 1 operation to solve a problem.

Ann called Steve in a nearby town. They talked on the phone for 24 minutes. The telephone rate is \$0.95 for the first 2 minutes and \$0.42 for each additional minute. How much did the call cost?

SOLVE Step 1 The cost for the first 2 minutes is \$0.95.

Step 2 The number of minutes not yet charged for is 22 minutes.

Find the cost of the next 22 minutes at \$0.42 a minute.

$$\begin{array}{r} \$0.42 \\ \times\ 22 \\ \hline \$9.24 \end{array}$$

Step 3 Find the total cost.

$$\begin{array}{r} \$\,0.95 \\ +\ 9.24 \\ \hline \$10.19 \end{array}$$

The call cost \$10.19.

A. Solve.

1. Ms. Valenti called Los Angeles person-to-person to speak to her mother. It cost \$3.55 for the first 3 minutes and \$0.38 for each additional minute. How much did a 10-minute call cost her?

2. Henry and Sue talked on the telephone for 40 minutes. The rate was 4 message units for the first 3 minutes and 1 message unit for each additional minute. Each message unit cost 8.2 cents. What did the call cost?

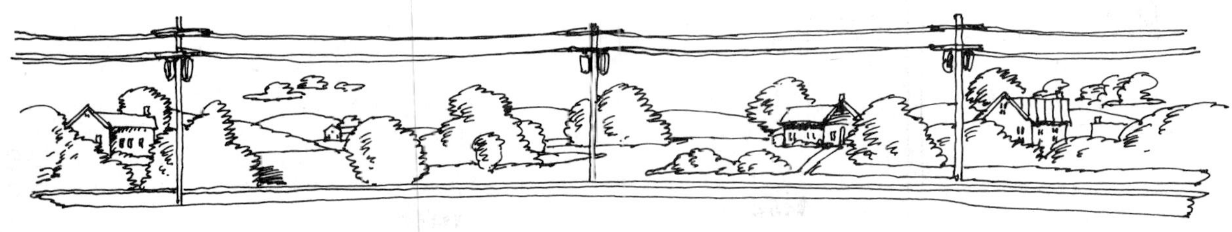

Practice

Solve.

1. Marcia called Henry in a nearby town. They spoke on the phone for 36 minutes. The rate is $0.54 for the first 2 minutes and $0.23 for each additional minute. How much did the call cost?

2. A lawyer called a client. They spoke for a half hour. The rate is $1.37 for the first 3 minutes and $0.23 for each additional minute. How much did the call cost?

3. The total cost of toll calls for 1 month was $16.16. Mrs. Perez made 1 toll call to New Jersey for $3.16. If the other 2 toll calls cost the same, how much did each cost?

4. The total cost of toll calls for one month was $35.07. Mr. Johnson's toll calls within his state totaled $22.16. He made another toll call to Nevada which cost $5.73. If the other 2 toll calls cost the same, how much did each cost?

5. Mr. Loo called a friend in the city and spoke for 25 minutes. The rate was 2 message units for the first 3 minutes and 2 message units for each additional minute. Each message unit costs 8.2 cents. What did the call cost?

6. Two friends spoke on the phone for 24 minutes. The rate was 6 message units for the first 2 minutes and 2 message units for each additional minute. Each message unit costs 8.2 cents. What did the call cost?

7. A direct-dial call of 20 minutes costs $1.35 for the first 2 minutes and $0.54 for each additional minute. The same call made person-to-person cost $3.29 for the first 3 minutes and $0.54 for each additional minute. How much is saved by a direct-dial call?

8. An operator-assisted call costs $2.15 for the first 3 minutes and $0.36 for each additional minute. A direct-dial call costs $0.52 for the first minute and $0.36 for each additional minute. How much is saved on a 10-minute call dialed direct?

Dividing Decimals by Whole Numbers

A piece of trim is 0.8 m long. It is cut into 4 equal parts. How long is each part?

$4\overline{)0.8}$ THINK $\begin{array}{r} 2\text{ tenths} \\ 4\overline{)8\text{ tenths}} \end{array}$, or $\begin{array}{r} 0.2 \\ 4\overline{)0.8} \end{array}$

To divide by a whole number, line up the decimal points in the dividend and the quotient. Divide as with whole numbers.

A. Divide.

1. $3\overline{)0.6}$ **2.** $4\overline{)1.2}$ **3.** $6\overline{)36.6}$ **4.** $7\overline{)13.3}$

B. Be careful with the zeros next to the decimal point.

Example $\begin{array}{r} 0.02 \\ 4\overline{)0.08} \end{array}$ $\begin{array}{r} 0.08 \\ 4\overline{)0.32} \end{array}$ $\begin{array}{r} 0.002 \\ 4\overline{)0.008} \end{array}$

Line up the decimal points.
Divide as with whole numbers.
Insert zeros if necessary.

Divide.

5. $2\overline{)0.06}$ **6.** $6\overline{)0.42}$ **7.** $7\overline{)1.47}$ **8.** $8\overline{)23.04}$

9. $3\overline{)0.009}$ **10.** $2\overline{)0.060}$ **11.** $5\overline{)0.500}$ **12.** $7\overline{)30.324}$

13. $31\overline{)148.8}$ **14.** $23\overline{)56.35}$ **15.** $46\overline{)1.058}$ **16.** $79\overline{)158.79}$

17. $27\overline{)13.689}$ **18.** $18\overline{)63.36}$ **19.** $23\overline{)10.373}$ **20.** $98\overline{)24.50}$

Practice

Divide.

1. $3\overline{)0.9}$	**2.** $3\overline{)0.3}$	**3.** $3\overline{)2.7}$	**4.** $7\overline{)3.5}$
5. $4\overline{)12.4}$	**6.** $4\overline{)24.8}$	**7.** $2\overline{)0.08}$	**8.** $6\overline{)0.36}$
9. $2\overline{)8.48}$	**10.** $4\overline{)1.64}$	**11.** $6\overline{)48.42}$	**12.** $3\overline{)48.45}$
13. $3\overline{)0.009}$	**14.** $2\overline{)0.014}$	**15.** $3\overline{)0.969}$	**16.** $3\overline{)0.159}$
17. $4\overline{)4.848}$	**18.** $2\overline{)8.124}$	**19.** $6\overline{)18.612}$	**20.** $3\overline{)42.012}$
21. $6\overline{)17.022}$	**22.** $4\overline{)1.624}$	**23.** $9\overline{)2.736}$	**24.** $4\overline{)34.136}$
25. $23\overline{)36.8}$	**26.** $41\overline{)98.4}$	**27.** $41\overline{)14.35}$	**28.** $59\overline{)18.88}$
29. $32\overline{)68.16}$	**30.** $18\overline{)60.12}$	**31.** $76\overline{)1{,}778.4}$	**32.** $27\overline{)1{,}379.7}$
33. $72\overline{)168.48}$	**34.** $86\overline{)145.34}$	**35.** $45\overline{)644.40}$	**36.** $56\overline{)113.68}$
37. $121\overline{)42.108}$	**38.** $142\overline{)59.214}$	**39.** $261\overline{)33.408}$	**40.** $343\overline{)29.498}$
41. $24\overline{)55.2}$	**42.** $86\overline{)318.2}$	**43.** $78\overline{)1.56}$	**44.** $24\overline{)14.232}$
45. $7\overline{)9.8}$	**46.** $9\overline{)0.117}$	**47.** $15\overline{)30.060}$	**48.** $92\overline{)100.28}$

Solve.

49. A piece of braid is 3.6 cm long. It is cut into 6 equal parts. How long is each part?

50. A bolt of fabric is 32.9 m long. It is cut into 47 equal parts. How long is each part?

51. A piece of seam binding is 97.2 cm long. It is cut into 12 equal pieces. How long is each piece?

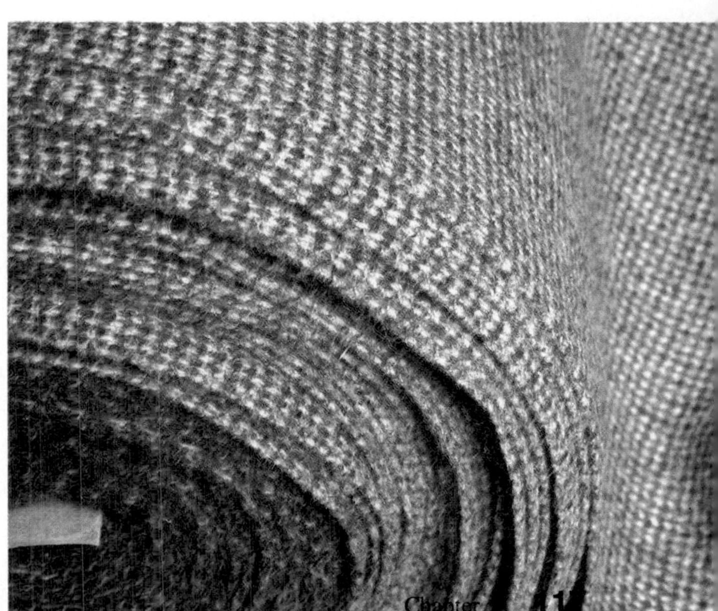

Dividing by Decimals

Jean has 3.5 m of wire for hanging pictures. She needs 0.5 m of wire for each picture. How many pieces of wire each 0.5 m long can be cut from the 3.5 m of wire?

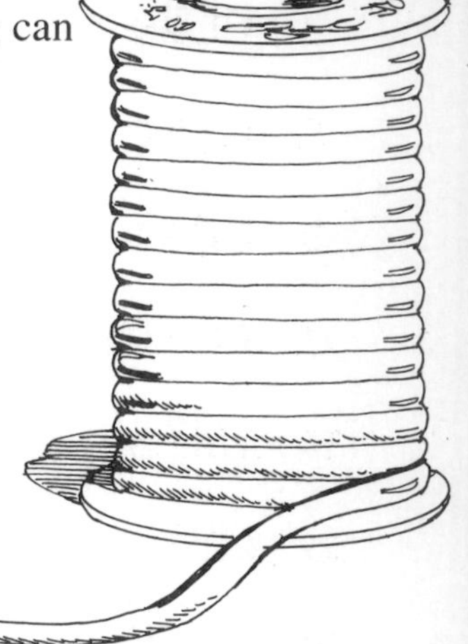

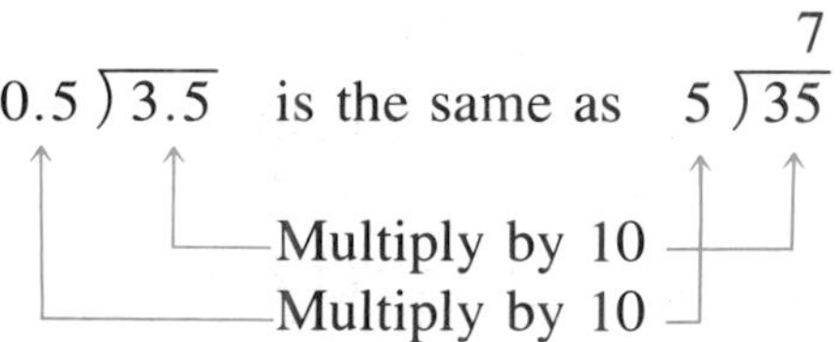

Multiplying the divisor (0.5) and the dividend (3.5) by the same number does not change the quotient.

A. Divide.

1. 0.2)0.8 **2.** 0.3)1.2 **3.** 0.9)4.5 **4.** 0.6)3.6

B. Sometimes you must multiply by a power of 10 to get a whole number divisor.

Examples 0.04)0.16 ⟶ 4)16 (multiplied by 100)
0.003)2.16 ⟶ 3)2,160 (multiplied by 1,000)

Divide.

5. 0.02)0.12 **6.** 0.08)0.32 **7.** 0.007)0.021 **8.** 0.006)0.126

> Here is a shortcut for multiplying by a power of 10.
>
> 0.5)3.5 Use a carat (∧) to "move" the decimal point.
>
> Multiplying 0.5 and 3.5 by 10 results in "moving" the decimal point 1 place to the right.
> To multiply 100, "move" 2 places to the right.
> To multiply by 1,000, "move" 3 places to the right.
>
> 0.04)0.16 0.003)2.160 ⟵ Insert zero.

C. Divide.

9. 1.2)0.144 **10.** 0.51)0.1173 **11.** 0.004)16 **12.** \$0.23)\$7.82

Practice

Divide.

1. $0.3\overline{)0.9}$
2. $0.4\overline{)0.8}$
3. $0.1\overline{)0.8}$
4. $0.2\overline{)0.6}$
5. $0.3\overline{)2.4}$
6. $0.6\overline{)2.4}$
7. $0.3\overline{)2.1}$
8. $0.5\overline{)3.0}$
9. $0.4\overline{)0.16}$
10. $0.6\overline{)0.42}$
11. $0.9\overline{)0.72}$
12. $0.8\overline{)0.48}$
13. $0.4\overline{)0.008}$
14. $0.8\overline{)0.032}$
15. $0.3\overline{)0.012}$
16. $0.9\overline{)0.027}$
17. $1.2\overline{)3.6}$
18. $2.4\overline{)5.52}$
19. $4.4\overline{)0.9328}$
20. $3.3\overline{)141.9}$
21. $0.3\overline{)6}$
22. $0.4\overline{)8}$
23. $0.9\overline{)18}$
24. $0.9\overline{)27}$
25. $0.03\overline{)0.9}$
26. $0.04\overline{)0.4}$
27. $0.01\overline{)0.1}$
28. $0.05\overline{)0.2}$
29. $0.05\overline{)0.30}$
30. $0.06\overline{)0.42}$
31. $0.08\overline{)0.72}$
32. $0.04\overline{)0.12}$
33. $0.03\overline{)0.009}$
34. $0.09\overline{)0.072}$
35. $0.07\overline{)0.217}$
36. $0.04\overline{)0.288}$
37. $6.04\overline{)193.28}$
38. $5.07\overline{)16.224}$
39. $4.04\overline{)1{,}292.8}$
40. $4.06\overline{)15.834}$
41. $0.003\overline{)0.009}$
42. $0.002\overline{)0.008}$
43. $0.003\overline{)0.06}$
44. $0.003\overline{)0.6}$
45. $0.004\overline{)0.32}$
46. $0.004\overline{)3.2}$
47. $0.004\overline{)32}$
48. $0.006\overline{)1.602}$
49. $0.012\overline{)0.48}$
50. $0.046\overline{)23}$
51. $0.109\overline{)0.4469}$
52. $0.427\overline{)3.4587}$
53. $2.3\overline{)3.68}$
54. $3.4\overline{)7.82}$
55. $0.1\overline{)2.6}$
56. $0.03\overline{)0.72}$
57. $\$0.12\overline{)\$3.00}$
58. $\$0.47\overline{)\$9.87}$
59. $\$0.36\overline{)\$15.12}$
60. $\$0.24\overline{)\$93.60}$

★ 61. $0.0006\overline{)3}$

★ 62. $0.0015\overline{)4.5}$

★ 63. $0.00025\overline{)0.8}$

Solve.

64. A roll of wire contains 1.26 m of wire. How many pieces 0.6 m long can be cut from the roll of wire?

65. Material for a fabric collage costs \$0.72 a yard. How many yards can be bought for \$8.64?

Rounding Quotients

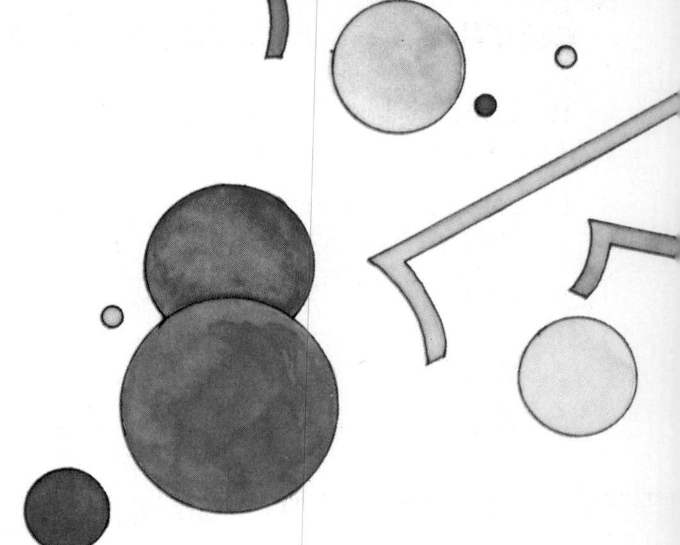

Sometimes quotients are rounded.

Divide 3.4 by 1.41. Round the quotient to the nearest tenth.

$1.41\overline{)3.4}$ $\qquad$ $1.41\overline{)3.40}$

To find a quotient to the nearest tenth, carry the division to hundredths. Then round to the nearest tenth.

$$\begin{array}{r} 2.41 \doteq 2.4 \\ 1.41\overline{)3.4000} \end{array}$$

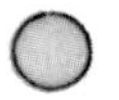

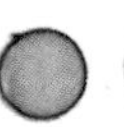

A. Find each quotient to the nearest tenth.

1. $0.3\overline{)0.5}$ **2.** $4\overline{)6.2}$ **3.** $1.9\overline{)3.4}$ **4.** $0.23\overline{)0.473}$

To find a quotient to the nearest hundredth, carry the division to thousandths. Then round to the nearest hundredth.

$0.08\overline{)0.2517}$ $\quad$ $0.08\overline{)0.2517}$ $\quad$ $0.08\overline{)0.25\ 170}$ $\quad$ $\begin{array}{r} 3.146 \doteq 3.15 \\ 0.08\overline{)0.25\ 170} \end{array}$

B. Find each quotient to the nearest hundredth.

5. $0.06\overline{)0.0257}$ **6.** $0.12\overline{)0.357}$ **7.** $13\overline{)0.946}$ **8.** $0.35\overline{)0.14897}$

Practice

Find each quotient to the nearest tenth.

1. $5\overline{)1.3}$ **2.** $7\overline{)2.6}$ **3.** $0.7\overline{)0.3}$ **4.** $0.9\overline{)0.6}$

5. $3.1\overline{)0.7}$ **6.** $4.2\overline{)5.34}$ **7.** $7.1\overline{)8.3}$ **8.** $0.34\overline{)0.789}$

Find each quotient to the nearest hundredth.

9. $0.04\overline{)0.3416}$ **10.** $0.23\overline{)0.516}$ **11.** $21\overline{)0.359}$ **12.** $15\overline{)0.746}$

13. $0.23\overline{)0.4768}$ **14.** $0.62\overline{)0.5049}$ **15.** $0.71\overline{)0.05617}$ **16.** $1.3\overline{)0.5163}$

Estimating Products and Quotients

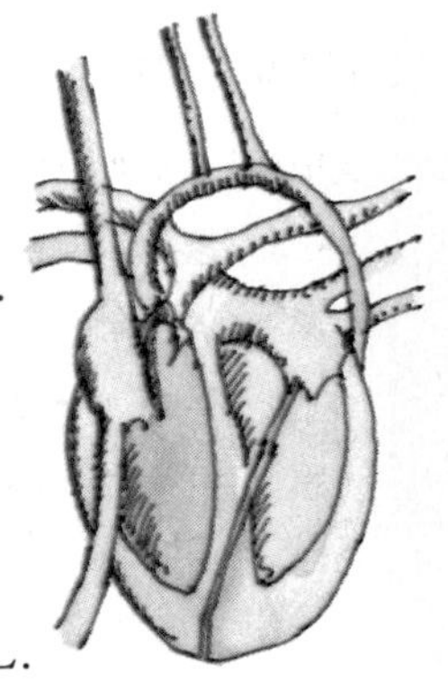

The heart pumps about 4.75 L of blood every minute. Estimate how many liters it pumps in 0.5 minutes.

To estimate a product with decimal factors:

Step 1 Round each number. Keep the decimal points if needed.
Step 2 Multiply.

	Step 1	Step 2	
4.75	5	5	
× 0.5	× 0.5	× 0.5	
		2.5	So, it pumps about 2.5 L.

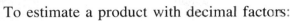

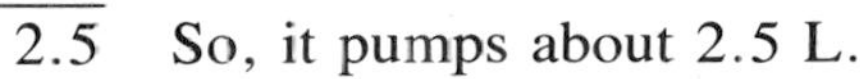

A. Estimate. Complete.

1. 5.7 → 6; × 3 → × 3

2. 3.5 → 4; × 6.4 → × 6

3. 0.31 → 0.3; × 6.8 → × 7

Here is how to estimate a quotient.

Step 1 Move the decimal points and place the decimal in the quotient as in dividing decimals.
Step 2 Round the divisor if more than 1 digit.
Step 3 Estimate the first digit in the quotient. Write 0's as needed.

Example	Step 1	Step 2	Step 3
$4.1\overline{)89.93}$	$4.1.\overline{)89.9.3}$	$40\overline{)899.3}$	$\overset{20.}{40\overline{)899.3}}$

B. Estimate.

4. $6\overline{)13.1}$ **5.** $2.8\overline{)1.82}$ **6.** $0.67\overline{)3.142}$ **7.** $0.49\overline{)31.14}$

Practice

Estimate.

1. 4.8 × 6 **2.** 3.1 × 8.2 **3.** 8.6 × 5.9 **4.** 0.21 × 4.1

5. $3\overline{)6.31}$ **6.** $4.2\overline{)0.439}$ **7.** $0.31\overline{)6.125}$ ★ **8.** $5.7\overline{)0.483}$

Equations with Decimals

Solving equations with decimals is just like solving equations with whole numbers.

$$x + 0.7 = 0.9$$
$$x + 0.7 - 0.7 = 0.9 - 0.7$$
$$x = 0.2$$

Check

$x + 0.7$	0.9
$0.2 + 0.7$	0.9
0.9	

$$3x = 1.2$$
$$\frac{3x}{3} = \frac{1.2}{3}$$
$$x = 0.4$$

Check

$3x$	1.2
$3(0.4)$	1.2
1.2	

A. Solve and check.

1. $x + 0.6 = 3.4$ **2.** $x + 3.7 = 5.9$ **3.** $x - 0.3 = 0.1$

4. $x - 0.9 = 1.7$ **5.** $5x = 0.25$ **6.** $0.4x = 2.4$

7. $\frac{x}{3} = 1.2$ **8.** $\frac{x}{0.2} = 0.2$ **9.** $\frac{x}{0.3} = 2.4$

B. Solve $2x + 0.3 = 1.5$. Complete.

10. $2x + 0.3 - \underline{\ ?\ } = 1.5 - \underline{\ ?\ }$

11. $2x = \underline{\ ?\ }$

12. $\frac{2x}{?} = \frac{1.2}{?}$

13. $x = \underline{\ ?\ }$

C. Solve and check.

14. $3x + 0.2 = 1.4$ **15.** $5x + 0.7 = 3.2$ **16.** $0.3x + 0.6 = 1.5$

17. $0.2x - 0.9 = 0.1$ **18.** $\frac{x}{4} + 0.3 = 0.6$ **19.** $\frac{x}{0.2} - 0.1 = 0.7$

Practice

Solve and check.

1. $x + 0.4 = 0.6$
2. $x + 0.3 = 0.9$
3. $x + 0.5 = 0.6$
4. $x + 0.5 = 2.3$
5. $x + 0.7 = 3.1$
6. $x + 0.9 = 2.3$
7. $x + 1.3 = 4.6$
8. $x + 2.3 = 4.7$
9. $x + 7.6 = 9.8$
10. $x - 0.4 = 0.3$
11. $x - 0.7 = 0.2$
12. $x - 0.1 = 0.4$
13. $x - 0.3 = 2.4$
14. $x - 0.9 = 3.4$
15. $x - 0.8 = 3.2$
16. $x - 1.4 = 3.9$
17. $x - 2.3 = 7.4$
18. $x - 14.7 = 32.9$
19. $2x = 0.8$
20. $3x = 0.9$
21. $4x = 0.8$
22. $3x = 2.4$
23. $8x = 3.2$
24. $4x = 0.16$
25. $0.4x = 0.8$
26. $0.9x = 8.1$
27. $0.6x = 42$
28. $\frac{x}{3} = 0.2$
29. $\frac{x}{4} = 0.1$
30. $\frac{x}{2} = 0.7$
31. $\frac{x}{0.3} = 4$
32. $\frac{x}{0.4} = 0.9$
33. $\frac{x}{2.4} = 0.7$
34. $7x + 1.6 = 3.0$
35. $0.3x + 0.4 = 2.5$
36. $0.6x + 1.2 = 3.6$
37. $2x - 0.7 = 0.3$
38. $0.3x - 0.4 = 1.4$
39. $0.5x - 1.6 = 2.9$
40. $\frac{x}{2} + 0.1 = 0.5$
41. $\frac{x}{3} + 0.3 = 0.5$
42. $\frac{x}{0.9} + 0.3 = 0.6$
43. $\frac{x}{3} - 0.1 = 0.4$
44. $\frac{x}{4} - 1.3 = 0.2$
45. $\frac{x}{0.5} - 0.8 = 0.2$
46. $x + 2.9 = 5.4$
47. $3x - 0.1 = 2$
48. $4x + 0.3 = 1.1$
49. $\frac{x}{1.3} = 6$
50. $\frac{x}{5} + 0.3 = 2.8$
51. $0.3x = 15$
52. The length of a display is 5.1 m. The length is 3 times the width. What is the width? [HINT: Use the equation $3x = 5.1$.]

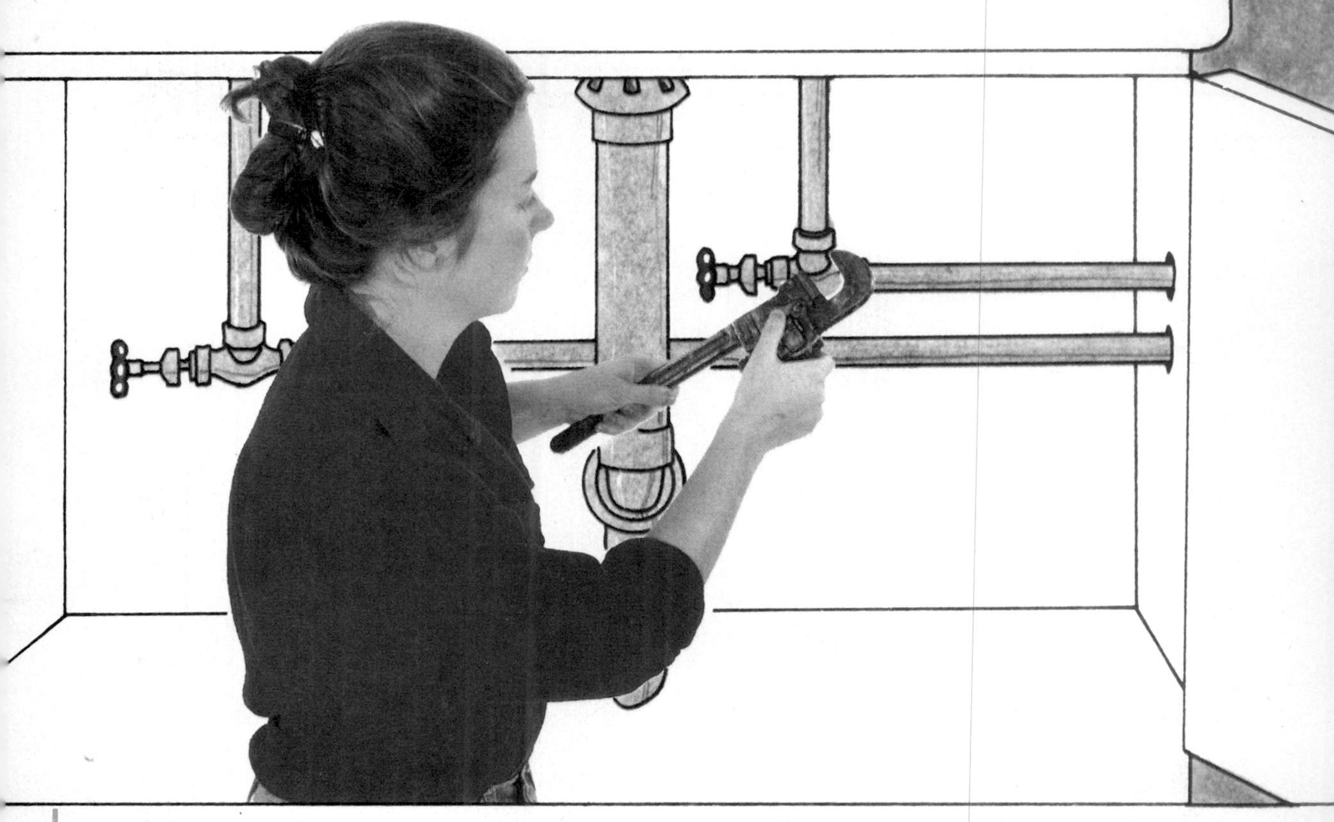

Career

Problem Solving • Plumbers and Pipefitters

Solve.

1. A plumber earns $11.41 an hour. How much does she earn in 35 hours? [HINT: Multiply.]

2. A plumber is paid bi-monthly. His yearly salary is $21,840. How much is each paycheck?

3. A force of 45 kg is applied to a pipe wrench. A force 17 times as much is applied to the pipe. How much is the force applied to the pipe?

4. A piece of copper tubing is 6.32 m long. A pipefitter cut 3 pieces each 1.17 m from the tubing. How long a piece of tubing remains?

5. The weight of 1 ft of a square steel bar is 11.95 lb per foot. Find the weight of 20 ft of the bar.

6. A plumber installed a new sink. He charged $17.50 to install the sink and $25.95 for the sink. What was the total charge?

★ 7. The outside diameter of a piece of copper tubing is 1.315 in. The thickness of the wall is 0.131 in. What is the length of the inside diameter?

★ 8. The inside diameter of a standard pipe is 26.62 mm. Its thickness is 3.38 mm. What is the length of the outside diameter?

Add. *(102)*

1. $\begin{array}{r} 4.37 \\ 1.68 \\ 3.49 \\ +\ 8.63 \\ \hline \end{array}$

2. $4 + 7.3 + 0.046$

3. $12 + 0.378 + 3.1$

Subtract. *(104)*

4. $\begin{array}{r} 8.406 \\ -\ 2.560 \\ \hline \end{array}$

5. $0.6 - 0.38$

6. $8 - 1.24$

Multiply. *(110, 112)*

7. $\begin{array}{r} 3.14 \\ \times\ 5 \\ \hline \end{array}$

8. $\begin{array}{r} 0.26 \\ \times\ 0.08 \\ \hline \end{array}$

9. 0.01×0.468

Divide. *(116, 118)*

10. $4\overline{)0.8}$

11. $0.6\overline{)0.18}$

12. $6.3\overline{)7.812}$

13. Give the quotient to the nearest tenth. $0.06\overline{)0.429}$
(120)

Estimate to the nearest whole number. *(106, 121)*

14. $\begin{array}{r} 6.317 \\ 4.936 \\ +\ 2.500 \\ \hline \end{array}$

15. $\begin{array}{r} 8.3169 \\ -\ 2.9042 \\ \hline \end{array}$

16. $\begin{array}{r} 3.6 \\ \times\ 7 \\ \hline \end{array}$

17. $3.1\overline{)6.176}$

18. Solve and check. $5x + 0.7 = 2.2$
(122)

Solve. *(114, 124)*

19. Two people spoke on the telephone for 25 minutes. The rate is $0.54 for the first 2 minutes and $0.23 for each additional minute. How much did the call cost?

20. A pipefitter needs 4 pieces of copper tubing, each 0.95 m long. How much copper tubing is needed in all?

Chapter Test

Add. *(102)*

1. $\begin{array}{r} 2.93 \\ 3.46 \\ 7.84 \\ +\ 6.52 \\ \hline \end{array}$

2. $6 + 4.9 + 0.024$

3. $9 + 0.234 + 11$

Subtract. *(104)*

4. $\begin{array}{r} 10.301 \\ -\ 1.876 \\ \hline \end{array}$

5. $0.4 - 0.31$

6. $5 - 1.23$

Multiply. *(110, 112)*

7. $\begin{array}{r} 7.82 \\ \times\ 3 \\ \hline \end{array}$

8. $\begin{array}{r} 0.15 \\ \times\ 0.09 \\ \hline \end{array}$

9. 0.15×0.03

Divide. *(116, 118)*

10. $3\overline{)0.6}$

11. $0.4\overline{)0.20}$

12. $3.1\overline{)6.51}$

13. Give the quotient to the nearest hundredth. $0.06\overline{)0.0255}$
(120)

Estimate to the nearest whole number. *(106, 121)*

14. $\begin{array}{r} 3.491 \\ 5.764 \\ +\ 4.500 \\ \hline \end{array}$

15. $\begin{array}{r} 7.4981 \\ -\ 3.6047 \\ \hline \end{array}$

16. $\begin{array}{r} 5.8 \\ \times\ 6.3 \\ \hline \end{array}$

17. $3.2\overline{)6.512}$

18. Solve and check. $\frac{x}{0.2} - 0.6 = 0.4$
(122)

Solve. *(114, 124)*

19. Jeremy called Louise and they spoke for 18 minutes. The rate was 4 message units for the first 3 minutes and 2 message units for each additional minute. Each message unit cost 8.2¢. What did the call cost?

20. A plumber charged the Browns $48 to hook up a dishwasher. The dishwasher cost $329.95. How much did the dishwasher cost in all?

Basic Skills Check

1. Solve.

$$3x - 4 = 29$$

A	B	C	D
6	7	9	11

2. What is the value of P on the number line?

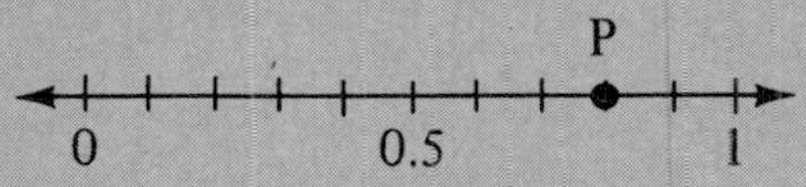

E	F	G	H
0.9	0.8	0.7	0.3

3. How many hours are there in 1,140 minutes?

A	B	C	D
23 hours	19 hours	15 hours	11 hours

4. How is the date September 26, 1979 written in numerical form?

E	F	G	H
9/26/79	26/9/79	9/79/26	10/26/79

5. Which percent has the same value as 0.3?

A	B	C	D
0.3%	3%	30%	300%

6. Which number has the same value as 53%?

E	F	G	H
0.53	53	5,300	0.0053

7. Which percent has the same value as $\frac{7}{10}$?

A	B	C	D
0.7%	7%	10%	70%

8. Which number does not have the same value as 60%?

E	F	G	H
$\frac{2}{5}$	$\frac{3}{5}$	$\frac{6}{10}$	$\frac{12}{20}$

9. Which percent of the region is shaded?

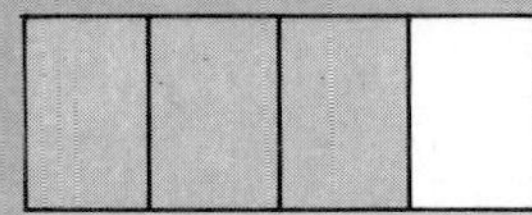

A	B	C	D
50%	60%	75%	80%

10. Which of the following decimals is equal to $\frac{5}{20}$?

E	F	G	H
0.25	0.46	0.85	0.92

11. What time is it?

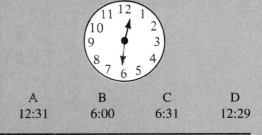

A	B	C	D
12:31	6:00	6:31	12:29

12. Which time is the same as half-past one?

E	F	G	H
12:30	12:45	1:15	1:30

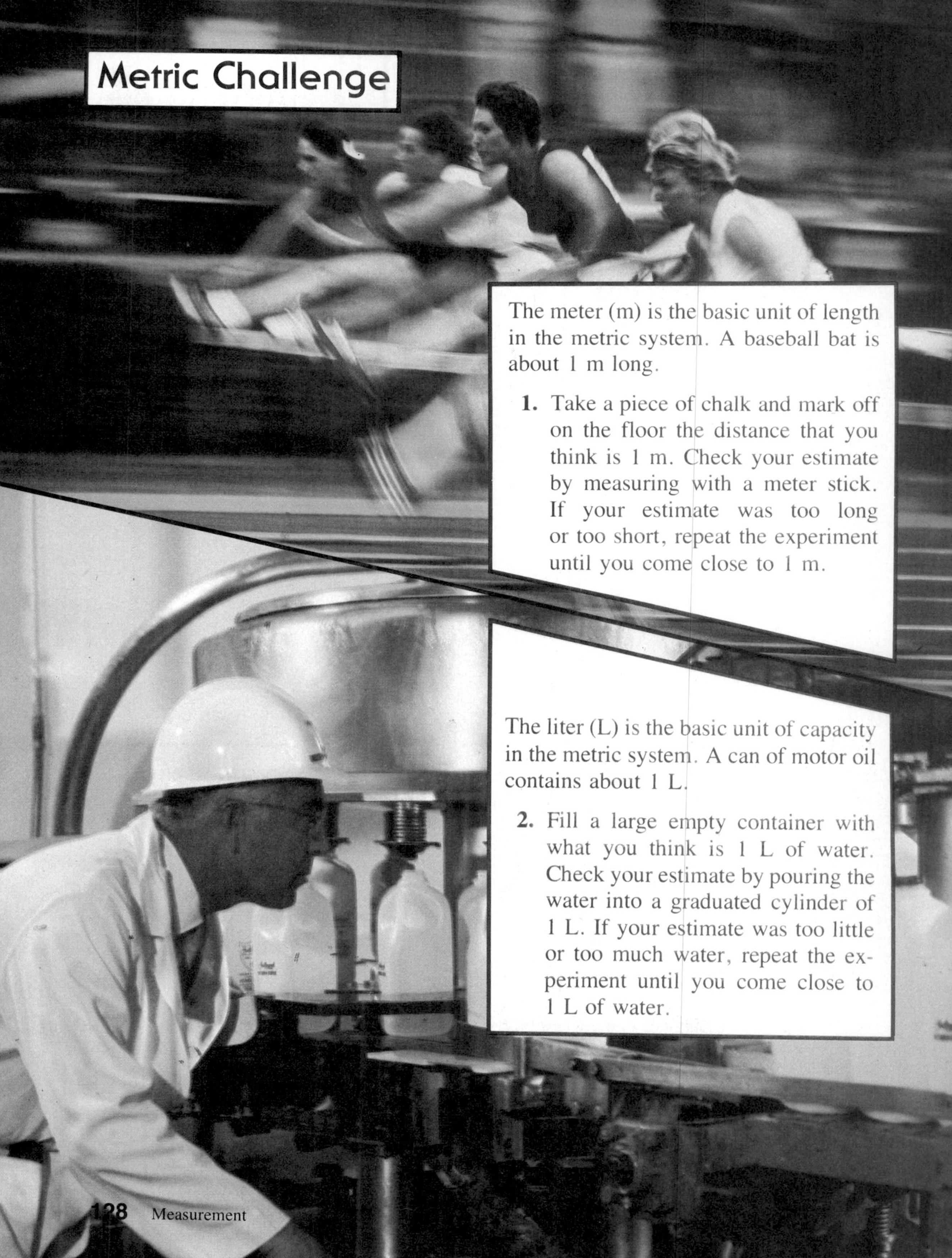

Metric Challenge

The meter (m) is the basic unit of length in the metric system. A baseball bat is about 1 m long.

1. Take a piece of chalk and mark off on the floor the distance that you think is 1 m. Check your estimate by measuring with a meter stick. If your estimate was too long or too short, repeat the experiment until you come close to 1 m.

The liter (L) is the basic unit of capacity in the metric system. A can of motor oil contains about 1 L.

2. Fill a large empty container with what you think is 1 L of water. Check your estimate by pouring the water into a graduated cylinder of 1 L. If your estimate was too little or too much water, repeat the experiment until you come close to 1 L of water.

CHAPTER
MEASUREMENT 6

The gram (g) is the basic unit of mass in the metric system. A kilogram (kg) contains 1,000 g. A paper clip has a mass of about 1 g. A book has a mass of about 1 kg.

3. Find an object in your classroom which you estimate to have a mass of 1 kg. Check your estimate by using a scale with metric weights. If your estimate was more or less than a kilogram, choose another object and repeat the experiment until you find an object close to 1 kg.

Length in the Metric System

The standard unit of length in the metric system is the meter. The other units are related to the meter. The prefix tells you its value. The most commonly used units are kilometer, meter, centimeter, and millimeter.

Unit of length	kilometer	hectometer	dekameter	meter	decimeter	centimeter	millimeter
Symbol	km	hm	dam	m	dm	cm	mm
Value	1,000 m	100 m	10 m	1 m	0.1 m	0.01 m	0.001 m
Prefix	kilo	hecto	deka		deci	centi	milli
Meaning	1,000	100	10		0.1	0.01	0.001

A. Complete.

Example 4 km = ___?___ m

4 km = 4 × 1 km
= 4 × 1,000 m
= 4,000 m

1. 7 km = ___?___ m **2.** 0.6 km = ___?___ m **3.** 5 m = ___?___ cm

4. 0.04 m = ___?___ cm **5.** 2 m = ___?___ mm **6.** 30 m = ___?___ mm

> Note the following relationships.
> Since 1 km = 1,000 m, 0.001 km = 1 m.
> Since 1 cm = 0.01 m, 100 cm = 1 m.
> Since 1 mm = 0.001 m, 1,000 mm = 1 m.

B. Complete.

Example 200 cm = ___?___ m

200 cm = 200 × 1 cm
= 200 × 0.01 m
= 2 m

7. 500 cm = ___?___ m **8.** 70 cm = ___?___ m **9.** 6,000 mm = ___?___ m

10. 2,500 mm = ___?___ m **11.** 9,000 m = ___?___ km **12.** 800 m = ___?___ km

Practice

Complete.

1. 5 km = ___?___ m
2. 90 km = ___?___ m
3. 0.8 km = ___?___ m
4. 0.07 km = ___?___ m
5. 26 km = ___?___ m
6. 6 m = ___?___ cm
7. 50 m = ___?___ cm
8. 0.8 m = ___?___ cm
9. 0.05 m = ___?___ cm
10. 0.32 m = ___?___ cm
11. 3 m = ___?___ mm
12. 50 m = ___?___ mm
13. 0.6 m = ___?___ mm
14. 0.02 m = ___?___ mm
15. 0.007 m = ___?___ mm
16. 200 cm = ___?___ m
17. 60 cm = ___?___ m
18. 9 cm = ___?___ m
19. 1,200 cm = ___?___ m
20. 700 cm = ___?___ m
21. 2,000 mm = ___?___ m
22. 600 mm = ___?___ m
23. 80 mm = ___?___ m
24. 10,000 mm = ___?___ m
25. 5,000 m = ___?___ km
26. 300 m = ___?___ km
27. 40 m = ___?___ km
28. 6 m = ___?___ km
29. ★ 50 dm = ___?___ m
30. ★ 7 hm = ___?___ m

FIND OUT!

Aid to Memory

Here is a quick way to multiply 2 numbers in the 90's.

Example 96 × 97

Step 1 Subtract each number from 100.
100 − 96 = 4   100 − 97 = 3

Step 2 Multiply the differences. Use this for the last 2 digits of the product.
4 × 3 = 12 The last 2 digits of the product are 12.

Step 3 Subtract the difference from 100 of one number from the other number. This is the first 2 digits of the product.
96 − 3 = 93 or 97 − 4 = 93
The first 2 digits of the product are 93.

Step 4 Write the product
9,312 So, 96 × 97 = 9,312

Find the products.

1. 92 × 91
2. 96 × 95
3. 93 × 98

Place Value and the Metric System

PLACE-VALUE CHART

Thousands	*Hundreds*	*Tens*	*Ones*	*Tenths*	*Hundredths*	*Thousandths*
1,000	100	10	1	0.1	0.01	0.001
km	hm	dam	m	dm	cm	mm
			2	3	4	5

This measure can be read in several ways. The unit of measure determines the placement of the decimal point.

2.345 m = 234.5 cm = 2,345 mm = 0.002345 km

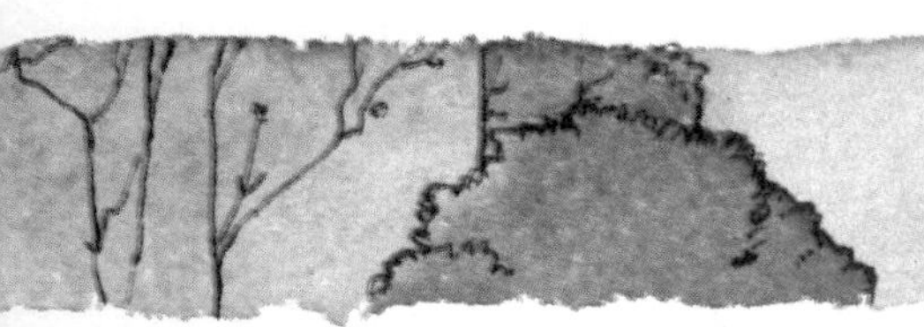

A. Complete.

1. 0.678 m = ___?___ cm
2. 0.678 m = ___?___ km
3. 0.678 m = ___?___ mm
4. 678 cm = ___?___ m

You can change units by "moving" the decimal point.	
3.4 cm = ___?___ mm	Since 1 cm = 10 mm, multiply by 10.
3.4 cm = 34 mm	Move the decimal point 1 place to the right.
342 cm = ___?___ m	Since 1 cm = 0.01 m, divide by 100.
342 cm = 3.42 m	Move the decimal point 2 places to the left.

B. Complete.

5. 5.21 m = ___?___ cm
6. 3.2 m = ___?___ mm
7. 2.4 km = ___?___ m
8. 24 mm = ___?___ cm
9. 432 mm = ___?___ m
10. 37 m = ___?___ km

Practice

Complete.

1. 4.1 cm = __?__ mm
2. 6.7 cm = __?__ mm
3. 2.34 cm = __?__ mm
4. 8.23 cm = __?__ mm
5. 7.42 m = __?__ cm
6. 8.32 m = __?__ cm
7. 6.2 m = __?__ cm
8. 9.1 m = __?__ cm
9. 4.67 km = __?__ m
10. 7.9 km = __?__ m
11. 2.7 m = __?__ mm
12. 3.64 m = __?__ mm
13. 24 mm = __?__ cm
14. 36 mm = __?__ cm
15. 6.7 cm = __?__ m
16. 16.4 cm = __?__ m
17. 416 mm = __?__ m
18. 2.13 mm = __?__ m
19. 63 m = __?__ km
20. 741.2 m = __?__ km
21. 9.3 cm = __?__ mm
22. 7.34 cm = __?__ mm
23. 12.41 m = __?__ cm
24. 4.364 m = __?__ cm
25. 8.34 km = __?__ m
26. 8.214 m = __?__ mm

★27. 9.4 km = __?__ mm

★28. 214.9 m = __?__ dam

Solve.

29. The Monroes are moving to another house 6.7 km away. How many meters are they moving?

FIND OUT!

Brainteaser

The number of bacteria in a test tube doubles each second. If the test tube is completely filled with bacteria after 10 seconds, after how many seconds was the test tube half full?

Precision and Greatest Possible Error

Materials: metric ruler

A. Measure each of the sides of triangle *ABC* to the given measure.

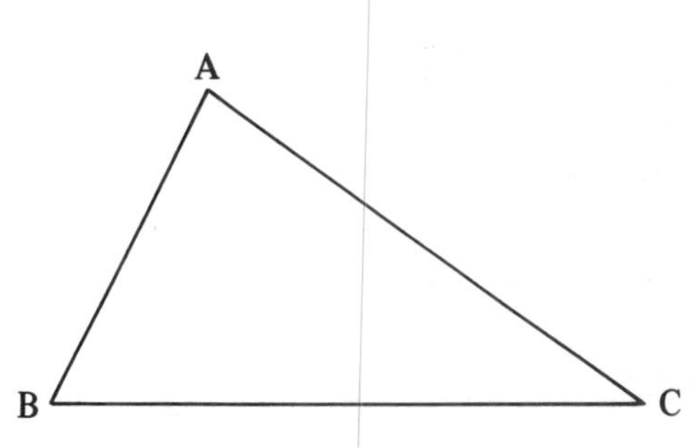

1. To the nearest centimeter

2. To the nearest millimeter

3. Which measurement is more precise?

▶ The smaller the unit of measure, the more *precise* (closer to the actual length) is the measurement.

B. Which measurement is more precise?

4. 3 cm or 8 mm **5.** 14 m or 600 m **6.** 4 mm or 7.4 mm

7. 0.3 cm or 2 cm **8.** 7 ft or 9 in. **9.** 0.4 mi or 0.04 mi

No measurement is ever exact. These 2 line segments are both measured to be 3 cm to the nearest centimeter. However, they are not the same length.

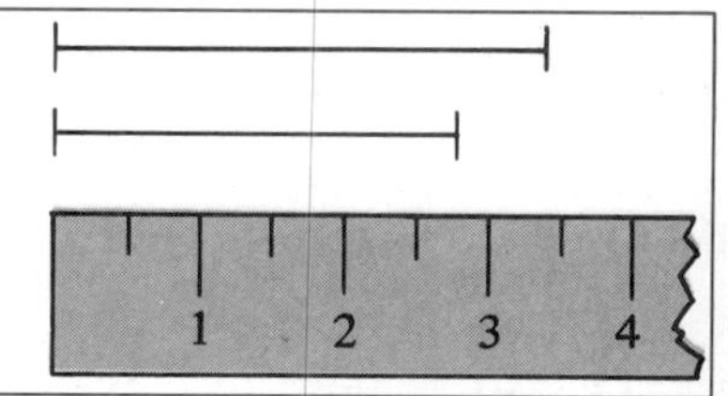

▶ The **greatest possible error of measurement** is the greatest possible difference between the actual length and the measurement. The greatest possible error is one-half of the unit of measurement.

C. The measured length of $\overline{AB}$ is 3.4 cm.

10. What is the unit of measure used?

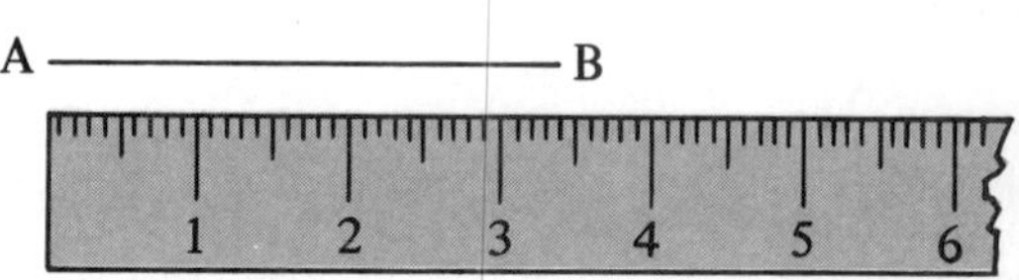

11. What is $\frac{1}{2}$ of 0.1 cm?

12. What is the greatest possible error of measurement?

D. Find the greatest possible error of measurement.

13. 4.2 cm **14.** 6 m **15.** 8 mm **16.** 6.04 km

Practice

Which measurement is more precise?

1. 5 cm or 5 mm
2. 6 m or 6 cm
3. 34 mm or 2 cm
4. 0.5 m or 5 m
5. 50 sec or 50 min
6. 15 mm or 0.16 m
7. 0.5 m or 0.5 mm
8. 5 cm or 50 mm
9. 7 mi or 1 ft
10. 0.3 in. or 0.03 in.

Find the greatest possible error of measurement.

11. 17 cm
12. 4 cm
13. 8 in.
14. 5 m
15. 2 cm
16. 8 m
17. 6.8 m
18. 18.5 km
19. 25.5 in.
20. 7.1 cm
21. 13.5 cm
22. 20.3 in.
23. 0.4 cm
24. 1.3 m
25. 2.8 in.
26. 0.003 cm
27. 0.3 in.
28. 0.90 m
29. 0.430 km
30. 6.05 cm
31. 8.6 m

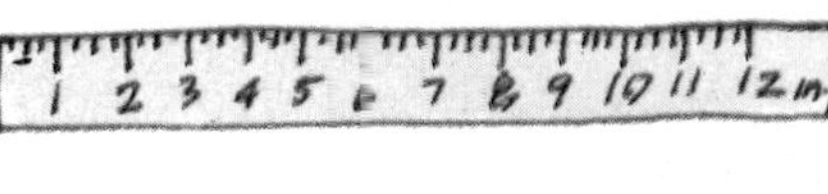

FIND OUT!

Brainteaser

Find 3 whole numbers greater than 10 so that when they are divided by 2 and by 3, the remainder in each case is 1.

Adding and Subtracting Lengths

What is the overall length?

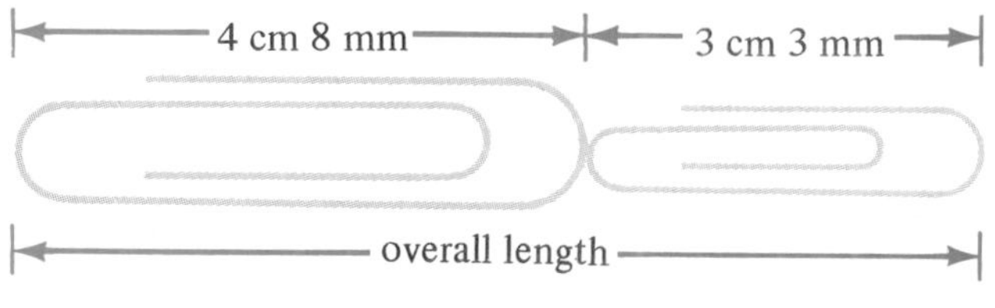

4 cm 8 mm →	4 cm + 0.8 cm →	4.8 cm
+ 3 cm 3 mm →	3 cm + 0.3 cm →	+ 3.3 cm
		8.1 cm

A. Add.

1. 8.7 cm + 6.5 cm

2. 6.34 m + 9.80 m

3. 4.982 km + 7.617 km

4. 0.612 m + 1.329 m

B. Subtract.

5. 6.5 cm − 2.8 cm

6. 8.41 m − 2.65 m

7. 9.700 km − 4.946 km

8. 56.412 km − 9.807 km

Practice

Add.

1. 9.4 cm + 8.9 cm

2. 14.8 cm + 8.2 cm

3. 26.8 m + 7.4 m

4. 16.29 km + 8.78 km

5. 9.73 m + 3.47 m

6. 3.66 km + 8.61 km

7. 12.751 km + 3.609 km

8. 3.295 km, 15.642 km + 1.820 km

Subtract.

9. 9.5 cm − 2.9 cm

10. 38.2 cm − 13.5 cm

11. 19.6 m − 2.8 m

12. 16.08 km − 11.81 km

13. 12.15 m − 3.89 m

14. 97.25 m − 72.80 m

15. 49.226 km − 32.454 km

16. 78.006 km − 9.314 km

Mid-Chapter Review

Complete. *(130, 132)*

1. 4,000 mm = ___?___ m   **2.** 640 m = ___?___ km   **3.** 32 cm = ___?___ mm

4. 3.02 km = ___?___ m   **5.** 7.3 cm = ___?___ m   **6.** 6.59 m = ___?___ mm

Which measurement is more precise? *(134)*

7. 7 cm or 7 m   **8.** 5 km or 8 m   **9.** 0.16 cm or 0.7 cm

Find the greatest possible error of measurement. *(134)*

10. 3.2 km   **11.** 4 mm   **12.** 6.05 cm   **13.** 0.2 m

Add or subtract. *(136)*

14. $\begin{array}{r} 5.6 \text{ cm} \\ + 2.8 \text{ cm} \\ \hline \end{array}$ **15.** $\begin{array}{r} 7.61 \text{ m} \\ + 3.90 \text{ m} \\ \hline \end{array}$ **16.** $\begin{array}{r} 5.7 \text{ cm} \\ - 2.8 \text{ cm} \\ \hline \end{array}$ **17.** $\begin{array}{r} 29.088 \text{ km} \\ - 15.327 \text{ km} \\ \hline \end{array}$

FIND OUT!

Aid to Memory

Here is an interesting way to multiply.

Example 41 × 28

Take half of each number. Ignore the remainder. Continue until the result is 1.

Double each number.

41	×	28
20		56
10		112
5		224
2		448
1		896

Cross out the rows with an even number in the left column. Add the remaining numbers in the right column.

41	28
~~20~~	~~56~~
~~10~~	~~112~~
5	224
~~2~~	~~448~~
1	896
	1,148

Find the products. Use the method above.

1. 73 × 54   **2.** 88 × 27   **3.** 135 × 93   **4.** 602 × 321

Problem Solving: Estimating Answers

A. Ms. Taxel is a traveling sales representative. One day, she drove 358 km using 76 L of gas. How many kilometers per liter (km/L) was this? Choose the best estimate.

300 km/L　　　　5 km/L　　　　50 km/L

Complete.

1. 358 km is __?__ km to the nearest hundred.
2. 76 L is __?__ L to the nearest ten.
3. Think: 400 km ÷ 80 L = 5 km/L, so __?__ is the best estimate.

B. Ms. Taxel drove 354.9 km the first day, 274.6 km the second day, and 136.0 km the third day. How many kilometers did she travel in all? Choose the best estimate.

600 km　　　　700 km　　　　800 km

4. 354.9 km is __?__ km to the nearest hundred.
5. 274.6 km is __?__ km to the nearest hundred.
6. 136.0 km is __?__ km to the nearest hundred.
7. 400 + 300 + 100 = __?__, so __?__ is the best estimate.

C. A liter of gasoline costs $0.29. What is the cost of 76.2 L? Choose the best estimate.

$14　　　　$21　　　　$24

8. $0.29 is __?__ to the nearest ten cents.
9. 76.2 L is __?__ L to the nearest ten liters.
10. $0.30 × 80 L = __?__, so __?__ is the best estimate.

Choose the best estimate.

1. On a car trip across the country, the driver kept a record of fuel used. One day she drove 283 mi and used 14 gal of gas. How many miles per gallon (mpg) was this?

   30 mpg 25 mpg 20 mpg

2. The family travel record showed that one day they drove 341.8 km during the hours from 7:00 am to noon. What was the average number of kilometers per hour (km/h) driven during that period of time?

   80 km/h 60 km/h 50 km/h

3. Mr. Avery drove 614.8 km one day, 553.9 km the second day, and 424.7 km the third day. How many kilometers did he travel in all?

   1,500 km 1,600 km 1,700 km

4. A gallon of gas costs 101.8 cents. A company expense record showed 284.3 gal was used during a trip. What was the cost of the gasoline during the trip?

   $140 $210 $300

5. Sandy averaged 77.2 km/h for 7 hours. How far did she travel in that time?

   7 km 490 km 560 km

6. During the 5-day trip the total cost of food and motels was $487.50. What was the average cost for food and motels for each day?

   $9 $90 $100

7. A family drove 280.8 km using 66.5 L of gasoline. How many kilometers per liter was this?

   40 km/L 50 km/L 60 km/L

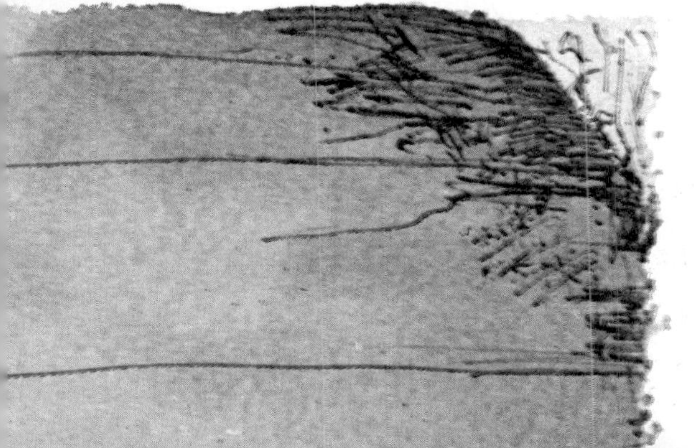

8. The distance between two cities is 3,142.8 km. A family has driven 1,874.9 km from one city toward the other. How much farther does the family need to drive to reach the other city?

   1,000 km 2,000 km 5,000 km

9. A liter of gasoline cost $0.27. A family used 1,256 L during a trip. What was the cost of gasoline for this trip?

   $2,400 $26.00 $300

Significant Digits

The length of the nail is 4.2 cm.
Unit of measure: 0.1 cm

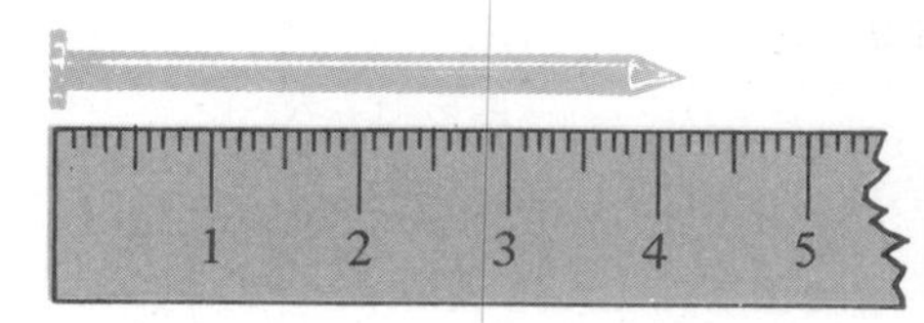

Units in measurement: 42 because $0.1\overline{)4.2}$ (quotient 42 ← 2 digits)
Number of significant digits: 2

▶ Significant digits are those digits in a measurement that give the number of times the unit is contained in the measurement.

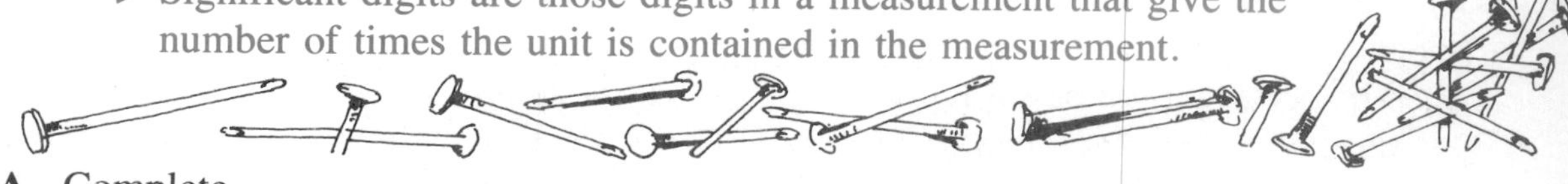

A. Complete.

	Measurement	*Unit of Measure*	*Units in Measurement*	*Number of Significant Digits*
1.	34 m	1 m		
2.	12 cm	1 cm		
3.	3 mm	1 mm		
4.	1.4 in.	0.1 in.		

B. When multiplying measures, the product should have the same number of significant digits as the measurements.

Example What is the area of this metal strip?

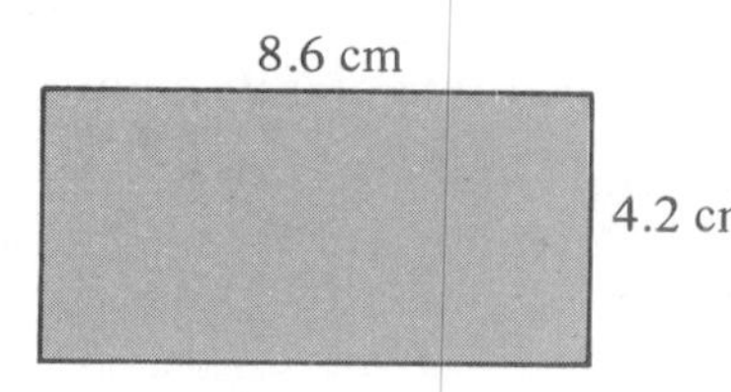

Each measurement, 8.6 and 4.2, has 2 significant digits. So, the area should have 2 significant digits.

$$\text{Area} = 8.6 \text{ cm} \times 4.2 \text{ cm} = 36.12 \text{ cm}^2$$

36.12 cm^2 rounded to 2 significant digits is 36 cm^2.

Find the area. Round to the correct number of significant digits.

5. Length: 4.7 m
Width: 3.6 m

6. Length: 22.3 cm
Width: 13.8 cm

Complete.

	Measurement	Unit of Measure	Units in Measurement	Number of Significant Digits
1.	12 km	1 km		
2.	7 m	1 m		
3.	103 m	1 m		
4.	1,302 mi	1 mi		
5.	205 km	1 km		
6.	24 cm	1 cm		
7.	600 ft	100 ft		
8.	0.40 mm	0.01 mm		
9.	0.400 yd	0.001 yd		
10.	0.3 ft	0.1 ft		
11.	2.04 in.	0.01 in.		
12.	0.423 km	0.001 km		
13.	63.52 cm	0.01 cm		

Find the areas. Round to the correct number of significant digits.

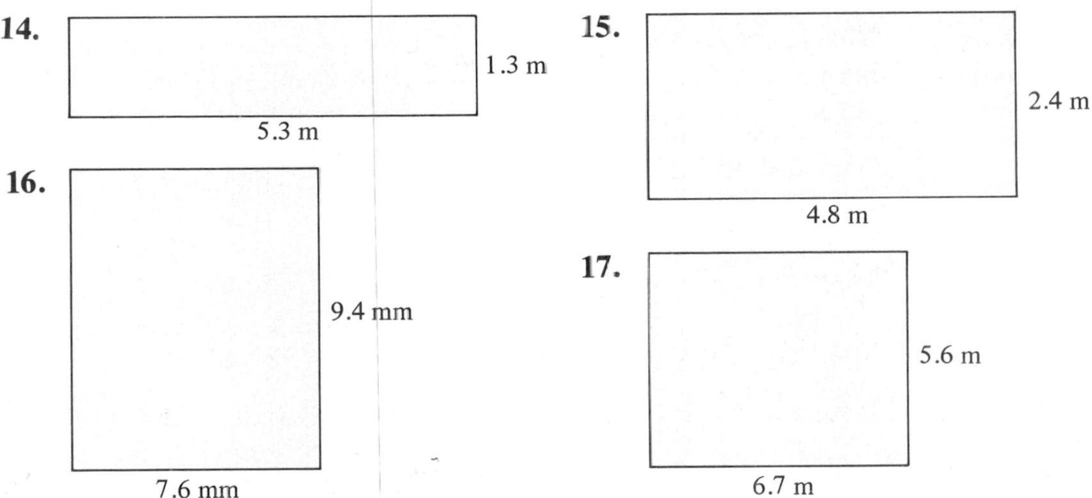

Metric Measures of Mass

In the metric system, the relationship between units of mass is based on 10. The most commonly used units are kilogram, gram, and milligram.

kilogram kg	hectogram hg	dekagram dag	gram g	decigram dg	centigram cg	milligram mg
1,000 g	100 g	10 g	1 g	0.1 g	0.01 g	0.001 g

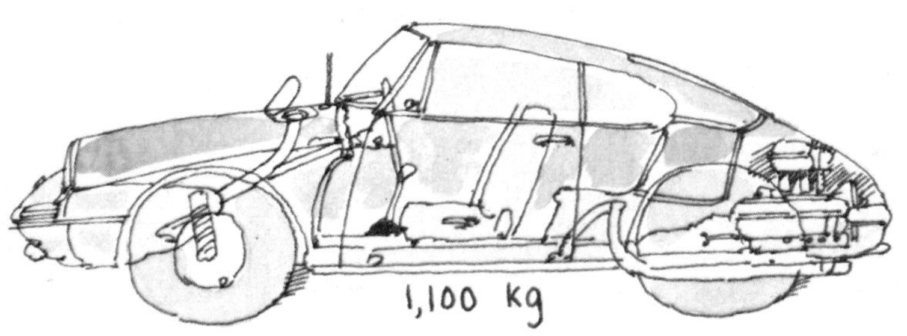

1 kg = 1,000 g

1 g = 0.001 kg

1 g = 1,000 mg

1 mg = 0.001 g

A. Complete.

Example 4.7 kg = __?__ g
4.7 kg = 4.7 × 1 kg
= 4.7 × 1,000 g
= 4,700 g

Move the decimal point 3 places to the right.

1. 3.5 kg = __?__ g

2. 42 g = __?__ mg

3. 5.6 g = __?__ mg

4. 25 kg = __?__ g

B. Complete.

Example 35 mg = __?__ g
35 mg = 35 × 1 mg
= 35 × 0.001 g
= 0.035 g

Move the decimal point 3 places to the left.

5. 125 mg = __?__ g

6. 50 g = __?__ kg

7. 225 g = __?__ kg

8. 5 mg = __?__ g

C. Another unit of mass is the ton (t). 1 t = 1,000 kg
Complete.

9. 7 t = __?__ kg

10. 4,500 kg = __?__ t

Practice

Complete.

1. 3 kg = __?__ g
2. 9 g = __?__ mg
3. 17 g = __?__ mg
4. 4.3 kg = __?__ g
5. 1.1 kg = __?__ g
6. 9.02 g = __?__ mg
7. 650 g = __?__ mg
8. 540 g = __?__ mg
9. 91 kg = __?__ g
10. 2.6 kg = __?__ g
11. 7.8 kg = __?__ g
12. 0.1 g = __?__ mg
13. 100 mg = __?__ g
14. 3,500 g = __?__ kg
15. 50 g = __?__ kg
16. 0.1 g = __?__ kg
17. 300 mg = __?__ g
18. 1 mg = __?__ g
19. 25 mg = __?__ g
20. 131 mg = __?__ g
21. 7 g = __?__ kg
22. 500 g = __?__ kg
23. 0.11 g = __?__ kg
24. 200 mg = __?__ g
25. 3 t = __?__ kg
26. 250 kg = __?__ t
27. 30,000 kg = __?__ t
28. 7,000 kg = __?__ t
29. 3.1 t = __?__ kg
30. 4.56 t = __?__ kg
31. 100 kg = __?__ t
32. 1,000 kg = __?__ t
33. 0.5 t = __?__ kg
34. ★ 325 mg = __?__ kg
35. ★ 6 t = __?__ g
36. ★ 0.03 t = __?__ mg

Solve.

37. A baby was 3.4 kg at birth. It gained 6.7 kg in 1 year. How heavy is the baby now?

38. A bag of potatoes is 5.1 kg. A bag of onions is 2.3 kg. How much heavier is the bag of potatoes?

FIND OUT!

Brainteaser

Choose the box that completes the sequence.

1. 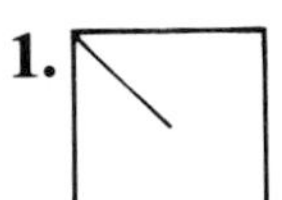   

a 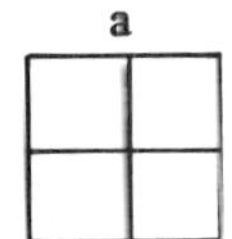 b 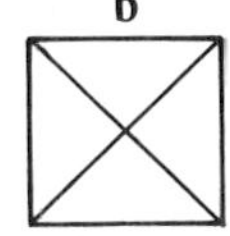 c 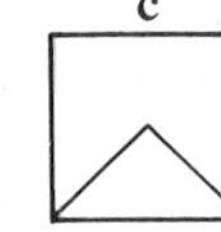 d 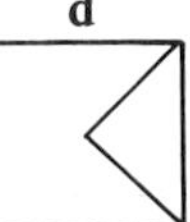

2. 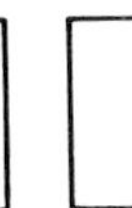  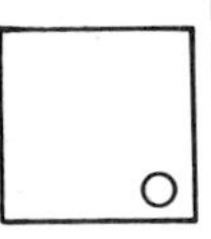 

a 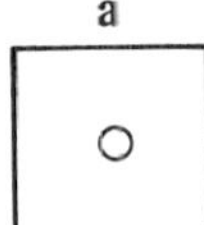 b 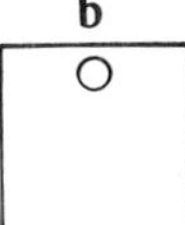 c 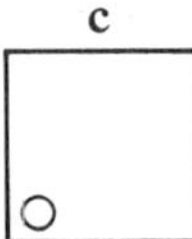 d 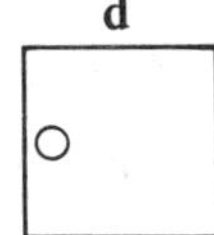

Metric Measures of Capacity

The most commonly used units of capacity in the metric system are the liter (L) and the milliliter (mL).

1 L = 1,000 mL   1 mL = 0.001 L

A. Here is a method for relating units.

Examples

3.7 L = __?__ mL
3.7 L = 3.7 × 1 L
= 3.7 × 1,000 mL
= 3,700 mL

73 mL = __?__ mL
73 mL = 73 × 1 mL
= 73 × 0.001 L
= 0.073 L

Complete.

1. 3 L = __?__ mL

2. 8 L = __?__ mL

3. 2 mL = __?__ L

4. 15 mL = __?__ L

5. 5.6 L = __?__ mL

6. 12.8 L = __?__ mL

7. 17 mL = __?__ L

8. 384 mL = __?__ L

Practice

Complete.

1. 4 L = __?__ mL

2. 12 L = __?__ mL

3. 4 mL = __?__ L

4. 20 mL = __?__ L

5. 8.7 L = __?__ mL

6. 24.9 L = __?__ mL

7. 27 mL = __?__ L

8. 412 mL = __?__ L

Keeping Fit

List all the factors of each number.

1. 15 **2.** 30 **3.** 36 **4.** 21

For each number tell whether it is prime or composite.

5. 16 **6.** 2 **7.** 13 **8.** 46

Add.

9. $16{,}254 + 9{,}751$

10. $\$9{,}826 + 7{,}249$

11. $383{,}109 + 265{,}355 + 841{,}712$

12. $62{,}527 + 9{,}438 + 116{,}019$

Subtract.

13. $71{,}324 - 9{,}836$

14. $90{,}000 - 13{,}143$

15. $742{,}561 - 400{,}698$

16. $165{,}329 - 92{,}561$

Multiply.

17. $5{,}024 \times 7$

18. 639×15

19. $7{,}042 \times 406$

20. $1{,}427 \times 219$

Divide.

21. $3\overline{)651}$

22. $27\overline{)297}$

23. $32\overline{)2{,}421}$

24. $135\overline{)3{,}645}$

Solve and check.

25. $x + 7 = 15$

26. $x - 11 = 39$

27. $x + 64 = 108$

28. $4x = 40$

29. $12x = 72$

30. $\frac{x}{6} = 18$

31. $3x + 1 = 16$

32. $9x - 2 = 25$

33. $\frac{x}{7} + 4 = 13$

Round.

34. 4.029 to the nearest tenth.

35. 5.601 to the nearest whole number.

36. 23.056 to the nearest hundredth.

37. 0.0015 to the nearest thousandth.

Multiply or divide.

38. $10^6 \cdot 10^3$

39. $10^5 \cdot 10^5$

40. $10^3 \cdot 10^4$

41. $\frac{10^8}{10^2}$

42. $\frac{10^{18}}{10^9}$

43. $10^{10} \div 10^3$

Customary Units of Length

A clock is 5 ft 3 in. high. Another clock is 64 in. high. Which is higher?

Change the height of the first clock to inches.

$$5 \text{ ft} = 5 \times (12 \text{ in.})$$
$$= 60 \text{ in.}$$
$$5 \text{ ft } 3 \text{ in.} = 60 \text{ in.} + 3 \text{ in.}$$
$$= 63 \text{ in.}$$

So, the second clock is higher.

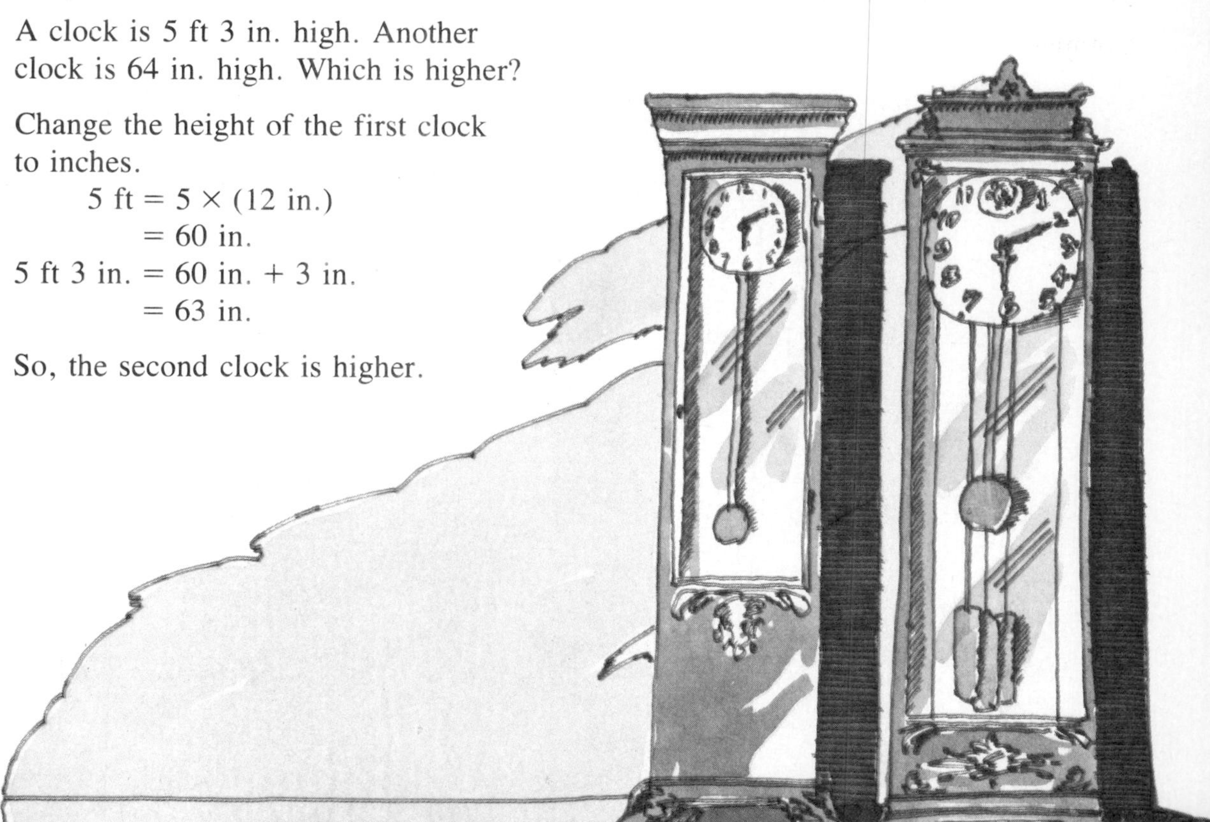

A. Complete. Use these relations between units of length.

1 foot (ft) = 12 inches (in.)　　1 yard (yd) = 3 ft　　1 yd = 36 in.
1 mile (mi) = 5,280 ft　　1 mi = 1,760 yd

1. 2 ft = _?_ in.　　**2.** 6 ft = _?_ in.　　**3.** 3 yd = _?_ in.

4. 3 yd = _?_ ft　　**5.** 2 mi = _?_ ft　　**6.** 3 mi = _?_ yd

7. 48 in. = _?_ ft　　**8.** 72 in. = _?_ ft　　**9.** 72 in. = _?_ yd

10. 6 ft = _?_ yd　　**11.** 12 ft = _?_ yd　　**12.** 108 in. = _?_ yd

13. $\frac{1}{2}$ ft = _?_ in.　　**14.** $\frac{1}{3}$ yd = _?_ in.　　**15.** $2\frac{1}{2}$ mi = _?_ ft

16. 3 ft 4 in. = _?_ in.　　**17.** 3 yd 1 ft = _?_ ft

18. 64 in. = _?_ ft _?_ in.　　**19.** 41 in. = _?_ yd _?_ in.

Practice

Complete.

1. 3 ft = ___?___ in.
2. 7 ft = ___?___ in.
3. 9 ft = ___?___ in.
4. 10 ft = ___?___ in.
5. 2 yd = ___?___ in.
6. 4 yd = ___?___ in.
7. 2 yd = ___?___ ft
8. 9 yd = ___?___ ft
9. 3 mi = ___?___ ft
10. 2 mi = ___?___ yd
11. $\frac{1}{4}$ ft = ___?___ in.
12. $\frac{1}{3}$ ft = ___?___ in.
13. $\frac{1}{3}$ yd = ___?___ ft
14. $\frac{1}{4}$ yd = ___?___ in.
15. $\frac{1}{2}$ mi = ___?___ ft
16. $\frac{1}{4}$ mi = ___?___ ft
17. $\frac{1}{2}$ mi = ___?___ yd
18. $\frac{1}{4}$ mi = ___?___ yd
19. 24 in. = ___?___ ft
20. 36 in. = ___?___ ft
21. 144 in. = ___?___ yd
22. 360 in. = ___?___ yd
23. 9 ft = ___?___ yd
24. 15 ft = ___?___ yd
25. 6 ft 3 in. = ___?___ in.
26. 7 ft 8 in. = ___?___ in.
27. 7 yd 2 ft = ___?___ ft
28. 6 yd 1 ft = ___?___ ft
29. 26 in. = ___?___ ft ___?___ in.
30. 53 in. = ___?___ ft ___?___ in.

Solve.

31. A heavy-duty canvas costs $8/yd. Tom needs 72 in. to make a new carrier for his carpentry tools. How much will the canvas cost him?

Customary Units of Weight and Capacity

Pedro bought 2 lb 8 oz of meat. The meat cost \$1.80/lb. How much did he pay for the meat?

2 lb at \$1.80/lb ⟶ \$1.80 × 2 = \$3.60

8 oz Think 16 oz = 1 lb,

so 8 oz = $\frac{1}{2}$ lb ⟶ \$1.80 × $\frac{1}{2}$ = \$0.90

\$3.60 + \$0.90 = \$4.50

Pedro paid \$4.50 for the meat.

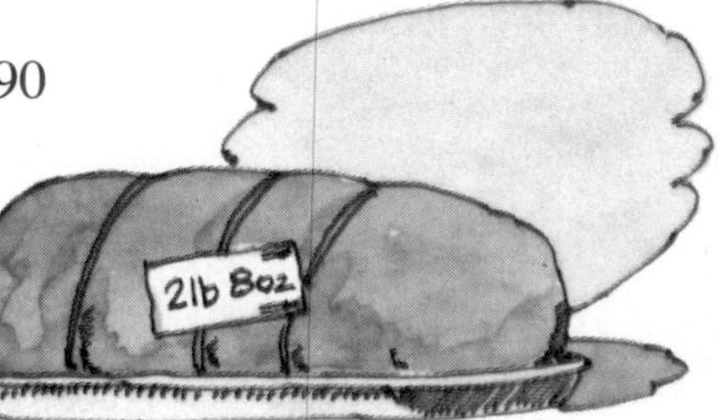

A. Complete. Use these relationships between units of weight.

1 pound (lb) = 16 ounces (oz) 1 ton = 2,000 lb

1. 3 lb = __?__ oz **2.** 2 tons = __?__ lb **3.** $\frac{1}{2}$ ton = __?__ lb

4. $\frac{1}{4}$ lb = __?__ oz **5.** 32 oz = __?__ lb **6.** 10,000 lb = __?__ tons

B. Complete. Use the relationships between units of capacity.

2 cups = 1 pint (pt) 1 quart (qt) = 2 pt 1 gallon (gal) = 4 qt

1 pt = 16 fluid ounces (fl oz) 1 fl oz = 2 tablespoons (tbs)

7. 3 pt = __?__ cups **8.** 2 pt = __?__ fl oz **9.** 3 qt = __?__ pt

10. 2 gal = __?__ qt **11.** 6 pt = __?__ qt **12.** 3 fl oz = __?__ tbs

Practice

Complete.

1. 4 lb = __?__ oz **2.** 6 tons = __?__ lb **3.** 64 oz = __?__ lb

4. $\frac{1}{4}$ ton = __?__ lb **5.** 70,000 lb = __?__ tons **6.** 4 oz = __?__ lb

7. 4 pt = __?__ fl oz **8.** 6 gal = __?__ qt **9.** 4 cups = __?__ pt

10. 8 qt = __?__ gal **11.** 9 pt = __?__ qt **12.** 32 fl oz = __?__ pt

13. 5 fl oz = __?__ tbs **14.** 12 qt = __?__ pt **15.** 10 tbs = __?__ fl oz

Celsius Temperature

Temperature may be measured using the Celsius scale. Two fixed points on the scale are the boiling point of water and the freezing point of water.

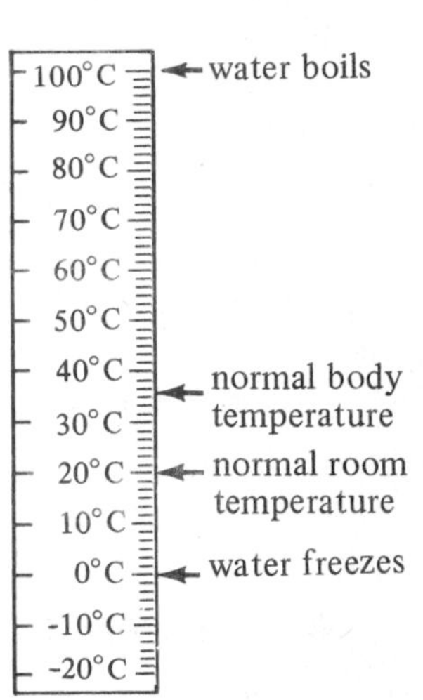

A. Look at the thermometer.

1. What is the temperature at which water boils?

2. What is the temperature at which water freezes?

3. What is the temperature difference between the boiling and the freezing points of water?

B. Comfortable, cold, or hot?

Example 21°C is a normal room temperature. So, 21°C is comfortable.

4. 4°C **5.** 65°C **6.** 19°C

C. Estimate the temperature for the following.

7. Swimming in a lake **8.** A refrigerated fruit

Practice

Comfortable, cold, or hot?

1. 5°C **2.** 94°C **3.** 18°C **4.** 39°C

5. 99°C **6.** $^{-}8$°C **7.** 74°C **8.** 61°C

Estimate the temperature for the following.

9. Ice skating on a lake **10.** Mowing a lawn

★ Cold, warm, or hot?

11. Gold melts at 1,063°C. **12.** Mercury freezes at $^{-}38.87$°C.

Time Zones

For each time zone you pass going west, the time changes to 1 hour earlier. For each time zone you pass going east, the time changes to 1 hour later.

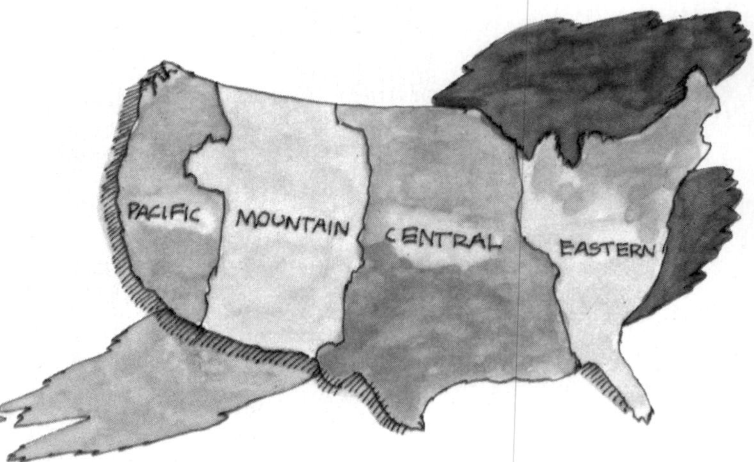

A. Bill is in the Pacific time zone at 11:00 am. He calls Jennifer in the Eastern time zone, 3 time zones to the east. What time is it for Jennifer?

1. Since the Eastern time zone is __?__ zones to the east, the time is 3 hours __?__.
2. 3 hours later than 11:00 am is __?__.
3. So, the time for Jennifer is __?__.

B. It is 4:30 pm in the Eastern time zone. What time is it in each of these zones?

4. 5 zones to the west
5. 8 zones to the east

> As you move across the International Date Line, in the Pacific Ocean, the date changes. If you are traveling eastward, the time stays the same but the date changes to one day earlier. If you are traveling westward, the time stays the same but the date changes to one day later.

C. On June 9th at 12:00 noon, Olga crossed the International Date Line going eastward.

6. Did the time on her watch change?
7. How did the date change?
8. What time and date did it become when Olga crossed the International Date Line?

Practice

It is 10:30 am in the Pacific time zone. What time is it in each of these zones?

1. 6 zones to the east
2. 10 zones to the west
3. 4 zones to the west
4. 8 zones to the east
5. Mrs. Wong is traveling westward in an airplane. As her plane approaches the International Date Line, her watch says Wednesday, September 15, 3:00 pm. How should she adjust her watch on the other side of the line?

★ 6. Mr. Goodman started traveling eastward in an airplane on April 27 at 9:00 am. His plane moved across 7 time zones and crossed the International Date Line. How did the time and date change for Mr. Goodman?

FIND OUT!

Brainteaser

Daylight Savings Time was instituted to increase the amount of daylight available in the evenings. During World War II, the United States used Daylight Savings Time all year long so as to save fuel. Today it is only used from spring until fall and not used in all the states. In the spring, the clocks are turned ahead 1 hour. In the fall, they are turned back 1 hour (back to Standard Time).

If it is 6:00 am Daylight Savings Time in the Eastern time zone, what is the Standard Time in the Mountain time zone?

Problem Solving

ESTIMATED POLLUTION CONTROL COSTS 1985

	Billions of dollars
Air pollution	
Public	0.8
Private	23.9
Water pollution	
Federal	0.2
State-local	12.6
Private	25.3

Answer the questions. Use the table.

1. What is the difference between estimated state-local and private costs for water pollution?

2. What is the estimated total amount to be spent on controlling air pollution in 1985?

3. What is the estimated total amount to be spent on controlling water pollution in 1985?

4. What is the total amount to be spent by the private sector in controlling air and water pollution in 1985?

5. How much more will the private sector spend on water pollution control than it will spend on air pollution control?

6. The estimated total cost for air pollution control is how many times the federal cost for water pollution control?

★ **7.** Assume there will be 225,000,000 people in 1985. How much per person will be spent for air pollution control by the public to the nearest dollar?

★ **8.** Use 225,000,000 as an estimated population in 1985. How much per person is spent by the private sector for air pollution to the nearest dollar?

Chapter Review

Complete. *(130, 132)*

1. 400 mm = ___?___ m **2.** 3.41 m = ___?___ cm **3.** 270 m = ___?___ km

Which measurement is more precise? *(134)*

4. 3 m or 3 mm **5.** 0.3 m or 0.45 m **6.** 6.3 km or 1 m

Find the greatest possible error of measurement. *(134)*

7. 3 m **8.** 4.7 cm **9.** 4.08 cm **10.** 9 mm

Add or subtract. *(136)*

11. 3.9 cm + 1.4 cm

12. 9.0 m + 8.3 m

13. 9.4 km − 1.8 km

Complete. *(142, 144)*

14. 1 kg = ___?___ g **15.** 300 mg = ___?___ g **16.** 1,600 g = ___?___ mg

17. 8 L = ___?___ mL **18.** 0.3 L = ___?___ mL **19.** 370 mL = ___?___ L

Comfortable, cold or hot? *(149)*

20. 7°C **21.** 37°C **22.** 61°C

Solve. *(150, 152)*

23. It is 7:00 pm in the Central time zone. What time is it in the zone 6 zones to the east?

24. The estimated federal cost of controlling water pollution in 1983 is 0.2 billion dollars. The state-local cost is 61 times as much. How much is the state-local cost?

Choose the best estimate. *(138)*

25. During a 10-day trip, the total cost of food and lodging was $681.45. What was the average cost for food and lodging per day?
$7 $70 $7,000

Chapter Test

Complete. *(130, 132)*

1. 600 cm = __?__ m **2.** 93.5 m = __?__ mm **3.** 550 m = __?__ km

Which measurement is more precise? *(134)*

4. 6 m or 6 mm **5.** 7 km or 9 m **6.** 0.23 m or 0.1 m

Find the greatest possible error of measurement. *(134)*

7. 2 cm **8.** 18 mm **9.** 4.2 m **10.** 3.06 cm

Add or subtact. *(136)*

11. $\begin{array}{r} 8.7 \text{ cm} \\ +\ 3.5 \text{ cm} \\ \hline \end{array}$ **12.** $\begin{array}{r} 8.3 \text{ m} \\ +\ 4.9 \text{ m} \\ \hline \end{array}$ **13.** $\begin{array}{r} 14.8 \text{ km} \\ -\ \ 4.9 \text{ km} \\ \hline \end{array}$

Complete. *(142, 144)*

14. 3 kg = __?__ g **15.** 500 mg = __?__ g **16.** 3,200 g = __?__ mg

17. 5 L = __?__ mL **18.** 750 mL = __?__ L **19.** 0.8 L = __?__ mL

Comfortable, cold or hot? *(149)*

20. 68°C **21.** 20°C **22.** 2°C

Solve. *(150, 152)*

23. It is 8:30 am in the Pacific time zone. What time is it in the zone 4 zones to the west?

24. The estimated private cost of controlling air pollution in 1985 is 23.9 billion dollars. The public cost is 23.1 billion dollars less. What is the public cost?

Choose the best estimate. *(138)*

25. A taxi driver drove 329 km one week and 573 km the second week. How many more kilometers did he travel the second week?
300 km 450 km 900 km

Basic Skills Check

1. Stella bought a blouse for $15 95. How much change did she receive from a twenty-dollar bill?

A $5.05 B $4.50

C $4.05 D $3.05

2. Ms. Glinka earns $175 a week. How much does she earn in a year?

E $9,100 F $9,000

G $8,900 H $1,225

3. It was ⁻3°C at 9:00 am and it was 7° warmer at noon. What was the temperature at noon?

A 10°C B 4°C

C ⁻4°C D ⁻10°C

4. Linda practices the guitar 45 minutes a day Monday through Friday. How long does she practice during the 5 days?

E 3 hours, 15 minutes

F 3 hours, 45 minutes

G 4 hours, 15 minutes

H 5 hours

5. What is the perimeter of a square with one side 22 mm?

A 484 mm B 88 mm

C 55 mm D 44 mm

6. Which of the 3 foods is the best source of vitamin C?

Food	*Vitamin C (mg)*
apple	8
grapefruit	40
milk	2

E apple F milk

G grapefruit H both apple and milk

7. A chef used 1 lb 3 oz of flour for bread, 12 oz of flour for muffins and 1 lb of flour for rolls. How much flour was used altogether?

A 6 lb 2 oz B 4 lb 6 oz

C 2 lb 15 oz D 1 lb 7 oz

8. A salesperson earned a total of $31,185 in one year. Estimate the average weekly income.

E $700 F $600

G $500 H $400

Greatest Common Factor

Find the greatest common factor of 12 and 18.

Method 1

List all the factors of each number. List the common factors. Find the greatest common factor (GCF).

Number	Factors	Common factors
12	①, ②, ③, 4, ⑥, 12	1, 2, 3, 6
18	①, ②, ③, ⑥, 9, 18	GCF 6

Method 2

Find the prime factorization of each number. Multiply the prime factors which are common to the numbers.

Number	Prime Factors	GCF
12	$2 \cdot 2 \cdot 3$	$2 \cdot 3$, or 6
18	$2 \cdot 3 \cdot 3$	

A. Find GCF of 20 and 30 using both methods above.

1. List the factors of 20 and of 30.
2. List the common factors of 20 and 30.
3. What is the GCF of 20 and 30?
4. Give prime factorizations of 20 and of 30.
5. Give the product of the common prime factors.
6. What is the GCF of 20 and 30?

CHAPTER 7
FRACTIONS

B. Find the GCF.

7. 12, 30 **8.** 18, 36 **9.** 7, 11 **10.** 18, 12, 24

▶ If the GCF of two numbers is 1, the numbers are relatively prime.

C. Which pairs of numbers are relatively prime?

11. 7, 13 **12.** 12, 15 **13.** 9, 16 **14.** 4, 5, 9

Practice

Find the GCF.

1. 15, 20 **2.** 20, 36 **3.** 42, 18

4. 12, 45 **5.** 70, 15 **6.** 18, 48

7. 8, 12, 20 **8.** 6, 15, 24 **9.** 14, 24, 48

10. 24, 30, 45 **11.** 42, 24, 72 **12.** 21, 63, 42

Which pairs of numbers are relatively prime?

13. 3, 4 **14.** 6, 8 **15.** 5, 10

16. 4, 6, 10 **17.** 3, 5, 7 **18.** 4, 8, 12

Equivalent Fractions

One loaf of bread is cut into 6 pieces. Another loaf of the same size is cut into 3 pieces. There is as much bread in 4 pieces of the first loaf as in 2 pieces of the second loaf.

$$\frac{4}{6} = \frac{2}{3}$$

$\frac{4}{6}$ and $\frac{2}{3}$ are equivalent fractions.

A. Equivalent fractions are formed by multiplying the numerator and denominator by the same number.

$\frac{1}{2}$	$\frac{2}{4}$	$\frac{3}{6}$	$\frac{4}{8}$	$\frac{5}{10}$	$\frac{6}{12}$
	↑	↑	↑	↑	↑
	$\frac{1 \cdot 2}{2 \cdot 2}$	$\frac{1 \cdot 3}{2 \cdot 3}$	$\frac{1 \cdot 4}{2 \cdot 4}$	$\frac{1 \cdot 5}{2 \cdot 5}$	$\frac{1 \cdot 6}{2 \cdot 6}$

1. Find 3 equivalent fractions for $\frac{1}{3}$.

2. Find 3 equivalent fractions for $\frac{2}{5}$.

B. Sometimes you need to find an equivalent fraction with a given denominator.

Example Find a fraction equivalent to $\frac{3}{4}$ with the denominator 20.

$\frac{3}{4} = \frac{x}{20}$ THINK $4 \cdot ? = 20$

$\frac{3}{4} = \frac{3 \cdot 5}{4 \cdot 5}$ $4 \cdot 5 = 20$

$\frac{3}{4} = \frac{15}{20}$

Find equivalent fractions with the given denominators.

3. $\frac{1}{3} = \frac{x}{6}$ **4.** $\frac{3}{5} = \frac{x}{20}$ **5.** $\frac{1}{2} = \frac{x}{16}$ **6.** $\frac{5}{6} = \frac{x}{18}$

Practice

Find 3 equivalent fractions for each.

1. $\frac{1}{9}$ **2.** $\frac{4}{9}$ **3.** $\frac{5}{6}$ **4.** $\frac{3}{10}$ **5.** $\frac{5}{12}$

6. $\frac{1}{4}$ **7.** $\frac{5}{2}$ **8.** $\frac{3}{5}$ **9.** $\frac{1}{10}$ **10.** $\frac{3}{1}$

Find equivalent fractions with the given denominators.

11. $\frac{1}{2} = \frac{x}{16}$ **12.** $\frac{1}{2} = \frac{x}{8}$ **13.** $\frac{2}{3} = \frac{x}{12}$ **14.** $\frac{2}{3} = \frac{x}{15}$

15. $\frac{3}{4} = \frac{x}{8}$ **16.** $\frac{3}{2} = \frac{x}{24}$ **17.** $\frac{5}{8} = \frac{x}{40}$ **18.** $\frac{3}{1} = \frac{x}{40}$

19. $\frac{5}{6} = \frac{x}{12}$ **20.** $\frac{5}{6} = \frac{x}{36}$ **21.** $\frac{3}{10} = \frac{x}{20}$ **22.** $\frac{5}{8} = \frac{x}{24}$

23. $\frac{2}{3} = \frac{x}{9}$ **24.** $\frac{1}{2} = \frac{x}{10}$ **25.** $\frac{3}{4} = \frac{x}{16}$ **26.** $\frac{3}{10} = \frac{x}{100}$

27. $\frac{1}{5} = \frac{x}{10}$ **28.** $\frac{1}{3} = \frac{x}{9}$ **29.** $\frac{5}{6} = \frac{x}{24}$ **30.** $\frac{3}{4} = \frac{x}{20}$

31. $\frac{2}{5} = \frac{x}{40}$ **32.** $\frac{1}{2} = \frac{x}{24}$ **33.** $\frac{1}{3} = \frac{x}{18}$ **34.** $\frac{1}{4} = \frac{x}{100}$

35. $\frac{3}{8} = \frac{x}{16}$ **36.** $\frac{4}{5} = \frac{x}{20}$ **37.** $\frac{3}{5} = \frac{x}{100}$ **38.** $\frac{2}{3} = \frac{x}{30}$

39. $\frac{1}{4} = \frac{x}{28}$ **40.** $\frac{5}{1} = \frac{x}{3}$ **41.** $\frac{2}{9} = \frac{x}{27}$ **42.** $\frac{1}{6} = \frac{x}{42}$

Simplifying Fractions

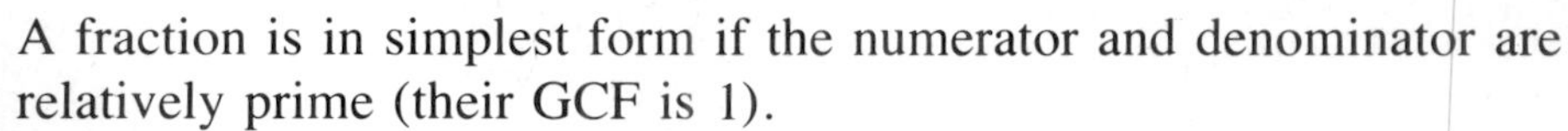

A fraction is in simplest form if the numerator and denominator are relatively prime (their GCF is 1).

$\frac{3}{5}$ is in simplest form.
The GCF of 3 and 5 is 1.

$\frac{6}{10}$ is *not* in simplest form.
The GCF of 6 and 10 is 2.

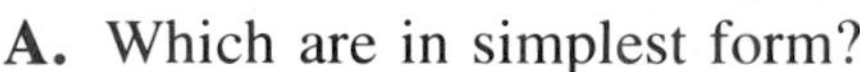

A. Which are in simplest form?

1. $\frac{3}{7}$ **2.** $\frac{3}{4}$ **3.** $\frac{9}{12}$ **4.** $\frac{6}{8}$ **5.** $\frac{3}{6}$

B. To simplify $\frac{4}{12}$, use the GCF of 4 and 12.

6. What is the GCF of 4 and 12?

7. Complete. $\frac{4 \div 4}{12 \div 4} = \underline{\ ?\ }$

8. Is $\frac{1}{3}$ in simplest form? Why?

C. Simplify.

9. $\frac{2}{4}$ **10.** $\frac{6}{8}$ **11.** $\frac{4}{10}$ **12.** $\frac{6}{15}$ **13.** $\frac{8}{12}$

14. $\frac{4}{6}$ **15.** $\frac{2}{10}$ **16.** $\frac{9}{12}$ **17.** $\frac{8}{20}$ **18.** $\frac{36}{48}$

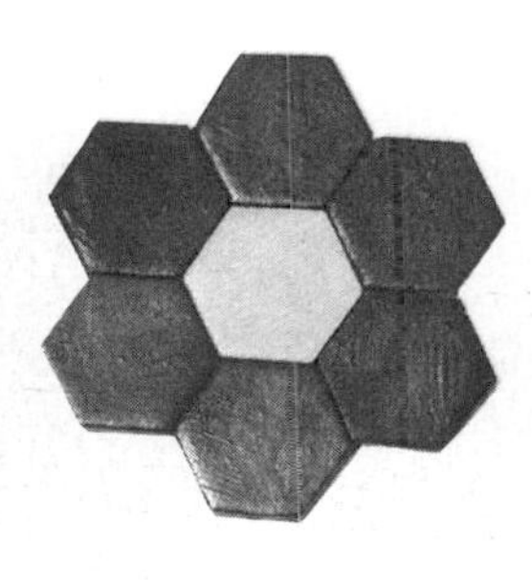

figure 1

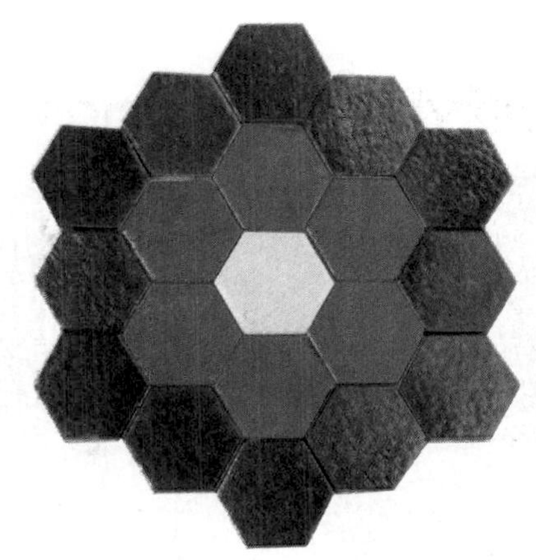

figure 2

Practice

Simplify.

1. $\frac{15}{30}$	**2.** $\frac{2}{4}$	**3.** $\frac{4}{6}$	**4.** $\frac{6}{10}$	**5.** $\frac{8}{24}$	**6.** $\frac{8}{12}$
7. $\frac{5}{25}$	**8.** $\frac{4}{16}$	**9.** $\frac{15}{18}$	**10.** $\frac{18}{20}$	**11.** $\frac{5}{10}$	**12.** $\frac{2}{6}$
13. $\frac{2}{8}$	**14.** $\frac{4}{20}$	**15.** $\frac{3}{4}$	**16.** $\frac{3}{9}$	**17.** $\frac{4}{8}$	**18.** $\frac{2}{10}$
19. $\frac{3}{12}$	**20.** $\frac{2}{15}$	**21.** $\frac{3}{5}$	**22.** $\frac{3}{8}$	**23.** $\frac{8}{10}$	**24.** $\frac{10}{12}$
25. $\frac{7}{9}$	**26.** $\frac{14}{28}$	**27.** $\frac{3}{6}$	**28.** $\frac{4}{12}$	**29.** $\frac{6}{9}$	**30.** $\frac{3}{15}$
31. $\frac{4}{6}$	**32.** $\frac{6}{12}$	**33.** $\frac{10}{15}$	**34.** $\frac{5}{15}$	**35.** $\frac{8}{10}$	**36.** $\frac{4}{10}$
37. $\frac{6}{15}$	**38.** $\frac{3}{24}$	**39.** $\frac{5}{6}$	**40.** $\frac{9}{27}$	**41.** $\frac{10}{12}$	**42.** $\frac{10}{24}$
43. $\frac{6}{18}$	**44.** $\frac{6}{24}$	**45.** $\frac{14}{21}$	**46.** $\frac{42}{48}$	**47.** $\frac{28}{36}$	**48.** $\frac{32}{40}$

★ Solve.

49. In figure 1, there are 6 red tiles with 12 sides that touch another. This ratio is $\frac{6}{12}$. Simplify this ratio.

50. Look at figure 2. Find and simplify this ratio for the blue tiles.

Comparing Fractions

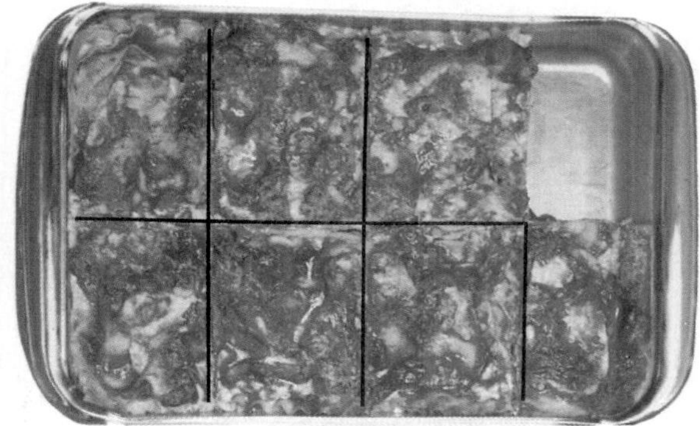

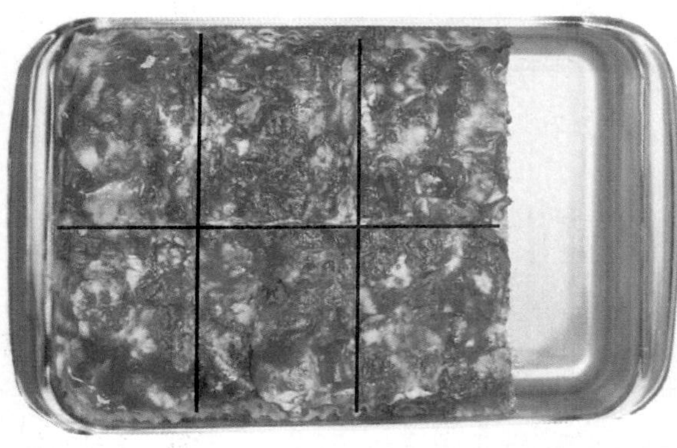

Inez wondered which pan contained more lasagna.

When comparing fractions with the same denominators, compare the numerators.

Example $\frac{7}{8} > \frac{6}{8}$ since $7 > 6$.

When comparing fractions with different denominators, first change them to equivalent fractions with the same denominators. Then compare numerators.

Example
$\frac{7}{8} \equiv \frac{3}{4}$
$\frac{7}{8} \equiv \frac{6}{8}$
$\frac{7}{8} > \frac{6}{8}$ so $\frac{7}{8} > \frac{3}{4}$.

The pan with $\frac{7}{8}$ contains more lasagna.

A. Compare. Use $>$, $<$, or $=$.

1. $\frac{5}{16} \equiv \frac{3}{16}$ **2.** $\frac{7}{10} \equiv \frac{9}{10}$ **3.** $\frac{5}{6} \equiv \frac{2}{3}$ **4.** $\frac{2}{3} \equiv \frac{8}{12}$

B. Compare $\frac{3}{8}$ and $\frac{1}{6}$.

5. What is the LCM of 8 and 6?

6. Find equivalent fractions for $\frac{3}{8}$ and for $\frac{1}{6}$ using the LCM.

7. Compare $\frac{9}{24} \equiv \frac{4}{24}$.

8. Compare $\frac{3}{8} \equiv \frac{1}{6}$.

C. Compare. Use $>$, $<$, or $=$.

9. $\frac{3}{4} \equiv \frac{1}{6}$ **10.** $\frac{3}{8} \equiv \frac{5}{12}$ **11.** $\frac{2}{3} \equiv \frac{10}{15}$ **12.** $\frac{3}{4} \equiv \frac{4}{5}$

Practice

Compare. Use $>$, $<$, or $=$.

1. $\frac{7}{8} \square \frac{1}{8}$
2. $\frac{2}{5} \square \frac{3}{5}$
3. $\frac{3}{10} \square \frac{9}{10}$
4. $\frac{5}{6} \square \frac{1}{6}$
5. $\frac{5}{12} \square \frac{7}{12}$
6. $\frac{7}{9} \square \frac{6}{9}$
7. $\frac{8}{24} \square \frac{8}{24}$
8. $\frac{3}{7} \square \frac{4}{7}$
9. $\frac{3}{8} \square \frac{3}{4}$
10. $\frac{1}{3} \square \frac{5}{6}$
11. $\frac{1}{2} \square \frac{3}{4}$
12. $\frac{3}{5} \square \frac{7}{10}$
13. $\frac{1}{6} \square \frac{2}{12}$
14. $\frac{3}{10} \square \frac{7}{20}$
15. $\frac{1}{3} \square \frac{3}{9}$
16. $\frac{3}{4} \square \frac{11}{12}$
17. $\frac{5}{6} \square \frac{23}{24}$
18. $\frac{2}{5} \square \frac{7}{30}$
19. $\frac{3}{7} \square \frac{6}{14}$
20. $\frac{3}{8} \square \frac{7}{24}$
21. $\frac{1}{2} \square \frac{1}{3}$
22. $\frac{2}{3} \square \frac{3}{4}$
23. $\frac{3}{4} \square \frac{4}{5}$
24. $\frac{1}{2} \square \frac{3}{3}$
25. $\frac{1}{3} \square \frac{2}{7}$
26. $\frac{1}{2} \square \frac{3}{5}$
27. $\frac{2}{3} \square \frac{4}{5}$
28. $\frac{3}{4} \square \frac{7}{9}$
29. $\frac{3}{4} \square \frac{5}{6}$
30. $\frac{3}{6} \square \frac{4}{8}$
31. $\frac{3}{8} \square \frac{1}{12}$
32. $\frac{7}{10} \square \frac{7}{15}$
33. $\frac{3}{4} \square \frac{7}{10}$
34. $\frac{2}{8} \square \frac{5}{20}$
35. $\frac{5}{12} \square \frac{7}{8}$
36. $\frac{3}{8} \square \frac{5}{6}$
37. $\frac{7}{15} \square \frac{5}{6}$
38. $\frac{3}{6} \square \frac{2}{4}$
39. $\frac{1}{12} \square \frac{1}{16}$
40. $\frac{3}{4} \square \frac{7}{10}$
41. $\frac{5}{6} \square \frac{2}{3}$
42. $\frac{6}{7} \square \frac{5}{7}$
43. $\frac{5}{12} \square \frac{3}{8}$
44. $\frac{2}{3} \square \frac{4}{5}$
45. $\frac{1}{2} \square \frac{14}{28}$
46. $\frac{3}{100} \square \frac{21}{100}$
47. $\frac{2}{10} \square \frac{3}{100}$
48. $\frac{3}{7} \square \frac{4}{9}$

Solve.

49. A brass rod has a diameter which is $\frac{3}{4}$ in. A second brass rod has a diameter of $\frac{1}{2}$ in. Which brass rod has the greater diameter?

50. Two pieces of lumber are each 1 yd long. $\frac{3}{4}$ yd is cut from one and $\frac{7}{8}$ yd from the second. Which piece remaining is longer?

Mixed Numbers

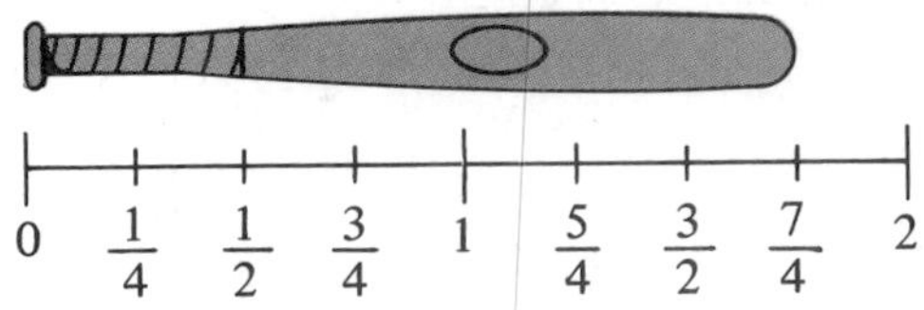

Joe says that the length of this bat is $\frac{7}{4}$ units. Maria says its length is $1\frac{3}{4}$ units.

$$\frac{7}{4} = 1\frac{3}{4}$$

fraction mixed number

$\frac{7}{4}$ means $7 \div 4$

$$\begin{array}{r} 1\frac{3}{4} \\ 4\overline{)7} \\ \underline{4} \\ 3 \end{array}$$

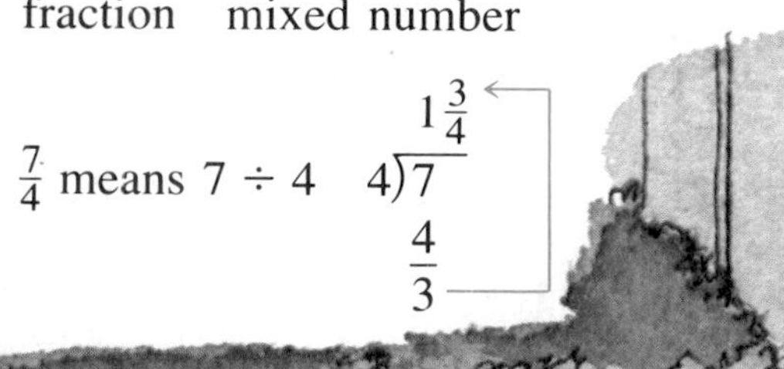

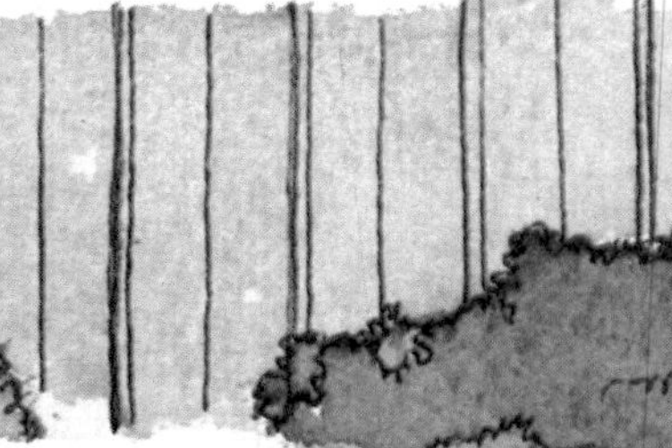

A. Write mixed numbers. Simplify if possible.

1. $\frac{3}{2}$ **2.** $\frac{6}{4}$ **3.** $\frac{7}{3}$ **4.** $\frac{9}{6}$ **5.** $\frac{13}{5}$

B. Write fractions.

6. $3\frac{1}{6} = 3 + \frac{1}{6}$
$= \frac{18}{6} + \frac{1}{6}$
$= \underline{\ ?\ }$

7. $5\frac{2}{3} = 5 + \frac{2}{3}$
$= \frac{15}{3} + \frac{2}{3}$
$= \underline{\ ?\ }$

8. $7\frac{2}{5}$ **9.** $1\frac{5}{6}$ **10.** $3\frac{3}{4}$ **11.** $6\frac{1}{2}$

C. Here's a quick way to write fractions for mixed numbers.

Examples

$6\frac{2}{3} = \frac{?}{3}$

$6\ \frac{2}{3} = \frac{3 \times 6 + 2}{3}$ (+, ×)

$= \frac{18 + 2}{3}$

$= \frac{20}{3}$

$5\frac{1}{2} = \frac{?}{2}$

$5\ \frac{1}{2} = \frac{2 \times 5 + 1}{2}$ (+, ×)

$= \frac{10 + 1}{2}$

$= \frac{11}{2}$

Write fractions.

12. $3\frac{1}{4}$ **13.** $5\frac{7}{8}$ **14.** $4\frac{1}{6}$ **15.** $2\frac{1}{2}$

Write mixed numbers. Simplify.

1. $\frac{5}{2}$ 2. $\frac{5}{4}$ 3. $\frac{5}{3}$ 4. $\frac{8}{6}$ 5. $\frac{12}{5}$

6. $\frac{8}{3}$ 7. $\frac{9}{4}$ 8. $\frac{10}{4}$ 9. $\frac{14}{6}$ 10. $\frac{18}{8}$

11. $\frac{18}{10}$ 12. $\frac{9}{7}$ 13. $\frac{13}{3}$ 14. $\frac{24}{5}$ 15. $\frac{26}{6}$

16. $\frac{16}{3}$ 17. $\frac{50}{20}$ 18. $\frac{56}{24}$ 19. $\frac{34}{4}$ 20. $\frac{30}{9}$

Write fractions.

21. $1\frac{1}{8}$ 22. $1\frac{2}{5}$ 23. $1\frac{3}{7}$ 24. $1\frac{5}{6}$ 25. $1\frac{6}{10}$

26. $2\frac{1}{8}$ 27. $2\frac{3}{8}$ 28. $2\frac{1}{3}$ 29. $2\frac{3}{4}$ 30. $2\frac{1}{5}$

31. $2\frac{3}{7}$ 32. $2\frac{1}{5}$ 33. $2\frac{4}{5}$ 34. $2\frac{5}{6}$ 35. $2\frac{6}{7}$

36. $3\frac{3}{4}$ 37. $3\frac{2}{3}$ 38. $3\frac{4}{5}$ 39. $3\frac{2}{10}$ 40. $3\frac{5}{9}$

41. $4\frac{3}{4}$ 42. $5\frac{7}{8}$ 43. $6\frac{5}{6}$ 44. $7\frac{3}{4}$ 45. $8\frac{1}{2}$

Solve.

46. A bench is $3\frac{5}{8}$ ft long. A second bench is $\frac{28}{8}$ ft long. Which bench is longer?

47. Lucy practiced batting for $3\frac{3}{4}$ hours. Jim practiced $\frac{13}{4}$ hours. Who practiced longer?

Adding Fractions

Anthony spent $\frac{3}{10}$ hour changing the tires on his bicycle. Then he spent $\frac{3}{10}$ hour pumping air into the tires. How much time did he spend on fixing his bike in all?

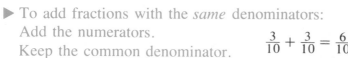

▶ To add fractions with the *same* denominators:
Add the numerators.
Keep the common denominator.

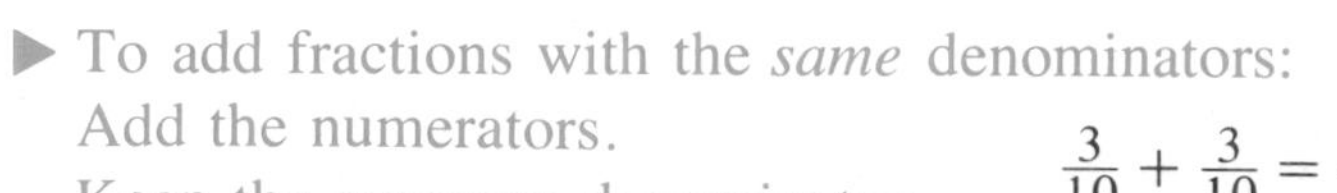

$\frac{3}{10} + \frac{3}{10} = \frac{6}{10}$, or $\frac{3}{5}$

So, Anthony spent $\frac{3}{5}$ hour fixing his bike.

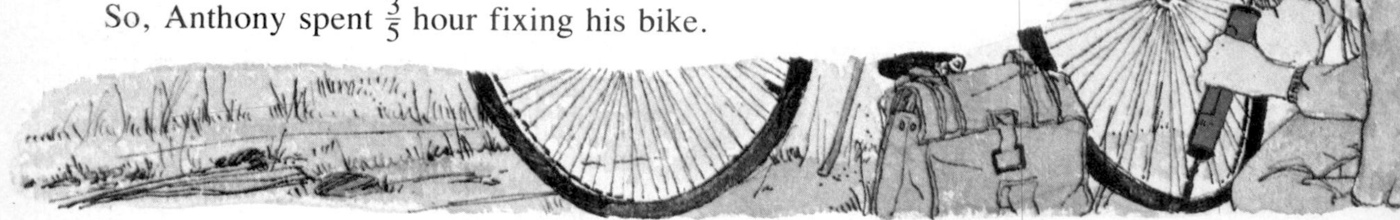

A. Add and simplify.

1. $\frac{3}{8} + \frac{2}{8}$ **2.** $\frac{3}{4} + \frac{1}{4}$ **3.** $\frac{1}{9} + \frac{2}{9}$ **4.** $\frac{9}{10} + \frac{4}{10}$ **5.** $\frac{5}{6} + \frac{3}{6}$

6. $\frac{3}{8} + \frac{1}{8}$ **7.** $\frac{3}{10} + \frac{4}{10} + \frac{2}{10}$ **8.** $\frac{3}{4} + \frac{3}{4} + \frac{3}{4}$

B. Add $\frac{1}{2} + \frac{2}{5}$. Complete.

Think: You want to rename each fraction so that both have the same denominator.

9. The LCM of 2 and 5 is __?__.

10. $\frac{1}{2} = \frac{?}{10}$ **11.** $\frac{2}{5} = \frac{?}{10}$

12. $\frac{5}{10} + \frac{4}{10} =$ __?__ **13.** So, $\frac{1}{2} + \frac{2}{5} =$ __?__

C. Add and simplify.

14. $\frac{1}{8} + \frac{3}{4}$ **15.** $\frac{1}{6} + \frac{3}{8}$ **16.** $\frac{1}{3} + \frac{5}{6}$ **17.** $\frac{3}{4} + \frac{7}{10}$ **18.** $\frac{1}{2} + \frac{1}{3} + \frac{1}{4}$

Practice

Add and simplify.

1. $\frac{4}{9} + \frac{1}{9}$

2. $\frac{3}{8} + \frac{4}{8}$

3. $\frac{5}{10} + \frac{2}{10}$

4. $\frac{3}{8} + \frac{3}{8}$

5. $\frac{1}{9} + \frac{2}{9}$

6. $\frac{7}{10} + \frac{4}{10}$

7. $\frac{3}{4} + \frac{3}{4}$

8. $\frac{1}{24} + \frac{7}{24} + \frac{5}{24}$

9. $\frac{3}{8} + \frac{3}{8} + \frac{3}{8}$

10. $\frac{3}{10} + \frac{5}{10} + \frac{8}{10}$

11. $\frac{3}{8} + \frac{6}{8}$

12. $\frac{3}{4} + \frac{2}{4} + \frac{3}{4}$

13. $\frac{5}{6} + \frac{1}{6} + \frac{4}{6}$

14. $\frac{1}{6} + \frac{3}{8}$

15. $\frac{2}{5} + \frac{1}{4}$

16. $\frac{1}{3} + \frac{1}{2}$

17. $\frac{3}{4} + \frac{1}{8}$

18. $\frac{3}{5} + \frac{2}{10}$

19. $\frac{3}{4} + \frac{1}{6}$

20. $\frac{7}{8} + \frac{3}{4}$

21. $\frac{7}{10} + \frac{1}{2}$

22. $\frac{1}{2} + \frac{2}{3}$

23. $\frac{3}{4} + \frac{4}{5}$

24. $\frac{3}{10} + \frac{1}{4} + \frac{1}{2}$

25. $\frac{3}{4} + \frac{1}{2} + \frac{1}{3}$

26. $\frac{1}{4} + \frac{3}{8} + \frac{1}{2}$

27. $\frac{1}{2} + \frac{2}{3} + \frac{5}{6}$

28. $\frac{5}{9} + \frac{1}{2} + \frac{1}{6}$

29. $\frac{5}{6} + \frac{1}{12}$

30. $\frac{2}{3} + \frac{3}{5} + \frac{1}{6}$

31. $\frac{3}{10} + \frac{1}{2} + \frac{3}{4}$

32. Audrey rode her bicycle for $\frac{3}{4}$ hour to the library and then for $\frac{3}{4}$ hour back home. How long did she ride in all?

33. Luis rode his bicycle $\frac{1}{2}$ mi to school, $\frac{3}{4}$ mi to a ballfield and $\frac{7}{10}$ mi home. How far did he ride in all?

Adding Mixed Numbers

Ms. Andrews owns a stock which advanced $1\frac{3}{8}$ points one week and advanced another $2\frac{1}{8}$ points the next week. What was the total advance for the 2 weeks?

To add mixed numbers:
Add the fractions.
Add the whole numbers.

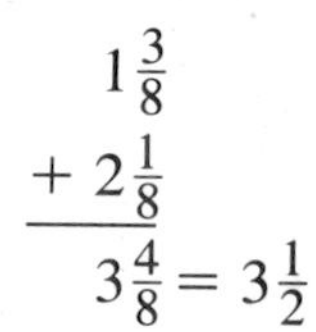

$$\begin{array}{r} 1\frac{3}{8} \\ +\ 2\frac{1}{8} \\ \hline 3\frac{4}{8} = 3\frac{1}{2} \end{array}$$

Answer: $3\frac{1}{2}$ points

A. Add and simplify.

1. $\begin{array}{r} 3\frac{3}{8} \\ +\ 2\frac{4}{8} \\ \hline \end{array}$ **2.** $\begin{array}{r} 1\frac{1}{4} \\ +\ 2\frac{1}{2} \\ \hline \end{array}$ **3.** $\begin{array}{r} 3\frac{4}{8} \\ +\ 2\frac{1}{4} \\ \hline \end{array}$ **4.** $\begin{array}{r} 4\frac{1}{6} \\ +\ 2\frac{3}{8} \\ \hline \end{array}$ **5.** $\begin{array}{r} 5\frac{2}{4} \\ +\ 2\frac{1}{6} \\ \hline \end{array}$

B. Sometimes the sum of the fractions is more than 1.

Examples

$\begin{array}{r} 2\frac{3}{8} \\ +\ 4\frac{5}{8} \\ \hline 6\frac{8}{8} = 7 \end{array}$ THINK: $\left[\frac{8}{8} = 1\right]$

$\begin{array}{r} 3\frac{5}{6} \\ +\ 2\frac{3}{6} \\ \hline 5\frac{8}{6} = 6\frac{2}{6} \\ = 6\frac{1}{3} \end{array}$ THINK: $\left[\frac{8}{6} = 1\frac{2}{6}\right]$

Add and simplify.

6. $\begin{array}{r} 1\frac{3}{4} \\ +\ 2\frac{2}{4} \\ \hline \end{array}$ **7.** $\begin{array}{r} 2\frac{3}{4} \\ +\ 3\frac{3}{4} \\ \hline \end{array}$ **8.** $\begin{array}{r} 4\frac{1}{2} \\ +\ 3\frac{5}{8} \\ \hline \end{array}$ **9.** $\begin{array}{r} 3\frac{1}{2} \\ 4\frac{1}{3} \\ +\ 5\frac{3}{4} \\ \hline \end{array}$ **10.** $\begin{array}{r} 1\frac{3}{4} \\ 3\frac{5}{8} \\ +\ 6\frac{1}{2} \\ \hline \end{array}$

C. Add and simplify.

11. $3\frac{3}{5} + 2\frac{3}{5}$ **12.** $4\frac{1}{2} + 3\frac{6}{8}$ **13.** $2\frac{1}{2} + 3\frac{3}{4} + 4$

Practice

Add and simplify.

1. $2\frac{1}{4} + 3\frac{2}{4}$

2. $3\frac{1}{8} + 2\frac{1}{8}$

3. $5\frac{1}{3} + 2\frac{2}{3}$

4. $6\frac{1}{10} + 3\frac{3}{10}$

5. $1\frac{2}{5} + 1\frac{2}{5}$

6. $4\frac{1}{2} + 3\frac{1}{4}$

7. $3\frac{3}{8} + 2\frac{1}{2}$

8. $6\frac{3}{8} + 2\frac{1}{4}$

9. $2\frac{2}{5} + 3\frac{1}{10}$

10. $1\frac{5}{6} + 2\frac{1}{3}$

11. $4\frac{3}{4} + 2\frac{1}{4}$

12. $6\frac{2}{3} + 2\frac{5}{6}$

13. $3\frac{1}{2} + 2\frac{4}{8}$

14. $7\frac{3}{8} + 4\frac{5}{6}$

15. $6\frac{2}{3} + 7\frac{2}{5}$

16. $3\frac{5}{6} + 2\frac{3}{4}$

17. $7\frac{1}{2} + 6\frac{7}{10}$

18. $6\frac{3}{5} + 4\frac{3}{4}$

19. $12\frac{3}{5} + 7\frac{11}{15}$

20. $4\frac{3}{4} + 2\frac{5}{6}$

21. $2\frac{3}{8}$, $3\frac{2}{8}$, $+ 4\frac{5}{8}$

22. $7\frac{1}{2}$, $3\frac{3}{4}$, $+ 2\frac{3}{4}$

23. $6\frac{1}{2}$, $3\frac{1}{3}$, $+ 4\frac{5}{6}$

24. $3\frac{3}{8}$, $3\frac{3}{4}$, $+ 2\frac{1}{2}$

25. $4\frac{3}{5}$, $2\frac{3}{10}$, $+ 1\frac{1}{2}$

26. $3\frac{3}{4} + 1\frac{1}{2}$

27. $7\frac{1}{2} + 3\frac{1}{2} + 1\frac{1}{4}$

28. $6\frac{3}{8} + 2\frac{1}{2} + 3\frac{3}{4}$

FIND OUT!

Brainteaser

Look at this sequence: $\frac{1}{2}, \frac{1}{4}, \frac{1}{8}, \frac{1}{16}, \ldots$

The number after $\frac{1}{16}$ is $\frac{1}{2} \times \frac{1}{16}$, or $\frac{1}{32}$.

1. What is the number after $\frac{1}{32}$?

2. Add $\frac{1}{2} + \frac{1}{4}$.

3. Add $\frac{1}{2} + \frac{1}{4} + \frac{1}{8}$.

4. Add $\frac{1}{2} + \frac{1}{4} + \frac{1}{8} + \frac{1}{16}$.

5. If you add more and more of the numbers of this sequence, the sum gets closer and closer to what number?

Mid-Chapter Review

Find the GCF. *(156)*

1. 10, 8 **2.** 15, 25 **3.** 18, 27 **4.** 12, 16, 28

Find the LCM. *(158)*

5. 2, 6 **6.** 4, 7 **7.** 9, 12 **8.** 3, 7, 2

Find equivalent fractions with the given denominators. *(160)*

9. $\frac{2}{3} = \frac{x}{9}$ **10.** $\frac{1}{2} = \frac{x}{12}$ **11.** $\frac{3}{4} = \frac{x}{16}$ **12.** $\frac{3}{5} = \frac{x}{25}$

Simplify. *(162)*

13. $\frac{3}{9}$ **14.** $\frac{6}{24}$ **15.** $\frac{6}{15}$ **16.** $\frac{12}{30}$

Compare. Use >, <, or =. *(164)*

17. $\frac{3}{8} \equiv \frac{1}{8}$ **18.** $\frac{3}{4} \equiv \frac{6}{8}$ **19.** $\frac{1}{2} \equiv \frac{2}{5}$ **20.** $\frac{5}{6} \equiv \frac{3}{4}$

Add and simplify. *(168, 170)*

21. $\frac{3}{9} + \frac{1}{9}$ **22.** $\frac{3}{8} + \frac{3}{8}$ **23.** $\frac{3}{4} + \frac{1}{6}$ **24.** $\frac{2}{3} + \frac{4}{5}$ **25.** $\frac{1}{2} + \frac{3}{4} + \frac{5}{8}$

16. $3\frac{1}{4} + 4\frac{1}{4}$ **27.** $3\frac{3}{8} + 6\frac{5}{8}$ **28.** $7\frac{5}{6} + 2\frac{3}{8}$ **29.** $5\frac{2}{5} + 3\frac{2}{3}$ **30.** $3\frac{1}{2} + 2\frac{5}{6} + 4\frac{2}{3}$

FIND OUT!

Calculator Activity

Find the following products: 1 × 142,857; 2 × 142,857; 3 × 142,857; 4 × 142,857; 5 × 142,857; and 6 × 142,857 using a calculator. What do you notice about the products?

Subtracting Fractions

Jan plays the piano $\frac{3}{4}$ hour each day. She has played for $\frac{1}{4}$ hour. How much longer will she play?

$$\begin{array}{r} \frac{3}{4} \\ -\frac{1}{4} \\ \hline \frac{2}{4}, \text{ or } \frac{1}{2} \end{array}$$

The denominators are the same. Subtract the numerators.

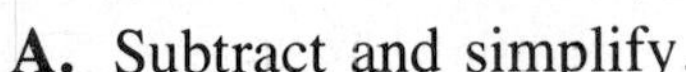

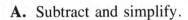

A. Subtract and simplify.

1. $\begin{array}{r} \frac{5}{6} \\ -\frac{1}{6} \\ \hline \end{array}$ **2.** $\begin{array}{r} \frac{9}{10} \\ -\frac{3}{10} \\ \hline \end{array}$ **3.** $\begin{array}{r} \frac{5}{8} \\ -\frac{1}{8} \\ \hline \end{array}$ **4.** $\frac{3}{5} - \frac{1}{5}$

5. $\frac{7}{9} - \frac{1}{9}$

B. When the denominators are not the same, rename each fraction so that the denominators are the same. Subtract and simplify.

6. $\begin{array}{r} \frac{3}{5} \\ -\frac{1}{4} \\ \hline \end{array}$ **7.** $\begin{array}{r} \frac{9}{10} \\ -\frac{2}{5} \\ \hline \end{array}$ **8.** $\begin{array}{r} \frac{3}{8} \\ -\frac{1}{6} \\ \hline \end{array}$ **9.** $\frac{2}{3} - \frac{1}{5}$

10. $\frac{3}{4} - \frac{1}{6}$

Practice

Subtract and simplify.

1. $\begin{array}{r} \frac{9}{12} \\ -\frac{5}{12} \\ \hline \end{array}$ **2.** $\begin{array}{r} \frac{4}{5} \\ -\frac{2}{5} \\ \hline \end{array}$ **3.** $\begin{array}{r} \frac{7}{8} \\ -\frac{1}{8} \\ \hline \end{array}$ **4.** $\frac{4}{6} - \frac{1}{6}$

5. $\frac{3}{4} - \frac{1}{6}$

6. $\begin{array}{r} \frac{1}{2} \\ -\frac{1}{4} \\ \hline \end{array}$ **7.** $\begin{array}{r} \frac{3}{4} \\ \frac{5}{8} \\ \hline \end{array}$ **8.** $\begin{array}{r} \frac{7}{8} \\ -\frac{3}{12} \\ \hline \end{array}$ **9.** $\frac{5}{6} - \frac{1}{12}$

10. $\frac{5}{6} - \frac{3}{10}$

Solve.

11. Steve ran for $\frac{7}{8}$ hour and walked for $\frac{1}{2}$ hour to practice for a race. How much longer did he run than walk?

Subtracting Mixed Numbers

Debbie had $4\frac{1}{2}$ boxes of books. She unpacked $2\frac{1}{4}$ of the boxes. How many boxes are still to be unpacked?

$$\begin{array}{r} 4\frac{1}{2} = 4\frac{2}{4} \\ -\ 2\frac{1}{4} = 2\frac{1}{4} \\ \hline 2\frac{1}{4} \end{array}$$

same denominator

So, $2\frac{1}{4}$ boxes are still to be unpacked.

A. Subtract and simplify.

1. $\begin{array}{r} 2\frac{3}{4} \\ -\ 1\frac{1}{4} \\ \hline \end{array}$ **2.** $\begin{array}{r} 6\frac{1}{2} \\ -\ 3\frac{1}{3} \\ \hline \end{array}$ **3.** $\begin{array}{r} 7\frac{3}{8} \\ -\ 4\frac{1}{6} \\ \hline \end{array}$ **4.** $6\frac{7}{12} - 3\frac{1}{4}$

5. $4\frac{3}{4} - 2\frac{1}{6}$

B. Whole numbers and fractions can be subtracted.

Examples

$$\begin{array}{r} 3\frac{1}{6} \\ -\ 2 \\ \hline 1\frac{1}{6} \end{array} \qquad \begin{array}{r} 6 = 5\frac{2}{2} \\ -\ 2\frac{1}{2} = 2\frac{1}{2} \\ \hline 3\frac{1}{2} \end{array}$$

THINK $6 = 5 + 1 = 5 + \frac{2}{2}$

Subtract.

6. $\begin{array}{r} 6 \\ -\ \frac{5}{8} \\ \hline \end{array}$ **7.** $\begin{array}{r} 9 \\ -\ 3\frac{5}{6} \\ \hline \end{array}$ **8.** $\begin{array}{r} 4\frac{1}{2} \\ -\ 2 \\ \hline \end{array}$ **9.** $2 - \frac{5}{8}$

10. $8 - 3\frac{4}{5}$

C. Sometimes you must rename the larger mixed number before you can subtract.

Example

$$\begin{array}{r} 5\frac{1}{3} = 4\frac{4}{3} \\ -\ 1\frac{2}{3} = 1\frac{2}{3} \\ \hline 3\frac{2}{3} \end{array}$$

THINK
$5 = 4\frac{3}{3}$
$5 + \frac{1}{3} = 4\frac{3}{3} + \frac{1}{3}$
$= 4\frac{4}{3}$

Subtract.

11. $\begin{array}{r} 7\frac{3}{5} \\ -\ 2\frac{4}{5} \\ \hline \end{array}$ **12.** $\begin{array}{r} 7\frac{1}{2} \\ -\ 3\frac{7}{8} \\ \hline \end{array}$ **13.** $\begin{array}{r} 4\frac{1}{3} \\ -\ 2\frac{3}{5} \\ \hline \end{array}$ **14.** $8\frac{1}{6} - 3\frac{3}{8}$

15. $9\frac{2}{3} - 6\frac{3}{4}$

Practice

Subtract. Simplify.

1. $3\frac{3}{8} - 2\frac{1}{8}$

2. $4\frac{4}{9} - 2\frac{2}{9}$

3. $6\frac{5}{6} - 2\frac{1}{6}$

4. $2\frac{3}{5} - 1\frac{2}{5}$

5. $8\frac{7}{10} - 3\frac{3}{10}$

6. $3\frac{3}{4} - 1\frac{2}{3}$

7. $6\frac{7}{8} - 3\frac{3}{4}$

8. $8\frac{5}{6} - 2\frac{1}{4}$

9. $7\frac{2}{3} - 3\frac{3}{5}$

10. $6\frac{5}{6} - 3\frac{3}{8}$

11. $7 - \frac{5}{6}$

12. $9 - 7\frac{3}{4}$

13. $5\frac{3}{4} - 3$

14. $6 - \frac{7}{8}$

15. $9 - 3\frac{5}{6}$

16. $6\frac{3}{8} - 2\frac{7}{8}$

17. $5\frac{1}{6} - 2\frac{5}{6}$

18. $8\frac{7}{9} - 3\frac{8}{9}$

19. $3\frac{1}{4} - 1\frac{3}{4}$

20. $8\frac{3}{5} - 2\frac{4}{5}$

21. $5\frac{1}{4} - 2\frac{7}{8}$

22. $6\frac{1}{2} - 4\frac{7}{20}$

23. $7\frac{1}{3} - 3\frac{5}{6}$

24. $5\frac{5}{12} - 3\frac{5}{6}$

25. $8\frac{2}{5} - 6\frac{2}{3}$

26. $6\frac{1}{5} - 2\frac{3}{4}$

27. $8\frac{1}{4} - 2\frac{1}{3}$

28. $9\frac{1}{6} - 6\frac{3}{8}$

★ **29.** $8\frac{1}{6} - 3\frac{3}{4} + 2\frac{1}{2}$

★ **30.** $9\frac{1}{12} - 5\frac{3}{8} - 1\frac{3}{4}$

Solve.

31. Frank had $2\frac{1}{2}$ cartons of orange juice. He used $\frac{3}{4}$ of a carton for breakfast. How much orange juice is left?

32. Blanche cut a $4\frac{1}{2}$ in. piece of metal for a machine from a piece $7\frac{3}{10}$ in. long. How long is the remaining piece?

Problem Solving

Sometimes a problem can have too much information.

A supermarket ordered 17 dozen packages of light bulbs. The light bulbs are sold at 2 packages for \$1.69. How much will 6 packages of light bulbs cost?

READ The problem asks:
How much will 6 packages cost?

PLAN The fact you need to know is:
2 packages cost \$1.69

SOLVE $6 \div 2 = 3$, so 6 packages cost $\$1.69 \times 3$, or \$5.07

You didn't need to know that the store had ordered 17 dozen packages.

A. There are 24 cans of corn in a case. The cans of corn are selling at 2 for \$0.79. What is the cost of 10 cans?

1. What are you asked to find?

2. What facts do you need to solve the problem?

3. What facts don't you need?

4. Solve.

B. At a sale a large bottle of apple juice sold for \$0.99. The next smaller size cost \$0.72. What is the cost of a dozen bottles of the large size?

5. What are you asked to find?

6. What facts do you need to solve the problem?

7. What facts don't you need?

8. Solve.

Practice

Identify only that information which is needed to solve each problem. Solve.

1. There are 48 cans of soup in a case. The cans of soup are selling at 3 for $0.89. What is the cost of a dozen cans of soup?

2. A package of a dozen muffins sells for $0.59. A package of 16 muffins sells for $0.75. What is the cost of 6 packages of a dozen muffins?

3. One brand of coffee is selling for $3.49 a can. A more expensive brand of coffee is selling for $4.19 a can. How much does a half dozen cans of the more expensive brand cost?

4. A 16-slice package of cheese is on sale for $0.99. A carton contains 48 of the 16-slice packages. How many slices of cheese are in a dozen packages?

5. Lu Chou bought peanuts at $0.69 a jar and cups at 2 packages for a dollar. The total purchases came to $3.38. How much change did she receive from a $10 bill?

6. Mr. Daniels bought 3 jars of mayonnaise at $0.89 each and 2 bottles of catsup at $0.86 each. How much change did he receive from a $20 bill?

7. At a sale a large bottle of shampoo was selling for $1.88. The next smaller size cost $1.29. Find the cost of 3 of the large size bottles of shampoo.

8. A can of tuna fish sells for $0.59 with a discount coupon. Without the coupon, the can of tuna costs $0.99. What is the cost of 8 cans of tuna without any coupons?

9. A brand of cat food is selling at 4 cans for $0.89. A brand of dog food is selling at 3 cans for $0.89. What does a half dozen cans of the dog food cost?

10. David bought milk for $0.51, cream cheese for $1.05, and butter for $2.00. What was the total cost of the milk and cream cheese?

Multiplying Fractions

Kaoni plays the violin $\frac{2}{3}$ hour a day. He has completed $\frac{1}{2}$ of his playing. What part of an hour has he played?

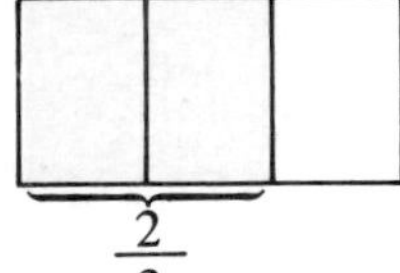

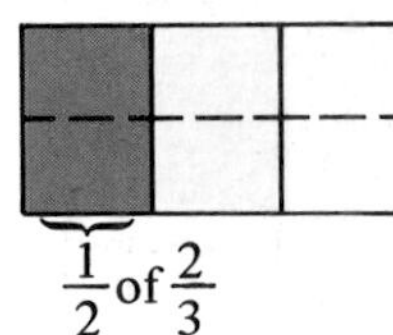

$\frac{1}{2}$ of $\frac{2}{3}$

$\frac{1}{2} \times \frac{2}{3} = \frac{1 \times 2}{2 \times 3}$ ← Multiply numerators. ← Multiply denominators.

$= \frac{2}{6}$, or $\frac{1}{3}$ Simplify.

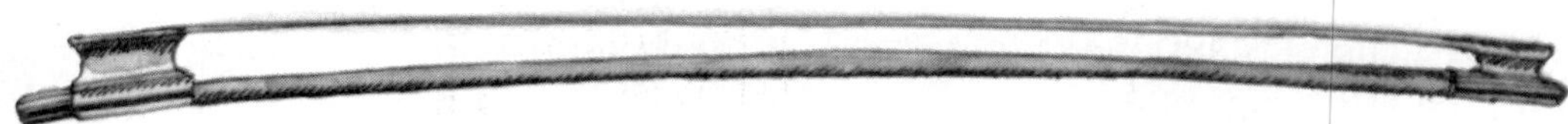

A. Multiply and simplify.

1. $\frac{1}{3} \times \frac{2}{5}$ **2.** $\frac{3}{4} \times \frac{1}{10}$ **3.** $\frac{2}{3} \times \frac{1}{8}$ **4.** $\frac{2}{5} \times \frac{1}{2} \times \frac{1}{4}$

B. Multiply and simplify.

Examples

$$\frac{2}{3} \times 9 = \frac{2}{3} \times \frac{9}{1} = \frac{2 \times 9}{3 \times 1} = \frac{18}{3}, \text{ or } 6$$

$$3 \times \frac{2}{5} = \frac{3}{1} \times \frac{2}{5} = \frac{3 \times 2}{1 \times 5} = \frac{6}{5}, \text{ or } 1\frac{1}{5}$$

5. $\frac{3}{4} \times 8$ **6.** $\frac{4}{5} \times 10$ **7.** $3 \times \frac{2}{5}$ **8.** $\frac{3}{10} \times 15$

> Here's a shortcut when multiplying fractions.
>
> *Long way*: $\frac{2}{3} \times \frac{1}{4} = \frac{2}{12}$, or $\frac{1}{6}$
>
> *Short way*: $\frac{\cancel{2}^{1}}{3} \times \frac{1}{\cancel{4}_{2}} = \frac{1}{6}$

C. Complete.

9. $\frac{5}{\cancel{9}_{3}} \times \frac{\cancel{3}^{1}}{8} =$ ___?___ **10.** $\frac{\cancel{9}^{3}}{10} \times \frac{7}{\cancel{12}_{4}} =$ ___?___ **11.** $\frac{\cancel{2}^{1}}{\cancel{3}_{1}} \times \frac{\cancel{9}^{3}}{\cancel{10}_{5}} =$ ___?___

D. Multiply and simplify.

12. $\frac{3}{4} \times \frac{5}{6}$ **13.** $\frac{3}{4} \times \frac{8}{9}$ **14.** $\frac{1}{2} \times \frac{8}{9} \times \frac{3}{5}$ **15.** $\frac{2}{3} \times 6$

Multiply and simplify.

1. $\frac{1}{3} \times \frac{1}{2}$
2. $\frac{1}{4} \times \frac{1}{8}$
3. $\frac{1}{3} \times \frac{1}{8}$
4. $\frac{1}{4} \times \frac{1}{6}$
5. $\frac{1}{2} \times \frac{3}{4}$
6. $\frac{1}{2} \times \frac{3}{5}$
7. $\frac{2}{3} \times \frac{5}{7}$
8. $\frac{3}{4} \times \frac{9}{10}$
9. $\frac{5}{6} \times \frac{7}{8}$
10. $\frac{7}{9} \times \frac{3}{5}$
11. $\frac{5}{6} \times \frac{11}{12}$
12. $\frac{5}{8} \times \frac{5}{9}$
13. $\frac{2}{3} \times 4$
14. $\frac{3}{4} \times 5$
15. $\frac{5}{6} \times 8$
16. $\frac{1}{2} \times 5$
17. $\frac{5}{7} \times 14$
18. $\frac{2}{3} \times 9$
19. $5 \times \frac{1}{3}$
20. $6 \times \frac{2}{3}$
21. $7 \times \frac{1}{2}$
22. $8 \times \frac{3}{4}$
23. $9 \times \frac{2}{3}$
24. $12 \times \frac{1}{4}$
25. $\frac{2}{3} \times \frac{6}{7}$
26. $\frac{3}{9} \times \frac{1}{2}$
27. $\frac{2}{5} \times \frac{1}{6}$
28. $\frac{4}{5} \times \frac{3}{8}$
29. $\frac{3}{5} \times \frac{2}{9}$
30. $\frac{3}{4} \times \frac{8}{11}$
31. $\frac{5}{6} \times \frac{7}{10}$
32. $\frac{2}{3} \times \frac{1}{4}$
33. $\frac{1}{2} \times \frac{4}{5}$
34. $\frac{3}{4} \times \frac{8}{9}$
35. $\frac{2}{3} \times \frac{9}{20}$
36. $\frac{3}{4} \times \frac{8}{9}$
37. $\frac{1}{5} \times \frac{2}{3} \times \frac{1}{4}$
38. $\frac{3}{4} \times \frac{1}{6} \times \frac{2}{5}$
39. $\frac{1}{2} \times \frac{9}{10} \times \frac{2}{3}$

★ 40. $\left(\frac{1}{2} + \frac{1}{3}\right) \times \left(\frac{1}{4} + \frac{1}{2}\right)$

★ 41. $\left(\frac{9}{10} - \frac{3}{5}\right) \times \left(1 - \frac{4}{9}\right)$

Solve.

42. Bill plays the piano $\frac{3}{4}$ hour a day. Cathy, his sister, plays $\frac{1}{2}$ as long. How long does Cathy play each day?

43. Jill signed up for 48 piano lessons. She took $\frac{2}{3}$ of them by September. How many piano lessons did she take by September?

Multiplying Mixed Numbers

Joe needs $3\frac{1}{2}$ cans of paint to paint each room in his house. How many cans of paint will he need for 8 rooms?

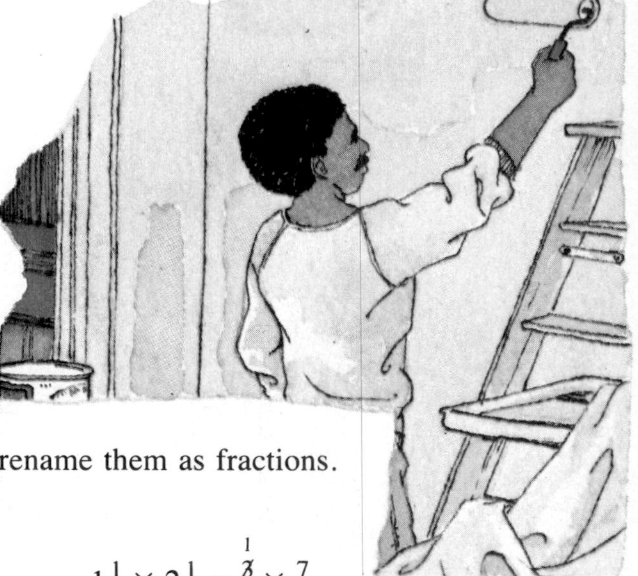

$$8 \times 3\frac{1}{2} = \frac{\overset{4}{\cancel{8}}}{1} \times \frac{7}{\underset{1}{\cancel{2}}}$$

$$= 28$$

So, 28 cans are needed for 8 rooms.

A. To multiply mixed numbers, first rename them as fractions. Then multiply.

Examples $\frac{3}{4} \times 1\frac{1}{2} = \frac{3}{4} \times \frac{3}{2}$ $= \frac{9}{8}$, or $1\frac{1}{8}$

$1\frac{1}{2} \times 2\frac{1}{3} = \frac{\overset{1}{\cancel{3}}}{2} \times \frac{7}{\underset{1}{\cancel{3}}}$ $= \frac{7}{2}$, or $3\frac{1}{2}$

1. $6 \times 4\frac{2}{3}$ **2.** $3\frac{2}{5} \times 8$ **3.** $7 \times 3\frac{3}{4}$ **4.** $\frac{2}{3} \times 2\frac{1}{2}$

5. $\frac{3}{4} \times 2\frac{1}{6}$ **6.** $2\frac{2}{3} \times \frac{5}{8} \times 6$ **7.** $3\frac{2}{3} \times 1\frac{1}{4}$ **8.** $2\frac{2}{5} \times 1\frac{5}{6} \times 1\frac{1}{2}$

Practice

Multiply.

1. $9 \times 1\frac{1}{3}$ **2.** $8 \times 3\frac{3}{4}$ **3.** $12 \times 6\frac{1}{2}$ **4.** $10 \times 5\frac{3}{10}$

5. $5 \times 1\frac{1}{4}$ **6.** $4 \times 2\frac{2}{3}$ **7.** $5 \times 3\frac{1}{2}$ **8.** $6 \times 5\frac{3}{5} \times 1\frac{2}{3}$

9. $2\frac{1}{2} \times 4$ **10.** $3\frac{1}{3} \times 4$ **11.** $1\frac{2}{5} \times 10$ **12.** $2\frac{1}{4} \times 8$

13. $2\frac{1}{2} \times 3$ **14.** $1\frac{1}{3} \times 4$ **15.** $3\frac{1}{4} \times 5$ **16.** $6\frac{2}{3} \times 7 \times 1\frac{1}{5}$

17. $\frac{3}{4} \times 1\frac{1}{2}$ **18.** $\frac{4}{5} \times 2\frac{1}{4}$ **19.** $\frac{7}{8} \times 3\frac{2}{3}$ **20.** $\frac{5}{6} \times 3\frac{1}{8}$

21. $2\frac{1}{2} \times 1\frac{1}{4}$ **22.** $3\frac{1}{3} \times 1\frac{3}{4}$ **23.** $4\frac{2}{3} \times 2\frac{3}{5}$ **24.** $2\frac{1}{6} \times 1\frac{7}{8} \times 5\frac{1}{3}$

Reciprocals

A. Multiply. What is true of each product?

1. $\frac{2}{3} \times \frac{3}{2}$ **2.** $\frac{5}{4} \times \frac{4}{5}$ **3.** $\frac{1}{2} \times 2$ **4.** $3\frac{1}{2} \times \frac{2}{7}$

▶ If the product of two numbers is 1, one number is the **reciprocal** of the other.

B. Find the reciprocals.

5. $\frac{2}{3}$ **6.** $\frac{5}{7}$ **7.** 6 **8.** $3\frac{1}{4}$

C. Fractions like $\frac{\frac{2}{7}}{\frac{3}{4}}$ are called **complex fractions.** Simplify $\frac{\frac{2}{7}}{\frac{3}{4}}$.

9. What is the reciprocal of the denominator?

10. Multiply the numerator and the denominator by $\frac{4}{3}$.

11. Simplify numerator and denominator. $\frac{\frac{2}{7} \times \frac{4}{3}}{\frac{3}{4} \times \frac{4}{3}} = \underline{\ \ ?\ \ }$

D. Simplify.

12. $\frac{\frac{1}{3}}{\frac{1}{2}}$ **13.** $\frac{\frac{2}{3}}{\frac{4}{3}}$ **14.** $\frac{\frac{1}{4}}{\frac{3}{2}}$ **15.** $\frac{\frac{1}{10}}{\frac{3}{5}}$

Practice

Find the reciprocals.

1. $\frac{1}{2}$ **2.** $\frac{1}{3}$ **3.** $\frac{3}{4}$ **4.** 3 **5.** $1\frac{1}{2}$

Simplify.

6. $\frac{\frac{3}{5}}{\frac{5}{9}}$ **7.** $\frac{\frac{2}{3}}{\frac{6}{9}}$ **8.** $\frac{\frac{3}{10}}{\frac{2}{5}}$ **9.** $\frac{\frac{5}{6}}{\frac{1}{2}}$ **10.** $\frac{\frac{1}{3}}{\frac{3}{5}}$

Dividing Fractions and Mixed Numbers

Multiplication can be used to divide fractions.

How many $\frac{1}{3}$'s in 1?

$1 \div \frac{1}{3}$

$1 \times \frac{3}{1} = \frac{3}{1} = 3$

reciprocals

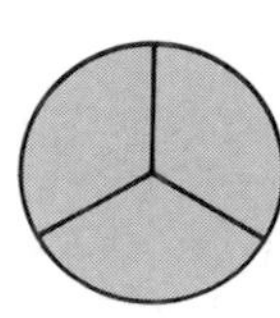

How many $\frac{1}{4}$'s in $\frac{1}{2}$?

$\frac{1}{2} \div \frac{1}{4}$

$\frac{1}{2} \times \frac{4}{1} = \frac{4}{2} = 2$

reciprocals

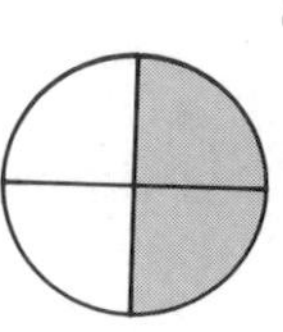

▶ To divide any number by a fraction, multiply by the reciprocal of the divisor.

A. Here's how to divide $\frac{2}{3} \div \frac{1}{6}$.

1. What is the reciprocal of $\frac{1}{6}$?
2. Rewrite the problem as multiplication.
   $\frac{2}{3} \div \frac{1}{6} = \frac{2}{3} \times \underline{\ ?\ }$
3. Multiply $\frac{2}{3} \times \frac{6}{1}$.
4. What is $\frac{2}{3} \div \frac{1}{6}$?

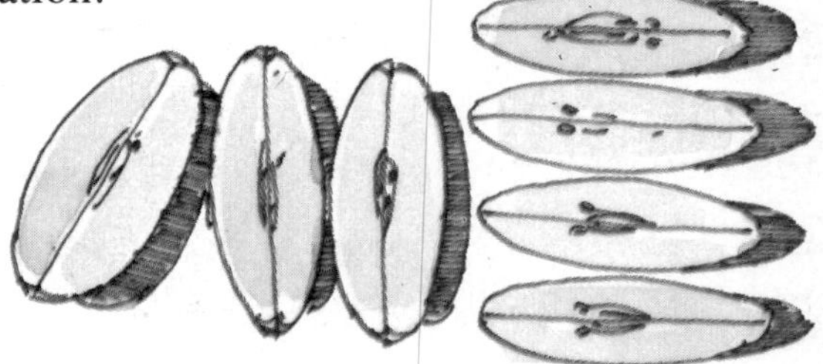

B. Divide.

5. $3 \div \frac{1}{2}$ **6.** $\frac{9}{10} \div 6$ **7.** $\frac{3}{4} \div \frac{1}{8}$ **8.** $\frac{3}{5} \div \frac{2}{3}$

C. To divide mixed numbers, change to fractions.

Examples

$2\frac{1}{2} \div \frac{3}{4} = \frac{5}{2} \div \frac{3}{4}$
$= \frac{5}{2} \times \frac{4}{3}$
$= \frac{10}{3}$, or $3\frac{1}{3}$

$3\frac{1}{2} \div 1\frac{1}{5} = \frac{7}{2} \div \frac{6}{5}$
$= \frac{7}{2} \times \frac{5}{6}$
$= \frac{35}{12}$, or $2\frac{11}{12}$

Divide.

9. $5\frac{3}{4} \div \frac{2}{3}$ **10.** $1\frac{2}{3} \div 6$ **11.** $2\frac{3}{4} \div 1\frac{1}{2}$ **12.** $5\frac{5}{6} \div 2\frac{2}{3}$

Divide.

1. $1 \div \frac{1}{2}$
2. $1 \div \frac{1}{5}$
3. $3 \div \frac{1}{3}$
4. $3 \div \frac{1}{10}$
5. $\frac{1}{4} \div \frac{1}{8}$
6. $\frac{1}{3} \div \frac{1}{6}$
7. $\frac{3}{4} \div \frac{1}{2}$
8. $\frac{5}{6} \div \frac{1}{3}$
9. $\frac{2}{3} \div \frac{1}{2}$
10. $\frac{3}{4} \div \frac{7}{8}$
11. $\frac{4}{5} \div \frac{7}{8}$
12. $\frac{5}{6} \div \frac{2}{3}$
13. $\frac{2}{3} \div \frac{3}{4}$
14. $\frac{9}{10} \div \frac{3}{5}$
15. $\frac{3}{8} \div \frac{3}{4}$
16. $\frac{7}{12} \div \frac{14}{15}$
17. $2\frac{1}{2} \div \frac{3}{4}$
18. $3\frac{1}{5} \div \frac{1}{2}$
19. $2\frac{3}{4} \div \frac{7}{8}$
20. $3\frac{5}{6} \div \frac{2}{3}$
21. $2\frac{3}{4} \div \frac{2}{5}$
22. $3\frac{5}{7} \div \frac{1}{2}$
23. $2\frac{5}{6} \div \frac{3}{4}$
24. $5\frac{1}{2} \div \frac{3}{5}$
25. $\frac{3}{4} \div 2$
26. $\frac{5}{6} \div 3$
27. $4 \div \frac{8}{9}$
28. $10 \div \frac{5}{6}$
29. $1\frac{4}{5} \div 3$
30. $2\frac{6}{7} \div 2$
31. $12 \div 1\frac{1}{7}$
32. $6 \div 2\frac{1}{4}$
33. $\frac{2}{3} \div 1\frac{1}{2}$
34. $\frac{5}{8} \div 1\frac{1}{4}$
35. $\frac{9}{10} \div 1\frac{3}{5}$
36. $\frac{8}{12} \div 1\frac{3}{4}$
37. $2\frac{1}{2} \div 2\frac{1}{2}$
38. $3\frac{3}{4} \div 1\frac{1}{2}$
39. $2\frac{1}{4} \div 3\frac{1}{3}$
40. $1\frac{3}{5} \div 1\frac{3}{5}$
41. $3\frac{1}{2} \div 4\frac{1}{2}$
42. $\frac{5}{6} \div 1\frac{1}{9}$
43. $9 \div \frac{3}{7}$
44. $\frac{7}{8} \div \frac{3}{4}$

★ 45. $\left(\frac{9}{10} \times \frac{5}{8}\right) \div \frac{3}{8}$

★ 46. $\left(3\frac{2}{3} \div 5\frac{1}{2}\right) \div \left(4\frac{1}{2} \div \frac{3}{4}\right)$

★ 47. $\left(\frac{3}{5} + \frac{1}{3}\right) \div \left(\frac{3}{4} - \frac{7}{10}\right)$

Solve.

48. Carl has 24 apples. He uses $2\frac{2}{3}$ apples to make a dessert. How many desserts can he make?

49. Gloria bought $40\frac{1}{2}$ ft of wire mesh to fence in her vegetable gardens. She cut the wire mesh into $4\frac{1}{2}$ ft pieces. How many pieces does she have?

Fractions and Decimals

Sue Ann is working in shop class. She is told to bore a hole $\frac{1}{2}$ in. wide. Is this the same as 0.5 in. wide?

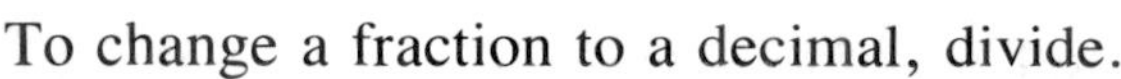

To change a fraction to a decimal, divide.

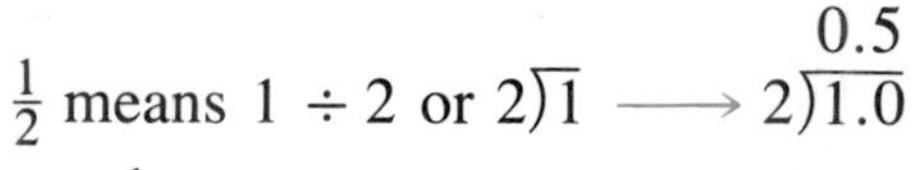

$\frac{1}{2}$ means $1 \div 2$ or $2\overline{)1} \longrightarrow \begin{array}{r} 0.5 \\ 2\overline{)1.0} \end{array}$

So, $\frac{1}{2} = 0.5$

A. Write decimals.

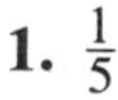

1. $\frac{1}{5}$ **2.** $\frac{2}{5}$ **3.** $\frac{3}{2}$ **4.** $\frac{6}{5}$ **5.** $\frac{7}{2}$

B. Sometimes you need to divide to hundredths.

Example $\frac{3}{4}$ means $3 \div 4$ or

$$\begin{array}{r} 0.75 \\ 4\overline{)3.00} \\ \underline{2\ 8} \\ 20 \\ \underline{20} \\ 0 \end{array}$$

Write decimals.

6. $\frac{1}{4}$ **7.** $\frac{1}{25}$ **8.** $\frac{2}{50}$ **9.** $\frac{4}{25}$ **10.** $\frac{5}{4}$

C. Sometimes you need to divide to thousandths.

Example $\frac{1}{8} \longrightarrow$

$$\begin{array}{r} 0.125 \\ 8\overline{)1.000} \\ \underline{8} \\ 20 \\ \underline{16} \\ 40 \\ \underline{40} \\ 0 \end{array}$$

Write decimals.

11. $\frac{3}{8}$ **12.** $\frac{5}{8}$ **13.** $\frac{1}{40}$ **14.** $\frac{3}{40}$ **15.** $\frac{1}{125}$

D. Write decimals.

Examples $1\frac{1}{2} = 1.5$ $2\frac{3}{4} = 2.75$

16. $2\frac{1}{2}$ **17.** $3\frac{3}{4}$ **18.** $4\frac{1}{5}$ **19.** $4\frac{1}{25}$ **20.** $3\frac{1}{8}$

Practice

Write decimals.

1. $\frac{5}{2}$ **2.** $\frac{7}{5}$ **3.** $\frac{7}{2}$ **4.** $\frac{7}{10}$ **5.** $\frac{7}{28}$

6. $\frac{3}{25}$ **7.** $\frac{3}{125}$ **8.** $\frac{7}{4}$ **9.** $\frac{9}{4}$ **10.** $\frac{7}{8}$

11. $\frac{5}{40}$ **12.** $\frac{27}{40}$ **13.** $2\frac{1}{5}$ **14.** $3\frac{1}{2}$ **15.** $4\frac{3}{10}$

16. $3\frac{1}{50}$ **17.** $1\frac{7}{25}$ **18.** $2\frac{3}{4}$ ★ **19.** $\frac{1}{80}$ ★ **20.** $2\frac{23}{80}$

Solve.

21. A drill size is $\frac{3}{4}$ in. Will the hole made by this drill be larger or smaller than 0.80 in.?

22. A drill size is $\frac{1}{8}$ in. A hole is made with this drill. Will it be larger or smaller than 0.1 in.?

Keeping Fit

1. Round 8,341,581 to the nearest million.

Solve.

2. $5x = 30$ **3.** $x + 9 = 24$

4. $7x + 2 = 23$ **5.** $\frac{x}{5} + 2 = 6$

Compare. Use $>$, $<$, or $=$.

6. 0.4 ▤ 0.9 **7.** 0.52 ▤ 0.520 **8.** 0.29 ▤ 0.3 **9.** 0.1 ▤ 0.08

Write in scientific notation.

10. 900 **11.** 12,000 **12.** 80,000 **13.** 4,620

Career

Problem Solving • Programmers

1. Information to a computer may be put on magnetic tape. The computer reads the information at a rate of 600,000 characters per second. How many characters can it read in a minute? [HINT: Multiply by 60.]

2. Early computers took 0.1 second to multiply two 10-digit numbers. A modern computer takes about 1 nanosecond (0.000000001) to find the same product. How many times faster is the modern computer?

3. Ms. Block worked 240 hours on a program. She is paid $25 per hour. How much did she earn?

4. A machine used to read punched cards can read 895 cards in 1 minute. How many cards can it read in an hour?

5. Computers are programmed to read the magnetic ink symbols found at the bottom of a check. A machine can sort 2,100 checks in one minute. How many checks can the machine sort in an 8-hour day?

6. Mr. Anderson worked $7\frac{3}{4}$ hours one day. He earned $124. How much was he paid per hour?

Chapter Review

Find equivalent fractions with the given denominators. (160)

1. $\frac{4}{5} = \frac{x}{15}$

2. $\frac{9}{10} = \frac{x}{20}$

Simplify. (162)

3. $\frac{4}{6}$

4. $\frac{15}{20}$

5. $\frac{18}{24}$

Compare. Use >, <, or =. (164)

6. $\frac{1}{2} \equiv \frac{2}{3}$

7. $\frac{3}{4} \equiv \frac{6}{8}$

8. $\frac{2}{3} \equiv \frac{3}{5}$

Add and simplify. (168, 170)

9. $\frac{3}{8} + \frac{4}{8}$

10. $11\frac{5}{8} + 5\frac{5}{6}$

11. $\frac{2}{3} + \frac{1}{6} + \frac{5}{12}$

Subtract and simplify. (173, 174)

12. $\frac{7}{16} - \frac{3}{16}$

13. $4\frac{3}{4} - 2\frac{2}{3}$

14. $3\frac{1}{2} - 1\frac{3}{4}$

Multiply and simplify. (178, 180)

15. $\frac{2}{5} \times \frac{1}{4}$

16. $\frac{3}{4} \times 12$

17. $\frac{1}{2} \times 3\frac{3}{4}$

Divide. (182)

18. $\frac{3}{4} \div \frac{3}{5}$

19. $5 \div 1\frac{2}{3}$

20. $3\frac{2}{3} \div 1\frac{1}{2}$

Write decimals. (184)

21. $\frac{9}{2}$

22. $\frac{7}{25}$

23. $6\frac{5}{8}$

Solve. (176, 186)

24. Lois bought juice at 6 cans for $1.59 and picnic plates at $0.89 a package. The total came to $6.74. How much change did she receive from a $20 bill?

25. A systems analyst earns $30,000 a year. To the nearest dollar, what is the weekly salary of the systems analyst?

Chapter Test

Find equivalent fractions with the given denominators. *(160)*

1. $\frac{5}{8} = \frac{x}{16}$

2. $\frac{7}{12} = \frac{x}{24}$

Simplify. *(162)*

3. $\frac{6}{8}$

4. $\frac{12}{15}$

5. $\frac{10}{12}$

Compare. Use >, <, or =. *(164)*

6. $\frac{2}{3} \equiv \frac{8}{12}$

7. $\frac{3}{8} \equiv \frac{5}{6}$

8. $\frac{3}{5} \equiv \frac{4}{7}$

Add and simplify. *(168, 170)*

9. $\frac{3}{4} + \frac{1}{5}$

10. $2\frac{1}{6} + 3\frac{3}{4}$

11. $\frac{5}{8} + \frac{3}{4} + \frac{1}{2}$

Subtract and simplify. *(173, 174)*

12. $\frac{5}{8} - \frac{1}{8}$

13. $7\frac{1}{3} - 2\frac{3}{4}$

14. $7 - 5\frac{2}{3}$

Multiply and simplify. *(178, 180)*

15. $\frac{2}{3} \times \frac{3}{4}$

16. $\frac{4}{5} \times 20$

17. $6\frac{1}{2} \times 4$

Divide. *(182)*

18. $\frac{2}{3} \div \frac{1}{2}$

19. $6 \div 2\frac{1}{3}$

20. $4\frac{1}{2} \div 2\frac{1}{3}$

Write decimals. *(184)*

21. $\frac{11}{4}$

22. $\frac{9}{125}$

23. $2\frac{11}{50}$

Solve. *(176, 186)*

24. The supermarket has 4 dozen cases of canned milk, 3 dozen cases of powdered milk, and 2 dozen cases of cocoa. How many cases of cocoa does it have?

25. A computer programmer earned \$18,000 last year. This year she got a raise of \$2,520. What is her salary now?

Basic Skills Check

1. Multiply.

$$\begin{array}{r} 0.347 \\ \times\ 0.36 \\ \hline \end{array}$$

A 0.12392 B 0.12492
C 1.2392 D 124.92

2. Multiply.

$$\begin{array}{r} \$423.62 \\ \times\ 24 \\ \hline \end{array}$$

E \$10,166.88 F \$8,166.78
G \$6,166.78 H none of the above

3. Divide.

$6\overline{)4.764}$

A 0.974 B 0.864
C 0.794 D 0.791

4. Divide.

$0.07\overline{)3.843}$

E 0.538 F 5.49
G 54.9 H 53,800

5. Divide.

$7\overline{)\$65.73}$

A \$4.93 B \$6.77
C \$8.63 D \$9.39

6. Add.

$$\begin{array}{r} \frac{3}{10} \\ +\ \frac{5}{6} \\ \hline \end{array}$$

E $3\frac{4}{15}$ F $2\frac{8}{15}$
G $2\frac{2}{15}$ H $1\frac{2}{15}$

7. Add.

$$\begin{array}{r} 3\frac{4}{9} \\ +\ 2\frac{5}{6} \\ \hline \end{array}$$

A $5\frac{3}{5}$ B $5\frac{5}{9}$
C $6\frac{5}{18}$ D $6\frac{5}{9}$

8. Subtract.

$$\begin{array}{r} \frac{19}{25} \\ -\ \frac{31}{50} \\ \hline \end{array}$$

E $3\frac{1}{3}$ F $2\frac{1}{6}$
G $\frac{7}{50}$ H $\frac{1}{50}$

9. Subtract.

$$\begin{array}{r} 4\frac{1}{2} \\ -\ 1\frac{3}{4} \\ \hline \end{array}$$

A $3\frac{1}{4}$ B $2\frac{3}{4}$
C $2\frac{1}{2}$ D $2\frac{1}{4}$

10. Subtract. $7 - 3\frac{2}{3}$

E $3\frac{1}{3}$ F $3\frac{5}{6}$
G $4\frac{1}{3}$ H $10\frac{2}{3}$

11. Multiply. $\frac{3}{4} \times \frac{8}{15}$

A $1\frac{2}{5}$ B $\frac{4}{5}$
C $\frac{2}{5}$ D $\frac{1}{5}$

12. Multiply. $6 \times \frac{4}{9}$

E $1\frac{1}{3}$ F $1\frac{2}{3}$
G $2\frac{1}{3}$ H $2\frac{2}{3}$

13. Multiply. $2\frac{1}{3} \times \frac{3}{4}$

A $7\frac{3}{4}$ B $2\frac{1}{4}$
C $1\frac{3}{4}$ D $1\frac{5}{12}$

14. Divide. $\frac{3}{5} \div \frac{9}{10}$

E $2\frac{1}{3}$ F $1\frac{2}{3}$
G $\frac{2}{3}$ H none of the above

15. Divide. $6 \div 1\frac{1}{2}$

A 4 B $4\frac{1}{2}$
C 9 D 12

16. Solve. 42% of 700

E 306 F 296
G 294 H 194

Geometric Figures

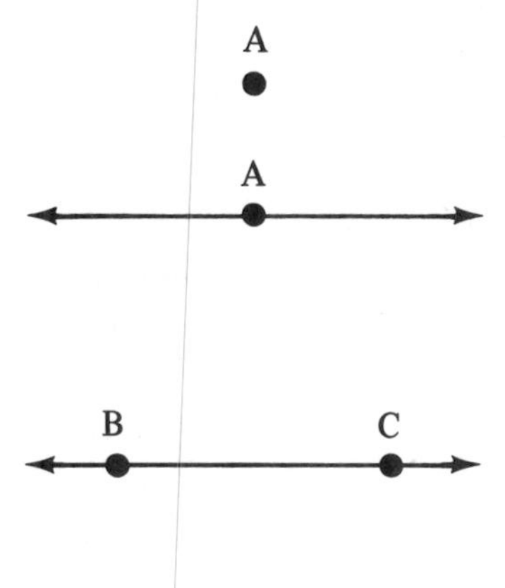

1. Draw a dot to picture a point. Label it point A.

2. Draw a line through point A.

3. How many other lines can be drawn through point A?

4. Draw two dots to picture points B and C.

5. How many lines can be drawn through both points B and C?

Three line segments form triangle DEF. $\overline{EF}$ means line segment EF.

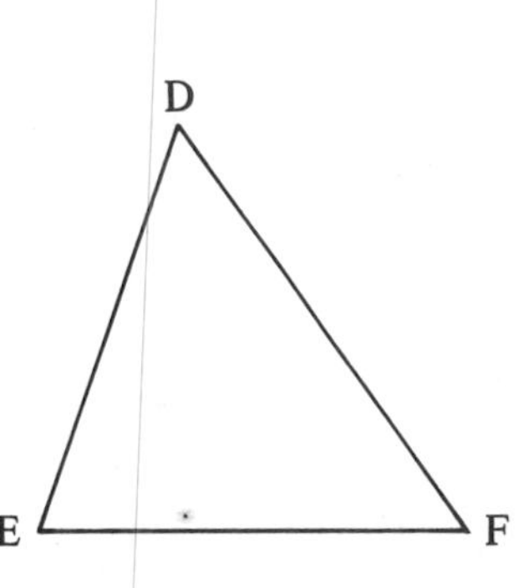

6. Name the other 2 line segments in $\triangle DEF$.

7. Measure $\overline{EF}$ and $\overline{ED}$ to the nearest millimeter. What do you notice?

   $\overline{ED} \cong \overline{EF}$

   ↑

   read: is congruent to

Measure the line segments.
Which pairs of line segments are congruent? Use $\cong$.

8.

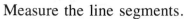

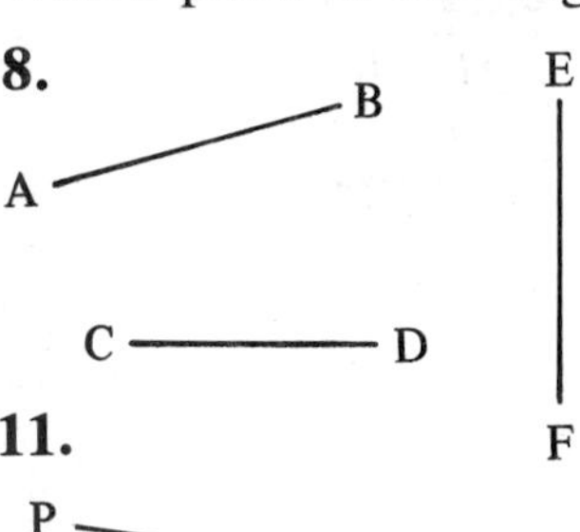

9.

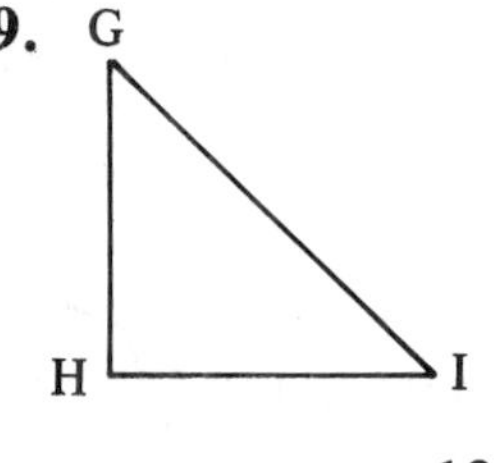

10.

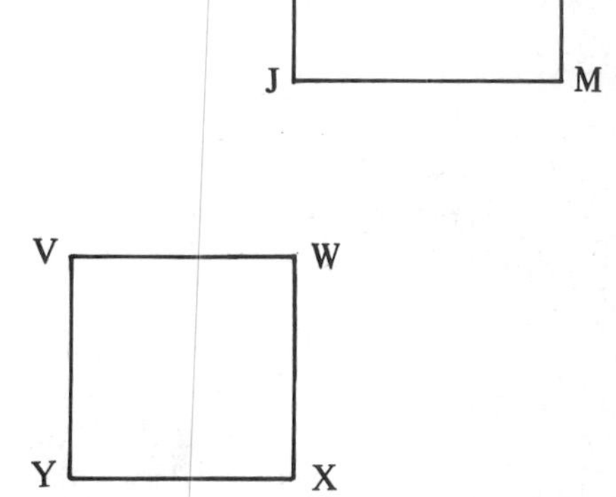

11.

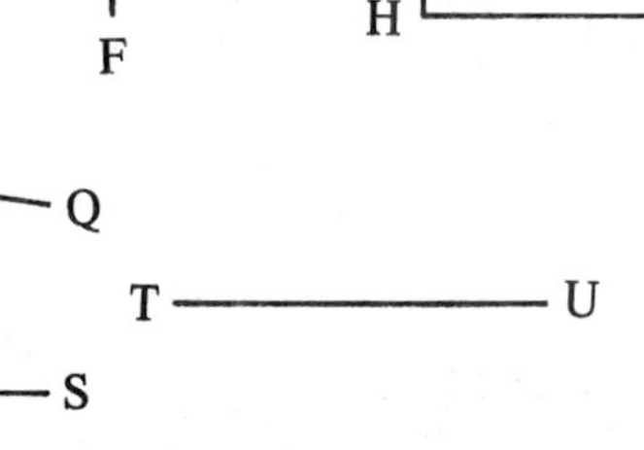

12.

CHAPTER 8 GEOMETRY

Angles

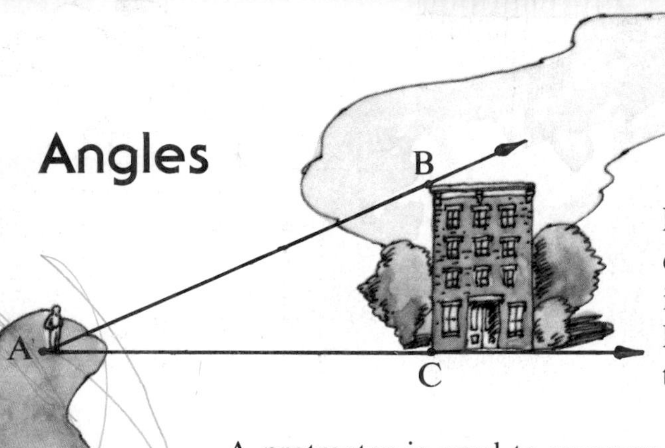

Ray AB ($\overrightarrow{AB}$) and ray AC ($\overrightarrow{AC}$) have a common endpoint. The angle formed is named $\angle BAC$, or $\angle CAB$, or $\angle A$. Point A is the vertex. $\overrightarrow{AB}$ and $\overrightarrow{AC}$ are the sides.

A protractor is used to measure angles. $m\angle COB = 50°$

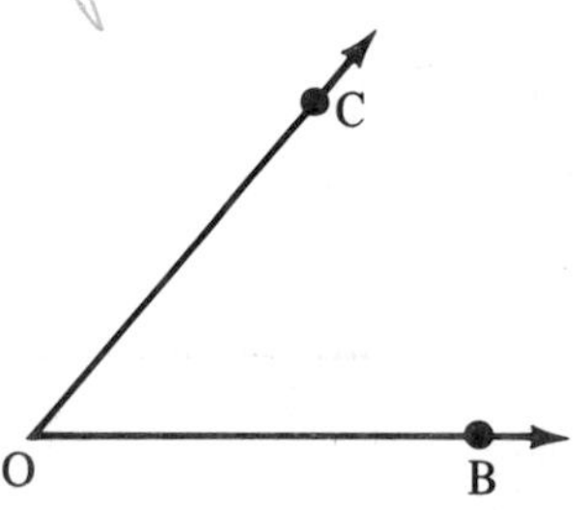

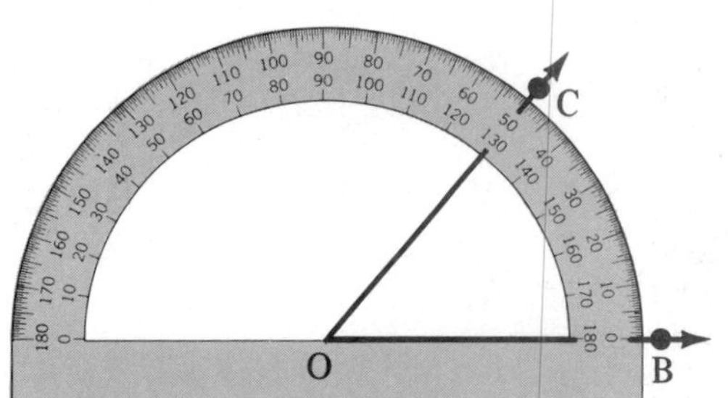

A. Look at the angle at the right.

1. Name the vertex.

2. Name the sides.

3. Name the angle in 3 ways.

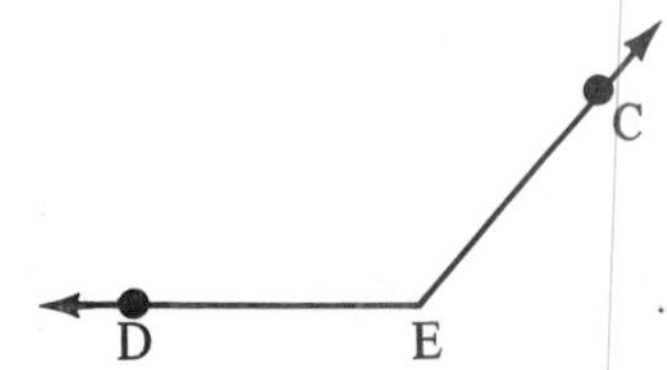

B. Draw angles with these measures.

4. 30° **5.** 90° **6.** 140° **7.** 65° **8.** 170°

C. Give the measures of the angles. $m\angle AOB$ is read measure of angle AOB.

9. $m\angle AOB =$ __?__ **10.** $m\angle AOC =$ __?__

11. $m\angle AOD =$ __?__ **12.** $m\angle AOE =$ __?__

13. $m\angle GOF =$ __?__ **14.** $m\angle GOE =$ __?__

15. $m\angle GOC =$ __?__ **16.** $m\angle DOG =$ __?__

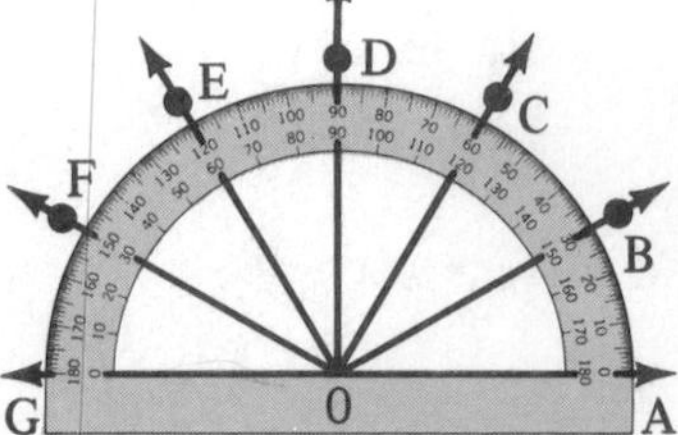

D. Two angles with the same measure are congruent. Measure these angles. Which are congruent?

17.

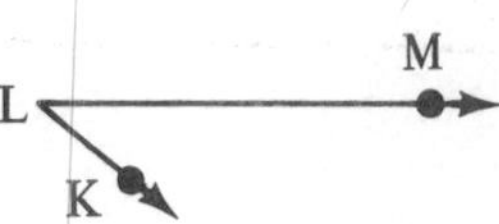

Practice

Name each angle in 3 ways.

1.

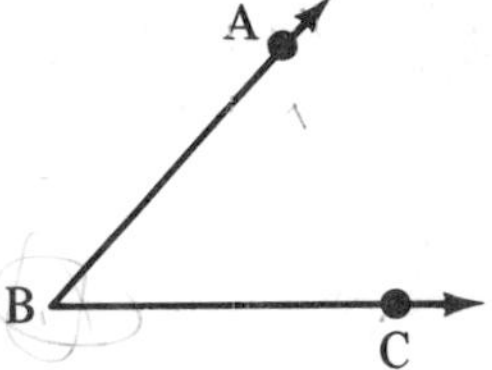

2.

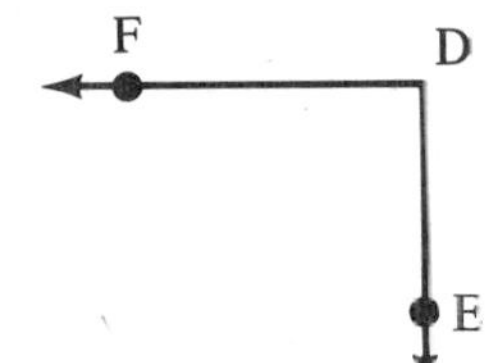

3.

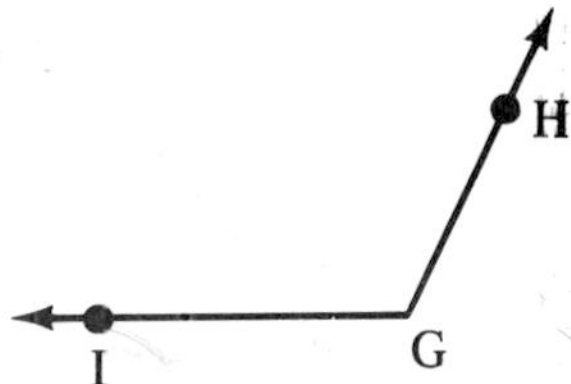

Draw angles with these measures.

4. 40° **5.** 80° **6.** 150° **7.** 62° **8.** 20°

Measure these angles.

9.

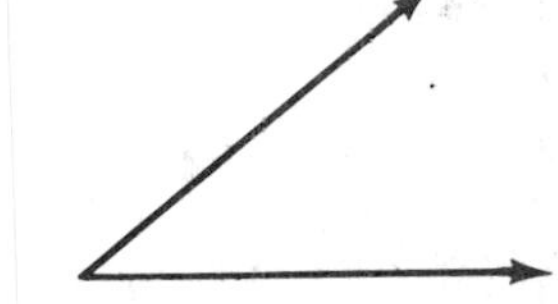

10.

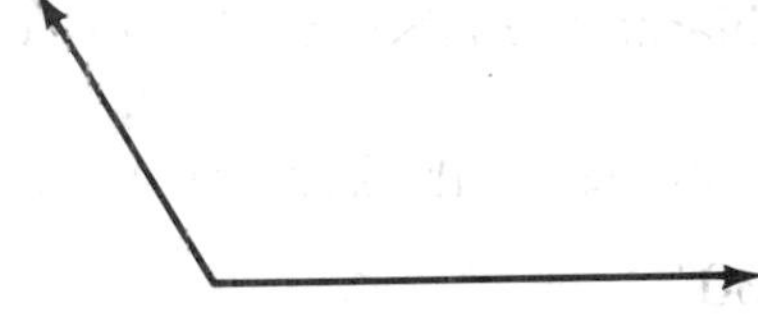

11.

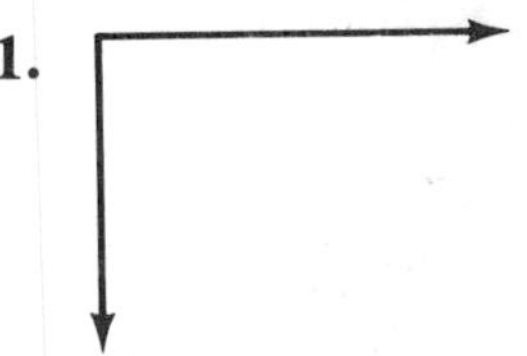

12.

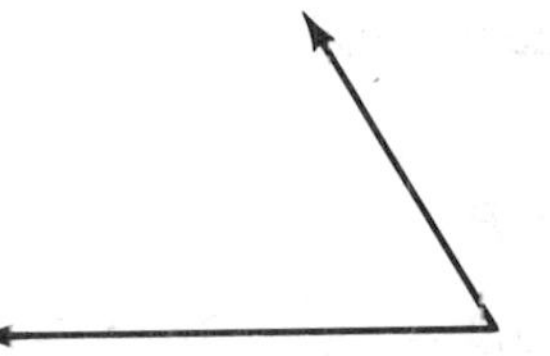

Which angles are congruent?

13.

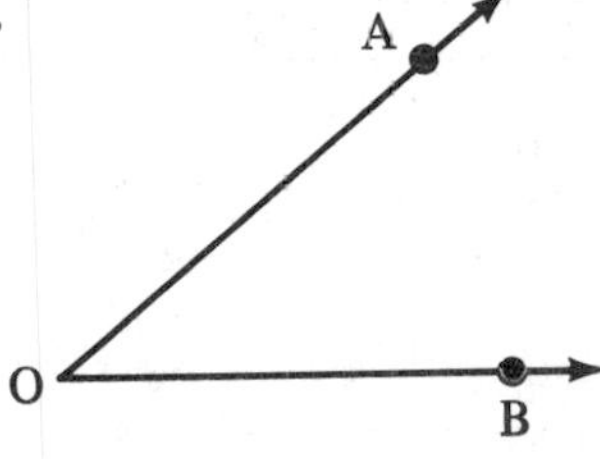

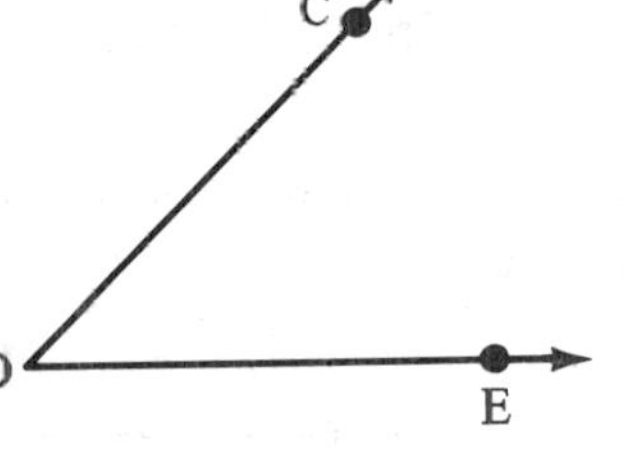

H I

J

Angles and Triangles

Angles and triangles can be classified by the measures of their angles.

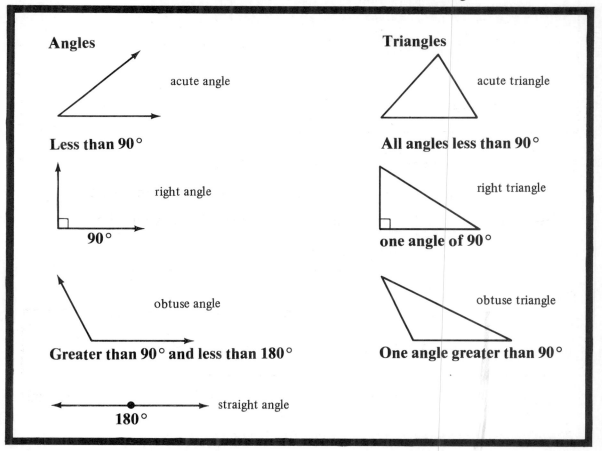

Angles	Triangles
acute angle **Less than 90°**	acute triangle **All angles less than 90°**
right angle **90°**	right triangle **one angle of 90°**
obtuse angle **Greater than 90° and less than 180°**	obtuse triangle **One angle greater than 90°**
straight angle **180°**	

A. Classify these angles.

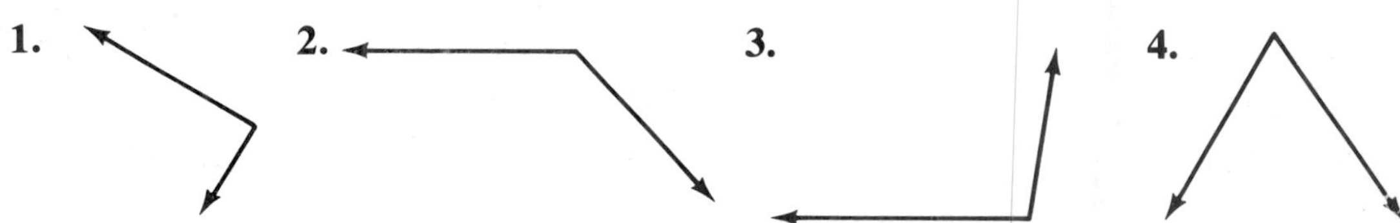

B. Classify these triangles by the measures of their angles.

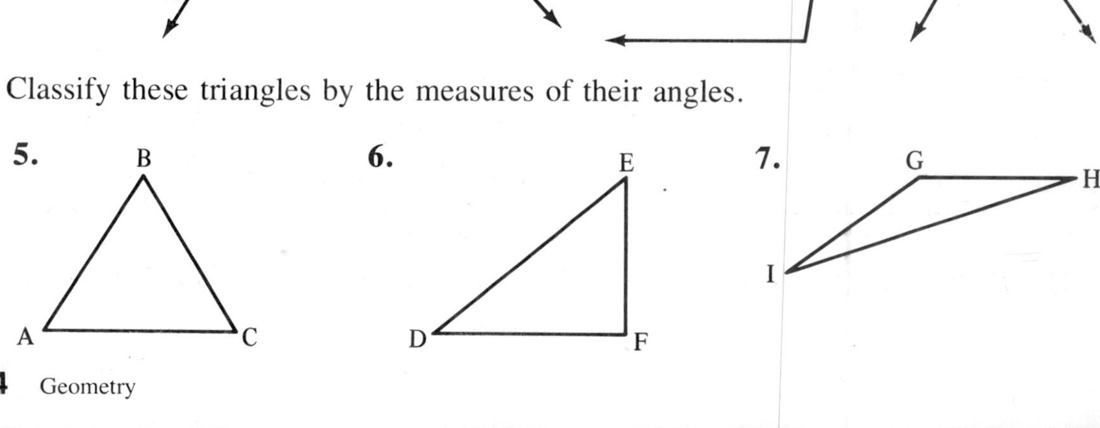

Triangles can also be classified by the measures of their sides.

scalene triangle

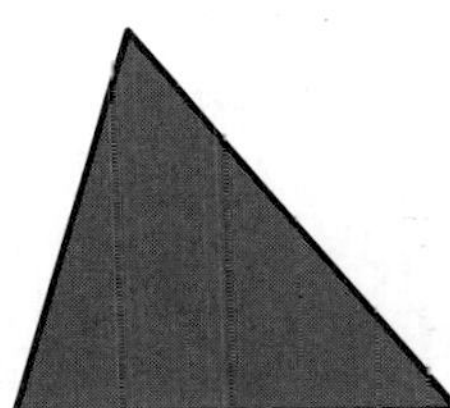

no sides congruent

isosceles triangle

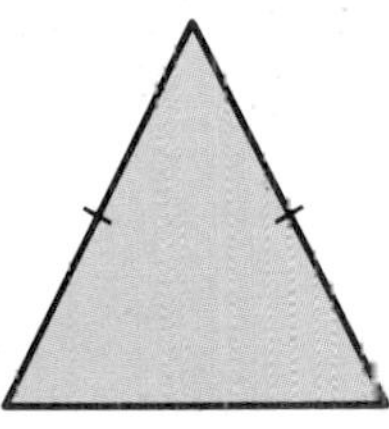

at least 2 sides congruent

equilateral triangle

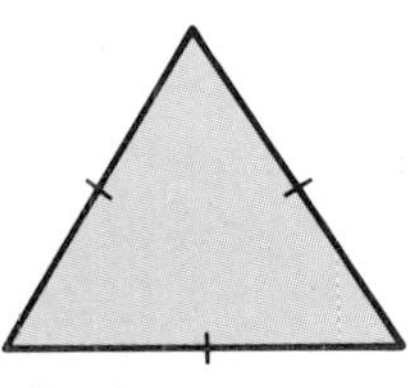

all sides congruent

C. Classify these triangles by the measures of their sides.

8. sides: 8 cm, 8 cm, 6 cm

9. sides: 2 in., 3 in., 4 in.

10. sides: 15 mm, 15 mm, 15 mm

11. sides: 3 cm, 4 cm, 5 cm

Practice

Classify these angles.

1. 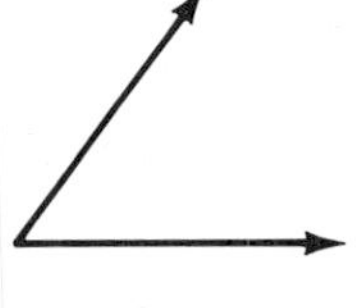

2. 

3. 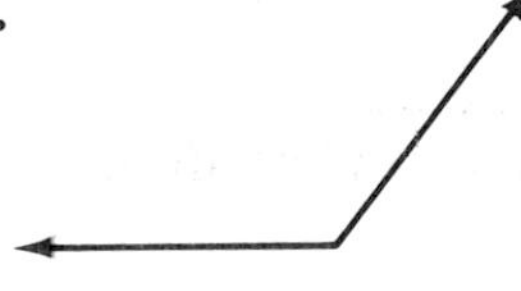

4. 

5. 153°

6. 12°

7. 90°

8. 180°

Classify these triangles by the measures of their angles.

9. 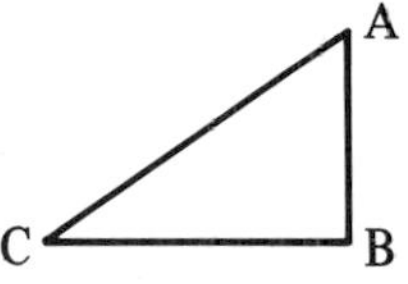

10. 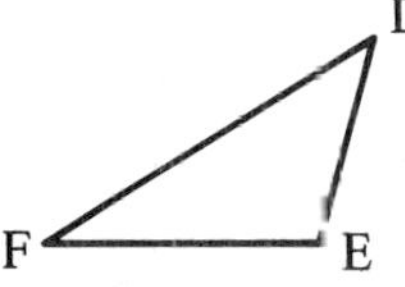

11. 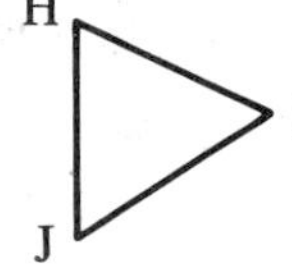

12. 40°, 40°, 100°

13. 30°, 60°, 90°

14. 24°, 85°, 71°

Classify these triangles by the measures of their sides.

15. 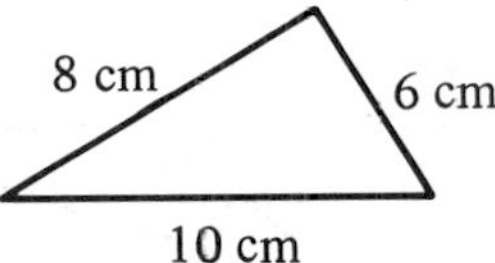

16. 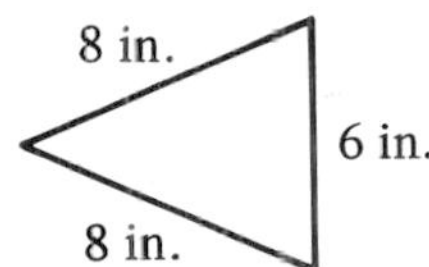

17. 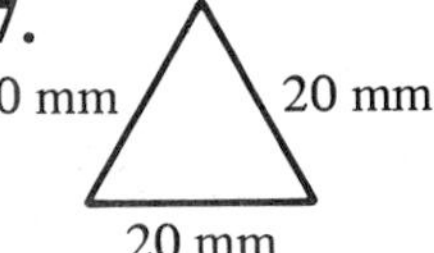

18. 10 cm, 10 cm, 10 cm

19. 4 ft, 6 ft, 8 ft

20. 3 m, 4 m, 3 m

Angle Construction

Materials: compass, paper, pencil

A. Here's how to construct an angle congruent to $\angle ACB$.

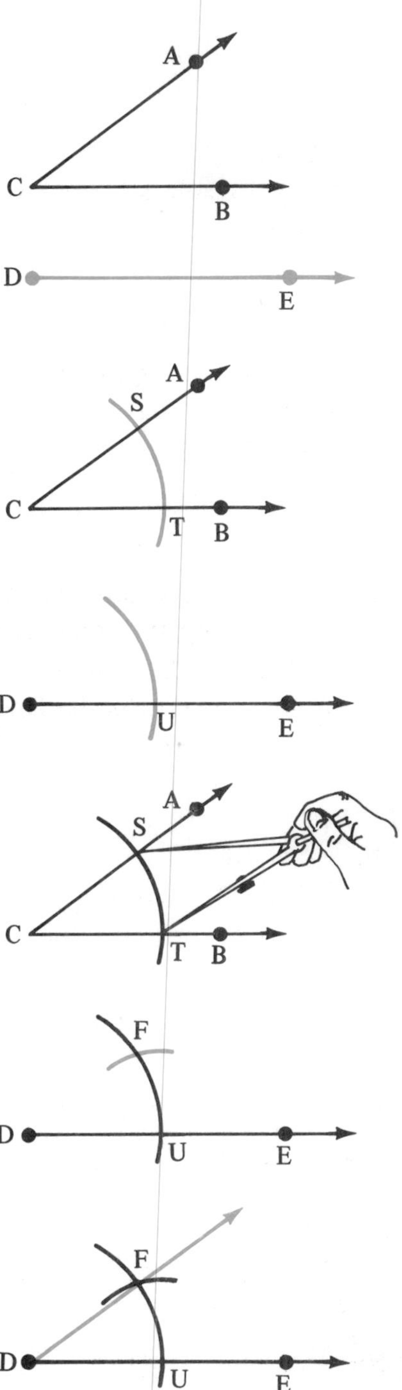

1. Draw $\overrightarrow{DE}$.

2. Put your compass point on C. Draw an arc. Mark points S and T.

3. Keep your compass open to the same distance. Now put the compass point on D and draw an arc. Mark point U.

4. Put your compass point on T and open it enough to reach S.

5. Using the distance from T to S, put your compass point on U and draw an arc. Mark point F.

6. Draw $\overrightarrow{DF}$.
$\angle FDE \cong \angle ACB$

B. Here's how to bisect $\angle XYZ$.

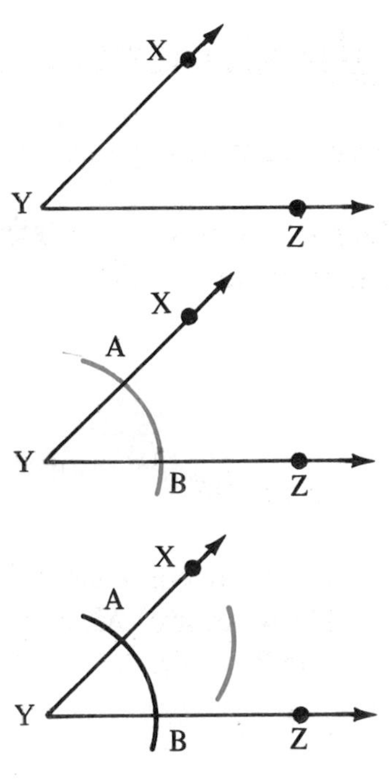

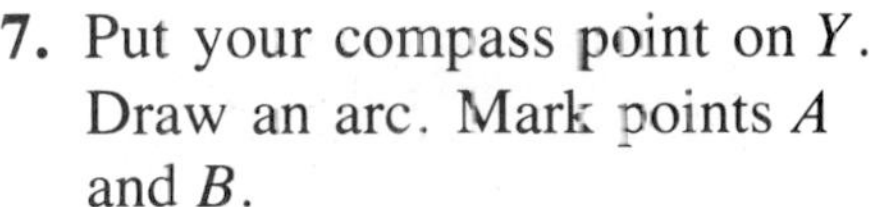

7. Put your compass point on Y. Draw an arc. Mark points A and B.

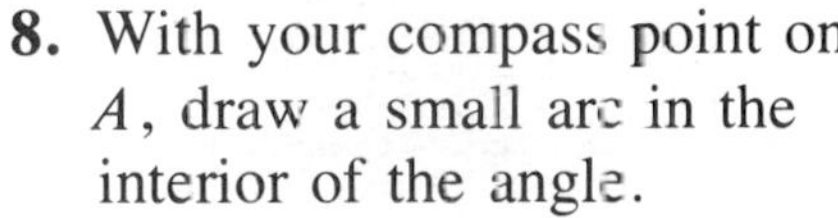

8. With your compass point on A, draw a small arc in the interior of the angle.

9. With your compass point on B and keeping the same distance on the compass, draw another arc that intersects the first arc. Mark point M.

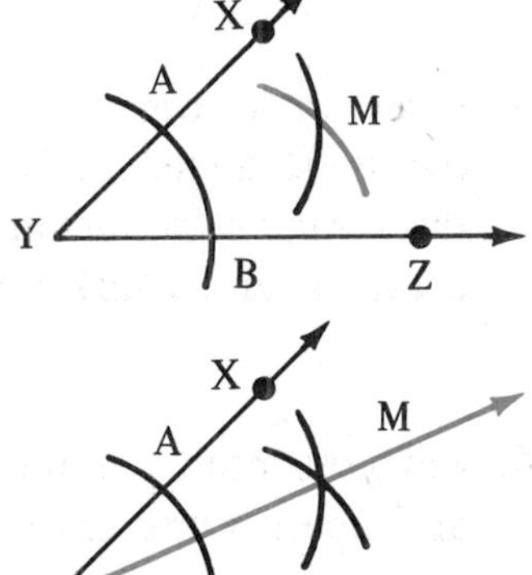

10. Draw $\overrightarrow{YM}$.
$\overrightarrow{YM}$ bisects $\angle XYZ$.

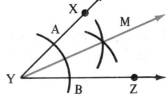

Practice

1. Copy $\angle MNO$.

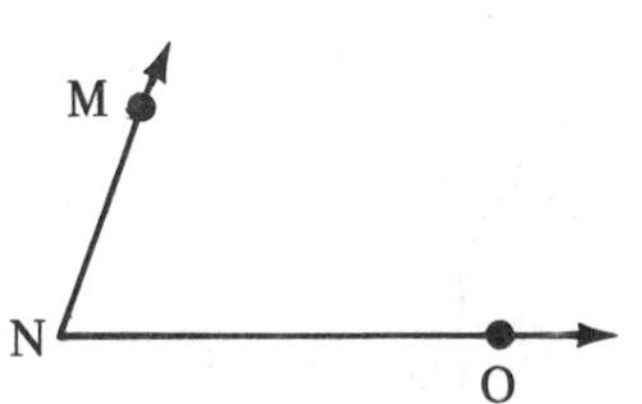

2. Draw an acute angle. Bisect it.

Polygons

Polygons are made up of line segments. They are classified by the number of line segments.

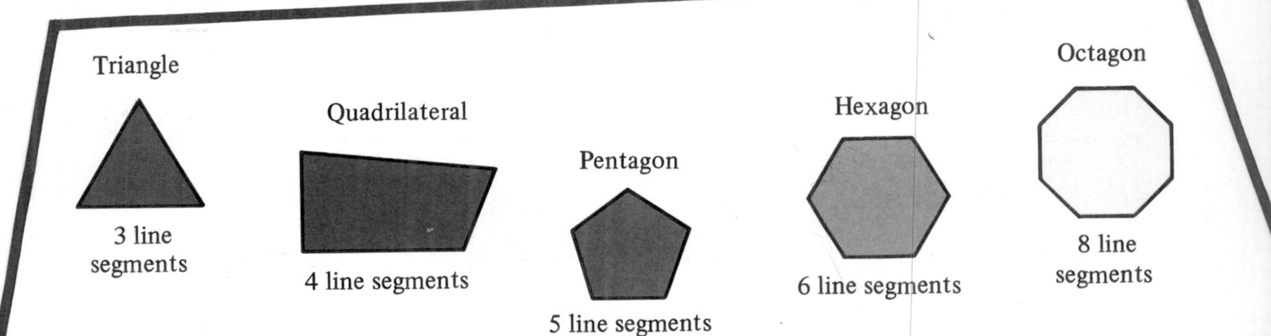

A. Name the polygons.

1. 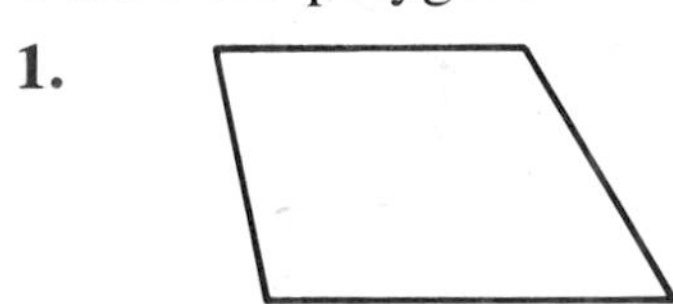

2. 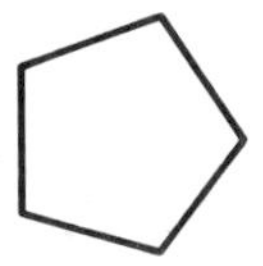

3. 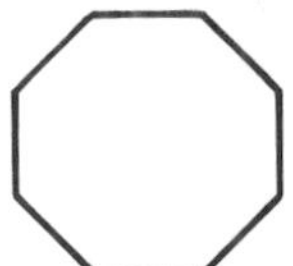

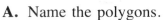

There are many special quadrilaterals.

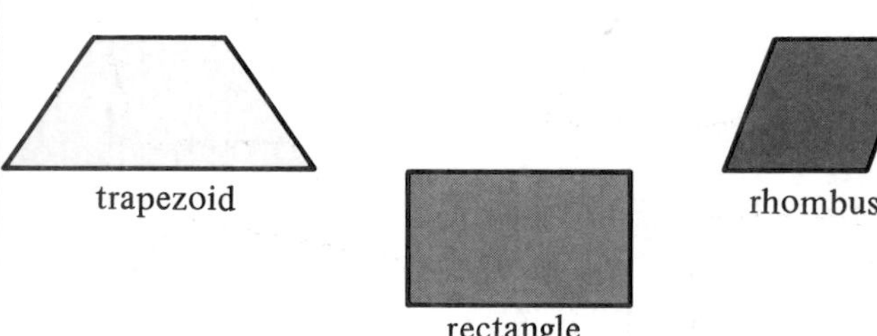

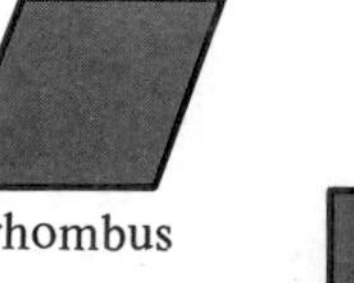

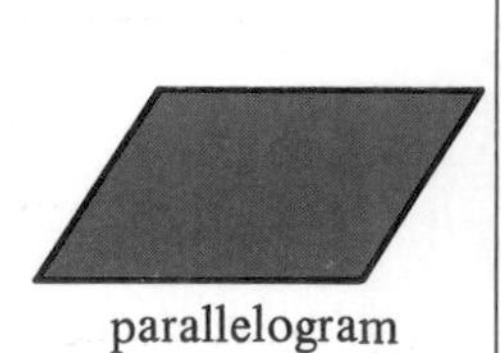

B. Look at the quadrilaterals above.

4. How many pairs of sides are parallel in a trapezoid?

5. In a parallelogram, how many pairs of sides are parallel?

6. In a parallelogram, what is true about the opposite sides and opposite angles?

7. In what way is a rhombus a special parallelogram?

8. In what way is a rectangle a special parallelogram?

9. In what way is a square a special rectangle?

C. Find x.

10. 

11. 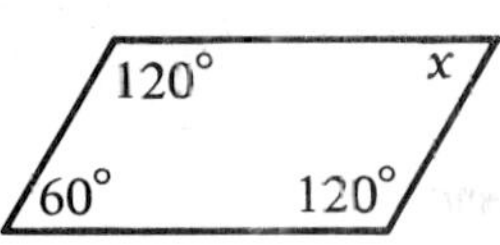

12. 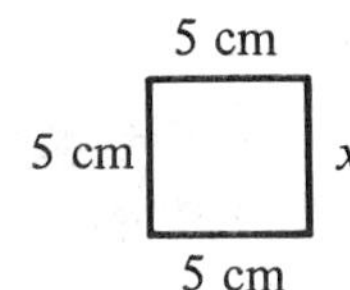

Practice

Name the polygons.

1. 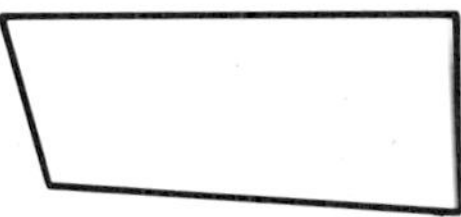

2. 

3. 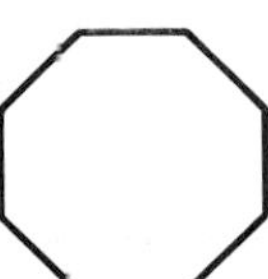

4. 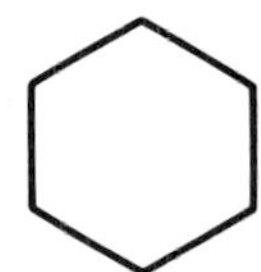

5. 

6. 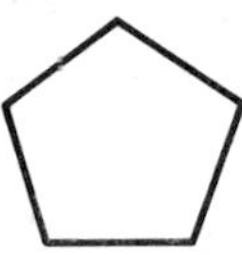

Name the quadrilaterals.

7. 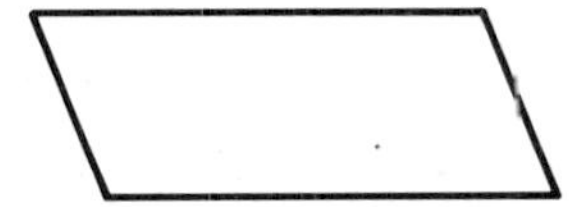

8. 

9. 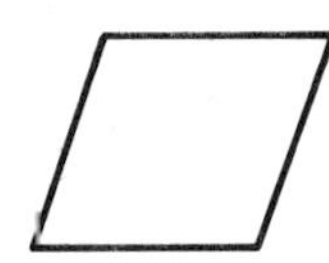

10. 

11. 

12. 

Find x.

13. 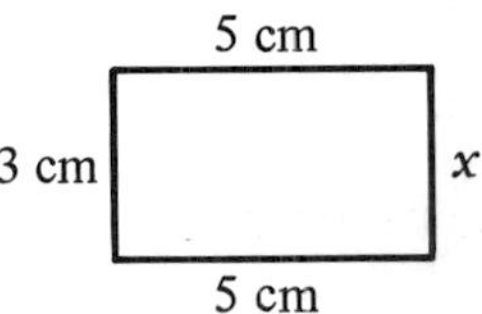

14. 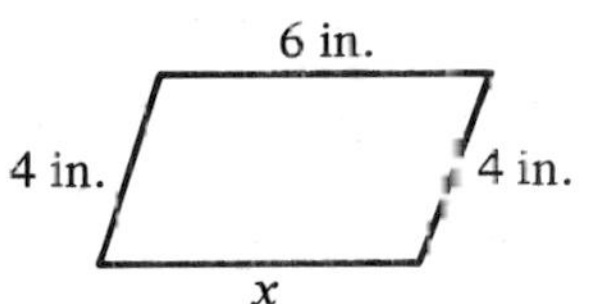

15. 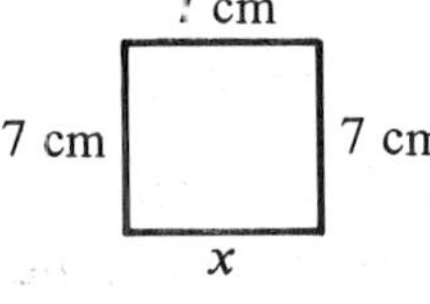

16. 

17. 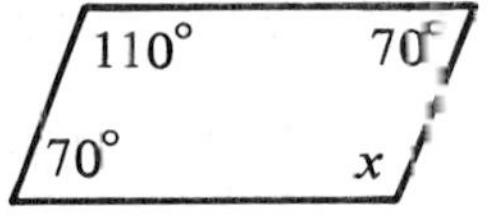

18. 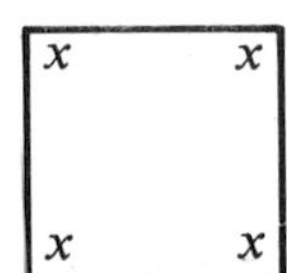

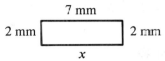

Angles of a Polygon

Discovery of geometric relationships may be made by experimentation.

Perform this experiment.

Draw a large triangle.

Cut out the triangle.

Cut off the 3 angles and place them side by side.

Notice that a straight angle is formed. The measure of a straight angle is 180°.

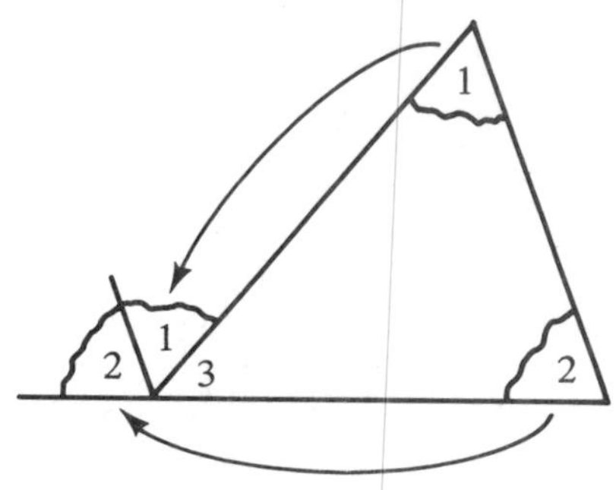

▶ The sum of the measures of the angles of a triangle is 180°.

A. In $\triangle ABC$, $m\angle A = 63°$ and $m\angle B = 59°$. What is $m\angle C$?

1. What is the sum of $m\angle A + m\angle B + m\angle C$?

2. What is the sum of $m\angle A + m\angle B$?

3. What is $m\angle C$?

B
59°
63°
A
C

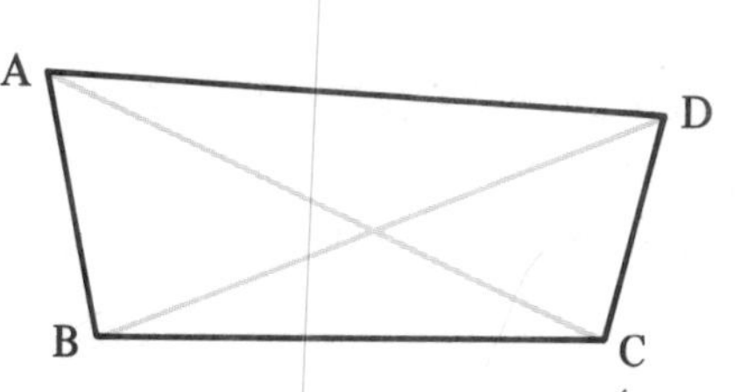

B. Quadrilateral *ABCD* has 4 vertices.

4. Name the 4 vertices of *ABCD*.

5. $\overline{AC}$ is a diagonal. Name the other diagonal.

C. Quadrilateral *ABCD* is divided into 2 triangles.

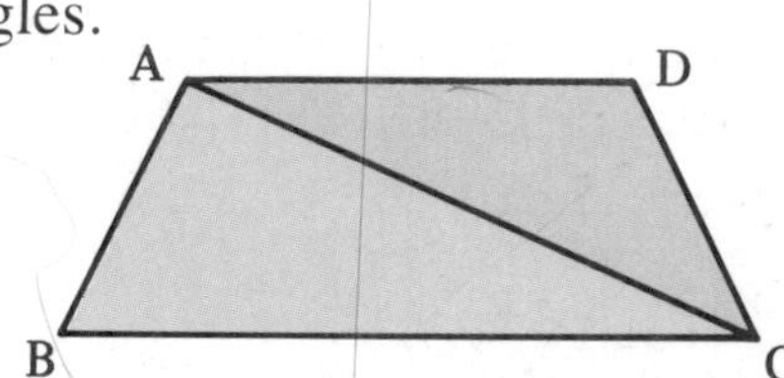

6. What is the sum of the measures of the angles of each triangle?

7. What is the sum of the measures of the angles of the quadrilateral?

D. A **regular polygon** has the same size angles and sides. Find the measures of each angle of these regular polygons.

8.

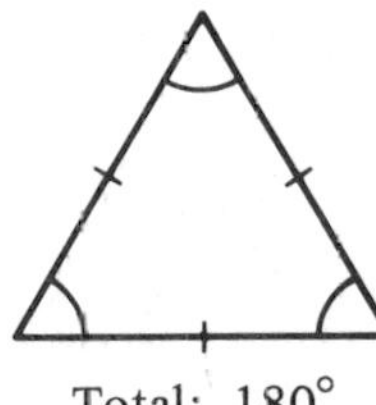

Total: 180°

9.

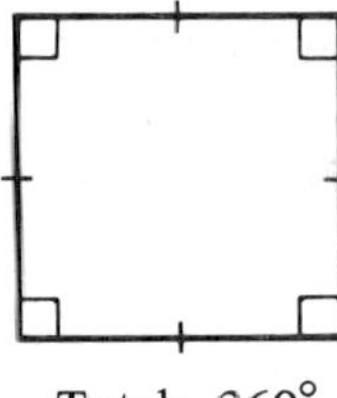

Total: 360°

10.

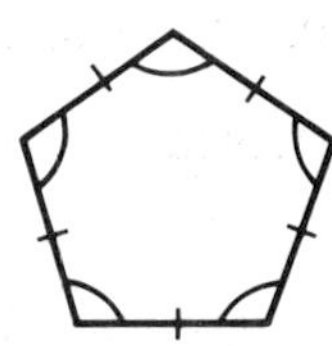

Total: 540°

Practice

The measures of 2 angles of a triangle are given. Find the measure of the third angle.

1. 50°, 50°

2. 10°, 140°

3. 90°, 50°

4. 60°, 70°

5. 24°, 37°

6. 18°, 90°

7. 73°, 46°

8. 131°, 17°

9. 47°, 101°

Draw diagonals. Find the sum of the measures of the angles of each polygon.

10.

11.

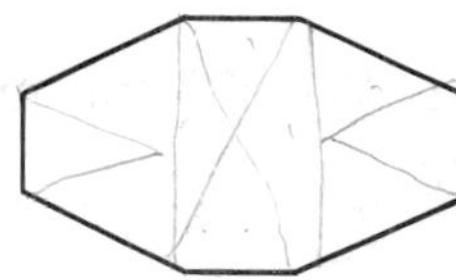

Solve.

12. One acute angle of a right triangle is 30°. What is the measure of the other acute angle?

13. An equilateral triangle is a regular polygon. What is the measure of each angle of an equilateral triangle?

14. One angle of a triangle measures 88°. The other 2 angles each have the same measure. What is the measure of each of the other 2 angles?

15. Each of 2 angles of a triangle measures 77°. What is the measure of the third angle of the triangle?

★**16.** What is the measure of each angle of a regular hexagon?

★**17.** What is the sum of the measures of the angles of a polygon with 10 sides?

Perimeter of a Polygon

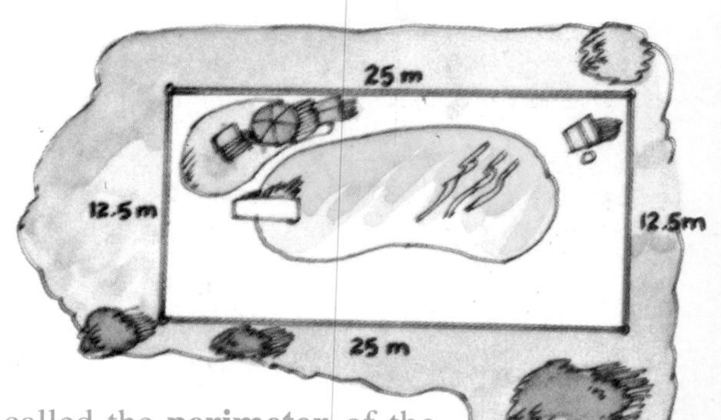

An iron fence will be placed around a pool as shown. How much fence will be needed?

perimeter = 25 + 12.5 + 25 + 12.5
= 75

The perimeter is 75 m.

▶ The distance around a polygon is called the **perimeter** of the polygon. The perimeter is found by adding the measures of the sides.

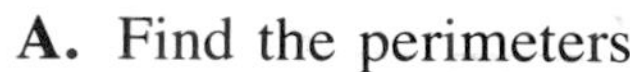

A. Find the perimeters.

1.

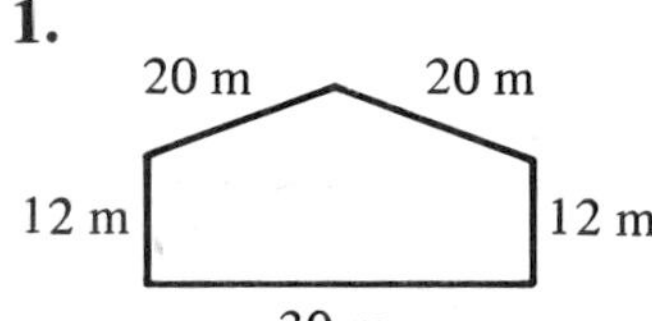

2.

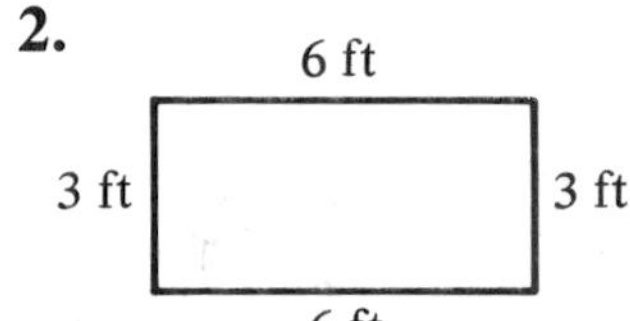

3.

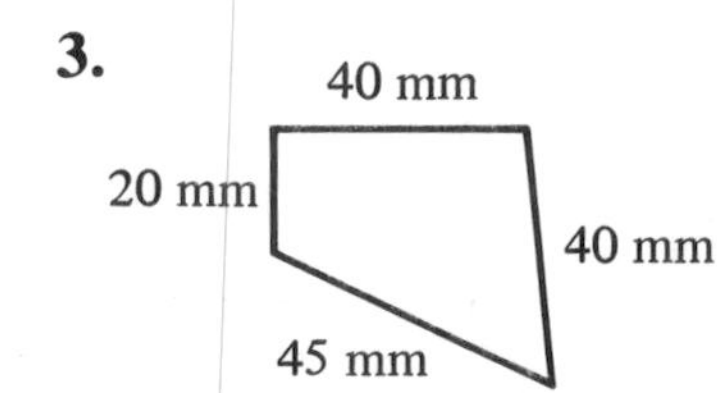

B. There are formulas to find the perimeters of some polygons.

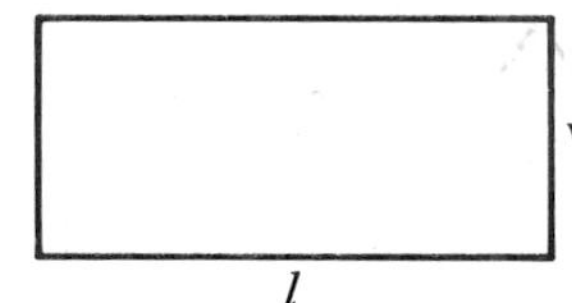

Rectangle
$p = 2l + 2w$

Square
$p = 4s$

Find the perimeters.

4.

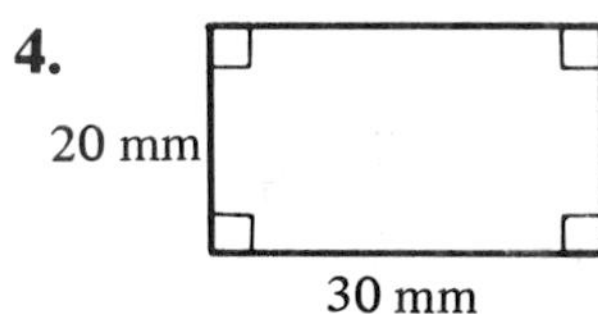

5. 1.4 cm, 3.7 cm

6.

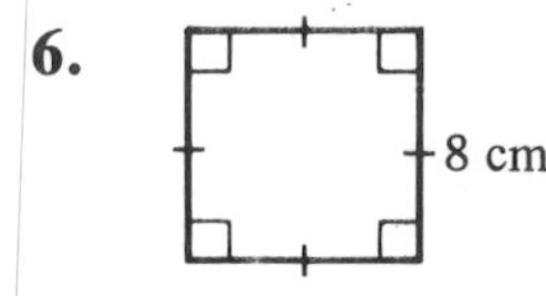

C. Here is an equilateral triangle.

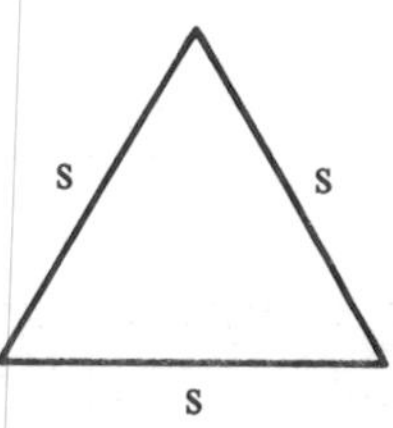

7. Write a formula for finding the perimeter of an equilateral triangle.

8. What is the perimeter of an equilateral triangle with one side 24 cm long?

Find the perimeters.

1.

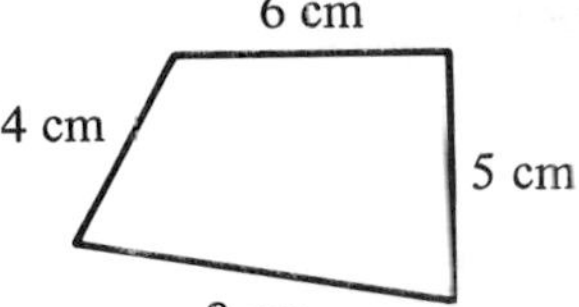

2.

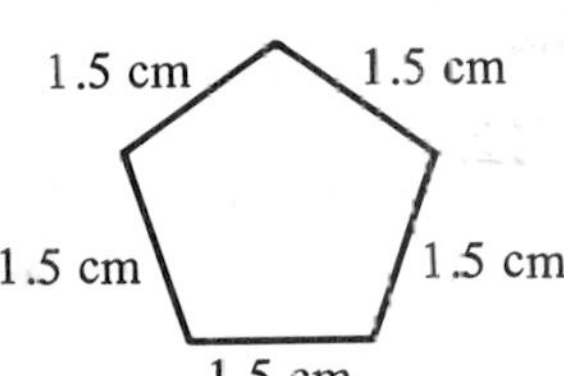

3.

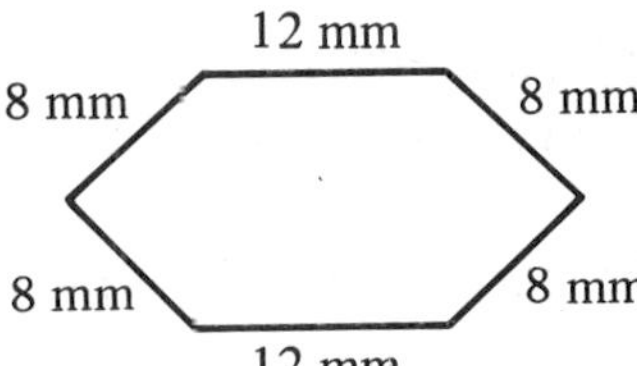

4.

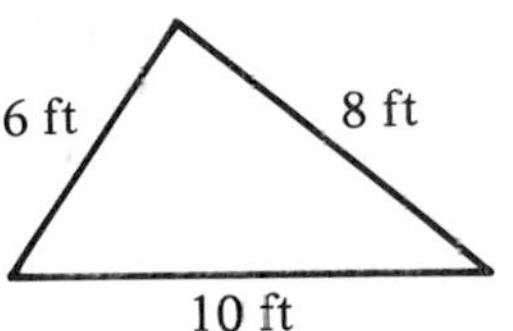

5.

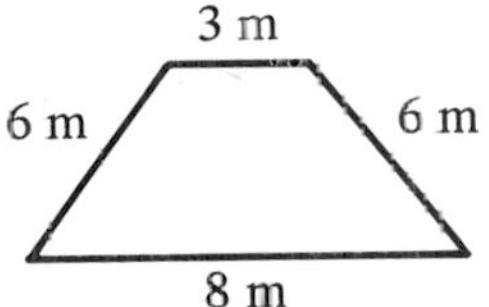

6.

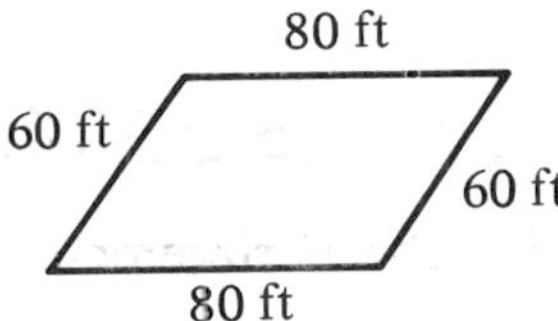

7.

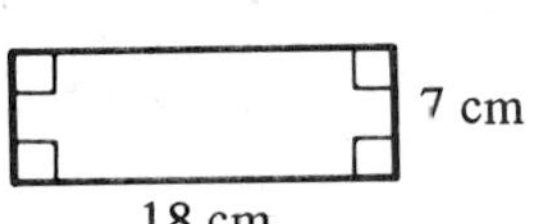

8.

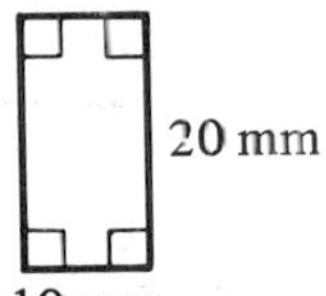

9.

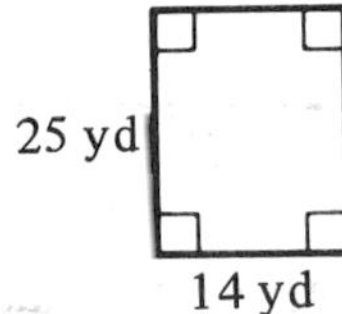

10.

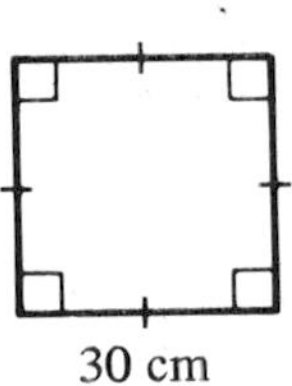

11.

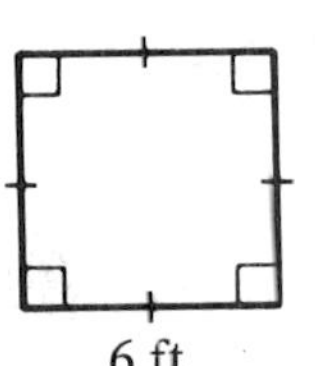

12.

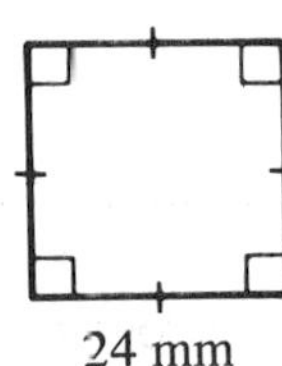

13.

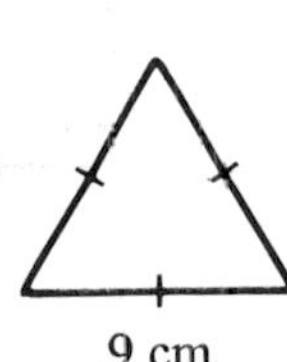

14.

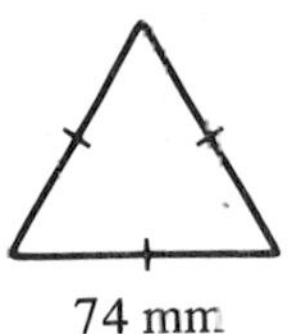

15.

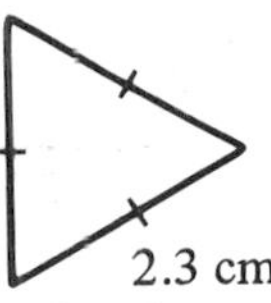

Solve.

16. How much fencing is needed to enclose a rectangular playground which is 90 ft by 120 ft?

Keeping Fit

Compare. Use >, <, or =.

1. 0.4 ▒ 0.8
2. 0.73 ▒ 0.730
3. 0.29 ▒ 0.3
4. 0.01 ▒ 0.009
5. Round 3.247 to the nearest tenth.

Add. Simplify when possible.

6. $\frac{3}{4} + \frac{2}{3}$
7. $3\frac{5}{6} + 2\frac{3}{8}$
8. $4\frac{1}{2} + 3\frac{3}{4}$
9. $\frac{5}{8} + 1\frac{1}{2} + 2\frac{5}{6}$

Subtract. Simplify when possible.

10. $\frac{4}{5} - \frac{1}{4}$
11. $5\frac{2}{3} - 2\frac{3}{8}$
12. $3\frac{1}{2} - 1\frac{3}{4}$
13. $8 - 3\frac{5}{6}$

Multiply.

14. 624×35
15. 427×30
16. $8{,}912 \times 605$
17. 286×542
18. 0.6×0.06
19. 0.6×0.9
20. 0.23×4.5
21. $\frac{1}{2} \times \frac{3}{4}$
22. $\frac{2}{3} \times \frac{9}{2}$
23. $\frac{4}{5} \times 2\frac{1}{7}$
24. $5\frac{1}{2} \times 1\frac{1}{3}$

Divide.

25. $7\overline{)364}$
26. $14\overline{)224}$
27. $33\overline{)10{,}032}$
28. $215\overline{)8{,}600}$
29. $0.3\overline{)495}$
30. $43\overline{)0.0129}$
31. $7.1\overline{)24.85}$
32. $0.34\overline{)32.81}$
33. $\frac{1}{2} \div \frac{4}{5}$
34. $\frac{3}{5} \div \frac{1}{5}$
35. $\frac{6}{7} \div \frac{3}{14}$
36. $2\frac{1}{4} \div 1\frac{1}{5}$

Divide. Round the quotient to the nearest tenth.

37. $6\overline{)1.4}$
38. $0.4\overline{)3.112}$
39. $1.6\overline{)57}$
40. $0.09\overline{)0.631}$

Divide. Round the quotient to the nearest hundredth.

41. $9\overline{)6.521}$
42. $0.7\overline{)16.056}$
43. $2.9\overline{)15.38}$
44. $0.52\overline{)0.976}$

Find equivalent fractions with the given denominators.

45. $\frac{1}{2} = \frac{x}{6}$
46. $\frac{5}{6} = \frac{x}{24}$
47. $\frac{3}{10} = \frac{x}{30}$
48. $\frac{7}{12} = \frac{x}{48}$

Mid-Chapter Review

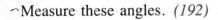

Measure these angles. *(192)*

1.

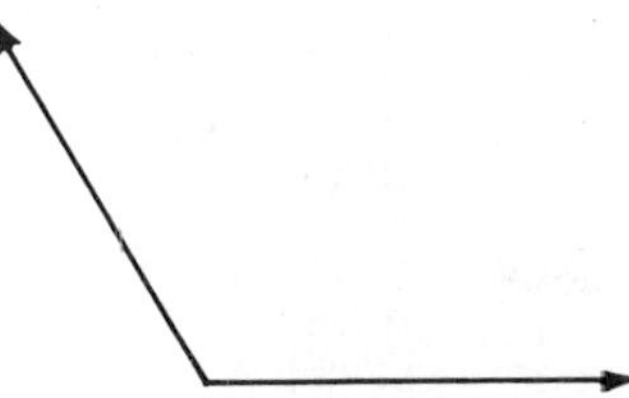

2.

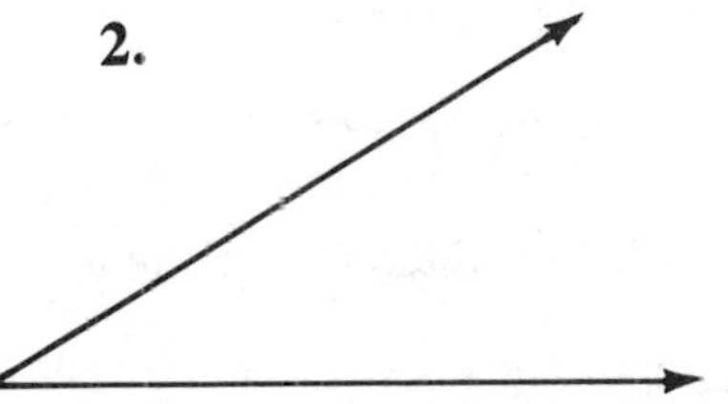

3.

Classify these triangles by the measures of their angles. *(194)*

4.

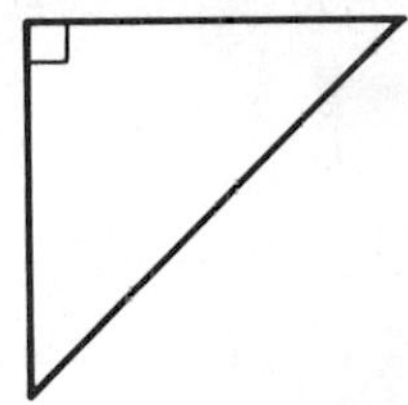

5.

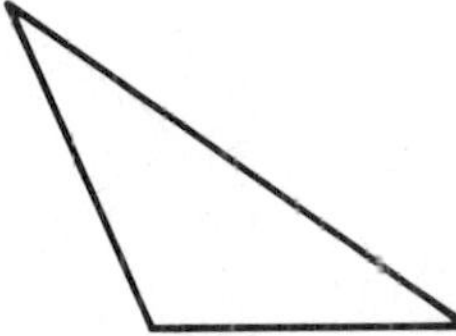

6.

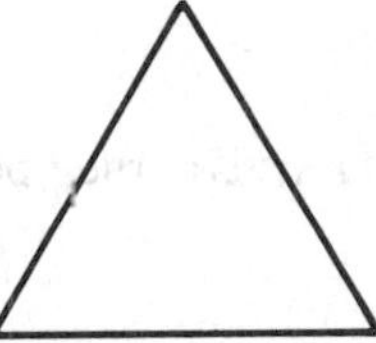

Classify these triangles by the measures of their sides. *(195)*

7.

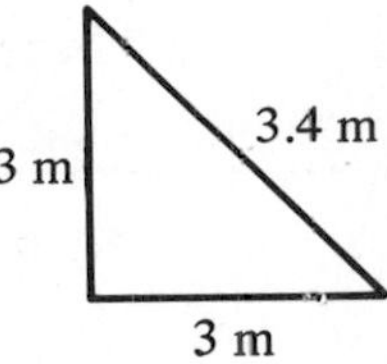

8.

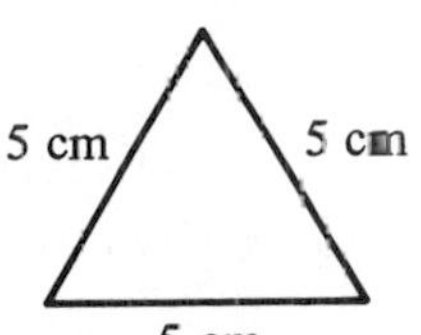

9.

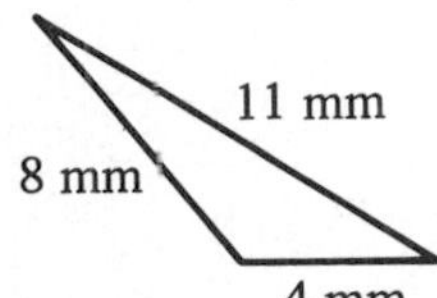

Find the missing measures. *(198, 200)*

10.

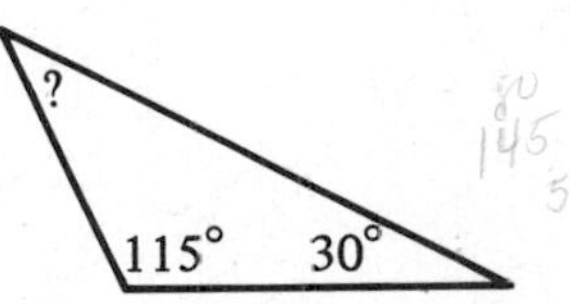

11.

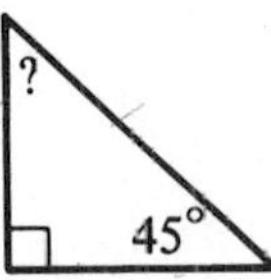

12.

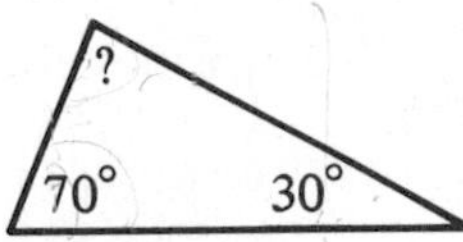

Find the perimeters. *(202)*

13.

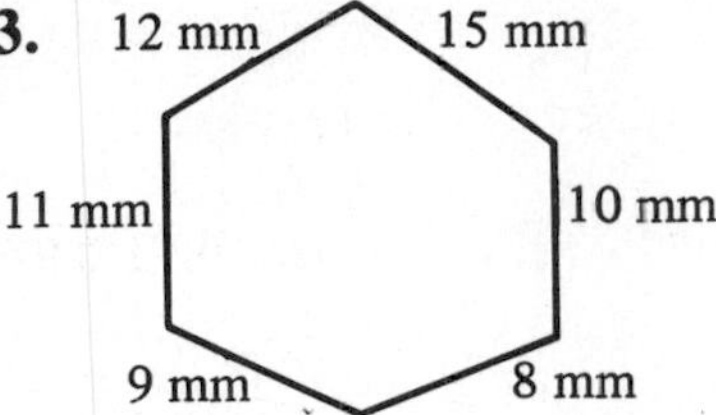

14.

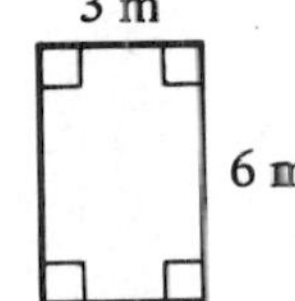

15.

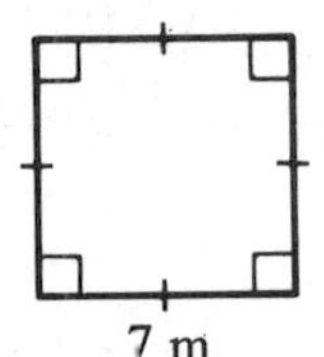

Problem Solving

40 mm

The length of a rectangle is 40 mm. What is the perimeter of the rectangle?

PLAN perimeter $= 2l + 2w$

You are told the length, but not the width. You don't have enough information to solve this problem.

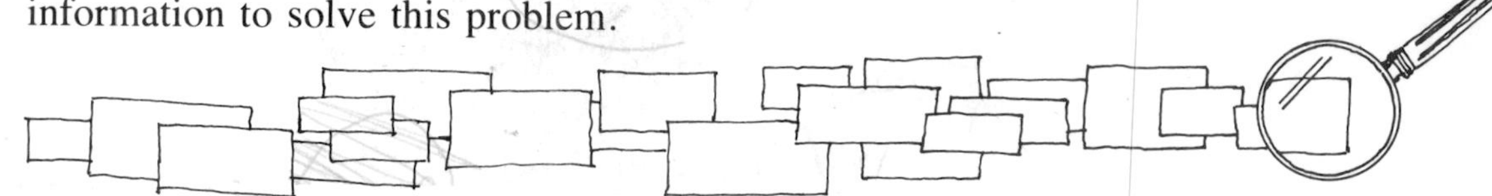

A. $\triangle RST$ is an acute triangle. $m\angle R = 43°$. What is the measure of $\angle S$?

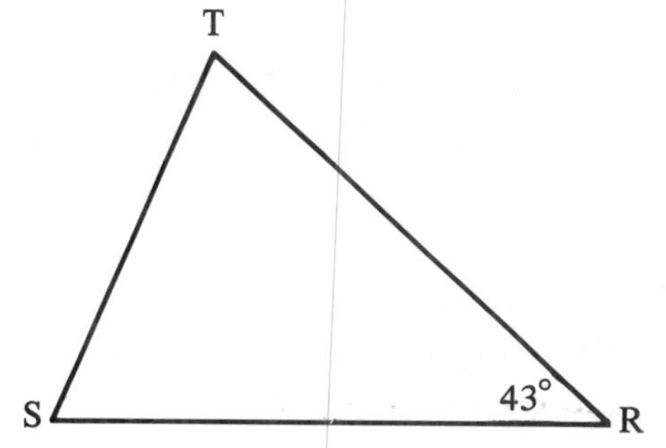

1. What information do you need to solve this problem?
2. What information is given?
3. Do you have enough information to solve the problem?

B. $\triangle UVW$ is a right triangle. $\angle U$ is a right angle and $m\angle V = 30°$. What is the measure of $\angle W$?

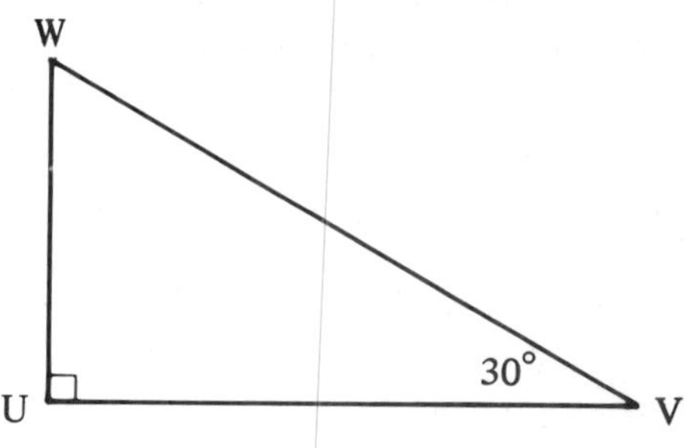

4. What information do you need to solve this problem?
5. What information is given?
6. Do you have enough information to solve the problem?
7. Solve.

C. The width of a rectangle is 34 cm. What is the perimeter of the rectangle?

8. Do you have enough information to solve this problem?
9. What information is missing?
10. Supply the missing information and solve.

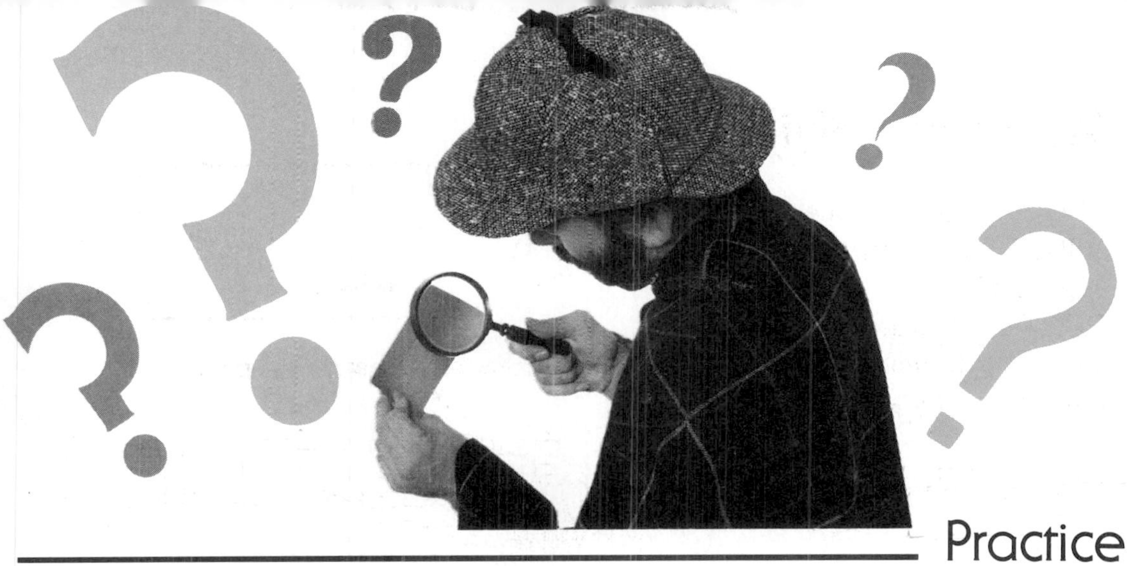

Practice

Decide if there is enough information to solve the problem. If so, solve.

1. The length of a rectangle is 30 mm. What is the perimeter of the rectangle?

2. In scalene triangle RST, RS = 1.5 cm. What is the perimeter of the triangle?

3. In right triangle DEF, $\angle D$ is a right angle. $m\angle E = 22$. What is the measure of $\angle F$?

4. In $\triangle ABC$, $m\angle A = 53$. What is the measure of $\angle B$?

5. A side of a regular pentagon is 10 cm long. What is the perimeter of the pentagon?

6. $\triangle ABC$ is a right triangle. $\angle C$ is a right angle. What is the sum of the measures of $\angle A$ and $\angle B$?

Tell what additional information is needed to solve the problem. Supply the information and solve.

7. The width of a rectangle is 24 cm. What is the perimeter of the rectangle?

8. In $\triangle ABC$, $\overline{AB} = 13$ mm and $\overline{AC} = 15$ mm. What kind of triangle is $\triangle ABC$?

9. The perimeter of a rectangle is 120 ft. What is the width?

10. In right triangle MNO, $\angle O$ is a right angle. What is the measure of $\angle M$?

11. A side of a hexagon is 12 cm long. What is the perimeter of the hexagon?

12. The perimeter of a triangle is 42 cm long. How long is each side?

Circles and Circumferences

Every point on this circle is 3 cm away from the center, O. $\overline{OA}$ is a radius. $\overline{BC}$ is a diameter. The length of the radius is 3 cm. The length of the diameter is 6 cm.

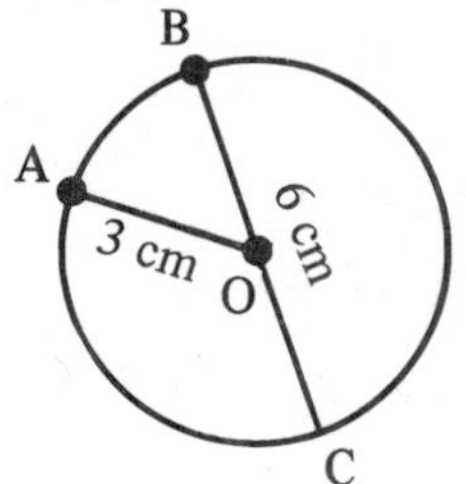

▶ The length of a diameter of a circle is twice the length of a radius of that circle.

A. Find the length of the diameter for the given radii.

1. 62 mm **2.** 0.5 m **3.** 2.1 cm **4.** 9.6 in.

B. Find the length of the radius for the given diameters.

5. 32 m **6.** 6 cm **7.** 15 mm **8.** 3.8 in.

The distance around a circle is called the **circumference.** The ratio of the circumference to the diameter is the same for all circles. $\frac{\text{circumference}}{\text{diameter}} = \pi$

$\pi \doteq 3.14$

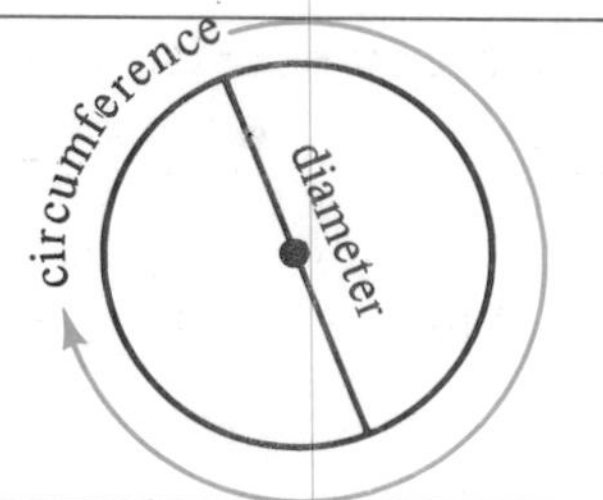

▶ The formula for finding the circumference is circumference = $\pi \cdot$ diameter, or $C = \pi \cdot d$. The formula $C = 2 \cdot \pi \cdot r$ is also used for finding the circumference of a circle.

C. Find the circumference. Give the answer in terms of π.

Examples

$d = 14$ mm
$C = \pi \cdot d$
$= \pi \cdot 14$, or 14π mm

$r = 6$ cm
$C = 2 \cdot \pi \cdot r$
$= 2 \cdot \pi \cdot 6$, or 12π cm

9. $d = 10$ m **10.** $d = 3.5$ cm **11.** $r = 4$ mm **12.** $r = 5.4$ m

D. Find the circumference. Use $\pi \doteq 3.14$.

Examples

$$d = 8 \text{ cm}$$
$$C = \pi \cdot d$$
$$= 3.14 \cdot 8$$
$$= 25.12 \text{ cm}$$

$$r = 5 \text{ mm}$$
$$C = 2 \cdot \pi \cdot r$$
$$= 2 \cdot 3.14 \cdot 5$$
$$= 31.4 \text{ mm}$$

13. $d = 11$ cm **14.** $d = 21$ mm **15.** $r = 9$ mm **16.** $r = 1.5$ in.

Practice

Find the length of the diameter for the given radii.

1. 7 cm **2.** 0.4 m **3.** 2.3 cm **4.** 1.3 ft

Find the length of the radius for the given diameters.

5. 24 mm **6.** 2.6 cm **7.** 8.6 m **8.** 27 in.

Find the circumferences. Give the answer in terms of π.

9. $d = 18$ cm **10.** $d = 9$ mm **11.** $d = 24$ m **12.** $d = 3.4$ in.

13. $r = 9$ m **14.** $r = 14$ cm **15.** $r = 31$ mm **16.** $r = 4.5$ ft

Find the circumferences. Use $\pi \doteq 3.14$.

17. $d = 3$ *m* **18.** $d = 50$ cm **19.** $d = 17$ cm **20.** $d = 1{,}000$ in.

21. $r = 10$ km **22.** $r = 25$ cm **23.** $r = 30$ mm **24.** $r = 3.5$ ft

Solve.

25. A wheel has a diameter which is 30.8 cm long. How long is a radius of the wheel?

26. A wheel has a diameter which is 50 cm long. How far will the wheel travel when it makes 1 complete turn?

★**27.** The circumference of a circle is 25.12 cm long. How long is the diameter of the circle?

★**28.** The circumference of a circle is 47.1 m long. How long is the radius of the circle?

Pairs of Angles

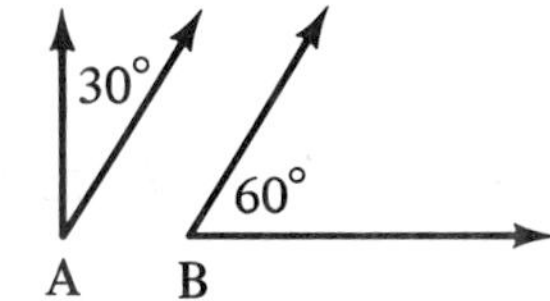

two complementary angles
sum = 90°
$\angle A$ is the complement of $\angle B$.

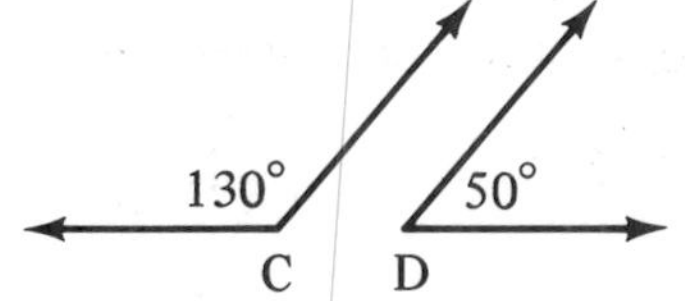

two supplementary angles
sum = 180°
$\angle C$ is the supplement of $\angle D$.

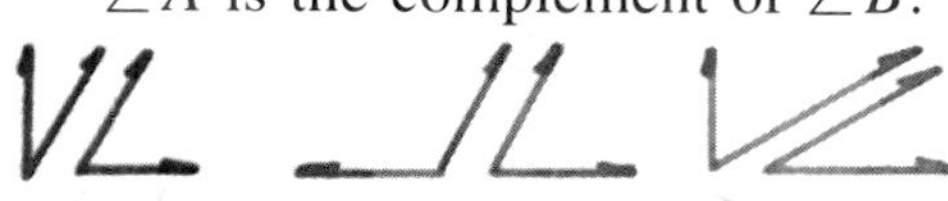

A. Complementary or supplementary?

1. 20°, 70° **2.** 146°, 34° **3.** 120°, 60° **4.** 88°, 2°

B. Find the complements.

5. 30° **6.** 24° **7.** 67° **8.** 54° **9.** 89°

C. Find the supplements.

10. 30° **11.** 120° **12.** 54° **13.** 117° **14.** 179°

D. $\triangle ABC$ is a right triangle. $\angle A$ is a right angle.

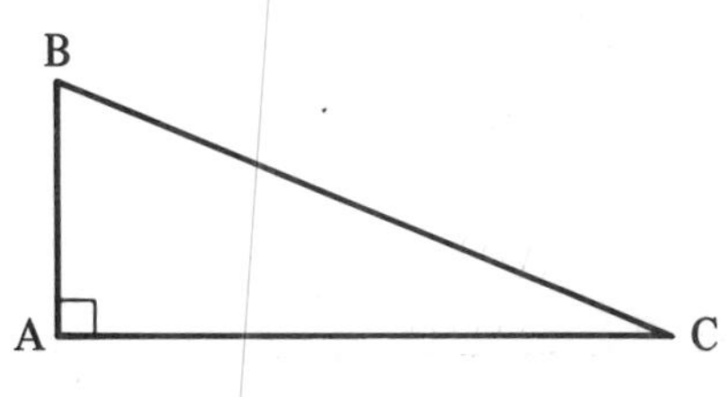

15. What is the measure of $\angle A$?

16. What is the sum of the measures of the angles in $\triangle ABC$?

17. What is the sum of the measures of $\angle B$ and $\angle C$?

▶ The two acute angles of a right triangle are complementary.
▶ Consecutive angles of a parallelogram are supplementary.

E. Find the missing measures.

18.

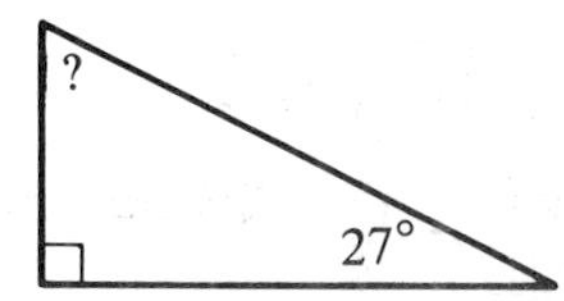

19.

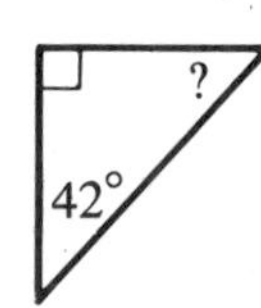

20.

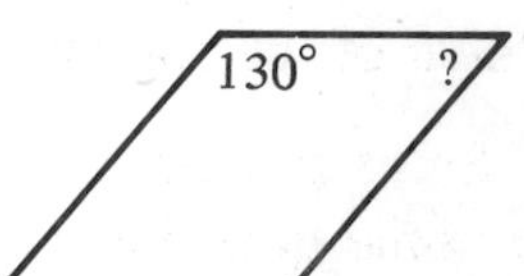

Practice

Complementary or supplementary?

1. 24°, 66°	**2.** 80°, 10°	**3.** 80°, 100°	**4.** 52°, 38°
5. 74°, 16°	**6.** 90°, 90°	**7.** 40°, 140°	**8.** 91°, 89°
9. 37°, 53°	**10.** 89°, 1°	**11.** 179°, 1°	**12.** 17°, 163°

Find the complements.

13. 14°	**14.** 62°	**15.** 71°	**16.** 17°	**17.** 49°
18. 64°	**19.** 24°	**20.** 53°	**21.** 81°	★ **22.** 90°

Find the supplements.

23. 80°	**24.** 75°	**25.** 141°	**26.** 74°	**27.** 114°
28. 178°	**29.** 40°	**30.** 125°	**31.** 119°	**32.** 0°

Find the missing measures.

33.

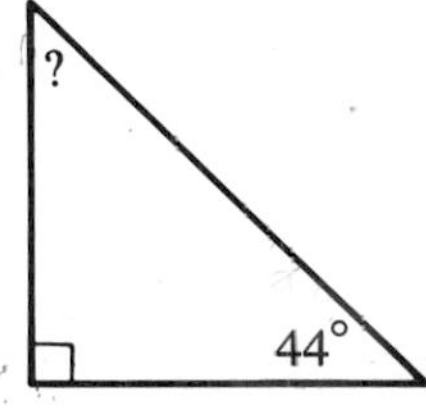

34.

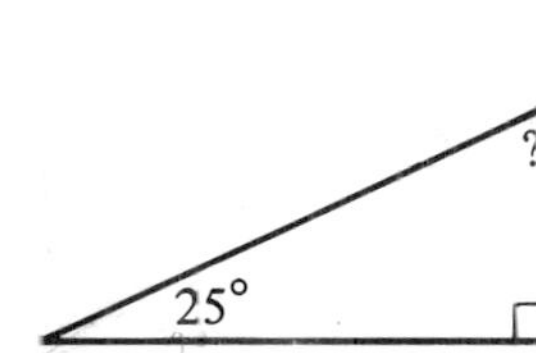

35.

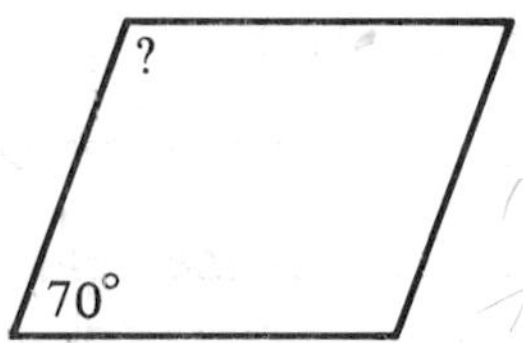

FIND OUT!
Brainteaser

The diagram shows that all triangles and all quadrilaterals are polygons. It also shows that some polygons are neither triangles nor quadrilaterals.

Which of the following are true?

a. Some polygons are triangles.
b. Some quadrilaterals are triangles.
c. Some triangles are quadrilaterals.
d. Some polygons are quadrilaterals.

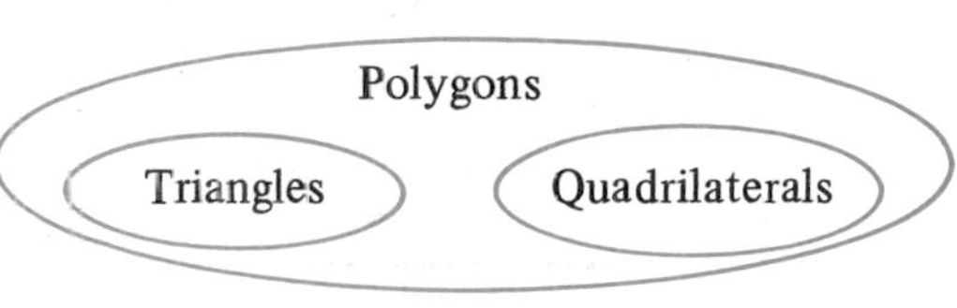

Parallel Lines

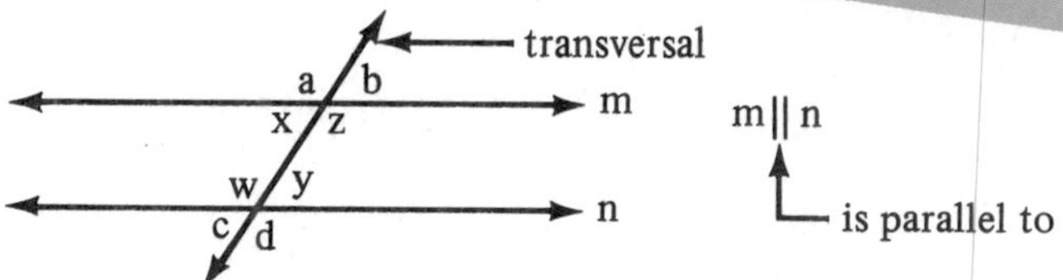

A. In the figure above, $m \parallel n$.

1. $\angle x$ and $\angle y$ are called **alternate interior angles.** Name another pair of alternate interior angles.

2. $\angle b$ and $\angle y$ are called **corresponding angles.** Name 3 more pairs of corresponding angles.

B. Draw a pair of parallel lines and a transversal.

3. Measure a pair of alternate interior angles. Measure another pair of alternate interior angles.

4. What is true of each pair of alternate interior angles?

5. Measure a pair of corresponding angles. Measure another pair of corresponding angles.

6. What is true of each pair of corresponding angles?

▶ If 2 parallel lines are cut by a transversal, the alternate interior angles are congruent.

▶ If 2 parallel lines are cut by a transversal, the corresponding angles are congruent.

C. Look at the figure above. Complete.

7. If $m\angle x = 50°$, $m\angle y =$ __?__ 8. If $m\angle a = 130°$, $m\angle w =$ __?__

D. When 2 lines intersect, vertical angles are formed.
$\angle a$ and $\angle b$ are vertical angles.
$\angle c$ and $\angle d$ are vertical angles.
Vertical angles are congruent.

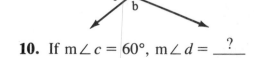

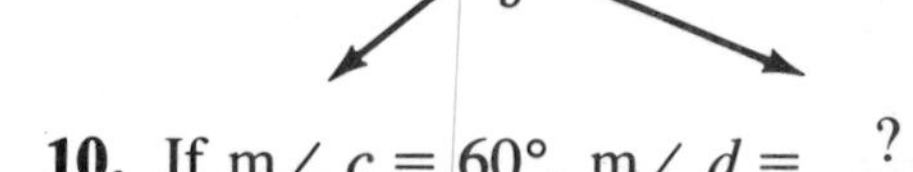

Complete.

9. If $m\angle a = 120°$, $m\angle b =$ __?__ 10. If $m\angle c = 60°$, $m\angle d =$ __?__

$l \parallel m$. t is a transversal.

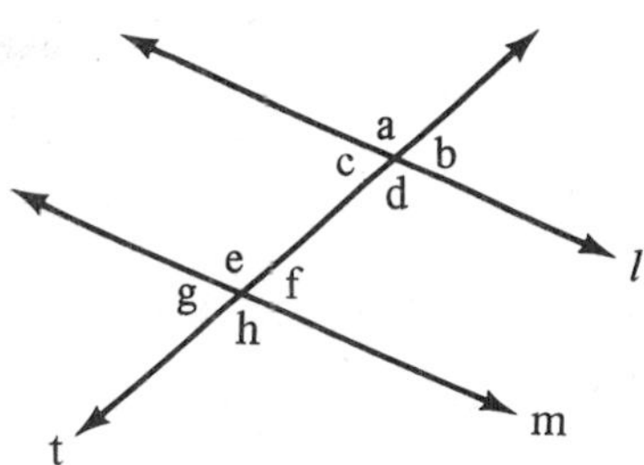

1. Name the pairs of alternate interior angles.

2. Name the pairs of corresponding angles.

3. Name the pairs of vertical angles.

$x \parallel y$. t is a transversal. True or false?

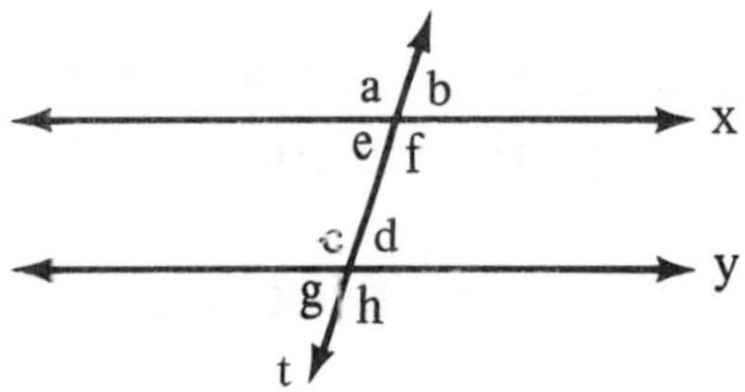

4. $\angle f \cong \angle c$
5. $\angle f \cong \angle b$
6. $\angle e \cong \angle d$
7. $\angle e \cong \angle g$
8. $\angle a \cong \angle g$
9. $\angle c \cong \angle h$

$p \parallel q$. Find m$\angle x$. Do not use a protractor.

10.

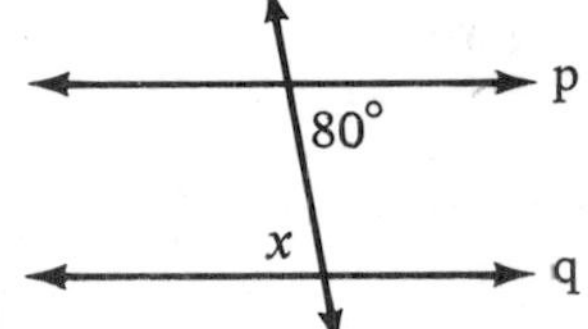

11.

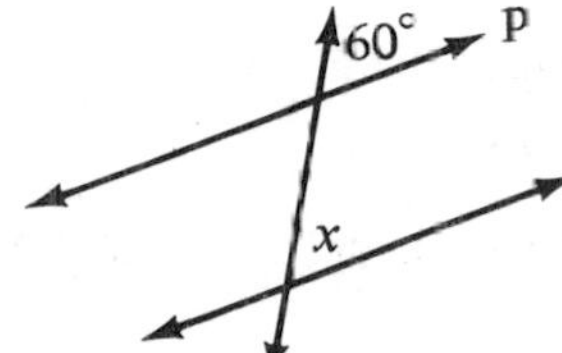

12.

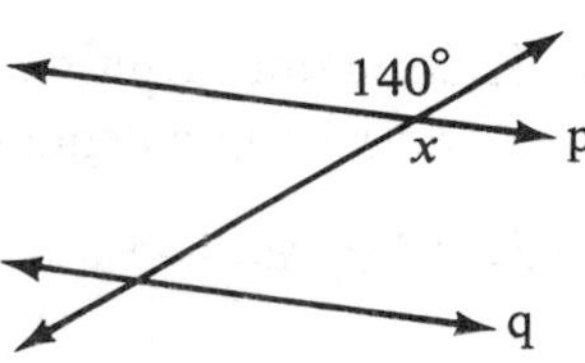

13.

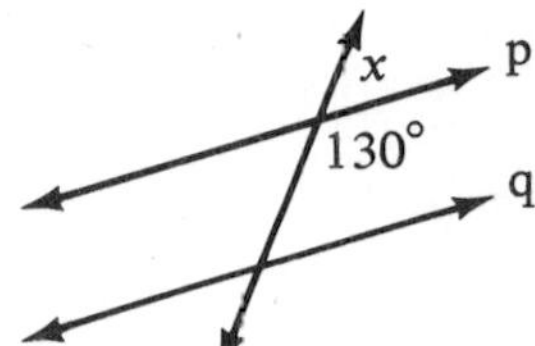

14.

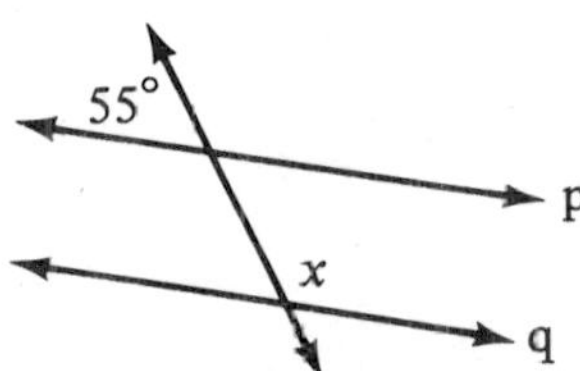

15.

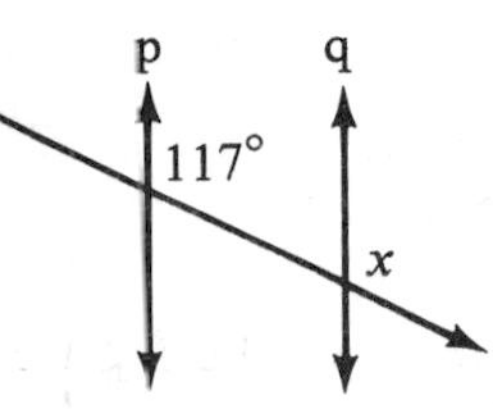

$s \parallel t$. m$\angle a = 112°$. Find the measures of the following angles.

16. $\angle b$
17. $\angle c$
18. $\angle d$
19. $\angle e$
20. $\angle f$
21. $\angle g$
22. $\angle h$

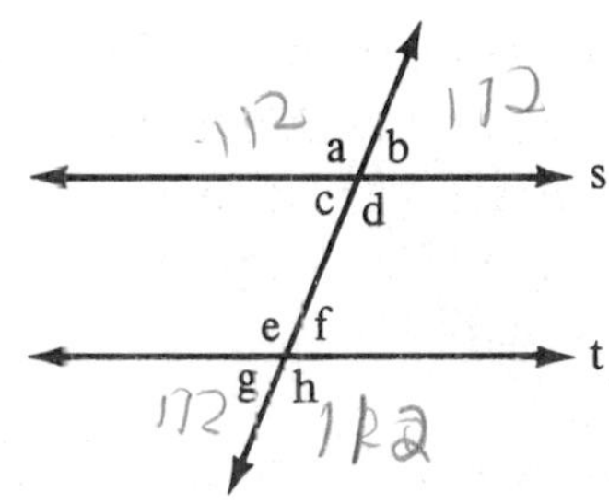

Perpendicular Lines

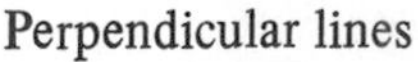

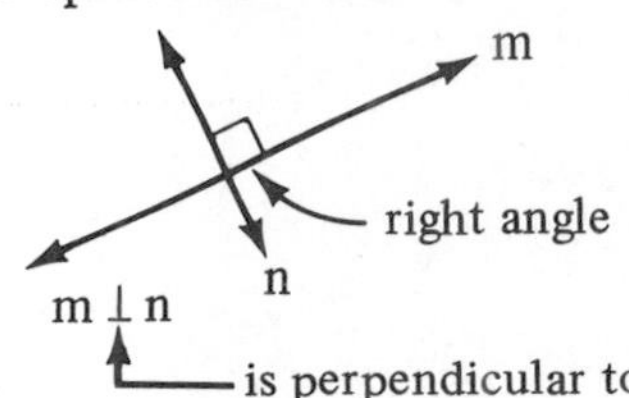

Perpendicular segments

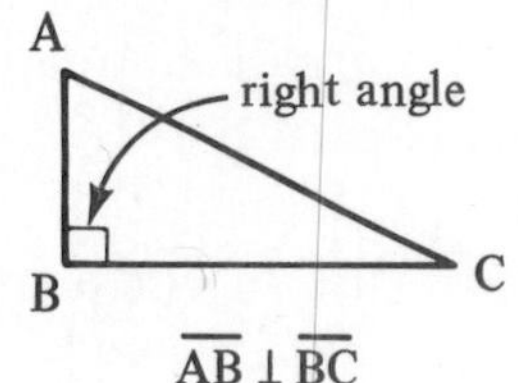

$\overline{AB} \perp \overline{BC}$

A. $\overleftrightarrow{UV} \perp \overleftrightarrow{WX}$.

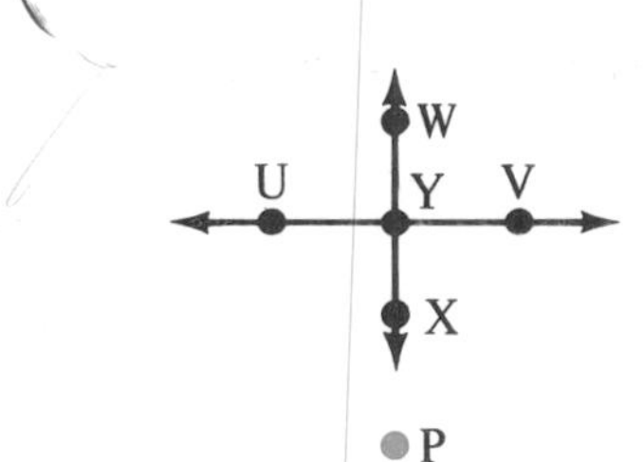

1. What is the measure of $\angle WYU$?

2. What is the measure of $\angle XYV$?

B. Construct the one line through point P perpendicular to line m.

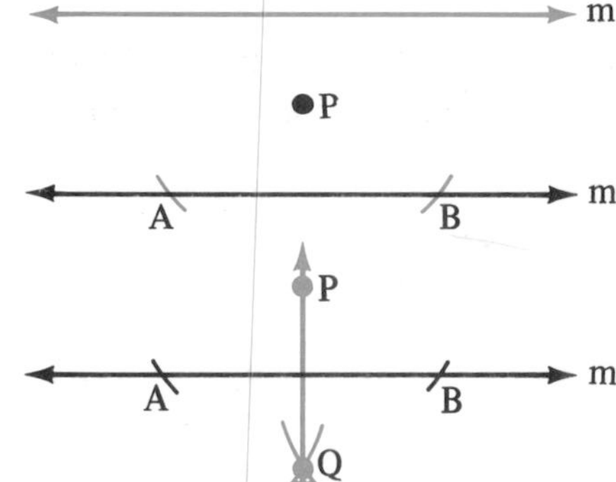

3. Draw line m and point P as shown.

4. Place the point of your compass at P and make arcs which cut line m.

5. Keep the opening of the compass the same. Place the point of the compass at A and draw an arc below the line. Do the same at B.

6. Draw $\overleftrightarrow{PQ}$. $\overleftrightarrow{PQ} \perp m$

C. Construct a line through point S perpendicular to line n.

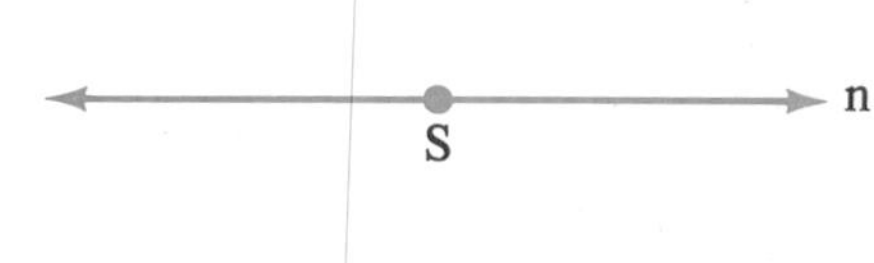

7. Draw line n and point S as shown.

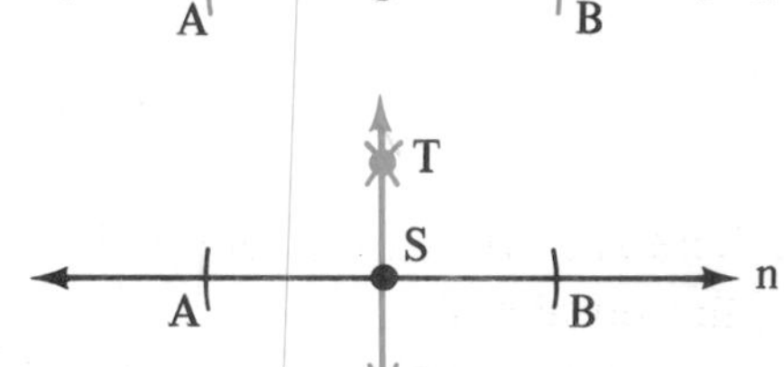

8. Place the point of your compass at S and make arcs which cut line n.

9. Keep the opening of the compass at A and draw arcs above and below the line. Do the same at B.

10. Draw $\overleftrightarrow{TU}$. $\overleftrightarrow{TU} \perp n$

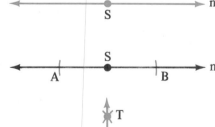

Which are perpendicular?

1.

2.

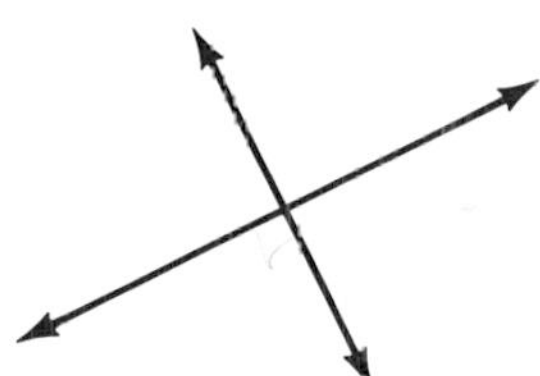

3.

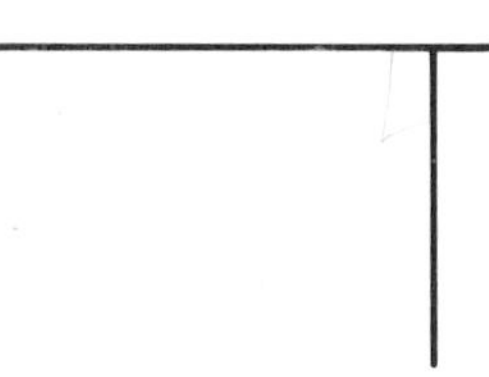

How many right angles are in each figure?

4.

5.

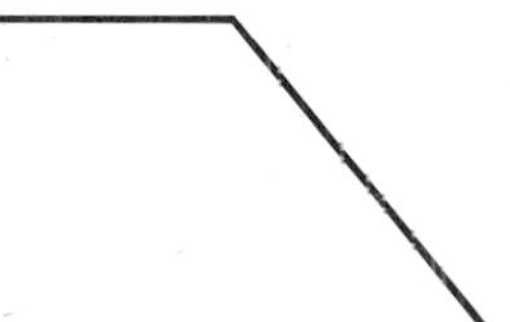

6.

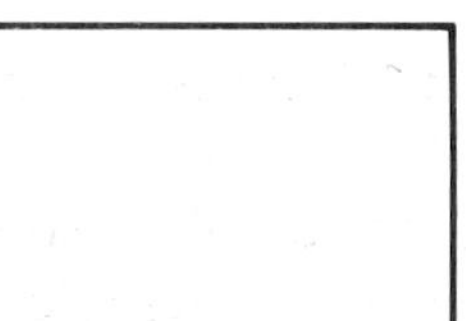

7. Draw line n and point P as shown. From point P construct a line perpendicular to line n.

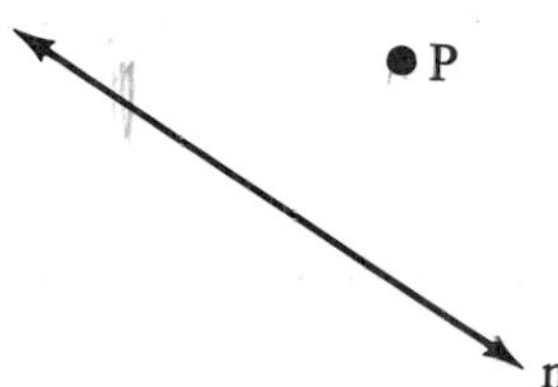

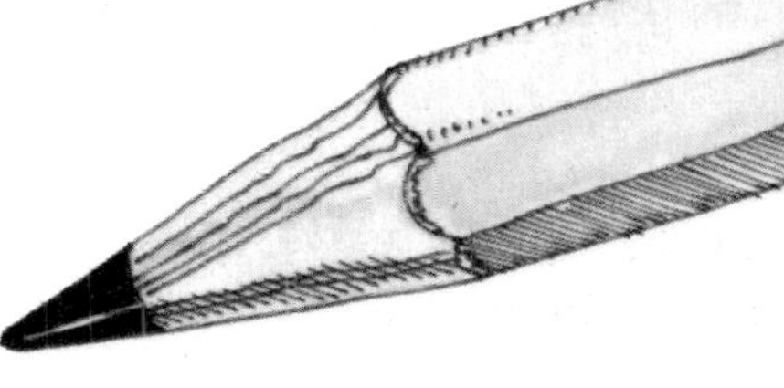

8. Draw line m and point S as shown. Construct a line perpendicular to line m through point S.

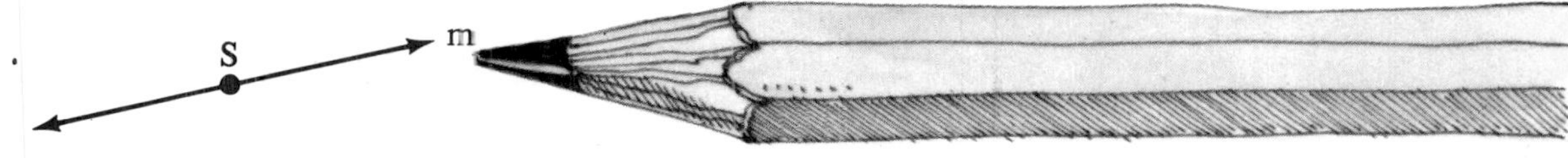

FIND OUT!
Brainteasers

1. The sum of 2 numbers is 60. Their difference is 24. What are the numbers?
2. The product of 2 numbers is 576. Their quotient is 16. What are the numbers?

Constructing Parallel Lines

There are 2 ways to construct parallel lines.

One way uses corresponding angles.

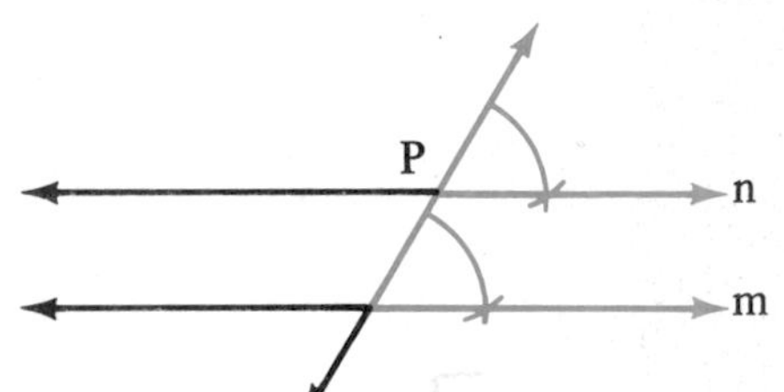

One way uses alternate interior angles.

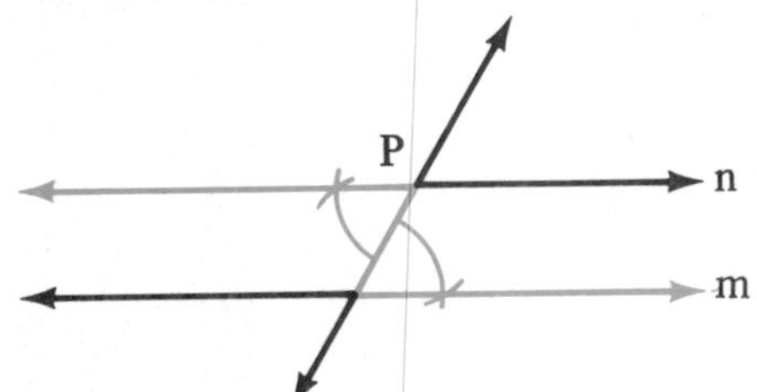

A. Look at the figure at the right.

1. How many possible lines through point P can be parallel to line m?

B. Construct the one line through P parallel to line m. Use the idea that corresponding angles are congruent.

2. Draw line m and point P as shown.
3. Through point P draw a transversal which intersects line m at Q.
4. Construct an angle congruent to $\angle PQR$ at point P.
5. Draw line n. Line n through point P is parallel to line m.

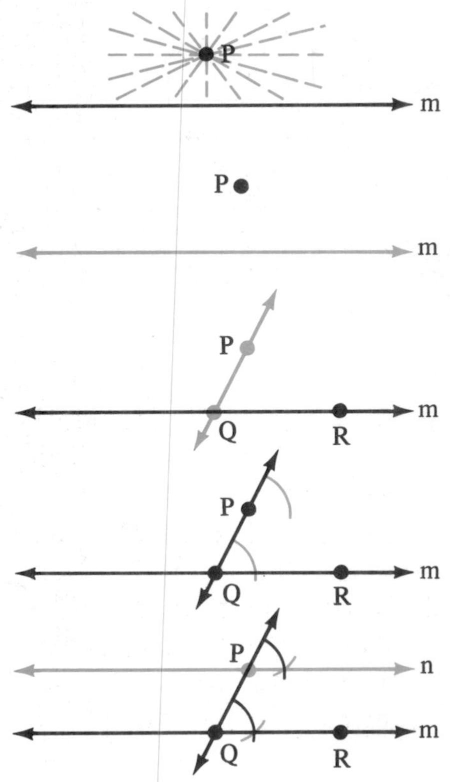

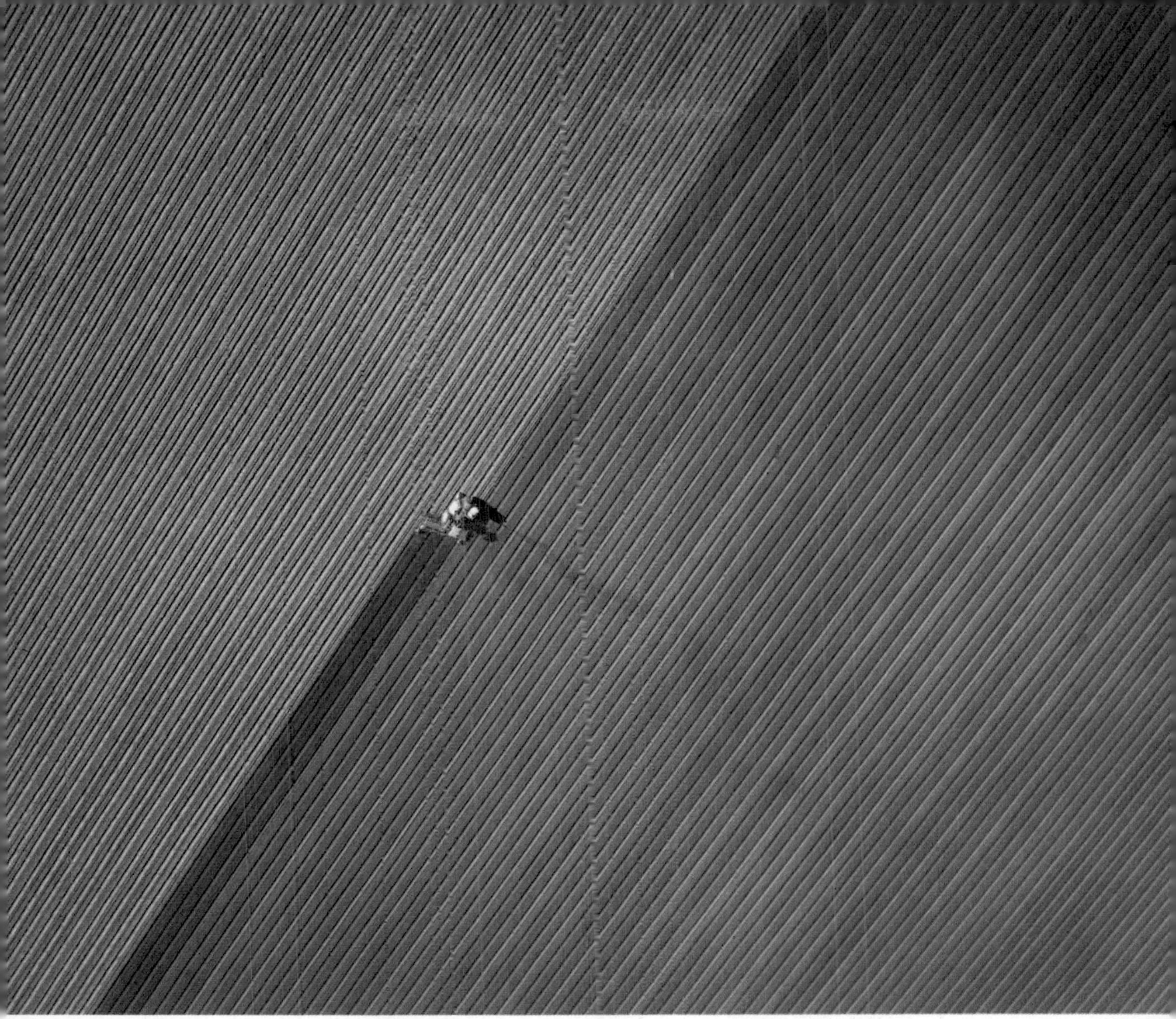

Practice

1. Draw a line n and point P as shown. Construct a line through point P parallel to line n using corresponding angles.

2. Draw a line n and point P as shown. Construct a line through point P parallel to line n using alternate interior angles.

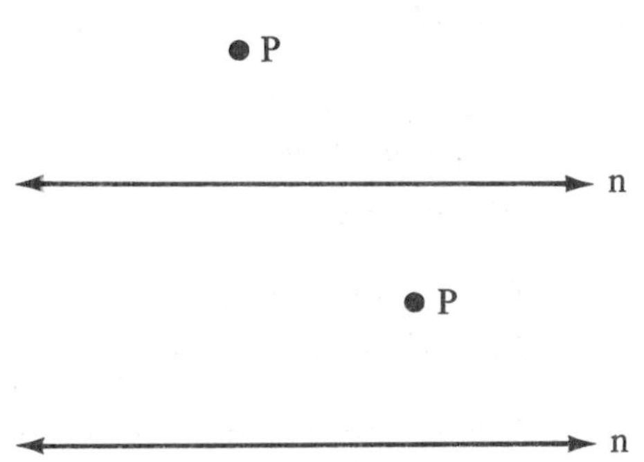

60-Month Car Loan Rates	
Amount Loaned	Monthly Payment
$3,500	$79.25
$4,400	$99.63
$6,600	$149.45

Problem Solving

1. Mr. Ames bought a $5,000 car. He put down $1,500. He took a $3,500 car loan for a 60-month period. What are his payments per month? [HINT: Look at the chart above.]

2. What will be Mr. Ames's total loan payments in 60 months?

3. What was the total amount that Mr. Ames paid for the car?

4. How much more did Mr. Ames pay for the car than the original cost of the car? (Note: This is called the finance charge.)

5. Mrs. Rodriguez bought a car for $7,500. How much cash must she put down if she wishes to take a $4,400 loan for 60 months?

6. How much must Mrs. Rodriguez put down if she wishes to take a $6,600 loan?

7. On a $4,400 loan, how much less cash will Mrs. Rodriguez pay each month than for a $6,600 loan?

8. What are the finance charges on the $4,400 loan for 60 months?

9. What are the finance charges on the $6,600 loan for 60 months?

10. How much will Mrs. Rodriguez save on finance charges with the $4,400 loan over the $6,600 loan?

Chapter Review

Measure these angles. *(192)*

1.
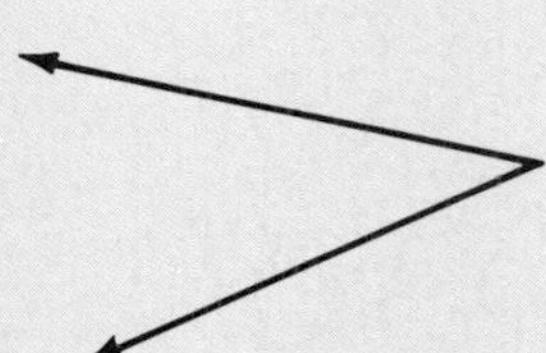

2.

3.
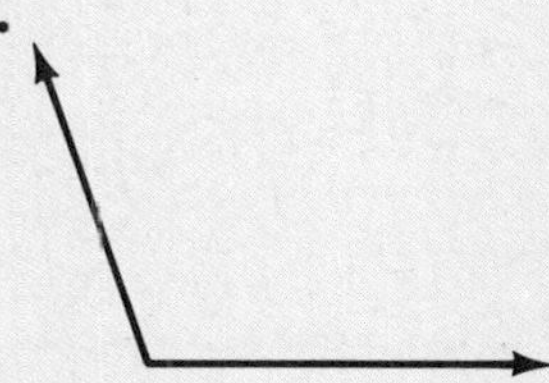

Classify these triangles by the measures of their angles. *(194)*

4.
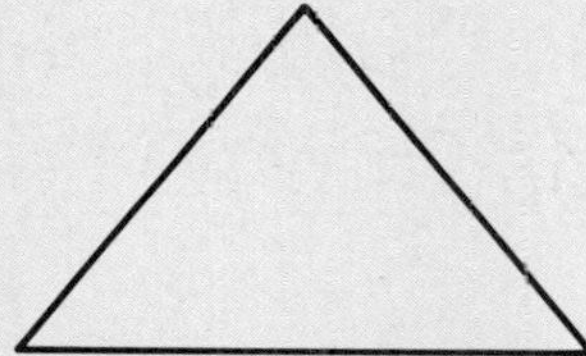

5.
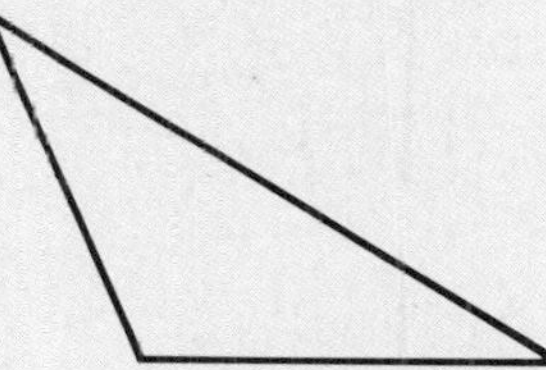

Classify these triangles by the measures of their sides. *(195)*

6.
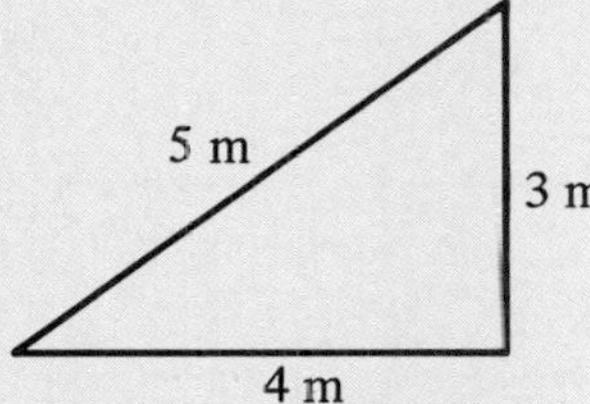

7.
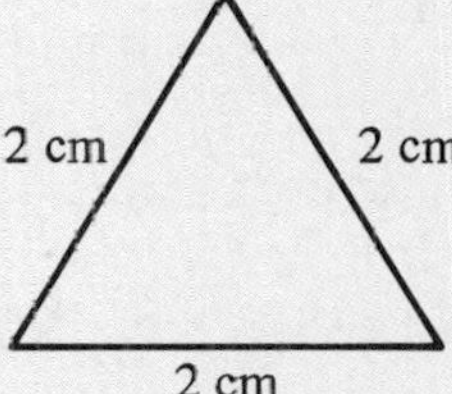

Identify these polygons. *(198)*

8.
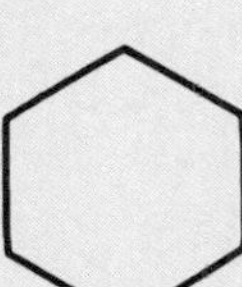

9.
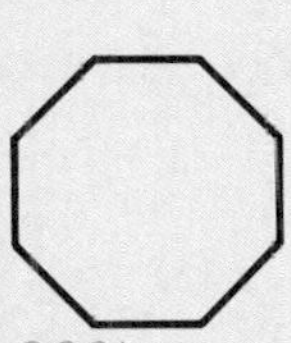

10.
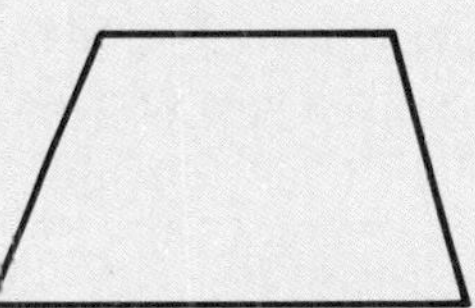

Find the missing measures. *(198, 200)*

11.
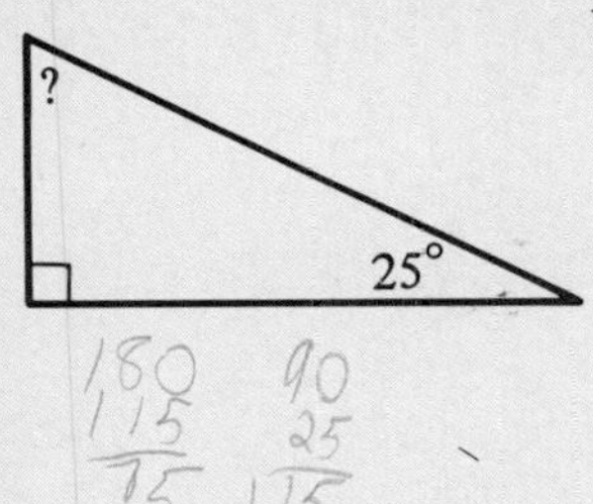

12.
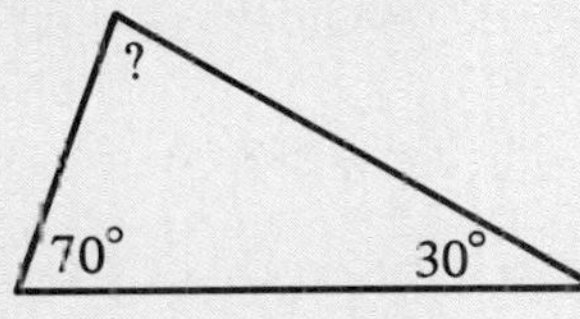

13.
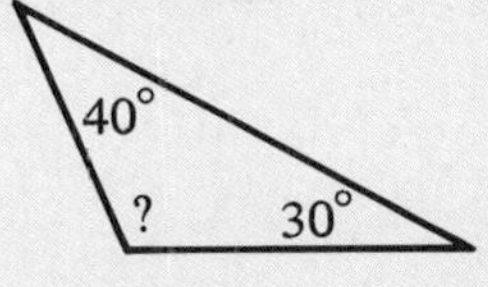

Review continues

Chapter Review continued

Find the perimeters. (202)

14.

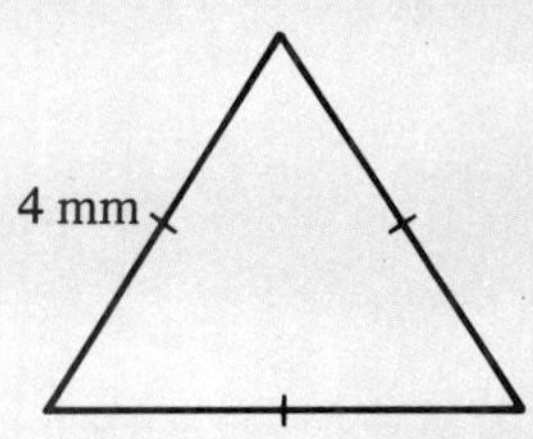

15.

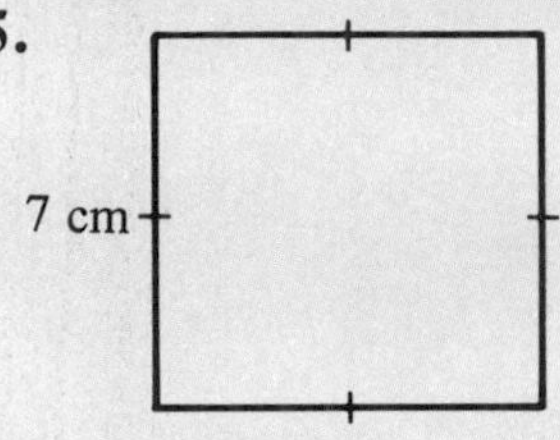

16.

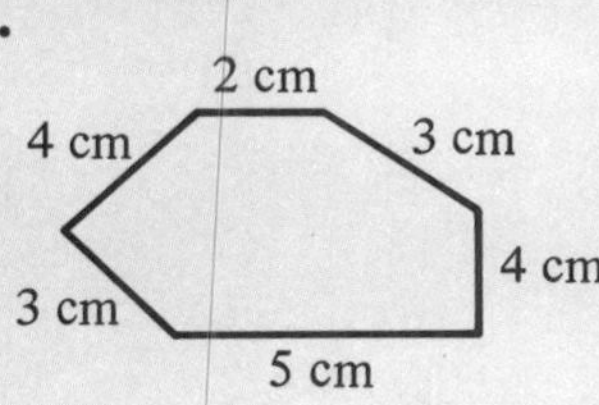

Find the circumference. Use $\pi \doteq 3.14$. (208)

17. $d = 3$ m **18.** $r = 1$ cm **19.** $r = 7$ mm

Find the complements. (210)

20. 45° **21.** 50° **22.** 3° **23.** 23°

Find the supplements. (210)

24. 45° **25.** 50° **26.** 103° **27.** 127°

$m \parallel n$ (212)

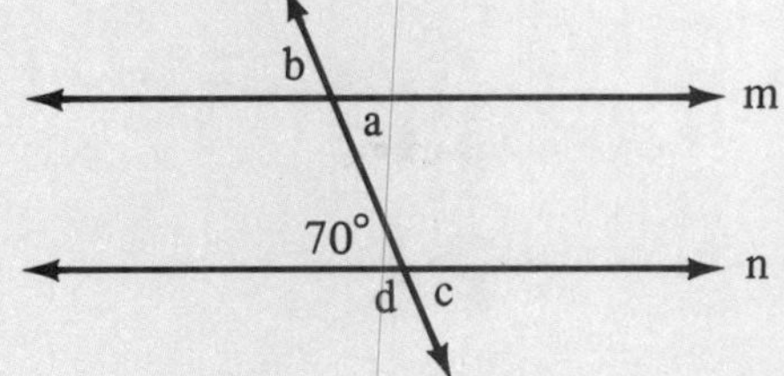

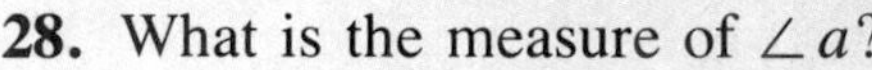

28. What is the measure of $\angle a$?

29. What is the measure of $\angle b$?

30. What is the measure of $\angle c$?

31. Draw a line l. Draw a point S on the line. Construct a
(214) perpendicular to line l through point S.

Solve, if possible. (206, 218)

32. The perimeter of a rectangle is 64 cm. The length is 20 cm. What is the width?

33. Ms. Citera pays $137.50 each month for her car loan. How much does she pay in 1 year?

Chapter Test

Measure these angles. *(192)*

1.

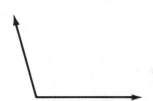

2.

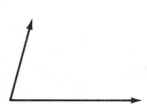

3.
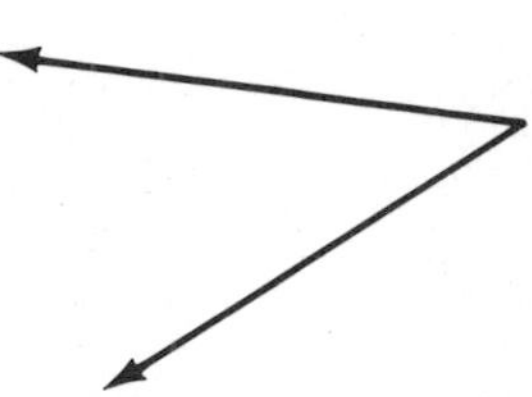

Classify these triangles by the measures of their angles. *(194)*

4.
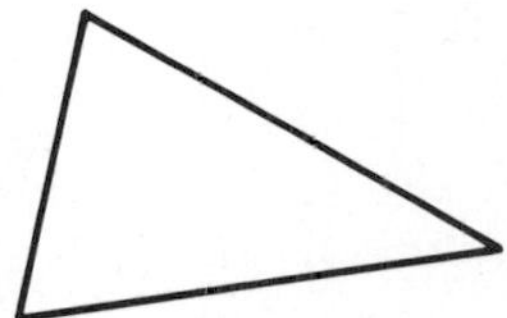

5.
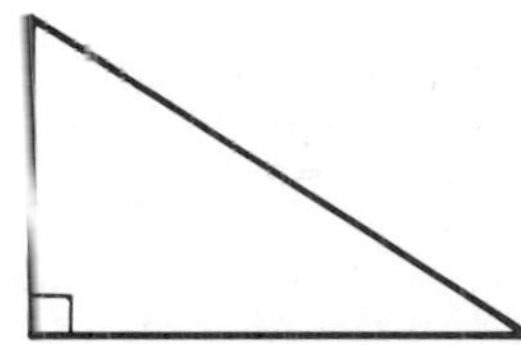

Classify these triangles by the measures of their sides. *(195)*

6.
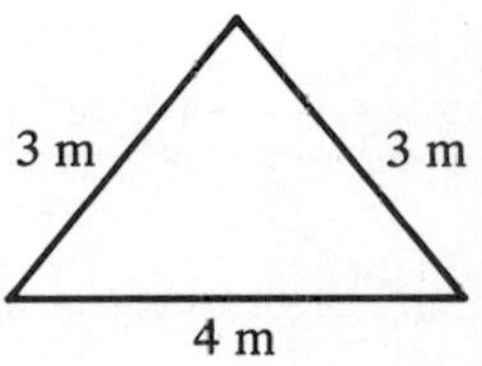

7.
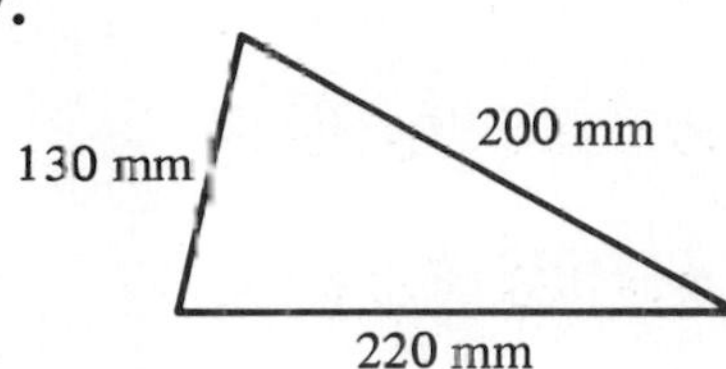

Identify these polygons. *(198)*

8.
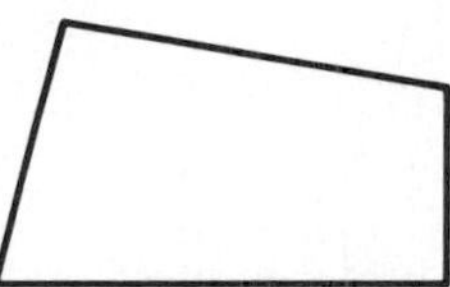

9.
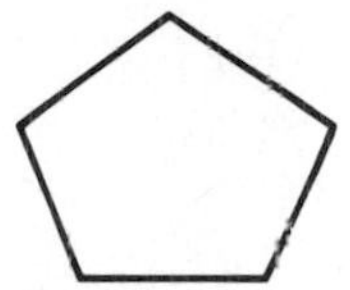

10.

Find the missing measures. *(198, 200)*

11.
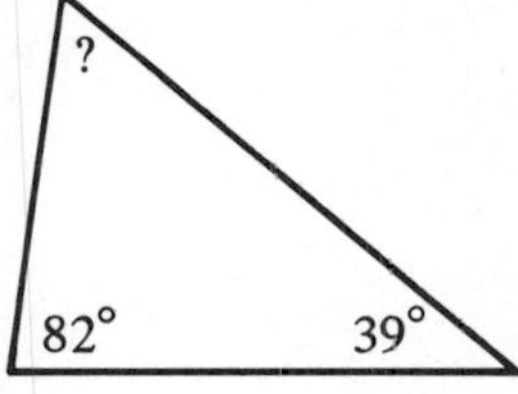

12.
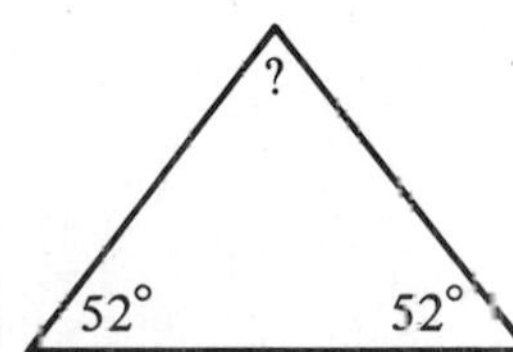

13.
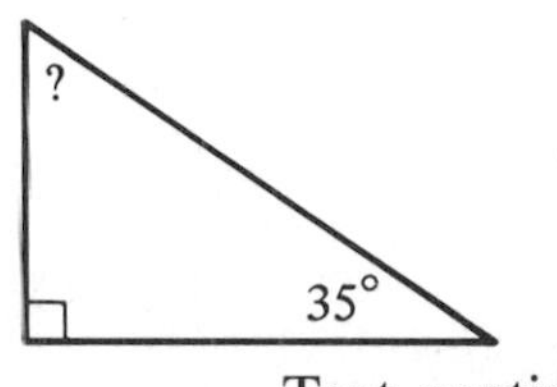

Test continues

Find the perimeters. *(202)*

14.

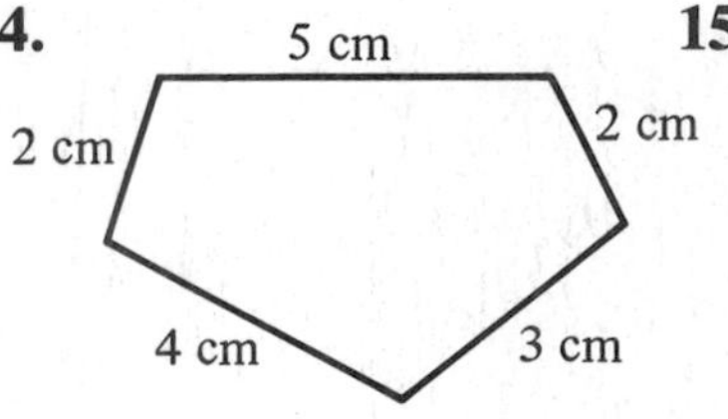

15.

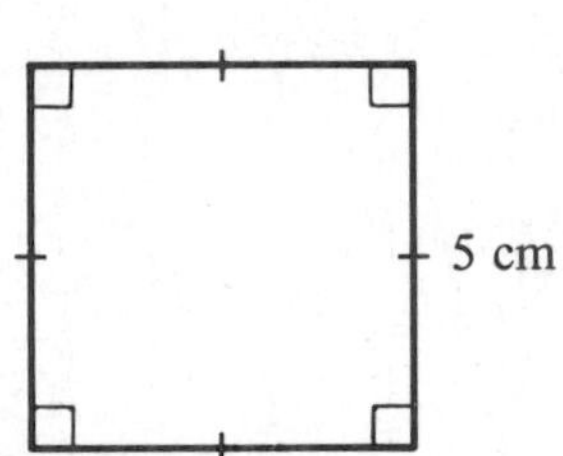

16.

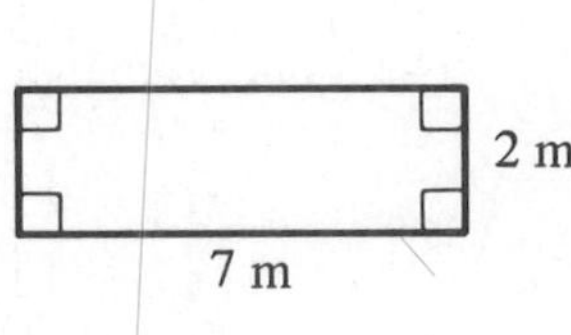

Find the circumference. Use $\pi \doteq 3.14$. *(208)*

17. $d = 11$ cm **18.** $r = 4$ mm **19.** $r = 6$ cm

Find the complements. *(210)*

20. 26° **21.** 35° **22.** 74° **23.** 41°

Find the supplements. *(210)*

24. 60° **25.** 80° **26.** 103° **27.** 135°

$m \parallel n$ *(212)*

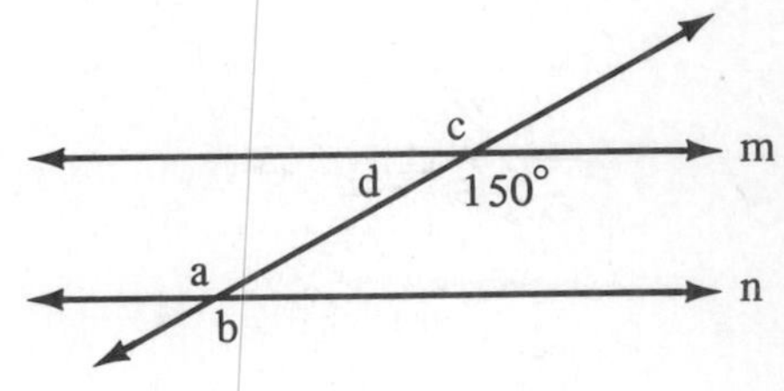

28. What is the measure of $\angle a$?

29. What is the measure of $\angle b$?

30. What is the measure of $\angle c$?

31. Draw a line m. Draw a point P above the line. Construct a *(214)* perpendicular to line m through point P.

Solve, if possible. *(206, 218)*

32. In right triangle PQR, $\angle Q$ is a right angle. What is the measure of $\angle R$?

33. Mr. Henn bought a car for $7,800. He put down $2,900. How much of a loan did he take?

Basic Skills Check

1. Bill has saved $56.95 for a bicycle that costs $88.50. How much more does he need to buy the bicycle?

   A $31.45 B $31.50
   C $31.55 D $32.55

2. Carla had $643.27 in her checking account. She made out a check for $37.29. What is the balance in her checking account?

   E $604.98 F $605.98
   G $606.98 H $680.56

3. It was ⁻23°F in Nome, Alaska when it was 23°F in New York City. How much colder was it in Nome?

   A 0° B 23°
   C 46° D 50°

4. October 2 is a Monday. What day of the week is October 17th?

   E Monday F Tuesday
   G Wednesday H Thursday

5. What is the perimeter of the rectangle?

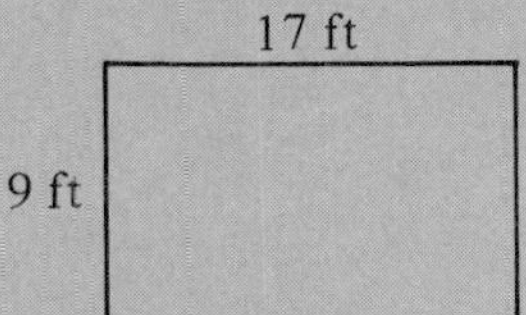

   A 153 ft B 52 ft
   C 34 ft D 26 ft

6. Bob jogged 850 m, 400 m, and 300 m one afternoon. How many kilometers did he jog altogether?

   E 1,550 km F 155 km
   G 15.5 km H 1.55 km

7. What seems to be the trend in the sale of magazines?

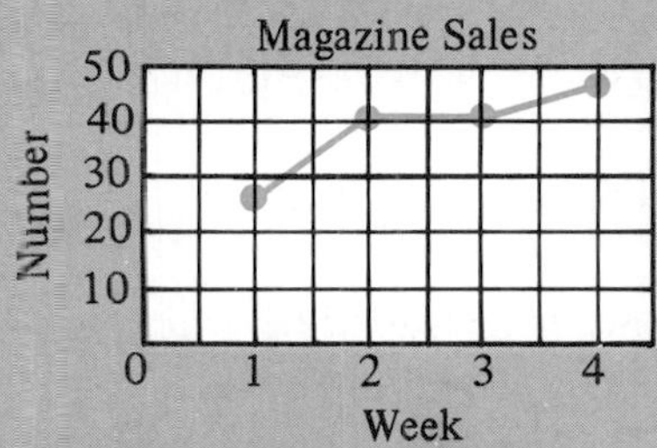

   A increasing B decreasing
   C constant D up and down

8. Which of the following units would you use to measure the amount of water in a raindrop?

   E mg F mL
   G L H kg

Evaluating Expressions

Two students computed $6 + 3 \cdot 4$.

Mona did it this way:

$$\begin{aligned} 6 + 3 \cdot 4 &= 9 \cdot 4 \\ &= 36 \end{aligned}$$

Sarah did it this way:

$$\begin{aligned} 6 + 3 \cdot 4 &= 6 + 12 \\ &= 18 \end{aligned}$$

Sarah's answer is correct. She used the rules for the order of operations.

▶ The rules for the order of operations are:
first, do operations within parentheses;
second, multiply and divide from left to right;
third, add and subtract from left to right.

CHAPTER
PROBLEM SOLVING 

A. Compute.

Examples

$2 \times (3 + 4)$
$= 2 \times 7$
$= 14$

$3 \times 6 + 4 \times 7$
$= 18 + 28$
$= 46$

1. $3 \times (2 + 4)$ **2.** $8 \times (7 - 1)$ **3.** $10 + 7 \cdot 2$ **4.** $14 \div 7 - 2$

B. Evaluate $\frac{n}{2} \cdot (a + l)$ if $n = 6$, $a = 2$, and $l = 12$.

Example

Step 1 Substitute the given values. $\frac{n}{2} \cdot (a + l) \longrightarrow \frac{6}{2} \cdot (2 + 12)$

Step 2 Compute.
First, compute within the parentheses.
Then, divide and multiply.

$\frac{6}{2} \cdot (2 + 12) = \frac{6}{2} \cdot (14)$
$= 3 \cdot (14)$
$= 42$

Evaluate.

5. $\frac{n}{2} \cdot (a + l)$ if $n = 8$, $a = 1$, and $l = 15$ **6.** $4a - b$ if $a = 6$, $b = 7$

Practice

Compute.

1. $7 \times (9 - 3)$ **2.** $5 \times (6 + 7)$ **3.** $(16 - 4) - (18 - 16)$

4. $5 \cdot 9 + 6$ **5.** $18 - 12 \div 6$ **6.** $9 \cdot (2 \cdot 5 - 3)$

Evaluate.

7. $\frac{n}{2} \cdot (a + l)$ if $n = 6$, $a = 4$, and $l = 9$ **8.** $6s + t$ if $s = 3$ and $t = 4$

9. $50 - 25p$ if $p = 2$ ★**10.** $\frac{w + 6}{z}$ if $w = 4$ and $z = 2$

Solve.

11. In a restaurant, the number of glasses can be found by computing $19 \cdot 6 + 4$. How many glasses are there?

Problem Solving: Open Expressions

In solving problems, it is often necessary to translate word expressions to algebraic expressions.

Let n be number of seconds of time for the first runner, then, $n + 2$ is number of seconds of time for the second runner.

Word expressions	*Algebraic expressions*
2 more than a number	$n + 2$
a number increased by 2	$n + 2$
the sum of a number and 2	$n + 2$
3 less than a number	$n - 3$
twice a number	$2n$
5 more than twice a number	$2n + 5$
a number divided by 2	$\frac{n}{2}$

A. Write algebraic expressions. Use n to represent a number.

1. 4 less than a number

2. 3 more than a number

3. the quotient of a number and 3

4. 3 more than twice a number

5. $\frac{1}{2}$ of a number

6. the square of a number

B. n represents a number. Translate these expressions into words.

Example $n - 3$ a number decreased by 3, or 3 less than a number

Translate these expressions into words.

7. $n + 8$ **8.** $n - 7$ **9.** $3n$ **10.** $\frac{n}{3}$

11. n^2 **12.** $2n + 3$ **13.** $3n - 4$ **14.** $\frac{1}{2}n + 3$

Practice

Write algebraic expressions. Use n to represent a number.

1. 5 more than a number

2. a number increased by 12

3. the sum of a number and 9

4. 6 less than a number

5. a number decreased by 6

6. the quotient of a number and 9

7. 6 more than twice a number

8. 4 less than three times a number

9. $\frac{1}{3}$ of a number

10. $\frac{2}{5}$ of a number

11. the square of a number increased by 1

12. 14 decreased by a number

13. two times a number, decreased by 7

14. 6 less than $\frac{1}{2}$ of a number

15. $\frac{1}{2}$ of a number, increased by 6

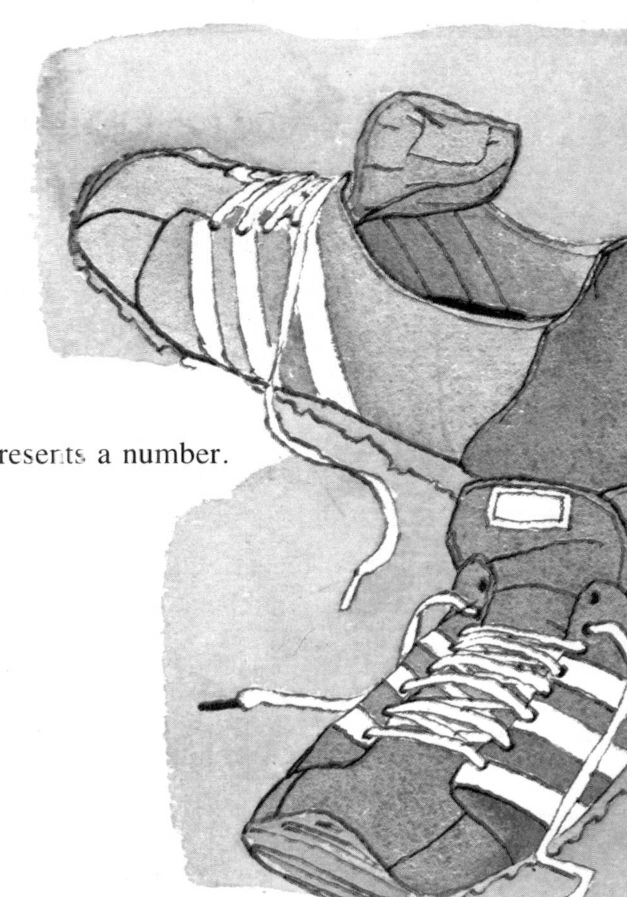

Translate these expressions into words. n represents a number.

16. $n + 3$

17. $n + 9$

18. $n - 4$

19. $n - 6$

20. $4n$

21. $\frac{n}{7}$

22. $\frac{2}{3}n$

23. $2n + 1$

24. $3n - 4$

25. $\frac{1}{2}n + 6$

26. $\frac{1}{2}n - 3$

27. $3 \cdot (n + 4)$

Writing Equations from Word Problems

Mrs. Jackson bought 3 containers of milk and a package of bread for \$2.18. The bread cost \$0.65. What was the cost of each container of milk?

PLAN Use x for the cost of each container of milk.
$3x$ is an expression to represent the cost of 3 containers of milk.

THINK the cost of 3 containers of milk + cost of bread = total cost

$$3x \quad + \quad 65 \quad = \quad 218$$

The equation is $3x + 65 = 218$.

SOLVE $3x + 65 = 218$

$$3x + 65 - 65 = 218 - 65$$
$$3x = 153$$
$$x = 51$$

Each container of milk costs \$0.51.

        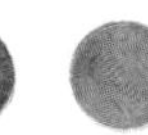     

A. Abe works in a supermarket. He receives \$4 an hour. Last week he earned \$92. How many hours did he work? Write an equation and solve.

1. What does the problem ask?
2. Let x represent the number of hours Abe worked. Write an expression to represent his pay for the week.
3. Write an equation and solve.

B. Ellen bought 3 shirts, each at the same price. She paid a \$5 deposit. This left a balance of \$43. What was the cost of each shirt? Write an equation and solve.

4. What does the problem ask?
5. Let n represent the cost of each shirt. Write an expression to represent the cost of 3 shirts.
6. Write an expression to represent the cost of 3 shirts less a \$5 deposit.
7. Write an equation and solve.

Practice

Write equations. Solve.

1. Josie bought 3 pens and a pencil for $2.08. The price of each pen was the same. The pencil cost $0.10. What was the cost of each pen?

2. Kathleen won a school election by receiving 17 more votes than Ken. Kathleen received 214 votes. How many votes did Ken receive?

3. Sam delivers papers and magazines. He has 43 customers for papers and 7 customers for magazines. Last week he received $14.25. He received $10.75 for delivering papers. How much does he receive from each of the 7 magazine customers?

4. Andy's father rented a car for a family trip. The car rented for $84 a week plus the cost of gas. Andy's father found it cost him $126 for the week. If he used 40 gal of gasoline, what was the cost of each gallon?

5. Ann's father is 50 years old. He is 8 years more than 3 times Ann's age. How old is Ann?

6. Marcia's bowling score was 28 pins more than Marty's score. Marcia's bowling score was 151. What was Marty's bowling score?

7. Gene bought a pair of shoes and 3 pairs of socks for $30.34. The shoes were $25 and the price of each pair of socks was the same. What was the cost of each pair of socks?

8. A wire was 20 m long. It was cut into 3 pieces of the same length and a piece 2 m long. How long was each of the 3 pieces of the same length?

Making up Problems from Equations

One equation may solve many problems. Here are 2 problems that can be solved by $2x + 4 = 10$.

Amy scored a total of 10 points in basketball. She scored 4 points for foul shots. How many baskets did she make? (Each basket is 2 points.) Let x be the number of baskets.

2 points for each basket	+	points for fouls	=	point total
$2x$	+	4	=	10

Jeff bought 2 records. The price of each is the same. He also bought a \$4 tape. The total cost was \$10. How much did each record cost? Use x for the cost of one record.

cost of 2 records	+	cost of tape	=	total cost
$2x$	+	4	=	10

Practice

Make up two problems for each equation.

1. $x + 24 = 37$

2. $x + 34 = 102$

3. $x - 5 = 18$

4. $x - 15 = 76$

5. $2x + 4 = 36$

6. $3x + 8 = 71$

7. $3x - 9 = 39$

8. $4x - 12 = 60$

9. $\frac{x}{3} + 2 = 5$

10. $\frac{x}{2} - 12 = 14$

Mid-Chapter Review

Compute. *(224)*

1. $4 \times (8 - 3)$

2. $24 \div (1 + 5)$

3. $18 - 6 \cdot 2$

Evaluate. *(224)*

4. $4a + b$ if $a = 6$ and $b = 7$

5. $n - n + k$ if $n = 14$ and $k = 3$

Write equations. Solve. *(228, 230)*

6. A number increased by 9 is 53.

7. Five less than a number is 37.

8. Three times a number, increased by 9 is 18.

9. Twice a number, decreased by 5 is 29.

10. Sonia wants to buy a radio for \$78. She earns \$7 a week baby sitting, and has saved \$43. How many more weeks must she work to buy the radio?

11. Henry bought 3 packs of notebook paper and a notebook for \$4.75. The notebook cost \$1.00. What is the price of each pack of notebook paper?

FIND OUT!
Brainteaser

Mike bought 3 shirts and 2 pairs of jeans. The cost of the 3 shirts was the same as the cost of the 2 pairs of jeans.

Which of the following can be determined from the above information?

a. The cost of 1 pair of jeans is the same as the cost of 1 shirt.

b. A pair of jeans costs less than a shirt.

c. A shirt costs $\frac{1}{3}$ of the cost of a pair of jeans.

d. A pair of jeans costs $1\frac{1}{2}$ times the cost of a shirt.

Reasoning

Given: All eighth grade students were present today. Henry is an eighth grade student.
Conclusion: Henry was present today.

A diagram can help you decide if the conclusion is necessarily true.

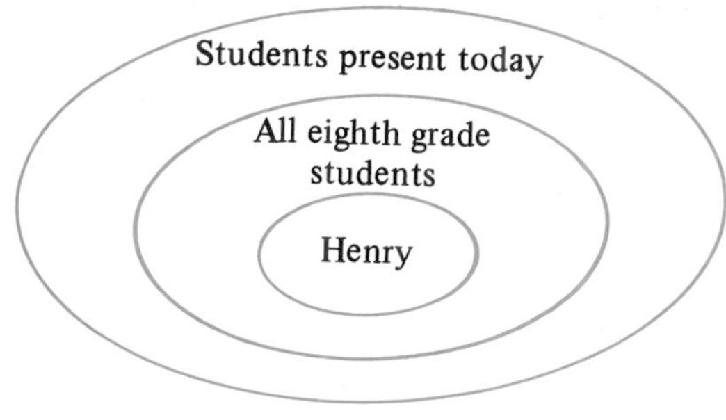

The conclusion is necessarily true.

A. Given: All baseball players eat "High Power."
Mary eats "High Power."
Conclusion: Mary is a baseball player.

1. Is it possible that Mary is a baseball player?
2. Is it possible that Mary is not a baseball player?
3. Is the conclusion necessarily true?

All people who eat "High Power"
All baseball players

B. Given: All movie stars use "Clean" toothpaste.
John uses "Clean."
Conclusion: John is a movie star.

4. Is the conclusion necessarily true?

All people who use "Clean" toothpaste
All movie stars

Practice

Decide whether the conclusions are necessarily true.

1. Given: All intelligent students can pass mathematics.
Maria is an intelligent student.
Conclusion: Maria can pass mathematics.

2. Given: All intelligent students can pass mathematics.
Walter can pass mathematics.
Conclusion: Walter is an intelligent student.

3. Given: All athletes eat "Strongies" for breakfast.
Jane is an athlete.
Conclusion: Jane eats "Strongies" for breakfast.

4. Given: All athletes eat "Strongies" for breakfast.
Tony eats "Strongies" for breakfast.
Conclusion: Tony is an athlete.

5. Given: All students on the math team are eighth grade students.
Adele is on the math team.
Conclusion: Adele is an eighth grade student.

6. Given: All students on the math team are eighth grade students.
Adele is an eighth grade student.
Conclusion: Adele is on the math team.

7. Given: All movie stars eat lunch at "Oscars."
Sonia eats lunch at "Oscars."
Conclusion: Sonia is a movie star.

8. Given: All movie stars eat soup for lunch.
Dan is a movie star.
Conclusion: Dan eats soup for lunch.

9. Given: All diameters are chords.
$\overline{AB}$ is a chord.
Conclusion: $\overline{AB}$ is a diameter.

Problem Solving: The Distance Formula

A jet plane flew at the rate of 950 km/h. How far did it fly in 9 hours?
Distance formula: distance = rate · time

$$d = r \cdot t$$

To solve the problem:

Step 1 Write the formula. $d = r \cdot t$

Step 2 Substitute the given information. $d = 950 \cdot 9$

Step 3 Solve the equation. $d = 8{,}550$ km

So the plane had flown 8,550 km.

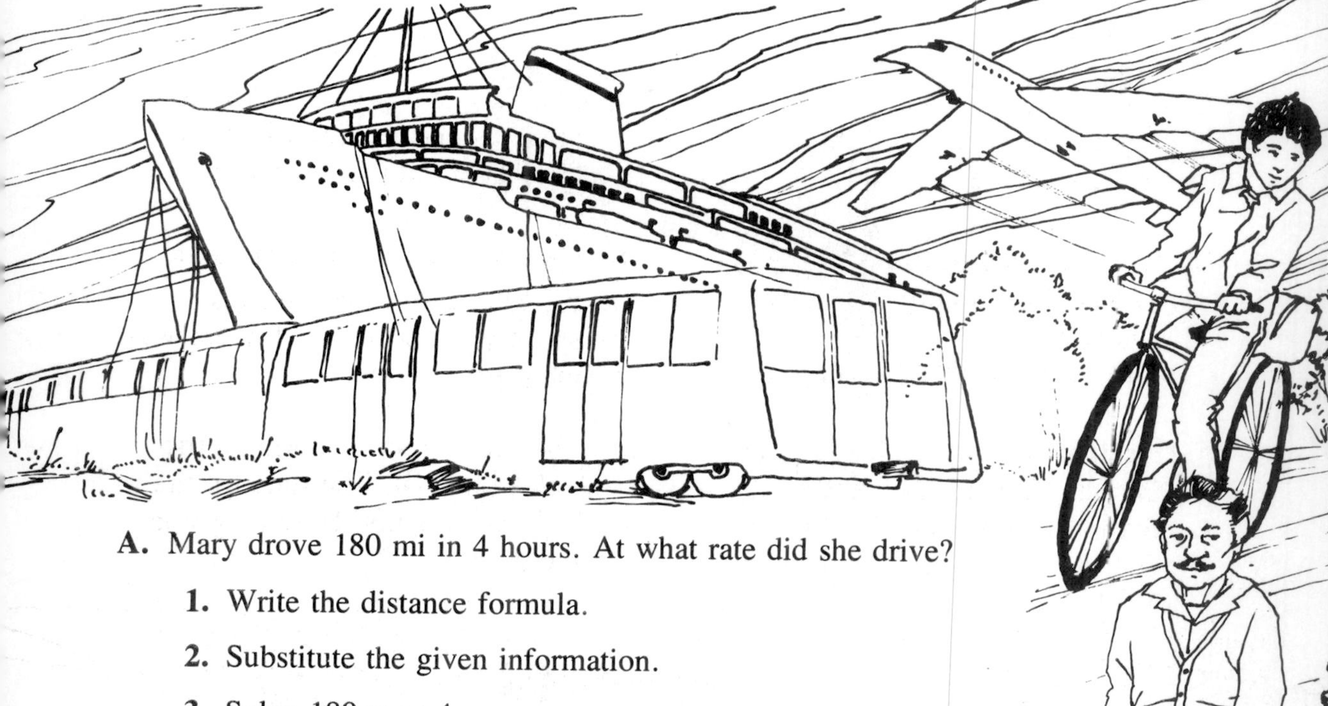

A. Mary drove 180 mi in 4 hours. At what rate did she drive?

1. Write the distance formula.
2. Substitute the given information.
3. Solve $180 = r \cdot 4$.

B. Dave drove 260 km at 65 km/h. How long did the trip take?

4. Write the distance formula.
5. Substitute the given information
6. Solve $260 = 65 \cdot t$.

Practice

Solve. Use the distance formula.

1. A commuter drove from her home to her place of work in $\frac{1}{2}$ hour. She drove at the rate of 76 km/h. What is the distance from her home to her office?

2. The highway distance from Chicago, Illinois, to Phoenix, Arizona, is 1,755 mi. Ms. Gomez made the trip in 30 hours over a 3-day period. What was her average speed for the trip?

3. May and Sam took a bicycle trip. They rode at the rate of 15 km/h. They rode from 8:00 am to 4:00 pm that afternoon. How far did they ride?

4. A ship left port at 9:00 pm and at 2:00 am the next morning was 80 mi out at sea. At what average rate of speed was the ship traveling?

5. A bus driver averaged 80 km/h during a 6-hour driving day. How far did he drive?

6. Ms. Joly rode a bicycle 96 km at an average rate of 16 km/h. How long did the trip take?

7. Mr. Perez walked from 8:30 am to noon along a hiking trail. He walked at an average rate of 3 mph. How far did he walk?

8. On a $4\frac{1}{2}$-hour air trip, the pilot announced that their average speed was 500 mph. How far was the trip?

9. Pete plans to take a car trip of 900 km. He plans to average 75 km/h. How long will the trip take?

10. The average speed during a trip was 54.7 mph. The time for the trip was 3 hours. How long was the trip?

Keeping Fit

Add.

1. $\begin{array}{r} 36.1 \\ 84.3 \\ 61.4 \\ +\ 81.4 \\ \hline \end{array}$

2. $\begin{array}{r} 64.183 \\ 2.409 \\ 31.604 \\ +\ \ 0.786 \\ \hline \end{array}$

3. $\begin{array}{r} 24.38162 \\ 0.48239 \\ 9.14613 \\ +\ \ 0.32007 \\ \hline \end{array}$

4. $1.4 + 6.39 + 0.7$

5. $0.7 + 0.06 + 0.931$

6. $\begin{array}{r} 3\frac{3}{8} \\ +\ 2\frac{1}{4} \\ \hline \end{array}$

7. $\begin{array}{r} 7\frac{1}{2} \\ +\ 2\frac{3}{4} \\ \hline \end{array}$

8. $\begin{array}{r} 4\frac{7}{8} \\ +\ 3\frac{1}{2} \\ \hline \end{array}$

9. $\begin{array}{r} 7\frac{3}{5} \\ +\ 2\frac{3}{4} \\ \hline \end{array}$

10. $\begin{array}{r} 25\frac{3}{4} \\ +\ 12\frac{1}{3} \\ \hline \end{array}$

Subtract.

11. $\begin{array}{r} 64.1 \\ -\ 38.9 \\ \hline \end{array}$

12. $\begin{array}{r} 815.6 \\ -\ 314.8 \\ \hline \end{array}$

13. $\begin{array}{r} 0.9004 \\ -\ 0.8966 \\ \hline \end{array}$

14. $\begin{array}{r} 6.3967 \\ -\ 2.6808 \\ \hline \end{array}$

15. $\begin{array}{r} 4.3578 \\ -\ 1.0681 \\ \hline \end{array}$

16. $0.8 - 0.5$

17. $0.017 - 0.009$

18. $5 - 0.87$

19. $9 - 0.656$

20. $\begin{array}{r} 5\frac{5}{8} \\ -\ 2\frac{1}{8} \\ \hline \end{array}$

21. $\begin{array}{r} 12\frac{3}{4} \\ -\ \ 9\frac{3}{8} \\ \hline \end{array}$

22. $\begin{array}{r} 5 \\ -\ 2\frac{1}{2} \\ \hline \end{array}$

23. $\begin{array}{r} 9 \\ -\ 8\frac{7}{9} \\ \hline \end{array}$

24. $\begin{array}{r} 8\frac{1}{3} \\ -\ 4\frac{5}{6} \\ \hline \end{array}$

Multiply.

25. $\begin{array}{r} 29.6 \\ \times\ 7 \\ \hline \end{array}$

26. $\begin{array}{r} 86.5 \\ \times\ 5 \\ \hline \end{array}$

27. $\begin{array}{r} 0.127 \\ \times\ 3 \\ \hline \end{array}$

28. $\begin{array}{r} 0.424 \\ \times\ 8 \\ \hline \end{array}$

29. $\begin{array}{r} 136.8 \\ \times\ 9 \\ \hline \end{array}$

30. $\begin{array}{r} 0.34 \\ \times\ 2.1 \\ \hline \end{array}$

31. $\begin{array}{r} 0.29 \\ \times\ 0.8 \\ \hline \end{array}$

32. $\begin{array}{r} 23.86 \\ \times\ 4.21 \\ \hline \end{array}$

33. $\begin{array}{r} 2.809 \\ \times\ 0.82 \\ \hline \end{array}$

34. $\begin{array}{r} 0.064 \\ \times\ 0.37 \\ \hline \end{array}$

35. $\frac{2}{3} \times \frac{5}{6}$

36. $\frac{2}{3} \times 12$

37. $3\frac{1}{2} \times 1\frac{2}{3}$

38. $4\frac{1}{8} \times 6\frac{1}{2}$

Divide.

39. $4\overline{)17.6}$

40. $9\overline{)0.081}$

41. $18\overline{)94.14}$

42. $26\overline{)241.8}$

43. $87\overline{)562.89}$

44. $0.3\overline{)0.24}$

45. $1.7\overline{)255}$

46. $0.08\overline{)0.048}$

47. $0.006\overline{)30}$

48. $6.9\overline{)310.5}$

49. $\frac{1}{2} \div \frac{1}{3}$

50. $\frac{7}{8} \div \frac{2}{5}$

51. $6 \div \frac{1}{4}$

52. $3\frac{1}{2} \div 2$

Ratio

6 girls and 8 boys joined the school running team. The ratio of the number of girls to the number of boys on the team is 6 to 8. The ratio 6 to 8 may be written as
$6:8$ or $\frac{6}{8}$.

A. Write each ratio in 2 ways.
The track team won 9 races and lost 3.

1. What is the ratio of the number of races won to the number of races lost?
2. What is the ratio of the number of races won to the total number of races?

B. Two ratios are equal if they can be written as equivalent fractions.

6 is to 8   3 is to 4

equal ratios since $\frac{6}{8} = \frac{3}{4}$

Which ratios are equal to 10 is to 15?

3. 6 is to 9   4. 5 is to 10   5. 20 is to 30

Practice

Leonard is on the basketball team. He played in 6 games and did not play in 4.

1. What is the ratio of the number of games played to the total number of games?
2. What is the ratio of the number of games not played to the number of games played?

Which ratios are equal to 7 is to 14?

3. 6 is to 42   4. 12 is to 24   5. 8 is to 15

Proportion

Steve's team won 7 games and lost 3 games.
Emma's team won 14 games and lost 6 games.
The ratios of games won to games lost are equal.
$\frac{7}{3} = \frac{14}{6}$ $7:3 = 14:6 \longleftarrow$ read 7 is to 3 as 14 is to 6

A. A proportion is a statement of equal ratios.
$\frac{7}{3} = \frac{14}{6}$ is a true proportion.

Which are true proportions?

1. $6:3 = 5:2$ **2.** $8:24 = 6:18$ **3.** $\frac{3}{10} = \frac{9}{30}$

B. A proportion has 2 means and 2 extremes.

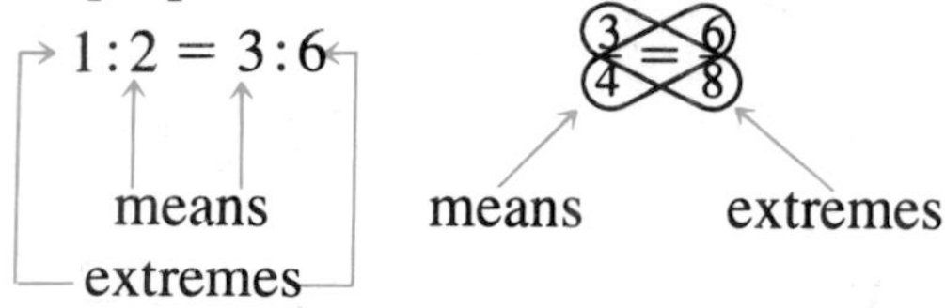

Identify the means. Identify the extremes.

4. $\frac{1}{2} = \frac{2}{4}$ **5.** $1:3 = 2:6$ **6.** $\frac{8}{4} = \frac{4}{2}$ **7.** $5:4 = 50:40$

C. In a true proportion, the product of the means equals the product of the extremes.

8. What is the product of the means in $\frac{8}{4} = \frac{4}{2}$?

9. What is the product of the extremes in $\frac{8}{4} = \frac{4}{2}$?

10. Are the products equal?

D. Solve the proportions.

Examples	$2:3 = 10:x$	$\frac{1}{2} = \frac{x}{10}$
Step 1 Find products.	$30 = 2x$	$10 = 2x$
Step 2 Solve.	$15 = x$	$5 = x$

11. $1:2 = 10:x$ **12.** $8:6 = x:3$ **13.** $\frac{x}{12} = \frac{3}{4}$

Practice

Which are true proportions?

1. $1:3 = 4:12$
2. $2:3 = 4:5$
3. $\frac{4}{6} = \frac{2}{3}$
4. $\frac{8}{3} = \frac{24}{9}$
5. $3:4 = 9:15$
6. $8:2 = 4:2$
7. $\frac{6}{8} = \frac{9}{12}$
8. $\frac{12}{8} = \frac{9}{6}$

Solve the proportions.

9. $1:2 = 2:x$
10. $2:3 = x:6$
11. $2:x = 4:10$
12. $x:3 = 6:9$
13. $5:4 = x:8$
14. $8:2 = 12:x$
15. $4:x = 3:6$
16. $x:9 = 4:6$
17. $6:5 = 12:x$
18. $8:x = 4:5$
19. $x:8 = 3:12$
20. $15:10 = 3:x$
21. $\frac{6}{8} = \frac{3}{x}$
22. $\frac{2}{3} = \frac{x}{6}$
23. $\frac{8}{x} = \frac{4}{5}$
24. $\frac{x}{8} = \frac{3}{2}$
25. $\frac{x}{6} = \frac{12}{9}$
26. $\frac{3}{x} = \frac{4}{8}$
27. $\frac{5}{4} = \frac{x}{8}$
28. $\frac{2}{6} = \frac{3}{x}$
29. $\frac{5}{x} = \frac{2}{4}$
30. $\frac{9}{6} = \frac{12}{x}$
31. $\frac{x}{28} = \frac{2}{7}$
32. ★ $\frac{x}{12} = \frac{3}{x}$

FIND OUT!
Calculator Activity

1. Find these products on a calculator.
   15,873 × 7 = ?
   15,873 × 14 = ?
   15,873 × 21 = ?
   15,873 × 28 = ?
   15,873 × 35 = ?
   15,873 × 42 = ?
   15,873 × 49 = ?
   15,873 × 56 = ?

2. What do you notice?
3. What would be the next problem in the sequence? What is the product?

Problem Solving: The Lever Formula

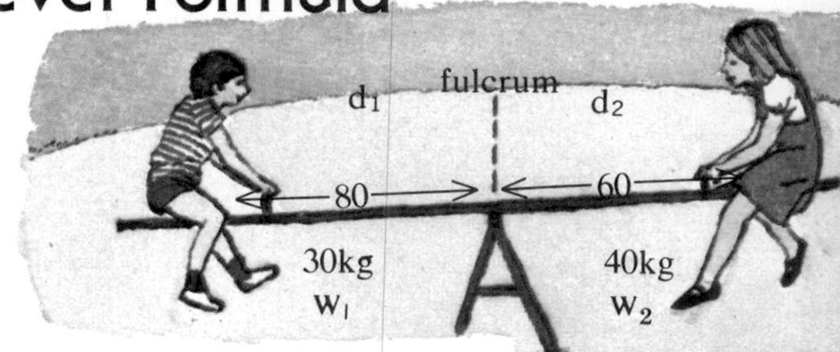

Two different masses can be balanced on a seesaw by adjusting their distances from the fulcrum.

The greater mass should be closer to the fulcrum.

The seesaw will be in balance when the masses and distances are in this proportion:

$$\frac{w_1}{w_2} = \frac{d_2}{d_1} \qquad \frac{30}{40} = \frac{60}{80}$$

Since the product of the extremes equals the product of the means, the lever formula can be written this way:

$$w_1 \cdot d_1 = w_2 \cdot d_2 \qquad 30 \cdot 80 = 40 \cdot 60$$
$$2{,}400 = 2{,}400$$

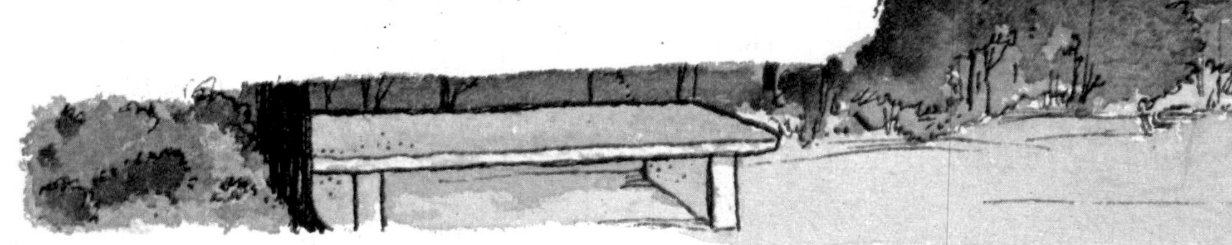

A. The scale is balanced. What is the mass of the rocks?

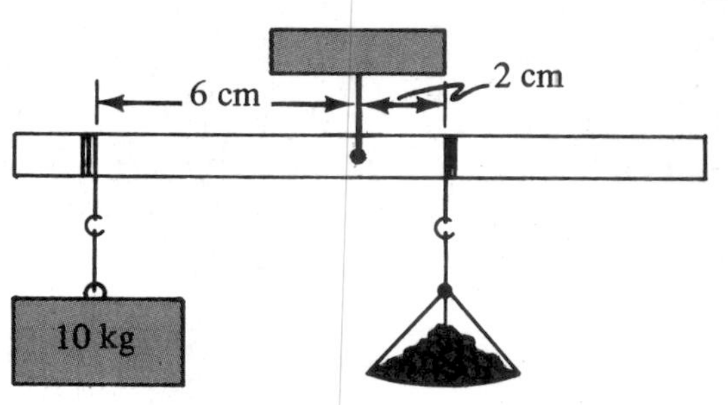

1. Write the lever formula in product form.
2. Substitute the given information in the formula.
3. Solve. $10 \cdot 6 = x \cdot 2$ or $60 = 2x$

B. A 16-kg mass is 5 cm from the fulcrum. What mass 4 cm from the fulcrum will balance it?

4. Write the lever formula in product form.
5. Substitute the given information in the formula.
6. Solve $16 \cdot 5 = x \cdot 4$.

Practice

The levers are balanced. Find x.

1\. 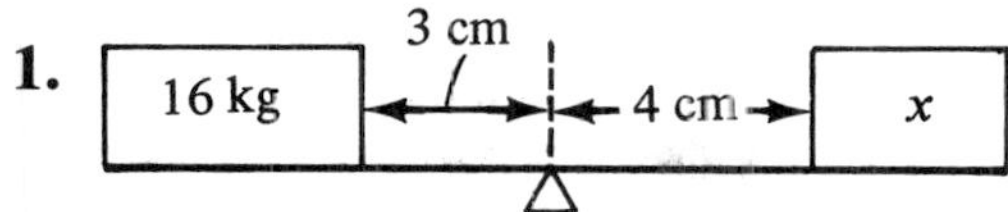

2\. 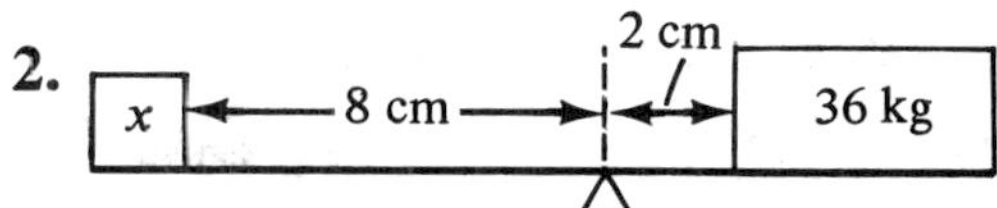

3\. 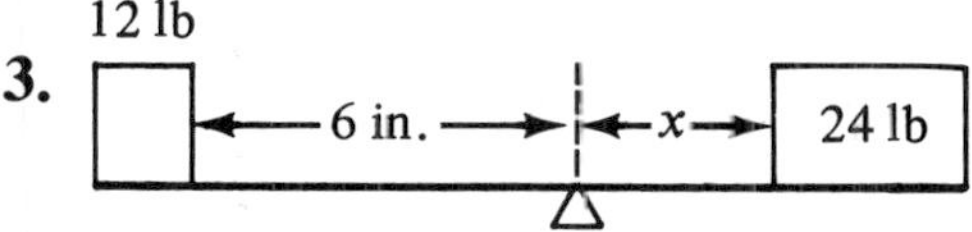

4\. 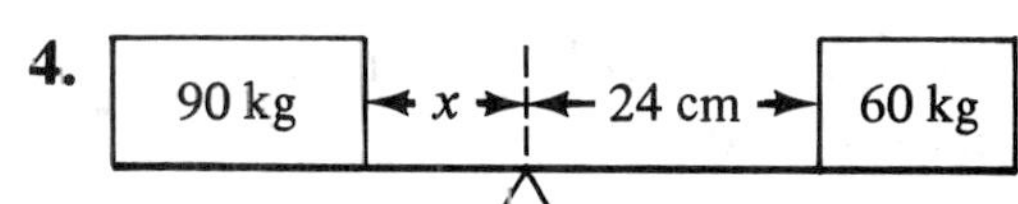

Solve. Use the lever formula.

5. A 36-g mass is 4 cm from the fulcrum. What mass 6 cm from the fulcrum will balance it?

6. An 81-lb weight is 2 yd from the fulcrum. What weight 3 yd from the fulcrum will balance it?

7. Mike has a mass of 32 kg. He is sitting 300 cm from the fulcrum. José has a mass of 24 kg. The seesaw is balanced. How far is José sitting from the fulcrum?

8. An 18-g mass 4 cm from the fulcrum balances a 12-g mass. How far from the fulcrum is the 12-g mass?

FIND OUT!
Brainteaser

Complete the sequences.

Ⓐ $\frac{1}{2}$, Ⓒ $\frac{1}{4}$, Ⓔ $\frac{1}{6}$, __?__, __?__

Ⓐ $1\frac{1}{2}$, Ⓑ $2\frac{1}{2}$, Ⓒ $3\frac{1}{2}$, __?__, __?__

Ⓩ $\frac{1}{5}$, Ⓨ $\frac{1}{10}$, Ⓧ $\frac{1}{20}$, Ⓦ $\frac{1}{40}$, __?__, __?__

Chapter Test

Compute. *(224)*

1. $5 \times (11 - 6)$

2. $18 \div 3 + 3$

Evaluate. *(224)*

3. $5x - y$ if $x = 8$ and $y = 9$

4. $\frac{p}{2} \cdot (q - 3)$ if $p = 8$ and $q = 4$

Write an equation. *(228)*

5. Six less than 7 times a number is 29.

Write an equation. Solve. *(230)*

6. Martha bought 4 cans of soup and a loaf of bread for $1.71. The loaf of bread cost $0.75. What was the price of each can of soup?

Solve. Use the distance formula. *(236)*

7. Ms. Miles drove from her home to work and back again. The total distance driven was 78 mi. She drove at an average speed of 52 mph. How long did she drive?

Solve the proportion. *(240)*

8. $3:2 = x:6$

Solve. Use the lever formula. *(242)*

9. An 18-g mass is 2 cm from the fulcrum. How far from the fulcrum must a 4-g mass be placed to balance it?

Solve. *(244)*

10. Eva needs 3 parts of red paint to 4 parts of blue paint to get a certain shade of purple. How much blue paint does she need to add to 24 L of red paint?

Basic Skills Check

1. What type of angle is $\angle ABC$?

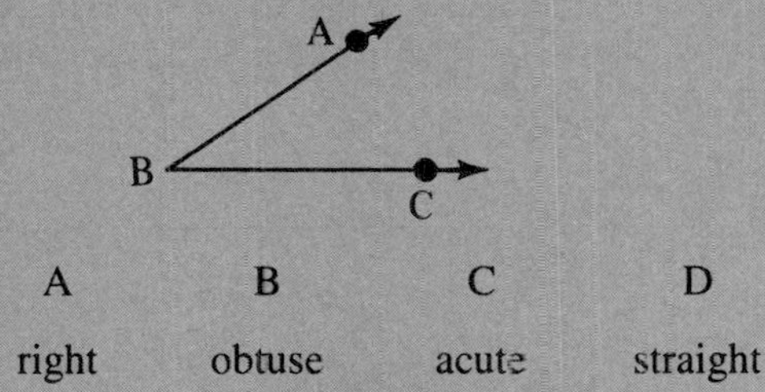

A	B	C	D
right	obtuse	acute	straight

2. Which line segment represents the edge of a cube?

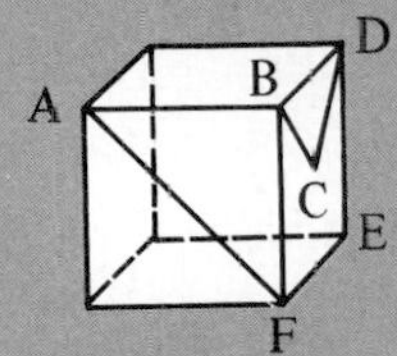

E	F	G	H
$\overline{AF}$	$\overline{AB}$	$\overline{BC}$	none of the above

3. What type of figure is shown?

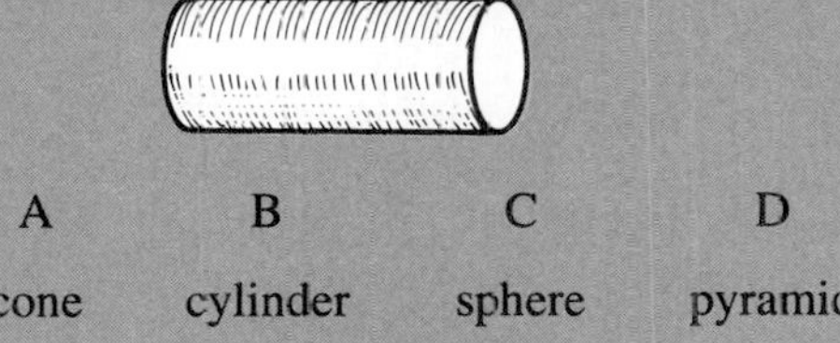

A	B	C	D
cone	cylinder	sphere	pyramid

4. Which is an isosceles triangle?

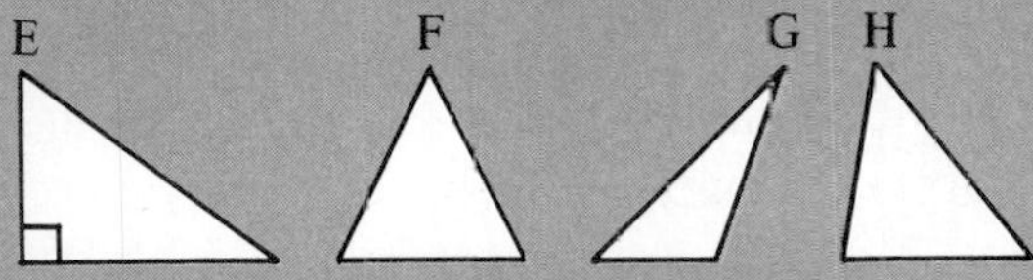

5. The radius of a circle is 24 mm. What is the diameter?

A	B	C	D
12 mm	24 mm	36 mm	48 mm

6. Which line segment is the altitude of $\triangle GHI$?

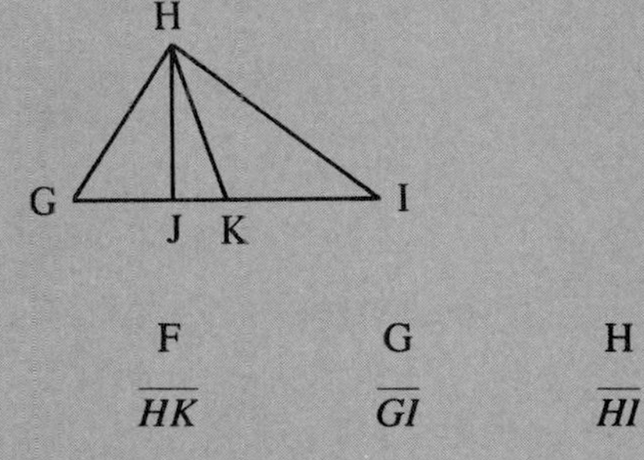

E	F	G	H
$\overline{HJ}$	$\overline{HK}$	$\overline{GI}$	$\overline{HI}$

7. Which angle is congruent to $\angle 1$?

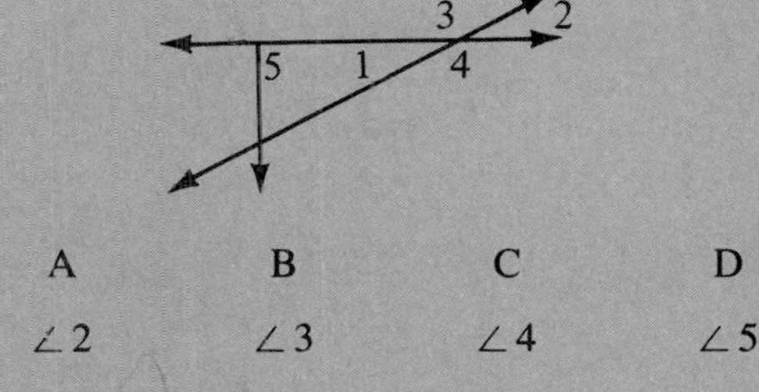

A	B	C	D
$\angle 2$	$\angle 3$	$\angle 4$	$\angle 5$

8. Which of the figures is not symmetric?

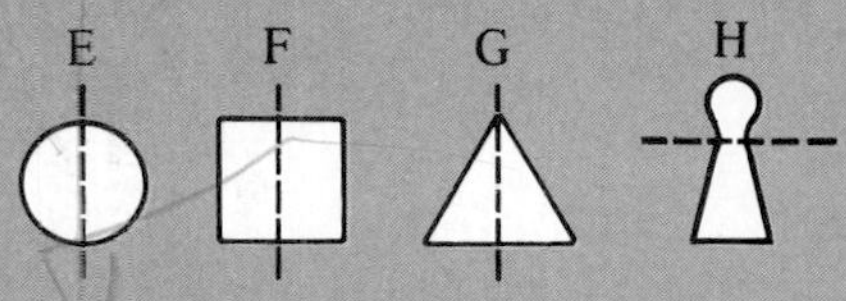

9. Which of the angles is 150°?

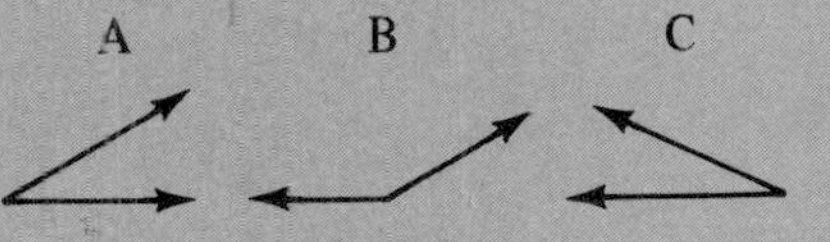

Meaning of Percent

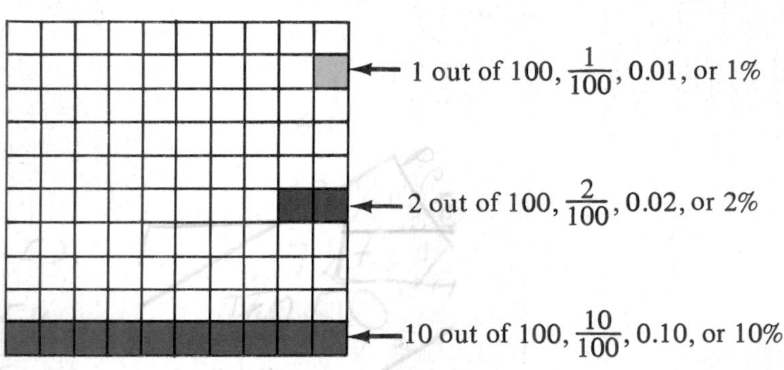

A. Write percents.

Examples $\frac{3}{100} = 3\%$ $\frac{18}{100} = 18\%$

1. $\frac{4}{100}$ **2.** $\frac{7}{100}$ **3.** $\frac{13}{100}$ **4.** $\frac{34}{100}$ **5.** $\frac{68}{100}$

B. Write fractions.

Examples $6\% = \frac{6}{100}$ $24\% = \frac{24}{100}$

6. 9% **7.** 12% **8.** 25% **9.** 63% **10.** 99%

C. Write percents.

Examples 0.03 = 3% 0.42 = 42%

(hundredths → hundredths)

11. 0.05 **12.** 0.07 **13.** 0.13 **14.** 0.29 **15.** 0.69

D. Write decimals.

Example 8% = 0.08 THINK: $8\% = \frac{8}{100} = 0.08$

16. 4% **17.** 7% **18.** 12% **19.** 39% **20.** 86%

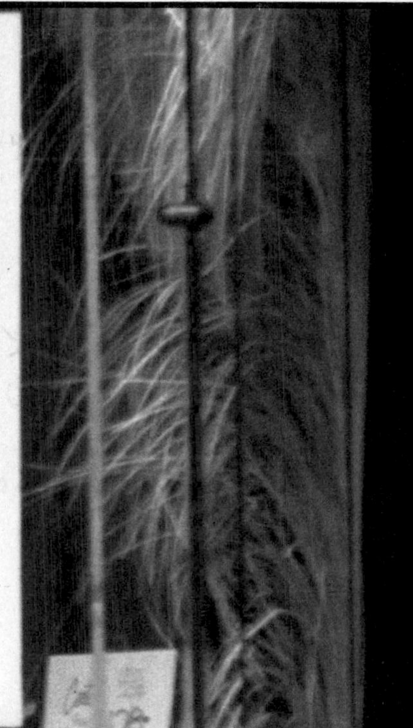

CHAPTER 10 PERCENT

Practice

Write percents.

1. $\frac{5}{100}$ **2.** $\frac{9}{100}$ **3.** $\frac{16}{100}$ **4.** $\frac{81}{100}$ **5.** $\frac{95}{100}$

6. 0.06 **7.** 0.08 **8.** 0.23 **9.** 0.53 **10.** 0.77

Write fractions.

11. 4% **12.** 8% **13.** 6% **14.** 5% **15.** 7%

16. 23% **17.** 37% **18.** 41% **19.** 81% **20.** 90%

Write decimals.

21. 1% **22.** 6% **23.** 18% **24.** 42% **25.** 89%

Fractions and Percent

JoAnn bought a stereo system marked 50% off. What fractional part of the marked price did she save?

$$50\% = \frac{50}{100}, \text{ or } \frac{1}{2}$$

She saved $\frac{1}{2}$ of the marked price.

A. Write the simplest fractions or whole numbers.

1. 10% **2.** 25% **3.** 40% **4.** 100% **5.** 200%

B. Write the simplest fractions.

Example

$$33\tfrac{1}{3}\% = 33\tfrac{1}{3} \cdot 1\% \leftarrow$$
$$= 33\tfrac{1}{3} \cdot \frac{1}{100} \leftarrow$$
$$= \frac{\overset{1}{\cancel{100}}}{3} \cdot \frac{1}{\underset{1}{\cancel{100}}}$$
$$= \frac{1}{3} \quad \text{So, } 33\tfrac{1}{3}\% = \frac{1}{3}$$

6. $12\frac{1}{2}\%$ **7.** $16\frac{2}{3}\%$ **8.** $4\frac{1}{2}\%$ **9.** $\frac{1}{4}\%$ **10.** $\frac{1}{2}\%$

Look at these methods for writing fractions as percents.

Method 1

$$\frac{3}{5} = \frac{3 \cdot 20}{5 \cdot 20}$$
$$= \frac{60}{100}$$
$$= 60\%$$

Method 2

$\frac{3}{5}$ or $5\overline{)3}$ $\quad$ $\begin{array}{r} 0.60 \\ 5\overline{)3.00} \end{array}$ ← hundredths

$\frac{3}{5} = 60\%$

11. Use both methods to change $\frac{3}{4}$ to a percent.

D. Write percents.

12. $\frac{1}{2}$ **13.** $\frac{1}{8}$ **14.** $\frac{1}{200}$ **15.** $\frac{300}{100}$ **16.** $\frac{7}{4}$

Practice

Write the simplest fractions or whole numbers.

1. 75%	**2.** 24%	**3.** 55%	**4.** 92%	**5.** 72%
6. 16%	**7.** 65%	**8.** 81%	**9.** 300%	**10.** 400%
11. $17\frac{1}{2}\%$	**12.** $8\frac{1}{3}\%$	**13.** $6\frac{1}{4}\%$	**14.** $\frac{2}{3}\%$	**15.** $\frac{1}{10}\%$
16. $\frac{1}{5}\%$	**17.** 250%	**18.** 12%	**19.** $\frac{1}{3}\%$	**20.** $14\frac{1}{2}\%$

Write percents.

21. $\frac{1}{4}$	**22.** $\frac{2}{5}$	**23.** $\frac{3}{5}$	**24.** $\frac{7}{10}$	**25.** $\frac{3}{25}$	**26.** $\frac{11}{50}$
27. $\frac{3}{8}$	**28.** $\frac{1}{12}$	**29.** $\frac{1}{3}$	**30.** $\frac{3}{200}$	**31.** $\frac{1}{400}$	**32.** $\frac{3}{400}$
33. $\frac{200}{100}$	**34.** $\frac{500}{100}$	**35.** $\frac{6}{5}$	**36.** $\frac{5}{4}$	★ **37.** $\frac{8}{1,000}$	★ **38.** $\frac{3}{10,000}$

Here are tables of commonly used percents. Complete.

	Percent	*Fraction*
39.	25%	
40.	50%	
41.	75%	
42.	$33\frac{1}{3}\%$	
43.	$66\frac{2}{3}\%$	
44.	10%	
45.	20%	

	Percent	*Fraction*
46.	30%	
47.	40%	
48.	60%	
49.	70%	
50.	80%	
51.	90%	
52.	100%	

	Percent	*Fraction*
53.	$12\frac{1}{2}\%$	
54.	$37\frac{1}{2}\%$	
55.	$62\frac{1}{2}\%$	
56.	$16\frac{2}{3}\%$	
57.	$83\frac{1}{3}\%$	
58.	$87\frac{1}{2}\%$	
★ **59.**	$\frac{1}{8}\%$	

Solve.

60. A record was marked $33\frac{1}{3}\%$ off. What fractional part of the cost is saved?

Decimals and Percents

Percent means hundredth. 1% = 0.01

Here is a method for changing percents to decimals:

$$140\% = 140 \cdot 1\% = 140 \cdot 0.01 = 1.40$$

$$0.3\% = 0.3 \cdot 1\% = 0.3 \cdot 0.01 = 0.003$$

A. Change to decimals.

1. 7% **2.** 81% **3.** 130% **4.** 0.4% **5.** 2.6%

B. Here is a quick way to change a percent to a decimal.

Examples 140% = 1.40; 0.3% = 0.003; 9% = 0.09

Step 1 Move the decimal point 2 places to the left.
Step 2 Drop the % sign.

Change to decimals.

6. 63% **7.** 150% **8.** 0.5% **9.** 2.3% **10.** 3.04%

C. Percents with fractions may be changed to decimals.

Example $\frac{1}{2}\%$

Step 1 Change the fraction to a decimal.
$\frac{1}{2}$ is $2\overline{)1.0}$ = 0.5   So, $\frac{1}{2}\% = 0.5\%$

Step 2 Change the percent to a decimal.
0.5% = 0.005   So, $\frac{1}{2}\% = 0.005$

Change to decimals.

11. $\frac{1}{4}\%$ **12.** $\frac{1}{5}\%$ **13.** $\frac{3}{4}\%$ **14.** $2\frac{1}{2}\%$ **15.** $5\frac{1}{4}\%$

D. The quick way is reversed to change decimals to percents.

Examples 0.06 → 0.06 = 6%; 0.3 → 0.30 = 30%

Step 1 Move the decimal point 2 places to the right.
Step 2 Write the % sign.

Change to percents.

16. 0.78 **17.** 0.5 **18.** 1 **19.** 2.4 **20.** 0.075

Practice

Change to decimals.

1. 2%	**2.** 6%	**3.** 9%	**4.** 10%	**5.** 23%
6. 34%	**7.** 42%	**8.** 60%	**9.** 80%	**10.** 100%
11. 120%	**12.** 140%	**13.** 210%	**14.** 250%	**15.** 300%
16. 0.2%	**17.** 0.6%	**18.** 0.9%	**19.** 3.1%	**20.** 8.6%
21. 9.5%	**22.** 0.03%	**23.** 0.06%	**24.** 2.04%	**25.** 5.25%
26. $\frac{1}{5}$%	**27.** $\frac{3}{10}$%	**28.** $2\frac{1}{4}$%	**29.** $5\frac{1}{2}$%	★ **30.** $6\frac{5}{8}$%

Change to percents.

31. 0.08	**32.** 0.64	**33.** 0.93	**34.** 0.6
35. 0.7	**36.** 0.9	**37.** 2	**38.** 2.8
39. 3.5	**40.** 4	**41.** 0.025	**42.** 0.050
43. 0.064	**44.** 0.001	**45.** 0.0075	**46.** 0.0061
★ **47.** $0.02\frac{1}{2}$	★ **48.** $0.05\frac{1}{4}$	★ **49.** $0.12\frac{1}{2}$	★ **50.** $0.66\frac{2}{3}$

FIND OUT!
Calculator Activity

1. Find 5 whole numbers greater than 10 so that when they are divided by 3 and 4, the remainder is 2 in each case.

2. Find 5 whole numbers greater than 100 which are divisible by 2, 3, and 7.

3. Find 5 whole numbers greater than 1,000 which are divisible by 2 and 3, but not by 4.

Finding a Percent of a Number

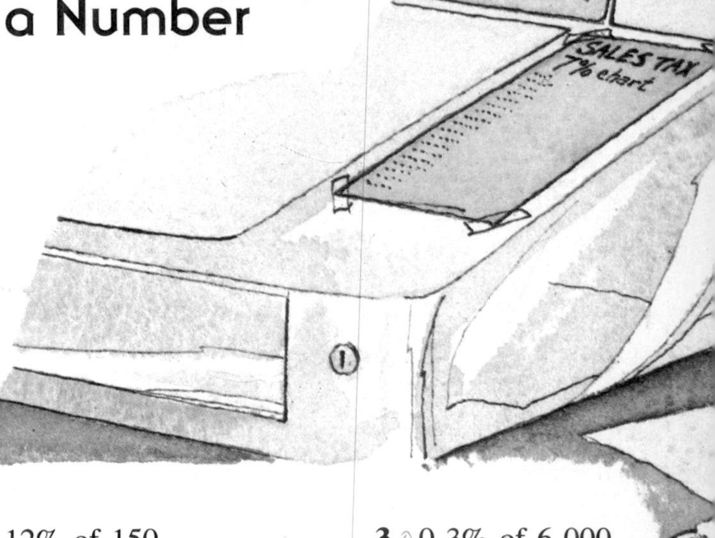

Mrs. Perez bought a bicycle for \$85. She had to pay 7% sales tax. How much sales tax did she pay?

THINK: 7% of \$85 is what?

Equation: $7\% \cdot 85 = n$

$0.07 \cdot 85 = n$

$5.95 = n$

The sales tax was \$5.95.

A. Compute.

1. 8% of 65 **2.** 12% of 150 **3.** 0.3% of 6,000

B. Find 140% of 65.

4. THINK: 140% of 65 is what? Write an equation.

5. Write a decimal for 140%.

6. Solve the equation $1.40 \cdot 65 = n$.

7. What is 140% of 65?

C. Compute.

Example $\frac{1}{4}\%$ of 600

$\frac{1}{4}\% \cdot 600 = n$

$0.0025 \cdot 600 = n$

$1.5 = n$

8. $\frac{1}{4}\%$ of 800 **9.** $\frac{1}{2}\%$ of 800 **10.** $3\frac{1}{2}\%$ of 450

D. Sometimes it is easier to change the percent to a fraction.

Example 25% of 60

$25\% \cdot 60 = n$

$\frac{1}{4} \cdot 60 = n$

$15 = n$

Compute.

11. 75% of 40 **12.** $12\frac{1}{2}\%$ of 72 **13.** $33\frac{1}{3}\%$ of 24

Practice

Compute.

1. 6% of 40
2. 9% of 100
3. 8% of 700
4. 10% of 45
5. 12% of 76
6. 56% of 850
7. 76% of 80
8. 87% of 240
9. 86% of 750
10. 100% of 80
11. 110% of 700
12. 120% of 40
13. 150% of 640
14. 225% of 80
15. 375% of 800
16. $\frac{1}{2}$% of 60
17. $\frac{1}{4}$% of 800
18. $\frac{3}{4}$% of 6,000
19. $2\frac{1}{2}$% of 80
20. $3\frac{1}{4}$% of 500
21. $5\frac{1}{4}$% of 2,500
22. 0.2% of 600
23. 0.5% of 950
24. 0.7% of $675
25. 0.06% of 842
26. 0.08% of 1,000
27. 0.07% of 8,000
28. 50% of 60
29. 5% of 200
30. 25% of 8
31. $33\frac{1}{3}$% of 9
32. $66\frac{2}{3}$% of 12
33. $12\frac{1}{2}$% of 16
34. $37\frac{1}{2}$% of 24
35. $62\frac{1}{2}$% of 80
36. $16\frac{2}{3}$% of 24
37. 25% of 120
38. 175% of 12
39. $\frac{1}{4}$% of 20
40. $2\frac{1}{2}$% of 90
41. 0.4% of 60
42. $87\frac{1}{2}$% of 100

★ 43. 20% of 0.5

★ 44. $33\frac{1}{2}$% of $16\frac{1}{2}$

★ 45. 400% of $\frac{1}{4}$

Solve.

46. Juan bought a television set for $685. The sales tax was 4% of the selling price. How much sales tax did he pay?

47. Maria bought a clock radio for $54. She paid a sales tax of 7% of the selling price. What was the total cost of the clock radio?

Finding Percents

At the Low Company, 16 of the 25 employees had perfect attendance records. What percent of the employees had perfect attendance records?

THINK: What percent of 25 is 16?

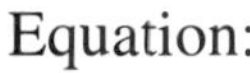

Equation: $n \cdot 25 = 16$

Solve: $n = \frac{16}{25} \longrightarrow 25\overline{)16.00}$ = 0.64

$n = 0.64$

$n = 64\%$

Answer: 64% of the employees had perfect attendance records.

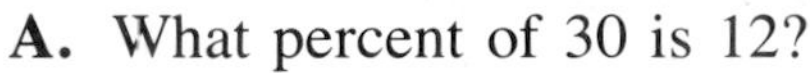

A. What percent of 30 is 12?

1. Write an equation for the problem.

2. Solve the equation $n \cdot 30 = 12$.

3. Write a percent for 0.40.

B. Compute.

4. What percent of 25 is 3?

5. 15 is what percent of 24?

C. Sometimes the percent is greater than 100%.

Example What percent of 4 is 8?

$n \cdot 4 = 8$

$n = \frac{8}{4}$

$n = 2$

$n = 200\%$

6. What percent of 3 is 9?

7. 21 is what percent of 4?

D. What percent of 10 is 0.05?

8. Write an equation for the problem.

9. Solve the equation $n \cdot 10 = 0.05$.

10. Write a percent for 0.005.

E. Compute.

11. What percent of 12 is 0.3?

12. 0.01 is what percent of 4?

Compute.

1. What percent of 2 is 1?
2. 4 is what percent of 8?
3. What percent of 10 is 3?
4. 2 is what percent of 5?
5. What percent of 25 is 4?
6. 6 is what percent of 8?
7. What percent of 15 is 9?
8. 1 is what percent of 8?
9. What percent of 3 is 1?
10. 9 is what percent of 16?
11. What percent of 4 is 12?
12. 24 is what percent of 12?
13. What percent of 9 is 18?
14. 10 is what percent of 2?
15. What percent of 2 is 15?
16. 9 is what percent of 4?
17. What percent of 5 is 7?
18. 9 is what percent of 5?
19. What percent of 100 is 0.05?
20. 0.3 is what percent of 10?
21. What percent of 15 is 0.3?
22. 0.4 is what percent of 5?
23. What percent of 100 is 0.08?
24. 0.07 is what percent of 14?
25. What percent of 5 is 8?
26. 0.8 is what percent of 16?
27. 24 is what percent of 42?
28. What percent of 7 is 14?
29. 0.02 is what percent of 12?
30. What percent of 7 is 3?
31. 9 is what percent of 16?
32. What percent of 20 is 0.5?

Solve.

33. At the company picnic, 40 of the 60 people came by car. What percent of the people came by car?
34. Team A made 7 baskets out of 25 tries. Team B made 10 baskets out of 30 tries. Who had a better scoring average?

Finding the Number

Ralph bought a sweater on sale. He saved \$6. During the sale everything was marked down 25%. What was the regular price of the sweater?

THINK: 25% of the regular price is saved.

Equation:

$$25\% \cdot n = 6$$

$$\frac{1}{4} \cdot n = 6$$

$$n = 24$$

Check: $\frac{1}{4} \cdot 24 = 6$

The regular price of the sweater was \$24.

A. Compute. 48 is 40% of what number?

1. Write an equation.
2. Write a decimal for 40%.
3. Solve the equation $48 = 0.40 \cdot n$.
4. Check the solution.

B. Compute.

5. 75% of what number is 18?
6. $33\frac{1}{3}\%$ of what number is 9?
7. 6.3 is 15% of what number?
8. 16.2 is 30% of what number?

C. Compute.

Examples

10 is 250% of what number?

$$250\% \cdot n = 10$$
$$2.5 \cdot n = 10$$
$$n = \frac{10}{2.5}$$
$$n = 4$$

$\frac{1}{2}\%$ of what number is 40?

$$\frac{1}{2}\% \cdot n = 40$$
$$0.005 \cdot n = 40$$
$$n = \frac{40}{0.005}$$
$$n = 8{,}000$$

9. 12 is 300% of what number?
10. 150% of what number is 6?
11. $1\frac{1}{2}\%$ of what number is 12?
12. 104 is 5.2% of what number?

Practice

Compute.

1. 25% of what number is 8?
2. 9 is 25% of what number?
3. 75% of what number is 9?
4. 30 is 50% of what number?
5. 10% of what number is 80?
6. 24 is 40% of what number?
7. $33\frac{1}{3}$% of what number is 3?
8. 80 is $66\frac{2}{3}$% of what number?
9. $12\frac{1}{2}$% of what number is 4?
10. 30 is $62\frac{1}{2}$% of what number?
11. 24% of what number is 15.6?
12. 36.1 is 38% of what number?
13. 100% of what number is 5?
14. 70 is 100% of what number?
15. 125% of what number is 6?
16. 18 is 150% of what number?
17. 220% of what number is 550?
18. 33 is 132% of what number?
19. $\frac{1}{4}$% of what number is 6?
20. 30 is $1\frac{1}{2}$% of what number?
21. 0.4% of what number is 3.8?
22. 12 is 2.4% of what number?
23. 0.1% of what number is 40?
24. 58.9 is 62% of what number?
25. 9 is $4\frac{1}{2}$% of what number?
26. 75% of what number is 9?
27. 8 is 250% of what number?
28. 2.5% of what number is 14?

Solve.

29. Ludmila bought a coat on sale. She saved $20. During the sale, everything was marked down $33\frac{1}{3}$%. What was the regular price of the coat?
30. Henry bought a jacket on sale. He saved $17. During the sale, everything was marked down 20%. What was the regular price of the jacket?

Keeping Fit

Add.

1. $\begin{array}{r} 6.3 \\ 4.0 \\ 8.6 \\ +\ 7.9 \\ \hline \end{array}$ **2.** $\begin{array}{r} 9.83 \\ 7.48 \\ 6.36 \\ +\ 5.79 \\ \hline \end{array}$ **3.** $\begin{array}{r} 3.10746 \\ 9.51387 \\ 6.71283 \\ +\ 4.00196 \\ \hline \end{array}$

4. $4 + 0.1 + 3.47 + 0.008$ **5.** $0.0164 + 0.24 + 0.9 + 5$

Subtract.

6. $\begin{array}{r} 7.804 \\ -\ 3.460 \\ \hline \end{array}$ **7.** $\begin{array}{r} 4.3160 \\ -\ 2.4094 \\ \hline \end{array}$ **8.** $0.5 - 0.291$ **9.** $7 - 2.23$

Multiply.

10. $\begin{array}{r} 4.06 \\ \times\ 7 \\ \hline \end{array}$ **11.** $\begin{array}{r} 0.349 \\ \times\ 18 \\ \hline \end{array}$ **12.** 10×0.8 **13.** 100×0.47

14. $\begin{array}{r} 0.46 \\ \times\ 0.19 \\ \hline \end{array}$ **15.** $\begin{array}{r} 2.13 \\ \times\ 4.01 \\ \hline \end{array}$ **16.** $\begin{array}{r} 61.4 \\ \times\ 0.923 \\ \hline \end{array}$ **17.** $\begin{array}{r} 40.01 \\ \times\ 1.90 \\ \hline \end{array}$

Divide.

18. $4\overline{)0.08}$ **19.** $6\overline{)0.126}$ **20.** $7\overline{)0.021}$ **21.** $9\overline{)0.0027}$

22. $0.3\overline{)2.4}$ **23.** $0.03\overline{)6}$ **24.** $0.4\overline{)2.88}$ **25.** $3.1\overline{)17.36}$

Divide. Give the quotient to the nearest tenth.

26. $0.6\overline{)0.8}$ **27.** $0.04\overline{)0.029}$ **28.** $5\overline{)3.2}$ **29.** $4.2\overline{)8.71}$

Divide. Give the quotient to the nearest hundredth.

30. $3\overline{)1.658}$ **31.** $0.9\overline{)0.3251}$ **32.** $1.1\overline{)8.346}$ **33.** $0.53\overline{)0.0972}$

Estimate to the nearest whole number.

34. $\begin{array}{r} 8.816 \\ 4.500 \\ +\ 9.319 \\ \hline \end{array}$ **35.** $\begin{array}{r} 7.4163 \\ -\ 2.9184 \\ \hline \end{array}$ **36.** $\begin{array}{r} 4.913 \\ \times\ 8.7 \\ \hline \end{array}$ **37.** $4.3\overline{)7.651}$

Write decimals.

38. $\frac{3}{5}$ **39.** $\frac{1}{4}$ **40.** $\frac{5}{8}$ **41.** $3\frac{1}{2}$

Mid-Chapter Review

Write percents.

1. $\frac{7}{100}$ (248) **2.** $\frac{86}{100}$ (248) **3.** $\frac{3}{4}$ (250) **4.** $\frac{7}{25}$ (250)

5. 0.07 (248) **6.** 0.74 (248) **7.** 3.4 (252) **8.** $0.04\frac{1}{4}$ (252)

Write simplest fractions or whole numbers. *(250)*

9. 25% **10.** 40% **11.** 200% **12.** $12\frac{1}{2}\%$

Write decimals. *(252)*

13. 100% **14.** 250% **15.** 5.3% **16.** $\frac{1}{4}\%$

Compute.

17. 8% of 60 *(254)*

18. 120% of 80 *(254)*

19. What percent of 12 is 4? *(256)*

20. 12 is what percent of 9? *(256)*

21. 25% of what number is 12? *(258)*

22. 39 is 0.3% of what number? *(258)*

FIND OUT!
Brainteaser

Choose the *opposite* of the first picture.

1.

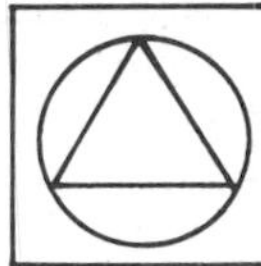

a
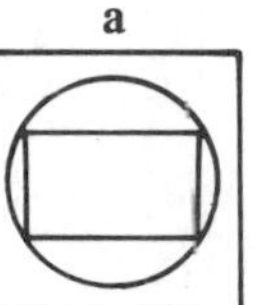

b
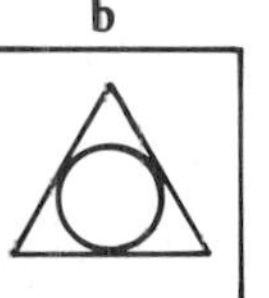

c
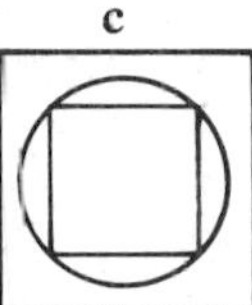

d
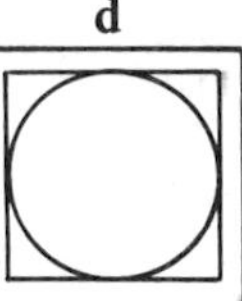

2.

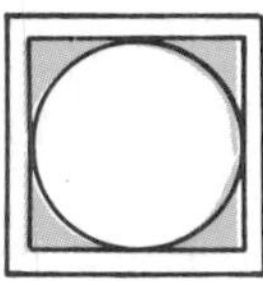

a
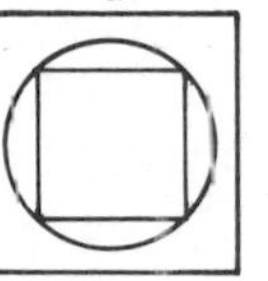

b
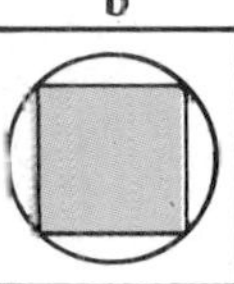

c
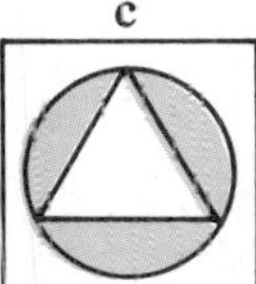

d
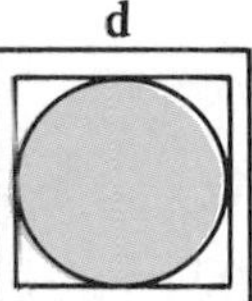

Problem Solving

Jean bought a pair of gloves for \$8.00. A day later she returned the gloves in exchange for a pair costing \$9.25. How much more must she pay?

PLAN Final pair cost \$9.25
Original pair cost \$8.00
How much more must she pay?

Write an equation.
$\$9.25 - \$8.00 = x$

SOLVE $\$9.25 - \$8.00 = x$
$\$1.25 = x$

Jean must pay \$1.25 more.

A. Write a mini-problem. Solve.

1. Mr. Guiterez bought a hammer for \$5.95. He found the handle was split. He returned the hammer and bought a screw driver for \$3.75. How much money was returned to him?

B. In multi-step problems, it helps to write more than 1 mini-problem.

Example Bill bought a radio for \$30. He exchanged it for a better radio costing \$37.50. How much change did he receive from a \$10 bill?

Mini-problem 1	Mini-problem 2
Second radio cost \$37.50	Gave \$10
First radio cost \$30	Additional cost \$7.50
Additional cost? \$7.50	Change? \$2.50

Write 2 mini-problems. Solve.

2. Mrs. Artuso bought a chair for \$125. It was damaged so she exchanged it for a chair which cost \$149.50. She gave the salesperson a \$50 bill. How much change did she receive?

EXCHANGE

Practice

Write mini-problems. Solve.

1. On Saturday Mrs. Glinka bought a lantern for \$16.95. On Monday she returned it and exchanged it for a lantern costing \$22. How much more did she pay?

2. Pete bought a record for \$5.95. He found that it was cracked. He returned it and was given a credit toward another album. He bought a record set for \$12. How much more did he pay?

3. Mr. Benitez bought a jacket for \$65. He returned it and bought a different jacket. 10% of his money was returned. How much money was returned to him?

4. The Stone family bought a 21″ television set for \$495. They returned it for a 17″ set. 5% of their money was returned. How much money was returned to the Stone family?

5. Mrs. Peterson bought a suit for \$39.50. She decided that she didn't like it and returned it. In exchange she bought a suit for \$45.75. She gave the salesperson a \$20 bill. How much change did she receive?

6. Mr. DeAngelo bought a box of 3 handkerchiefs for \$2.49. He exchanged them for a box of 3 handkerchiefs for \$4.75. He gave the salesperson a \$10 bill. How much change did he receive?

7. Paula bought 3 pairs of knee socks at \$1.25 each. She decided to exchange them for 3 pairs of pantyhose costing \$1.75 each. She gave the salesperson a \$5 bill. How much change did she receive?

Discounts and Sales

At a sale, every item is sold at a discount of 20%. What is the sale price of a belt marked $8?

Step 1 Find the discount.

discount = rate of discount · price

$x = 20\% \cdot 8$

$x = 0.20 \cdot 8$

$x = 1.60$

discount = $1.60

Step 2 Find the sale price.

$8.00 − $1.60 = $6.40

The sale price is $6.40.

A. Find the discount and the sale price. The rate of discount is 25%.

1. Pocketbook: $48
2. Skirt: $31
3. Shirt: $17.80

B. Here is a quick way to find the sale price.

Example The marked price of sneakers is $40 at a 30% sale.

THINK: You save 30%, so you must pay 70% (100% − 30%).

sale price = rate · marked price

$n = 70\% \cdot 40$

$n = 0.70 \cdot 40$

$n = 28$

sale price = $28

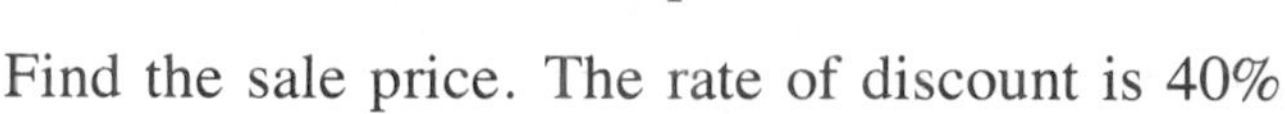

Find the sale price. The rate of discount is 40%.

4. Hat: $24
5. Shoes: $28
6. Pants: $32

C. A sweater was marked $16. It sells for $12 during a sale. Find the rate of discount as a percent.

7. Find the discount in dollars.
8. Write an equation. [HINT: discount = rate of discount · marked price]
9. Solve the equation.
10. Write the rate of discount as a percent.

Find the discount and the sale price.
The rate of discount is 10%.

1. Jacket: $85
2. Coat: $95
3. Shirt: $18.50

Find the sale price. Use the quick way.

4. Shoes marked $28 at a 25% off sale
5. Tie marked $8 at a 20% off sale
6. Sweater marked $18.10 at a 30% off sale

Find the rate of discount as a percent.

7. Hat: was $15, now $10
8. Jacket: was $50, now $40
9. Skirt: was $32, now $24

Complete.

	Marked Price	*Rate of discount*	*Discount*	*Sales Price*
10.	$80	20%		
11.	$60		$12	
12.	$40			$30
13.	$28.50	40%		
14.	$150		$50	
★ **15.**		25%		$72

Solve.

16. At a sale every item was sold at a discount of 30%. What is the sale price of a blouse marked $12?

17. A pair of gloves was $10. It sold for $8 during a sale. Find the rate of discount as a percent.

Borrowing Money

Edna's father loaned her \$200 to buy an electric guitar. Edna is to pay back the loan in 3 years at an interest rate of 6% per year. How much interest will she pay?

▶ interest = principal · rate (per year) · time (in years)

$$
\begin{aligned}
i &= p \cdot r \cdot t \\
&= 200 \cdot 6\% \cdot 3 \\
&= 200 \cdot 0.06 \cdot 3 \\
&= 36.00
\end{aligned}
$$

So, Edna will pay \$36 interest.

A. Find the interest.

1. \$6,300 at 8% for 2 years
2. \$2,000 at 5.5% for 3 years

B. Find the total amount to be paid back.

Example Borrowed \$800 at 8% per year for 3 months

Step 1

$$
\begin{aligned}
i &= p \cdot r \cdot t \\
&= 800 \cdot 0.08 \cdot 0.25 \qquad \text{[HINT: 3 months = 0.25 year]} \\
&= 16.00 \\
&= \$16
\end{aligned}
$$

Step 2

$$
\begin{aligned}
\text{Total amount} &= p + i \\
&= \$800 + \$16 \\
&= \$816
\end{aligned}
$$

3. \$3,500 at 9% for 1 year
4. \$4,550 at 8.5% for 1 year
5. \$1,200 for 7.5% for 2 years
6. \$500 at 7% for 6 months
7. \$6,500 at 12% for 3 months
8. \$2,400 at $5\frac{1}{4}\%$ for 6 months

Find the interest.

1. $600 at 7% for 2 years
2. $4,800 at 8% for 6 months
3. $3,000 at 7.5% for 4 years
4. $8,000 at $7\frac{1}{4}$% for 3 months

Find the total amount to be paid back.

	Principal	*Rate per year*	*Time*
5.	$500	6%	1 year
6.	$800	5%	2 years
7.	$1,000	12%	3 years
8.	$1,200	6%	6 months
9.	$1,600	8%	3 months
10.	$2,100	12%	4 months
11.	$600	6.5%	2 years
12.	$1,000	17.25%	3 years
13.	$200	$5\frac{1}{2}$%	2 years
14.	$4,000	8%	6 months

Solve.

15. Bill borrowed $90 to buy a tape recorder. He agreed to pay back the loan at 7% interest in 2 years. How much interest must he pay?

16. Joanne's mother loaned her $8,000 for college. Joanne paid back her mother at 5% interest after 4 years. What was the total amount she repaid?

17. Ms. Smith borrowed $4,500 for a new car. The rate of interest was $1\frac{1}{2}$% per month. How much would she pay if the money was borrowed for 6 months?

★ **18.** Mr. Boone charged $200 at a local department store. The rate of interest was $1\frac{1}{2}$% per month. How much interest would he pay if the money was borrowed for 2 months?

Compound Interest

Mr. Chin deposited \$530 in a bank savings account that pays 6% interest per year compounded annually. How much did Mr. Chin have in his account at the end of 2 years?

First year

$i = p \cdot r \cdot t$
$= 530 \cdot 0.06 \cdot 1$
$= 31.80$

new amount $= 530 + 31.80$
$= \$561.80$

Second year

$i = p \cdot r \cdot t$
$= 561.80 \cdot 0.06 \cdot 1$
$= 33.708 \rightarrow 33.71$

new amount $= 561.80 + 33.71$
$= \$595.51$

At the end of 2 years, Mr. Chin had \$595.51 in his account.

A. \$1,000 is deposited in an account that pays 7% interest per year compounded annually.

1. How much interest is earned in 1 year?
2. What amount is in the account at the end of 1 year?
3. The \$1,070 is left in the account for another year. How much interest is earned the second year?
4. What amount is in the account at the end of 2 years?
5. What amount is in the account at the end of 3 years?

B. Interest may be compounded quarterly. This means that the interest is compounded every 3 months, or 4 times a year. Interest may also be compounded semiannually. This means that the interest is compounded every 6 months, or 2 times a year. What amount is in the account at the end of 1 year if the interest rate is 6% per year?

Example \$1,000, compounded semiannually

Six months

$i = p \cdot r \cdot t$
$= 1{,}000 \cdot 0.06 \cdot 0.5$
$= 30$

new amount $= 1{,}000 + 30$
$= \$1{,}030$

One year

$i = p \cdot r \cdot t$
$= 1{,}030 \cdot 0.06 \cdot 0.5$
$= 30.90$

new amount $= 1{,}030 + 30.90$
$= \$1{,}060.90$

6. \$800, compounded semiannually
7. \$250, compounded quarterly

Find the amount at the end of 3 years. The interest rate is 5% per year compounded annually.

1. \$600 **2.** \$900 **3.** \$1,500 **4.** \$6,000

Find the amount at the end of 3 years. The interest rate is $5\frac{1}{4}\%$ per year compounded annually.

5. \$1,000 **6.** \$2,000 **7.** \$3,000 **8.** \$4,000

Find the amount at the end of 1 year. The interest rate is 8% per year compounded semiannually.

9. \$800 **10.** \$1,000 **11.** \$3,000 **12.** \$5,000

Find the amount at the end of 1 year. The interest rate is 7% per year compounded quarterly.

13. \$400 **14.** \$800 **15.** \$1,600 **16.** \$2,400

Solve.

17. Ted deposited \$300 in a bank that pays 6% interest compounded annually. How much will Ted have in his account at the end of 3 years?

18. Ms. Luzinski opened a savings account with \$1,000. The bank pays 5.5% interest compounded semiannually. How much will Ms. Luzinski have in her account at the end of 1 year?

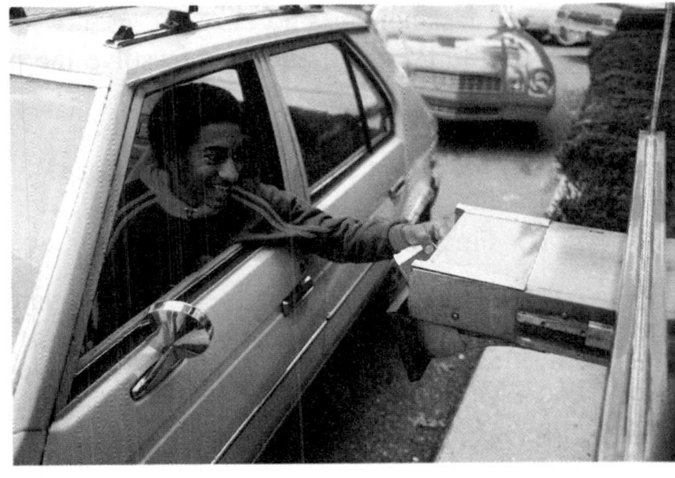

FIND OUT!
Brainteaser

Five friends joined a club. When the club meets, each member shakes the right hand of every other member. How many handshakes take place when the five members hold a club meeting?

Problem Solving

1. Ilga sold $4,000 worth of dental supplies to dentists. Her rate of commission is 9%. How much commission did she receive?
[HINT: commission = rate of commission · sales]

2. Mr. Valenti earns commission at the rate of 40% of his sales. Last week he sold an insurance policy costing $500. What was his commission?

3. Peggy earns a commission of 12% of her total sales of office equipment. Last week she sold $84 worth of office equipment. What was her commission?

4. Mr. Gomez earns 6% commission for selling houses. He sold a house for $64,500. What was his commission?

5. Mr. Spalding receives $100 a week salary plus 4% of all sales over $5,000. Last week he sold $9,000 worth of groceries to supermarkets. How much did he earn last week?

6. Mrs. Janeway receives $50 a week salary plus 7% of total sales above $3,000. Last week her total sales amounted to $4,500. How much did she earn last week?

7. Ms. Soberjeski received $200 in commission. Her rate of commission was 25%. What were her total sales?

8. Pedro received $95 commission last week. His rate of commission is 10%. What were his total sales?

Chapter Review

Write percents.

1. $\frac{10}{100}$ (248) **2.** 0.24 (248) **3.** $\frac{1}{4}$ (250) **4.** 0.047 (252)

Write simplest fractions or whole numbers. (248, 250)

5. 7% **6.** 75% **7.** 300% **8.** $37\frac{1}{2}$%

Write decimals. (248, 252)

9. 9% **10.** 350% **11.** 6.7% **12.** $\frac{1}{2}$% **13.** 0.2%

Compute.

14. 7% of 80 (254)

15. $\frac{1}{2}$% of 60 (254)

16. What percent of 16 is 4? (256)

17. 0.5 is what percent of 50? (256)

18. 75% of what number is 90? (258)

19. 6% of what number is 4.8? (258)

Solve.

20. (264) At a sale a jacket marked $75 was sold at a discount of 30%. What was the sale price of the jacket?

21. (264) A shirt marked $15 was sold for $12 during a sale. What was the rate of discount during the sale?

22. (266) Fred borrowed $800 at 8% annual interest for 2 years. How much interest did he pay for the use of the money?

23. (270) The price for a can of soup was 24¢ last year. This year the same can costs 30¢. What is the percent increase in the cost of the can of soup?

Write a mini-problem. Solve. (262)

24. Jennifer bought a sweater for $12.50 last Friday. On Monday she returned it for a sweater costing $19.75. How much more did she pay?

Solve. (272)

25. Ms. Klein sold $6,500 worth of watchbands. Her rate of commission is 8%. How much commission did she receive?

Chapter Test

Write percents.

1. $\frac{5}{100}$ (248) **2.** 0.42 (248) **3.** $\frac{2}{5}$ (250) **4.** 0.074 (252)

Write simplest fractions or whole numbers. *(248, 250)*

5. 3% **6.** 25% **7.** 400% **8.** $66\frac{2}{3}$%

Write decimals *(248, 252)*

9. 8% **10.** 250% **11.** 7.6% **12.** $\frac{1}{4}$% **13.** 0.7%

Compute.

14. 13% of 70 *(254)*

15. 0.9% of 300 *(254)*

16. What percent of 24 is 18? *(256)*

17. 0.2 is what percent of 50? *(256)*

18. 25% of what number is 60? *(258)*

19. 8% of what number is 7.2? *(258)*

Solve.

20. *(264)* At a sale a dress marked $60 was sold at a discount of 25%. What was the sale price of the dress?

21. *(264)* A tie marked $12 was sold for $10 during a sale. What was the rate of discount during the sale?

22. *(266)* Gwen borrowed $750 at 6% annual interest for 2 years. How much interest did she pay for the use of the money?

23. *(270)* A supermarket sold 300 boxes of tissues last week. This week the supermarket sold 250 boxes of tissues. What is the percent decrease in sale of tissues?

Write a mini-problem. Solve. *(262)*

24. Mr. Sanko bought a set of drinking glasses for $12.95. Some of the glasses were cracked, so he returned them for a set costing $15.25. How much more did he pay?

Solve. *(272)*

25. Miss Lowenthal received $360 in commission. Her rate of commission was 8%. What were her total sales?

Basic Skills Check

1. Soup is selling at 2 cans for 45¢. About how much will 6 cans of soup cost?

A $3.00 B $2.00

C $1.50 D $1.00

2. One year tests showed 23.9, 28.9, 22.3, and 19.7 units of radioactive materials in milk. What was the average number of radioactive units in the milk?

E 23.4 F 23.6

G 23.7 H 24.8

3. Five eggs contain 400 calories. Sue ate 2 eggs for breakfast. How many calories are in 2 eggs?

A 100 calories B 150 calories

C 160 calories D 200 calories

4. What is the area of a square with one side 12 cm?

E 144 cm^2 F 96 cm^2

G 48 cm^2 H 24 cm^2

5. What is the circumference of a circle with a radius of 14 cm? Use 3.14 for π. Round to the nearest whole number.

A 616 cm B 88 cm

C 41 cm D 22 cm

6. To tell the distance between two cities, which unit is used?

E cm F m

G mm H km

7. About how much money was spent on clothing?

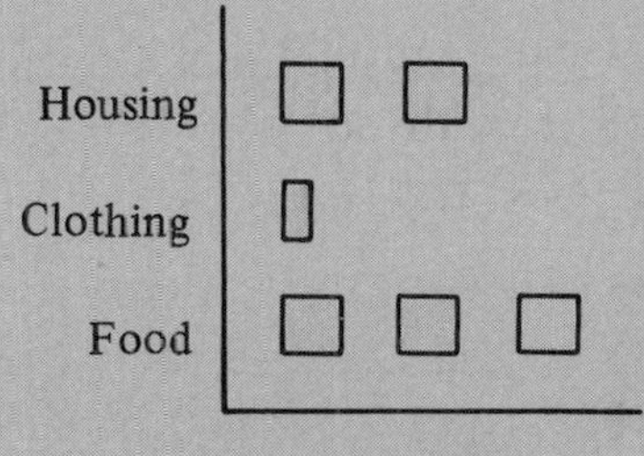

A $100 B $75

C $50 D $25

8. Mr. Jimenez bought 1.5 L of bleach and 750 mL of fabric softener. How much did he buy in all?

E 2.25 mL F 751.5 mL

G 2.25 L H 751.5 L

Integers on the Number Line

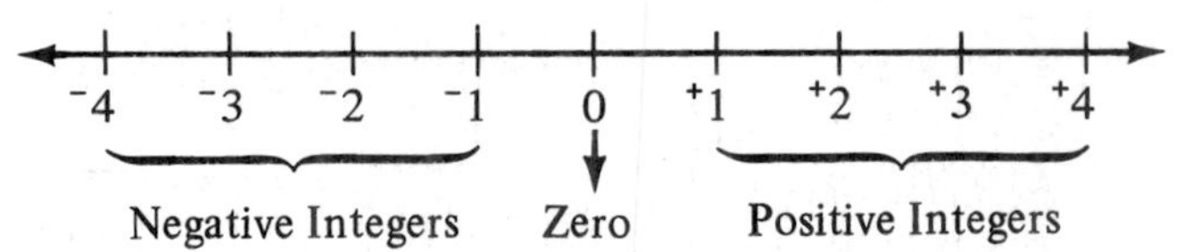

The integers are the numbers . . . , $^{-}5$, $^{-}4$, $^{-}3$, $^{-}2$, $^{-}1$, 0, $^{+}1$, $^{+}2$, $^{+}3$, $^{+}4$, $^{+}5$, . . .

A. $^{+}3$ is read positive three. $^{-}3$ is read negative three. Read these.

1. $^{+}4$ **2.** $^{-}4$ **3.** $^{+}1$ **4.** $^{-}13$ **5.** $^{+}28$

B. Integers can be paired with points on a number line. The point matched with 0 is called the **origin.** A unit of length is marked off to the right and to the left of the origin. The points to the right represent positive integers. The points to the left represent negative integers.

What integers match these points?

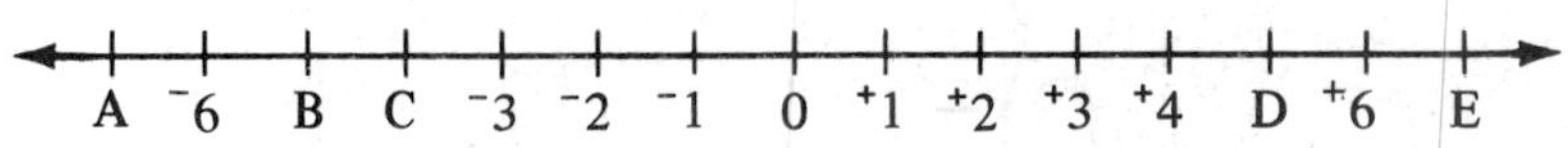

6. *A* **7.** *B* **8.** *C* **9.** *D* **10.** *E*

C. When comparing numbers, the greater of two integers is paired with a point farther to the right on a number line.

Examples $^{-}7 > {}^{-}10$ $^{+}4 > {}^{+}2$ $^{-}3 < {}^{+}1$

Compare. Use > or <.

11. $^{+}3$ ▒ $^{+}1$ **12.** $^{+}2$ ▒ $^{+}5$ **13.** 0 ▒ $^{-}3$ **14.** $^{-}4$ ▒ $^{-}1$

Practice

Compare. Use > or <.

1. $^{+}1$ ▒ $^{+}4$ **2.** $^{+}7$ ▒ $^{+}4$ **3.** $^{-}6$ ▒ $^{-}7$ **4.** $^{+}4$ ▒ 0

5. $^{-}1$ ▒ 0 **6.** $^{-}4$ ▒ $^{-}2$ **7.** $^{+}3$ ▒ $^{-}7$ **8.** $^{-}6$ ▒ $^{-}8$

CHAPTER 11
INTEGERS

Dallas, Texas
32° North Latitude ($^{+}32$)

Rio de Janiero
22° South Latitude ($^{-}22$)

Mt. McKinley
$^{+}6,194$ m
Above Sea Level
$^{-}52$° C

Death Valley
$^{-}86$ m
Below Sea Level
$^{+}52$° C

Opposites and Absolute Value

A. Perform the following experiment.

1. Draw a number line.

2. Fold the paper vertically through the origin, 0.

3. Where does the point $^{-}1$ fall?

4. Where does the point $^{+}4$ fall?

▶ $^{-}1$ and $^{+}1$ are called **opposites.** $^{+}4$ and $^{-}4$ are opposites. Their points are on opposite sides of the origin and each point is the same distance from the origin.

B. Give the opposites.

5. $^{+}6$ **6.** $^{-}7$ **7.** $^{+}15$ **8.** $^{-}11$ **9.** $^{-}43$ **10.** $^{+}73$

▶ The **absolute value** of an integer is the number or its opposite, whichever is positive.

C. $|^{-}4|$ is read absolute value of negative 4. It is equal to positive 4.

11. What is $|^{-}5|$?

12. What is $|^{+}5|$?

D. Find the absolute value.

13. $|^{-}9|$ **14.** $|^{+}7|$ **15.** $|^{-}21|$ **16.** $|^{+}16|$ **17.** $|^{+}37|$ **18.** $|^{-}86|$

E. Compare. Use >, <, or =.

19. $|^{+}5|$ ≣ $|^{-}6|$ **20.** $|^{-}15|$ ≣ $|^{+}11|$ **21.** $|^{-}22|$ ≣ $|^{+}22|$

Practice

Give the opposites.

1. $^{+}3$ 2. $^{-}9$ 3. $^{+}8$ 4. $^{+}7$ 5. $^{-}6$ 6. 0

7. $^{-}14$ 8. $^{+}27$ 9. $^{+}56$ 10. $^{-}83$ 11. $^{-}124$ 12. $^{+}253$

Find the absolute value.

13. $|^{+}8|$ 14. $|^{-}3|$ 15. $|^{-}5|$ 16. $|^{+}2|$ 17. $|^{+}9|$

18. $|0|$ 19. $|^{-}15|$ 20. $|^{+}11|$ 21. $|^{-}26|$ 22. $|^{-}52|$

23. $|^{+}86|$ 24. $|^{-}75|$ 25. $|^{+}37|$ 26. $|^{-}248|$ 27. $|^{+}374|$

Compare. Use $>$, $<$, or $=$.

28. $|^{+}4|$ ≡ $|^{-}2|$ 29. $|^{-}8|$ ≡ $|^{+}7|$ 30. $|^{+}9|$ ≡ $|^{+}15|$ 31. $|^{-}4|$ ≡ $|^{-}10|$

32. $|^{-}6|$ ≡ $|^{+}9|$ 33. $|^{+}10|$ ≡ $|^{-}18|$ 34. $|^{-}12|$ ≡ $|^{+}6|$ 35. $|^{+}13|$ ≡ $|^{-}14|$

36. $|^{+}25|$ ≡ $|^{-}25|$ 37. $|^{-}13|$ ≡ $|^{-}15|$ 38. $|^{+}18|$ ≡ $|^{-}16|$ 39. $|^{-}9|$ ≡ $|^{+}6|$

40. $|^{-}11|$ ≡ $|^{+}8|$ 41. $|^{+}20|$ ≡ $|^{-}16|$ 42. $|^{-}12|$ ≡ $|^{-}9|$ 43. $|^{-}7|$ ≡ $|^{-}9|$

★ The equation $|n| = {}^{+}2$ has two solutions, $^{+}2$ and $^{-}2$, since $|^{+}2| = {}^{+}2$ and $|^{-}2| = {}^{+}2$. Find the solutions.

44. $|n| = {}^{+}5$ 45. $|n| = {}^{+}6$ 46. $|n| = 0$ 47. $|n| = {}^{+}18$

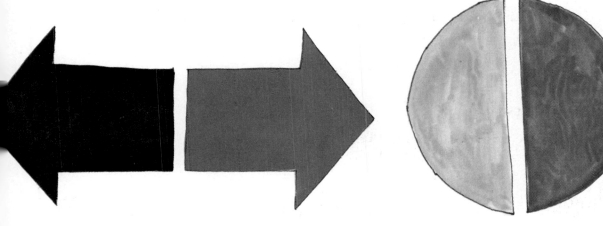

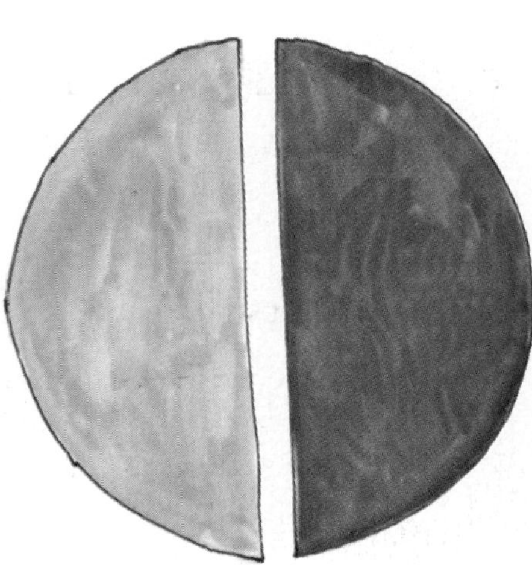

Adding Integers

To add $^{+}2 + {}^{+}3$:

Start at 0.

Move 2 units to the right.

From $^{+}2$, move 3 units to the right.

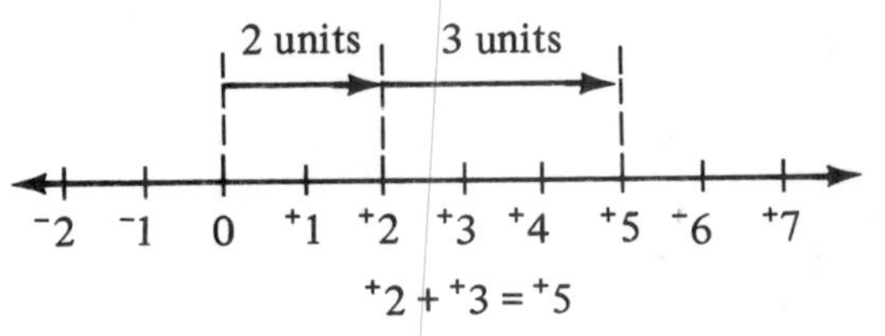

▶ The sum of two positive integers is a positive integer.

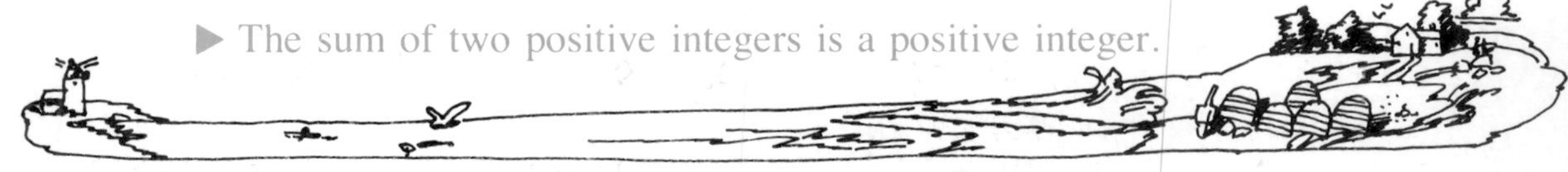

A. Add. Use a number line.

1. $^{+}3 + {}^{+}1$ **2.** $^{+}2 + {}^{+}5$ **3.** $0 + {}^{+}3$ **4.** $^{+}4 + {}^{+}2$

B. Add.

5. $^{+}36 + {}^{+}51$ **6.** $^{+}24 + {}^{+}17$ **7.** $^{+}31 + {}^{+}41$ **8.** $^{+}16 + {}^{+}15$

Here is how to find the sum of 2 negative numbers.

Add $^{-}3 + {}^{-}4$.

Start at 0.

Move 3 units to the left.

From $^{-}3$, move 4 units to the left.

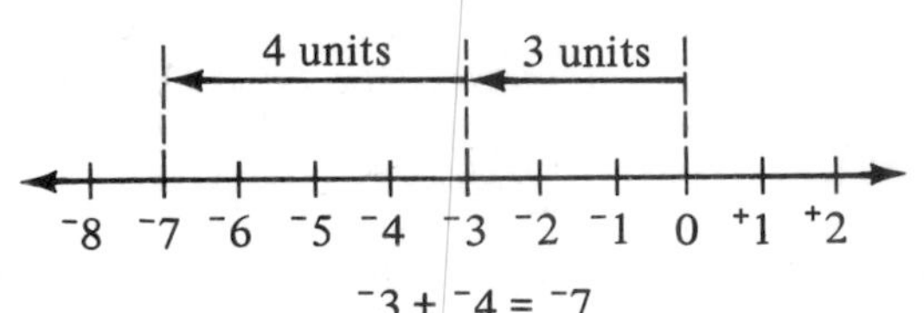

▶ The sum of two negative integers is a negative integer.

C. Add. Use a number line.

9. $^{-}2 + {}^{-}2$ **10.** $^{-}1 + {}^{-}5$ **11.** $0 + {}^{-}4$ **12.** $^{-}2 + {}^{-}4$

D. Add.

13. $^{-}16 + {}^{-}13$ **14.** $^{+}35 + {}^{+}47$ **15.** $^{-}22 + {}^{-}34$ **16.** $^{+}56 + {}^{+}17$

17. $^{+}7 + {}^{+}8 + {}^{+}9$ **18.** $^{+}11 + {}^{+}24 + {}^{+}9$ **19.** $^{-}12 + {}^{-}43 + {}^{-}24$

Practice

Add.

1. $^{+}2 + ^{+}1$
2. $^{+}3 + ^{+}2$
3. $^{+}6 + ^{+}2$
4. $^{+}3 + ^{+}7$
5. $^{+}8 + ^{+}3$
6. $^{+}4 + ^{+}8$
7. $^{+}7 + ^{+}6$
8. $^{+}8 + ^{+}9$
9. $^{-}2 + ^{-}1$
10. $^{-}3 + ^{-}2$
11. $^{-}1 + ^{-}4$
12. $^{-}7 + ^{-}3$
13. $^{-}3 + ^{-}8$
14. $^{-}4 + ^{-}7$
15. $^{-}9 + ^{-}8$
16. $^{-}5 + ^{-}5$
17. $^{+}10 + ^{+}12$
18. $^{+}19 + ^{+}21$
19. $^{+}21 + ^{+}31$
20. $^{+}24 + ^{+}31$
21. $^{+}41 + ^{+}53$
22. $^{+}32 + ^{+}49$
23. $^{+}56 + ^{+}29$
24. $^{+}20 + ^{+}86$
25. $^{-}22 + ^{-}14$
26. $^{-}24 + ^{-}15$
27. $^{-}15 + ^{-}29$
28. $^{-}32 + ^{-}24$
29. $^{-}27 + ^{-}38$
30. $^{-}62 + ^{-}14$
31. $^{-}74 + ^{-}18$
32. $^{-}65 + ^{-}19$
33. $^{-}4 + ^{-}9$
34. $^{-}6 + ^{-}7$
35. $^{+}15 + ^{+}6$
36. $^{+}26 + ^{+}7$
37. $^{-}12 + ^{-}21$
38. $^{+}35 + ^{+}43$
39. $^{-}46 + ^{-}37$
40. $^{+}38 + ^{+}77$
41. $\begin{array}{r} ^{+}3 \\ +\ ^{+}2 \\ \hline \end{array}$
42. $\begin{array}{r} ^{+}3 \\ +\ ^{+}4 \\ \hline \end{array}$
43. $\begin{array}{r} ^{+}6 \\ +\ ^{+}5 \\ \hline \end{array}$
44. $\begin{array}{r} ^{+}8 \\ +\ ^{+}9 \\ \hline \end{array}$
45. $\begin{array}{r} ^{+}57 \\ +\ ^{+}29 \\ \hline \end{array}$
46. $\begin{array}{r} ^{+}64 \\ +\ ^{+}37 \\ \hline \end{array}$
47. $\begin{array}{r} ^{+}81 \\ +\ ^{+}29 \\ \hline \end{array}$
48. $\begin{array}{r} ^{+}46 \\ +\ ^{+}28 \\ \hline \end{array}$
49. $\begin{array}{r} ^{-}34 \\ +\ ^{-}17 \\ \hline \end{array}$
50. $\begin{array}{r} ^{-}64 \\ +\ ^{-}29 \\ \hline \end{array}$
51. $\begin{array}{r} ^{-}64 \\ +\ ^{-}59 \\ \hline \end{array}$
52. $\begin{array}{r} ^{-}67 \\ +\ ^{-}74 \\ \hline \end{array}$
53. $^{+}2 + ^{+}6 + ^{+}7$
54. $^{+}29 + ^{+}17 + ^{+}8$
55. $^{-}3 + ^{-}4 + ^{-}5$
56. $^{-}17 + ^{-}3 + ^{-}5$

Solve.

57. In Maine the average temperature was $^{+}5°C$ on Monday. The average temperature on Tuesday was 8° higher. What was the average temperature on Tuesday?

Adding Positive and Negative Integers

To add ${}^{+}3 + {}^{-}2$:

Start at 0.

Move 3 units to the right.

From ${}^{+}3$, move 2 units to the left.

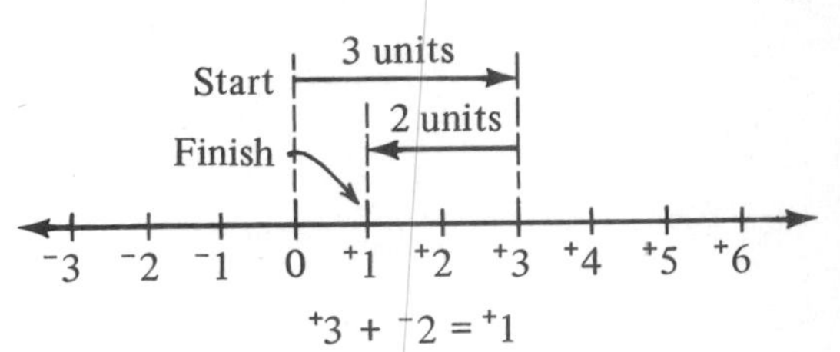

VOLUME ISSUES UP UNCH ISSUES OFF S & P INDUSTRIALS RAILS UTILITIES COMPOSITE
7.0000 866 320 204 +939 +268 +021 +281

A. To add ${}^{-}5 + {}^{+}2$:

1. Draw a number line from ${}^{-}5$ to ${}^{+}5$.
2. Start at 0. Show ${}^{-}5$ by a move on the number line.
3. From ${}^{-}5$, move ${}^{+}2$ units or 2 units to the right.
4. The sum ${}^{-}5 + {}^{+}2 =$ __?__.

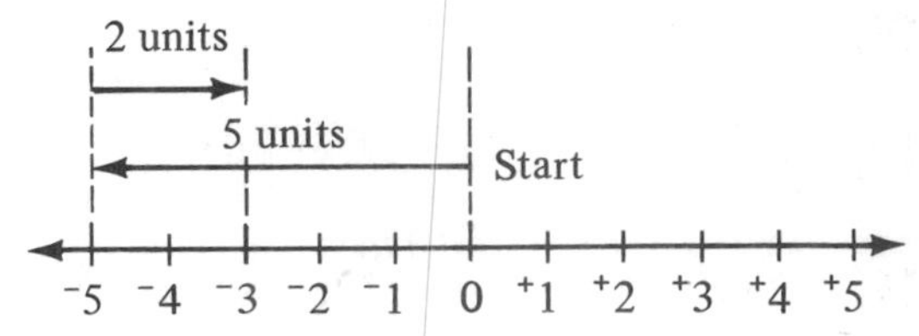

B. Add. Use a number line.

5. ${}^{+}4 + {}^{-}3$ **6.** ${}^{+}4 + {}^{-}7$ **7.** ${}^{-}3 + {}^{+}5$

> Notice a pattern for adding positive and negative integers.
>
> ${}^{+}3 + {}^{-}2 = {}^{+}1$ The greater move, ${}^{+}3$, is in the positive direction. This is the difference of the number of units moved. $3 - 2 = 1$
>
> ${}^{+}2 + {}^{-}5 = {}^{-}3$ The greater move, ${}^{-}5$, is in the negative direction. This is the difference of the number of units moved. $5 - 2 = 3$

C. Add ${}^{+}17 + {}^{-}9$.

8. Is the greater move in a positive or negative direction?

9. Find the difference of the number of units moved, $17 - 9$.

10. Complete. ${}^{+}17 + {}^{-}9 =$ __?__

D. Add.

11. ${}^{+}5 + {}^{-}1$ **12.** ${}^{-}7 + {}^{+}4$ **13.** ${}^{+}3 + {}^{-}18$ **14.** ${}^{-}3 + {}^{-}4 + {}^{-}5$

E. Add to find the sum of opposites.

15. $^{+}1 + ^{-}1$ **16.** $^{-}2 + ^{+}2$ **17.** $^{+}4 + ^{-}4$ **18.** $^{-}5 + ^{+}5$

▶ The sum of opposites is zero.

Practice

Add.

1. $^{+}5 + ^{-}1$ **2.** $^{+}4 + ^{-}5$ **3.** $^{+}1 + ^{-}5$

4. $^{+}23 + ^{-}12$ **5.** $^{+}44 + ^{-}27$ **6.** $^{+}63 + ^{-}55$

7. $^{+}43 + ^{-}51$ **8.** $^{+}65 + ^{-}61$ **9.** $^{+}84 + ^{-}93$

10. $^{-}2 + ^{+}5$ **11.** $^{-}3 + ^{+}8$ **12.** $^{-}1 + ^{+}4$

13. $^{-}65 + ^{+}11$ **14.** $^{-}94 + ^{+}13$ **15.** $^{-}73 + ^{+}86$

16. $^{-}21 + ^{+}15$ **17.** $^{-}15 + ^{+}16$ **18.** $^{-}12 + ^{+}14$

19. $^{+}13 + ^{-}7$ **20.** $^{+}15 + ^{-}11$ **21.** $^{-}19 + ^{+}14$

22. $^{+}17 + ^{-}24$ **23.** $^{-}21 + ^{+}16$ **24.** $^{-}19 + ^{+}26$

25. $\begin{array}{r} ^{+}3 \\ + \; ^{-}1 \\ \hline \end{array}$ **26.** $\begin{array}{r} ^{-}7 \\ + \; ^{+}4 \\ \hline \end{array}$ **27.** $\begin{array}{r} ^{-}8 \\ + \; ^{+}9 \\ \hline \end{array}$ **28.** $\begin{array}{r} ^{+}6 \\ + \; ^{-}2 \\ \hline \end{array}$

29. $\begin{array}{r} ^{+}24 \\ + \; ^{-}19 \\ \hline \end{array}$ **30.** $\begin{array}{r} ^{-}18 \\ + \; ^{+}12 \\ \hline \end{array}$ **31.** $\begin{array}{r} ^{-}25 \\ + \; ^{+}19 \\ \hline \end{array}$ **32.** $\begin{array}{r} ^{+}34 \\ + \; ^{-}51 \\ \hline \end{array}$

33. $^{-}1 + ^{+}2 + ^{+}3$ **34.** $^{-}8 + ^{+}14 + ^{-}3$ **35.** $^{-}2 + ^{+}3 + ^{-}4$

36. $^{+}7 + ^{-}7 + ^{+}3$ **37.** $^{+}5 + ^{+}7 + ^{-}3$ **38.** $^{-}3 + ^{-}8 + ^{+}5$

★ **39.** $^{+}3 + ^{-}9 + ^{+}2 + ^{+}3$ ★ **40.** $^{-}6 + ^{+}4 + ^{+}1 + ^{+}5$

Solve.

41. One week the price of a stock went up \$2, then down \$3, and then up \$4. What was the net change in the price of the stock?

Subtracting Integers

Examine these related subtraction and addition sentences.

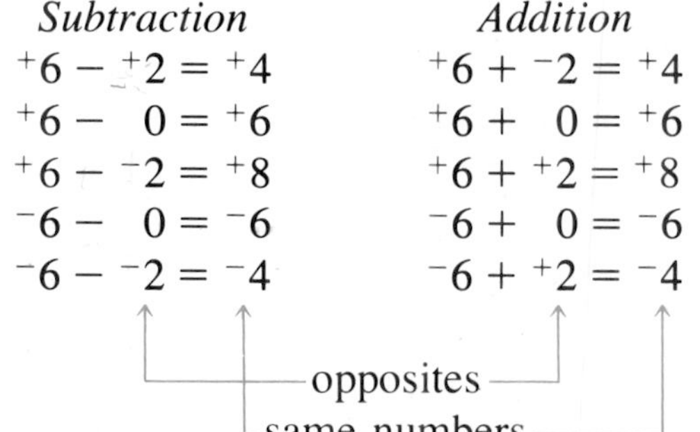

Subtraction	*Addition*
$^{+}6 - {}^{+}2 = {}^{+}4$	$^{+}6 + {}^{-}2 = {}^{+}4$
$^{+}6 - 0 = {}^{+}6$	$^{+}6 + 0 = {}^{+}6$
$^{+}6 - {}^{-}2 = {}^{+}8$	$^{+}6 + {}^{+}2 = {}^{+}8$
$^{-}6 - 0 = {}^{-}6$	$^{-}6 + 0 = {}^{-}6$
$^{-}6 - {}^{-}2 = {}^{-}4$	$^{-}6 + {}^{+}2 = {}^{-}4$

▶ To subtract an integer, add its opposite.

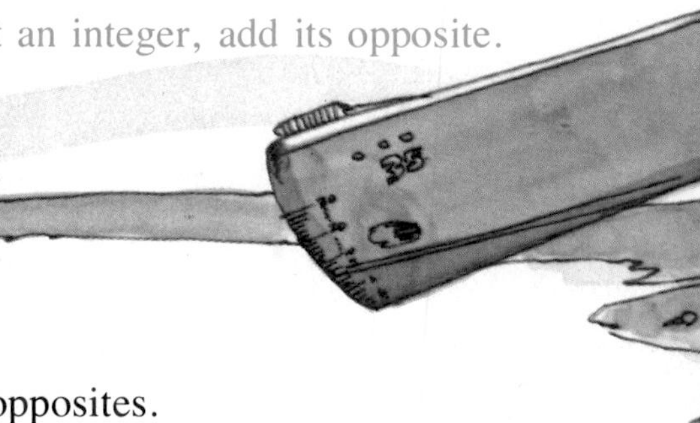

A. Give the opposites.

1. $^{+}6$ **2.** $^{-}14$ **3.** $^{-}3$

B. Subtract $^{+}7 - {}^{+}3$.

4. What is the opposite of $^{+}3$?

5. Complete. $^{+}7 - {}^{+}3 = {}^{+}7 +$ __?__

6. Add $^{+}7 + {}^{-}3$.

7. What is $^{+}7 - {}^{+}3$?

Subtract.

8. $^{+}9 - {}^{+}1$ **9.** $^{+}4 - {}^{+}9$ **10.** $^{+}6 - {}^{+}14$ **11.** $^{+}15 - {}^{+}8$

C. Subtract $^{+}9 - {}^{-}2$.

12. What is the opposite of $^{-}2$?

13. Complete. $^{+}9 - {}^{-}2 = {}^{+}9 +$ __?__

14. Add $^{+}9 + {}^{+}2$.

15. What is $^{+}9 - {}^{-}2$?

Subtract.

16. $^{+}8 - {}^{-}3$ **17.** $^{-}8 - {}^{-}4$ **18.** $^{-}7 - {}^{-}14$ **19.** $^{-}6 - {}^{+}9$

Practice

Subtract.

1. $^{+}8 - ^{+}3$ **2.** $^{-}4 - ^{+}1$ **3.** $^{+}6 - ^{+}2$ **4.** $^{+}8 - ^{+}6$

5. $^{+}14 - ^{+}9$ **6.** $^{+}16 - ^{+}3$ **7.** $^{+}14 - ^{+}81$ **8.** $^{+}92 - ^{+}54$

9. $^{+}36 - ^{+}62$ **10.** $^{+}27 - ^{+}58$ **11.** $^{+}76 - ^{+}14$ **12.** $^{+}36 - ^{+}10$

13. $^{+}6 - ^{-}1$ **14.** $^{+}4 - ^{-}3$ **15.** $^{+}8 - ^{-}4$ **16.** $^{+}7 - ^{-}3$

17. $^{+}14 - ^{-}3$ **18.** $^{+}16 - ^{-}7$ **19.** $^{+}18 - ^{-}96$ **20.** $^{+}57 - ^{-}38$

21. $^{+}51 - ^{-}88$ **22.** $^{+}79 - ^{-}10$ **23.** $^{+}64 - ^{-}80$ **24.** $^{+}32 - ^{-}26$

25. $^{-}4 - ^{+}1$ **26.** $^{-}8 - ^{+}5$ **27.** $^{-}7 - ^{+}6$ **28.** $^{-}8 - ^{+}2$

29. $^{-}41 - ^{+}28$ **30.** $^{-}91 - ^{+}76$ **31.** $^{-}82 - ^{+}44$ **32.** $^{-}92 - ^{+}37$

33. $^{-}12 - ^{+}81$ **34.** $^{-}17 - ^{+}32$ **35.** $^{-}24 - ^{+}78$ **36.** $^{-}41 - ^{+}20$

37. $^{-}5 - ^{-}8$ **38.** $^{-}3 - ^{-}7$ **39.** $^{-}4 - ^{-}6$ **40.** $^{-}3 - ^{-}4$

41. $^{-}8 - ^{-}92$ **42.** $^{-}16 - ^{-}20$ **43.** $^{-}81 - ^{-}31$ **44.** $^{-}71 - ^{-}29$

45. $^{-}81 - ^{-}31$ **46.** $^{-}42 - ^{-}17$ **47.** $^{-}86 - ^{-}52$ **48.** $^{-}30 - ^{-}45$

49. $^{-}71 - ^{-}12$ **50.** $^{-}14 - ^{+}92$ **51.** $^{+}16 - ^{-}78$ **52.** $^{-}36 - ^{-}54$

53. $^{-}3 - ^{+}8$ **54.** $^{+}41 - ^{-}92$ **55.** $^{+}16 - ^{+}14$ **56.** $^{-}58 - ^{-}82$

Solve.

57. A submarine 85 m below sea level fires a rocket, which rises 215 m. How far above sea level is the rocket?

★ Simplify.

58. $^{+}6 + ^{-}5 - ^{-}4 - ^{-}2 - ^{-}3$ **59.** $^{-}3 + ^{-}5 - ^{+}2 - ^{-}1 - ^{-}5$

Using Absolute Value to Add Integers

Here's a way to use absolute value when adding integers.

Use these steps to add 2 integers with the same signs.

Step 1 Find the sum of the absolute values of the integers.
Step 2 Use the sign of the integer with the greater absolute value.

Examples

	$^{+}5 + {}^{\oplus}7$		$^{-}6 + {}^{\ominus}9$
Step 1	$\lvert ^{+}5 \rvert + \lvert ^{+}7 \rvert$	**Step 1**	$\lvert ^{-}6 \rvert + \lvert ^{-}9 \rvert$
Step 2	$^{+}12$	**Step 2**	$^{-}15$

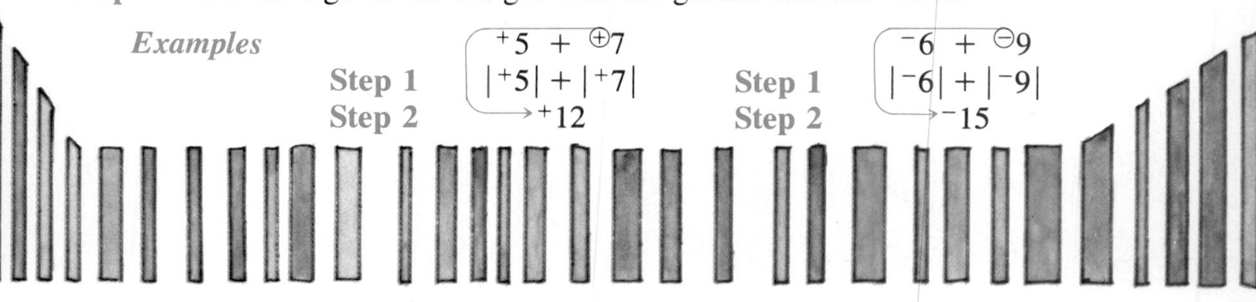

A. Add.

1. $^{+}8 + {}^{+}3$ **2.** $^{+}4 + {}^{+}9$ **3.** $^{-}7 + {}^{-}6$ **4.** $^{-}5 + {}^{-}5$

Use these steps to add 2 integers with different signs.

Step 1 Find the difference of the absolute values of the integers.
Step 2 Use the sign of the integer with the greater absolute value.

Examples

	${}^{\oplus}17 + {}^{-}9$		${}^{\ominus}15 + {}^{+}8$
Step 1	$\lvert ^{+}17 \rvert - \lvert ^{-}9 \rvert$	**Step 1**	$\lvert ^{-}15 \rvert - \lvert ^{+}8 \rvert$
Step 2	$^{+}8$	**Step 2**	$^{-}7$

B. Add.

5. $^{+}11 + {}^{-}3$ **6.** $^{+}9 + {}^{-}12$ **7.** $^{-}6 + {}^{+}10$ **8.** $^{-}14 + {}^{+}7$

Practice

Add.

1. $^{+}6 + {}^{+}2$ **2.** $^{+}9 + {}^{+}9$ **3.** $^{-}8 + {}^{-}4$ **4.** $^{-}10 + {}^{-}7$

5. $^{+}8 + {}^{-}5$ **6.** $^{+}6 + {}^{-}12$ **7.** $^{-}4 + {}^{+}13$ **8.** $^{-}15 + {}^{+}12$

9. $^{+}4 + {}^{+}7 + {}^{+}5$ **10.** $^{-}3 + {}^{-}8 + {}^{-}2$ **11.** $^{+}9 + {}^{-}6 + {}^{-}5$

Mid-Chapter Review

Compare. Use >, <, or =. *(276, 278)*

1. $^{+}2$ ▒ $^{+}6$ **2.** $^{-}9$ ▒ $^{-}5$ **3.** $^{-}4$ ▒ $^{+}5$ **4.** $^{+}3$ ▒ $^{-}8$

5. $|^{+}4|$ ▒ $|^{-}7|$ **6.** $|^{-}3|$ ▒ $|^{+}5|$ **7.** $|^{+}8|$ ▒ $|^{-}8|$ **8.** $|^{-}3|$ ▒ $|0|$

Add. *(280, 282)*

9. $^{+}7 + {}^{+}8$ **10.** $^{-}4 + {}^{-}6$ **11.** $^{-}8 + {}^{-}9$ **12.** $^{-}7 + {}^{-}4$

13. $^{-}7 + {}^{+}9$ **14.** $^{+}5 + {}^{-}1$ **15.** $^{-}6 + {}^{+}3$ **16.** $^{+}4 + {}^{-}8$

17. $^{+}4 + {}^{-}4$ **18.** $^{-}12 + {}^{+}12$ **19.** $^{-}2 + {}^{-}3$ **20.** $^{-}6 + {}^{-}4$

21. $^{+}6 + {}^{+}2 + {}^{+}4$ **22.** $^{-}3 + {}^{-}2 + {}^{-}9$ **23.** $^{+}5 + {}^{-}7 + {}^{+}8$ **24.** $^{-}10 + {}^{-}4 + {}^{+}7$

Subtract. *(284)*

25. $^{+}7 - {}^{+}3$ **26.** $^{+}6 - {}^{+}8$ **27.** $^{+}7 - {}^{-}1$ **28.** $^{+}9 - {}^{-}7$

29. $^{+}5 - {}^{-}8$ **30.** $^{-}3 - {}^{-}4$ **31.** $^{-}4 - {}^{-}9$ **32.** $^{-}8 - {}^{-}3$

33. $^{-}4 - {}^{+}6$ **34.** $^{-}5 - {}^{+}1$ **35.** $^{-}4 - {}^{-}4$ **36.** $^{+}5 - {}^{-}5$

FIND OUT!

Brainteasers

1. Use only the numbers 1, 3, 9, and 27 with addition and subtraction to name the numbers from 1 to 25. Each number may be used at most once.

Example $20 = 27 - 9 + 3 - 1$

2. Use only prime numbers with addition to name the positive even integers from 4 to 50.

Example $24 = 11 + 13$

3. Use only the numbers 3, 4, 5, 6, and 7 with addition and multiplication to name the number 100.

Problem Solving: Circle Graphs

Jennifer interviewed 60 people. She asked each of them which of 3 television programs was his or her favorite. The results are shown by the circle graph.

The entire graph represents 100%, or all 60 choices.

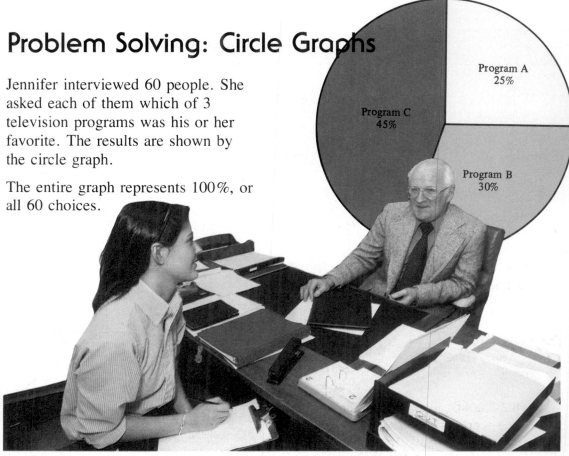

Program A
25%

Program B
30%

Program C
45%

A. Look at the graph above and answer these questions.

1. Which program was selected as the favorite by the people?

2. What percent of the people selected Program A?

3. How many people selected Program A?
Complete. 25% of 60 = __?__

4. How many people selected Program B?

5. How many people selected Program C?

B. There are 400 workers in Middle Village.

6. What percent of the labor force is represented by the graph?

7. Are most workers union or non-union?

8. How many union workers are there?

9. How many non-union workers are there?

Labor Force in Middle Village

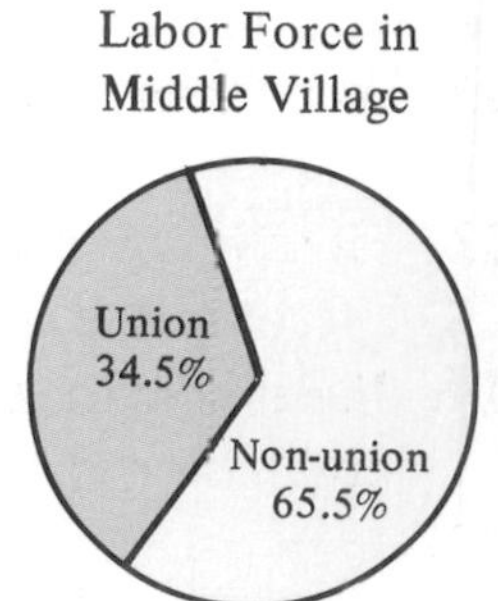

The Alitos' weekly income is $400.

1. What percent of the budget is represented by the graph?
2. What takes up the largest part of the budget?
3. How much is spent on housing?
4. How much is spent on food?
5. How much is spent on each of the other items in the budget?

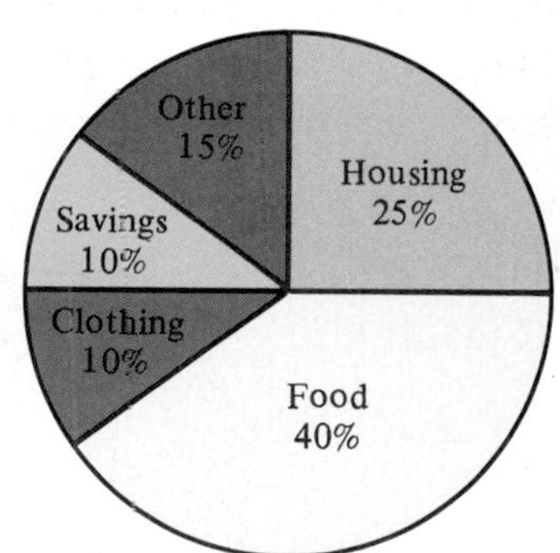

The Field factory employs 1,200 people.

6. Which is the largest group of field employees?
7. What fractional part of the employees are the office workers?
8. How many factory workers are employed?
9. How many supervisors are employed?

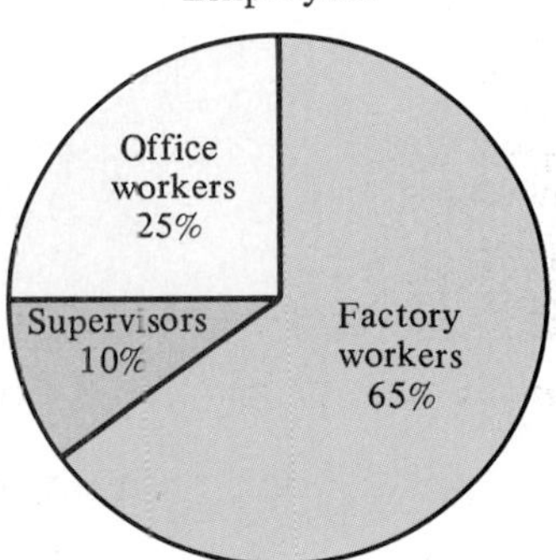

Two thousand high school graduates were asked what they did after graduation.

10. What did most of the high school graduates do?
11. How many went to college?
12. How many went to work?
13. How many could not find jobs?

★ 14. What fractional part of the graduates went to college or are working?

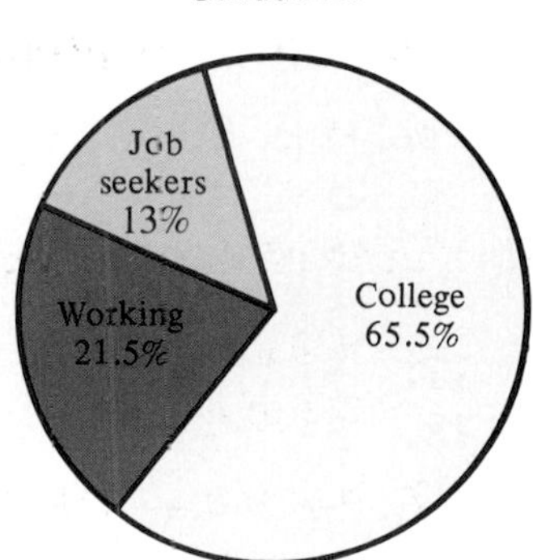

Multiplying Integers

Multiplying whole numbers

$3 \cdot 4 = 12$

$6 \cdot 9 = 54$

Multiplying integers

$^{+}3 \cdot {}^{+}4 = {}^{+}12$

$^{+}6 \cdot {}^{+}9 = {}^{+}54$

▶ The product of two positive integers is a positive integer.

A. Multiply.

1. $^{+}7 \cdot {}^{+}8$ **2.** $^{+}6 \cdot {}^{+}1$ **3.** $^{+}9 \cdot {}^{+}7$ **4.** $^{+}7 \cdot {}^{+}5$

B. Complete. Study the pattern.

$^{+}6 \cdot {}^{+}2 = {}^{+}12$

$^{+}6 \cdot {}^{+}1 = {}^{+}6$

$^{+}6 \cdot 0 = 0$

5. $^{+}6 \cdot {}^{-}1 =$ __?__

6. $^{+}6 \cdot {}^{-}2 =$ __?__

▶ The product of a positive integer and a negative integer is a negative integer.

Multiply.

7. $^{+}7 \cdot 0$ **8.** $^{+}6 \cdot {}^{-}3$ **9.** $^{+}7 \cdot {}^{-}4$ **10.** $^{+}9 \cdot {}^{-}6$

C. Complete.

11. $^{+}6 \cdot {}^{-}3 = {}^{-}18$; $^{-}3 \cdot {}^{+}6 =$ __?__

12. $^{+}4 \cdot {}^{-}5 = {}^{-}20$; $^{-}5 \cdot {}^{+}4 =$ __?__

▶ The product of a negative integer and a positive integer is a negative integer.

Multiply.

13. $^{-}2 \cdot {}^{+}4$ **14.** $^{-}1 \cdot {}^{+}8$ **15.** $^{-}7 \cdot {}^{+}6$ **16.** $^{-}9 \cdot {}^{+}6$

D. Complete. Study the pattern.

$^{-}5 \cdot {}^{+}2 = {}^{-}10$

$^{-}5 \cdot {}^{+}1 = {}^{-}5$

$^{-}5 \cdot 0 = 0$

17. $^{-}5 \cdot {}^{-}1 =$ __?__

18. $^{-}5 \cdot {}^{-}2 =$ __?__

▶ The product of two negative integers is a positive integer.

Multiply.

19. $^{-}3 \cdot {}^{-}9$ **20.** $^{-}4 \cdot {}^{-}8$ **21.** $^{-}7 \cdot {}^{-}9$ **22.** $^{-}8 \cdot {}^{-}7$

Practice

Multiply.

1. $^{+}3 \cdot {}^{-}9$ **2.** $^{+}7 \cdot {}^{+}6$ **3.** $^{+}8 \cdot {}^{+}3$ **4.** $^{+}7 \cdot {}^{+}9$

5. $^{-}6 \cdot {}^{-}7$ **6.** $^{-}4 \cdot {}^{-}5$ **7.** $^{-}8 \cdot {}^{-}9$ **8.** $^{-}6 \cdot {}^{-}4$

9. $^{+}3 \cdot {}^{-}4$ **10.** $^{+}8 \cdot {}^{-}3$ **11.** $^{+}7 \cdot {}^{-}5$ **12.** $^{+}9 \cdot {}^{-}8$

13. $^{-}4 \cdot {}^{+}8$ **14.** $^{-}7 \cdot {}^{+}7$ **15.** $^{-}9 \cdot {}^{+}5$ **16.** $^{-}6 \cdot {}^{+}7$

17. $0 \cdot {}^{+}8$ **18.** $0 \cdot {}^{-}7$ **19.** $^{+}3 \cdot 0$ **20.** $^{-}41 \cdot 0$

21. $^{-}1 \cdot {}^{-}18$ **22.** $^{-}1 \cdot {}^{+}1$ **23.** $^{-}1 \cdot {}^{+}8$ **24.** $^{-}11 \cdot {}^{+}10$

25. $^{+}1 \cdot {}^{+}96$ **26.** $^{+}11 \cdot {}^{-}38$ **27.** $^{+}1 \cdot 0$ **28.** $^{+}1 \cdot {}^{-}1$

29. $^{+}4 \cdot {}^{+}12$ **30.** $^{-}30 \cdot {}^{+}8$ **31.** $^{-}40 \cdot {}^{-}9$ **32.** $^{+}20 \cdot {}^{-}9$

Solve.

33. In the first quarter, the Lions lost 14 yd a minute for the first 4 minutes. What was the net change in yardage?

★ Multiply.

34. $^{+}3 \cdot {}^{+}4 \cdot {}^{-}1$ **35.** $^{-}4 \cdot {}^{-}8 \cdot {}^{-}1$

36. $^{+}2 \cdot {}^{-}3 \cdot {}^{+}4$ **37.** $^{-}4 \cdot {}^{+}2 \cdot {}^{-}8$

38. $^{-}1 \cdot {}^{+}5 \cdot {}^{-}6$ **39.** $^{+}1 \cdot {}^{-}1 \cdot {}^{-}3$

FIND OUT!
Brainteaser

Is this a true or false conclusion? Give reasons.

Given: If a person is 17 years old, the person may obtain a driver's license.
Jeff has a driver's license.

Conclusion: Jeff is 17 years old.

Properties of Integers

A. Complete.

ADDITION PROPERTIES

	Property	Illustration check	Does the property hold? Yes	No
1.	Commutative	$^{+}7 + {}^{-}6 = {}^{-}6 + {}^{+}7$	?	?
2.	Associative	$({}^{+}3 + {}^{-}2) + {}^{-}4 = {}^{+}3 + ({}^{-}2 + {}^{-}4)$	?	?
3.	of Zero	${}^{-}7 + 0 = {}^{-}7$	?	?
4.	Opposite or Inverse	${}^{-}6 + {}^{+}6 = 0$	?	?

MULTIPLICATION PROPERTIES

	Property	Illustration check	Does the property hold? Yes	No
5.	Commutative	${}^{-}3 \cdot {}^{+}4 = {}^{+}4 \cdot {}^{-}3$	?	?
6.	Associative	$({}^{-}3 \cdot {}^{-}4) \cdot {}^{+}2 = {}^{-}3 \cdot ({}^{-}4 \cdot {}^{+}2)$	?	?
7.	of One	${}^{-}3 \cdot {}^{+}1 = {}^{-}3$	?	?
8.	Distributive	${}^{+}2 \cdot ({}^{-}3 + {}^{+}4) = ({}^{+}2 \cdot {}^{-}3) + ({}^{+}2 \cdot {}^{+}4)$	?	?
9.	of Zero	${}^{-}4 \cdot 0 = 0$	?	?

Practice

Solve. Then name the properties shown.

1. $({}^{-}1 + {}^{-}1) + {}^{-}3 = n + ({}^{-}1 + {}^{-}3)$

2. ${}^{+}7 + n = {}^{+}9 + {}^{+}7$

3. $n + {}^{-}3 = {}^{-}3$

4. ${}^{+}5 + {}^{-}5 = n$

5. ${}^{+}6 \cdot {}^{+}2 = {}^{+}2 \cdot n$

6. ${}^{-}8 \cdot {}^{+}1 = n$

7. $({}^{+}4 \cdot {}^{-}1) \cdot {}^{-}3 = n \cdot ({}^{-}1 \cdot {}^{-}3)$

8. ${}^{-}3 \cdot ({}^{+}7 + {}^{-}5) = ({}^{-}3 \cdot {}^{+}7) + ({}^{-}3 \cdot n)$

9. ${}^{+}7 \cdot n = 0$

Keeping Fit

Compare. Use $>$, $<$, or $=$.

1. $\frac{3}{8} \equiv \frac{7}{8}$
2. $\frac{3}{5} \equiv \frac{12}{20}$
3. $\frac{3}{4} \equiv \frac{5}{6}$

Simplify.

4. $\frac{6}{10}$
5. $\frac{12}{21}$
6. $\frac{8}{12}$

Write fractions.

7. $2\frac{3}{4}$
8. $4\frac{1}{2}$
9. $6\frac{2}{3}$
10. $9\frac{3}{7}$
11. $8\frac{3}{10}$

Write mixed numbers.

12. $\frac{7}{4}$
13. $\frac{3}{2}$
14. $\frac{13}{3}$
15. $\frac{26}{5}$
16. $\frac{54}{11}$

Add. Simplify when possible.

17. $\frac{3}{8} + \frac{2}{8}$
18. $\frac{5}{16} + \frac{1}{2}$
19. $\frac{3}{5} + \frac{1}{4}$
20. $\frac{5}{11} + \frac{2}{3}$
21. $\frac{5}{8} + \frac{7}{12}$
22. $2\frac{3}{4} + 1\frac{5}{8}$
23. $3\frac{3}{4} + 2\frac{5}{6}$
24. $7\frac{1}{2} + 8\frac{7}{10}$
25. $7\frac{2}{3} + 3\frac{1}{5}$
26. $16\frac{3}{4} + 2\frac{1}{2}$

Subtract. Simplify when possible

27. $12\frac{7}{8} - 6\frac{1}{8}$
28. $6\frac{3}{4} - 3\frac{3}{5}$
29. $5\frac{1}{3} - 2\frac{3}{4}$
30. $7\frac{4}{5} - 2\frac{1}{2}$
31. $6\frac{2}{5} - 3\frac{9}{10}$
32. $8\frac{1}{3} - 5$
33. $4 - 2\frac{2}{3}$
34. $7 - 3\frac{4}{5}$
35. $8 - 6\frac{1}{8}$

Multiply. Simplify when possible.

36. $\frac{3}{4} \times \frac{1}{5}$
37. $\frac{3}{5} \times \frac{2}{3}$
38. $\frac{3}{4} \times 12$
39. $\frac{7}{8} \times 24$
40. $1\frac{1}{2} \times 6$
41. $1\frac{1}{2} \times 2\frac{3}{4}$
42. $7\frac{2}{3} \times 6$
43. $2\frac{2}{5} \times 4\frac{3}{4}$

Divide. Simplify when possible.

44. $\frac{3}{4} \div \frac{1}{2}$
45. $4 \div 1\frac{1}{2}$
46. $2\frac{2}{3} \div 1\frac{1}{4}$
47. $6 \div \frac{3}{4}$

Dividing Integers

Multiplication and division are related.

Multiplication	Division
$^{+}6 \cdot {}^{+}3 = {}^{+}18$	$^{+}18 \div {}^{+}6 = {}^{+}3; \frac{^{+}18}{^{+}6} = {}^{+}3$
$^{-}5 \cdot {}^{+}4 = {}^{-}20$	$^{-}20 \div {}^{-}5 = {}^{+}4; \frac{^{-}20}{^{-}5} = {}^{+}4$
$^{-}2 \cdot {}^{-}7 = {}^{+}14$	$^{+}14 \div {}^{-}2 = {}^{-}7; \frac{^{+}14}{^{-}2} = {}^{-}7$
$^{+}8 \cdot {}^{-}9 = {}^{-}72$	$^{-}72 \div {}^{+}8 = {}^{-}9; \frac{^{-}72}{^{+}8} = {}^{-}9$

Division Rules for Integers

positive ÷ positive = positive
negative ÷ negative = positive
positive ÷ negative = negative
negative ÷ positive = negative

A. Divide.

1. $^{+}12 \div {}^{+}3$ **2.** $^{+}4 \div {}^{+}1$ **3.** $\frac{^{+}9}{^{+}3}$

4. $^{-}24 \div {}^{-}3$ **5.** $^{-}8 \div {}^{-}1$ **6.** $\frac{^{-}12}{^{-}6}$

7. $^{+}36 \div {}^{-}6$ **8.** $^{+}42 \div {}^{-}7$ **9.** $\frac{^{+}18}{^{-}3}$

10. $^{-}24 \div {}^{+}8$ **11.** $^{-}17 \div {}^{+}1$ **12.** $\frac{^{-}42}{^{+}7}$

B. Complete.

13. $^{+}6 \cdot 0 = 0; 0 \div {}^{+}6 =$ ___?___ ▶ Zero divided by a non-zero integer is zero.

14. $^{-}3 \cdot 0 = 0; 0 \div {}^{-}3 =$ ___?___

15. $0 \cdot$ ___?___ $= {}^{+}3;\ {}^{+}3 \div 0 =$ ___?___ ▶ Division by zero has no answer.

16. $0 \cdot$ ___?___ $= {}^{-}4;\ {}^{-}4 \div 0 =$ ___?___

C. Divide if possible.

17. $0 \div {}^{-}1$ **18.** $^{-}1 \div {}^{+}1$ **19.** $^{+}5 \div 0$ **20.** $\frac{0}{^{+}8}$

Divide.

1. $^{+}8 \div {}^{+}2$
2. $^{+}12 \div {}^{+}6$
3. $^{+}15 \div {}^{+}3$
4. $^{+}20 \div {}^{+}5$
5. $^{+}36 \div {}^{+}6$
6. $^{+}45 \div {}^{+}9$
7. $^{+}50 \div {}^{+}10$
8. $^{+}80 \div {}^{+}16$
9. $^{-}36 \div {}^{-}4$
10. $^{-}36 \div {}^{-}9$
11. $^{-}56 \div {}^{-}7$
12. $^{-}56 \div {}^{-}8$
13. $^{-}27 \div {}^{-}9$
14. $^{-}36 \div {}^{-}3$
15. $^{-}36 \div {}^{-}12$
16. $^{-}64 \div {}^{-}16$
17. $^{+}24 \div {}^{-}3$
18. $^{+}40 \div {}^{-}5$
19. $^{+}72 \div {}^{-}8$
20. $^{+}36 \div {}^{-}4$
21. $^{-}42 \div {}^{+}6$
22. $^{-}28 \div {}^{+}7$
23. $^{-}48 \div {}^{+}6$
24. $^{-}40 \div {}^{+}5$
25. $0 \div {}^{-}3$
26. $0 \div {}^{+}5$
27. $0 \div {}^{-}2$
28. $^{+}9 \div {}^{-}3$
29. $^{+}16 \div {}^{-}4$
30. $^{-}8 \div {}^{+}1$
31. $^{-}30 \div {}^{-}5$
32. $^{+}45 \div {}^{-}9$
33. $^{+}30 \div {}^{-}5$
34. $^{-}63 \div {}^{-}9$
35. $^{-}42 \div {}^{-}3$
36. $^{-}60 \div {}^{-}10$
37. $^{+}80 \div {}^{-}20$
38. $^{-}45 \div {}^{-}15$
39. $^{-}60 \div {}^{+}15$
40. $^{+}80 \div {}^{-}40$
41. $\frac{^{+}18}{^{+}6}$
42. $\frac{^{+}56}{^{+}8}$
43. $\frac{^{+}6}{^{+}6}$
44. $\frac{^{+}55}{^{+}55}$
45. $\frac{^{-}27}{^{-}9}$
46. $\frac{^{-}48}{^{-}8}$
47. $\frac{^{-}24}{^{-}3}$
48. $\frac{^{-}64}{^{-}8}$
49. $\frac{^{+}36}{^{-}4}$
50. $\frac{^{+}40}{^{-}8}$
51. $\frac{^{+}30}{^{-}5}$
52. $\frac{^{+}40}{^{-}10}$
53. $\frac{^{-}21}{^{+}7}$
54. $\frac{^{-}35}{^{+}5}$
55. $\frac{^{-}42}{^{+}6}$
56. $\frac{^{-}42}{^{+}14}$
57. $\frac{0}{^{-}3}$
58. $\frac{0}{^{+}4}$
59. $\frac{0}{^{-}10}$
60. $\frac{^{-}7}{^{-}7}$
61. $\frac{^{+}17}{^{-}17}$
62. $\frac{^{-}56}{^{-}1}$
63. $\frac{^{-}60}{^{+}10}$
64. $\frac{^{-}46}{^{+}23}$

★ Solve.

65. The height of Mount Everest is $^{+}8,848$ m. The height of Lao Shan is $^{+}1,130$ m. About how many times higher is Mount Everest than Lao Shan?

Equations with Integers

Solve and check.

$$x + {}^{+}3 = {}^{+}7$$
$$x + {}^{+}3 - {}^{+}3 = {}^{+}7 - {}^{+}3$$
$$x = {}^{+}4$$

Strategy: You want x alone.
You need to undo ${}^{+}3$ from x.
Use the subtraction property for equations.

Check:

$x + {}^{+}3$	${}^{+}7$
${}^{+}4 + {}^{+}3$	${}^{+}7$
${}^{+}7$	${}^{+}7$

Is ${}^{+}4$ a solution of $x + {}^{+}3 = {}^{+}7$?

Yes, ${}^{+}4$ is the solution of $x + {}^{+}3 = {}^{+}7$.

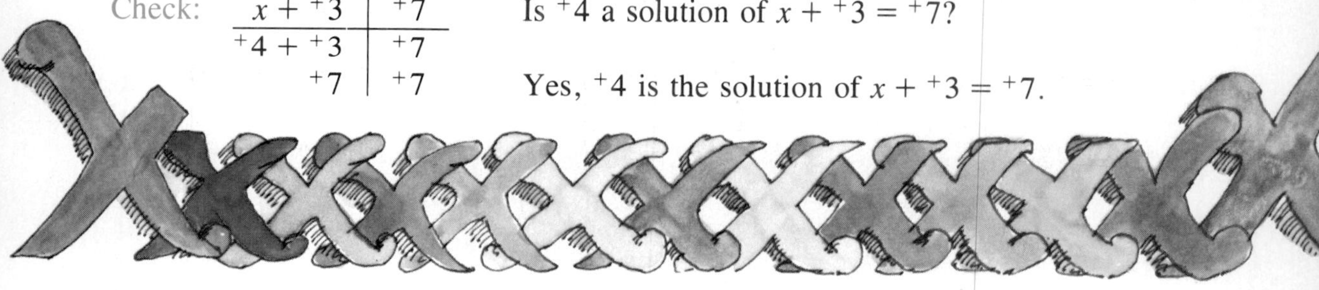

A. Solve and check.

1. $x + {}^{+}4 = {}^{-}3$ **2.** $x - {}^{+}4 = {}^{+}7$ **3.** $x - {}^{-}3 = {}^{-}9$

Solve and check.

$${}^{+}2x = {}^{-}18$$
$$\frac{{}^{+}2x}{{}^{+}2} = \frac{{}^{-}18}{{}^{+}2}$$
$$x = {}^{-}9$$

Strategy: You want x alone.
You need to undo ${}^{+}2$ from x.
Use the division property for equations.
The solution of $x = {}^{-}9$ is ${}^{-}9$.

Check:

${}^{+}2x$	${}^{-}18$
${}^{+}2 \cdot {}^{-}9$	${}^{-}18$
${}^{-}18$	${}^{-}18$

Is ${}^{-}9$ a solution of ${}^{+}2x = {}^{-}18$?

Yes, ${}^{-}9$ is the solution of ${}^{+}2x = {}^{-}18$.

B. Solve and check.

4. ${}^{+}3x = {}^{+}24$ **5.** ${}^{-}5x = {}^{-}40$ **6.** ${}^{-}7x = {}^{+}35$

C. Solve and check. Use the multiplication property for equations.

7. $\frac{x}{{}^{+}3} = {}^{-}7$ **8.** $\frac{x}{{}^{-}4} = {}^{-}8$ **9.** $\frac{x}{{}^{-}9} = {}^{+}6$

D. Solve. Use 2 properties of equations. Check.

10. ${}^{+}3x + {}^{-}3 = {}^{+}9$ **11.** $\frac{x}{{}^{-}2} + {}^{+}1 = {}^{+}3$ **12.** ${}^{-}5x - {}^{-}2 = {}^{-}13$

Practice

Solve and check.

1. $x + {}^{+}7 = {}^{+}9$
2. $x + {}^{+}8 = {}^{+}3$
3. $x + {}^{-}3 = {}^{-}5$
4. $x + {}^{-}1 = {}^{+}7$
5. $x + {}^{-}4 = {}^{-}8$
6. $x - {}^{+}1 = {}^{+}7$
7. $x - {}^{+}3 = {}^{+}1$
8. $x - {}^{-}5 = {}^{-}9$
9. $x - {}^{-}7 = {}^{+}3$
10. ${}^{+}3x = {}^{+}27$
11. ${}^{+}7x = {}^{+}42$
12. ${}^{+}5x = {}^{-}30$
13. ${}^{+}7x = {}^{-}35$
14. ${}^{-}3x = {}^{+}12$
15. ${}^{-}6x = {}^{+}48$
16. ${}^{-}7x = {}^{-}14$
17. ${}^{-}3x = {}^{-}15$
18. $\frac{x}{{}^{+}4} = {}^{+}7$
19. $\frac{x}{{}^{+}9} = {}^{+}6$
20. $\frac{x}{{}^{-}5} = {}^{-}4$
21. $\frac{x}{{}^{+}8} = {}^{-}2$
22. $\frac{x}{{}^{-}3} = {}^{+}8$
23. $\frac{x}{{}^{-}7} = {}^{+}6$
24. $\frac{x}{{}^{-}5} = {}^{-}6$
25. $\frac{x}{{}^{-}8} = {}^{-}8$
26. ${}^{+}2x + {}^{+}4 = {}^{+}12$
27. ${}^{+}3x + {}^{+}7 = {}^{+}19$
28. ${}^{+}3x + {}^{-}3 = {}^{+}12$
29. ${}^{+}4x + {}^{-}8 = {}^{+}4$
30. ${}^{+}4x + {}^{-}8 = {}^{-}20$
31. ${}^{+}7x + {}^{-}2 = {}^{-}23$
32. ${}^{+}3x - {}^{-}5 = {}^{+}23$
33. ${}^{+}2x - {}^{+}1 = {}^{+}1$
34. $\frac{x}{{}^{+}2} + {}^{+}3 = {}^{+}5$
35. $\frac{x}{{}^{+}3} + {}^{+}7 = {}^{+}8$
36. ${}^{+}2x = {}^{+}32$
37. $\frac{x}{{}^{-}3} + {}^{+}4 = {}^{+}6$
38. $\frac{x}{{}^{+}5} = {}^{+}8$
39. $\frac{x}{{}^{-}2} - {}^{+}3 = {}^{-}5$

★ Solve. Replacements for x: ${}^{-}10, {}^{-}9, \ldots, {}^{-}9, {}^{+}10$

40. $x + {}^{+}3 < {}^{+}6$
41. $x + {}^{-}4 > {}^{-}3$
42. ${}^{+}4x > {}^{+}12$
43. ${}^{-}3x > {}^{-}21$
44. ${}^{+}3x + {}^{+}4 > {}^{+}31$
45. ${}^{+}8x + {}^{-}4 > {}^{+}4$

Negative Exponents and Decimals

Examine the pattern for the meaning of negative exponents.

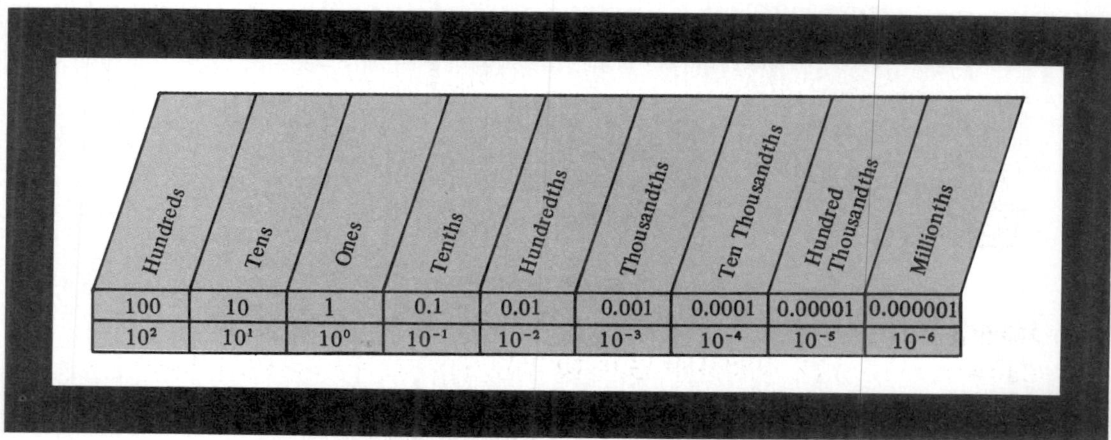

A. Complete.

1. $\frac{1}{10} = 0.1 = 10^{\underline{?}}$ **2.** $\frac{1}{100} = 0.01 = 10^{\underline{?}}$ **3.** $\frac{1}{10{,}000} = 0.0001 = 10^{\underline{?}}$

4. $10^{-1} = 0.1 = \frac{1}{\underline{?}}$ **5.** $10^{-2} = 0.01 = \frac{1}{\underline{?}}$ **6.** $10^{-5} = 0.00001 = \frac{1}{\underline{?}}$

B. Write standard numerals.

7. 10^2 **8.** 10^{-2} **9.** 10^1 **10.** 10^{-1} **11.** 10^6 **12.** 10^{-6}

C. Write in exponential notation.

13. 10 **14.** 0.1 **15.** 1,000 **16.** 0.001 **17.** 100 **18.** 0.01

Practice

Write standard numerals.

1. 10^4 **2.** 10^{-4} **3.** 10^5 **4.** 10^{-5} **5.** 10^3

6. 10^{-3} **7.** 10^{-1} **8.** 10^{-2} **9.** 10^{-6} ★ **10.** 10^{-7}

Write in exponential notation.

11. 1,000 **12.** 0.001 **13.** 100,000 **14.** 0.00001 **15.** 1,000,000

16. 0.000001 **17.** 100 **18.** 10 **19.** 10,000 **20.** 10,000,000

Expanded Numerals with Exponents

Exponents may be used to write numbers in expanded form.

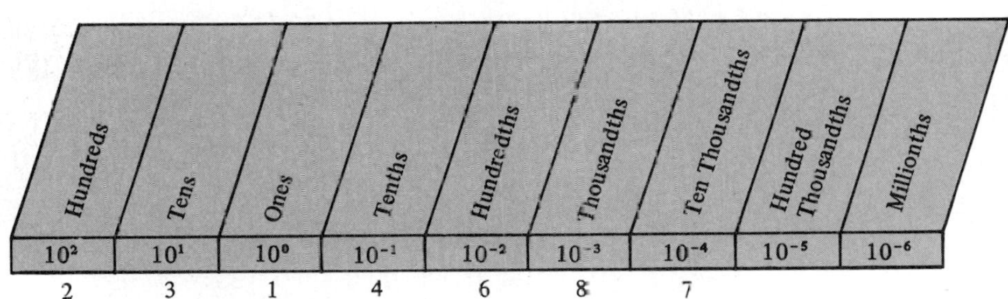

Standard numeral 231.4687 = Expanded numeral using exponents

$$231.4687 = (2 \times 10^2) + (3 \times 10^1) + (1 \times 10^0) + (4 \times 10^{-1}) + (6 \times 10^{-2}) + (8 \times 10^{-3}) + (7 \times 10^{-4})$$

A. Complete for the standard numeral 358.46127.

1. The digit 3 has the value $3 \times 10^{?}$.
2. The digit 4 has the value $4 \times 10^{?}$.
3. The digit 1 has the value $1 \times 10^{?}$.
4. The digit 7 has the value $7 \times 10^{?}$.

B. Write expanded numerals. Use exponents.

5. 3.467
6. 28.5106
7. 374.691802

C. Write standard numerals.

8. $(3 \times 10^2) + (4 \times 10^1) + (6 \times 10^0) + (8 \times 10^{-1}) + (7 \times 10^{-2}) + (8 \times 10^{-3})$
9. $(4 \times 10^3) + (2 \times 10^2) + (0 \times 10^1) + (0 \times 10^0) + (6 \times 10^{-1}) + (3 \times 10^{-2}) + (4 \times 10^{-3})$

Practice

Write expanded numerals. Use exponents.

1. 64.37
2. 5,416.2743
3. 43.61371
4. 151.016341

Write standard numerals.

5. $(6 \times 10^0) + (3 \times 10^{-1}) + (8 \times 10^{-2}) + (7 \times 10^{-3}) + (2 \times 10^{-4})$
6. $(4 \times 10^1) + (0 \times 10^0) + (3 \times 10^{-1}) + (8 \times 10^{-2}) + (9 \times 10^{-3}) + (8 \times 10^{-4})$

Problem Solving • Wholesalers

The job of a wholesaler is to buy items from a manufacturer and then sell them to a retailer or store.

1. A salesperson from the Dale Wholesale Company sold 12 beds to the Most Attractive Furniture Store. The store paid $180 per bed. How much did the store pay for the beds? [HINT: multiply.]

2. The store listed the beds for $450 each and put them on sale at 40% off. Mrs. Rome bought a bed. What was the cost to her?

3. The Stanley Appliance Store paid a wholesale price of $203 for an air conditioner. The store sold it for $298 after a 20% off sale. How much profit did the store make on the air conditioner?

4. Mr. Jackson paid $125 wholesale for a television. He sold it for $200. What was Mr. Jackson's percent of profit on the sale based on the cost of the television?

5. Ms. Klein sold ties to a store at the wholesale price of $50.40 a dozen. The store sold each tie for $7.50. How much did the store make on the dozen ties?

6. Mr. Johnson sold 8 television sets to a store at the wholesale price of $216 each. The storeowner sold the television sets at double the wholesale price. How much did the owner make on the sale of the 8 television sets?

★ 7. Chris sells books wholesale to a bookstore. She sells books marked $8.95 to the store at a 40% discount. If the owner pays for the books within 10 days, he gets a 2% discount. What does the owner pay for a book if payment is made within 10 days?

Chapter Review

Compare. Use >, <, or =. *(276, 278)*

1. $^{+}3 \equiv {}^{-}4$

2. $^{-}6 \equiv {}^{-}1$

3. $|^{+}3| \equiv |^{-}6|$

Add. *(280, 282)*

4. $^{+}6 + {}^{-}8$

5. $^{-}4 + {}^{-}6$

6. $^{+}3 + {}^{-}5$

Subtract. *(284)*

7. $^{+}6 - {}^{+}2$

8. $^{-}6 - {}^{-}4$

9. $^{+}4 - {}^{+}9$

Multiply. *(290)*

10. $^{+}4 \cdot {}^{+}6$

11. $^{-}8 \cdot {}^{-}5$

12. $^{+}8 \cdot {}^{-}6$

Divide. *(294)*

13. $^{+}16 \div {}^{+}4$

14. $^{-}56 \div {}^{-}8$

15. $\frac{^{+}56}{^{-}7}$

Solve. *(296)*

16. $x + {}^{-}6 = {}^{+}8$

17. $\frac{x}{^{-}3} = {}^{-}5$

18. $^{+}2x + {}^{+}3 = {}^{+}27$

Write the exponential notation. *(298)*

19. 10

20. 10,000

21. 0.001

Write expanded numerals. Use exponents. *(299)*

22. 78.21

23. 3,419.102

Solve. *(289, 300)*

24. The Langs' yearly income is $24,000. They spend 30% of it on food. How much do they spend a year on food?

25. Mr. Wong paid a wholesale price of $1,380 for 6 chairs. He sold each of them for $348. How much profit did he make on all the chairs?

Chapter Test

Compare. Use >, <, or =. *(276, 278)*

1. $^{+}4 \equiv {}^{-}5$ **2.** $^{-}5 \equiv {}^{-}2$ **3.** $|{}^{+}6| \equiv |{}^{-}6|$

Add. *(280, 282)*

4. $^{+}6 + {}^{-}3$ **5.** $^{-}8 + {}^{-}5$ **6.** $^{+}6 + {}^{-}8$

Subtract. *(284)*

7. $^{-}3 - {}^{-}7$ **8.** $^{+}8 - {}^{-}3$ **9.** $^{+}3 - {}^{+}8$

Multiply. *(290)*

10. $^{+}3 \cdot {}^{+}8$ **11.** $^{-}9 \cdot {}^{-}6$ **12.** $^{+}7 \cdot {}^{-}8$

Divide. *(294)*

13. $^{+}24 \div {}^{+}3$ **14.** $^{-}56 \div {}^{-}7$ **15.** $\frac{0}{^{-}5}$

Solve. *(296)*

16. $x - {}^{+}2 = {}^{-}5$ **17.** $^{+}4x = {}^{-}20$ **18.** $\frac{x}{^{-}2} + {}^{+}1 = {}^{+}4$

Write in exponential notation. *(298)*

19. 100 **20.** 1,000 **21.** 0.0001

Write expanded numerals. Use exponents. *(299)*

22. 30.15 **23.** 526.1234

Solve. *(289, 300)*

24. Andy receives $3.00 for an allowance each week. He saves 15% of it. How much does he save each week?

25. Mr. Allen paid $250 wholesale for a stereo. He sold it for $375. What was his percent of profit on the sale based upon the cost of the stereo?

Basic Skills Check

1. Which is not the same as 562 cm?

   A 56.2 m　　B 5,620 mm

   C 5.62 m　　D 0.00562 km

2. Which is the same as 42 in.?

   E $2\frac{1}{2}$ ft　　F 3 ft

   G $3\frac{1}{2}$ ft　　H none of the above

3. Which is the same as 659 g?

   A 659 kg　　B 65.9 kg

   C 6.59 kg　　D 0.659 kg

4. Which is the same as 56 oz?

   E $3\frac{1}{2}$ lb　　F 4 lb

   G $4\frac{1}{2}$ lb　　H 5 lb

5. Which is the same as 1,256 mL?

   A 125.6 L　　B 12.56 L

   C 1.256 L　　D 0.1256 L

6. Which is not a factor of 42?

   E 14　　F 6

   G 4　　H 2

7. What is the next number in this sequence? 2.1, 1.8, 1.5, . . .

   A 0.12　　B 1.2

   C 1.4　　D 1.6

8. Add.

$$\begin{array}{r} 4 \text{ lb } 9 \text{ oz} \\ + \, 2 \text{ lb } 8 \text{ oz} \\ \hline \end{array}$$

   E 9 lb 2 oz　　F 8 lb 4 oz

   G 7 lb 1 oz　　H 6 lb 3 oz

9. What is the length of $\overline{AB}$ to the nearest $\frac{1}{2}$ inch?

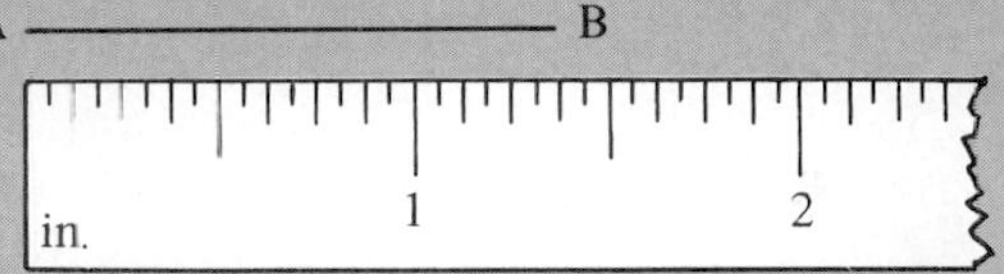

   A $2\frac{1}{2}$ in.　　B 2 in.

   C $1\frac{1}{2}$ in.　　D 1 in.

10. What is the length of $\overline{CD}$ to the nearest centimeter?

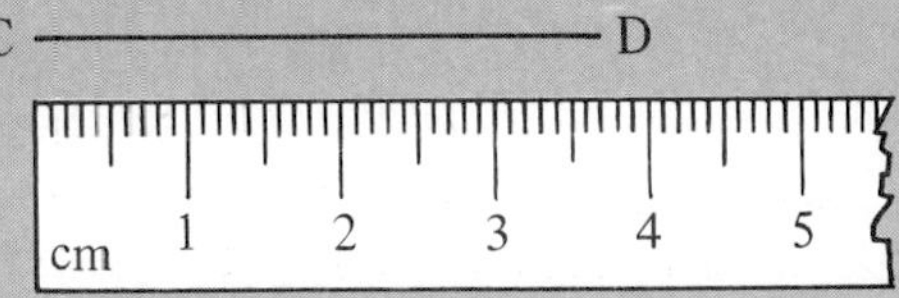

   E 4 cm　　F 5 cm

   G 6 cm　　H none of the above

Rational Numbers

▶ A rational number is a number that can be written in the form $\frac{a}{b}$, where a and b are integers and b is not zero.

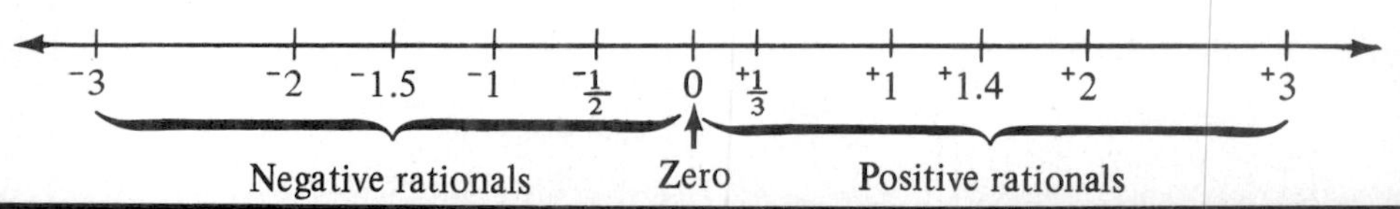

A. Integers are rational numbers. Write in the form $\frac{a}{b}$.

Examples $^{+}3 = \frac{^{+}3}{^{+}1}$ $^{-}3 = \frac{^{-}3}{^{+}1}$

1. $^{+}8$ **2.** $^{-}8$ **3.** $^{-}5$ **4.** $^{+}5$ **5.** 0

B. There are decimals which are rational numbers. Positive numbers can be written without a plus sign. Write in the form $\frac{a}{b}$.

Examples $1.4 = \frac{14}{10}$ $^{-}3.74 = \frac{^{-}374}{100}$

6. 0.6 **7.** 3.3 **8.** $^{-}0.1$ **9.** $^{-}6.28$ **10.** $^{-}7.82$

C. Compare. Use >, <, or =.

11. $^{-}2 \equiv {}^{-}1\frac{1}{2}$ **12.** $\frac{^{-}2}{3} \equiv 0$ **13.** $^{-}1.4 \equiv 0.7$ **14.** $\frac{^{-}1}{2} \equiv \frac{^{-}3}{4}$

CHAPTER 12
REAL NUMBERS

Practice

Write in the form $\frac{a}{b}$.

1. 4
2. $^-3$
3. 6
4. $^-13$
5. 17
6. $^-0.3$
7. 2.64
8. $^-1.5$
9. 3.102
10. ★ $\frac{\frac{1}{2}}{3}$

Compare. Use >, <, or =.

11. $^-6$ ▤ $5\frac{3}{4}$
12. 4 ▤ $^-3.6$
13. $^-1.7$ ▤ $^-2.8$
14. $\frac{^-1}{3}$ ▤ 0
15. $\frac{^-4}{5}$ ▤ $\frac{^-8}{10}$
16. $^-0.3$ ▤ $^-1.2$
17. $^-2\frac{1}{2}$ ▤ $1\frac{3}{4}$
18. $^-7.3$ ▤ 8.1
19. A diver went down 50 m below sea level, or $^-50$ m. Write $^-50$ in the form $\frac{a}{b}$.

Adding Rational Numbers

Adding positive and negative rational numbers is like adding integers.

Integers	*Rational Numbers*
$5 + 2 = 7$	$\frac{5}{9} + \frac{2}{9} = \frac{7}{9}$
${}^-3 + {}^-4 = {}^-7$	$\frac{{}^-3}{8} + \frac{{}^-4}{8} = \frac{{}^-7}{8}$
${}^-14 + {}^-6 = {}^-20$	${}^-1.4 + {}^-0.6 = {}^-2.0$

A. Add and simplify.

1. $\frac{{}^-1}{7} + \frac{{}^-3}{7}$ **2.** $\frac{1}{10} + \frac{3}{10}$ **3.** $\frac{{}^-5}{8} + \frac{{}^-5}{8}$ **4.** ${}^-3.7 + {}^-2.1$

B. Adding a positive and a negative rational number is like adding positive and negative integers.

Integers

Rational Numbers

$3 + {}^-2 = 1$

$\frac{3}{7} + \frac{{}^-2}{7} = \frac{1}{7}$

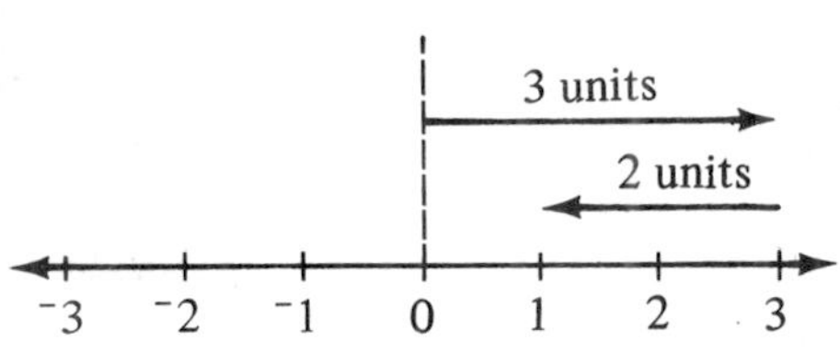

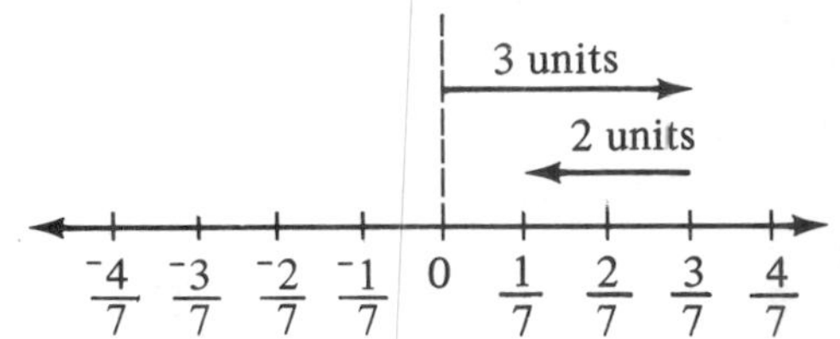

Add and simplify.

5. $\frac{{}^-5}{9} + \frac{2}{9}$ **6.** $\frac{{}^-3}{4} + \frac{1}{4}$ **7.** $\frac{{}^-7}{8} + \frac{3}{8}$ **8.** ${}^-2.6 + 4.0$

9. $\frac{3}{4} + \frac{{}^-1}{2}$ **10.** $\frac{2}{3} + \frac{{}^-1}{6}$ **11.** $\frac{3}{4} + \frac{{}^-5}{6}$ **12.** $3.1 + {}^-5.6$

C. Give the opposites.

13. $\frac{{}^-1}{2}$ **14.** $\frac{3}{4}$ **15.** $\frac{{}^-5}{6}$ **16.** 1.2

D. Add.

17. $\frac{1}{2} + \frac{{}^-1}{2}$ **18.** $\frac{3}{4} + \frac{{}^-3}{4}$ **18.** $\frac{{}^-5}{6} + \frac{5}{6}$ **20.** $1.2 + {}^-1.2$

Practice

Add and simplify.

1. $\frac{4}{9} + \frac{1}{9}$
2. $\frac{3}{8} + \frac{4}{8}$
3. $\frac{5}{10} + \frac{2}{10}$
4. $0.3 + 0.6$
5. $\frac{^-6}{12} + \frac{^-1}{12}$
6. $\frac{^-3}{7} + \frac{^-2}{7}$
7. $\frac{^-4}{12} + \frac{^-3}{12}$
8. $^-0.06 + {}^-0.09$
9. $\frac{3}{8} + \frac{^-3}{8}$
10. $\frac{1}{9} + \frac{^-2}{9}$
11. $\frac{3}{10} + \frac{^-3}{10}$
12. $6.2 + {}^-8.1$
13. $\frac{^-3}{10} + \frac{5}{10}$
14. $\frac{^-5}{6} + \frac{1}{6}$
15. $\frac{^-3}{4} + \frac{3}{4}$
16. $^-9.8 + 8.4$
17. $\frac{1}{6} + \frac{3}{8}$
18. $\frac{^-2}{5} + \frac{^-1}{4}$
19. $\frac{1}{3} + \frac{^-1}{2}$
20. $\frac{^-3}{4} + \frac{1}{8}$
21. $\frac{^-3}{8} + \frac{2}{8}$
22. $\frac{4}{5} + \frac{^-3}{5}$
23. $\frac{7}{12} + \frac{^-2}{12}$
24. $0.7 + {}^-0.3$
25. $\frac{7}{8} + \frac{^-3}{8}$
26. $\frac{^-3}{6} + \frac{1}{6}$
27. $\frac{5}{12} + \frac{^-1}{12}$
28. $1.6 + {}^-0.9$
29. $\frac{1}{2} + \frac{^-2}{6}$
30. $^-4.5 + 8.1$
31. $\frac{^-1}{4} + \frac{3}{8}$
32. $\frac{3}{4} + \frac{^-1}{2}$
33. $\frac{^-3}{10} + \frac{1}{4}$
34. $\frac{1}{2} + \frac{^-5}{6}$
35. $^-0.2 + {}^-4.1$
36. $\frac{5}{6} + \frac{^-5}{9}$
37. $\frac{3}{6} + \frac{5}{6}$
38. $6.9 + {}^-4.8$
39. $\frac{^-5}{8} + \frac{2}{3}$
40. $\frac{^-7}{10} + \frac{^-3}{10}$

★ 41. $\frac{^-9}{10} + \frac{3}{5} + \frac{1}{2}$
★ 42. $\frac{^-5}{6} + \frac{3}{4} + \frac{^-1}{2}$
★ 43. $\frac{^-1}{3} + \frac{1}{6} + \frac{^-5}{6}$

Solve.

44. A stock decreased in value in January $\frac{3}{4}$ of a point $\left(\frac{^-3}{4}\right)$. In February, the stock increased in value $\frac{7}{8}$ of a point $\left(\frac{^+7}{8}\right)$. What was the total change in value for the 2 months?

Subtracting Rational Numbers

Integers			*Rational Numbers*		
Subtract.		Add opposites.	Subtract.		Add opposites.
$4 - 3$	or	$4 + {}^-3 = 1$	$\frac{4}{7} - \frac{3}{7}$	or	$\frac{4}{7} + \frac{^-3}{7} = \frac{1}{7}$
$^-8 - {}^-6$	or	$^-8 + 6 = {}^-2$	$\frac{^-8}{9} - \frac{^-6}{9}$	or	$\frac{^-8}{9} + \frac{6}{9} = \frac{^-2}{9}$
$^-5 - 3$	or	$^-5 + {}^-3 = {}^-8$	$^-0.5 - 0.3$	or	$^-0.5 + {}^-0.3 = {}^-0.8$

▶ To subtract a rational number, add its opposite.

A. Subtract $\frac{1}{8} - \frac{^-3}{8}$.

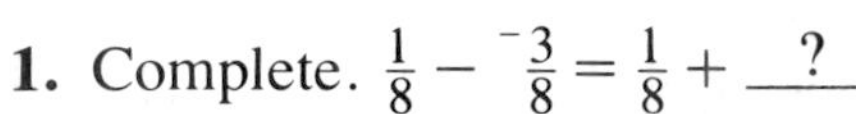

1. Complete. $\frac{1}{8} - \frac{^-3}{8} = \frac{1}{8} + \underline{\ \ ?\ \ }$

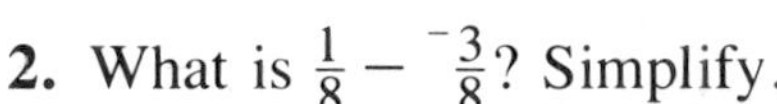

2. What is $\frac{1}{8} - \frac{^-3}{8}$? Simplify.

B. Subtract and simplify.

3. $\frac{^-3}{4} - \frac{1}{4}$ **4.** $\frac{^-9}{10} - \frac{^-3}{10}$ **5.** $^-0.8 - {}^-0.4$ **6.** $3.8 - {}^-1.9$

C. Subtract $\frac{1}{2} - \frac{^-3}{4}$.

7. Complete. $\frac{1}{2} - \frac{^-3}{4} = \frac{?}{4} - \frac{^-3}{4}$ ← 4 is the least common denominator.

8. Complete. $\frac{2}{4} - \frac{^-3}{4} = \frac{2}{4} + \underline{\ \ ?\ \ }$

9. What is $\frac{1}{2} - \frac{^-3}{4}$?

D. Subtract and simplify.

10. $\frac{7}{8} - \frac{^-3}{4}$ **11.** $\frac{^-2}{3} - \frac{3}{4}$ **12.** $\frac{^-5}{6} - \frac{^-3}{8}$ **13.** $^-3\frac{1}{2} - 5\frac{2}{3}$

E. Subtract.

14. $\frac{^-1}{2} - 0$ **15.** $0 - \frac{^-2}{3}$ **16.** $0 - \frac{1}{3}$ **17.** $0 - 0.4$

18. $\frac{2}{3} - \frac{2}{3}$ **19.** $\frac{^-4}{5} - \frac{^-4}{5}$ **20.** $^-0.9 - {}^-0.9$ **21.** $^-0.8 - {}^-0.8$

Practice

Subtract and simplify.

1. $\frac{3}{5} - \frac{1}{5}$
2. $\frac{5}{8} - \frac{2}{8}$
3. $\frac{7}{10} - \frac{6}{10}$
4. $\frac{9}{12} - \frac{4}{12}$
5. $0.8 - 0.6$
6. $1.0 - 0.8$
7. $0.13 - 0.04$
8. $2.46 - 1.19$
9. $\frac{3}{5} - \frac{^-1}{5}$
10. $\frac{3}{8} - \frac{^-2}{8}$
11. $\frac{1}{6} - \frac{^-4}{6}$
12. $\frac{7}{12} - \frac{^-4}{12}$
13. $0.9 - {}^-0.6$
14. $0.7 - {}^-0.3$
15. $0.9 - {}^-0.3$
16. $1.6 - {}^-1.6$
17. $\frac{^-3}{8} - \frac{1}{8}$
18. $\frac{^-2}{5} - \frac{2}{5}$
19. $\frac{^-1}{6} - \frac{2}{6}$
20. $\frac{^-2}{10} - \frac{3}{10}$
21. ${}^-0.6 - 0.4$
22. ${}^-0.6 - 0.9$
23. ${}^-0.6 - 0.8$
24. ${}^-2.3 - 1.4$
25. $\frac{^-1}{8} - \frac{^-3}{8}$
26. $\frac{^-1}{12} - \frac{^-3}{12}$
27. $\frac{^-3}{4} - \frac{^-2}{4}$
28. $\frac{^-5}{6} - \frac{^-5}{6}$
29. ${}^-0.8 - {}^-0.3$
30. ${}^-1.9 - {}^-0.8$
31. ${}^-3.4 - {}^-2.9$
32. ${}^-4.1 - {}^-2.1$
33. $\frac{1}{2} - \frac{1}{4}$
34. $\frac{3}{4} - \frac{2}{5}$
35. $\frac{5}{6} - \frac{^-3}{8}$
36. $\frac{2}{3} - \frac{^-3}{12}$
37. $\frac{^-3}{4} - \frac{5}{8}$
38. $\frac{^-3}{5} - \frac{3}{4}$
39. $\frac{^-1}{8} - \frac{^-3}{12}$
40. $\frac{^-5}{8} - \frac{^-4}{6}$
41. $\frac{^-3}{4} - 0$
42. ${}^-0.4 - 0$
43. $0 - \frac{3}{4}$
44. $0 - \frac{^-1}{2}$
45. ${}^-3.2 - {}^-4.8$
46. $\frac{^-2}{3} - \frac{1}{3}$
47. $\frac{2}{10} - \frac{^-4}{100}$
48. $5.6 - {}^-4.9$

FIND OUT!
Brainteasers

Choose the correct answer.

1.  is to ⅂ as  is to

a.  b.  c.  d. 

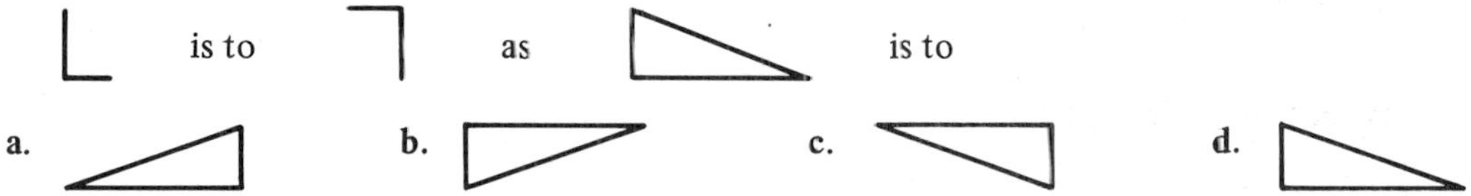

2. S is to Ƨ as  is to

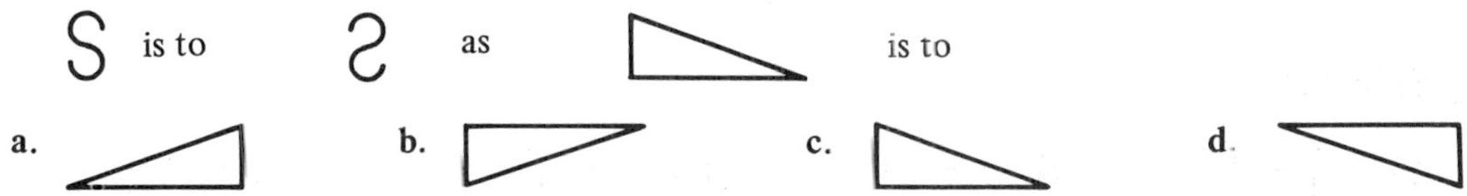

a. b.  c.  d. 

Multiplying and Dividing Rational Numbers

Integers	*Rational Numbers*
$2 \cdot 3 = 6$	$\frac{1}{3} \cdot \frac{5}{6} = \frac{5}{18}$
$^-2 \cdot {}^-3 = 6$	$\frac{^-2}{3} \cdot \frac{^-1}{5} = \frac{2}{15}$
$2 \cdot {}^-3 = {}^-6$	$\frac{5}{8} \cdot \frac{^-3}{4} = \frac{^-15}{32}$
$^-2 \cdot 3 = {}^-6$	$^-0.7 \cdot 0.8 = {}^-0.56$

▶ The product of 2 positive or of 2 negative numbers is positive.

▶ The product of a negative and a positive number is negative.

A. Multiply and simplify.

1. $\frac{^-3}{5} \cdot \frac{2}{3}$ **2.** $\frac{^-3}{4} \cdot \frac{^-1}{2}$ **3.** $2\frac{1}{2} \cdot \frac{^-4}{5}$ **4.** $^-1.4 \cdot 2.3$

B. Multiply. Use a shortcut.

Example $\frac{^-3}{4} \cdot \frac{2}{3} = \frac{^-\overset{1}{\cancel{3}}}{\underset{2}{\cancel{4}}} \cdot \frac{\overset{1}{\cancel{2}}}{\underset{3}{\cancel{3}}} = \frac{^-1}{2}$

5. $\frac{^-3}{4} \cdot \frac{^-6}{9}$ **6.** $\frac{^-2}{5} \cdot \frac{7}{12}$ **7.** $\frac{8}{10} \cdot \frac{^-5}{6}$ **8.** $^-1\frac{1}{2} \cdot \frac{^-5}{6}$

▶ Two numbers are **reciprocals** if their product is 1.

C. Give the reciprocals.

9. $\frac{^-3}{4}$ **10.** $\frac{^-5}{8}$ **11.** $\frac{3}{4}$ **12.** $^-1\frac{1}{2}$

D. Divide and simplify.

Example $\frac{^-3}{4} \div \frac{^-1}{2} = \frac{^-3}{\underset{2}{\cancel{4}}} \cdot \frac{^-\overset{1}{\cancel{2}}}{1}$

$= \frac{3}{2}$, or $1\frac{1}{2}$

13. $\frac{^-5}{8} \div \frac{^-2}{3}$ **14.** $10 \div {}^-2\frac{1}{2}$ **15.** $\frac{7}{8} \div {}^-3\frac{1}{2}$ **16.** $^-1.6 \div {}^-0.8$

Practice

Multiply and simplify.

1. $\frac{2}{3} \cdot \frac{1}{3}$
2. $\frac{3}{4} \cdot \frac{1}{5}$
3. $\frac{5}{6} \cdot \frac{1}{3}$
4. $1\frac{1}{2} \cdot 1\frac{1}{3}$
5. ${}^-\frac{3}{4} \cdot {}^-\frac{1}{2}$
6. ${}^-\frac{4}{5} \cdot {}^-\frac{7}{9}$
7. ${}^-\frac{4}{5} \cdot {}^-\frac{2}{3}$
8. ${}^-\frac{6}{7} \cdot {}^-\frac{3}{5}$
9. ${}^-\frac{5}{6} \cdot \frac{2}{3}$
10. ${}^-\frac{3}{4} \cdot \frac{5}{8}$
11. ${}^-\frac{6}{7} \cdot \frac{3}{7}$
12. ${}^-\frac{5}{8} \cdot \frac{7}{12}$
13. $\frac{7}{8} \cdot {}^-\frac{3}{5}$
14. $\frac{5}{12} \cdot {}^-\frac{5}{6}$
15. $\frac{7}{10} \cdot {}^-\frac{3}{4}$
16. $\frac{2}{3} \cdot {}^-\frac{4}{5}$
17. ${}^-0.4 \cdot {}^-0.8$
18. ${}^-0.8 \cdot 0.3$
19. ${}^-1.6 \cdot {}^-0.7$
20. $8.4 \cdot {}^-3.4$
21. $\frac{3}{4} \cdot {}^-\frac{8}{9}$
22. ${}^-\frac{5}{6} \cdot \frac{3}{4}$
23. ${}^-\frac{3}{10} \cdot {}^-\frac{2}{3}$
24. $\frac{5}{6} \cdot {}^-\frac{3}{10}$
25. ${}^-1\frac{1}{2} \cdot 3$
26. $2\frac{1}{6} \cdot {}^-8$
27. ${}^-\frac{3}{4} \cdot {}^-4$
28. ${}^-1\frac{2}{5} \cdot 2\frac{1}{3}$

★ 29. ${}^-\frac{1}{2} \cdot \frac{2}{3} \cdot {}^-6$

★ 30. ${}^-0.1 \cdot {}^-0.2 \cdot {}^-0.4$

★ 31. $\frac{3}{4} \cdot \frac{1}{3} \cdot {}^-\frac{2}{3}$

Divide and simplify.

32. $0.6 \div 0.3$
33. ${}^-0.09 \div {}^-0.03$
34. ${}^-1.6 \div 0.4$
35. $0.72 \div {}^-0.9$
36. $\frac{5}{6} \div \frac{3}{4}$
37. $\frac{3}{8} \div \frac{3}{10}$
38. ${}^-\frac{2}{3} \div {}^-\frac{1}{3}$
39. ${}^-\frac{4}{5} \div {}^-\frac{7}{9}$
40. ${}^-\frac{3}{4} \div \frac{1}{2}$
41. ${}^-\frac{5}{8} \div \frac{3}{4}$
42. $\frac{1}{4} \div {}^-\frac{5}{12}$
43. $\frac{5}{6} \div {}^-\frac{2}{3}$
44. $\frac{3}{4} \div 2$
45. ${}^-\frac{8}{10} \div {}^-4$
46. $\frac{7}{8} \div {}^-4$
47. ${}^-\frac{15}{24} \div 8$
48. $8 \div \frac{3}{4}$
49. ${}^-6 \div {}^-\frac{1}{2}$
50. $7 \div {}^-\frac{1}{3}$
51. ${}^-4 \div \frac{5}{6}$
52. $1\frac{1}{2} \div \frac{3}{4}$
53. ${}^-2\frac{1}{3} \div {}^-\frac{1}{4}$
54. $3\frac{2}{5} \div {}^-\frac{3}{5}$
55. ${}^-2\frac{3}{4} \div \frac{7}{8}$
56. $2\frac{1}{2} \div 1\frac{1}{4}$
57. ${}^-3\frac{1}{3} \div {}^-1\frac{1}{4}$
58. ${}^-2\frac{3}{4} \div 1\frac{1}{2}$
59. $5\frac{1}{2} \div {}^-1\frac{3}{4}$

Problem Solving: Bar Graphs

Information can be pictured by a bar graph.

This bar graph shows that in September the 8th grade borrowed more books than the 7th grade borrowed.

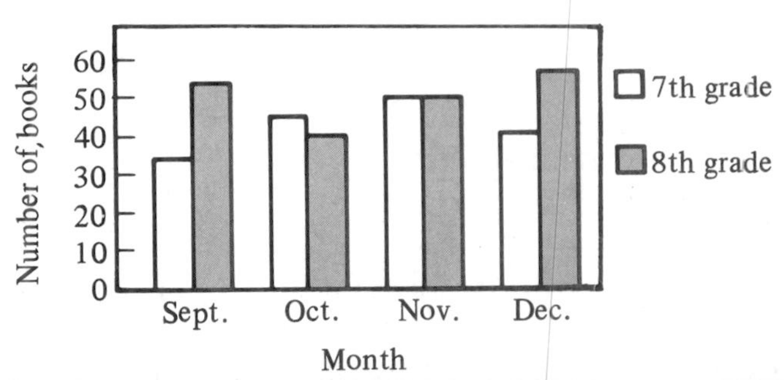

A. Look at the bar graph above.

1. How many books did the 7th grade borrow in September?
2. How many books did the 8th grade borrow in September?
3. In which month did the 7th grade borrow more books than the 8th grade?
4. In which month did the 2 grades borrow the same number of books?
5. How many more books did the 8th grade borrow than the 7th grade in December?

B. Sometimes a bar may be used to give 2 pieces of information.

Example In September, 15 fiction and 10 (25-15) biographies were borrowed.

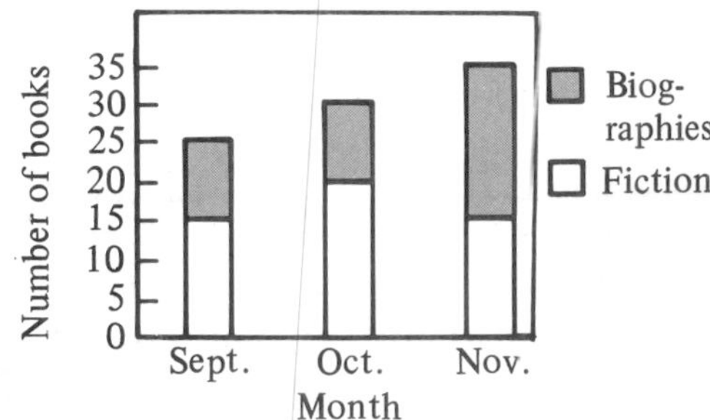

6. How many fiction and how many biographies were borrowed in November?
7. In which month were the most fiction books borrowed?
8. In which month was the total number of fiction and biographies borrowed greatest?

Practice

Use this bar graph to answer Exercises 1 to 4.

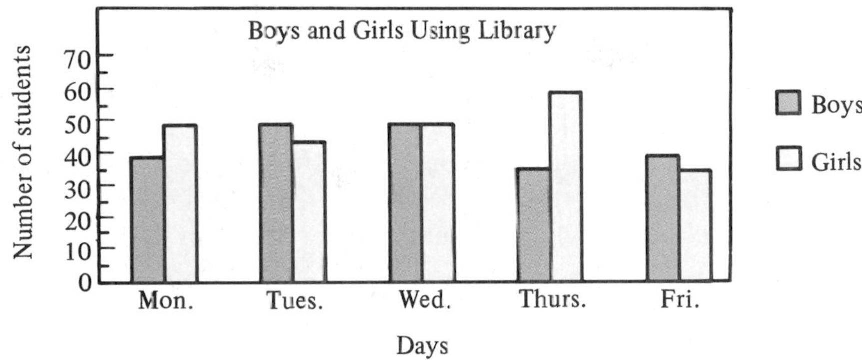

1. On what day did the most girls use the library?

2. On what days did more boys than girls use the library?

3. On what day did the same number of boys and girls use the library?

4. How many more girls than boys used the library on Monday?

Use this bar graph to answer Exercises 5 to 8.

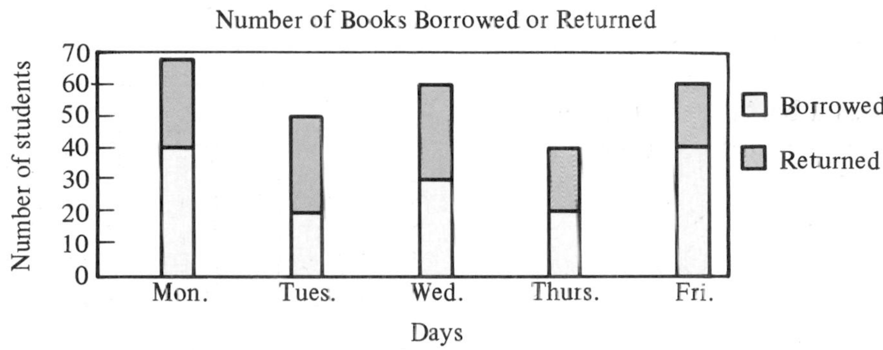

5. Which was the busiest day for borrowing and returning books?

6. On which 3 days were the greatest number of books returned?

7. How many more books were borrowed than returned on Monday?

8. How many more books were returned than borrowed on Tuesday?

Working With Repeating Decimals

Observe these patterns.

Multiplying Decimals	*Multiplying Repeating Decimals*
$10 \times 0.44 = 4.4$	$10 \times 0.4\overline{4} = 4.4\overline{4}$
$100 \times 0.1818 = 18.18$	$100 \times 0.18\overline{18} = 18.18\overline{18}$

A. Every repeating decimal names a rational number. Write in the form $\frac{a}{b}$.

Example $0.3\overline{3}$

Step 1	Multiply by a power of 10 (10^1 since 1 digit repeats).	$10 \times 0.3\overline{3} = 3.3\overline{3}$ (SUBTRACT)
Step 2	Write an equation using 1.	$1 \times 0.3\overline{3} = 0.3\overline{3}$
Step 3	Subtract the equations.	$9 \times 0.3\overline{3} = 3$
Step 4	Divide each side by 9.	$\frac{9 \times 0.3\overline{3}}{9} = \frac{3}{9}$
Step 5	Simplify.	$0.3\overline{3} = \frac{1}{3}$

1. $0.1\overline{1}$ **2.** $0.8\overline{8}$ **3.** $0.6\overline{6}$

B. Write in the form $\frac{a}{b}$.

Example $0.27\overline{27}$

Step 1	Multiply by a power of 10 (10^2 since 2 digits repeat).	$100 \times 0.27\overline{27} = 27.27\overline{27}$ (SUBTRACT)
Step 2	Write an equation using 1.	$1 \times 0.27\overline{27} = 0.27\overline{27}$
Step 3	Subtract the equations.	$99 \times 0.27\overline{27} = 27$
Step 4	Divide each side by 99.	$\frac{99 \times 0.27\overline{27}}{99} = \frac{27}{99}$
Step 5	Simplify.	$0.27\overline{27} = \frac{3}{11}$

4. $0.18\overline{18}$ **5.** $0.09\overline{09}$ **6.** $0.54\overline{54}$

Practice

Write in the form $\frac{a}{b}$.

1. $0.4\overline{4}$ **2.** $0.5\overline{5}$ **3.** $0.2\overline{2}$ **4.** $0.9\overline{9}$

5. $0.01\overline{01}$ **6.** $0.72\overline{72}$ **7.** $0.63\overline{63}$ **8.** $0.45\overline{45}$

Squares of Numbers

To square a number means to multiply it by itself.
Read 7^2 : 7 squared or second power of 7

$7^2 = 7 \cdot 7 = 49$ $\qquad$ $(^-7)^2 = {^-7} \cdot {^-7} = 49$

$\left(\frac{3}{4}\right)^2 = \frac{3}{4} \cdot \frac{3}{4} = \frac{9}{16}$ $\qquad$ $\left(\frac{^-3}{4}\right)^2 = \frac{^-3}{4} \cdot \frac{^-3}{4} = \frac{9}{16}$

Squares of rational numbers, except 0, are positive.

A. Compute.

1. 4^2 **2.** 8^2 **3.** $(^-3)^2$ **4.** $\left(\frac{2}{3}\right)^2$ **5.** $\left(\frac{^-2}{3}\right)^2$

6. 0.4^2 **7.** 2.3^2 **8.** 1.9^2 **9.** 3.1^2 **10.** $(^-4.2)^2$

B. The square of 5 is 25.

11. What other number is there whose square is 25?

12. Give 2 numbers whose square is 100.

C. Some numbers are squares of whole numbers. 36 is the square of 6. 36 is called a **perfect square.** Which of these numbers are perfect squares?

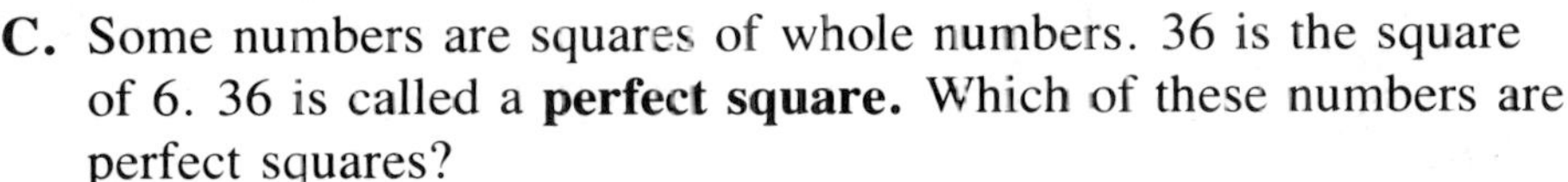

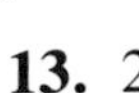

13. 2 **14.** 4 **15.** 16 **16.** 49 **17.** 80

Practice

Compute.

1. 5^2 **2.** 9^2 **3.** 12^2 **4.** 20^2 **5.** $(^-9)^2$

6. $(^-10)^2$ **7.** $(^-15)^2$ **8.** $(^-100)^2$ **9.** $\left(\frac{2}{5}\right)^2$ **10.** $\left(\frac{^-2}{5}\right)^2$

11. $\left(\frac{3}{5}\right)^2$ **12.** $\left(\frac{^-3}{5}\right)^2$ **13.** 0.3^2 **14.** 1.1^2 **15.** $(^-2.1)^2$

Give 2 numbers whose square is the given number.

16. 16 **17.** 9 **18.** 4 **19.** 49 ★**20.** 2.25

Which of these numbers are perfect squares?

21. 25 **22.** 50 **23.** 64 **24.** 100 **25.** 500

Finding Square Roots

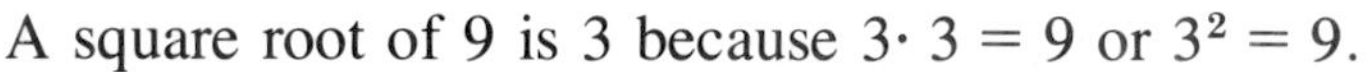

A square root of 9 is 3 because $3 \cdot 3 = 9$ or $3^2 = 9$.
A square root of 9 is $^-3$ because $^-3 \cdot {^-3} = 9$ or $(^-3)^2 = 9$.

▶ A positive rational number has 2 square roots.
$\sqrt{9} = 3$ and $^-\sqrt{9} = {^-3}$.
$\sqrt{\ }$ means positive square root $\quad$ $^-\sqrt{\ }$ means negative square root

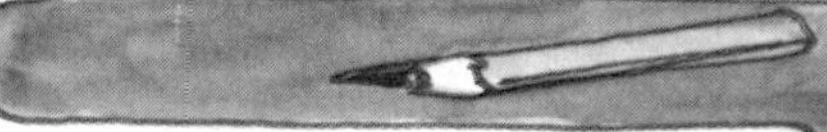

A. Give 2 square roots.

1. 25 **2.** 100 **3.** $\frac{4}{9}$ **4.** 0.09 **5.** 0.64

B. Find the square roots.

6. $\sqrt{36}$ **7.** $\sqrt{81}$ **8.** $\sqrt{\frac{1}{36}}$ **9.** $^-\sqrt{0.16}$ **10.** $^-\sqrt{400}$

C. Estimate $\sqrt{289}$, and then find the exact square root.

THINK: $\sqrt{100} < \sqrt{289}$ and $\sqrt{289} < \sqrt{400}$
So, $10 < \sqrt{289}$ and $\sqrt{289} < 20$, or
$\sqrt{289}$ is between 10 and 20 $\quad 10 < \sqrt{289} < 20$ ⟵ Estimate

11. Try whole numbers between 10 and 20 to find one whose square is 289. What is $\sqrt{289}$?

D. Estimate, and then find the exact square root.

12. $\sqrt{225}$ **13.** $\sqrt{529}$ **14.** $\sqrt{961}$ **15.** $\sqrt{2{,}809}$ **16.** $\sqrt{8{,}464}$

E. Estimate $\sqrt{5}$, and then find the square root to the nearest tenth.

THINK: $\sqrt{4} < \sqrt{5}$ and $\sqrt{5} < \sqrt{9}$
So, $2 < \sqrt{5}$ and $\sqrt{5} < 3$, or
$\sqrt{5}$ is between 2 and 3 $\quad 2 < \sqrt{5} < 3$ ⟵ Estimate

17. Try tenths between 2 and 3. Try $2.1 \cdot 2.1$, $2.2 \cdot 2.2$, $2.3 \cdot 2.3$, and so on. What is $\sqrt{5}$ to the nearest tenth?

F. Estimate, and then find the square root to the nearest tenth.

18. $\sqrt{7}$ **19.** $\sqrt{11}$ **20.** $\sqrt{24}$ **21.** $\sqrt{73}$ **22.** $\sqrt{95}$

Practice

Give 2 square roots.

1. 4 **2.** 16 **3.** 1 **4.** 25

5. 81 **6.** 64 **7.** 100 **8.** 49

9. $\frac{1}{9}$ **10.** $\frac{4}{25}$ **11.** $\frac{36}{49}$ **12.** $\frac{81}{100}$

13. 0.04 **14.** 0.01 **15.** 0.49 **16.** 0.0025

Find the square roots.

17. $\sqrt{49}$ **18.** $\sqrt{100}$ **19.** $\sqrt{1}$ **20.** $\sqrt{4}$

21. $^-\sqrt{16}$ **22.** $^-\sqrt{36}$ **23.** $^-\sqrt{100}$ **24.** $^-\sqrt{4}$

25. $\sqrt{\frac{4}{81}}$ **26.** $\sqrt{\frac{1}{100}}$ **27.** $^-\sqrt{\frac{9}{25}}$ **28.** $^-\sqrt{\frac{49}{64}}$

29. $\sqrt{0.36}$ **30.** $\sqrt{0.81}$ **31.** $^-\sqrt{0.0064}$ **32.** $^-\sqrt{0.01}$

33. $\sqrt{2,500}$ **34.** $\sqrt{3,600}$ **35.** $^-\sqrt{4,900}$ **36.** $^-\sqrt{6,400}$

Estimate, and then find the exact square root.

37. $\sqrt{196}$ **38.** $\sqrt{361}$ **39.** $\sqrt{625}$ **40.** $\sqrt{784}$

41. $\sqrt{1,024}$ **42.** $\sqrt{2,209}$ **43.** $\sqrt{4,624}$ **44.** $\sqrt{5,041}$

Estimate, and then find the square root to the nearest tenth.

45. $\sqrt{2}$ **46.** $\sqrt{8}$ **47.** $\sqrt{12}$ **48.** $\sqrt{20}$

49. A square board has an area of 91 cm^2. How long is each side to the nearest tenth?

FIND OUT!
Brainteaser

A bottle and a bottle cap cost S1.10. What is the cost of each if the bottle costs \$1 more than the cap?

The Square Root Table

$(1.4)^2 = 1.96$ $\qquad$ $(1.5)^2 = 2.25$
So, $\sqrt{2} = 1.4$ to the nearest tenth.

$\sqrt{2}$ may be found to the nearest hundredth.
$(1.41)^2 = 1.9881$ $\qquad$ $(1.42)^2 = 2.0164$
So, $\sqrt{2} = 1.41$ to the nearest hundredth.

You can continue this process endlessly. You will not find a number whose square is exactly 2.

$\sqrt{2}$ is a non-terminating, non-repeating decimal.

A. The square root table below gives square roots to 3 decimal places.

Example $\quad \sqrt{5} = 2.236$

Find the square roots. Use the table.

1. $\sqrt{7}$ **2.** $\sqrt{10}$ **3.** $\sqrt{29}$ **4.** $\sqrt{41}$

TABLE OF SQUARE ROOTS

Number	*Square Root*	*Number*	*Square Root*	*Number*	*Square Root*	*Number*	*Square Root*
1	1	13	3.606	26	5.099	38	6.164
2	1.414	14	3.742	27	5.196	39	6.245
3	1.732	15	3.873	28	5.292	40	6.325
4	2	16	4	29	5.385	41	6.403
5	2.236	17	4.123	30	5.477	42	6.481
6	2.449	18	4.243	31	5.568	43	6.557
7	2.646	19	4.359	32	5.657	44	6.633
8	2.828	20	4.472	33	5.745	45	6.708
9	3	21	4.583	34	5.831	46	6.782
10	3.162	22	4.690	35	5.916	47	6.856
11	3.317	23	4.796	36	6	48	6.928
12	3.464	24	4.899	37	6.083	49	7
		25	5			50	7.071

Some square roots are rational numbers, such as $\sqrt{1}$, $\sqrt{4}$, and $\sqrt{9}$. Some square roots are irrational numbers. $\sqrt{2}$, $\sqrt{3}$, and $\sqrt{5}$.

▶ If the square root of a whole number is not a whole number, then it is an irrational number.

B. Rational or irrational?

5. $\sqrt{16}$ **6.** $\sqrt{10}$ **7.** $\sqrt{24}$ **8.** $\sqrt{25}$

Practice

Find the square roots. Use the table on page 322.

1. $\sqrt{8}$ **2.** $\sqrt{12}$ **3.** $\sqrt{23}$ **4.** $\sqrt{25}$ **5.** $\sqrt{37}$

6. $\sqrt{48}$ **7.** $\sqrt{31}$ **8.** $\sqrt{15}$ **9.** $\sqrt{35}$ **10.** $\sqrt{43}$

Rational or irrational?

11. $\sqrt{6}$ **12.** $\sqrt{20}$ **13.** $\sqrt{31}$ **14.** $\sqrt{36}$ **15.** $\sqrt{64}$

Keeping Fit

Write percents.

1. 0.7 **2.** 0.23 **3.** 0.148

4. 3.6 **5.** $\frac{47}{100}$ **6.** $\frac{6}{100}$

7. $\frac{3}{4}$ **8.** $\frac{1}{25}$ **9.** $\frac{1}{8}$

Compute.

10. 10% of 80 **11.** 50% of 36 **12.** 25% of 96 **13.** 45% of 75

14. 0.5% of 60 **15.** 6.8% of 24 **16.** 13.2% of 15 **17.** 52.3% of 40

18. $1\frac{1}{2}$% of 34 **19.** $2\frac{1}{4}$% cf 43 **20.** $4\frac{3}{4}$% of 24 **21.** $9\frac{1}{2}$% of 61

Solve.

22. What percent of 10 is 6? **23.** What percent of 50 is 28?

24. What percent of 80 is 46? **25.** What percent of 4 is 8?

The Real Number Line

The length of a side can be rational or irrational.

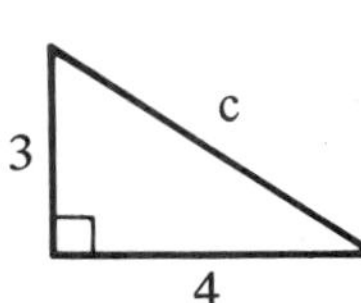

$$a^2 + b^2 = c^2$$
$$3^2 + 4^2 = c^2$$
$$9 + 16 = c^2$$
$$25 = c^2$$
$$5 = c$$

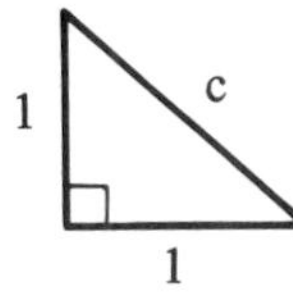

$$a^2 + b^2 = c^2$$
$$1^2 + 1^2 = c^2$$
$$1 + 1 = c^2$$
$$2 = c^2$$
$$\sqrt{2} = c$$

▶ The real numbers are all the rational numbers and all the irrational numbers.

A. Find the missing lengths. Write the answers as square roots.

1.

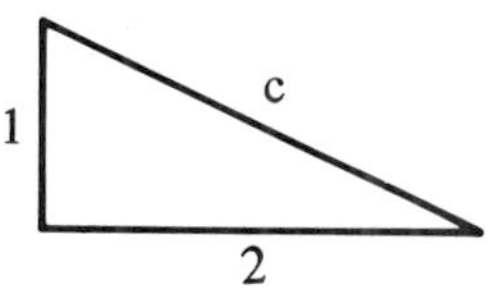

2.

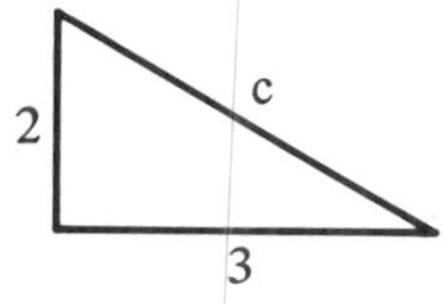

B. Each point on a line may be associated with a rational or an irrational number. This is the real number line. To associate the irrational number $\sqrt{2}$ with a point on a number line, you can use the Pythagorean relationship.

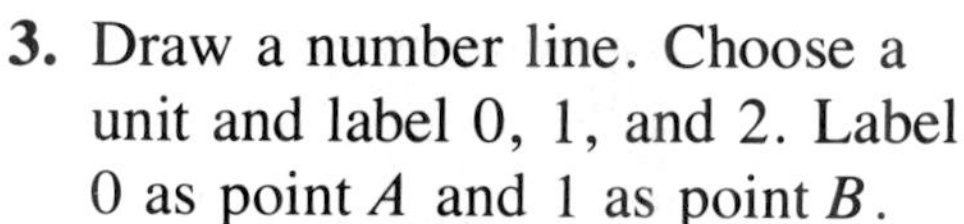

3. Draw a number line. Choose a unit and label 0, 1, and 2. Label 0 as point A and 1 as point B.

4. Construct a perpendicular to $\overline{AB}$ at B.

5. Mark point C on the perpendicular so that $BC = 1$ unit.

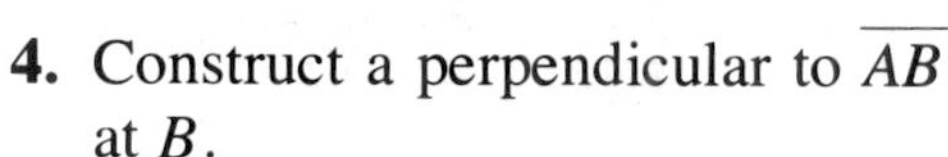

6. Draw $\overline{AC}$.

7. What is the length of $\overline{AC}$? [HINT: see display.]

8. Use your compass and mark off $\overline{AC}$ on the number line. (Put the compass point on 0.)

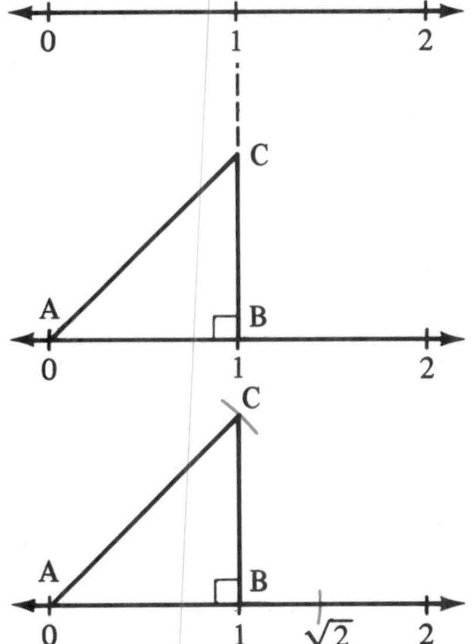

C. Look at the numbers shown on this number line.

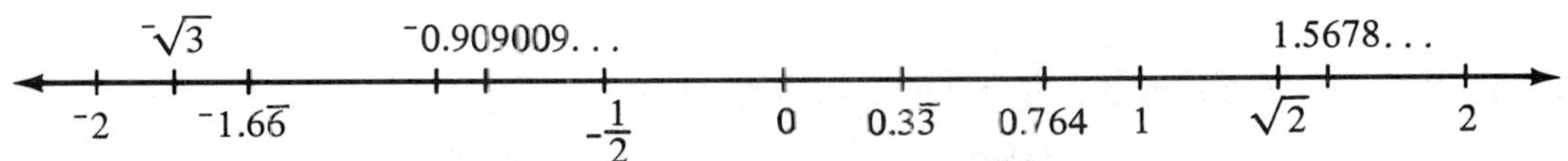

9. Which are rational?

10. Which are irrational?

Practice

Find the missing lengths. Write the answers as square roots.

1.

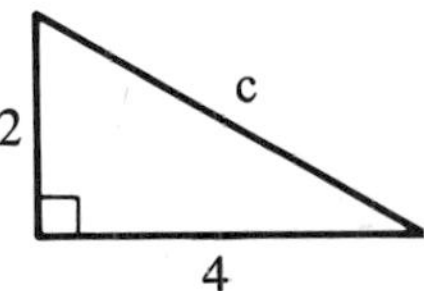

2.

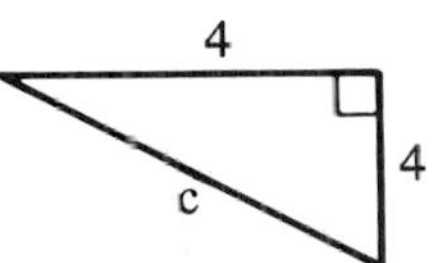

3.

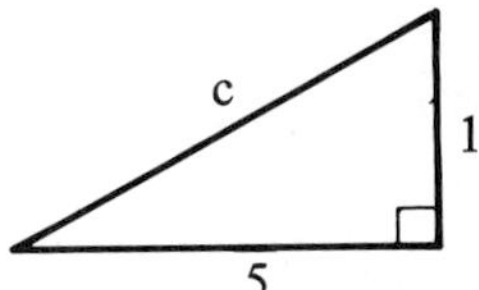

4.

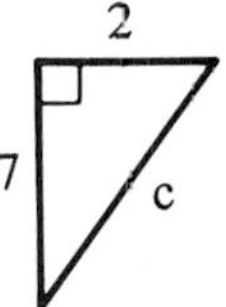

5.

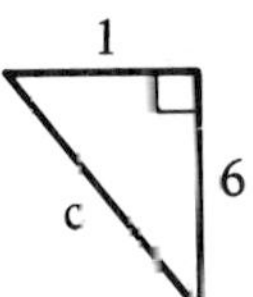

6.

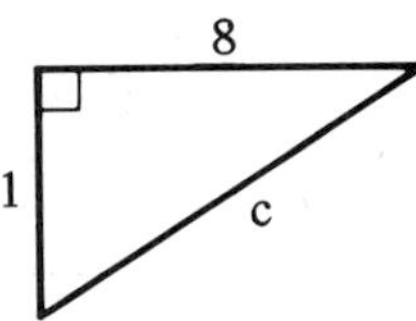

Draw a number line. Use the method in Item B on page 326 to find the points associated with these real numbers.

7. $\sqrt{8}$ **8.** $\sqrt{13}$ **9.** $\sqrt{17}$ ★ **10.** $^-\sqrt{8}$

Consider this number line. What points are matched with the numbers listed below?

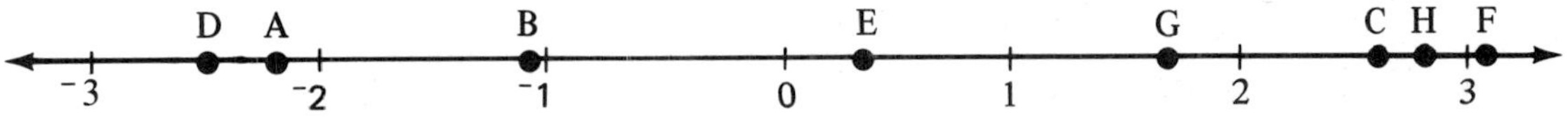

11. $\sqrt{8}$ **12.** $^-2.5$ **13.** $^-1.010010001\ldots$ **14.** $\sqrt{10}$

15. $^-\sqrt{5}$ **16.** 1.7 **17.** $0.3\overline{3}$ **18.** $\sqrt{7}$

19. Which of the numbers in Exercises **11–18** are rational numbers?

20. Which of the numbers in Exercises **11–18** are real numbers?

21. Which of the numbers in Exercises **11–18** are irrational numbers?

Problem Solving • Astronomers

Astronomers are people who study the universe.

1. Astronomers have estimated that there are 200 billion stars in our galaxy. They believe that only 1 star in 25 might have planets suitable for life. About how many stars in our galaxy might have planets suitable for life? [HINT: divide.]

2. Light travels about 3×10^5 km per second. It takes light about $1\frac{1}{3}$ seconds to reach the earth from the moon. About how far is the Earth from the moon?

3. Neptune rotates on its axis in 15 hours 8 minutes. The Earth rotates on its axis once every 24 hours. How much longer does it take Earth to rotate than Neptune?

4. Light travels about 9 trillion km per year. The distance is called a light year by astronomers. The nearest star to us is Alpha Centauri. It is $4\frac{1}{3}$ light years from us. How many kilometers from Earth is the star?

5. Astronomers believe that the nearest star which might have planets suitable for life is 10.8 light years away. How long would it take for a signal from such a planet to be received on Earth and then an answer to be sent back to the planet?

6. One year there were about 2,000 astronomers. About 85% of these were involved in research. How many were not involved in research?

★ 7. The distance from Pluto to the sun is about 3.67×10^9 mi. The distance from Neptune to the sun is about 2.79×10^9 mi. How much farther away from the sun is Pluto?

Chapter Review

Compare. Use < or >. *(304)*

1. $^{-}\frac{2}{3} \equiv 0$ **2.** $^{-}3.4 \equiv {}^{-}4.1$ >

Write as a decimal.

3. $\frac{1}{2}$

Add or subtract and simplify. *(308, 310)*

4. $^{-}\frac{5}{8} + {}^{-}\frac{5}{8}$ **5.** $\frac{3}{4} + {}^{-}\frac{5}{8}$ **6.** $^{-}3.46 + 2.19$

7. $^{-}\frac{2}{3} - \frac{1}{2}$ **8.** $0 - \frac{3}{4}$ **9.** $^{-}3.16 - 5.87$

Multiply or divide and simplify. *(312)*

10. $^{-}\frac{3}{4} \cdot \frac{1}{3}$ **11.** $^{-}1\frac{1}{2} \cdot \frac{3}{8}$ **12.** $^{-}6.3 \cdot {}^{-}1.9$

13. $\frac{5}{8} \div {}^{-}\frac{1}{2}$ **14.** $^{-}\frac{2}{3} \div 2$ **15.** $^{-}0.72 \div {}^{-}0.9$

Compute. *(319)*

16. 8^2 **17.** $(^{-}5)^2$ **18.** $\left(^{-}\frac{4}{5}\right)^2$ **19.** 1.3^2

Find square roots. *(320)*

20. $\sqrt{64}$ **21.** $^{-}\sqrt{4}$ **22.** $\sqrt{\frac{9}{49}}$ **23.** $\sqrt{0.36}$

24. $\sqrt{1{,}600}$ **25.** $\sqrt{4{,}900}$ **26.** $\sqrt{196}$ **27.** $\sqrt{576}$

Rational or irrational? *(314, 322)*

28. $0.34\overline{4}$ **29.** 0.4040040004 . . . **30.** $\sqrt{10}$ **31.** $\sqrt{81}$

Solve.

32. *(324)* Two sides of a right triangle are 5 cm and 12 cm. How long is the hypotenuse?

33. *(328)* The distance from the Earth to the sun is 9.3×10^7 mi. The distance from Mercury to the sun is 3.6×10^7 mi. How much farther away from the sun is the Earth?

Chapter Test

Compare. Use < or >. *(304)*

1. $^{-}\frac{1}{4}$ ▒ 0

2. $^{-}2.9$ ▒ $^{-}3.1$

Write as a decimal.

3. $\frac{2}{3}$

Add or subtract and simplify. *(308, 310)*

4. $\frac{^{-}3}{4} + \frac{^{-}3}{4}$

5. $\frac{2}{3} + \frac{^{-}5}{6}$

6. $^{-}5.36 + 4.08$

7. $\frac{^{-}3}{4} - \frac{2}{3}$

8. $0 - \frac{^{-}1}{2}$

9. $^{-}4.08 - 6.73$

Multiply or divide and simplify. *(312)*

10. $\frac{^{-}5}{6} \cdot \frac{1}{5}$

11. $^{-}2\frac{1}{2} \cdot \frac{2}{3}$

12. $^{-}3.9 \cdot {}^{-}2.5$

13. $\frac{5}{6} \div \frac{^{-}1}{3}$

14. $\frac{^{-}3}{4} \div 3$

15. $^{-}0.81 \div 0.9$

Compute. *(319)*

16. 6^2

17. $(^{-}3)^2$

18. $\left(\frac{^{-}2}{3}\right)^2$

19. 2.1^2

Find the square roots. *(320)*

20. $\sqrt{36}$

21. $^{-}\sqrt{16}$

22. $\sqrt{\frac{9}{64}}$

23. $\sqrt{0.04}$

24. $\sqrt{900}$

25. $\sqrt{6,400}$

26. $\sqrt{256}$

27. $\sqrt{441}$

Rational or irrational? *(314, 322)*

28. $0.45\overline{5}$

29. $\sqrt{8}$

30. $\sqrt{64}$

31. 0.3131131113 . . .

Solve.

32. *(324)* The hypotenuse of a right triangle is 15 m. One side is 12 m. What is the length of the other side?

33. *(328)* The distance from Mercury to the sun is 3.6×10^7 mi. The distance from Mercury to Venus is 3.1×10^7 mi. How much farther away from Mercury is the sun?

Basic Skills Check

1. What is the least number of bills and coins to make change from a 20 dollar bill for a purchase of $13.40?

   A one $5, one $1, one 50¢, two 5¢

   B one $5, one $1, two 25¢, one 10¢

   C six $1, one 50¢, one 10¢

   D one $5, one $1, one 50¢, one 10¢

2. Sue Ellen bought clothing for $146. The sales tax was 5%. How much tax did she pay?

   E $7.30 F $73

   G $153.30 H $219

3. Sneakers marked $21.25 are sold at a 20% discount during a sale. How much is saved during the sale?

   A $0.43 B $4.25

   C $5.31 D $17.00

4. What is the area of a rectangle with a length of 23 in. and a width of 14 in.?

   E 37 in.^{2} F 74 in.^{2}

   G 322 in.^{2} H 422 in.^{2}

5. Which program received the most votes?

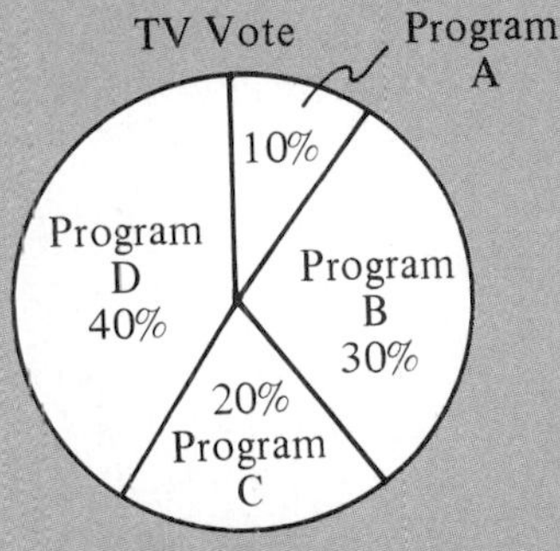

   A program A B program B

   C program C D program D

6. A 6 lb 8 oz piece of meat became 4 lb 14 oz after cooking. How much was lost during cooking?

   E 2 lb 6 oz F 1 lb 10 oz

   G 1 lb 8 oz H 1 lb 4 oz

7. A machine produces 6,000 radio parts an hour. On the average, 5% of the parts are defective. How many are defective?

   A 3 B 30

   C 300 D 3,000

8. Vegetable soup is selling at 2 cans for $0.39. What is the cost of a dozen cans of vegetable soup?

   E $4.68 F $2.48

   G $2.34 H $1.17

Congruent Triangles

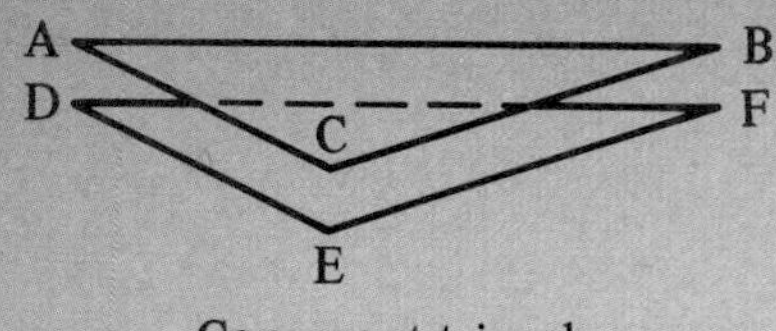

Congruent triangles

Corresponding Sides	*Corresponding Angles*
$\overline{AB} \cong \overline{DF}$	$\angle C \cong \angle E$
$\overline{AC} \cong \overline{DE}$	$\angle B \cong \angle F$
$\overline{CB} \cong \overline{EF}$	$\angle A \cong \angle D$

▶ Congruent triangles are triangles which can be matched so that corresponding sides are congruent and corresponding angles are congruent.

A. $\triangle LMN$ and $\triangle PQR$ are congruent.

1. Name the corresponding sides.

2. Name the corresponding angles.

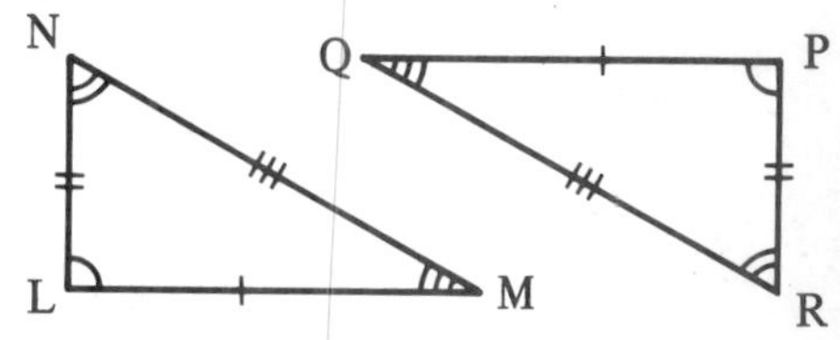

B. Find x.

3. $\triangle ABC \cong \triangle DEF$

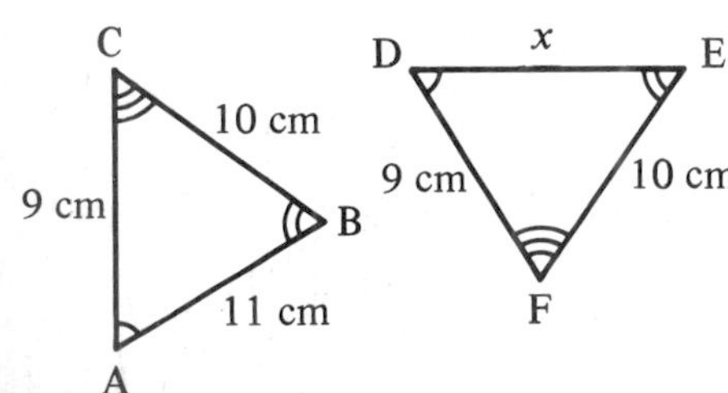

4. $\triangle TUV \cong \triangle XYZ$

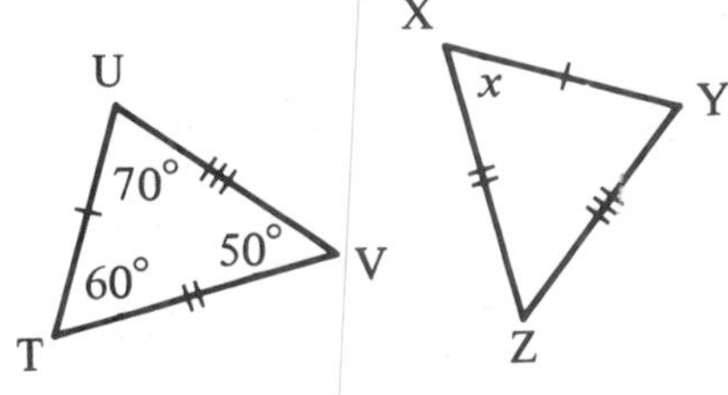

CHAPTER 13
USING GEOMETRY

Practice

Complete. $\triangle ABC \cong \triangle DEF$

1. $\overline{BC} \cong$ __?__

2. $\angle A \cong$ __?__

3. $\overline{DF} \cong$ __?__

4. $\angle E \cong$ __?__

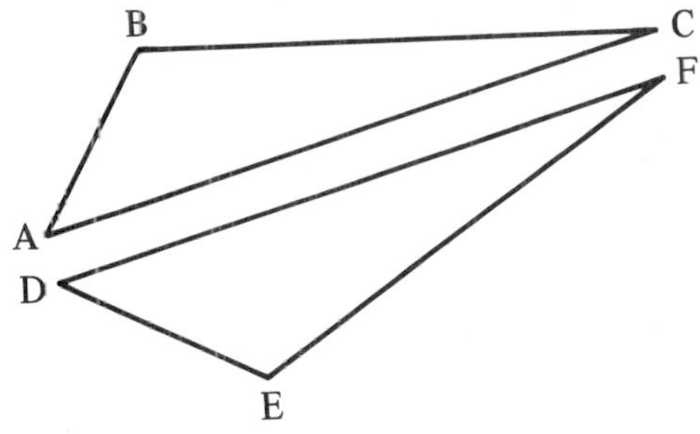

Find x.

5. $\triangle ABC \cong \triangle DEF$

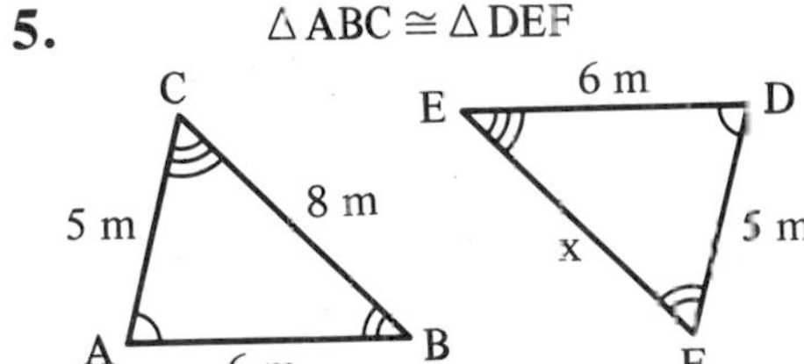

6. $\triangle LMN \cong \triangle PQR$

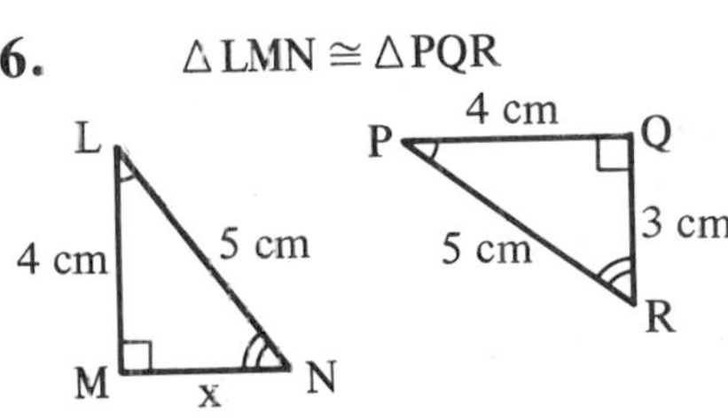

Constructing Congruent Triangles

Materials: compass, paper, straightedge, pencil, scissors

A. Construct a triangle congruent to $\triangle ABC$ by copying its sides.

1. Draw a triangle and label it $\triangle ABC$.
2. Draw a working segment and copy $\overline{AB}$. Label it $\overline{DE}$.
3. Measure $\overline{AC}$ with your compass. With your compass point on D, make an arc the measure of $\overline{AC}$.
4. Measure $\overline{BC}$ with your compass. With your compass point on E, make an arc the measure of $\overline{BC}$. Label the point where the 2 arcs meet point F.
5. Draw $\overline{DF}$ and $\overline{EF}$.
6. Cut out $\triangle DEF$ and place it on $\triangle ABC$. Are all the parts congruent?

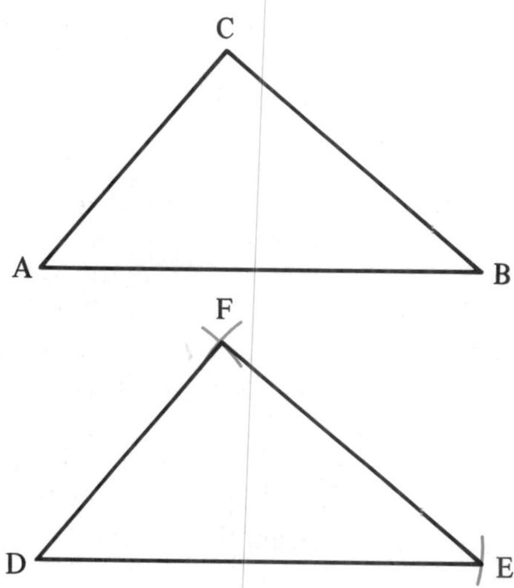

▶ Two triangles are congruent if their corresponding sides are congruent. This principle is called SSS (side-side-side).

B. Construct a triangle congruent to $\triangle ABC$ by copying 2 sides and the included angle ($\angle A$ is the included angle of sides $\overline{AB}$ and $\overline{AC}$.)

7. Draw a triangle and label it $\triangle ABC$.
8. Draw a working segment and copy $\overline{AC}$. Label it $\overline{DF}$.
9. Copy $\angle A$ using point D as the vertex.
10. On the ray you drew to copy $\angle A$, copy $\overline{AB}$. Label it $\overline{DE}$.
11. Draw $\overline{EF}$.
12. Cut out $\triangle DEF$ and place it on $\triangle ABC$. Are all the parts congruent?

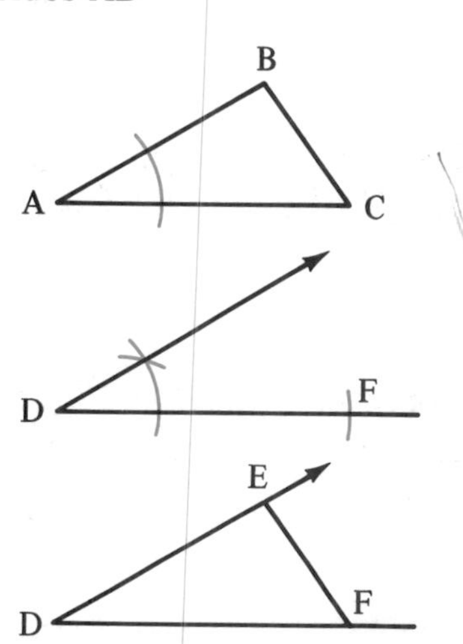

▶ Two triangles are congruent if 2 sides and the included angle of 1 triangle are congruent to 2 sides and the included angle of the other. This principle is called SAS (side-angle-side).

C. Construct a triangle congruent to $\triangle DEF$ by copying 2 angles and the included side. ($\overline{DE}$ is the included side of angles D and E.)

13. Draw a triangle and label it $\triangle DEF$.

14. Draw a working segment and copy $\overline{DE}$. Label it $\overline{GH}$.

15. Copy $\angle D$ using point G as the vertex.

16. Copy $\angle E$ using point H as the vertex. Label the point where the 2 rays intersect point I.

17. Cut out $\triangle GHI$ and place it on $\triangle DEF$. Are all the parts congruent?

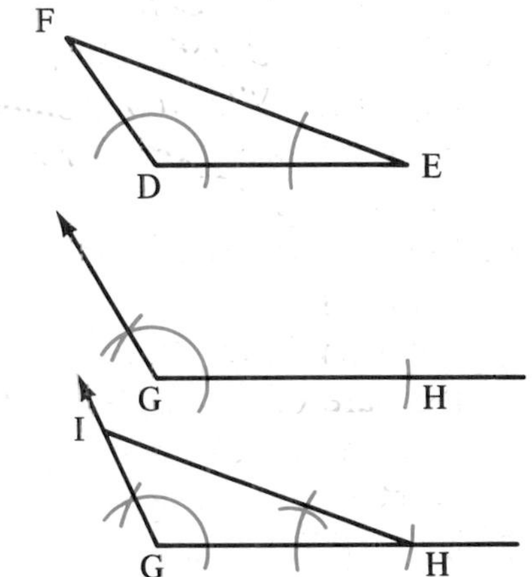

▶ Two triangles are congruent if 2 angles and the included side of 1 triangle are congruent to 2 angles and the included side of the other. This principle is called ASA (angle-side-angle).

Practice

1. Construct a triangle congruent to $\triangle JKL$. Use the SSS principle.

2. Construct a triangle congruent to $\triangle PQR$. Use the SAS principle.

3. Construct a triangle congruent to $\triangle XYZ$. Use the ASA principle.

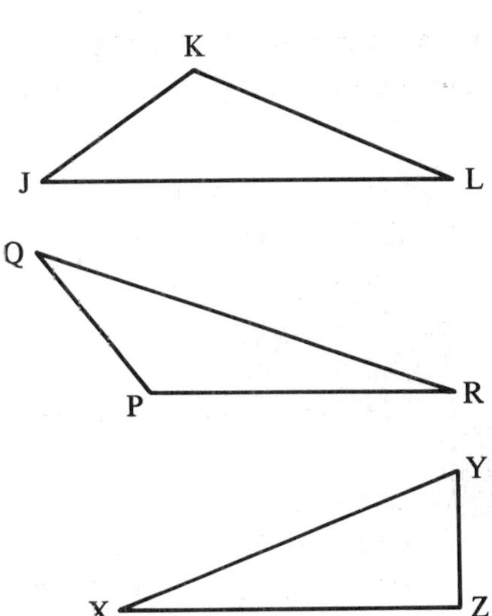

Similar Triangles

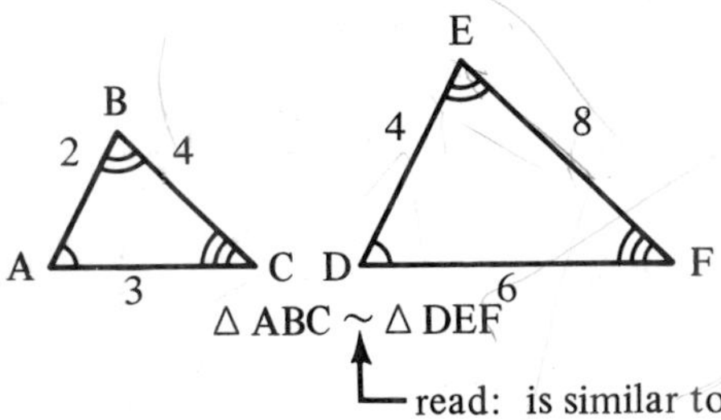

Corresponding Angles

$\angle A \cong \angle D$

$\angle B \cong \angle E$

$\angle C \cong \angle F$

Corresponding Sides

$\frac{BC}{EF} = \frac{4}{8}$ or $\frac{1}{2}$

$\frac{AC}{DF} = \frac{3}{6}$ or $\frac{1}{2}$

$\frac{AB}{DE} = \frac{2}{4}$ or $\frac{1}{2}$

$\frac{BC}{EF} = \frac{AC}{DF} = \frac{AB}{DE}$

▶ Similar triangles have:

1. corresponding angles congruent, and
2. corresponding sides in proportion.

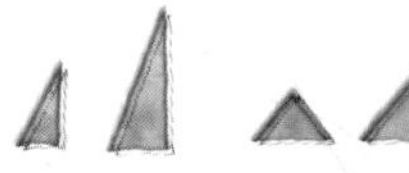

A. Decide if the triangles are similar.

1. Are the corresponding angles congruent?
2. Are the corresponding sides in proportion?
3. Are the triangles similar?

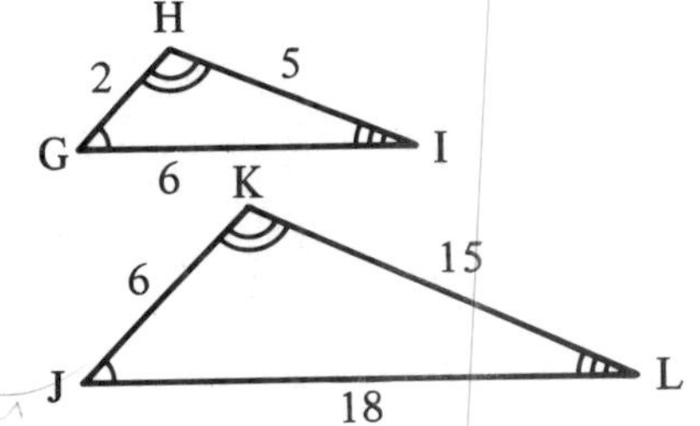

B. $\triangle MNO \sim \triangle PQR$. Find x. Complete.

4. $\frac{NM}{QP} = \frac{MO}{?}$
5. $\frac{4}{2} = \frac{?}{x}$
6. $4x =$ __?__
7. $x =$ __?__

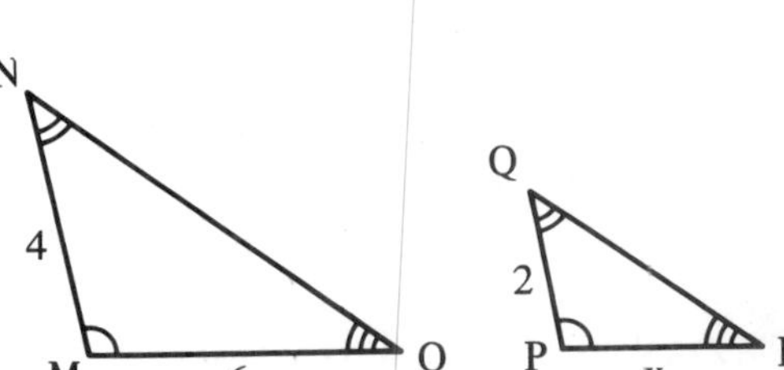

C. $\triangle STU \sim \triangle WVU$

8. Find x.

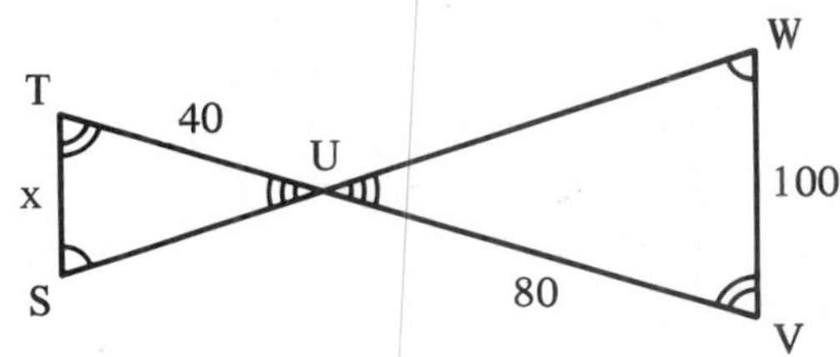

Practice

Are the triangles similar? Why?

1.

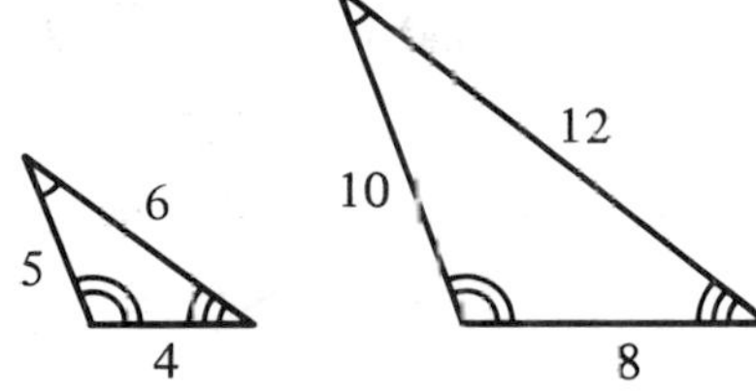

2.

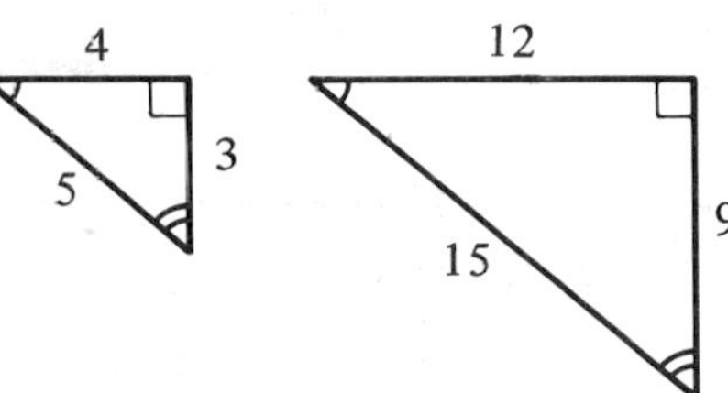

Each pair of triangles is similar. Find x.

3.

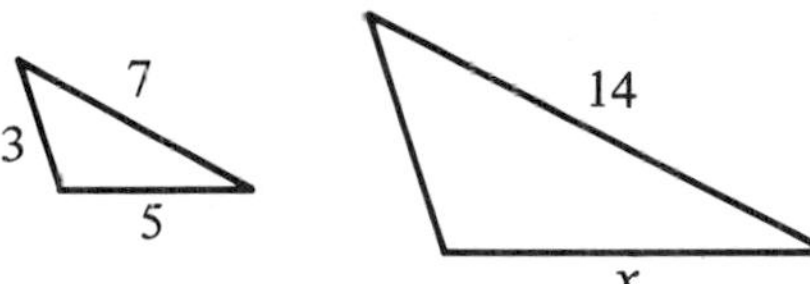

4.

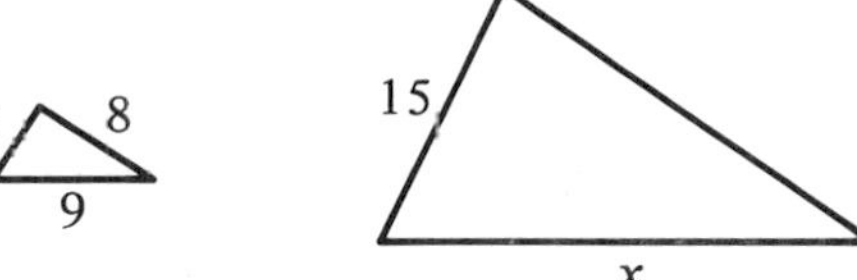

5.

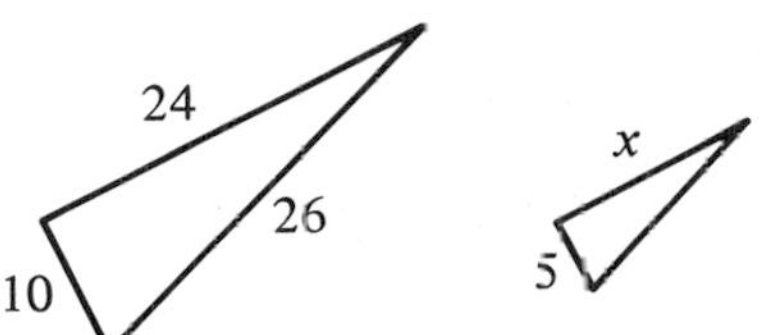

6.

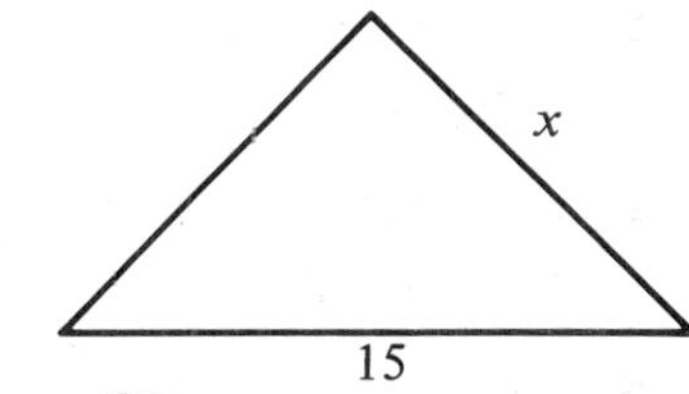

7.

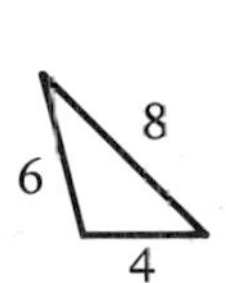

9 x

8.

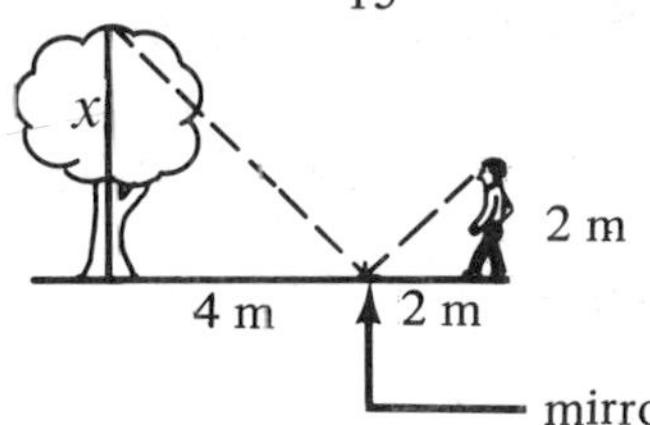

Solve.

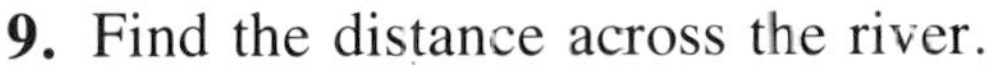

9. Find the distance across the river.

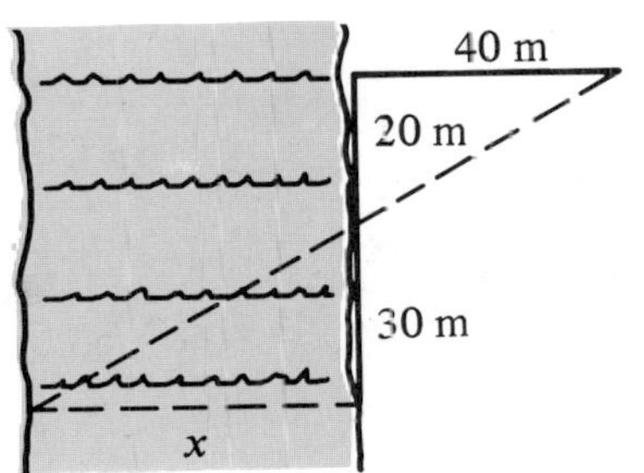

★ **10.** Assume that the sun's rays form similar triangles. Find the height of the school building.

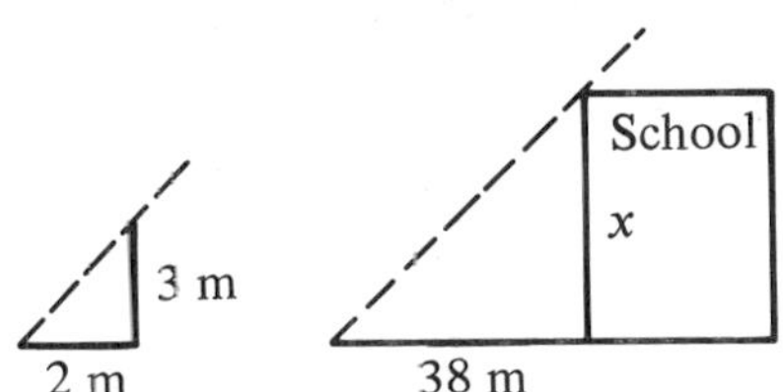

Scale Drawings

A scale drawing is similar to the actual object. The scale may be shown in different ways.

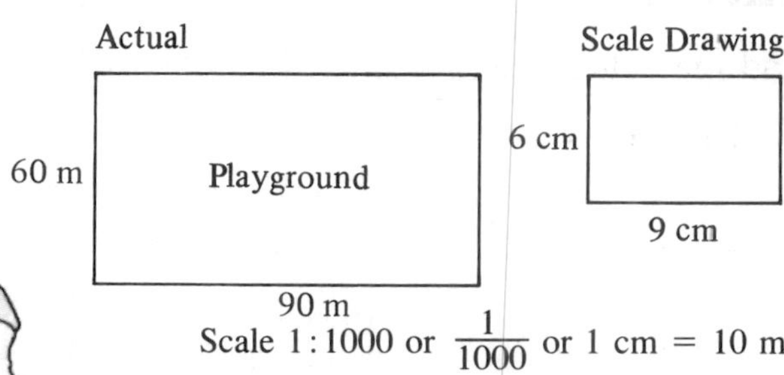

Scale 1:1000 or $\frac{1}{1000}$ or 1 cm = 10 m

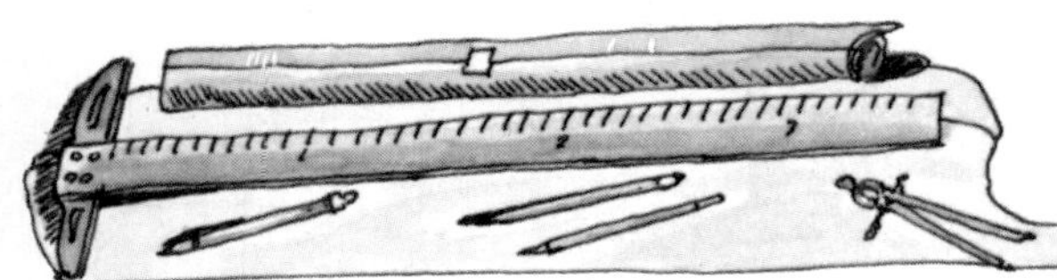

A. Find the actual length of the living room.

Scale: 0.5 cm = 1 m

1. Measure the length of the scale drawing.

2. Write a proportion and solve.

Scale Length   Actual Length

$$\frac{0.5 \text{ cm}}{3 \text{ cm}} = \frac{1 \text{ m}}{x}$$

3. What is the actual length of the living room?

B. Find the actual length.

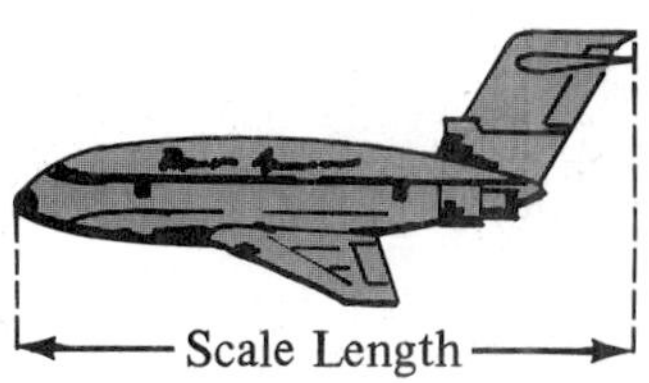

Scale 1:800

4. Measure the scale length to the nearest centimeter.

5. Complete the proportion. $\frac{1}{800} = \frac{?}{}$

6. Solve. $\frac{1}{800} = \frac{4 \text{ cm}}{x}$

7. Change 3,200 cm to m.

C. Use the scale 0.5 cm represents 1 m to make a scale drawing of a room 4.8 m by 6.6 m.

8. What length is represented by 1 cm?

9. How many centimeters on the drawing will represent 4.8 m?
Solve. $\frac{1 \text{ cm}}{2 \text{ m}} = \frac{x}{4.8 \text{ m}}$

10. How many centimeters on the drawing will represent 6.6 m?

11. What are the dimensions of the drawing?

12. Draw the scale drawing of the room.

Practice

Find the actual length and width. Measure to the nearest centimeter.

1. Living room
2. Kitchen
3. Bedroom 1
4. Bedroom 2

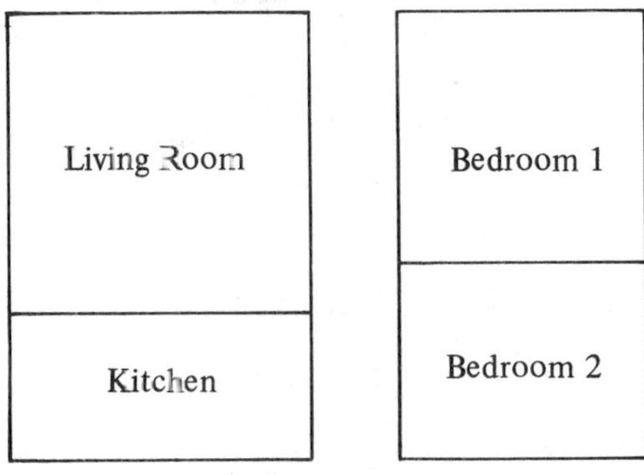

Scale 0.5 cm = 1 m

Find the actual lengths. Measure to the nearest centimeter.

5.

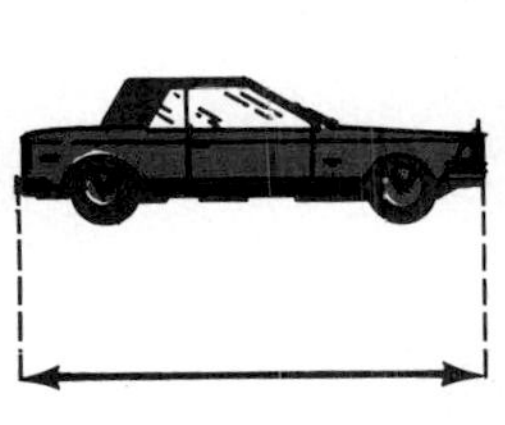

Scale 1:100

6.

Scale $\frac{1}{36}$

7.

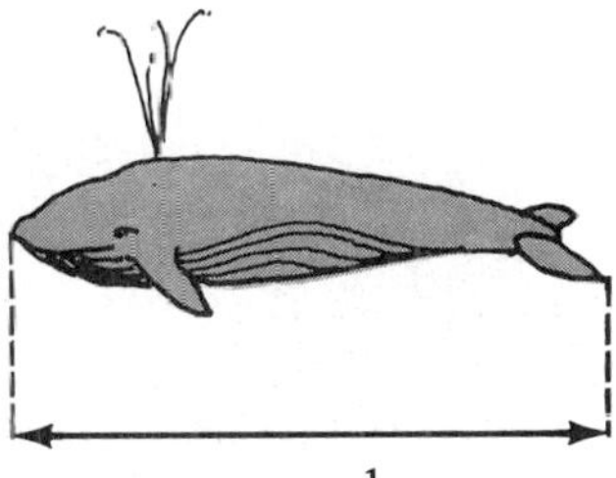

Scale $\frac{1}{500}$

Make scale drawings.

	Item	*Dimensions*	*Scale*
8.	Table top	1.5 m by 2.5 m	6 cm = 1 m
9.	Door	1 m by 2 m	0.5 cm = 1 m
10.	Playground	160 m by 300 m	1 cm = 40 m
11.	Room	2.3 m by 3 m	1:100

Trigonometric Ratios *(Optional)*

In right $\triangle ABC$,
the ratio $\frac{a}{c}$ is the sine of $m\angle A$,
the ratio $\frac{b}{c}$ is the cosine of $m\angle A$, and
the ratio $\frac{a}{b}$ is the tangent of $m\angle A$.

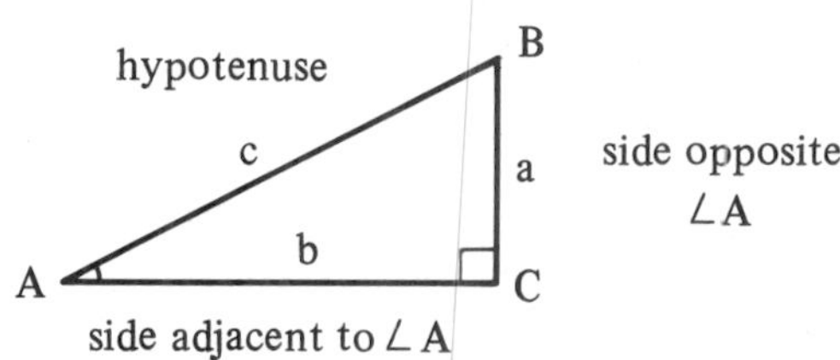

These abbreviations are used:

$\sin A = \frac{a}{c}$ $\cos A = \frac{b}{c}$ $\tan A = \frac{a}{b}$

▶ The sine, cosine, and tangent are trigonometric ratios. The word **trigonometry** means triangle measurement.

A. Find the lengths of these sides of $\triangle DEF$.

1. The hypotenuse

2. The side opposite $\angle D$

3. The side adjacent to $\angle D$

B. Find the ratios. Use $\triangle DEF$ at the right.

4. tan D **5.** sin D

6. cos D **7.** tan E

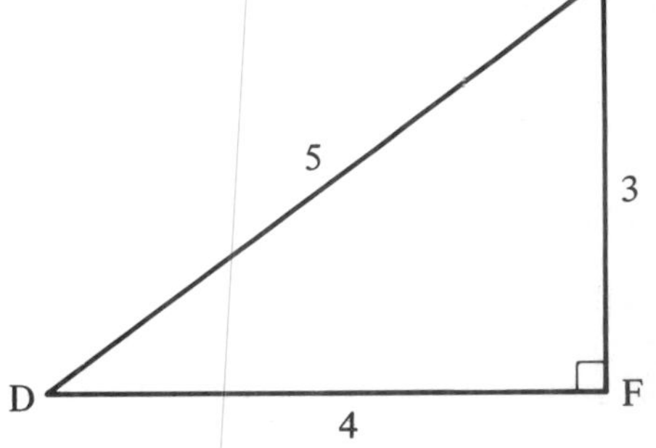

C. The trigonometric ratios are the same for a certain angle, no matter what the size of the triangle. The trigonometric ratios for angles measuring 0° through 90° are given in the table on page 402.

Find the ratios. Use the table on page 402.

8. sin 38° **9.** cos 21° **10.** tan 74°

D. You can use trigonometric ratios to find the height of a building.

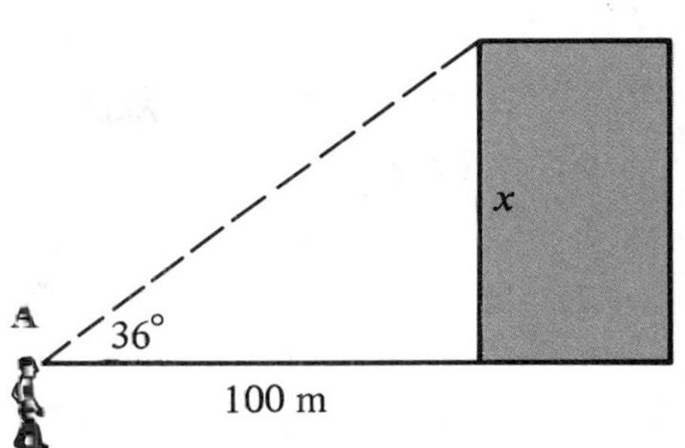

11. m$\angle A$ is given. Which length is given, opposite, adjacent, or hypotenuse?

12. Which length is x, opposite, adjacent, or hypotenuse?

13. Which ratio involves adjacent and opposite?

14. Complete.

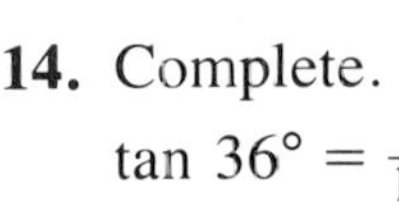

$$\tan 36° = \frac{x}{100}$$

$$0.727 = \frac{x}{100}$$

$$x = \underline{\quad ? \quad}$$

15. What is the height of the building?

Practice

Find the ratios. Use the table on page 402.

1. sin 54° **2.** sin 16° **3.** sin 87°

4. cos 27° **5.** cos 45° **6.** cos 71°

7. tan 38° **8.** tan 4° **9.** tan 69°

Find x.

10.

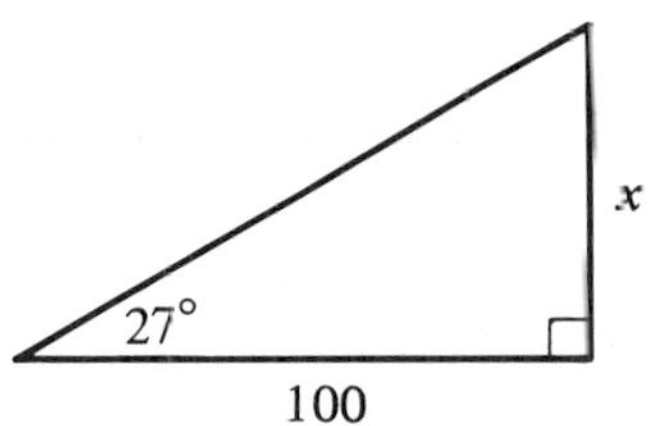

11.

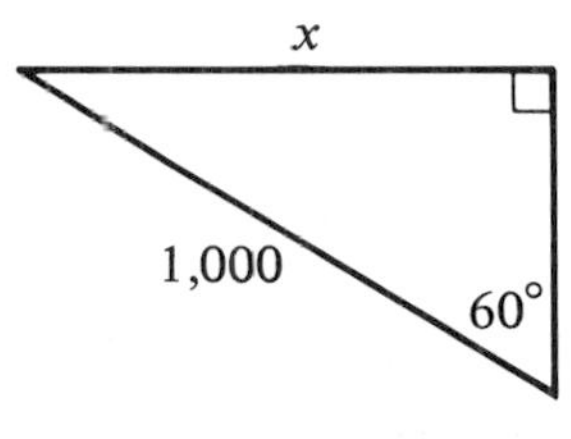

12.

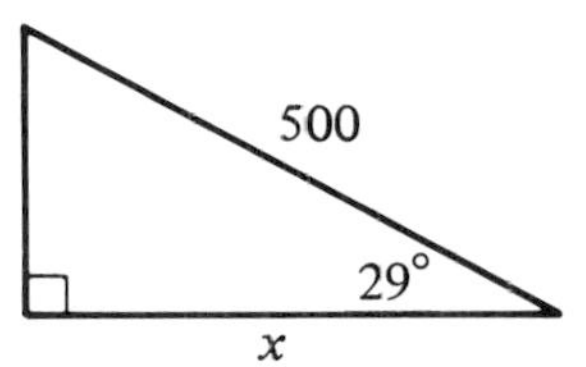

13.

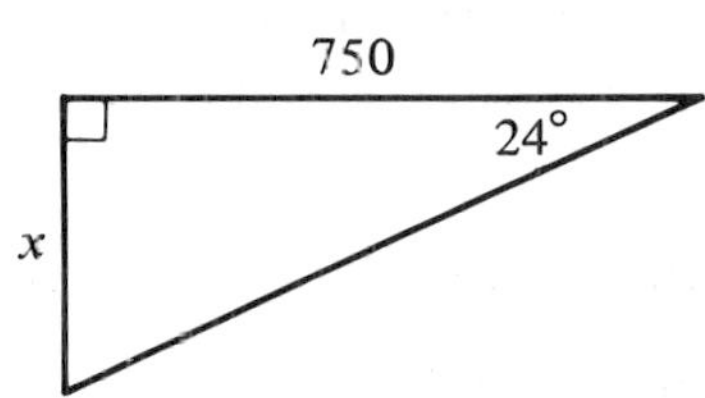

Area

Rectangle

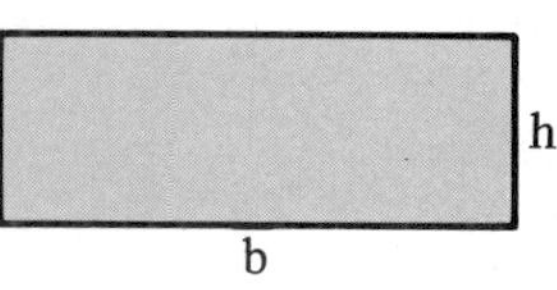

$A = b \cdot h$

Parallelogram

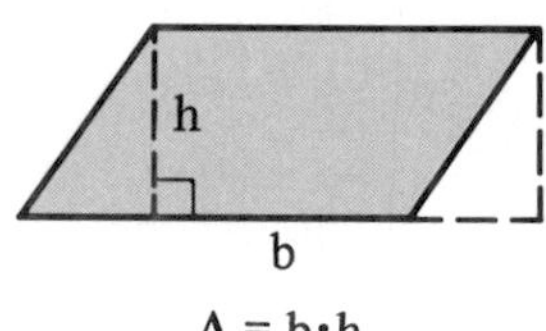

$A = b \cdot h$

Triangles

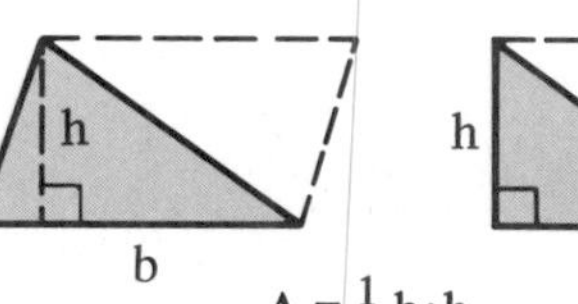

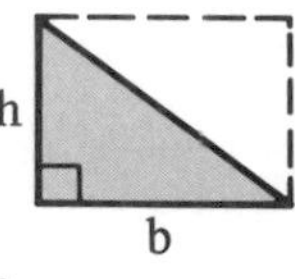

$A = \frac{1}{2} b \cdot h$

A. Find the areas.

1.

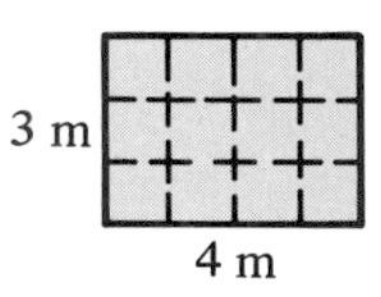

2.

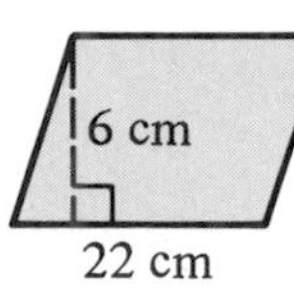

3.

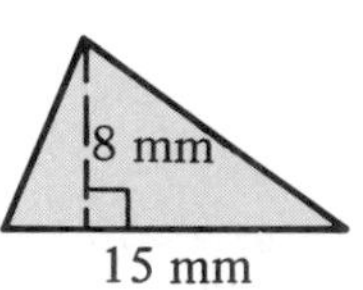

4.

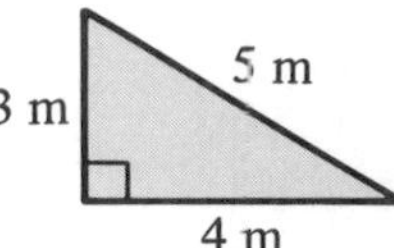

B. A square is a rectangle. Find the areas of these squares.

5.

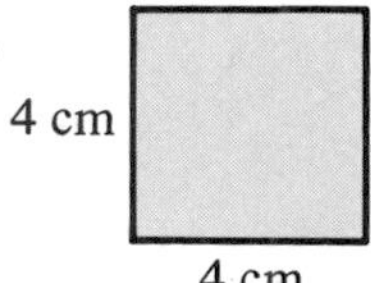

6.

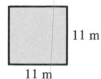

C. Here's how to find a formula for the area of a trapezoid.

7. Copy this trapezoid on square-ruled paper.

8. Double the trapezoid as shown.

9. What figure results?

10. The base of the parallelogram is $a + b$, or ___?___.

11. What is the area of the parallelogram?

a = 3
h = 2
b = 5

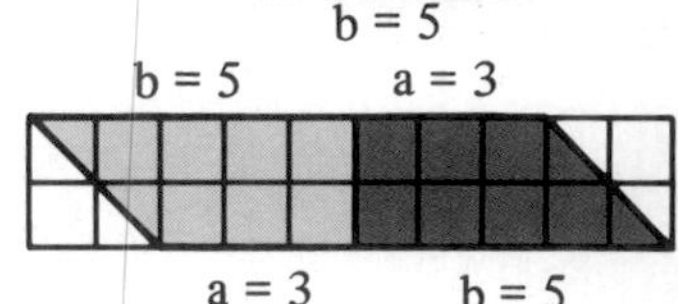

12. How does the area of the trapezoid compare with that of the parallelogram?

13. What is the area of the trapezoid?

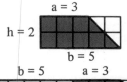

▶ The area of a trapezoid is $\frac{1}{2}$ the height times the sum of the bases.
$A = \frac{1}{2}h \cdot (a + b)$

D. Find the areas of the trapezoids.

14.

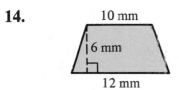

10 mm

6 mm

12 mm

15.

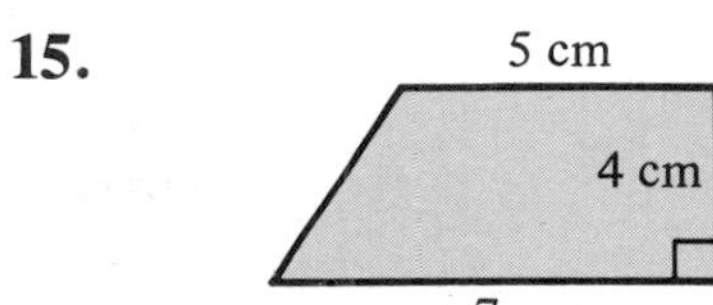

Practice

Find the areas.

1.

5 m

7 m

2.

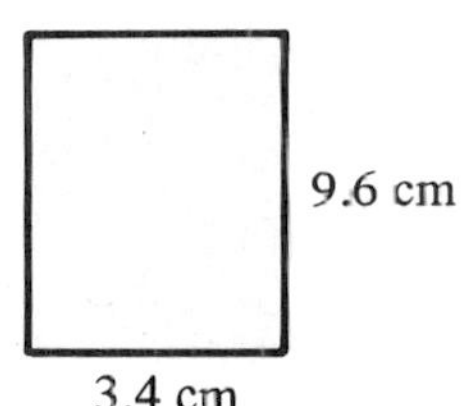

3.

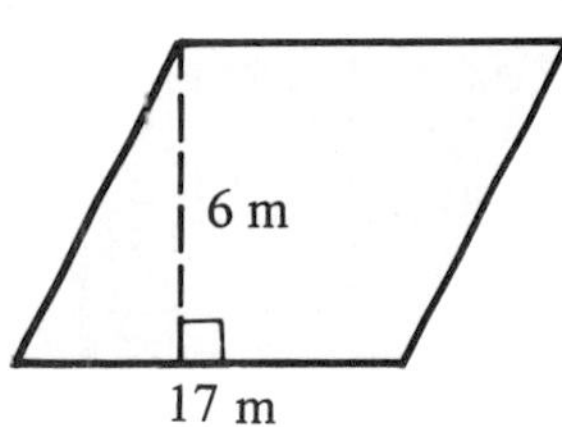

4.

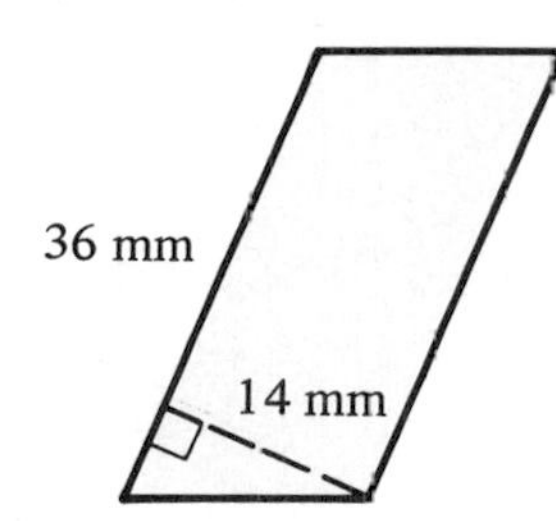

5.

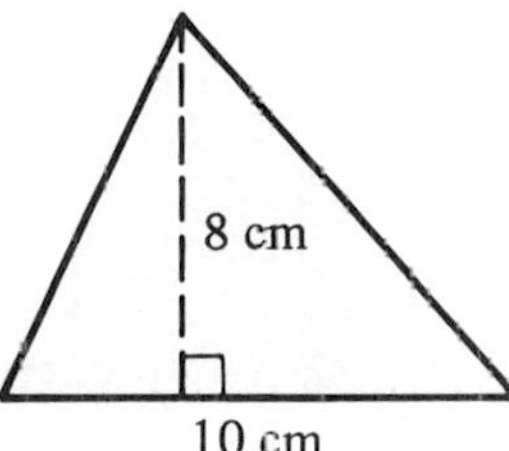

6.

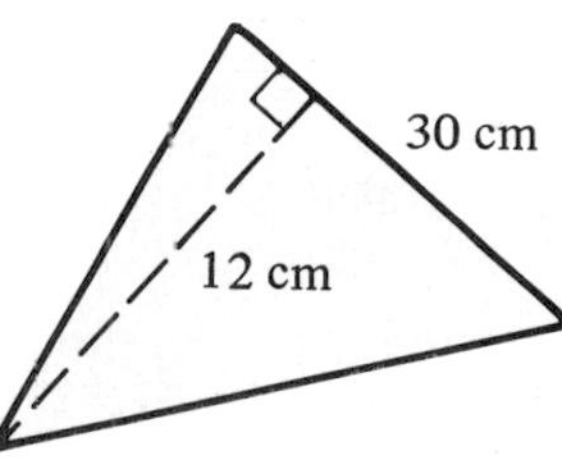

7.

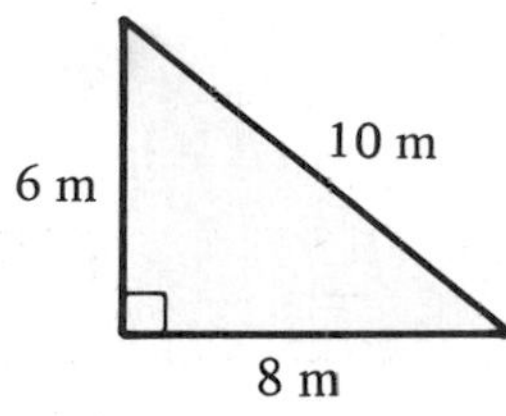

8.

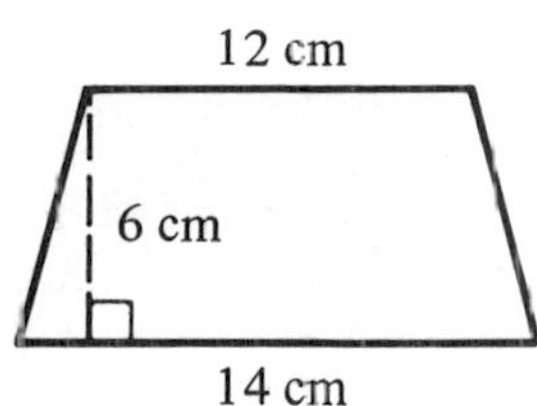

9.

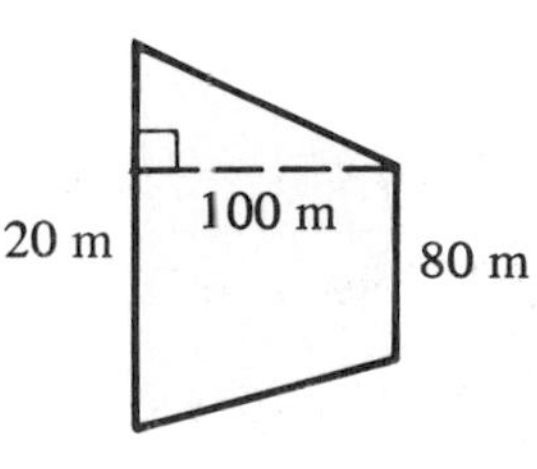

Solve.

10. Ms. Stone bought a carpet for a rectangular living room that is 6 m by 4 m. The carpet sold for $14.95/m². How much did she pay to carpet her living room?

★ **11.** What happens to the area of a square when a side is doubled?

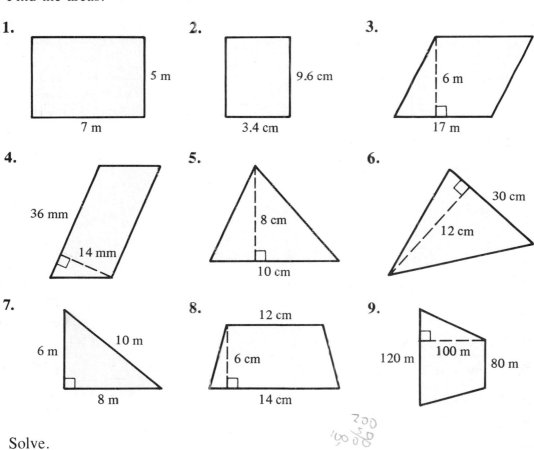

Area in Metric System

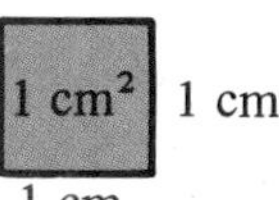

A square centimeter (cm^2) is a unit of area.

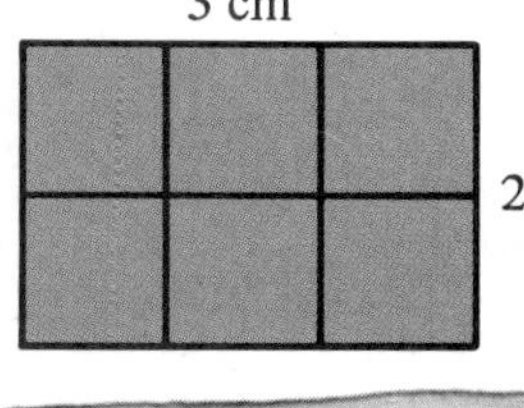

The area of this rectangle is 6 cm^2.

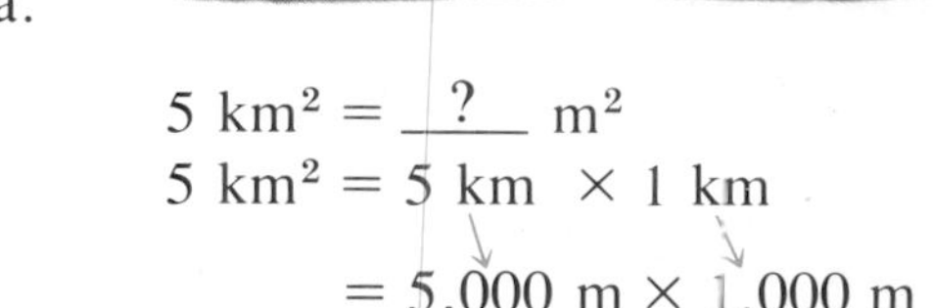

A. You can change between metric units of area.

Examples

$1 \text{ m}^2 = \underline{\ ?\ } \text{ cm}^2$
$1 \text{ m}^2 = 1 \text{ m} \times 1 \text{ m}$
$= 100 \text{ cm} \times 100 \text{ cm}$
$= 10{,}000 \text{ cm}^2$

$5 \text{ km}^2 = \underline{\ ?\ } \text{ m}^2$
$5 \text{ km}^2 = 5 \text{ km} \times 1 \text{ km}$
$= 5{,}000 \text{ m} \times 1{,}000 \text{ m}$
$= 5{,}000{,}000 \text{ m}^2$

Complete.

1. $1 \text{ cm}^2 = \underline{\ ?\ } \text{ mm}^2$ **2.** $1 \text{ km}^2 = \underline{\ ?\ } \text{ m}^2$ **3.** $2 \text{ m}^2 = \underline{\ ?\ } \text{ cm}^2$

4. $4 \text{ cm}^2 = \underline{\ ?\ } \text{ mm}^2$ **5.** $3 \text{ km}^2 = \underline{\ ?\ } \text{ m}^2$ **6.** $1 \text{ m}^2 = \underline{\ ?\ } \text{ mm}^2$

B. Use decimals to change from a smaller unit to a larger unit.

Examples

$1 \text{ cm}^2 = \underline{\ ?\ } \text{ m}^2$
$1 \text{ cm}^2 = 1 \text{ cm} \times 1 \text{ cm}$
$= 0.01 \text{ m} \times 0.01 \text{ m}$
$= 0.0001 \text{ m}^2$

$5 \text{ mm}^2 = \underline{\ ?\ } \text{ cm}^2$
$5 \text{ mm}^2 = 5 \text{ mm} \times 1 \text{ mm}$
$= 0.5 \text{ cm} \times 0.1 \text{ cm}$
$= 0.05 \text{ cm}^2$

Complete.

7. $1 \text{ mm}^2 = \underline{\ ?\ } \text{ cm}^2$ **8.** $1 \text{ m}^2 = \underline{\ ?\ } \text{ km}^2$ **9.** $1 \text{ mm}^2 = \underline{\ ?\ } \text{ m}^2$

10. $25 \text{ cm}^2 = \underline{\ ?\ } \text{ m}^2$ **11.** $500 \text{ m}^2 = \underline{\ ?\ } \text{ km}^2$ **12.** $400 \text{ mm}^2 = \underline{\ ?\ } \text{ cm}^2$

C. The units of area commonly used for measuring land are the are (a) and hectare (ha).

1 are (a) = 100 m^2 1 hectare (ha) = 10,000 m^2

Complete.

13. $2 \text{ ha} = \underline{\ ?\ } \text{ m}^2$ **14.** $40{,}000 \text{ m}^2 = \underline{\ ?\ } \text{ ha}$ **15.** $4 \text{ a} = \underline{\ ?\ } \text{ m}^2$

D. Which unit of area would you use to measure the following? Choose km^2, ha, m^2, cm^2, or mm^2.

16. Alaska

17. Fabric for a suit

18. The school property

19. An arm bandage

20. A shirt button

21. A rug

Practice

Complete.

1. $2\ m^2 = \underline{\ ?\ }\ cm^2$

2. $6\ m^2 = \underline{\ ?\ }\ mm^2$

3. $900\ m^2 = \underline{\ ?\ }\ km^2$

4. $4\ km^2 = \underline{\ ?\ }\ m^2$

5. $6\ cm^2 = \underline{\ ?\ }\ mm^2$

6. $400\ cm^2 = \underline{\ ?\ }\ m^2$

7. $30{,}000\ cm^2 = \underline{\ ?\ }\ m^2$

8. $\underline{\ ?\ }\ m^2 = 7{,}000{,}000\ mm^2$

9. $2\ cm^2 = \underline{\ ?\ }\ m^2$

10. $4\ m^2 = \underline{\ ?\ }\ km^2$

11. $3\ mm^2 = \underline{\ ?\ }\ cm^2$

12. $53\ mm^2 = \underline{\ ?\ }\ m^2$

13. $3\ ha = \underline{\ ?\ }\ m^2$

14. $70{,}000\ m^2 = \underline{\ ?\ }\ ha$

15. $5\ a = \underline{\ ?\ }\ m^2$

16. $700\ m^2 = \underline{\ ?\ }\ a$

Solve.

17. A rectangular piece of land is 300 m long and 200 m wide. Express its area in hectares.

18. The side of a square is 50 cm. Express its area in m^2.

Which unit of measure would you use? Choose km^2, ha, m^2, cm^2, or mm^2.

19. Draperies

20. New York City

21. The playground

Brainteaser

What are all the possible whole numbers for x such that $x^2 = x + x$?

Area of a Circle

A goat is tied to a stake with a rope 7 m long. Over how many square meters can the goat graze?

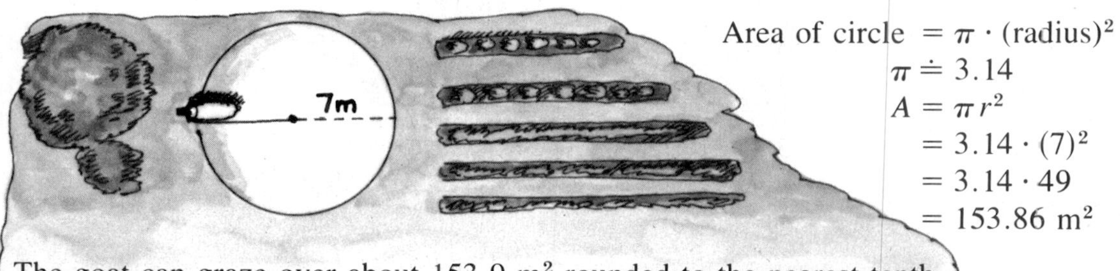

Area of circle $= \pi \cdot (\text{radius})^2$

$\pi \doteq 3.14$

$A = \pi r^2$

$= 3.14 \cdot (7)^2$

$= 3.14 \cdot 49$

$= 153.86 \text{ m}^2$

The goat can graze over about 153.9 m^2 rounded to the nearest tenth.

A. Find the areas. Use $\pi \doteq 3.14$. Round the answer to the nearest tenth.

1. $r = 10$ cm **2.** $r = 4$ m **3.** $d = 10$ cm **4.** $d = 18$ cm

B. Here's how to find the area of the shaded portion (ring). Use $\pi \doteq 3.14$.

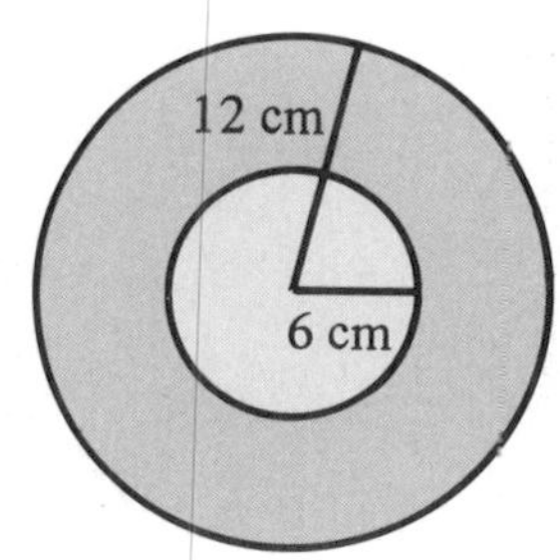

5. What is the area of the large circle?

6. What is the area of the small circle?

7. Subtract the area of the small circle from the area of the large circle.

8. What is the area of the ring?

Practice

Find the areas. Use $\pi \doteq 3.14$. Round the answer to the nearest tenth.

1. $r = 8$ mm **2.** $r = 14$ m **3.** $d = 12$ cm **4.** $d = 24$ cm

Find the area of the shaded region.

5.

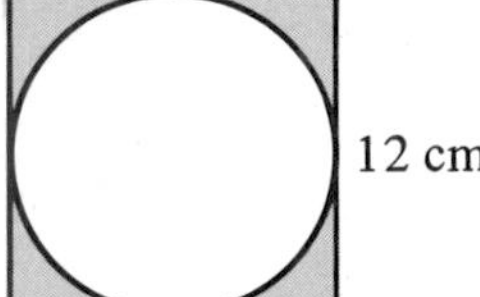

6.

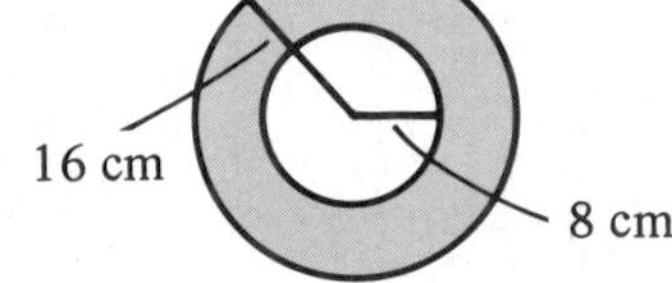

7.

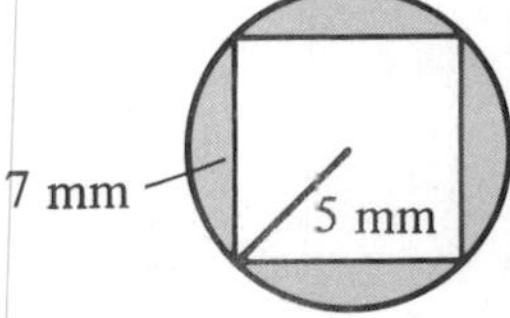

Mid-Chapter Review

Find x. *(332, 336)*

1. $\triangle ABC \cong \triangle DEF$

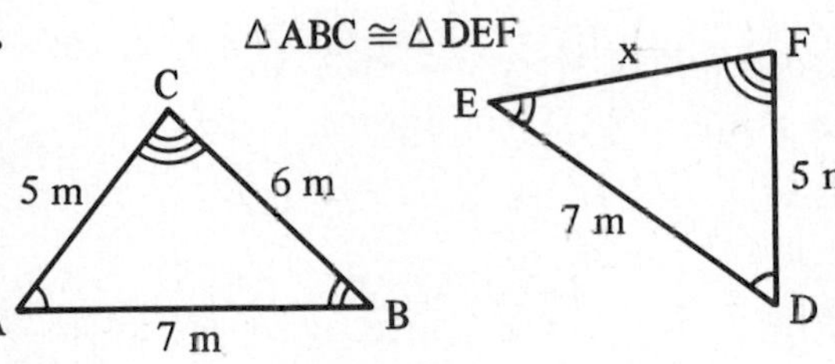

2. $\triangle XYU \cong \triangle STU$

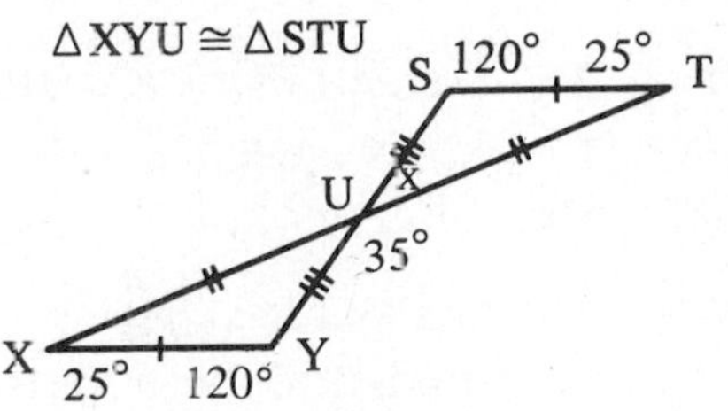

3. $\triangle LMN \sim \triangle PQR$

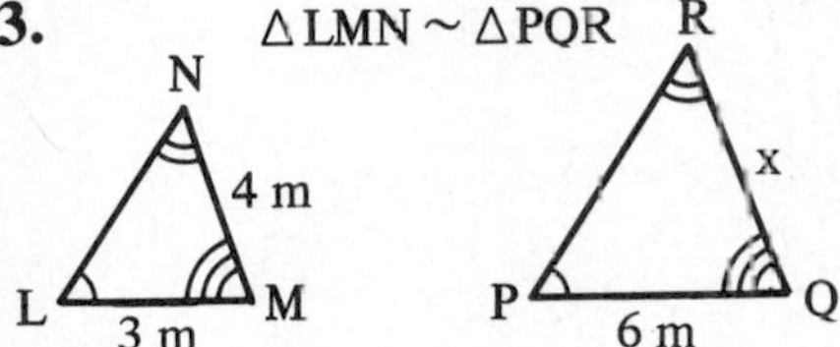

4. $\triangle GHI \sim \triangle JKI$

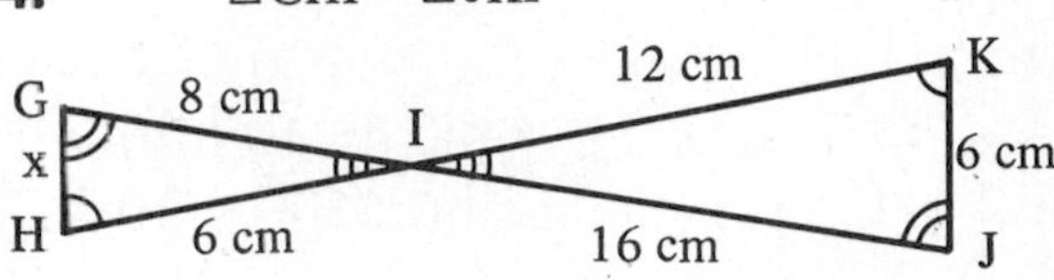

Find the actual lengths. Measure to the nearest centimeter. *(338)*

5.

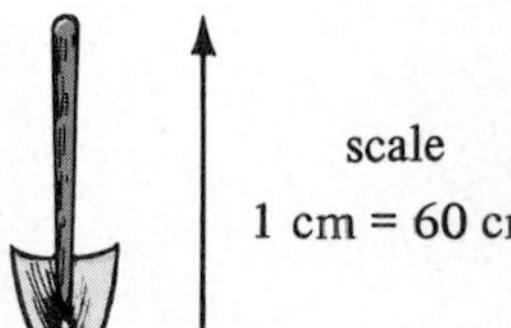

6.

scale 1:5

7.

scale 1:300

Complete. *(344)*

8. 3 m^2 = __?__ cm^2

9. 4 m^2 = __?__ mm^2

10. 8 cm^2 = __?__ m^2

11. 8 ha = __?__ m^2

Find the areas. Use $\pi \doteq 3.14$. *(342, 346)*

12.

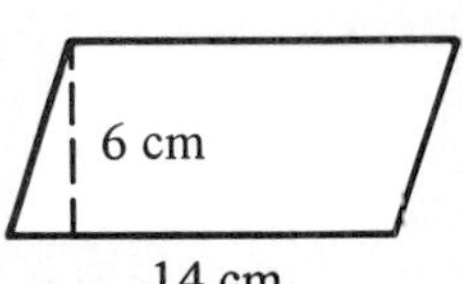

13.

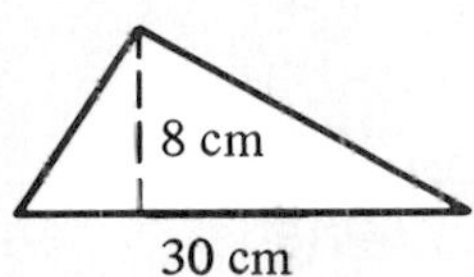

14.

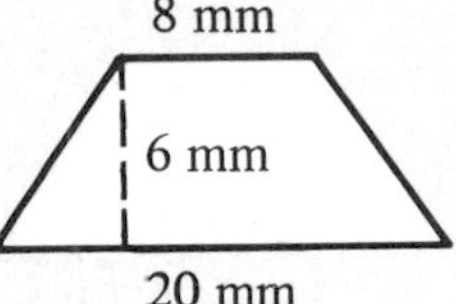

15.

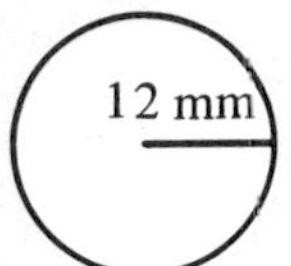

16.

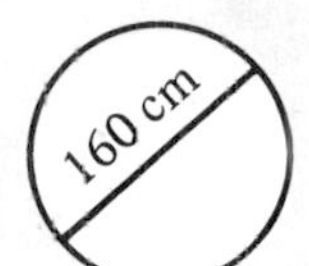

17.

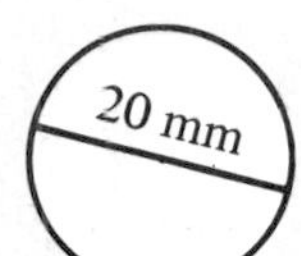

Problem Solving

Rounded numbers can be used in order to find a method to solve problems and check if your answer is reasonable.

READ Mr. Valenti owns a sporting goods store. He paid \$328.44 for a dozen jogging suits. What is the cost of 1 jogging suit?

PLAN 1 dozen = 12
12 rounded to the nearest ten is 10.
\$328.44 rounded to the nearest hundred dollars is \$300.

Think of a method to solve the problem.
Divide \$300 by 10 to find the approximate cost of 1 jogging suit. \$300 ÷ 10 = \$30

SOLVE Use the original numbers to find the exact cost.
\$328.44 ÷ 12 = \$27.37

CHECK \$27.37 is close to \$30, so the answer is reasonable.

A can of 3 tennis balls sells for \$1.99. Sue bought 24 cans for her tennis club. What was the total cost of the tennis balls?

PLAN Complete.

1. \$1.99 rounded to the nearest dollar is ___?___.
2. 24 rounded to the nearest ten is ___?___.
3. To find the approximate total cost, use the operation of ___?___.
4. \$2.00 × 20 = ___?___

SOLVE Complete.

5. Use the original numbers to find the exact cost.
   \$1.99 × 24 = ___?___

CHECK

6. Is \$47.76 close to \$40.00?

Solve. First use rounded numbers.

1. A barbell set of weights is on sale for $68.99. After the sale the set will sell for $84.25. How much more will the set cost after the sale?

2. A box of a dozen golf balls costs a store owner $4.92. What is the cost to the store owner of 75 boxes of these golf balls?

3. The school basketball team bought a new basketball on sale for $13.99. They saved $2.98 off the regular price. What was the regular price of the basketball?

4. Mr. Hawthorne bought a tennis racket for $24.90, a pair of tennis shorts for $19.95, sneakers for $24.25, and a warm-up suit for $26.95. How much did he spend in all?

5. A soccer ball costs $17.49 during a sale. A soccer club bought 18 balls at the beginning of the soccer season. How much did they pay for the soccer balls?

6. A store owner pays $46.19 for a basketball backboard. She sells it for $61.25 during a sale. How much does the store owner make if a backboard is sold during the sale?

7. A rod and reel combination is on sale for $29.99. When the sale ends, it will cost $41.50. How much is saved by buying during the sale?

8. The jogging club has 17 members. They want to buy jogging shoes, which sell for $24.99 a pair. If they all buy their shoes at once, the price will be $21.25 a pair. How much will they save by buying the shoes together?

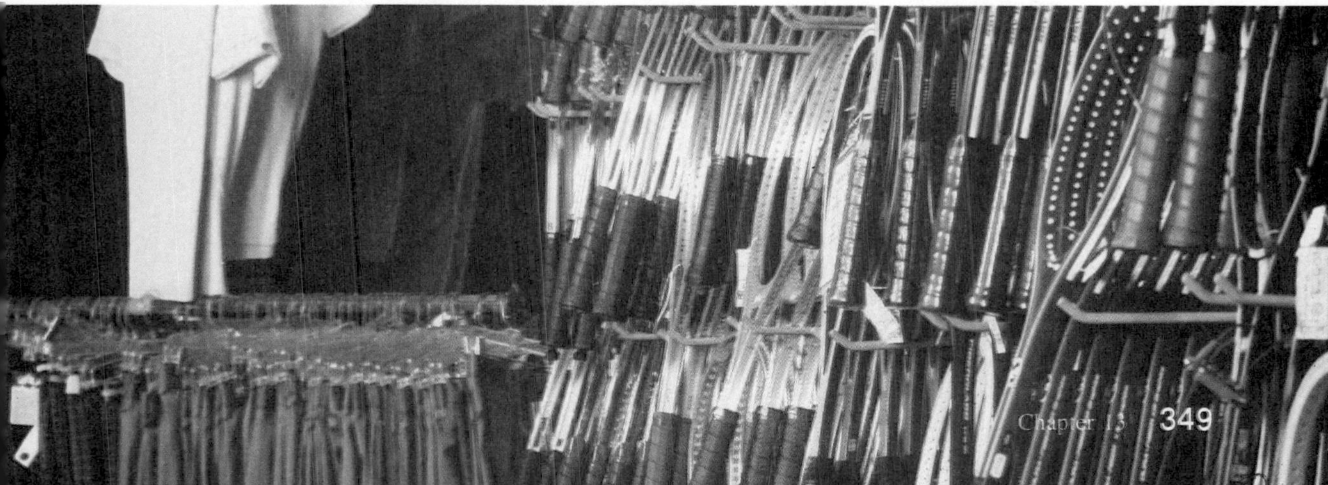

Using Customary Units of Area

Doug wants to carpet a hall that measures 4 ft by 9 ft. Carpeting costs $5.95/yd². What will carpeting for the hall cost?

$$1 \text{ yd} = 3 \text{ ft}$$
$$1 \text{ yd}^2 = 9 \text{ ft}^2$$

$$\text{Area of the hall} = 4 \text{ ft} \times 9 \text{ ft}$$
$$= 36 \text{ ft}^2$$
$$= 4 \text{ yd}^2 \longleftarrow (36 \text{ ft} \div 9 \text{ ft})$$

Carpeting will cost 4 × $5.95, or $23.80.

A. Complete. Use these relationships.

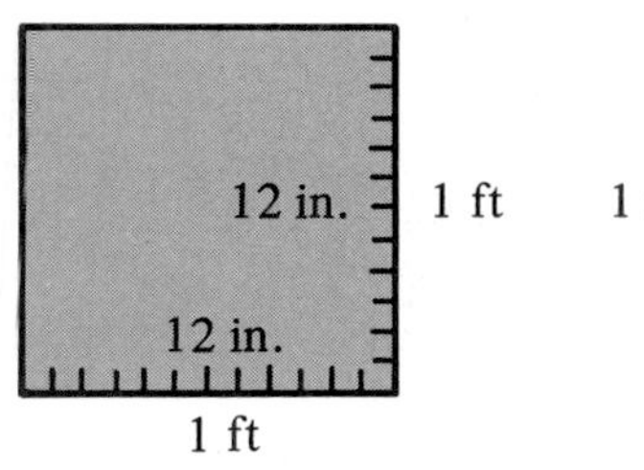

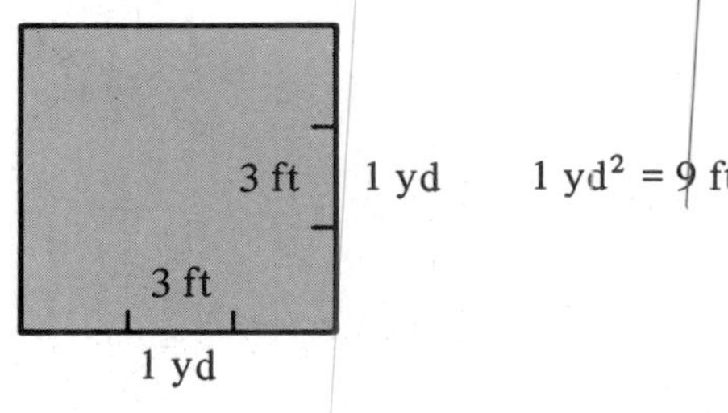

1. $3 \text{ ft}^2 = \underline{\ ?\ } \text{ in.}^2$

2. $4 \text{ yd}^2 = \underline{\ ?\ } \text{ ft}^2$

3. $72 \text{ ft}^2 = \underline{\ ?\ } \text{ yd}^2$

4. $288 \text{ in.}^2 = \underline{\ ?\ } \text{ ft}^2$

B. Give the areas in square yards.

5.

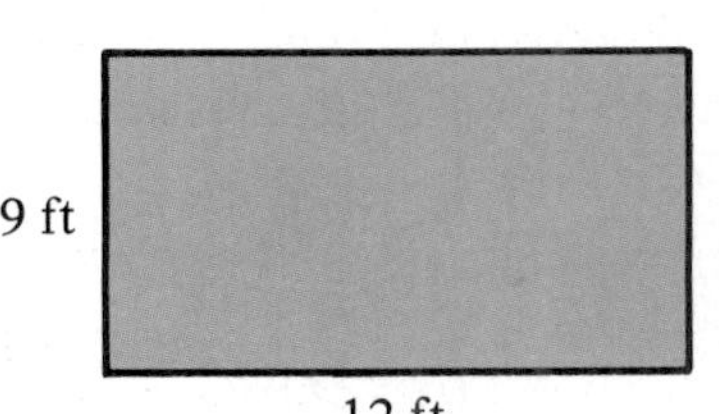

6.

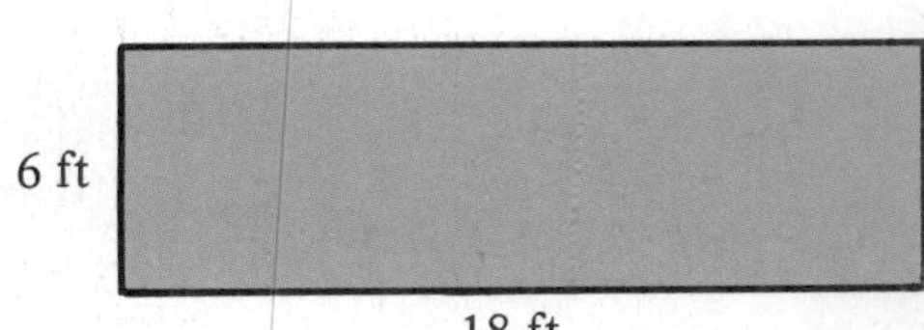

C. Complete. Use these relationships.

1 acre = 43,560 ft²　　　640 acres = 1 mi²

7. $2 \text{ acres} = \underline{\ ?\ } \text{ ft}^2$

8. $2 \text{ mi}^2 = \underline{\ ?\ } \text{ acres}$

Complete.

1. 5 ft^2 = ___?___ $in.^2$

2. 7 ft^2 = ___?___ $in.^2$

3. 10 ft^2 = ___?___ $in.^2$

4. 20 ft^2 = ___?___ $in.^2$

5. 6 yd^2 = ___?___ ft^2

6. 10 yd^2 = ___?___ ft^2

7. 12 yd^2 = ___?___ ft^2

8. 20 yd^2 = ___?___ ft^2

9. 432 $in.^2$ = ___?___ ft^2

10. 1,440 $in.^2$ = ___?___ ft^2

11. 18 ft^2 = ___?___ yd^2

12. 45 ft^2 = ___?___ yd^2

13. 81 ft^2 = ___?___ yd^2

14. 270 ft^2 = ___?___ yd^2

15. 3 acres = ___?___ ft^2

16. 10 acres = ___?___ ft^2

17. 6 mi^2 = ___?___ acres

18. 10 mi^2 = ___?___ acres

Give the areas in square yards.

19.

20.

21.

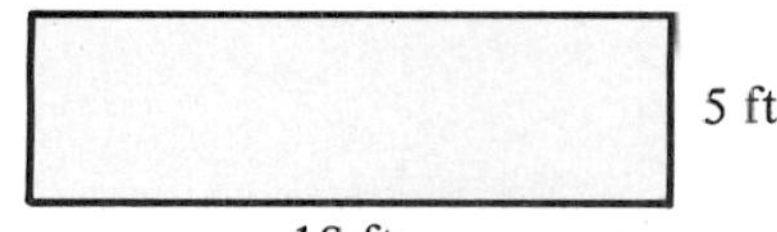

22.

23.

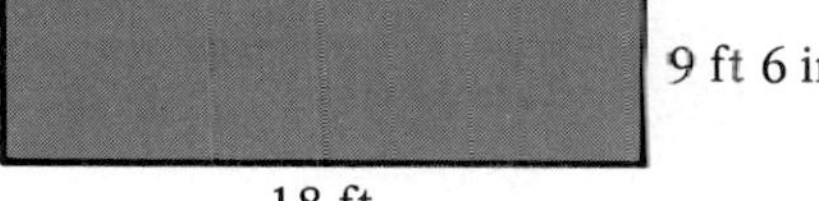

24.

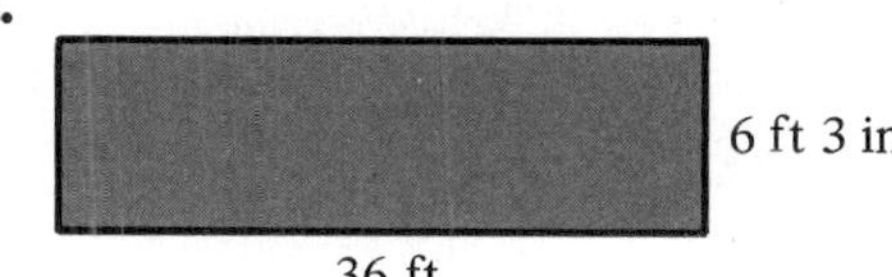

Solve.

25. Carpeting sells for $17.65/$yd^2$. Find the cost of carpeting for a room 12 ft by 18 ft.

Surface Area

The surface area of a solid is the sum of the areas of its faces.

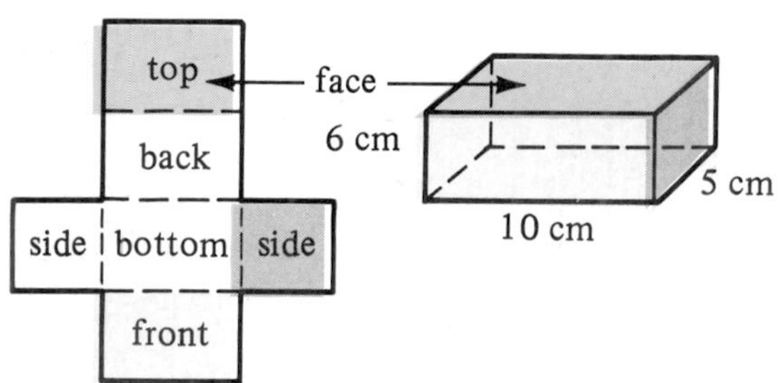

Area of bottom	=	$10 \cdot 5$ or 50 cm^2
Area of top	=	$10 \cdot 5$ or 50 cm^2
Area of side	=	$5 \cdot 6$ or 30 cm^2
Area of side	=	$5 \cdot 6$ or 30 cm^2
Area of front	=	$10 \cdot 6$ or 60 cm^2
Area of back	=	$10 \cdot 6$ or 60 cm^2
Surface Area		280 cm^2

A. Find the surface areas.

1.

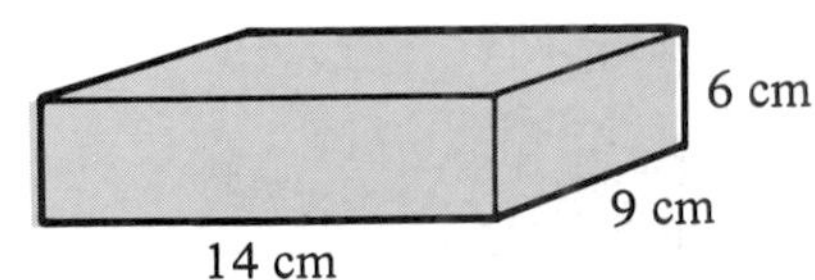

2.

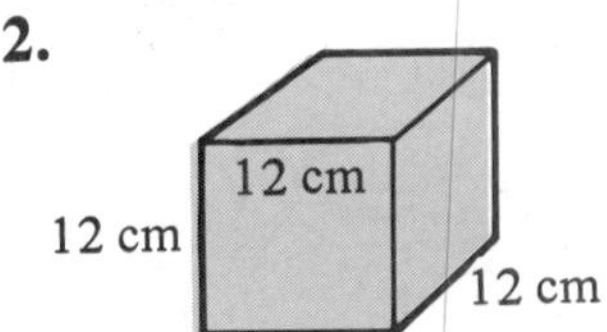

B. Here's a way to find the surface area of the cylinder.

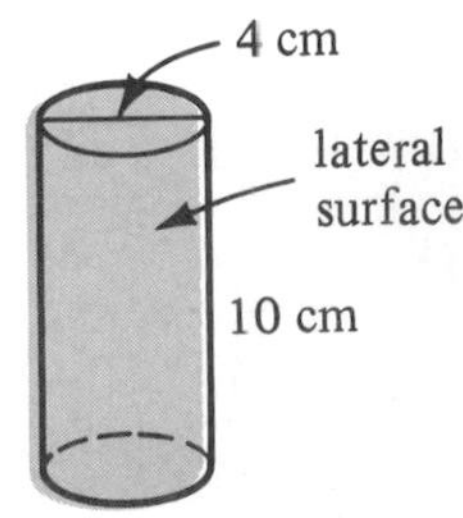

3. What kind of figure is each base?

4. Find the area of one base. Use $\pi \doteq 3.14$.

5. What is the area of both bases?

6. When the lateral surface is unfolded, what figure is formed?

7. What is the width of this rectangle?

8. Find the length of this rectangle. (It's the same as the circumference of the circle. Use $\pi \doteq 3.14$.)

9. Find the area of the lateral surface.

10. What is the surface area of the cylinder?

C. Here's a way to find the surface area of the pyramid.

11. The base is a square. Find its area.

12. What is the area of one face?

13. What is the area of the 4 faces?

14. What is the surface area of the pyramid?

Practice

Find the surface areas.

1\.

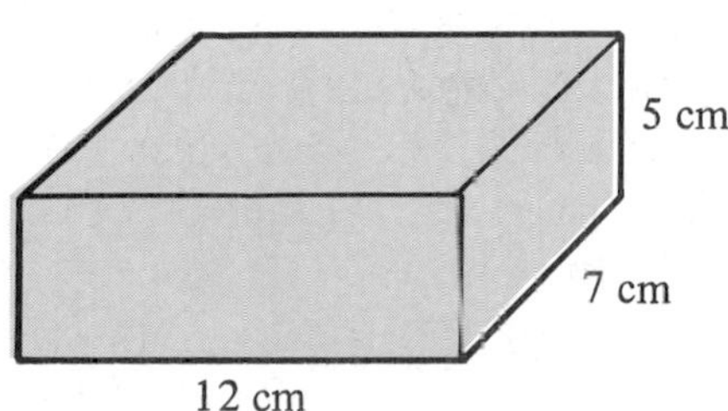

2\.

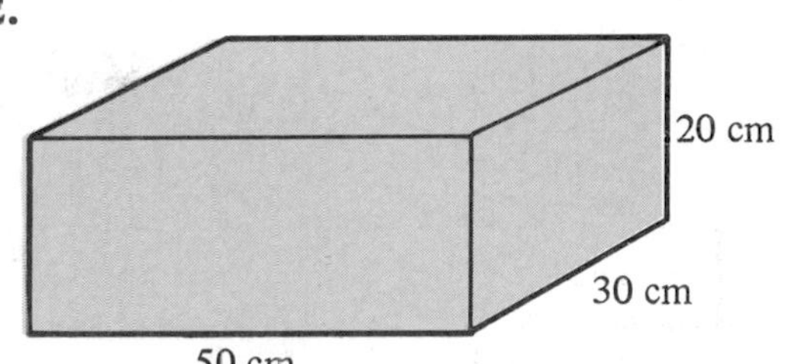

3\.

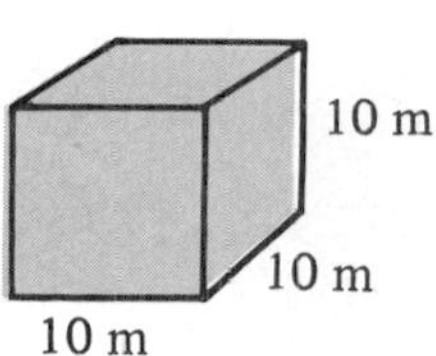

4\.

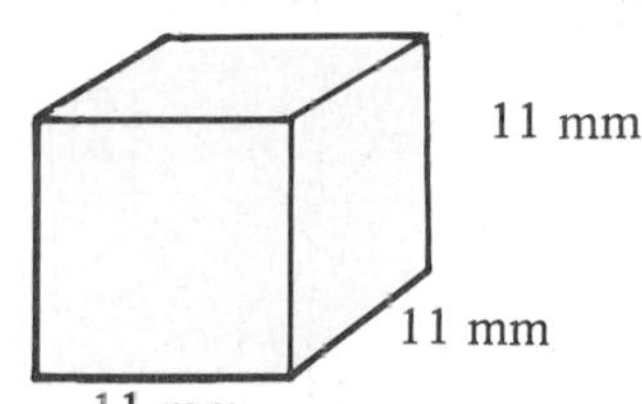

5\.

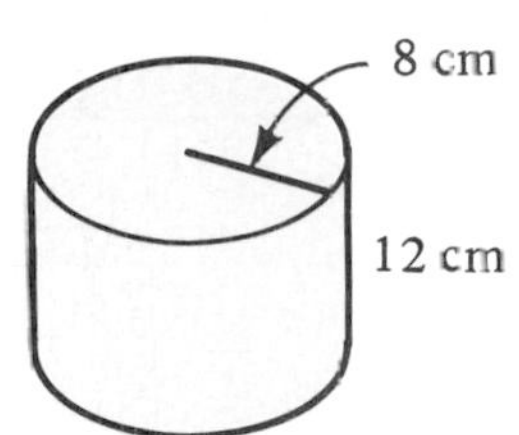

6\.

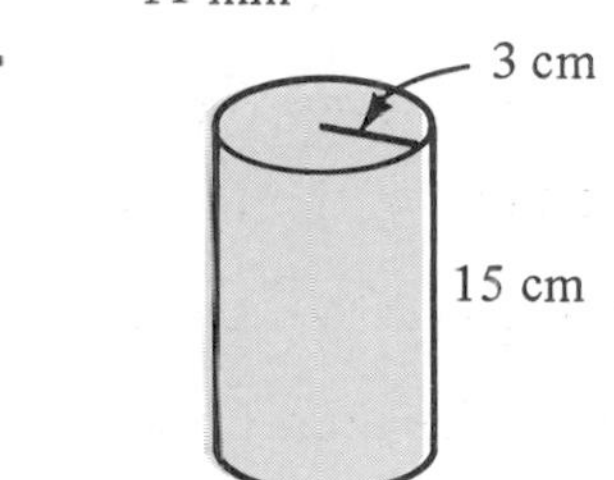

7\.

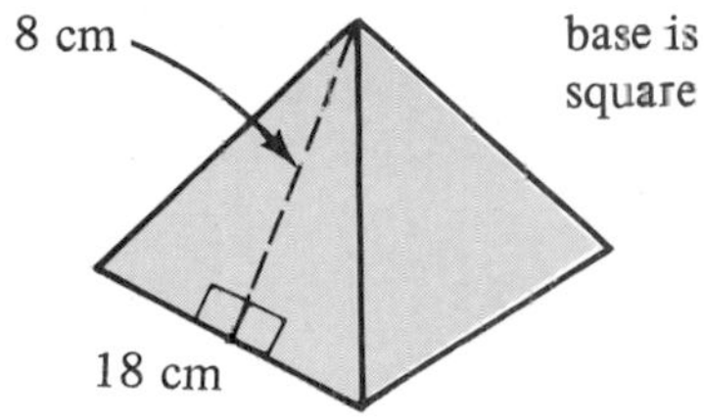

8\.

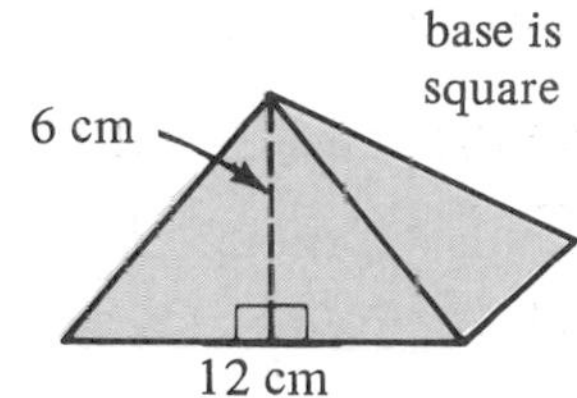

Solve.

9\. A liter of paint will cover about $12\ m^2$. How much paint is needed to paint the walls and ceiling of a room which is 7 m long, 6 m wide, and 3 m high?

10\. Which can needs more material to cover it completely?

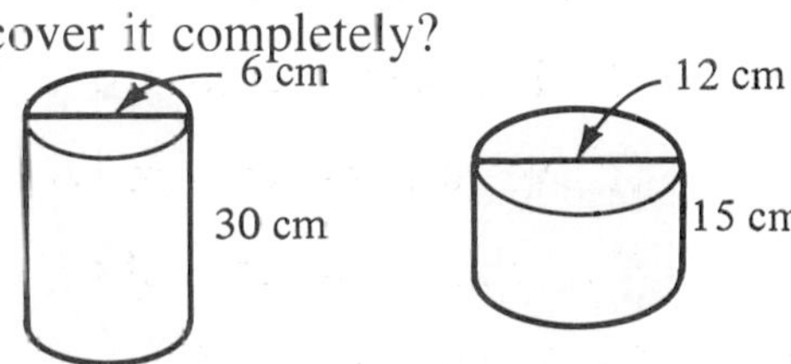

Volume in the Metric System

A cubic centimeter (cm³) is a unit of volume.

A. You can change between metric units of volume.

Example $2 \text{ cm}^3 = \underline{\ ?\ } \text{ mm}^3$

$$2 \text{ cm}^3 = 2 \text{ cm} \times 1 \text{ cm} \times 1 \text{ cm}$$
$$\downarrow \qquad \downarrow \qquad \downarrow$$
$$= 20 \text{ mm} \times 10 \text{ mm} \times 10 \text{ mm}$$
$$= 2{,}000 \text{ mm}^3$$

Complete.

1. $4 \text{ m}^3 = \underline{\quad\quad} \text{ cm}^3$ **2.** $7 \text{ cm}^3 = \underline{\ ?\ } \text{ mm}^3$ **3.** $1 \text{ m}^3 = \underline{\ ?\ } \text{ mm}^3$

B. Use decimals to change from a smaller unit of volume to a larger unit of volume.

Example $3 \text{ mm}^3 = \underline{\ ?\ } \text{ cm}^3$

$$3 \text{ mm}^3 = 3 \text{ mm} \times 1 \text{ mm} \times 1 \text{ mm}$$
$$\downarrow \qquad \downarrow \qquad \downarrow$$
$$= 0.3 \text{ cm} \times 0.1 \text{ cm} \times 0.1 \text{ cm}$$
$$= 0.003 \text{ cm}^3$$

Complete.

4. $8 \text{ cm}^3 = \underline{\ ?\ } \text{ m}^3$ **5.** $500 \text{ cm}^3 = \underline{\ ?\ } \text{ m}^3$ **6.** $9 \text{ mm}^3 = \underline{\ ?\ } \text{ cm}^3$

7. $5{,}000 \text{ mm}^3 = \underline{\ ?\ } \text{ cm}^3$ **8.** $7{,}000{,}000 \text{ mm}^3 = \underline{\ ?\ } \text{ m}^3$

Practice

Complete.

1. $2\ m^3 =$ ___?___ cm^3
2. $80\ m^3 =$ ___?___ cm^3
3. $8\ cm^3 =$ ___?___ mm^3
4. $60\ cm^3 =$ ___?___ mm^3
5. $5{,}000\ cm^3 =$ ___?___ mm^3
6. $3\ m^3 =$ ___?___ mm^3
7. $7\ m^3 =$ ___?___ mm^3
8. $2\ cm^3 =$ ___?___ m^3
9. $8{,}000\ cm^3 =$ ___?___ m^3
10. $6\ mm^3 =$ ___?___ cm^3
11. $4{,}000\ mm^3 =$ ___?___ cm^3
12. $5{,}000{,}000\ mm^3 =$ ___?___ m^3
13. $9{,}000\ mm^3 =$ ___?___ m^3
14. $20\ cm^3 =$ ___?___ mm^3
15. $30{,}000\ mm^3 =$ ___?___ m^3
16. $5\ m^3 =$ ___?___ cm^3

★ 17. $25\ m^3 =$ ___?___ mm^3

★ 18. $1\ km^3 =$ ___?___ m^3

Solve.

19. A tank has a volume of 4,000 cm^3. Express its volume in cubic millimeters.
20. In excavating a cellar, 70 m^3 of dirt were removed. How many cubic centimeters of dirt is this?

FIND OUT!
Brainteaser

Choose the missing box.

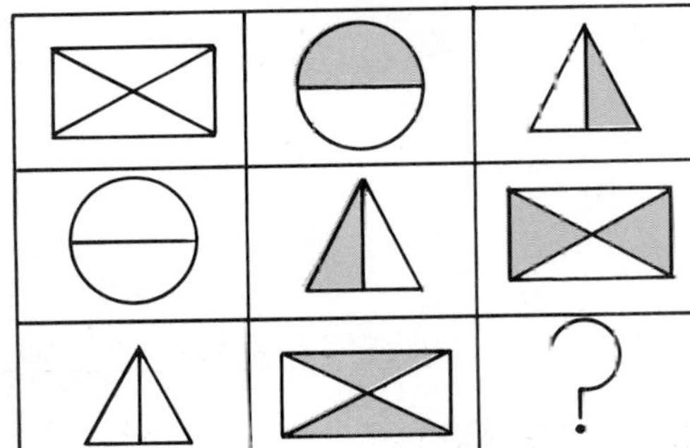

a

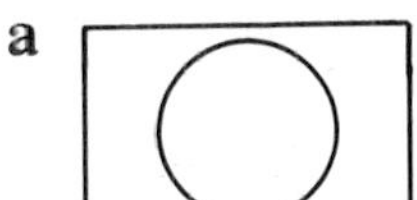

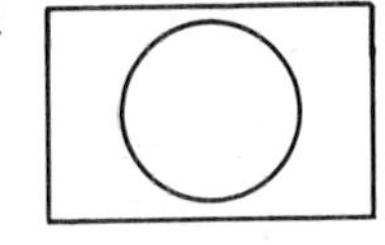

b

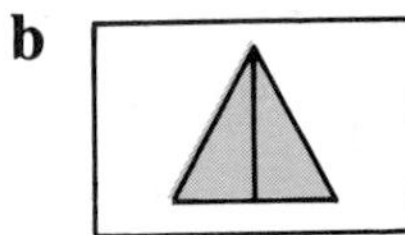

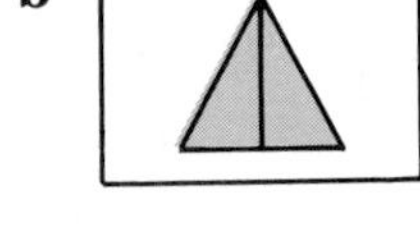

c

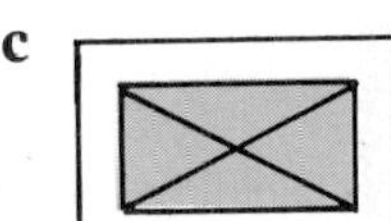

d

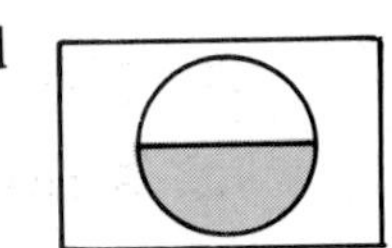

Volumes of Prisms and Cylinders

The volume of a solid is the number of cubic units it contains.

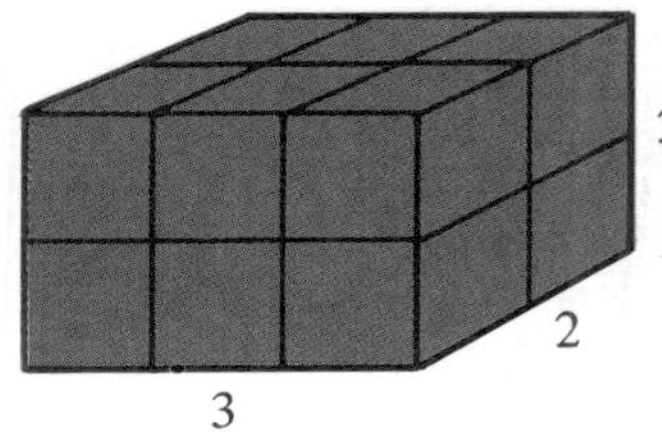

Volume is
12 cubic units

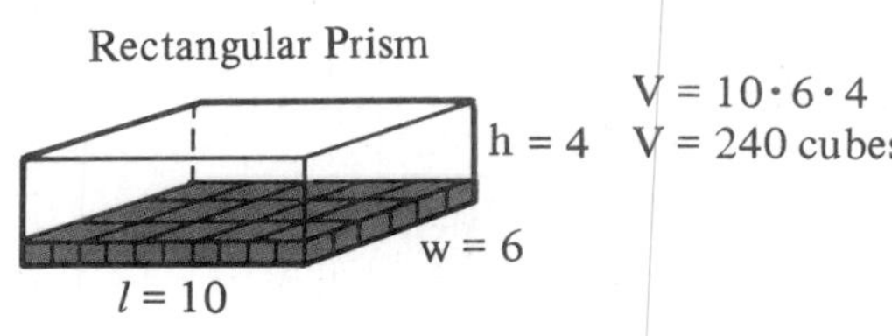

V = 10·6·4
V = 240 cubes

V = l · w · h or
V = B · h

A. Find the volumes. Use $V = l \cdot w \cdot h$ or $V = B \cdot h$.

1.

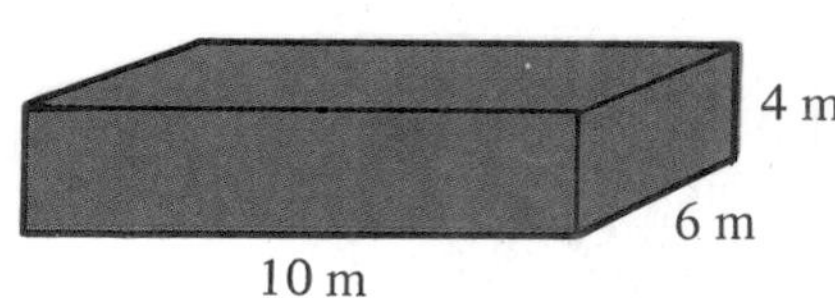

2.

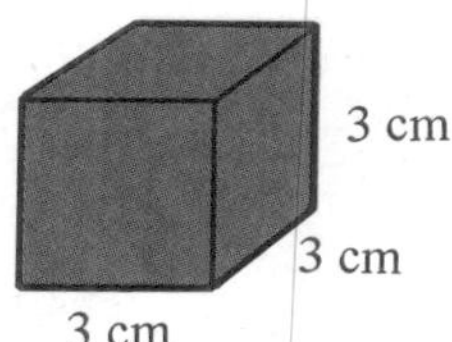

B. Find the volume. Use $V = B \cdot h$.

3. What kind of figure is the base?

4. What is B (area of the base)?

5. What is the volume?

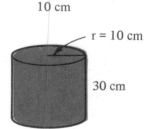

18 cm
6 cm
10 cm

C. Find the volume. Use $V = B \cdot h$.

6. What kind of figure is the base?

7. Find B. Use $\pi \doteq 3.14$.

8. Find the volume.

r = 10 cm
30 cm

D. Find the volumes.

9.

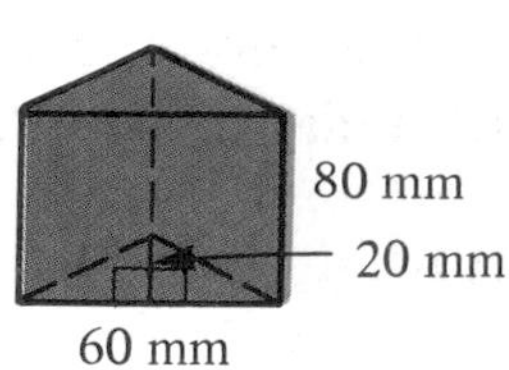

10.

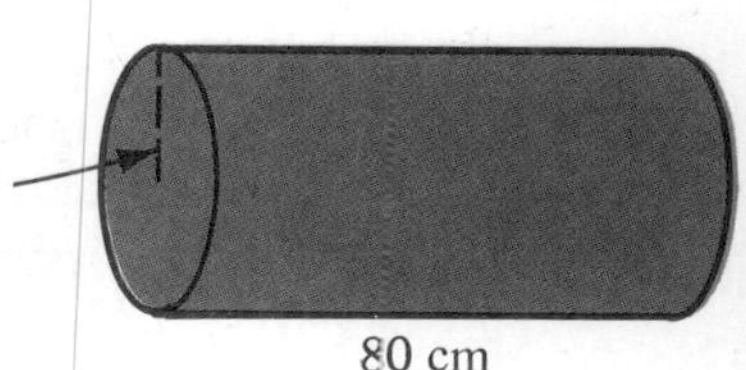

Practice

Find the volumes.

1.

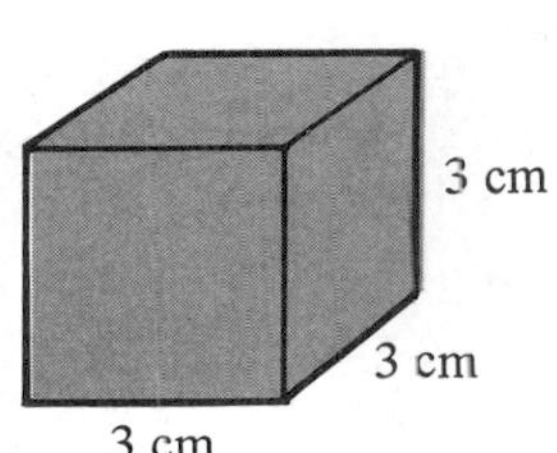

2.

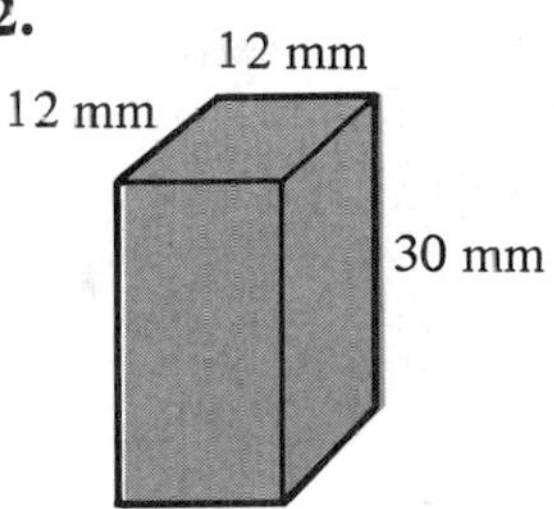

3.

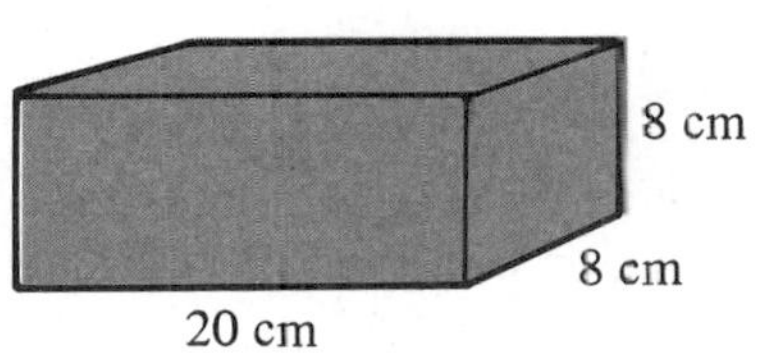

4.

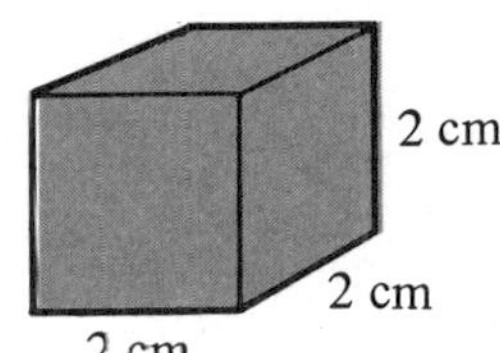

5.

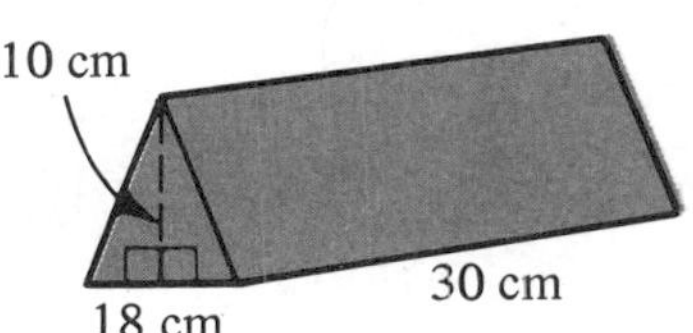

6.

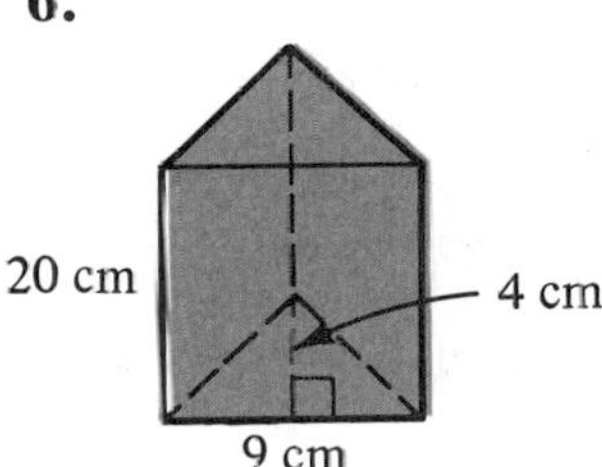

7.

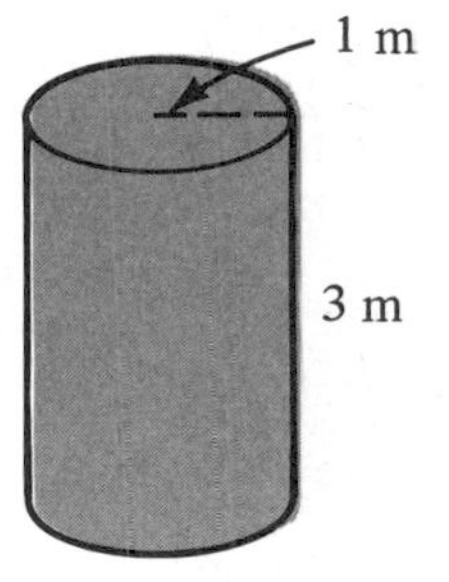

8.

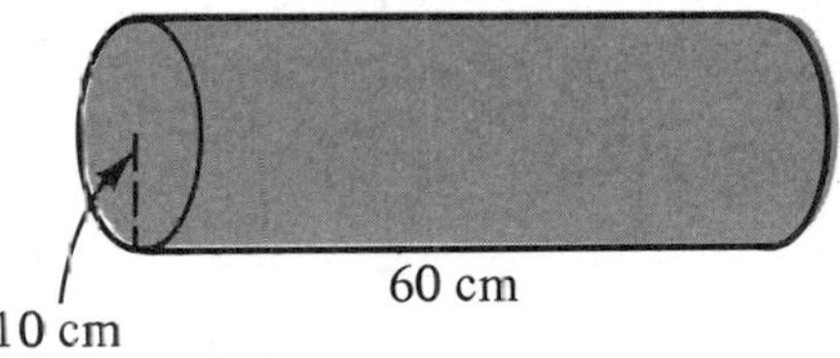

★Solve.

9. 1 cm^3 of lead is 11.3 g. What is the mass of a lead bar 20 cm long, 5 cm wide, and 5 cm high?

10. 1 cm^3 of iron is 7.8 g. What is the mass of an iron bar 300 cm long with a diameter of 20 cm?

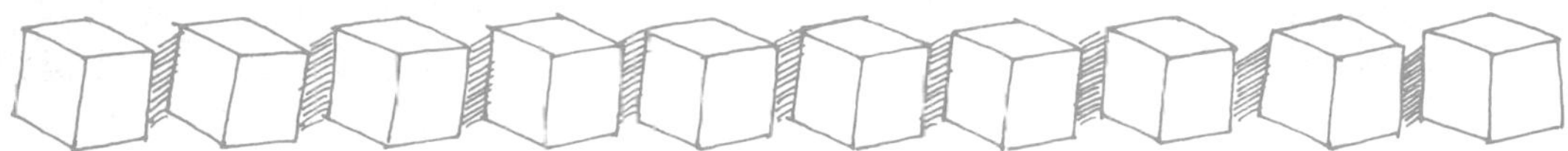

Relating Metric Measures

In the metric system, a liter is defined in terms of cubic centimeters.

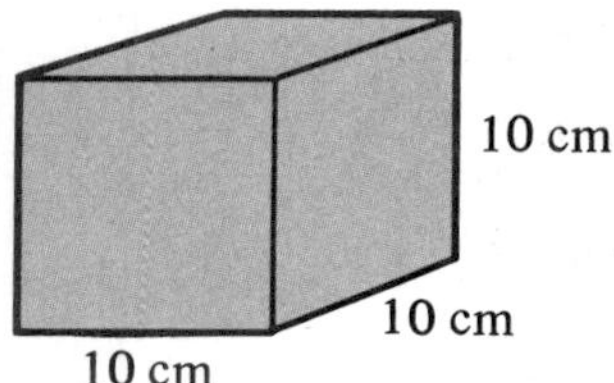

This cube holds 1 liter, so 1 L = 1,000 cm^3

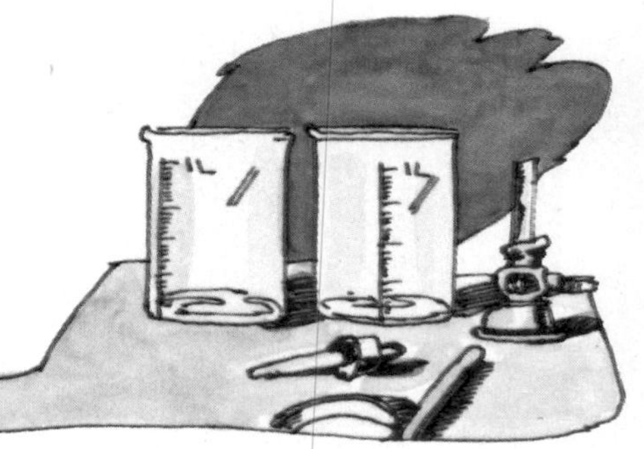

A. Change to liters. Complete.

1. 5,000 cm^3 = 5 × 1,000 cm^3
= 5 × 1 L
= ___?___ L

2. 2,500 cm^3 = 2.5 × 1,000 cm^3
= 2.5 × 1 L
= ___?___ L

3. 10,000 cm^3 = ___?___ L

4. 650 cm^3 = ___?___ L

B. Change to cubic centimeters. Complete.

5. 8 L = 8 × 1 L
= 8 × 1,000 cm^3
= ___?___ cm^3

6. 7.3 L = 7.3 × 1 L
= 7.3 × 1,000 cm^3
= ___?___ cm^3

7. 3 L = ___?___ cm^3

8. 2.5 L = ___?___ cm^3

C. 1 L = 1,000 cm^3, so 1 mL = 1 cm^3. Complete.

9. 3 mL = ___?___ cm^3

10. 400 mL = ___?___ cm^3

11. 240 cm^3 = ___?___ mL

12. 7.4 cm^3 = ___?___ mL

▶ 1,000 cm^3 of water is 1 kg.
1 cm^3 of water is 1 g.

D. How many grams of water?

13. 7 cm^3 **14.** 34.1 cm^3 **15.** 2,300 cm^3 **16.** 3,400 cm^3

E. How many cubic centimeters of water?

17. 3 kg **18.** 8 g **19.** 341.7 g **20.** 4,600 g

Practice

Complete.

1. $2{,}000 \text{ cm}^3 = \underline{\quad ? \quad} \text{ L}$
2. $7{,}000 \text{ cm}^3 = \underline{\quad ? \quad} \text{ L}$
3. $3{,}500 \text{ cm}^3 = \underline{\quad ? \quad} \text{ L}$
4. $4{,}800 \text{ cm}^3 = \underline{\quad ? \quad} \text{ L}$
5. $6{,}140 \text{ cm}^3 = \underline{\quad ? \quad} \text{ L}$
6. $8{,}345 \text{ cm}^3 = \underline{\quad ? \quad} \text{ L}$
7. $350 \text{ cm}^3 = \underline{\quad ? \quad} \text{ L}$
8. $413 \text{ cm}^3 = \underline{\quad ? \quad} \text{ L}$
9. $7 \text{ L} = \underline{\quad ? \quad} \text{ cm}^3$
10. $4 \text{ L} = \underline{\quad ? \quad} \text{ cm}^3$
11. $12 \text{ L} = \underline{\quad ? \quad} \text{ cm}^3$
12. $40 \text{ L} = \underline{\quad ? \quad} \text{ cm}^3$
13. $5.7 \text{ L} = \underline{\quad ? \quad} \text{ cm}^3$
14. $8.1 \text{ L} = \underline{\quad ? \quad} \text{ cm}^3$
15. $4 \text{ mL} = \underline{\quad ? \quad} \text{ cm}^3$
16. $30 \text{ mL} = \underline{\quad ? \quad} \text{ cm}^3$
17. $600 \text{ mL} = \underline{\quad ? \quad} \text{ cm}^3$
18. $7.4 \text{ mL} = \underline{\quad ? \quad} \text{ cm}^3$
19. $350 \text{ cm}^3 = \underline{\quad ? \quad} \text{ mL}$
20. $17.6 \text{ cm}^3 = \underline{\quad ? \quad} \text{ mL}$
21. $3{,}700 \text{ cm}^3 = \underline{\quad ? \quad} \text{ L}$
22. $18 \text{ L} = \underline{\quad ? \quad} \text{ cm}^3$
23. $850 \text{ cm}^3 = \underline{\quad ? \quad} \text{ mL}$
24. $8.2 \text{ mL} = \underline{\quad ? \quad} \text{ cm}^3$

How many grams of water?

25. 8 cm^3
26. 50 cm^3
27. 300 cm^3
28. $4{,}100 \text{ cm}^3$
29. 42.3 cm^3
30. 117.9 cm^3

How many cubic centimeters of water?

31. 12 kg
32. 6 g
33. 53 g
34. 2,400 g
35. 46.7 g
36. 131.7 g

Solve.

37. What is the mass in kilograms of the water in the fish tank?

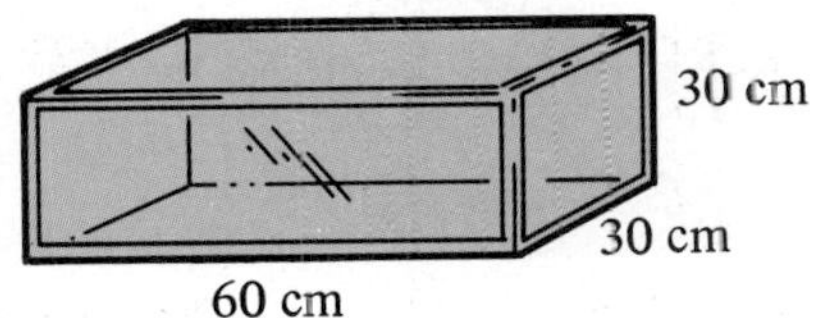

38. How many liters of water can this tank hold?

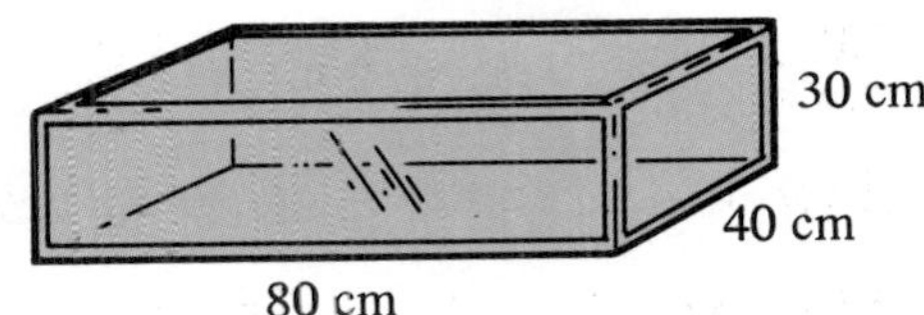

Volumes of Cones and Pyramids

Materials: cardboard, scissors, sand or salt

A. The formula for the volume of a rectangular prism can be used to find a formula for the volume of a pyramid.

1. Make a model of a rectangular prism out of cardboard.

2. Make a model of a pyramid out of cardboard. Use the same base and height for both figures.

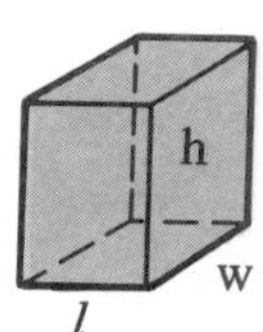

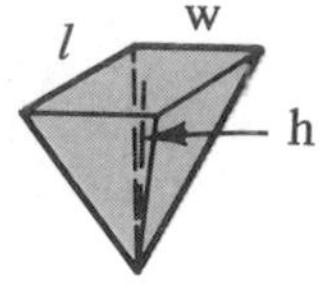

3. Fill the pyramid with sand or salt.

4. Pour the contents of the pyramid into the rectangular prism.

5. Appproximately how full is the rectangular prism?

6. The volume of the pyramid is what part of the volume of the rectangular prism?

▶ Volume of a pyramid: $V = \frac{1}{3}B \cdot h$

B. Find the volumes.

7.

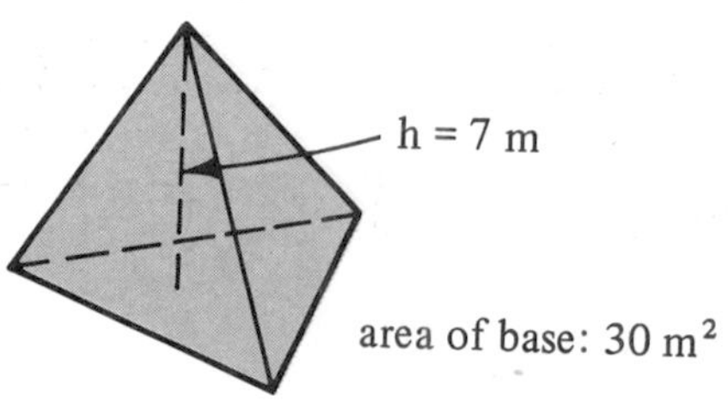

8.

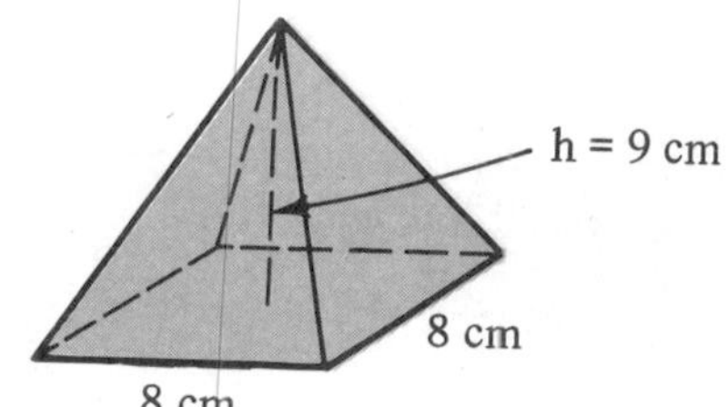

C. Examine these diagrams.

9. The volume of the pyramid is what part of the volume of the rectangular prism?

10. The volume of the cone appears to be what part of the volume of the cylinder?

▶ Volume of a cone: $V = \frac{1}{3}B \cdot h$

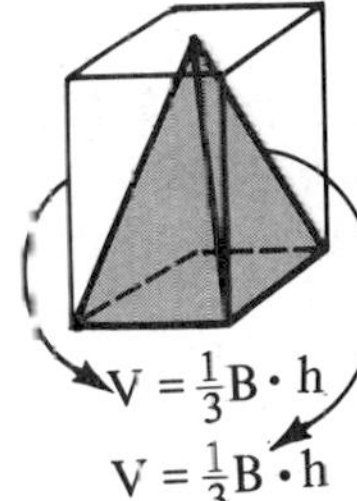

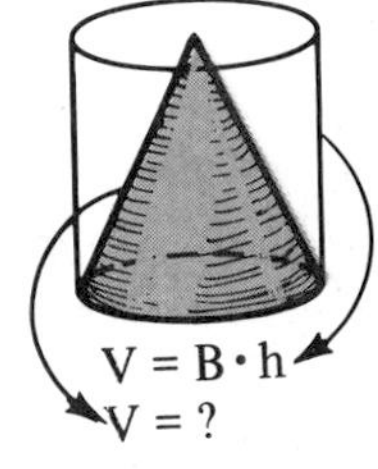

D. Find the volumes. Use $\pi \doteq 3.14$. Give the answers to the nearest whole number.

11.

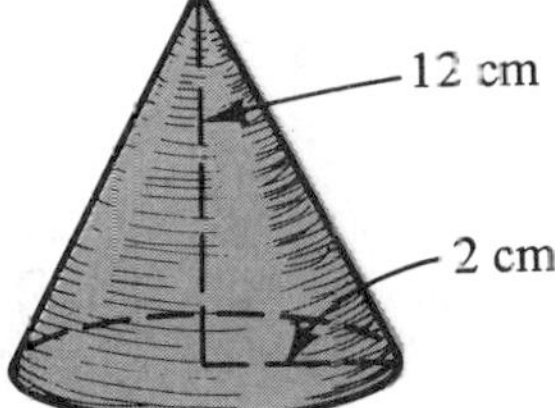

12.

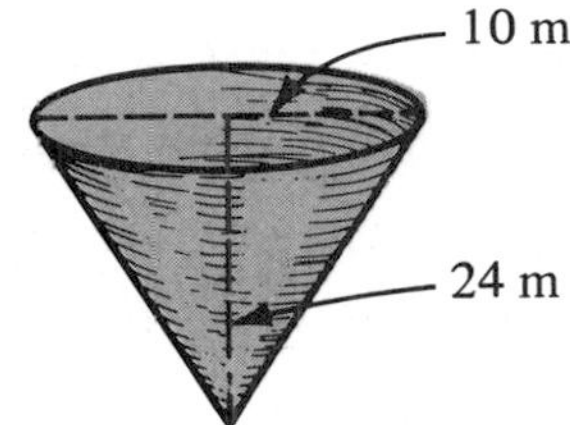

Practice

Find the volumes.

1.

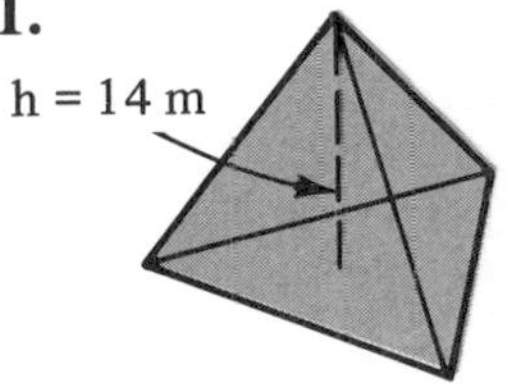

2.

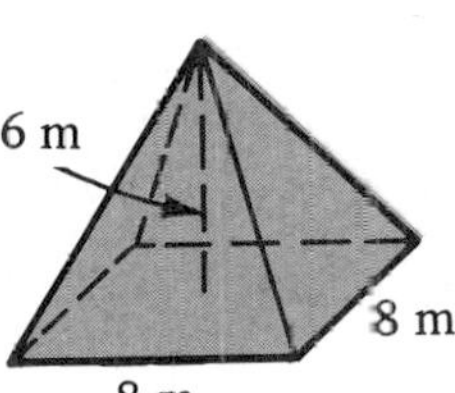

3.

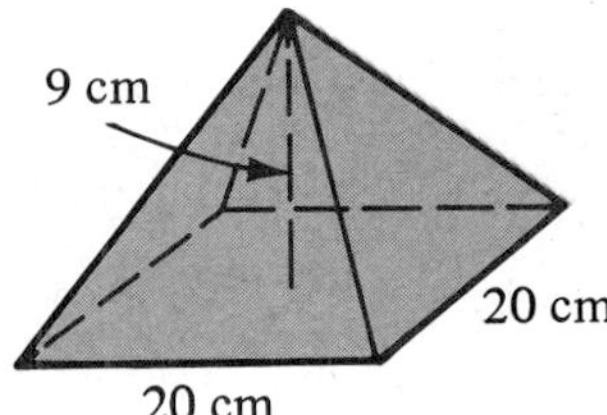

Find the volumes. Use $\pi \doteq 3.14$. Give the answers to the nearest whole number.

4.

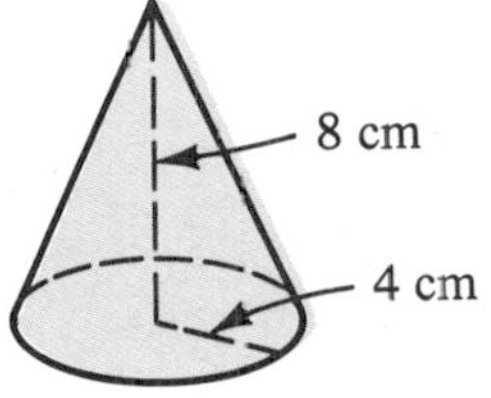

5.

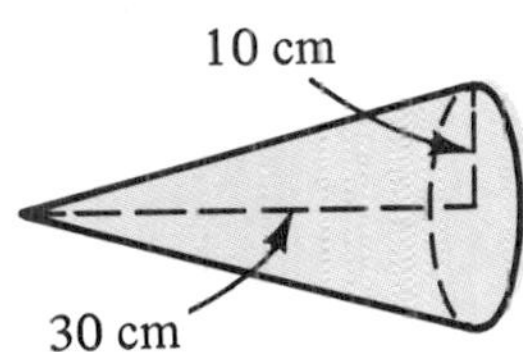

6.

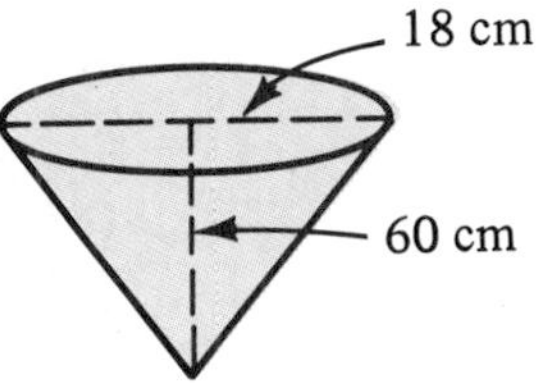

Using Customary Units of Volume

Find the number of cubic yards of coal removed in digging out a hole 9 ft by 15 ft by 21 ft in a mine.

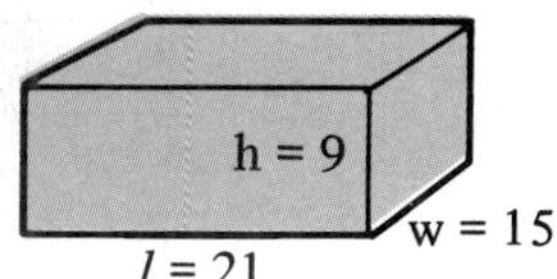

$$
\begin{aligned}
V &= l \cdot w \cdot h \\
&= 21 \cdot 15 \cdot 9 \\
&= 2{,}835 \text{ ft}^3 \\
&= 105 \text{ yd}^3 \longleftarrow 1 \text{ yd}^3 = 27 \text{ ft}^3 \text{ and } 2{,}835 \div 27 = 105
\end{aligned}
$$

105 yd^3 of coal are removed.

A. Complete. Use these relationships.

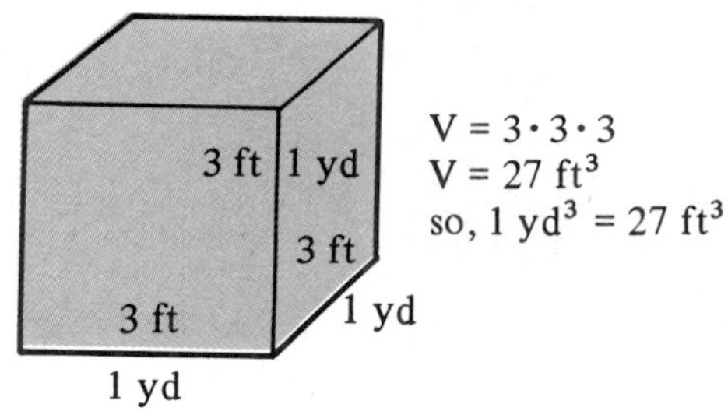

12 in. 1 ft
12 in.
1 ft
12 in.
1 ft

V = 12 · 12 · 12
V = 1,728 in.^{3}
so, 1 ft^3 = 1,728 in.^{3}

1. 2 yd^3 = __?__ ft^3
2. 10 yd^3 = __?__ ft^3
3. 3 ft^3 = __?__ in.^{3}
4. 10 ft^3 = __?__ in.^{3}
5. 54 ft^3 = __?__ yd^3
6. 8,640 in.^{3} = __?__ ft^3

Practice

Complete.

1. 4 yd^3 = __?__ ft^3
2. 8 yd^3 = __?__ ft^3
3. 6 ft^3 = __?__ in.^{3}
4. 20 ft^3 = __?__ in.^{3}
5. 270 ft^3 = __?__ yd^3
6. 5,184 in.^{3} = __?__ ft^3

Solve.

7. A bin 8 ft wide and 7 ft 6 in. long is filled to a depth of 5 ft with coal. One ton of coal occupies about 50 ft^3. How many tons of coal are in the bin?

Keeping Fit

Multiply.

1. $\begin{array}{r} 2.16 \\ \times 7 \\ \hline \end{array}$

2. $\begin{array}{r} 0.34 \\ \times 0.9 \\ \hline \end{array}$

3. $\begin{array}{r} 1.46 \\ \times 2.4 \\ \hline \end{array}$

4. $\begin{array}{r} 0.37 \\ \times 0.09 \\ \hline \end{array}$

5. $\begin{array}{r} 2.57 \\ \times 0.60 \\ \hline \end{array}$

6. $\begin{array}{r} 34.1 \\ \times 2.40 \\ \hline \end{array}$

Divide.

7. $6\overline{)0.6}$
8. $3\overline{)15.3}$
9. $4\overline{)0.0016}$
10. $33\overline{)4.95}$
11. $0.6\overline{)2.4}$
12. $0.03\overline{)9}$
13. $2.4\overline{)0.744}$
14. $0.87\overline{)78.3}$

Multiply. Simplify when possible.

15. $\frac{2}{5} \times \frac{5}{6}$
16. $\frac{4}{9} \times \frac{3}{16}$
17. $\frac{3}{4} \times 20$
18. $7\frac{1}{2} \times 8$
19. $1\frac{1}{2} \times 4$
20. $\frac{2}{3} \times 1\frac{1}{2}$
21. $1\frac{1}{2} \times 1\frac{1}{2}$
22. $3\frac{3}{4} \times \frac{8}{9} \times 6$

Divide. Simplify when possible.

23. $\frac{3}{4} \div \frac{1}{2}$
24. $4 \div 1\frac{1}{2}$
25. $\frac{2}{3} \div 4$
26. $4\frac{2}{3} \div 1\frac{1}{6}$

Write percents.

27. $\frac{7}{100}$
28. 0.38
29. $\frac{3}{5}$
30. 0.069

Write simplest fractions or whole numbers.

31. 6%
32. 25%
33. 200%
34. $12\frac{1}{2}$%

Write decimals.

35. 7%
36. 150%
37. 6.7%
38. $\frac{1}{2}$%

Compute.

39. 12% of 60
40. $\frac{1}{2}$% of 400
41. 0.7% of 6,000
42. 20% of what number is 75?
43. What percent of 12 is 9?
44. 0.3 is what percent of 25?

Solve.

45. At a sale, a dress marked $90 was sold at a discount of 30%. What was the sale price?

Problem Solving • Architects

1. Mr. Engel, an architect, made a scale drawing of a house that he designed. The living room is to be 7 m long. The scale on the drawing is 0.5 cm = 1 m. What is the scale length of the living room? [HINT: Write a proportion and solve.]

2. Mr. Bendler used a scale of 1 cm for 10 m on a scale drawing of a playground. The distance of the playground to the school building is 14.5 cm. What is the actual distance of the playground to the school building?

3. Of all the architects that work in a certain city, 30% are women. There are 150 architects in the city. How many of the architects are men?

4. Ms. Koch designs schools. A classroom is to have 35 students. Each student needs 3 m^2 of floor space. What should the area of the classroom be?

5. An architect designed a house to cost $80,000 to build. The actual cost of building the house was $90,000. What was the percent increase in the cost of building the house?

6. Mrs. Gonzalez made a scale drawing of a house. She used the scale 0.5 cm = 1 m. The scale length of the bedroom is 2.5 cm and the width is 2 cm. What is the actual area of the bedroom?

Chapter Review

Find x. *(332, 336)*

1. $\triangle GHI \cong \triangle JKL$

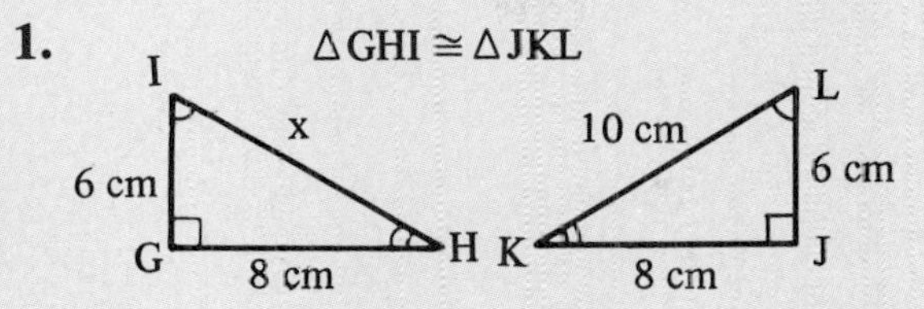

2. $\triangle ABC \cong \triangle DEC$

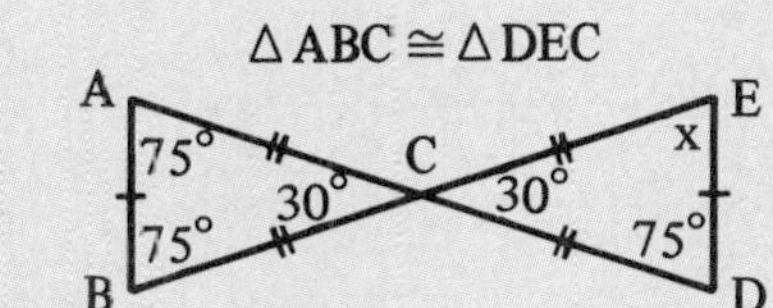

3. $\triangle XYZ \sim \triangle UVW$

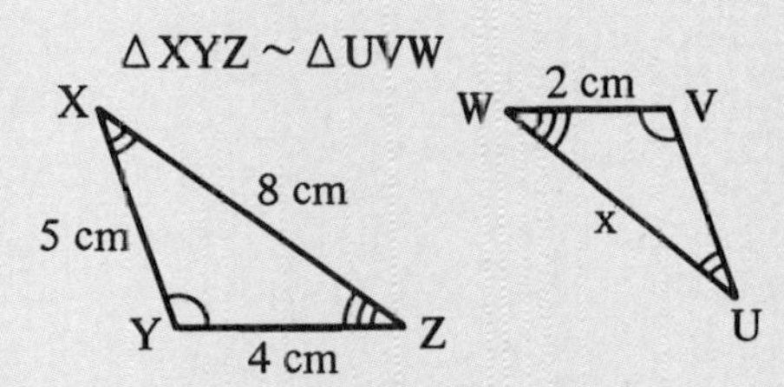

4. $\triangle PQR \sim \triangle STU$

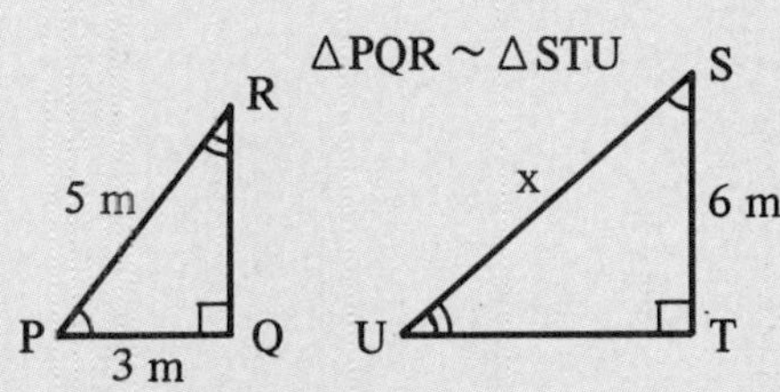

Find the actual lengths. Measure the scale lengths to the nearest centimeter. *(338)*

5.

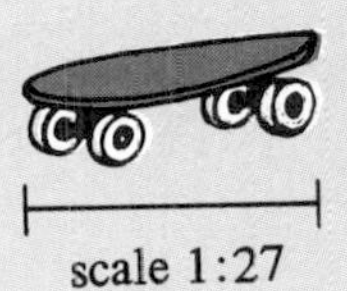

scale 1:27

6.

scale 1:9

7.

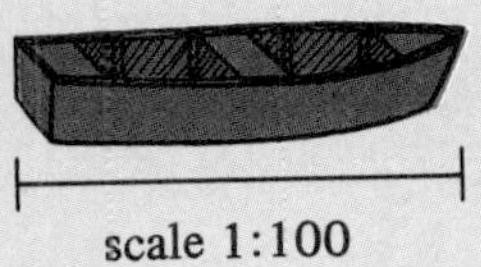

scale 1:100

Complete. *(344)*

8. $4 \text{ m}^2 = \underline{\quad ? \quad} \text{ cm}^2$

9. $6 \text{ ha} = \underline{\quad ? \quad} \text{ m}^2$

10. $10 \text{ cm}^2 = \underline{\quad ? \quad} \text{ m}^2$

11. $50 \text{ mm}^2 = \underline{\quad ? \quad} \text{ cm}^2$

Find the areas. Use $\pi \doteq 3.14$. *(342, 346)*

12.

12 m

25 m

13.

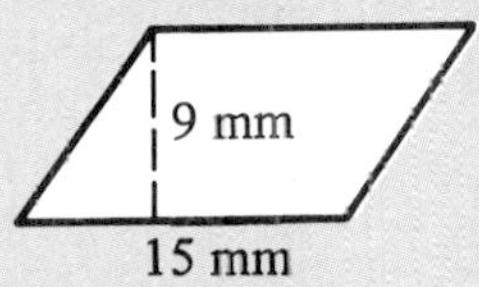

14.

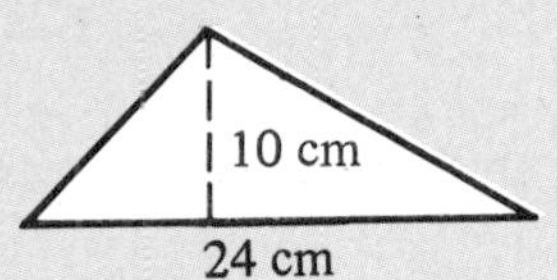

15.

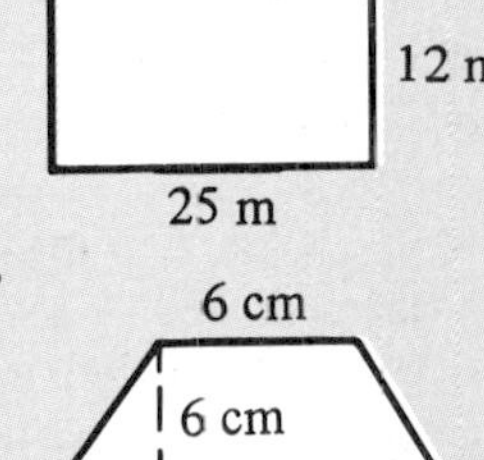

16.

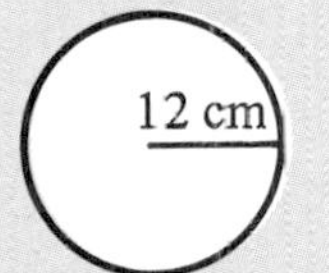

17.

Review continues

Chapter Review (continued)

Find the surface areas. *(352)*

18.

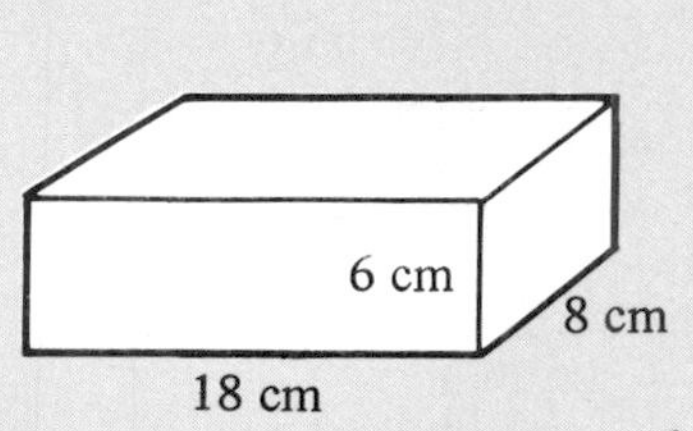

19.

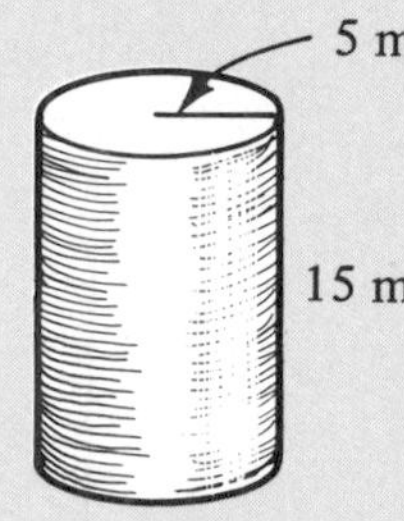

20.

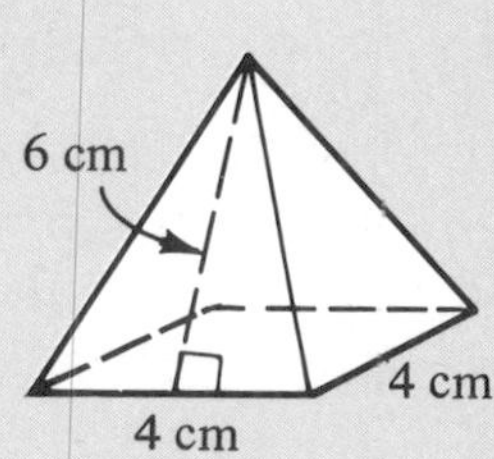

Complete. *(354)*

21. $2\ m^3 = \underline{\ ?\ }\ cm^3$

22. $4\ cm^3 = \underline{\ ?\ }\ m^3$

23. $300\ cm^3 = \underline{\ ?\ }\ m^3$

24. $10{,}000\ mm^3 = \underline{\ ?\ }\ cm^3$

Find the volumes. *(356)*

25.

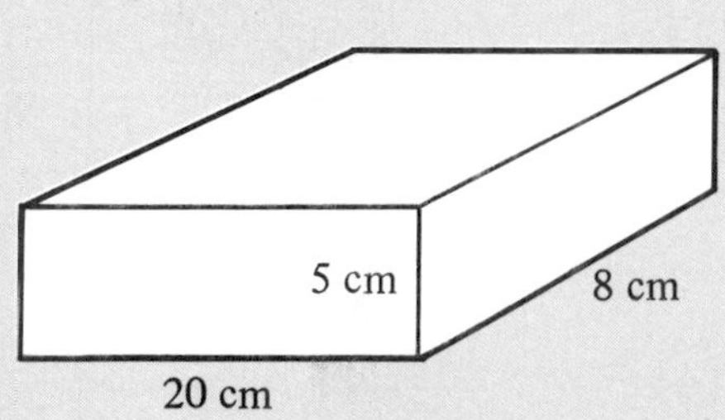

26.

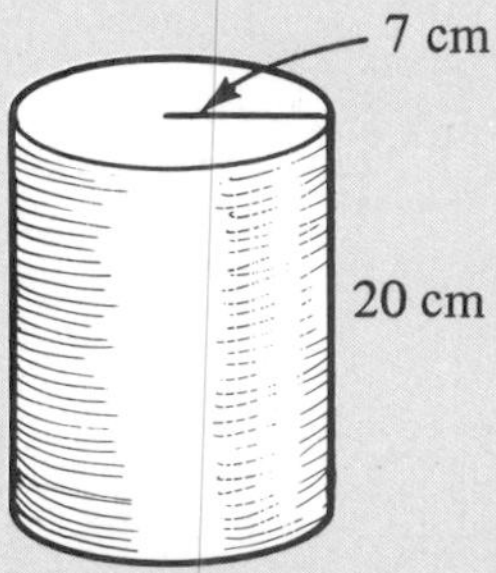

Complete. *(358)*

27. $4{,}000\ cm^3 = \underline{\ ?\ }\ L$

28. $6.2\ L = \underline{\ ?\ }\ cm^3$

29. $7.5\ mL = \underline{\ ?\ }\ cm^3$

30. How many grams of water in $10.5\ cm^3$? *(358)*

31. How many cubic centimeters of water in 3 kg? *(358)*

Solve. *(348, 364)*

32. A dozen fielder's gloves cost a store owner $145.44. What is the cost of 1 glove?

33. Jody used a scale of 0.4 cm = 1 m. What is the actual length of a room which is 1.6 cm on the scale drawing?

Find x. *(332, 336)*

1. $\triangle ABC \cong \triangle DEF$

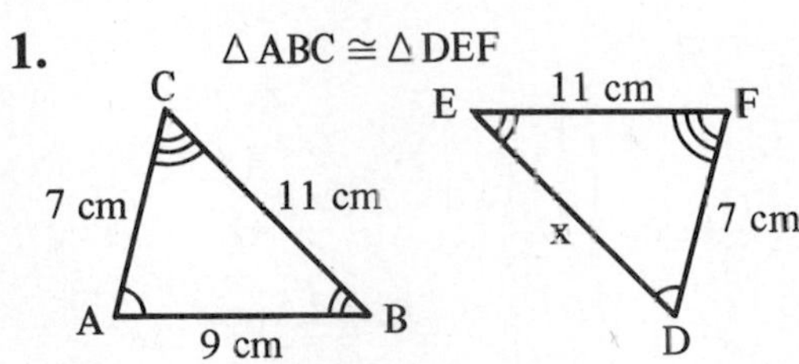

2. $\triangle LMP \cong \triangle NMP$

P
x
54°
36°
36°
L
M
N

3. $\triangle QRS \sim \triangle TUV$

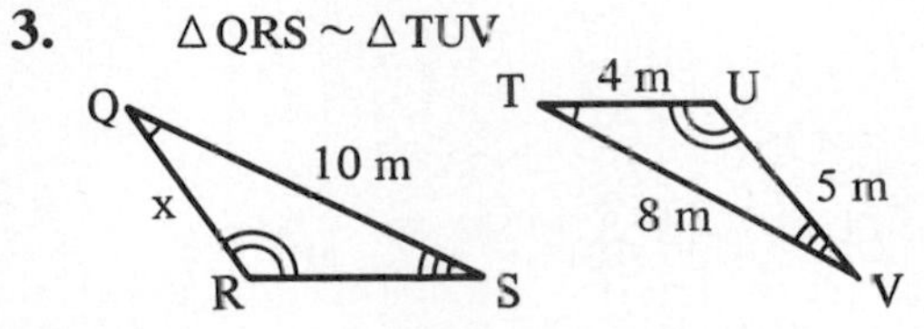

4. $\triangle GHI \sim \triangle JHK$

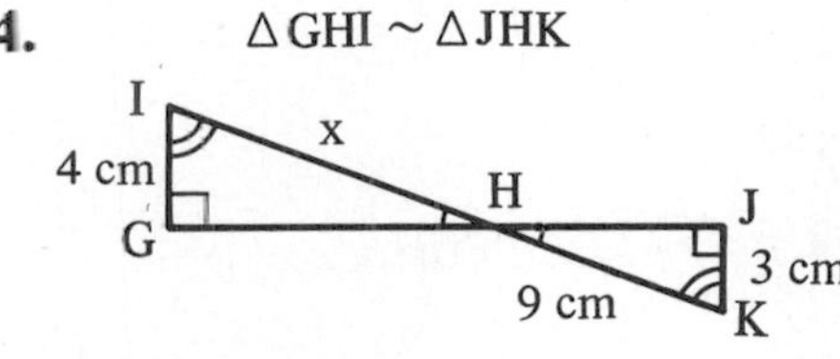

Find the actual lengths. Measure the scale lengths to the nearest centimeter. *(338)*

5.

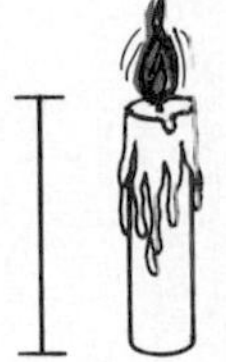

scale
1 cm = 5 cm

6.

scale 1:20

7.

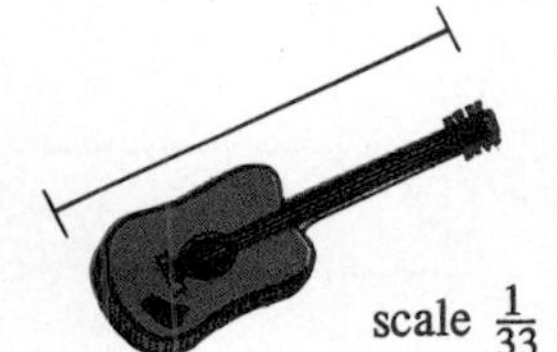

scale $\frac{1}{33}$

Complete. *(344)*

8. $8 \text{ m}^2 = \underline{\ ?\ } \text{ cm}^2$

9. $4 \text{ ha} = \underline{\ ?\ } \text{ m}^2$

10. $100 \text{ mm}^2 = \underline{\ ?\ } \text{ cm}^2$

11. $30 \text{ cm}^2 = \underline{\ ?\ } \text{ m}^2$

Find the areas. Use $\pi \doteq 3.14$. *(342, 346)*

12.

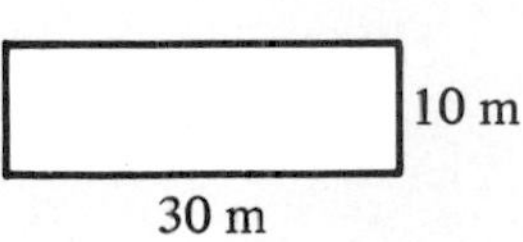

13.

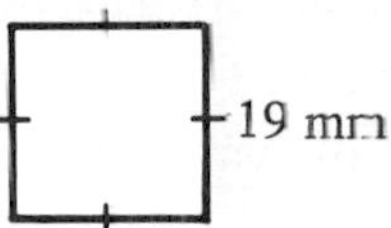

14.

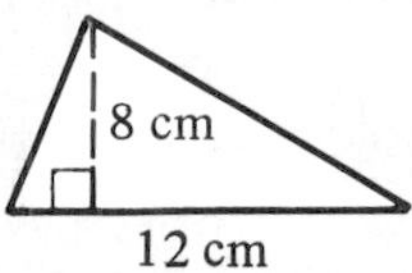

15.

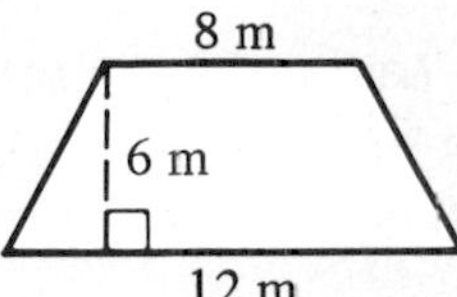

16.

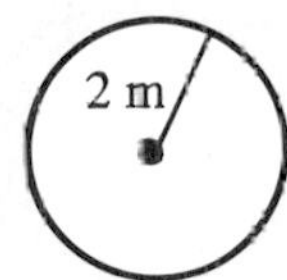

17.

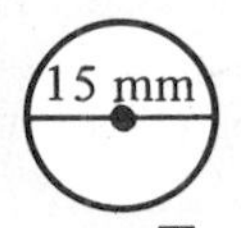

Test continues

Chapter Test (continued)

Find the surface areas. *(352)*

18.

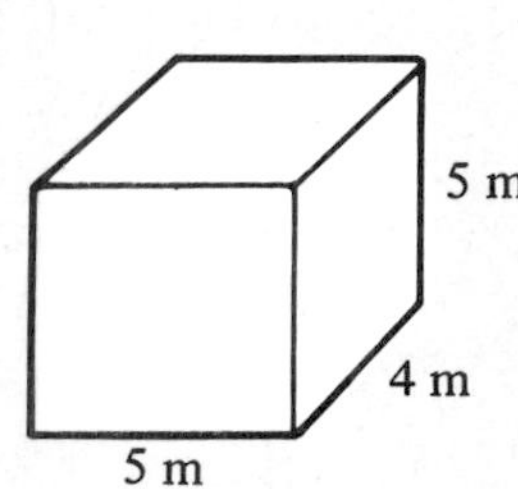

19.

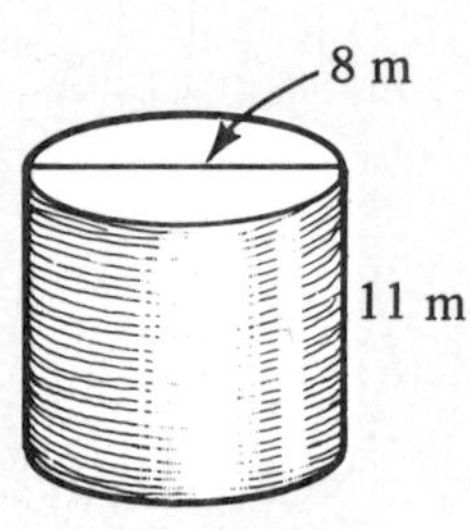

20.

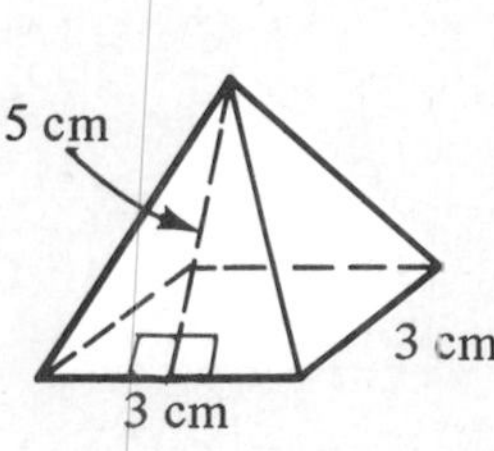

Complete. *(354)*

21. 3 m³ = __?__ cm³

22. 7,000 cm³ = __?__ m³

23. 4 cm³ = __?__ mm³

24. 20,000 mm³ = __?__ cm³

Find the volumes. *(356)*

25.

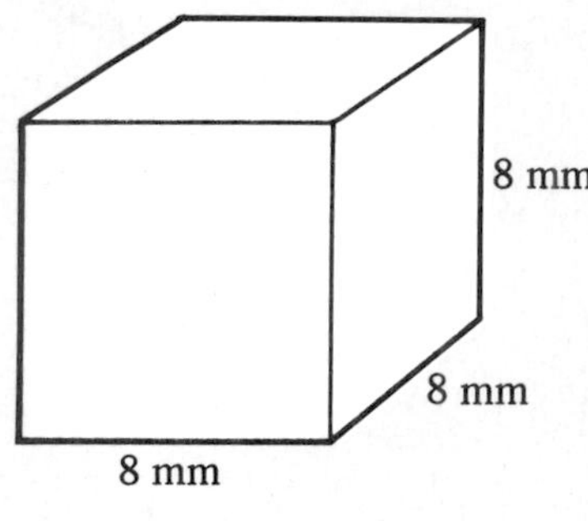

26.

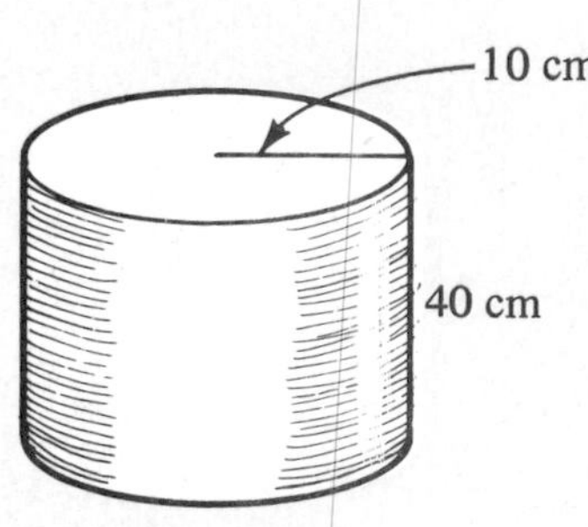

Complete. *(358)*

27. 4,150 cm³ = __?__ L

28. 19 L = __?__ cm³

29. 8.7 mL = __?__ cm³

30. How many grams of water in 14 cm³? *(358)*

31. How many cubic centimeters of water in 4.5 kg? *(358)*

Solve. *(348, 364)*

32. A jump rope sells for $4.99. A gym bought 55 jump ropes. How much did they pay for the ropes?

33. Jim used a scale of 1.5 cm = 1 m on a drawing. What is the scale length of a distance of 9 m?

Basic Skills Check

1. The people working in Ann's department earn \$134, \$256, \$176, and \$158 per week. What is their average weekly earnings?

A \$181　　B \$191

C \$201　　D \$211

2. A radio marked \$64 is sold at a discount of 25% during a sale. How much does it cost during the sale?

E \$12.80　　F \$16

G \$48　　H \$51.20

3. Mr. Green drove his car a distance of 484 km at an average speed of 88 km/h. How long did he drive?

A 4 hours　　B 5 hours

C $5\frac{1}{2}$ hours　　D 6 hours

4. What is the volume of the rectangular solid?

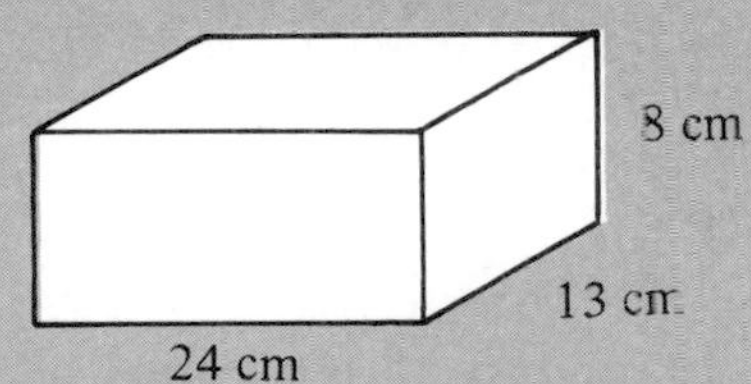

E 2,496 cm^3　　F 312 cm^3

G 104 cm^3　　H 45 cm^3

5. What is the area of the right triangle?

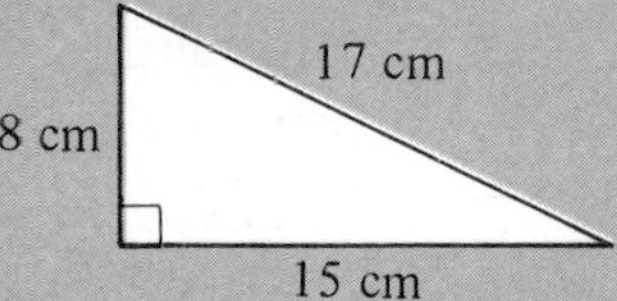

A 40 cm^2　　B 60 cm^2

C 120 cm^2　　D 136 cm^2

6. Ms. Levy bought 2 bags of onions. One bag was marked 1.3 kg. The other bag was marked 820 g. How much heavier was the first bag?

E 480 g　　F 818.7 g

G 480 kg　　H 818.7 kg

7. There are 5 black checkers and 6 red checkers in a box. A checker is drawn. What is the probability that it is red?

A $\frac{1}{11}$　　B $\frac{5}{11}$

C $\frac{6}{11}$　　D $\frac{11}{11}$

8. Which class has the best attendance record?

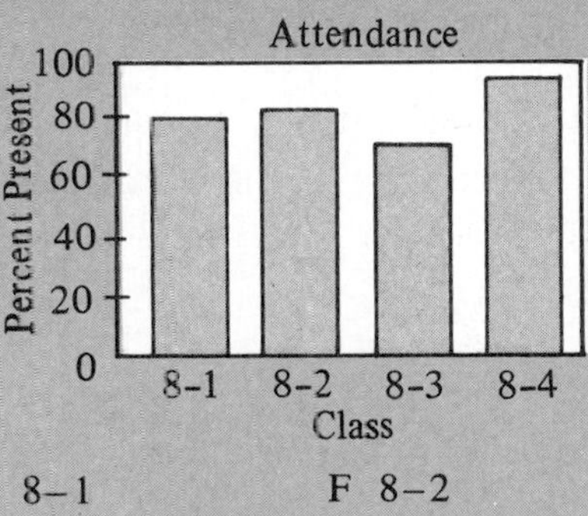

E 8–1　　F 8–2

G 8–3　　H 8–4

Graphing on a Number Line

This is the graph of $x = 3$.

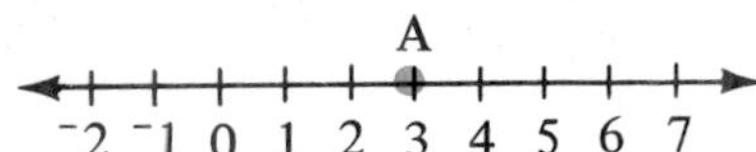

A. Graph.

1. $x = 2$ **2.** $x = 0$ **3.** $x = {}^{-}1$

B. Graph $x + 2 = 5$.

4. Solve $x + 2 = 5$.
What is the solution?

5. Graph the solution.

C. Graph.

6. $x + 3 = 9$ **7.** $x - 5 = 2$ **8.** $2x = 4$

9. $\frac{x}{2} = 1$ **10.** $3x + 4 = 1$ **11.** $2x - 3 = 3$

CHAPTER

GRAPHING, PROBABILITY, AND STATISTICS

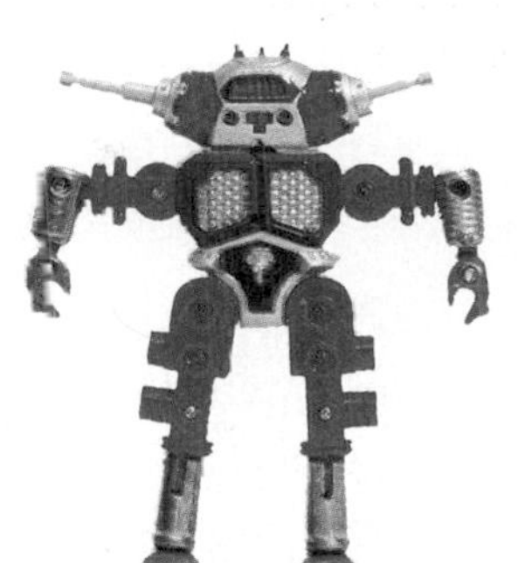

Practice

Graph.

1. $x = 4$ **2.** $x = 1$ **3.** $x = {}^-3$

4. $x + 1 = 5$ **5.** $x - 2 = 1$ **6.** $x - 7 = {}^-11$

7. $3x = 6$ **8.** $2x = {}^-4$ **9.** $\frac{x}{2} = {}^-1$

10. $3x - 1 = 14$ **11.** $2x + 5 = 7$ **12.** $4x + 6 = 2$

★ Graph. Replacements for x: integers

Example This is the graph of $x > {}^-2$.

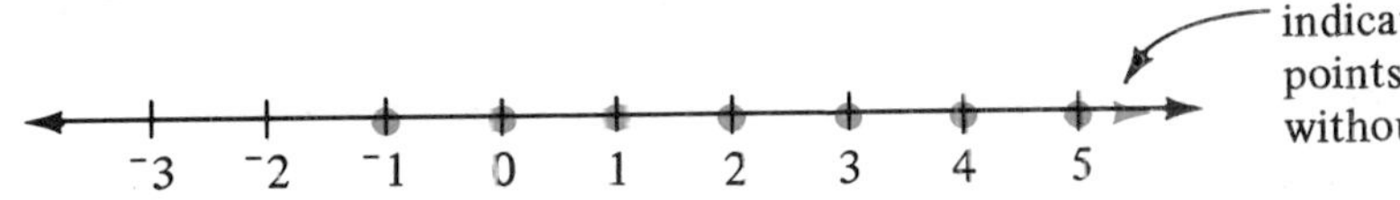

13. $x < 3$ **14.** $x > {}^-4$ **15.** $x + 1 < {}^-2$

16. $x - 5 > {}^-2$ **17.** $2x > 10$ **18.** $4x < {}^-8$

19. ${}^-3x > {}^-9$ **20.** $5x + 2 > 2$ **21.** $3 < x < 7$

22. A robot can graph the solution of $2x + 3 = 19$ in 0.5 seconds. How fast can you do it?

Ordered Pairs

A point may be located by an ordered pair of numbers. Two perpendicular number lines called axes are used.

The horizontal number line is called the **x-axis.**

The vertical number line is called the **y-axis.**

The point where the axes intersect is called the **origin.**

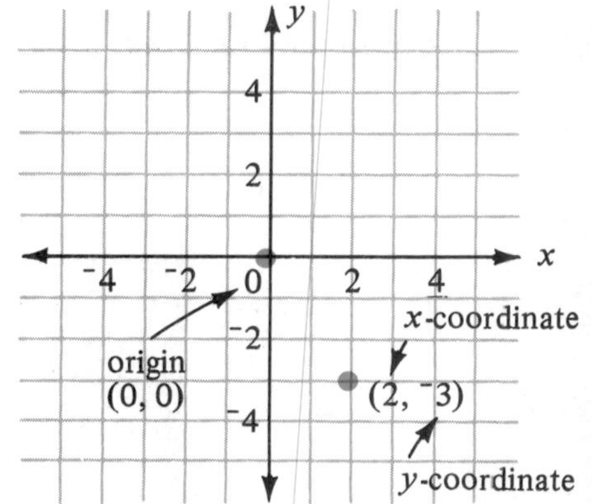

A. Give the coordinates.

1. A **2.** B **3.** C

4. D **5.** E **6.** F

7. G **8.** H **9.** I

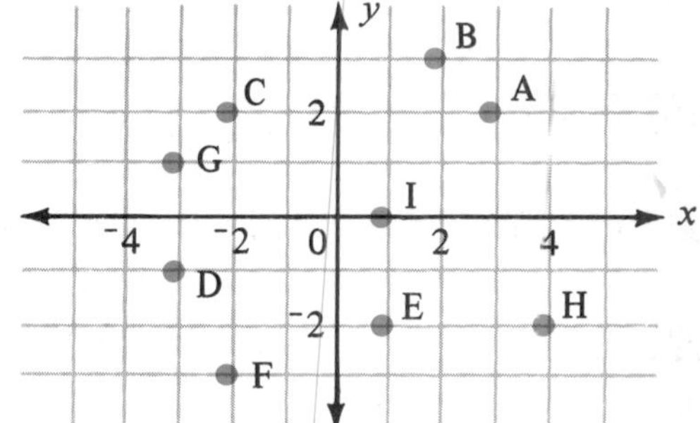

B. To plot the point $(4, {}^-2)$, count 4 units to the right of the origin, then 2 units down.

Plot these points.

10. $(1, 2)$ **11.** $({}^-2, 3)$ **12.** $({}^-1, {}^-1)$ **13.** $(4, {}^-5)$ **14.** $(0, {}^-4)$

C. The axes divide the plane into 4 parts called **quadrants.**

In which quadrant is each point?

15. $(1, 2)$ **16.** $(1, {}^-2)$

17. $({}^-1, 2)$ **18.** $({}^-1, {}^-2)$

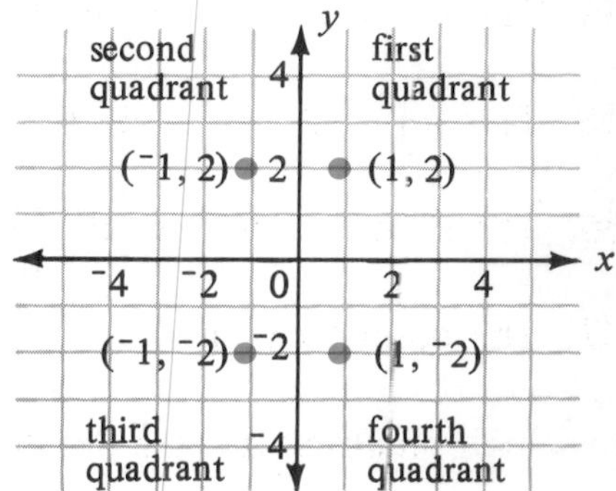

Practice

Give the coordinates of these points.

1. *A* **2.** *B* **3.** *C*

4. *D* **5.** *E* **6.** *F*

7. *G* **8.** *H* **9.** *I*

10. *J* **11.** *K* **12.** *L*

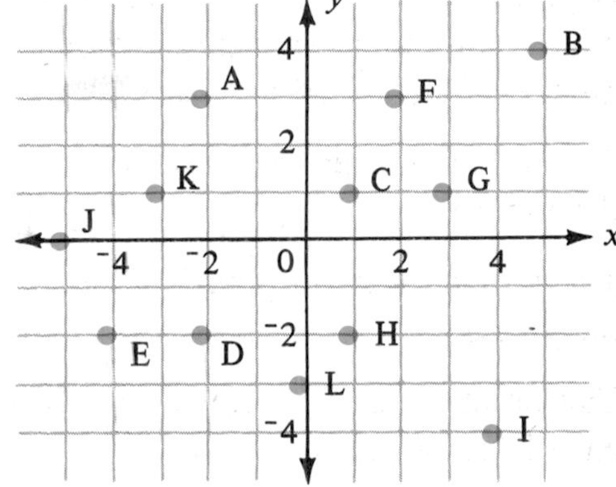

Plot these points.

13. $(3, 1)$ **14.** $(4, 0)$ **15.** $(3, {}^{-}1)$ **16.** $({}^{-}2, 2)$

17. $({}^{-}2, {}^{-}2)$ **18.** $(0, 2)$ **19.** $(5, {}^{-}3)$ **20.** $(2, 2)$

21. $({}^{-}1, 3)$ **22.** $(0, {}^{-}1)$ **23.** $({}^{-}1, 0)$ **24.** $({}^{-}3, 4)$

25. $(1, 1.5)$ **26.** $\left(2\frac{1}{2}, {}^{-}1\right)$ **27.** $({}^{-}3, {}^{-}0.5)$ **28.** $(0, {}^{-}0.5)$

In which quadrant is each point?

29. $({}^{-}1, 2)$ **30.** $(3, 4)$ **31.** $({}^{-}4, 2)$ **32.** $(4, {}^{-}1)$

Complete.

33. The point $(0, 1)$ lies on the __?__ axis.

34. The point $(0, {}^{-}1)$ lies on the __?__ axis.

35. The point $(2, 0)$ lies on the __?__ axis.

36. The point $({}^{-}3, 0)$ lies on the __?__ axis.

37. The point $(0, 0)$ is the __?__.

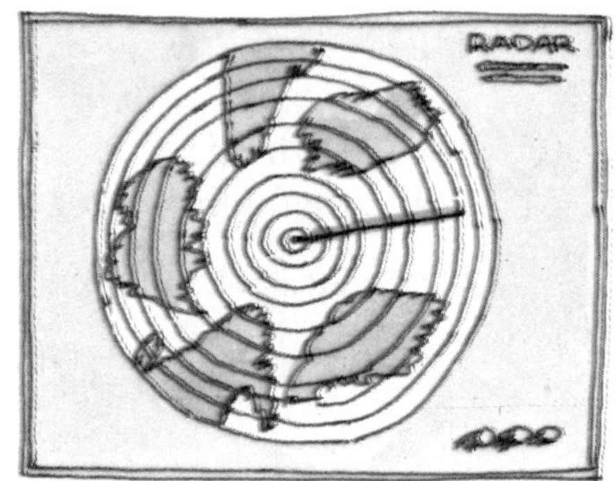

★ In which quadrant are the points with these signs of coordinates?

38. $(+, +)$ **39.** $(-, -)$ **40.** $(+, -)$ **41.** $(-, +)$

Graphing Integer Pairs for Equations

The sum of two numbers is 6. What are the numbers?
Let x = one number
y = other number
Equation: $x + y = 6$
There are many number pairs which are solutions of the equation.
Three of them are (0, 6), (1, 5), and (2, 4).

A. Find the number pair solutions of $y = 2x$. Complete the table.

Select any value for x.
Let $x = 1$.
Then: $y = 2x$
$y = 2 \cdot 1$
$y = 2$

$y = 2x$

x	y
1	2
2	
3	

1. Let $x = 2$. Find the corresponding value for y.

2. Let $x = 3$. Find the corresponding value for y.

B. Complete this table for the equation $y = x + 4$.

	x	y
3.	0	
4.	1	
5.	2	
6.	3	

C. Graph integer pairs for the equation $y = 2x + 1$.

7. Make a table of x and y values. Let $x = {}^-2, {}^-1, 0$, and 1.

8. Write each pair as an ordered pair. **9.** Graph the 4 pairs on a set of axes.

Example

x	y
$^-2$	$^-3$

⟶ $(^-2, {}^-3)$

Practice

Find integer pair solutions for each equation. Let $x = 0, 1, 2, 3, 4$ and 5. Place the integer pairs in table form.

1. $y = 3x$ **2.** $y = x + 1$ **3.** $y = x + 2$

4. $y = x - 1$ **5.** $y = x - 2$ **6.** $y = 2x + 2$

7. $y = 2x + 4$ **8.** $y = 3x - 2$ **9.** $y = 3x - 3$

Graph integer pairs for each equation. Let $x = {}^-2, {}^-1, 0, 1,$ and 2.

10. $y = 2x$ **11.** $y = 3x$ **12.** $y = x + 3$

13. $y = x + 5$ **14.** $y = 3x - 1$ ★ **15.** $y = x^2$

Keeping Fit

Compare. Use >, <, or =.

1. $\frac{5}{8} \equiv \frac{3}{8}$ **2.** $\frac{3}{4} \equiv \frac{9}{12}$ **3.** $\frac{5}{6} \equiv \frac{7}{8}$

Simplify.

4. $\frac{6}{10}$ **5.** $\frac{9}{12}$ **6.** $\frac{12}{16}$

Add. Simplify when possible.

7. $\frac{5}{8} + \frac{1}{4}$ **8.** $\frac{9}{10} + 1\frac{4}{5}$ **9.** $2\frac{3}{4} + 1\frac{2}{5}$ **10.** $3\frac{5}{6} + 2\frac{2}{3}$ **11.** $4\frac{3}{8} + 5\frac{5}{6}$

Subtract. Simplify when possible.

12. $\frac{7}{12} - \frac{1}{3}$ **13.** $3\frac{5}{8} - 2$ **14.** $4\frac{5}{8} - 1\frac{1}{2}$ **15.** $6\frac{1}{4} - 2\frac{3}{8}$ **16.** $7 - 3\frac{5}{6}$

Add.

17. $5 + 9.6 + 0.029$ **18.** $17 + 0.019 + 4.3$ **19.** $0.03 + 0.146 + 7 + 0.1$

Subtract.

20. $0.5 - 0.38$ **21.** $7 - 1.36$ **22.** $0.4 - 0.019$

Graphing Equations with Two Variables

Equation: $y = x + 1$

Step 1 Make a table of values.

x	0	1	2	$^-1$	$^-2$	$2\frac{1}{2}$
y	1	2	3	0	$^-1$	$3\frac{1}{2}$

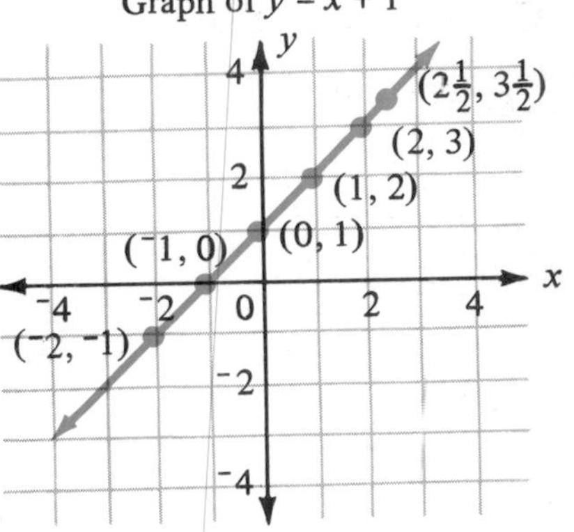

Step 2 Plot the number pairs.

Step 3 Draw a line through the plotted points.

A. Look at the graph of $y = x + 1$.

1. The point with coordinates (4, 5) is on the graph of $y = x + 1$. Is (4, 5) a solution of $y = x + 1$?
2. The point with coordinate (3, 1) is not on the graph of $y = x + 1$. Is (3, 1) a solution of $y = x + 1$?

B. Graph the equation $y = 2x$.

3. Make a table of x and y values for $y = 2x$.
4. Write ordered pairs from the table of values.
5. Plot the ordered pairs.
6. Draw a line through the plotted points.

C. Complete the tables. Then graph the equations.

7. $y = 2x - 1$

x	y
2	
1	
0	
$^-1$	
$^-2$	

8. $y = \frac{1}{2}x$

x	y
2	
0	
$^-2$	
$^-4$	
$^-6$	

9. $y = {}^-2x + 1$

x	y
2	
1	
0	
$^-1$	
$^-2$	

Practice

Complete the tables. Then graph the equations.

1. $y = x + 2$

x	y
3	
2	
1	
0	
$^-1$	
$^-2$	

2. $y = 3x$

x	y
3	
2	
1	
0	
$^-1$	
$^-2$	

3. $y = x - 1$

x	y
3	
2	
1	
0	
$^-1$	
$^-2$	

4. $y = 3x - 1$

x	y
3	
2	
1	
0	
$^-1$	
$^-2$	

5. $y = \frac{1}{3}x$

x	y
9	
6	
3	
0	
$^-3$	
$^-6$	

6. $y = {}^-2x + 2$

x	y
3	
2	
1	
0	
$^-1$	
$^-2$	

Graph.

7. $y = x + 3$

8. $y = 5x$

9. $y = x - 2$

10. $y = 2x - 3$

11. $y = \frac{1}{2}x + 1$

12. $y = {}^-x + 7$

★ **13.** $y = x^2$

★ **14.** $y = x^2 - 1$

★ **15.** $x + y = 9$

★ **16.** $x = y - 4$

Graphing Inequalities

Graph $y > x + 1$.

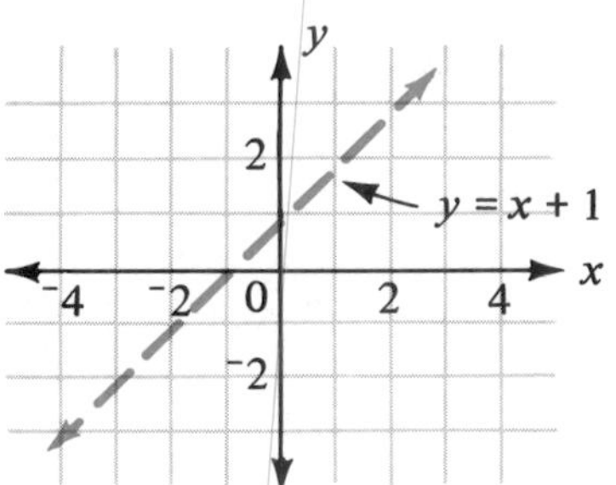

Step 1 Make a table of values for the related equation $y = x + 1$.

Step 2 Graph $y = x + 1$ as a dashed line.

Step 3 Test a point on one side of the line.

$A(2, 1)$ $\quad y > x + 1$

$1 > 2 + 1$

$1 > 3$ False

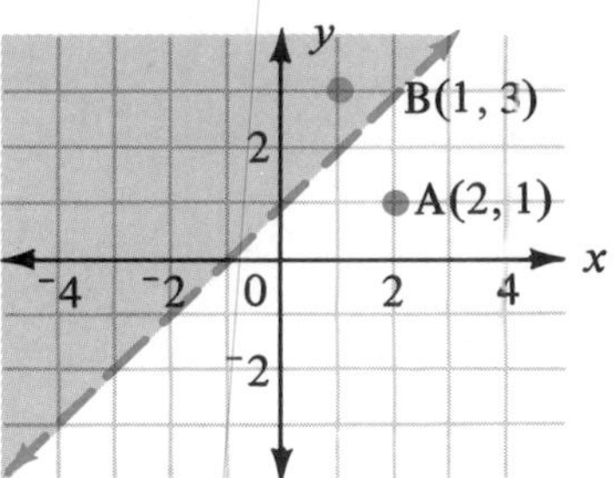

Step 4 Test a point on the other side of the line.

$B(1, 3)$ $\quad y > x + 1$

$3 > 1 + 1$

$3 > 2$ True

Step 5 Shade the side containing the point that tested true.

A. Graph $y > 2x - 1$.

1. Make up a table of values for the related equation $y = 2x - 1$.
2. Use square-ruled paper and plot $y = 2x - 1$ with a dashed line.
3. Test a point on one side of the line. $A(3, 1)$ Is the inequality true?
4. Test a point on the other side of the line. $B(^-2, 3)$ Is the inequality true?
5. Shade the side containing point B. This is the graph of $y > 2x - 1$.

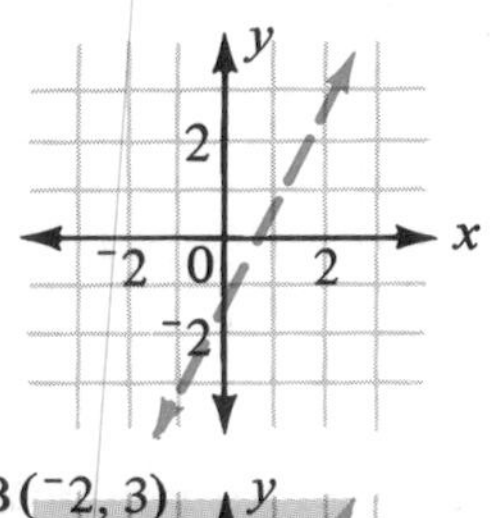

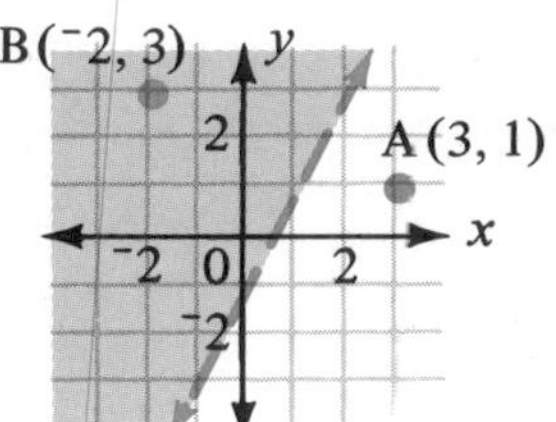

B. Graph these inequalities.

6. $y > x + 2$
7. $y > 3x$
8. $y < x$
9. $y < x - 1$

Practice

Test a point on each side of the line. Complete the graph.

1. $y > 2x + 1$

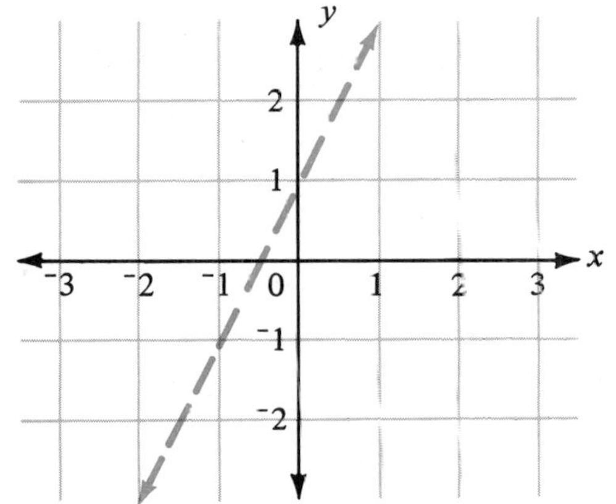

2. $y < 2x + 1$

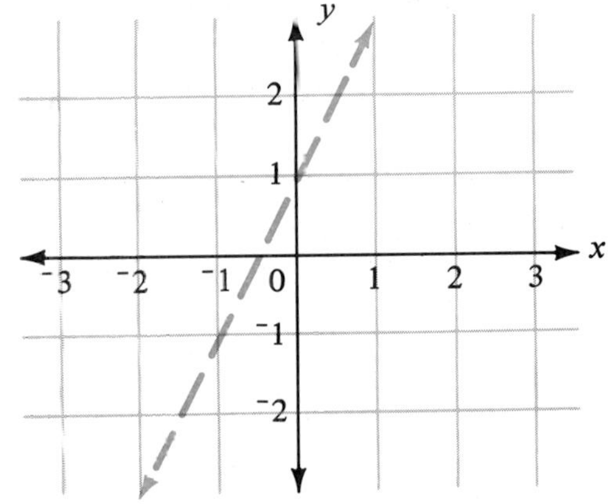

3. $y > {}^{-}x + 2$

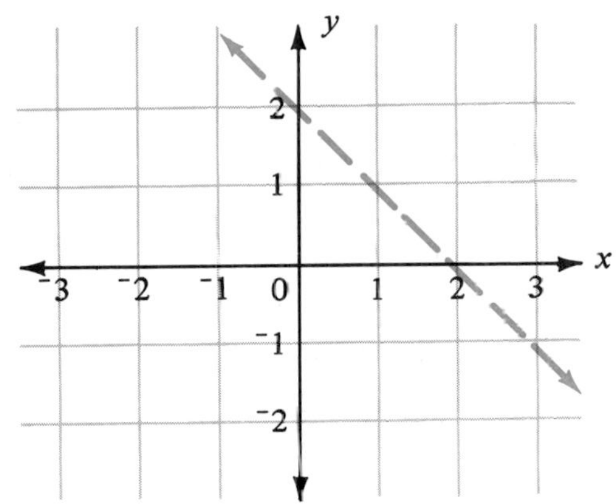

4. $y < {}^{-}2x - 1$

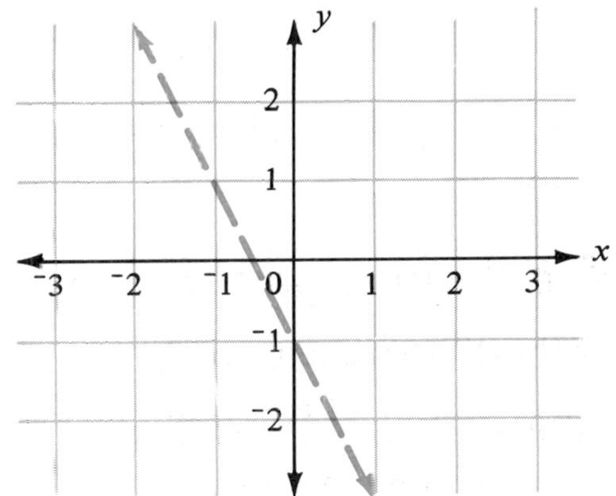

Graph these inequalities.

5. $y > x + 3$

6. $y > 2x$

7. $y < x + 3$

8. $y < 2x$

9. $y > 2x - 3$

10. $y < 3x - 4$

11. $y < {}^{-}3x + 3$

12. $y > {}^{-}\frac{1}{2}x + 2$

Mid-Chapter Review

Plot these points. *(372)*

1. $A(3, 0)$ **2.** $B(1, ^-2)$ **3.** $C(^-1, ^-1)$ **4.** $D(^-4, 5)$

Graph. *(376)*

5. $y = x + 4$ **6.** $y = 2x$ **7.** $y = 3x - 2$

FIND OUT!

Brainteasers

1. Here are the steps of a flow chart for getting the mail. Put the steps in order and make a flow chart.

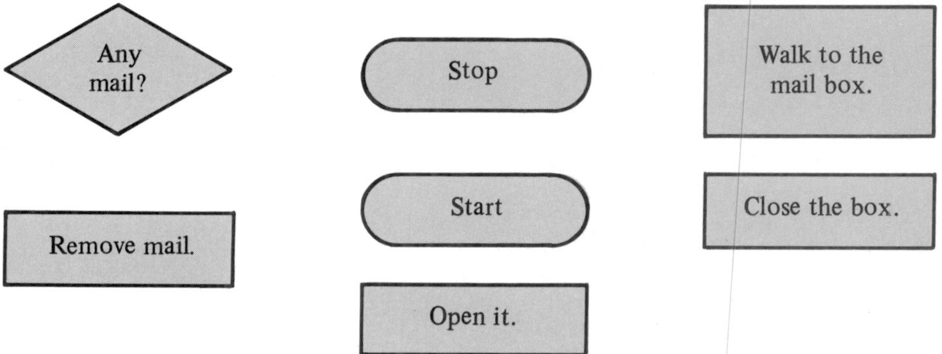

2. Here are the steps to decide if a triangle is a right triangle given the lengths of the sides. Put the steps in order and make a flow chart.

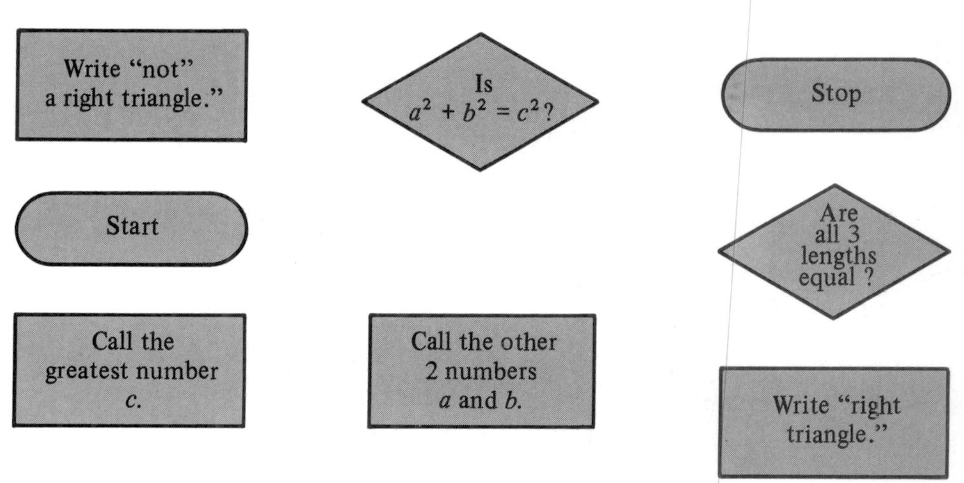

Symmetry and Coordinates

A figure is symmetric if its parts on either side of a line of symmetry are congruent.

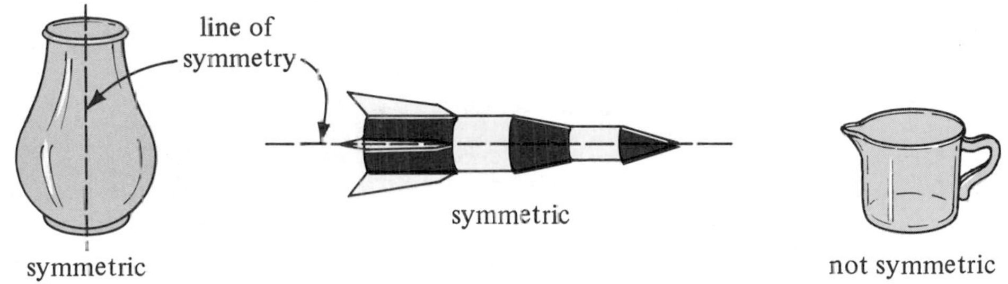

$\overline{CD}$ is a mirror image of $\overline{AB}$ about the x-axis.

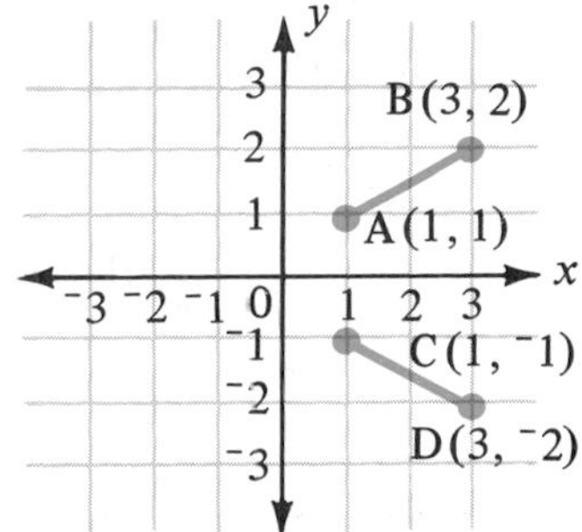

1. What are the coordinates of point C?
2. How do the coordinates of A and C compare?
3. What are the coordinates of point D?
4. How do the coordinates of B and D compare?
5. What is true of the distances of points A and C from the x-axis?
6. What is true of the distances of points B and D from the x-axis?

Find the mirror image of $\triangle ABC$ about the y-axis.

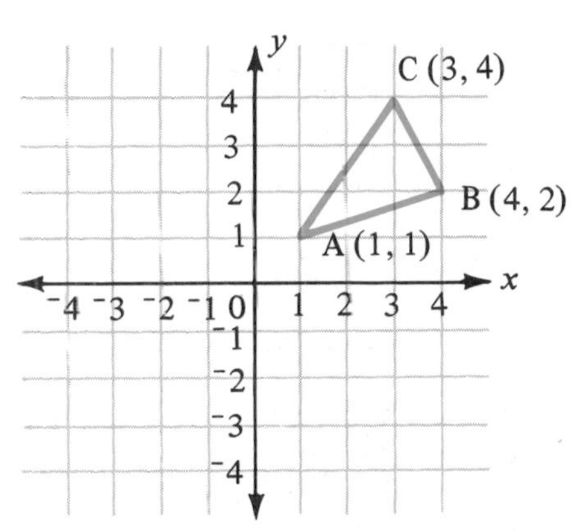

7. What are the coordinates of the point that is directly across from point A and the same distance from the y-axis?
8. What is the mirror image of point B about the y-axis?
9. What is the mirror image of point C about the y-axis?
10. Copy the graph and draw in the mirror image of $\triangle ABC$.

Solving Problems by Graphs

Under Plan 1 a salesperson can earn \$100 per week plus 10% of sales. Under Plan 2 the salesperson can earn 20% of sales. How much must be sold so that both plans give the same earnings?

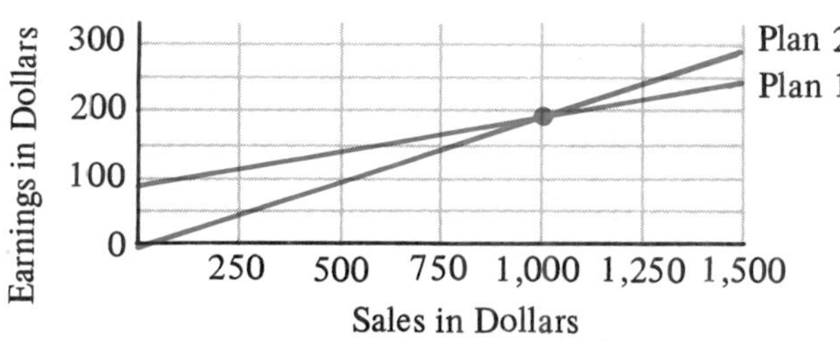

Answer: If sales are \$1,000, the earnings under either plan are the same.

A. Mr. Leff left his house at 8:00 am and drove 60 km/h on a business trip. His son left at 9:00 am. To overtake his father, the son drove at 80 km/h. At what time will the son overtake his father?

1. Copy the graph at the right.
2. Plot Mr. Leff's trip.

Time	*Distance*
8:00 am	0 km
9:00 am	60 km
10:00 am	120 km
11:00 am	180 km
12:00 noon	240 km

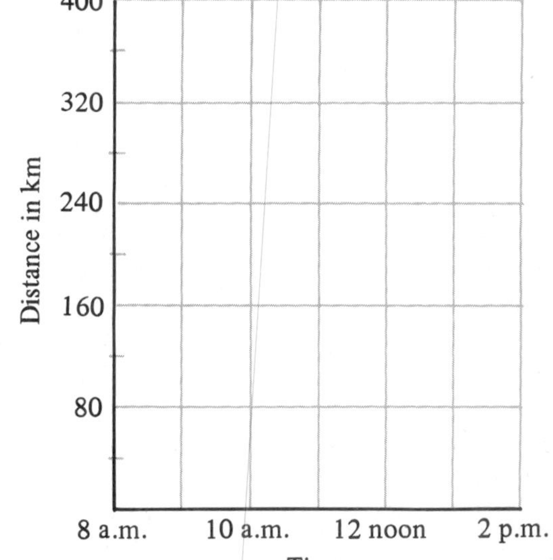

3. Plot the son's trip.
4. Where do the lines intersect?
5. Answer the problem.

B. Draw a graph and solve.

6. José has 24 records. Each week he adds 2 records to his collection. Susan has no records, but she is beginning to collect them. She is collecting 4 records a week. In how many weeks will she have as many as José?

Practice

A ship leaves New York harbor at 6:00 am. It goes at an average speed of 10 knots per hour. Another ship leaves New York at 9:00 am. It follows the first ship at an average speed of 15 knots per hour.

1. Draw a graph.
2. At what time will the second ship overtake the first ship?
3. How far from New York will they meet?

Joan has $60 in the bank. Each week she deposits $5. Bill has no money in the bank, but he is working part time. He deposits $10 a week.

4. Draw a graph.
5. In how many weeks will Joan and Bill have deposited the same amount of money?
6. How much money will each have saved?

Draw a graph and solve.

7. A company has 2 pay plans for salespersons. Under Plan 1, a salesperson earns $100 a week plus 25% of sales. Under Plan 2, a salesperson earns 50% of sales. How much must be sold so that a salesperson would earn the same amount under either plan?

Interpreting Data

The scores made by the school basketball team were 47, 68, 50, 34, 64, 47, and 54. The scores are arranged below from highest to lowest.

highest →	68	
	64	
	54	
	50	*Median* (50), or middle number
	47	*Mode* (47), or number that occurs most often
	47	
lowest →	34	
	364	*Mean,* or average: $7\overline{)364}$ = 52

Range: 34 to 68

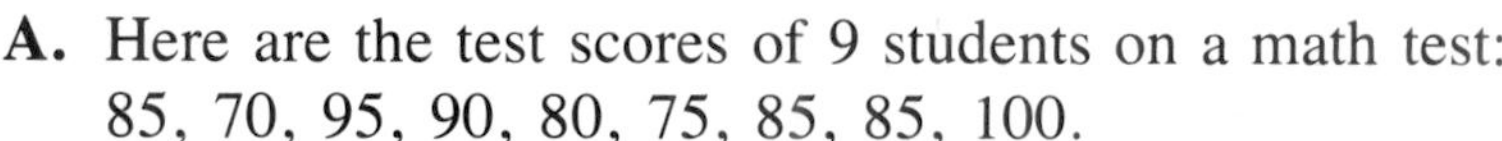

A. Here are the test scores of 9 students on a math test: 85, 70, 95, 90, 80, 75, 85, 85, 100.

1. Arrange the scores in order from highest to lowest.

2. What is the range of the scores?

3. What is the mode of the scores?

4. What is the median of the scores?

5. What is the mean of the scores?

B. Here are Jeremy's bowling scores: 100, 120, 114, 118, 94, 102.

6. Find the mean of the bowling scores.

7. Jeremy's average for 7 bowling games is 112. What was his total for the 7 games?

C. Find the median of these salaries: \$75, \$105, \$246, \$156, \$182, \$98.

8. How many salaries are there? Arrange them in order.

9. Is there a middle salary?

10. What are the 2 middle salaries?

11. What is their mean? This is the median.

Practice

Find the ranges.

1. 32, 52, 72, 92, 13

2. 20, 14, 23, 35, 7, 6

3. 34, 41, 33, 12, 18, 31, 29, 28, 13, 16, 18, 31, 49, 18

Find the modes.

4. 34, 21, 22, 34, 29

5. 85, 90, 85, 90, 75, 65

6. 86, 92, 81, 90, 59, 85, 69, 81, 39, 64, 100, 99, 79

Find the means.

7. 81, 88, 87, 89, 69

8. 135, 146, 119, 124, 138, 148

9. 34, 22, 36, 49, 38, 29, 40, 51, 48, 38, 43, 22

Find the medians.

10. 8, 5, 13, 16, 9

11. 22, 31, 41, 29, 34, 38

12. 81, 96, 87, 75, 68, 78, 90, 90, 100, 75, 87, 61, 58, 60

These are the salaries of 9 people working in a store:
\$150, \$110, \$210, \$180, \$220, \$185, \$180, \$180, \$250.

13. Arrange the salaries in order. What is the range?

14. What is the mode of the salaries?

15. What is the median of the salaries?

16. What is the mean of the salaries?

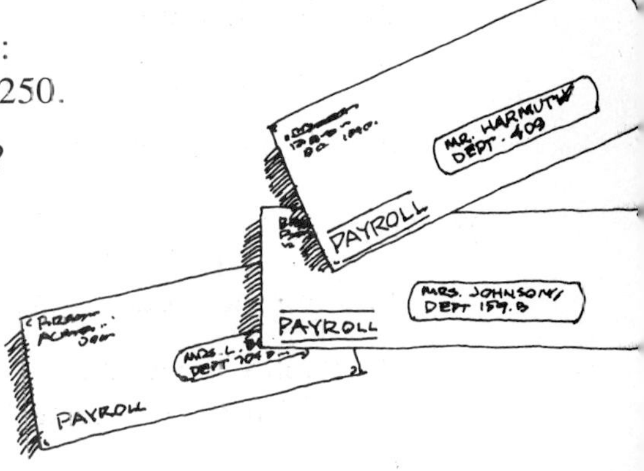

Solve.

17. The ages of the workers in an office are 48, 29, 32, 41, 37, 39, 43, 23, and 26. What is the mean of the ages of these office workers?

★ **18.** In 7 games, a team averaged 6 runs. In 6 games, the team scored 39 runs. How many runs did they score in the seventh game?

Graphing Data

A survey was made of the number of people using the tennis courts on Brown Boulevard. The data may be shown in table form or by a graph.

PEOPLE USING TENNIS COURTS

Week	*Number of People*
1	300
2	150
3	250
4	200

Step 1 Select axes and scales.

Step 2 Draw bars. Use information in the table.

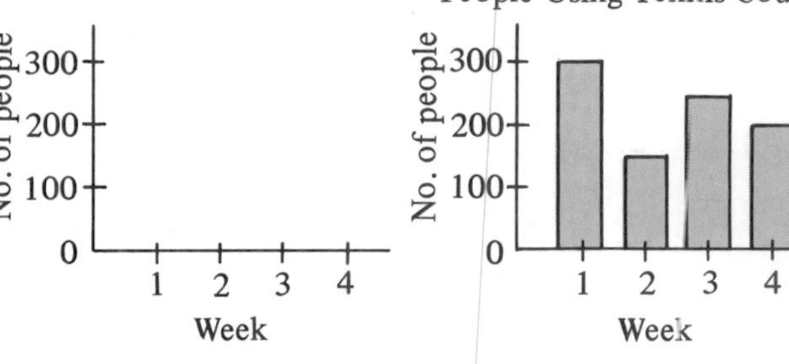

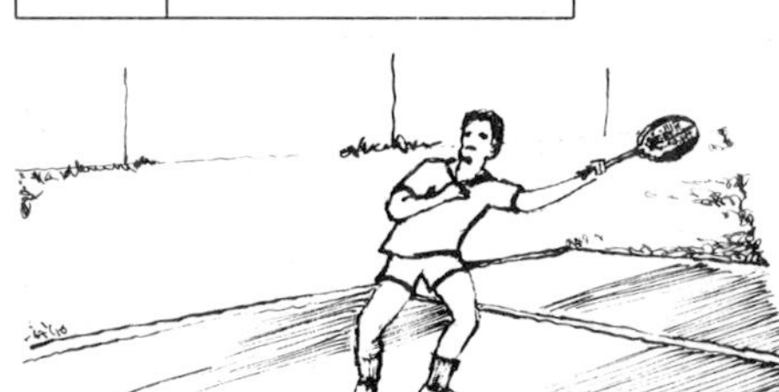

A. On square-ruled paper construct a bar graph of the data in the table.

1. Draw a vertical and a horizontal axis.
2. From numbers in the table, decide upon a scale for each axis.
3. Construct each bar equally wide and equally spaced.
4. Label the graph.

VOTES FOR CLASS PRESIDENT

Name	*Votes*
Gene	70
Maria	60
Randy	80

B. Construct bar graphs from the tables.

5. TICKETS SOLD TO SCHOOL DANCE

Grade	*Number of Tickets*
7th	110
8th	150
9th	180

6. TELEPHONES PER 100 PEOPLE

Country	*Number of Telephones*
United States	45
Canada	35
Norway	25

The number of people using the tennis courts may also be shown by a broken-line graph.

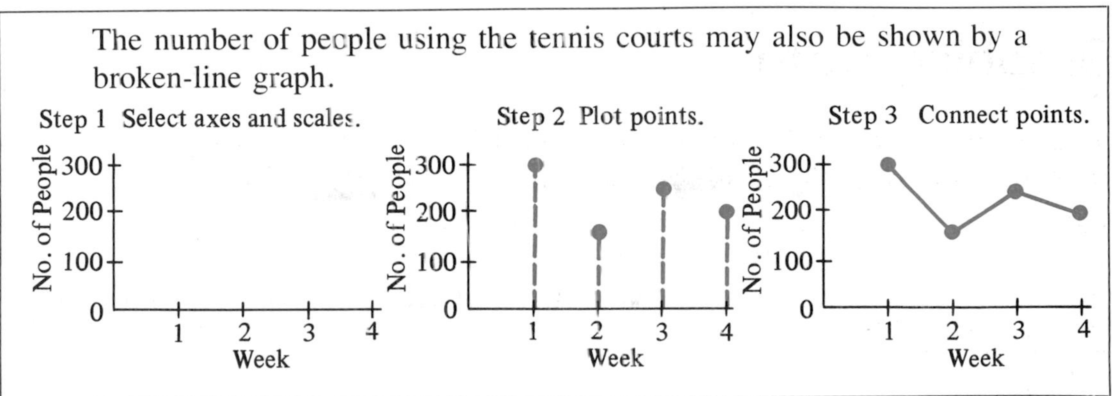

C. Construct broken-line graphs from the tables.

7. BETH'S SCHOOL MARKS

Test	*Mark*
1	90
2	95
3	80

8. TEMPERATURE RECORD

Time	*Temperature*
8 am	20° C
10 am	20° C
noon	23° C

Practice

Construct bar graphs.

1. TED'S PAPER ROUTE

Day	*Papers sold*
1	40
2	35
3	60

★ **2.** POPULATION 100 YEARS AGO

State	*Population*
California	864,694
Georgia	1,542,180
Illinois	3,077,871

Construct broken-line graphs.

3. HAROLD'S TEST SCORES

Test	*Score*
1	90
2	75
3	80

4. SIZE OF SENIOR CLASS

Year	*Number*
1960	350
1970	300
1980	500

Frequency Tables and Histograms

Here are the test scores of a class on a mathematics test: 100, 91, 83, 70, 100, 95, 82, 70, 83, 100, 90, 85, 72, 77, 81, 76, 64, 91, 82, 77, 87, 66, 82, 70, 50, 82, 85, 89, 73, 87.

Tables and graphs are used to organize and visualize data.

FREQUENCY TABLE

Score	*Tally*	*Frequency*
100	|||	3
95	|	1
91	||	2
90	|	1
89	|	1
87	||	2
85	||	2
83	||	2
82	||||	4
81	|	1
77	||	2
76	|	1
73	|	1
72	|	1
70	|||	3
66	|	1
64	|	1
50	|	1
	Total	30

The table can be organized like this.

Scores	*Frequency*
50–60	1
61–70	5
71–80	5
81–90	13
91–100	6
Total	30

A histogram can be made from this table.

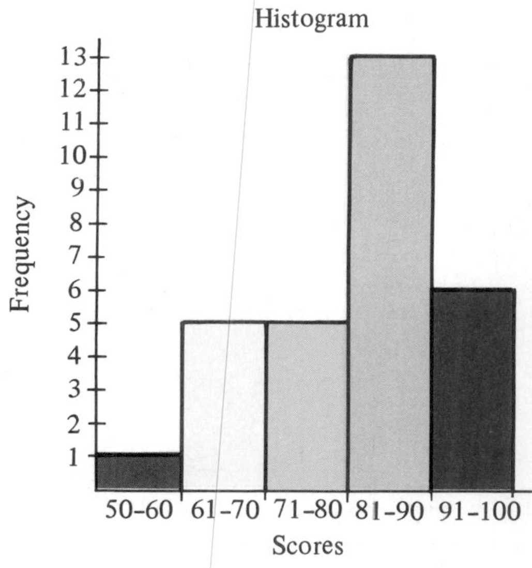

A. Answer these questions about the test scores. Use the frequency tables and the histogram.

1. What is the mode of the test scores?

2. Did more students receive scores between 70 and 85 than between 85 and 100?

B. Use the frequency table on the left to find the mean of the test scores.

3. Multiply each score by its frequency.

4. Add the products.

5. Divide by 30.

Practice

Here are the number of people using Steve's Racquetball Club each day for a month: 110, 110, 125, 130, 150, 100, 115, 130, 125, 130, 150, 100, 125, 150, 130, 110, 120, 140, 135, 145, 130, 105, 130, 145, 115, 130, 140, 130, 145, 100.

1. Make frequency tables.
2. What is the mode?
3. What is the mean?
4. Complete the histogram.
5. From the histogram, the range of the number of people using Steve's Racquetball Club most often is between what 2 numbers?

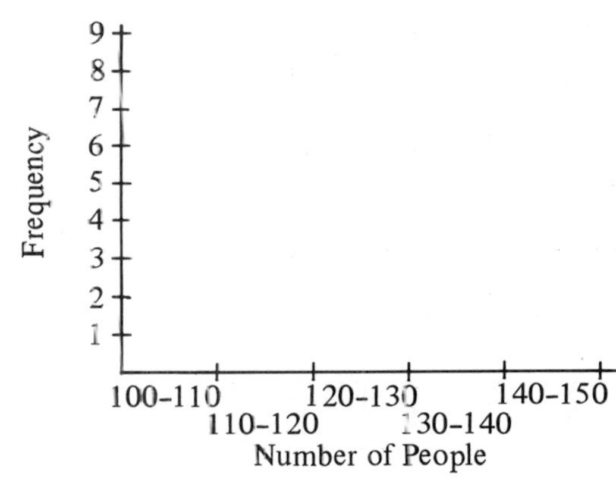

Make histograms.

6.

Salaries	*Frequency*
\$276–300	2
\$251–275	3
\$226–250	4
\$201–225	6
\$176–200	12
\$150–175	8

7.

Years of service	*Frequency*
1–5	9
6–10	10
11–15	6
16–20	8
21–25	2
26–30	3

Circle Graphs

Ilga interviewed 40 students. She asked each which of 4 popular records was his or her favorite. The results are in the first 2 columns of the table. The next 2 columns are used to construct a circle graph of the results.

Record	*Number*	*Fractional Part of Circle*	*Measure of Central Angle*
A	10	$\frac{10}{40}$ or $\frac{1}{4}$	$\frac{1}{4} \times 360° = 90°$
B	20	$\frac{20}{40}$ or $\frac{1}{2}$	$\frac{1}{2} \times 360° = 180°$
C	4	$\frac{4}{40}$ or $\frac{1}{10}$	$\frac{1}{10} \times 360° = 36°$
D	6	$\frac{6}{40}$ or $\frac{3}{20}$	$\frac{3}{20} \times 360° = 54°$
Total	40		360°

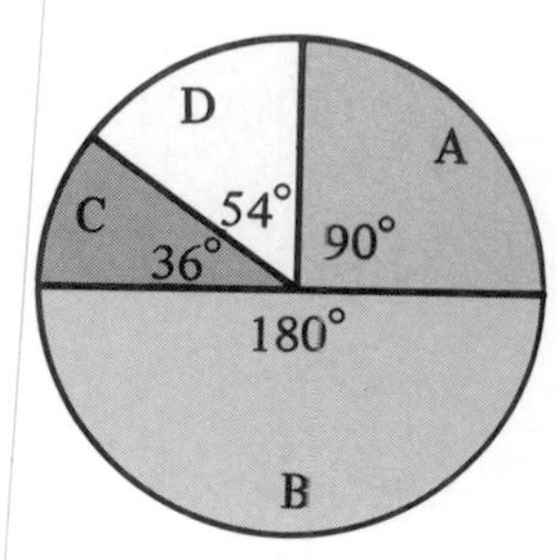

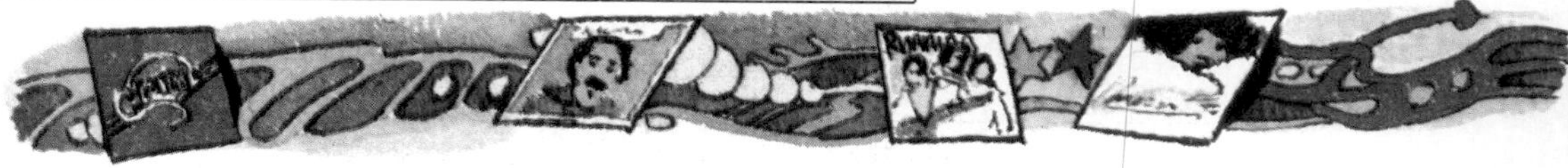

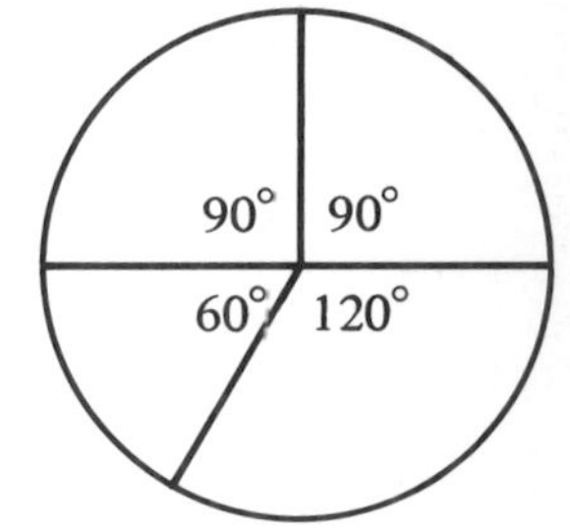

A. A central angle is formed by 2 radii of a circle.

1. How many central angles are shown?

2. What is the sum of the central angles?

▶ The sum of the central angles of a circle is 360°.

B. Complete the table.

	Days Absent	*No. of Students*	*Fractional Part of Circle*	*Measure of Central Angle*
Example	0	10	$\frac{10}{30}$ or $\frac{1}{3}$	$\frac{1}{3} \times 360° = 120°$
3.	1	4		
4.	2	8		
5.	3	5		
6.	4	3		
	Total	30		360°

7. Make a circle graph.

Practice

Complete the tables. Make circle graphs.

1. CEREAL PREFERENCE SURVEY

Cereal	*Number*	*Fractional Part of Circle*	*Measure of Central Angle*
A	4		
B	3		
C	10		
D	8		
E	9		
F	2		
Total	36		

2. STUDENT QUIZ

Score	*Number*	*Fractional Part of Circle*	*Measure of Central Angle*
100	10		
80	24		
60	15		
40	6		
20	5		
Total	60		

Make circle graphs.

3. The Jackson sisters sold 1,200 boxes of shoes. Ann sold 200 boxes, Peg sold 350 boxes, Ruby sold 250 boxes, and Kay sold 400 boxes.

4. In Mrs. Spencer's mathematics class, 30% received A's, 40% received B's, 20% received C's, and 10% just passed.

Probability

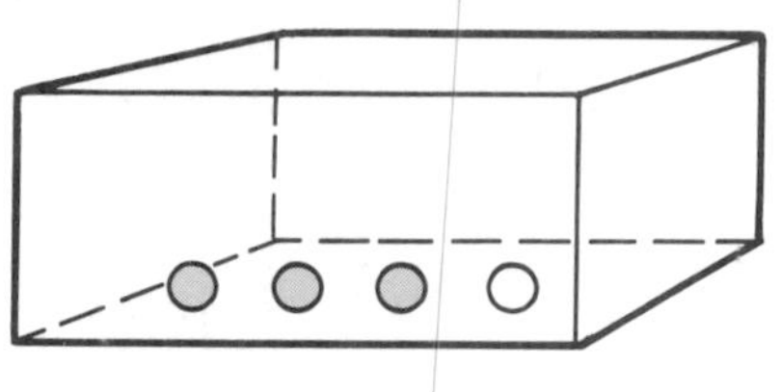

Lee is going to draw 1 marble from the box. It is equally likely that any of the 4 marbles will be drawn. 1 of the 4 marbles is white. The probability of drawing a white marble is $\frac{1}{4}$.

Probability of drawing a white marble = $\frac{\text{number of white marbles}}{\text{number of marbles}}$

A. Find the probability of spinning a 2.

1. How many 2's are there? This is the number of *favorable outcomes*.

2. How many *possible outcomes* are there?

3. What is the ratio $\frac{\text{number of favorable outcomes}}{\text{number of possible outcomes}}$?

4. What is the probability of spinning a 2?

   Write P (2) = $\frac{4}{8}$, or $\frac{1}{2}$.

B. This box contains 5 checkers. One checker is black, 3 are red, and 1 is white.

5. What is P (black)?

6. What is the probability of *not* getting black?

C. Look at the spinner.

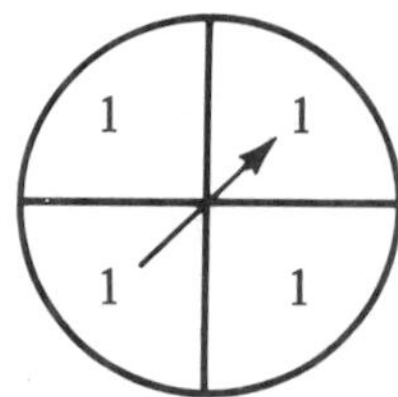

7. What is P (1)?

8. What is P (2)?

▶ A probability of 1 indicates certainty.
A probability of 0 indicates impossibility.

Practice

Assume that all outcomes are equally likely.

The box shown at the right contains numbered blocks. Find the probabilities.

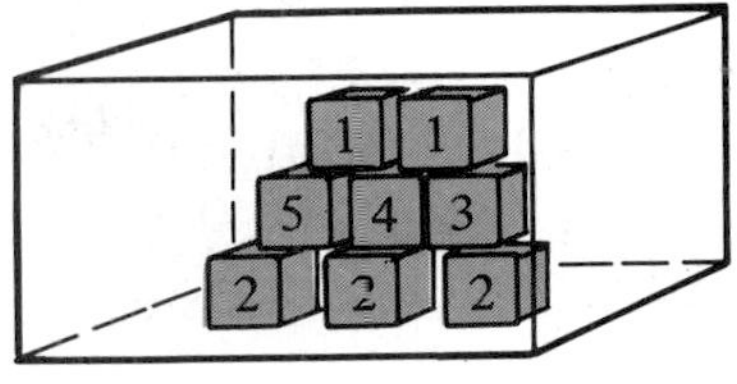

1. P(2)
2. P(3)
3. P(4)
4. P(5)
5. P(6)
6. P(1)

Use the spinner at the right. Find the probabilities.

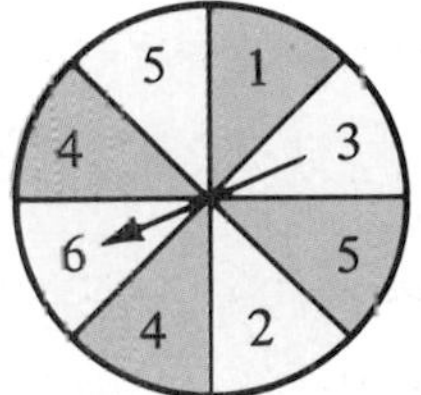

7. P(6)
8. P(5)
9. P(4)

An envelope contains six \$1 bills, eight \$5 bills, and three \$10 bills.

10. What is the probability of drawing a \$1 bill?

11. What is the probability of drawing a \$5 bill?

12. What is the probability of drawing a \$10 bill?

A penny is tossed.

13. What is the probability that it will fall heads up?

14. What is the probability that it will fall tails up?

A die is tossed.

15. What is the probability the face with 2 dots will be on top?

★ 16. What is the probability that 3 or fewer dots will be on top?

★ 17. What is the probability that an odd number of dots will be on top?

★ 18. What is the probability that an even number of dots will be on top?

Sample Space

The sample space of an experiment consists of all the possible outcomes. For tossing a die, the sample space consists of 1, 2, 3, 4, 5, 6. P(1 or 2) means the probability of getting a number less than 3.

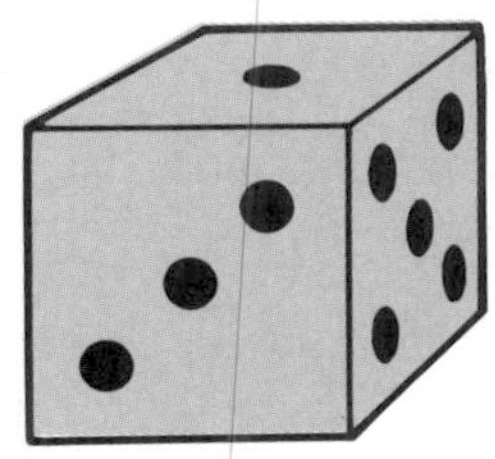

$$P(1 \text{ or } 2) = \frac{2}{6} \begin{array}{l} \leftarrow \text{number of favorable outcomes} \\ \leftarrow \text{number of possible outcomes} \end{array}$$

A. For tossing a die, the sample space consists of 1, 2, 3, 4, 5, 6. Find the probabilities.

1. P(1)　　**2.** P(2 or 4 or 6)　　**3.** P(number $>$ 3)

B. Find the sample space for tossing 2 coins. Use H for heads and T for tails. Complete the table of possible outcomes.

	1st coin	*2nd coin*	*Ordered Pair*
	H	H	(H, H)
4.	H		
5.	T		
6.		H	

▶ The sample space for tossing 2 coins consists of (H, H), (H, T), (T, T), (T, H).

C. Two coins are tossed 100 times. Predict how many times the outcome will be (H, H).

7. What is $P(H, H)$?

8. Multiply $\frac{1}{4} \times 100$.

Practice

A slip of paper is drawn at random from the box.

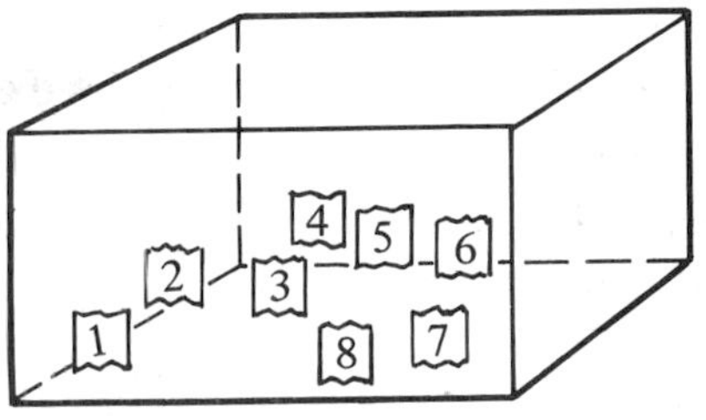

1. What is the sample space?

Find the probabilities.

2. P(3)
3. P(3 or 4)
4. P(even number)
5. P(number > 8)
6. Predict the number of times 3 would be drawn in 40 draws.

The pointers on the red and white spinners are spun at the same time.

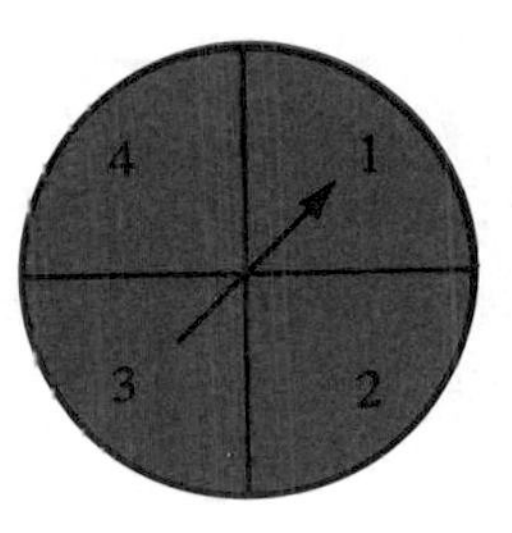

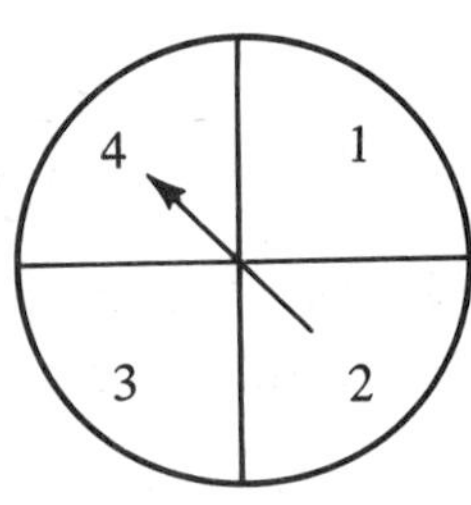

7. Give the ordered pairs in the sample space. Use (red, white).

Find the probabilities.

8. P(2, 3)
9. P(4, 4)
10. P(sum of both numbers is 3)
11. Predict how many times (1, 2) will occur in 400 spins.

Keeping Fit

Compute.

1. 10% of 80
2. 25% of 12
3. 30% of 70
4. 68% of 97
5. 45% of 75
6. 15% of 50
7. 20% of 150
8. 175% of 300
9. 25% of what is 8?
10. 30% of what is 12?
11. 8% of what is 16?
12. 3% of what is 60?
13. 150% of what is 72?
14. 160% of what is 32?
15. What percent of 20 is 5?
16. What percent of 100 is 84?
17. What percent of 40 is 24?
18. What percent of 16 is 2?
19. What percent of 230 is 69?
20. What percent of 32 is 48?

Compound Probability

The probability that an M or an E is drawn is $\frac{2}{11} + \frac{1}{11}$, or $\frac{3}{11}$.

$P(M \text{ or } E) = P(M) + P(E)$

A. A bag contains 4 red marbles, 7 blue marbles, and 1 yellow marble. One marble is drawn. Find the probabilities.

1. P(blue)

2. P(yellow)

3. P(blue or yellow)

▶ If 2 events cannot occur at the same time, then the probability that one or the other of them will occur is the *sum* of their probabilities.

B. You can discuss the probability of events which occur one after another.

Here is how to find the probability that on 2 successive tosses of a coin 2 heads result.

4. What is $P(H)$ on the first toss?

5. What is $P(H)$ on the second toss?

6. Give the ordered pairs for the sample space for 2 successive tosses. Use (1st toss, 2nd toss).

7. What is $P(H, H)$?

8. True or false? $P(H, H) = P(H) \cdot P(H)$

▶ If an event can occur and then afterward a second event can occur, then the probability that both events can occur is the product of their probabilities.

C. One box contains 3 red checkers and 4 black checkers. A second box contains 5 red checkers and 3 black checkers. One is drawn from each box.

9. What is the probability that they are both red?

Practice

A card is drawn from the box. Find the probabilities.

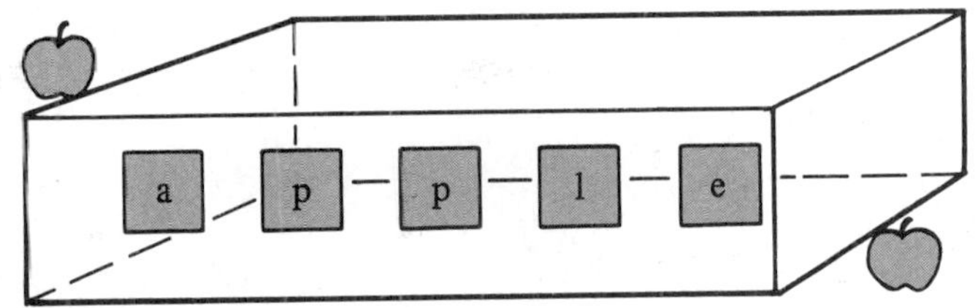

1. P(p)

2. P(a)

3. P(p or a)

A jar contains seven $1 bills, eight $5 bills, and six $10 bills. A bill is drawn from the jar. Find the probabilities.

4. P($1)
5. P($5)
6. P($10)
7. P($1 or $10)
8. P($1 or S5)
9. P($5 or $10)

A box contains 3 red balls and 5 black balls. A second box contains 2 red balls and 4 black balls. One ball is drawn from each box. Find the probabilities.

10. P(black) on drawing from first box
11. P(black) on drawing from second box
12. P(black and black)
13. P(red) on drawing from first box
14. P(red) on drawing from second box
15. P(red and red)

A bag contains 4 red blocks and 6 white blocks. One block is drawn, then replaced. A second block is drawn. Find the probabilities.

16. P(red and red)
17. P(white and white)
18. P(red and white), red drawn first and then white drawn
19. P(white and red), white drawn first and then red drawn

★ 20. The arrow is spun 3 times. What is the probability of getting 3 ones?

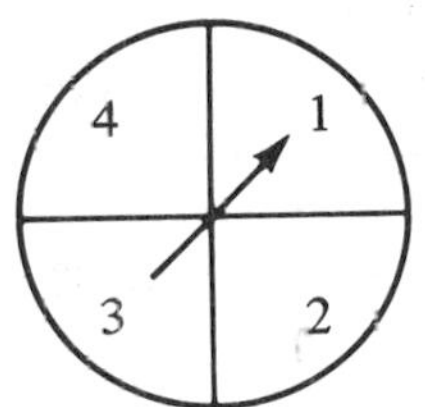

Problem Solving • Research Analysts

A research analyst made the bar graph at the right.

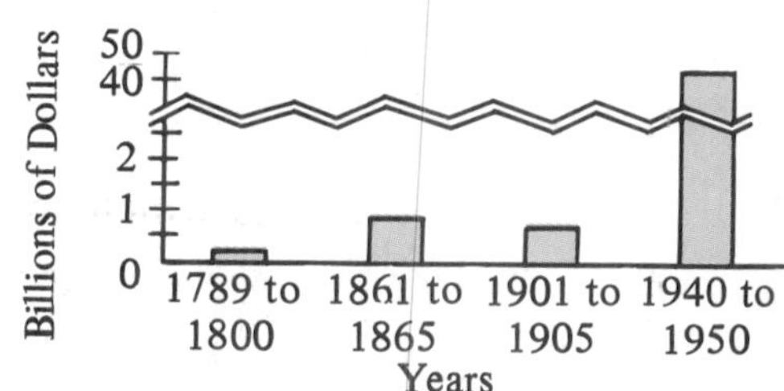

1. Approximately how much was spent by the U.S. government during each period shown on the graph?

2. During which 2 periods shown were U.S. expenditures about the same?

A research analyst made the circle graph at the right for her company.

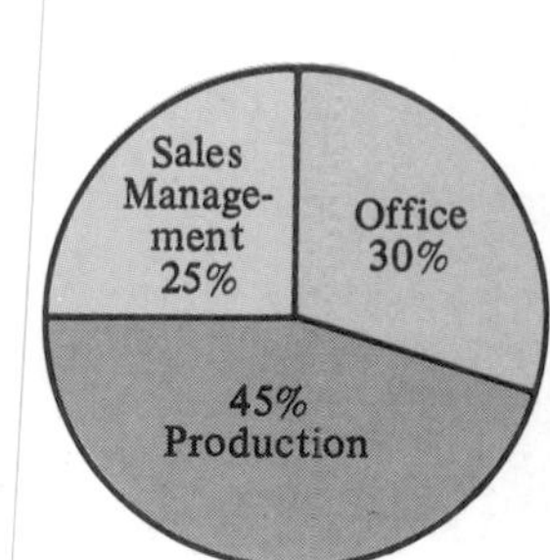

3. There are 600 people employed by the XY Company. How many work in production?

4. How many do office work?

5. The number of people in production are about how many times the number in sales and management?

A research analyst made the broken-line graph at the right for his company.

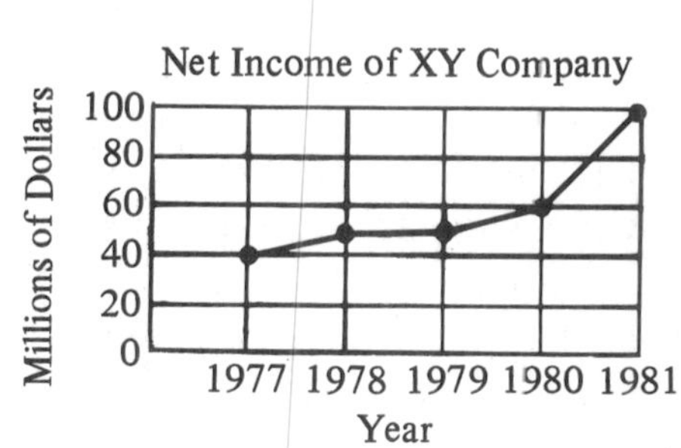

6. What was the net income of the company during 1980?

7. During which 2 years was the net income about the same?

8. What is the trend in the net income of the company?

Career

Chapter Review

Plot these points. (372)

1. $A(4, 2)$
2. $B(^{-}1, 0)$
3. $C(^{-}2, ^{-}1)$

Graph. (376)

4. $y = x + 3$
5. $y = 2x + 2$
6. $y = 3x - 1$

Daily attendance at the handball court one week was 31, 29, 36, 48, 48, 71, 76. (384)

7. Find the range.
8. Find the mean.
9. Find the median.
10. Find the mode.

11. Construct a bar graph.
(386) Sales: Mon. \$300; Tues. \$400; Wed. \$215; Thurs. \$525; Fri. \$809; Sat. \$1,200

12. Construct a broken-line graph.
(386) Attendance: August, 23,000; September, 40,000; October, 35,000; November, 24,000; December, 18,000.

13. Lena asked 20 students which sport they like to play most,
(390) baseball, football or soccer. 5 people said baseball, 3 people said football and 12 people said soccer. Make a circle graph.

A box contains 4 red marbles, 2 green marbles, 1 white marble and 5 black marbles. Find the probabilities. (392)

14. P(red)
15. P(not green)
16. P(yellow)

Two spinners are spun at the same time. (394)

17. Give the ordered pairs in the sample space.
18. Predict how many times (1, 4) will occur in 300 spins.

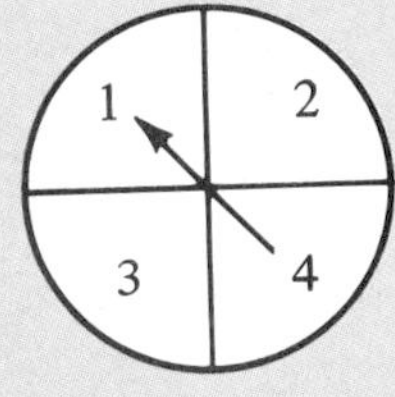

Solve. (382, 398)

19. Opi has \$50 in the bank. Each week she deposits \$7. Steve has no money in the bank, but plans to deposit \$12 a week. In how many weeks will they have the same amount of money in the bank?

20. A research analyst found that of the 250 employees at the Bright Company, 10% are secretaries. How many secretaries are there at the Bright Company?

Chapter Test

Plot these points. *(372)*

1. $A(3, 1)$ **2.** $B(0, 3)$ **3.** $C(^-3, 2)$

Graph. *(376)*

4. $y = x - 1$ **5.** $y = x + 4$ **6.** $y = 4x - 3$

The average daily temperatures for 5 days were 23°C, 21°C, 23°C, 27°C, 26°C. *(384)*

7. Find the range.

8. Find the mean.

9. Find the median.

10. Find the mode.

11. Construct a bar graph. Sales:
(386) Howard, \$600; Mimi, \$720; Daniel, \$525; Isaac, \$410; Kate, \$475

12. Construct a broken-line graph.
(386) Quiz scores: Mon., 86%; Tues., 85%; Wed., 90%; Thurs., 94%; Fri., 97%

13. Jorge noted the colors of the first 100 cars to drive pass his
(390) house. 25 were blue, 15 were black, 20 were yellow, 10 were white, 15 were green, 15 were red. Make a circle graph.

A box contains 7 blue blocks, 3 white blocks, and 6 red blocks. Find the probabilities. *(392)*

14. P(white) **15.** P(not green) **16.** P(red)

Two spinners are spun at the same time. *(394)*

17. Give the ordered pairs in the sample space.

18. Predict how many times (1, 1) will occur in 400 spins.

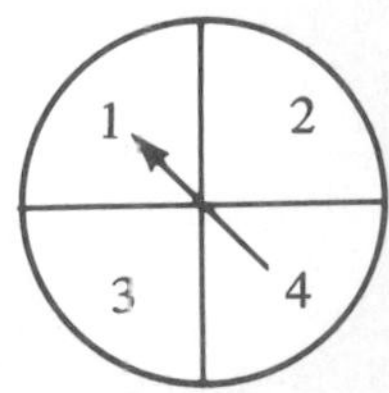

Solve. *(382, 398)*

19. Mr. James left his home at 7:00 am driving at a speed of 60 km/h. Mrs. James left at 8:00 am and followed him driving at a speed of 80 km/h. At what time will she overtake him?

20. A research analyst found that out of 500 persons polled, 275 prefer Smile toothpaste. What percent prefer Smile toothpaste?

Basic Skills Check

1. Which is the best buy?

A 2 rolls for 25¢ B 3 rolls for 36¢

C 4 rolls for 46¢ D 5 rolls for 55¢

---

2. Bill borrowed $500 from his uncle for 2 years at 6% interest. What was the interest at the end of the 2 years?

E $30 F $60

G $300 H $600

---

3. For which of the following times will the hands of a clock form right angles?

A noon B 6:00 am

C 3:00 am D 2:00 am

---

4. The radius of a magnifying glass is 30 mm. What is the area of the magnifying glass? Use 3.14 for π.

E 282,600 mm^2 F 2,826 mm^2

G 188.400 mm^2 H 94.20 mm^2

---

5. What point is located at (3, 4)?

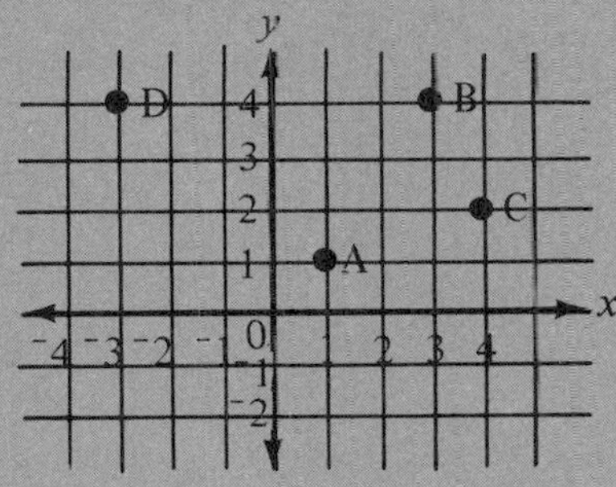

A A B B

C C D D

6. Weekly income is $400. How much is budgeted for food?

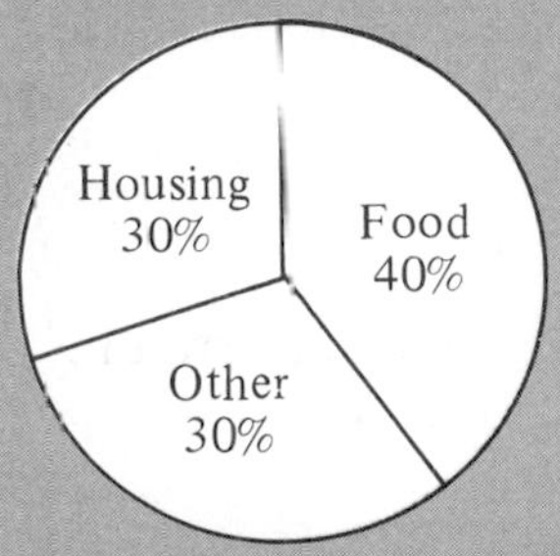

E $40 F $160

G $200 H $400

---

7. The scale on a map is 1 cm = 50 km. Two cities are 3 cm apart on the map. How many kilometers apart are the cities?

A 50 km B 150 km

C 175 km D 200 km

---

8. A sports car gets 34 miles per gallon of gasoline. How far can it go on 9 gal of gasoline?

E 340 mi F 306 mi

G 296 mi H 25 mi

---

9. The Blass family drove for 3 hours at an average speed of 65 km/h to their cousins' house. How far is it to their cousins' house?

A 68 km B 185 km

C 195 km D 245 km

TRIGONOMETRIC RATIOS

Angle Measure	*Sin*	*Cos*	*Tan*	*Angle Measure*	*Sin*	*Cos*	*Tan*
0°	0.00	1.00	0.00	**46°**	.719	.695	1.04
1°	.017	1.00	.017	**47°**	.731	.682	1.07
2°	.035	.999	.035	**48°**	.743	.669	1.11
3°	.052	.999	.052	**49°**	.755	.656	1.15
4°	.070	.998	.070	**50°**	.766	.643	1.19
5°	.087	.996	.087	**51°**	.777	.629	1.23
6°	.105	.995	.105	**52°**	.788	.616	1.28
7°	.122	.993	.123	**53°**	.799	.602	1.33
8°	.139	.990	.141	**54°**	.809	.588	1.38
9°	.156	.988	.158	**55°**	.819	.574	1.43
10°	.174	.985	.176	**56°**	.829	.559	1.48
11°	.191	.982	.194	**57°**	.839	.545	1.54
12°	.208	.978	.213	**58°**	.848	.530	1.60
13°	.225	.974	.231	**59°**	.857	.515	1.66
14°	.242	.970	.249	**60°**	.866	.500	1.73
15°	.259	.966	.268	**61°**	.875	.485	1.80
16°	.276	.961	.287	**62°**	.883	.469	1.88
17°	.292	.956	.306	**63°**	.891	.454	1.96
18°	.309	.951	.325	**64°**	.899	.438	2.05
19°	.326	.946	.344	**65°**	.906	.423	2.15
20°	.342	.940	.364	**66°**	.914	.407	2.25
21°	.358	.934	.384	**67°**	.921	.391	2.36
22°	.375	.927	.404	**68°**	.927	.375	2.48
23°	.391	.921	.424	**69°**	.934	.358	2.61
24°	.407	.914	.445	**70°**	.940	.342	2.75
25°	.423	.906	.466	**71°**	.946	.326	2.90
26°	.438	.899	.488	**72°**	.951	.309	3.08
27°	.454	.891	.510	**73°**	.956	.292	3.27
28°	.469	.883	.532	**74°**	.961	.276	3.49
29°	.485	.875	.554	**75°**	.966	.259	3.73
30°	.500	.866	.577	**76°**	.970	.242	4.01
31°	.515	.857	.601	**77°**	.974	.225	4.33
32°	.530	.848	.625	**78°**	.978	.208	4.71
33°	.545	.839	.649	**79°**	.982	.191	5.15
34°	.559	.829	.675	**80°**	.985	.174	5.67
35°	.574	.819	.700	**81°**	.988	.156	6.31
36°	.588	.809	.727	**82°**	.990	.139	7.12
37°	.602	.799	.754	**83°**	.993	.122	8.14
38°	.616	.788	.781	**84°**	.995	.105	9.51
39°	.629	.777	.810	**85°**	.996	.087	11.4
40°	.643	.766	.839	**86°**	.998	.070	14.3
41°	.656	.755	.869	**87°**	.999	.052	19.1
42°	.669	.743	.900	**88°**	.999	.035	28.6
43°	.682	.731	.933	**89°**	1.00	.017	57.3
44°	.695	.719	.966	**90°**	1.00	0.00	
45°	.707	.707	1.00				

EXTRA PRACTICE

Solve. *(Use with page 8.)*

1. Ed ran 35 minutes on Sunday, 25 minutes on Monday, and 48 minutes on Tuesday. How long did he run in all?

2. Jamie bought 4 ribbons, each 32 in. long. How much ribbon did she buy in all?

3. Joan bought shoes for $28.95, a sweater for $17.98, and a shirt for $17.50. How much did she spend in all?

4. Al handed out 158 flyers for a play. Pat handed out 63 more flyers than Al. How many flyers did Pat hand out?

5. Miss Marsh bought 4 rolls of paper. The paper cost $32.16. What was the cost of 1 roll of paper?

6. Tickets for a movie were $3.00 each. Mr. Lang bought $135 worth of tickets. How many tickets did he buy?

Add. *(Use with page 24.)*

1. 754 + 35

2. 3,654 + 2,543

3. $5,189 + 2,675

4. 36,136 + 52,375

5. 47,967 + 31,358

6. 736,184 + 124,819

7. $359,487 + 427,891

8. 4,189 + 7,156 + 5,398

9. 7,157 + 3,984 + 5,619 + 3,487

10. $89,167 + 42,789 + 3,487 + 9,135

11. 416,871 + 39,375 + 182,468 + 51,009 + 237,861

12. $2,386,143 + 1,194,865 + 544,328 + 167,246 + 4,891,387

★ **13.** 15,489,163 + 27,564 + 39,986,115 + 656,789 + 8,132,108

★ **14.** 31,376,181 + 497,275 + 73,891,476 + 65,971,183 + 1,246,971

Subtract. *(Use with page 26.)*

1. 5,896 − 2,589

2. 36,738 − 12,394

3. 48,971 − 26,489

4. 342,462 − 113,931

5. 7,321 − 3,496

6. 29,148 − 13,889

7. $56,782 − 24,395

8. 563,436 − 351,189

9. 4,618,497 − 2,948,699

10. $58,324.75 − 17,496.98

11. 8,006 − 3,849

12. 80,000 − 14,679

★ Find the missing numbers.

13. 358,647 − □ = 149,867

14. 3,674,187 − □ = 1,897,379

Estimate the sums. *(Use with page 28.)*

1. 634 + 798
2. 3,486 + 5,714
3. 71,863 + 13,974
4. 31,489 + 8,437
5. $67,874 + 1,396
6. 879 + 7,253 + 189
7. 13,875 + 9,684 + 57,183
8. $5,712 + 6,410 + 481 + 759
9. ★ 489,398 + 217,167
10. ★ 87,189 + 2,788 + 1,473 + 8,689 + 9,267

Estimate the differences.

11. 864 − 395
12. 738 − 53
13. 5,329 − 1,875
14. 7,467 − 89
15. 84,675 − 32,198
16. 36,489 − 8,114
17. 73,298 − 1,640
18. 37,317 − 3,843
19. ★ 467,483 − 279,156
20. ★ 458,175 − 37,137

Draw a diagram for each picture. Solve. *(Use with page 32.)*

1. A 65-ft television wire is cut into two pieces. The shorter piece is 27 ft long. How long is the longer piece?
2. The length of a garden is 72 ft longer than the width. The width is 94 ft. What is the length of the garden?
3. Ms. Gold bought a radio on sale for $98.98. She saved $50.95 of the original price. What was the original price of the radio?
4. Jan and Pietro drove toward each other from towns 146 km apart. When they met, Jan had driven 57 km. How far had Pietro driven?
5. Mr. Olin's fence is 240 ft long. He has painted 138 ft. How many feet does he have left to paint?
6. Sam walked south from a store for 460 m. Ilga walked north from the store 519 m. How far apart were they?

Multiply. *(Use with page 34.)*

1. 73 × 9
2. 246 × 5
3. $4,237 × 7
4. 39,467 × 6
5. $864.27 × 8
6. 56 × 28
7. 37 × 89
8. 450 × 25
9. $604 × 34
10. 3,596 × 72
11. 6,743 × 67
12. $77.39 × 41
13. 84,163 × 74
14. 35,186 × 29
15. $763.85 × 37
16. 7 × 836
17. 85 × 31
18. 27 × 562
19. ★ 36 × 4 × 93
20. ★ 56 × 8 × 37
21. ★ 37 × 6 × 82 × 4

Multiply. *(Use with page 36.)*

1. 346×121 **2.** 482×326 **3.** 507×827 **4.** 429×495 **5.** 360×128

6. $3{,}460 \times 423$ **7.** $8{,}067 \times 212$ **8.** $4{,}163 \times 409$ **9.** $3{,}170 \times 604$ **10.** $8{,}234 \times 740$

11. $42{,}316 \times 819$ **12.** $6{,}816 \times 4{,}118$ **13.** $3{,}939 \times 2{,}617$ **14.** $4{,}070 \times 2{,}061$ **15.** $14{,}152 \times 2{,}020$

16. $347 \times 1{,}803$ **17.** $1{,}830 \times 4{,}072$ ★ **18.** $31{,}463 \times 2{,}004$

★ **19.** $56 \times 87 \times 109$ ★ **20.** $74 \times 28 \times 15 \times 9$ ★ **21.** $136 \times 18 \times 9 \times 25$

Divide. *(Use with page 38.)*

1. $4\overline{)96}$ **2.** $3\overline{)87}$ **3.** $6\overline{)83}$ **4.** $6\overline{)79}$ **5.** $5\overline{)86}$

6. $4\overline{)168}$ **7.** $3\overline{)159}$ **8.** $7\overline{)219}$ **9.** $6\overline{)\$126}$ **10.** $5\overline{)183}$

11. $9\overline{)6{,}831}$ **12.** $8\overline{)7{,}580}$ **13.** $7\overline{)9{,}430}$ **14.** $6\overline{)7{,}594}$ **15.** $7\overline{)3{,}687}$

16. $6\overline{)8{,}172}$ **17.** $6\overline{)4{,}614}$ **18.** $8\overline{)\$9{,}072}$ **19.** $4\overline{)5{,}073}$ **20.** $5\overline{)8{,}172}$

21. $6\overline{)24{,}738}$ **22.** $5\overline{)10{,}070}$ **23.** $8\overline{)26{,}183}$ **24.** $9\overline{)35{,}703}$ **25.** $8\overline{)26{,}924}$

★ Find the missing numbers.

26. $\square \div 8 = 476\text{r}3$ **27.** $\square \div 7 = 4{,}587\text{r}6$ **28.** $\square \div 6 = 25{,}187\text{r}5$

Divide. *(Use with page 40.)*

1. $25\overline{)75}$ **2.** $36\overline{)72}$ **3.** $34\overline{)67}$ **4.** $24\overline{)75}$

5. $21\overline{)756}$ **6.** $23\overline{)667}$ **7.** $33\overline{)\$825}$ **8.** $27\overline{)189}$

9. $34\overline{)9{,}678}$ **10.** $44\overline{)9{,}618}$ **11.** $56\overline{)9{,}817}$ **12.** $25\overline{)6{,}718}$

13. $84\overline{)7{,}916}$ **14.** $73\overline{)5{,}629}$ **15.** $24\overline{)\$1{,}584}$ **16.** $37\overline{)2{,}679}$

17. $382\overline{)9{,}168}$ **18.** $627\overline{)8{,}787}$ **19.** $148\overline{)8{,}436}$ **20.** $439\overline{)9{,}239}$

21. $875\overline{)55{,}175}$ **22.** $287\overline{)80{,}387}$ **23.** $676\overline{)13{,}008}$ **24.** $555\overline{)92{,}130}$

★ Find the missing numbers.

25. $\square \div 37 = 29\text{r}36$ **26.** $\square \div 89 = 436\text{r}75$ **27.** $\square \div 189 = 374\text{r}59$

Extra Practice

Multiply. *(Use with page 44.)*

1. 50×7
2. 70×60
3. 300×50
4. 800×600
5. $50{,}000 \times 2$
6. $50{,}000 \times 20$
7. $50{,}000 \times 200$
8. $50{,}000 \times 2{,}000$
★9. $60{,}000 \times 50{,}000$
★10. $700{,}000 \times 20{,}000$

Divide.

11. 30)180
12. 40)1,600
13. 30)12,000
14. 60)24,000
15. 300)6,000
16. 400)28,000
17. 700)42,000
★18. 4,000)16,000

Estimate the products. *(Use with page 46.)*

1. 38×41
2. 350×29
3. $\$179 \times 68$
4. 479×881
5. $3{,}869 \times 43$
6. $8{,}704 \times 56$
7. $7{,}500 \times 418$
8. $\$8{,}164 \times 893$
★9. $15{,}675 \times 536$
★10. $38{,}471 \times 986$

Estimate the quotients.

11. 31)94
12. 36)418
13. 39)8,242
14. 51)$4,606
15. 42)29,416
16. 269)61,419
17. 289)16,681
★18. 837)334,198

Add or subtract. *(Use with page 51.)*

1. $8{,}734 + 3{,}978$
2. $75{,}349 + 26{,}863$
3. $\$526{,}679 + 29{,}187$
4. $86{,}183 + 5{,}967 + 15{,}363$
5. $418{,}379 + 67{,}186 + 153{,}208$
6. $5{,}673 - 3{,}192$
7. $6{,}837 - 2{,}988$
8. $52{,}126 - 28{,}378$
9. $\$7{,}003 - 5{,}394$
10. $60{,}000 - 38{,}145$

Multiply.

11. $3{,}918 \times 7$
12. $\$483 \times 96$
13. $5{,}670 \times 72$
14. $\$676 \times 137$
15. $5{,}379 \times 802$

Divide.

16. 5)975
17. 8)5,483
18. 27)189
19. 37)5,617
20. 64)$28,096

Estimate the answers.

21. $8{,}719 + 324$
22. $63{,}495 - 8{,}961$
23. 786×39
24. $6{,}917 \times 257$
25. 78)26,187

Select the equation to solve the problem. *(Use with page 88.)*

1. The regular price of a table is $269.50. On sale it is $199.25. How much is saved by buying the table on sale?

   a. $269.50 + 199.25 = c$
   b. $269.50 - 199.25 = c$
   c. $c - 269.50 = 199.25$
   d. $c - 199.25 = 269.50$

2. During a sale a person buying a plant for $7.50 received a second plant free. What is the average cost of each plant?

   a. $2 \times 7.50 = c$
   b. $7.50 + 7.50 = c$
   c. $7.50 + 7.50 = 2 \times c$
   d. $7.50 \div 2 = c$

3. Two cans of paint cost $13.96. How much do 12 cans of paint cost?

   a. $6 \times 13.96 = c$
   b. $12 \times 13.96 = c$
   c. $2 \times c = 13.96$
   d. $13.96 - 12 = c$

4. Baseballs cost $7.75 and footballs cost $9.98. How much more are footballs?

   a. $9.98 + 7.75 = c$
   b. $9.98 \times 7.75 = c$
   c. $c - 9.98 = 7.75$
   d. $9.98 - 7.75 = c$

5. Eighteen rulers cost $10.62. What is the cost of 1 ruler?

   a. $10.62 \div 18 = c$
   b. $18 \times 10.62 = c$
   c. $18 + 10.62 = c$
   d. $18 \div 10.62 = c$

6. Sara paid $11.98 for a book and $.59 for a card. How much did she pay in all?

   a. $11.98 - 0.59 = c$
   b. $c + 0.59 = 11.98$
   c. $0.59 \times 11.98 = c$
   d. $11.98 + 0.59 = c$

7. Five chairs, marked $36.75 a chair, were on sale at $5.00 off for each chair. How much did the five chairs cost on sale?

   a. $5 \times 36.75 = c$
   b. $36.75 - 5.00 = c$
   c. $5 \times 31.75 = c$
   d. $36.75 + 5.00 = c$

★ 8. Roses are 6 for $1.98, with 50¢ off if you buy more than a dozen. How much would 3 dozen roses cost?

   a. $3 \times (1.98 - 0.50) = c$
   b. $6 \times (1.98 - 0.50) = c$
   c. $2 \times (1.98 - 0.50) = c$
   d. $18 \times (1.98 - 0.50) = c$

Which is the better buy? *(Use with page 96.)*

1. A package of 6 rolls is marked $1.05, and a package of 8 rolls is marked $1.30. Which is the better buy?

2. At store A, 3 cans of soup cost $0.59. At store B, the same soup is 2 for $0.43. Which is the better buy?

3. A store sold 6 pencils for $0.55 or 10 pencils for $0.85. Which is the better buy?

4. A box of 6 cupcakes costs $1.71, and a box of 10 cupcakes costs $2.90. Which is the better buy?

5. A box of 100 paper clips costs $0.39. A box of 1,000 costs $3.50. Which is the better buy?

6. Jill bought socks, 3 pairs for $2.98. Ann bought the same socks, 2 pairs for $1.89. Which was the better buy?

Add. *(Use with page 102.)*

1. 1.3 + 4.4 **2.** 7.5 + 8.9 **3.** 56.72 + 13.25 **4.** \$8.72 + 3.19 **5.** 15.364 + 53.524

6. 0.5, 0.8, + 0.4 **7.** 0.624, 0.896, + 0.471 **8.** 0.1245, 0.7862, + 0.1459 **9.** 8.6, 3.4, + 3.6 **10.** \$15.63, 25.08, + 19.75

11. 3.6, 8.9, 7.4, + 6.7 **12.** \$2.67, 8.95, 7.07, + 8.88 **13.** 3.561, 1.089, 7.364, + 8.516 **14.** 0.1465, 0.3897, 0.1642, + 0.3875 **15.** 35.4179, 6.1175, 9.2874, + 3.1579

16. 3.4 + 8 + 9.31 **17.** 9 + 1.5 + 0.011 ★ **18.** 0.6 + 0.095 + 0.48751

★ **19.** 8 + 1.606 + 9.5 + 7.0031 ★ **20.** 6.5 + 0.11316 + 8.145 + 6

Find the answers. *(Use with page 104.)*

1. 12.7 − 9.3 **2.** 358.7 − 149.8 **3.** \$10.98 − 8.79 **4.** \$45.73 − 24.89 **5.** 0.074 − 0.065

6. 0.897 − 0.648 **7.** 8.786 − 3.347 **8.** 0.0008 − 0.0005 **9.** 0.0074 − 0.0038 **10.** 8.1674 − 6.9848

11. 6.7 − 0.46 **12.** 0.7 − 0.56 **13.** 0.04 − 0.008 **14.** 0.83 − 0.079

15. 8.4 − 7.83 **16.** 7.3 − 2.186 **17.** 8 − 0.94 ★ **18.** 9 − 6.18765

★ **19.** 9.1 − 3.46153 ★ **20.** 8 − 2.6 + 0.451 ★ **21.** 7.6 − 0.43 + 9

Estimate to the nearest whole number or dollar. *(Use with page 106.)*

1. 0.98 + 3.063 **2.** 7.623, 2.417, + 3.986 **3.** 3.1684, 6.1875, + 9.7864 **4.** \$6.75, 2.09, + 3.86 **5.** \$9.64, 3.75, + 8.67

6. 8.5 − 0.76 **7.** 7.86 − 2.34 **8.** 8.3146 − 2.9108 **9.** \$6.75 − 2.86 **10.** \$37.89 − 5.98

Estimate the answers to the nearest tenth.

11. 0.75 + 0.81 **12.** 8.36, 0.4, 1.98, + 0.153 **13.** 8.167, 9.4, 3.046, + 6.13 **14.** 0.75 − 0.38 **15.** 7.496 − 2.1873

Multiply. *(Use with page 110.)*

1. 0.8 × 6	**2.** 4.7 × 5	**3.** 13.6 × 3	**4.** 256.7 × 8	**5.** 0.08 × 7	**6.** 0.37 × 4
7. 3.96 × 9	**8.** 4.08 × 7	**9.** 0.009 × 6	**10.** 0.034 × 2	**11.** 6.044 × 8	**12.** 3.497 × 3
13. 7.35 × 89	**14.** 6.103 × 48	**15.** 3.1463 × 32	★**16.** 8.49 × 186	★**17.** 0.1897 × 245	★**18.** 7.18164 × 136

Multiply. *(Use with page 112.)*

1. 0.4 × 0.6	**2.** 3.4 × 0.8	**3.** 0.06 × 0.5	**4.** 3.86 × 0.4	**5.** 0.634 × 0.7
6. 0.83 × 0.45	**7.** 0.635 × 0.49	**8.** 7.865 × 0.32	**9.** 1.483 × 0.08	**10.** 2.59 × 0.006
11. 0.018 × 0.005	**12.** 6.508 × 0.038	**13.** 83.6 × 0.9	**14.** 0.8 × 0.65	**15.** 7.453 × 0.345

★**16.** 3.03 × 0.7 × 7.14 ★**17.** 8.1 × 3.07 × 4.214 ★**18.** 0.08 × 3.45 × 1.111

★**19.** 6.8 × 0.413 × 0.3 ★**20.** 0.61 × 7.3 × 0.043 ★**21.** 0.083 × 1.2 × 6.49

Solve. *(Use with page 114.)*

1. Ellen had 230 stamps. Bob had 4 times as many stamps as Ellen, but he gave 325 of his stamps away. How many stamps does he have now?

2. Mr. Howard bought 144 pens that cost $3 a dozen. How much did he pay in all?

3. Adam bought a shirt for $8.98, a suit for $87.50, and a tie for $4.75. He paid with 6 twenty-dollar bills. How much change did he receive?

4. Heather bought 225 m of movie film. The film is on 15 m rolls which cost $2.75 a roll. How much did Heather spend for the film?

5. Eric earns $2.35 an hour and averages $1.25 an hour in tips. He worked 4 hours on Saturday. How much did he earn?

6. Five pencils and 2 pens cost $3.73. Each pencil cost 7¢. How much does a pen cost?

7. At a sale, old records cost 24¢ each or 5 for $1.00. What is the greatest number of records that Hernandez can buy for $6.75?

8. Maria bought 3 kg of meat for $4.98 a kilogram and 5 kg of chicken for $3.79 a kilogram. How much change did she receive from a $50-bill?

Divide. *(Use with page 116.)*

1. $2\overline{)5.8}$ **2.** $4\overline{)1.2}$ **3.** $8\overline{)1.20}$ **4.** $7\overline{)3.57}$

5. $6\overline{)1.836}$ **6.** $5\overline{)47.855}$ **7.** $15\overline{)4.5}$ **8.** $23\overline{)29.9}$

9. $86\overline{)144.48}$ **10.** $72\overline{)169.20}$ **11.** $32\overline{)2.144}$ **12.** $39\overline{)2.184}$

★ **13.** $75\overline{)158.4225}$ ★ **14.** $253\overline{)89.056}$ ★ **15.** $418\overline{)883.9028}$ ★ **16.** $302\overline{)136.2322}$

Divide. *(Use with page 118.)*

1. $0.3\overline{)1.2}$ **2.** $0.3\overline{)0.06}$ **3.** $0.6\overline{)0.024}$ **4.** $0.4\overline{)8}$

5. $0.07\overline{)0.42}$ **6.** $0.09\overline{)0.036}$ **7.** $0.03\overline{)0.6}$ **8.** $0.008\overline{)0.016}$

9. $0.004\overline{)16}$ **10.** $0.003\overline{)1.503}$ **11.** $2.7\overline{)91.8}$ **12.** $2.8\overline{)169.12}$

★ **13.** $0.0005\overline{)10}$ ★ **14.** $0.0036\overline{)0.234}$ ★ **15.** $0.00025\overline{)0.375}$

Find each quotient to the nearest tenth. *(Use with page 120.)*

1. $6\overline{)1.9}$ **2.** $4\overline{)3.5}$ **3.** $8\overline{)6.2}$ **4.** $0.6\overline{)0.4}$

5. $0.8\overline{)0.5}$ **6.** $0.4\overline{)0.2}$ **7.** $2.3\overline{)0.9}$ **8.** $4.2\overline{)6.35}$

9. $6.8\overline{)5.96}$ **10.** $0.43\overline{)0.382}$ ★ **11.** $0.076\overline{)0.937}$ ★ **12.** $1.37\overline{)0.4364}$

Find each quotient to the nearest hundredth.

13. $0.04\overline{)0.2317}$ **14.** $0.32\overline{)0.397}$ **15.** $0.45\overline{)0.618}$ **16.** $32\overline{)0.469}$

17. $13\overline{)0.674}$ **18.** $0.23\overline{)0.5631}$ **19.** $0.26\overline{)0.7019}$ **20.** $1.9\overline{)0.2136}$

21. $4.2\overline{)3.0169}$ **22.** $3.8\overline{)6.452}$ ★ **23.** $0.026\overline{)0.1387}$ ★ **24.** $0.187\overline{)2.6179}$

Estimate the products to the nearest whole number. *(Use with page 121.)*

1. 7.6×2.3 **2.** 4.019×8.35 **3.** 0.491×6.8 **4.** 8.634×2.9 **5.** 0.876×0.735

6. 2.8×3.7 **7.** 6.41×7.13 **8.** 8.34×0.913 ★ **9.** $6.45 \times 0.719 \times 3.6$

Estimate the quotients to the nearest whole number, if possible.

10. $1.6\overline{)6.116}$ **11.** $4.2\overline{)8.4132}$ **12.** $0.83\overline{)7.364}$ **13.** $6.7\overline{)0.3178}$ **14.** $0.23\overline{)6.251}$

15. $2.7\overline{)9.145}$ **16.** $0.41\overline{)0.863}$ **17.** $5.6\overline{)0.483}$ **18.** $0.39\overline{)8.67}$ ★ **19.** $4.19\overline{)8239.5}$

Extra Practice

Solve for x and check. (*Use with page 122.*)

1. $x + 0.5 = 0.9$ **2.** $x - 2.4 = 6.7$ **3.** $0.3x + 0.4 = 3.1$ **4.** $0.5x - 2.4 = 0.6$

5. $4x - 3.1 = 4.1$ **6.** $3x + 5.6 = 9.5$ ★ **7.** $3x + 9.5 = 3 + 4x$ ★ **8.** $2.4x - 1.8 = 5.4 - 1.2x$

9. $3x = 0.6$ **10.** $0.9x = 7.2$ **11.** $\frac{x}{4} = 0.2$ **12.** $\frac{x}{3.1} = 0.5$

13. $\frac{x}{3} + 0.4 = 0.7$ **14.** $\frac{x}{0.5} - 0.8 = 0.2$ ★ **15.** $\frac{x}{3} + 1.5 = 9.5 - x$

Add or subtract. (*Use with page 125.*)

1. $\begin{array}{r} 5.73 \\ 2.89 \\ +\ 1.57 \\ \hline \end{array}$ **2.** $\begin{array}{r} 7.437 \\ -\ 3.879 \\ \hline \end{array}$ **3.** $5 + 9.7 + 0.648$ **5.** $0.8 - 0.57$

4. $7 + 0.486 + 9.4$ **6.** $9 - 2.74$

Multiply.

7. $\begin{array}{r} 4.56 \\ \times\ 8 \\ \hline \end{array}$ **8.** $\begin{array}{r} 3.9 \\ \times\ 0.4 \\ \hline \end{array}$ **9.** $\begin{array}{r} 0.37 \\ \times\ 0.09 \\ \hline \end{array}$ **10.** 0.04×0.362 **11.** 0.7×0.005

Divide.

12. $3\overline{)0.90}$ **13.** $9\overline{)1.53}$ **14.** $0.8\overline{)0.32}$ **15.** $7.1\overline{)25.915}$ **16.** $0.25\overline{)6.25}$

Solve.

17. It snowed 8.56 cm on Monday and 12.85 cm on Tuesday. How much did it snow on both days?

18. Bill needs 5 pieces of rope each 24.5 cm long. How much will be left over from a piece 146.9 cm long?

Choose the best estimate. (*Use with page 138.*)

1. Ms. Kowalski drove 397 mi and used 21 gal of gas. How many miles per gallon (mpg) was this?
15 mpg 20 mpg 30 mpg

2. Mr. Stern drove 541.9 km in 10 h. What was his average kilometers per hour (km/h)?
50 km/h 60 km/h 70 km/h

3. Ms. Jackson used 114.9 gal of gasoline at a cost of $1.08 per gallon. What was the cost of the gasoline?
$50 $75 $100

4. Amy drove at an average speed of 78.7 km per hour for 12 hours. How far did she travel in that time?
600 km 700 km 800 km

5. The cost for food for a 5-day trip was $209.85. What was the average cost for food per day?
$4 $40 $400

6. Alex drove 213.9 km one day, 347.3 km the next day, and 186.4 km the third day. How far did he drive in all?
700 km 750 km 800 km

Solve. *(Use with page 152.)*

1. Mr. Garcia bought 1.8 kg of fish and 2.3 kg of meat. How much fish and meat did he buy in all?
2. A thickness of a piece of paper is 0.8 mm. How high is a pile of 2,000 sheets of this paper?
3. A box holds 7.6 kg of raisins. How many of these boxes are needed for 250 kg?
4. Jessie ran a race in 32.8 sec. Adam ran the same race in 28.9 sec. How much faster did Adam run the race?
5. Mrs. Kahn bought 11.5 yd of drapery material and 17.84 yd of dress fabric. How many yards did she buy in all?
6. Chad had a board 30.64 cm long. How many 7.66-cm pieces can be cut from it?
7. A plant was 4.8 ft high. The next year it was 5.03 ft high. How much did it grow?
8. A certain steel bar weighs 0.044 kg per centimeter. How much will a 28-cm length of this steel bar weigh?

Add and simplify. *(Use with page 168.)*

1. $\frac{2}{7} + \frac{5}{7}$
2. $\frac{2}{9} + \frac{4}{9}$
3. $\frac{3}{5} + \frac{1}{5}$
4. $\frac{5}{8} + \frac{3}{8}$
5. $\frac{3}{4} + \frac{2}{4}$
6. $\frac{5}{8} + \frac{3}{8}$
7. $\frac{1}{3} + \frac{1}{2}$
8. $\frac{3}{5} + \frac{1}{4}$
9. $\frac{1}{8} + \frac{1}{5}$
10. $\frac{3}{4} + \frac{5}{6}$
11. $\frac{1}{4} + \frac{7}{8}$
12. $\frac{4}{5} + \frac{3}{10}$
13. $\frac{3}{10} + \frac{4}{10} + \frac{2}{10}$
14. $\frac{3}{4} + \frac{1}{2} + \frac{1}{5}$
15. $\frac{1}{2} + \frac{3}{4} + \frac{5}{8}$
16. $\frac{3}{8} + \frac{1}{6} + \frac{7}{12}$

★17. $\frac{2}{3} + \frac{3}{4} + \frac{5}{6} + \frac{1}{2}$

★18. $\frac{5}{9} + \frac{4}{5} + \frac{5}{6}$

★19. $\frac{1}{2} + \frac{4}{7} + \frac{5}{9}$

★20. $\frac{2}{3} + \frac{1}{5} + \frac{5}{6} + \frac{7}{9}$

Add and simplify. *(Use with page 170.)*

1. $2\frac{2}{7} + 3\frac{3}{7}$
2. $2\frac{1}{6} + 5\frac{1}{6}$
3. $2\frac{1}{3} + 5\frac{2}{5}$
4. $6\frac{2}{3} + 5\frac{1}{4}$
5. $2\frac{1}{5} + 4\frac{3}{7}$
6. $4\frac{3}{8} + 3\frac{5}{8}$
7. $6\frac{4}{9} + 7\frac{8}{9}$
8. $5\frac{7}{12} + 7\frac{5}{8}$
9. $7\frac{2}{5} + 4\frac{3}{4}$
10. $3\frac{2}{3} + 4\frac{5}{6}$
11. $1\frac{1}{2} + 3\frac{2}{3}$
12. $3\frac{7}{8} + 4\frac{3}{4}$
13. $2\frac{3}{7} + 1\frac{2}{7} + 4\frac{1}{7}$
14. $5\frac{4}{9} + 1\frac{2}{9} + 1\frac{7}{9}$
15. $7\frac{2}{3} + 6\frac{5}{6} + 3\frac{4}{9}$
16. $2\frac{3}{5} + 4\frac{7}{10} + 2\frac{1}{2}$

★17. $1\frac{3}{4} + 3\frac{2}{3} + 1\frac{3}{5} + 2\frac{1}{2}$

★18. $4\frac{1}{3} + 2\frac{5}{14} + 3\frac{11}{21}$

★19. $2\frac{7}{24} + 1\frac{5}{18} + 3\frac{7}{9}$

★20. $3\frac{5}{12} + 6\frac{7}{18} + 1\frac{4}{15}$

Subtract and simplify. *(Use with page 173.)*

1. $\frac{7}{8} - \frac{3}{8}$
2. $\frac{5}{6} - \frac{1}{5}$
3. $\frac{5}{9} - \frac{1}{3}$
4. $\frac{7}{8} - \frac{3}{4}$
5. $\frac{1}{2} - \frac{1}{3}$
6. $\frac{5}{6} - \frac{2}{3}$
7. $\frac{5}{8} - \frac{1}{6}$
8. $\frac{7}{10} - \frac{2}{5}$
9. $\frac{7}{9} - \frac{1}{6}$
10. $\frac{2}{3} - \frac{1}{4}$
11. $\frac{9}{10} - \frac{1}{3}$
12. $\frac{4}{5} - \frac{1}{6}$

★13. $\frac{11}{15} - \frac{7}{18}$ ★14. $\left(\frac{11}{12} - \frac{2}{9}\right) - \frac{1}{2}$ ★15. $\left(\frac{3}{8} + \frac{2}{3}\right) - \frac{2}{3}$ ★16. $\left(\frac{7}{9} - \frac{1}{4}\right) - \left(\frac{2}{3} - \frac{5}{8}\right)$

Subtract and simplify. *(Use with page 174.)*

1. $6\frac{3}{8} - 2\frac{1}{8}$
2. $7\frac{5}{12} - 2\frac{1}{12}$
3. $9\frac{7}{8} - 2\frac{3}{4}$
4. $8\frac{5}{6} - 2\frac{3}{4}$
5. $5 - 1\frac{4}{5}$
6. $5\frac{3}{8} - 2$
7. $7\frac{3}{8} - 2\frac{7}{8}$
8. $8\frac{1}{12} - 3\frac{5}{12}$
9. $7\frac{1}{2} - 3\frac{3}{4}$
10. $8\frac{1}{3} - 2\frac{3}{4}$
11. $3\frac{1}{4} - 1\frac{2}{5}$
12. $4\frac{1}{9} - 3\frac{5}{6}$

★13. $7\frac{5}{24} - 3\frac{11}{18}$ ★14. $9\frac{7}{15} - 5\frac{9}{40}$ ★15. $7\frac{2}{9} - 2\frac{4}{5} + 4\frac{1}{2}$ ★16. $8\frac{3}{8} - 4\frac{11}{12} - 1\frac{5}{6}$

Identify only that information which is needed to solve each problem. Solve. *(Use with page 176.)*

1. Francisca lost 3 kg during an illness. She now weighs 47 kg. Her sister weighs 53 kg. How much did Francisca weigh before she was ill?

2. Mr. Bryan spent $350 during his vacation for motel and food. He stayed at the motel for 2 weeks for $220. How much did he spend for food?

3. A dozen eggs cost $0.98 and a liter of milk costs $0.48. How much do 7 dozen eggs cost?

4. Bob earns $18 a week. He saves $3 a week to buy a guitar. How long will it take him to save $45?

5. A regular box of cereal costs $0.96. The giant size costs $1.29. What is the cost of a dozen boxes of the regular size?

6. A bottle of shampoo costs $2.15. There are 24 bottles in a case. What is the cost of a dozen bottles of shampoo?

7. Cherries sell for $1.59 a kg and plums sell for $0.98 a kg. Andy bought 2.1 kg of cherries and 3.4 kg of plums. How much fruit did he buy in all?

8. Jodi ran 2.5 km on Sunday, 3.4 km on Monday and 1.9 km on Tuesday. How much farther did she run on Sunday than on Tuesday?

Multiply and simplify. *(Use with page 178.)*

1. $\frac{1}{4} \times \frac{1}{5}$ **2.** $\frac{1}{8} \times \frac{1}{3}$ **3.** $\frac{2}{5} \times \frac{3}{7}$ **4.** $\frac{3}{4} \times \frac{1}{2}$ **5.** $\frac{1}{3} \times \frac{2}{5}$ **6.** $\frac{1}{2} \times 7$

7. $\frac{3}{4} \times 12$ **8.** $5 \times \frac{1}{4}$ **9.** $15 \times \frac{3}{5}$ **10.** $\frac{5}{8} \times \frac{6}{7}$ **11.** $\frac{5}{8} \times \frac{2}{5}$ **12.** $\frac{2}{3} \times \frac{9}{10}$

13. $\frac{1}{3} \times \frac{1}{2} \times \frac{1}{4}$ **14.** $\frac{2}{3} \times \frac{3}{4} \times \frac{1}{8}$ **15.** $\frac{3}{5} \times \frac{1}{4} \times \frac{5}{6}$

★ **16.** $\left(\frac{1}{2} \times \frac{1}{4}\right) + \left(\frac{1}{3} \times \frac{1}{3}\right)$ ★ **17.** $\left(\frac{3}{4} - \frac{1}{5}\right) \times \left(1 - \frac{2}{3}\right)$ ★ **18.** $\left(\frac{7}{8} - \frac{3}{4}\right) \times \left(\frac{4}{9} - \frac{1}{3}\right)$

Multiply and simplify. *(Use with page 180.)*

1. $8 \times 1\frac{1}{2}$ **2.** $12 \times 2\frac{3}{4}$ **3.** $10 \times 6\frac{1}{5}$ **4.** $4 \times 2\frac{1}{3}$ **5.** $2\frac{1}{2} \times 6$

6. $3\frac{1}{3} \times 6$ **7.** $1\frac{3}{5} \times 15$ **8.** $6\frac{3}{4} \times 5$ **9.** $\frac{1}{3} \times 1\frac{1}{2}$ **10.** $\frac{2}{5} \times 3\frac{1}{4}$

11. $\frac{3}{8} \times 2\frac{1}{3}$ **12.** $1\frac{1}{2} \times 2\frac{1}{3}$ **13.** $3\frac{1}{4} \times 2\frac{1}{5}$ **14.** $6\frac{2}{3} \times 1\frac{1}{2}$ **15.** $5\frac{2}{5} \times 2\frac{1}{4}$

16. $3 \times 1\frac{1}{2} \times 2\frac{1}{4}$ **17.** $4\frac{3}{4} \times 8 \times 1\frac{2}{5}$ ★ **18.** $3\frac{1}{6} \times 2\frac{1}{2} \times 1\frac{3}{4} \times 2\frac{2}{3}$

★ **19.** $\left(\frac{3}{5} + \frac{1}{2}\right) \times \left(\frac{3}{8} + \frac{1}{4}\right)$ ★ **20.** $\left(3\frac{1}{2} - 1\frac{7}{8}\right) \times \left(4\frac{3}{4} - 2\frac{5}{6}\right)$ ★ **21.** $\left(\frac{7}{8} + \frac{4}{5}\right) \times \left(4 - 3\frac{1}{5}\right)$

Divide. *(Use with page 182.)*

1. $\frac{1}{5} \div \frac{1}{3}$ **2.** $\frac{3}{4} \div \frac{2}{5}$ **3.** $\frac{5}{6} \div \frac{1}{8}$ **4.** $\frac{7}{8} \div \frac{1}{2}$ **5.** $\frac{3}{4} \div \frac{2}{3}$

6. $\frac{3}{8} \div \frac{9}{10}$ **7.** $1\frac{3}{5} \div \frac{2}{5}$ **8.** $2\frac{5}{6} \div \frac{2}{6}$ **9.** $\frac{5}{8} \div 3$ **10.** $\frac{3}{4} \div 3$

11. $4 \div \frac{3}{4}$ **12.** $3 \div \frac{6}{7}$ **13.** $3\frac{4}{5} \div 2$ **14.** $8 \div 2\frac{5}{6}$ **15.** $\frac{7}{8} \div 1\frac{1}{2}$

16. $\frac{8}{9} \div 2\frac{2}{3}$ **17.** $1\frac{1}{2} \div 1\frac{3}{4}$ **18.** $2\frac{1}{3} \div 3\frac{1}{2}$ **19.** $6\frac{2}{3} \div 3\frac{1}{6}$ ★ **20.** $\left(4\frac{5}{6} \div 1\frac{7}{8}\right) \div \frac{4}{5}$

★ **21.** $\left(\frac{4}{5} \times \frac{7}{8}\right) \div \frac{5}{6}$ ★ **22.** $\left(4\frac{1}{4} \div 3\frac{2}{3}\right) \div \left(5\frac{2}{7} \div \frac{4}{7}\right)$ ★ **23.** $\left(\frac{7}{9} + \frac{5}{6}\right) \div \left(\frac{2}{3} - \frac{3}{8}\right)$

Write decimals. *(Use with page 184.)*

1. $\frac{9}{2}$ **2.** $\frac{9}{8}$ **3.** $\frac{3}{10}$ **4.** $\frac{6}{25}$ **5.** $\frac{17}{50}$ **6.** $\frac{11}{40}$ **7.** $\frac{23}{125}$

8. $3\frac{3}{5}$ **9.** $5\frac{7}{50}$ **10.** $4\frac{9}{40}$ **11.** $6\frac{7}{10}$ ★ **12.** $\frac{3}{80}$ ★ **13.** $4\frac{9}{80}$ ★ **14.** $\frac{1}{160}$

Add or subtract. Simplify. *(Use with page 188.)*

1. $\frac{3}{7} + \frac{2}{7}$
2. $\frac{3}{4} + \frac{1}{3}$
3. $3\frac{4}{5} + 4\frac{5}{6}$
4. $\frac{7}{8} - \frac{3}{8}$
5. $5\frac{7}{9} - 3\frac{2}{3}$
6. $4\frac{2}{3} - 1\frac{4}{5}$
7. $\frac{3}{4} + \frac{1}{8} + \frac{5}{6}$
8. $2\frac{2}{3} + 4\frac{1}{4} + 3\frac{3}{5}$

Multiply or divide. Simplify.

9. $\frac{3}{5} \times \frac{2}{7}$
10. $\frac{2}{3} \times 6$
11. $\frac{4}{5} \div \frac{4}{9}$
12. $6 \div 3\frac{1}{6}$
13. $4\frac{3}{4} \div 2\frac{3}{8}$

Solve.

14. Sara bought 3 tennis balls for $2.98 and 3 baseballs for $11.98. How much did she spend in all?
15. Sal had $\frac{3}{4}$ of a pizza. He ate $\frac{1}{2}$ of it. How much of the pizza did he eat?

Solve, if possible. *(Use with page 206.)*

1. The perimeter of a rectangle is 60 mm. What is the length?
2. The perimeter of a square is 40 mm. What is the length of a side?
3. In right triangle *ABC*, *C* is a right angle. $m\angle A = 34°$. What is $m\angle B$?
4. The perimeter of a triangle is 36 cm. How long is each side?
5. The width of a garden is 6 ft. At $3.59 a foot, what is the cost of fencing the garden?
6. A yard is in the shape of a scalene triangle. One side is 86 ft. What is the perimeter of the yard?

Solve. *(Use with page 218.)*

1. Ms. Best spent $167.98 for a car radio, $37.75 for carpet protectors and $486.95 for air-conditioning. How much did she spend in all?
2. The average gas mileage for a certain car is 23 miles per gallon. The car has an 18-gal gas tank. How far can it go on a tank of gas?
3. Mr. Joseph spent $\frac{1}{2}$ h with one car dealer and $1\frac{1}{4}$ h with a second dealer. How much more time did he spend with the second dealer?
4. One dealer charged $7,186.78 for a certain car. Another dealer charged $6,794.89 for the same car. How much more did the first dealer charge?
5. Mrs. Genzoff will pay $8,256 in 12 equal payments for a new car. How much will each payment be?
6. Bill's new car had 4.8 mi on the odometer when he bought it. A week later the odometer read 142.6 mi. How far had he gone that week?

Compute. *(Use with page 224.)*

1. $7 \times (5 + 8)$ **2.** $9 \times (7 - 3)$ **3.** $(8 + 16) - (2 \times 6)$ **4.** $8 \times 6 + 5$

5. $25 - 3 \times 6$ **6.** $6 \times (3 \times 4 - 8)$ ★**7.** $\left(\frac{8+7}{3}\right) \times \left(\frac{9+9}{9}\right)$ ★**8.** $\left[(6 + 8) - \left(\frac{7-3}{4}\right)\right]$

Evaluate.

9. $2a + 7$ if $a = 3$ **10.** $6x - 7$ if $x = 9$

11. $5a + b$ if $a = 3, b = 6$ **12.** $\frac{a+7}{b}$ if $a = 3, b = 2$

13. $\frac{n}{2} \cdot (a + b)$ if $n = 8, a = 1, b = 13$ **14.** $\frac{n}{2} \cdot (a + l)$ if $n = 100, a = 1, l = 20$

15. $\frac{a(2+b)}{c} \cdot ab$ if $a = 2, b = 3, c = 5$ ★**16.** $abc \cdot \frac{(2a + 3b - c)}{d}$ if $a = 3, b = 4, c = 6, d = 2$

Write equations. Solve. *(Use with page 230.)*

1. Tickets for a concert are $3 each. Jeff's club paid $69 for tickets. How many boys bought tickets?

2. Sam bought twice as many stamps as Charlie. Sam bought 54 stamps. How many stamps did Charlie buy?

3. Maria bought 4 greeting cards, each the same price, and a book for a total of $6.58. The book cost $3.98. What was the cost of each card?

4. Mrs. Hill bought a chair and a desk. The desk was $34.98 more than the chair. The chair was $148.79. How much was the desk?

5. Danny's mother is 38. She is 2 years more than 4 times Danny's age. How old is Danny?

6. A string was 45 cm long. It was cut into 6 pieces of the same length and a piece 3 cm long. How long was each of the 6 pieces?

Solve. Use the distance formula. *(Use with page 236.)*

1. Mrs. Alms averaged 80 km/h during a 4-hour trip. How far did she drive?

2. Amanda drove 135 mi in 3 hours. What was her average speed?

3. Ms. Ruff drove 840 km at an average speed of 70 km/h. How long did it take her?

4. A plane flew 3,840 km at an average speed of 640 km/h. How long was the trip?

5. Juan rode a bicycle $18\frac{3}{4}$ mi. It took him $2\frac{1}{2}$ hours. What was his average speed?

6. A plane flew $2\frac{1}{2}$ hours at an average speed of 540 mph. How far was the trip?

Find the ratios. *(Use with page 239.)*
Jim planted 12 tulip bulbs. Seven of them sprouted.

1. What is the ratio of the number of bulbs planted to the number which sprouted?

2. What is the ratio of the number of bulbs which sprouted to the number of bulbs planted?

Eight girls and 10 boys joined a club.

3. What is the ratio of the number of girls to the number of boys.

4. What is the ratio of the number of boys to the total number in the club?

Which ratios are equal to 6 is to 18?

5. 1 is to 3 **6.** 5 is to 15 **7.** 8 is to 16

Solve the proportions. *(Use with page 240.)*

1. $1:3 = 3:x$ **2.** $2:3 = x:9$ **3.** $2:x = 6:12$ **4.** $x:3 = 8:12$

5. $5:3 = x:9$ **6.** $4:1 = x:5$ **7.** $3:x = 4:8$ **8.** $x:6 = 4:3$

9. $\frac{9}{12} = \frac{6}{x}$ **10.** $\frac{2}{3} = \frac{8}{x}$ **11.** $\frac{8}{x} = \frac{12}{3}$ **12.** $\frac{2}{9} = \frac{6}{x}$ **13.** $\frac{x}{3} = \frac{12}{9}$

14. $\frac{x}{12} = \frac{10}{5}$ **15.** $\frac{x}{12} = \frac{8}{6}$ **16.** $\frac{10}{x} = \frac{5}{4}$ **17.** $\frac{9}{54} = \frac{2}{x}$ **18.** $\frac{14}{16} = \frac{x}{24}$

19. $\frac{x}{18} = \frac{2}{3}$ **20.** $\frac{5}{9} = \frac{x}{27}$ **21.** $\frac{6}{x} = \frac{9}{15}$ **22.** $\frac{4}{7} = \frac{20}{x}$ **23.** $\frac{12}{15} = \frac{x}{5}$

★**24.** $\frac{4}{3} = \frac{10}{x}$ ★**25.** $\frac{x}{9} = \frac{4}{5}$ ★**26.** $\frac{x}{4} = \frac{16}{x}$ ★**27.** $\frac{x}{0.6} = \frac{1.5}{0.2}$ ★**28.** $\frac{1.8}{0.2} = \frac{x}{2.3}$

Solve. Use the lever formula. *(Use with page 242.)*

1. A 9-g mass is 8 cm from the fulcrum. What mass 12 cm from the fulcrum will balance it?

2. A 33-lb weight is 3 ft from the fulcrum. What weight 9 feet from the fulcrum will balance it?

3. A 6-g mass is 28 cm from the fulcrum. How far from the fulcrum is a 21-g mass which balances the 6-gram mass?

4. Val has a mass of 36 kg. She is sitting 3 m from the fulcrum. Mike has a mass of 54 kg. The seesaw is balanced. How far is Mike from the fulcrum?

5. A 24-lb weight 14 inches from the fulcrum balances a 16-lb weight. How far from the fulcrum is the 16-lb weight?

6. Josh has a mass of 42 kg. He is sitting 2 m from the fulcrum. He is balanced by his sister who is 3 m from the fulcrum. What is the mass of his sister?

Extra Practice

Solve. *(Use with page 244.)*

1. Shirts are selling at 3 for \$42. What is the cost of 1 dozen shirts?

2. Ann saves \$4 of each \$15 she earns. If she earned \$75, how much did she save?

3. Mrs. Gleason earned \$80 by selling 2 television sets. How many sets would she have to sell to earn \$200?

4. The ratio of the width of a rectangle to its length is 3 to 5. The length is 30 in. What is the width?

5. Tires are selling at 2 for \$75. How much will 8 cost?

6. Mr. Hu's gas bill was \$45 for 2 months. What will his gas bill be for 1 year?

7. At a party there were 4 boys to every 5 girls. There were 320 boys. How many girls were there?

8. At a school there were 3 bicycles for every 5 children. There were 45 children. How many bicycles were there?

Write the simplest fractions, whole numbers or mixed numbers. *(Use with page 250.)*

1. 60% **2.** 28% **3.** 65% **4.** 17% **5.** 800% **6.** 500%

7. $66\frac{2}{3}\%$ **8.** $37\frac{1}{2}\%$ **9.** $\frac{2}{5}\%$ **10.** 350% **11.** $\frac{1}{4}\%$ **12.** 175%

13. $2\frac{1}{5}\%$ **14.** $3\frac{1}{2}\%$ ★ **15.** $\frac{3}{8}\%$ ★ **16.** $2\frac{5}{8}\%$ ★ **17.** 1,040% ★ **18.** $1{,}250\frac{3}{5}\%$

Write percents.

19. $\frac{3}{4}$ **20.** $\frac{4}{5}$ **21.** $\frac{7}{25}$ **22.** $\frac{3}{10}$ **23.** $\frac{2}{3}$ **24.** $\frac{7}{200}$

25. $\frac{300}{100}$ **26.** $\frac{13}{50}$ **27.** $\frac{3}{2}$ **28.** $\frac{8}{5}$ **29.** $\frac{17}{20}$ **30.** $\frac{29}{400}$

31. $\frac{5}{12}$ **32.** $\frac{7}{8}$ ★ **33.** $\frac{23}{1{,}000}$ ★ **34.** $\frac{15}{10{,}000}$ ★ **35.** $\frac{382}{600}$ ★ **36.** $\frac{240}{400}$

Change to decimals. *(Use with page 252.)*

1. 4% **2.** 8% **3.** 15% **4.** 36% **5.** 150% **6.** 180%

7. 200% **8.** 340% **9.** 0.4% **10.** 2.4% **11.** 0.08% **12.** 6.14%

13. $\frac{7}{10}\%$ **14.** $3\frac{1}{4}\%$ ★ **15.** $3\frac{7}{8}\%$ ★ **16.** 1350% ★ **17.** $9\frac{5}{6}\%$ ★ **18.** $1000\frac{1}{8}\%$

Change to percents.

19. 0.06 **20.** 0.53 **21.** 0.2 **22.** 4 **23.** 3.7 **24.** 0.031

25. 0.004 **26.** 0.0086 ★ **27.** $0.05\frac{1}{2}$ ★ **28.** $0.08\frac{3}{4}$ ★ **29.** $0.37\frac{1}{2}$ ★ **30.** $0.33\frac{1}{3}$

Compute. *(Use with page 254.)*

1. 8% of 20
2. 36% of 100
3. 100% of 40
4. 150% of 90
5. 300% of 500
6. 0.7% of 240
7. $2\frac{1}{2}$% of 60
8. $33\frac{1}{3}$% of 90
9. $\frac{1}{4}$% of 1,200
10. 1.8% of $4,000
11. 0.05% of 200
12. 0.08% of 350

★ 13. 40% of 0.8

★ 14. $66\frac{2}{3}$% of $5\frac{5}{6}$

★ 15. 300% of $\frac{1}{2}$

Compute. *(Use with page 256.)*

1. What percent of 18 is 12?
2. 6 is what percent of 12?
3. What percent of 10 is 6?
4. 7 is what percent of 4?
5. What percent of 6 is 10?
6. 8 is what percent of 8?
7. What percent of 3 is 4?
8. 0.3 is what percent of 10?
9. What percent of 100 is 0.5?
10. 0.08 is what percent of 24?

★ 11. What percent of 20 is 200?

★ 12. 2,500 is what percent of 200?

★ 13. What percent of $\frac{1}{2}$ is $\frac{1}{6}$?

★ 14. $\frac{1}{5}$ is what percent of $\frac{1}{10}$?

Compute. *(Use with page 258.)*

1. 75% of what number is 150?
2. 12 is 6% of what number?
3. $66\frac{2}{3}$% of what number is 64?
4. 56 is $87\frac{1}{2}$% of what number?
5. 35% of what number is 24.5?
6. 18 is 120% of what number?
7. 300% of what number is 36?
8. 64 is 3.2% of what number?
9. $1\frac{1}{2}$% of what number is 72?
10. 8 is 0.1% of what number?

★ 11. 25% of what number is $\frac{1}{16}$?

★ 12. 2% of what number is $1\frac{3}{5}$?

★ 13. $66\frac{2}{3}$% of what number is 1?

★ 14. $16\frac{1}{2}$% of what number is $\frac{5}{24}$?

Write mini-problems. Solve. *(Use with page 262.)*

1. Betsy worked 6 hours on Saturday and 8 hours on Sunday. She earns $2.90 an hour. How much did she earn in all?

2. Ms. Frankel bought 3 dozen roses at $2.95 a dozen. How much change did she receive from a $10-bill?

3. Joe bought 4 shirts for $63.80. If he exchanges one for a tie costing $8.79, how much change will he receive?

4. Kim has 18 records more than Beth, who has 78 records. If Kim stacks them in piles of eight, how many piles will she have?

5. A theater has 18 rows with 32 seats in a row. For one movie all the seats were taken except the first two rows. How many people saw the movie?

6. Jim typed 34 pages of 70 pages on Sunday and finished the rest in 4 hours on Monday. How many pages did he type per hour on Monday?

Find the discount and the sale price. *(Use with page 264.)*
The rate of discount is 25%. The regular prices are given.

1. Radio: $40
2. Television: $150
3. Stereo: $200

Find the sale prices. The regular prices are given.

4. Hat marked $15 at a 10%-off sale
5. Gloves marked $8 at a 30%-off sale
6. Shoes marked $32 at a 25%-off sale
7. Tie marked $12 at a 20%-off sale

Find the rate of discount as a percent.

8. Bat: was $9, now $6
9. Ball: was $4, now $3
10. Mitt: was $10, now $8

Solve.

11. A tire selling for $45 was on sale at 20% off. What was the sale price?

12. An $8 book was sold for $5.60 during a sale. What was the rate of discount?

Find the interest. *(Use with page 266.)*

1. $120 at 8% for 2 years
2. $5,000 at 6.5% for 3 years
3. $600 at 6% for 4 months
4. $600 at $8\frac{1}{2}$% for 6 months

Find the total amount to be paid back.

5. $6,000 at 9% for 5 years
6. $2,000 at 9.5% for 4 years
7. $2,000 at 10% for 10 years
8. $400 at 8% for 6 months
9. $200 at $5\frac{1}{2}$% for 3 months
10. $5,000 at 11.25% for 3 years

Find the percent increase. *(Use with page 270.)*

1. Last year: 40 games won
This year: 52 games won

2. Last week: 16 dolls sold
This week: 28 dolls sold

3. 1st math test: 75
2nd math test: 100

4. Last year: gloves cost $8
This year: gloves cost $10

Find the percent decrease.

5. Sold 250 records last week
Sold 125 records this week

6. Last month's telephone bill: $20
This month's telephone bill: $15

7. Population 10 years ago: 2,000
Population now: 800

8. 600 customers last year
450 customers this year

Write percents. *(Use with page 273.)*

1. $\frac{8}{100}$ **2.** 0.06 **3.** 0.58 **4.** $\frac{3}{4}$ **5.** $2\frac{1}{2}$ **6.** 0.089 **7.** 2.75

Write simplest fractions, whole numbers, or mixed numbers.

8. 2% **9.** 35% **10.** 200% **11.** 325% **12.** $16\frac{1}{2}\%$ **13.** $\frac{3}{5}\%$

Write decimals.

14. 5% **15.** 275% **16.** 8.6% **17.** $\frac{3}{4}\%$ **18.** 0.8% **19.** $\frac{6}{10}\%$

Compute.

20. 8% of 70 **21.** $\frac{1}{4}\%$ of 20 **22.** 0.6% of 200

23. What percent of 20 is 5?

24. 0.4 is what percent of 80?

25. 50% of what number is 16?

26. 9% of what number is 40.5?

Solve.

27. A radio selling for $85 was on sale at 20% off. What was the sale price?

28. Al borrowed $1,200 at 8% interest for 4 years. How much interest did he pay?

29. A $150 stereo was sold for $105 during a sale. What was the rate of discount?

30. Jill borrowed $500 at 7.5% for 6 months. How much did she pay back at the end of 6 months?

31. Last year a hat cost $12. This year the hat cost $16. What is the percent increase?

32. Last week a store sold 200 books. This week the store sold 150 books. What is the percent decrease?

Add. *(Use with page 280.)*

1. $^{+}4 + {}^{+}7$ **2.** $^{+}8 + {}^{+}6$ **3.** $^{+}15 + {}^{+}16$ **4.** $^{+}56 + {}^{+}12$

5. $^{-}3 + {}^{-}7$ **6.** $^{-}8 + {}^{-}7$ **7.** $^{-}31 + {}^{-}14$ **8.** $^{-}23 + {}^{-}47$

9. $\begin{array}{r} ^{+}9 \\ + \; ^{+}3 \\ \hline \end{array}$ **10.** $\begin{array}{r} ^{+}17 \\ + \; ^{+}19 \\ \hline \end{array}$ **11.** $\begin{array}{r} ^{-}6 \\ + \; ^{-}7 \\ \hline \end{array}$ **12.** $\begin{array}{r} ^{-}81 \\ + \; ^{-}10 \\ \hline \end{array}$

13. $^{+}4 + {}^{+}8 + {}^{+}3$ **14.** $^{+}35 + {}^{+}18 + {}^{+}11$ **15.** $^{-}5 + {}^{-}1 + {}^{-}3$

16. $^{-}13 + {}^{-}6 + {}^{-}19$ ★ **17.** $^{+}4 + {}^{+}9 + {}^{+}13 + {}^{+}8$ ★ **18.** $^{+}35 + {}^{+}16 + {}^{+}7 + {}^{+}1$

★ **19.** $^{-}8 + {}^{-}6 + {}^{-}2 + {}^{-}1$ ★ **20.** $^{-}11 + {}^{-}24 + {}^{-}6 + {}^{-}3$ ★ **21.** $^{-}15 + {}^{-}31 + {}^{-}64 + {}^{-}32$

Add. *(Use with page 282.)*

1. $^{+}3 + {}^{-}1$ **2.** $^{+}6 + {}^{-}5$ **3.** $^{+}12 + {}^{-}18$ **4.** $^{+}63 + {}^{-}49$

5. $^{-}3 + {}^{+}5$ **6.** $^{-}34 + {}^{+}25$ **7.** $^{-}23 + {}^{+}47$ **8.** $^{-}46 + {}^{+}31$

9. $\begin{array}{r} ^{+}8 \\ + \; ^{-}5 \\ \hline \end{array}$ **10.** $\begin{array}{r} ^{-}9 \\ + \; ^{+}6 \\ \hline \end{array}$ **11.** $\begin{array}{r} ^{-}5 \\ + \; ^{+}7 \\ \hline \end{array}$ **12.** $\begin{array}{r} ^{+}6 \\ + \; ^{-}4 \\ \hline \end{array}$ **13.** $\begin{array}{r} ^{+}10 \\ + \; ^{-}8 \\ \hline \end{array}$

14. $\begin{array}{r} ^{-}15 \\ + \; ^{+}38 \\ \hline \end{array}$ **15.** $\begin{array}{r} ^{-}35 \\ + \; ^{+}14 \\ \hline \end{array}$ **16.** $\begin{array}{r} ^{+}46 \\ + \; ^{-}29 \\ \hline \end{array}$ **17.** $\begin{array}{r} ^{+}83 \\ + \; ^{-}96 \\ \hline \end{array}$ **18.** $\begin{array}{r} ^{-}57 \\ + \; ^{+}48 \\ \hline \end{array}$

19. $^{+}3 + {}^{-}4 + {}^{+}8$ **20.** $^{-}8 + {}^{+}4 + {}^{+}5$ **21.** $^{+}6 + {}^{+}3 + {}^{-}9$

22. $^{-}6 + {}^{+}3 + {}^{-}5$ ★ **23.** $^{-}6 + {}^{-}8 + {}^{+}4 + {}^{-}2$ ★ **24.** $^{+}3 + {}^{-}4 + {}^{-}3 + {}^{+}6$

★ **25.** $^{+}8 + {}^{-}6 + {}^{+}1 + {}^{+}3$ ★ **26.** $^{+}4 + {}^{-}3 + {}^{+}1 + {}^{+}2$ ★ **27.** $^{-}3 + {}^{+}4 + {}^{+}5 + {}^{-}2$

Subtract. *(Use with page 284.)*

1. $^{+}9 - {}^{+}4$ **2.** $^{+}4 - {}^{+}6$ **3.** $^{+}23 - {}^{+}47$ **4.** $^{+}53 - {}^{+}38$

5. $^{+}3 - {}^{-}1$ **6.** $^{+}6 - {}^{-}9$ **7.** $^{+}16 - {}^{-}12$ **8.** $^{+}13 - {}^{-}15$

9. $^{-}3 - {}^{+}7$ **10.** $^{-}12 - {}^{+}3$ **11.** $^{-}16 - {}^{+}4$ **12.** $^{-}24 - {}^{+}36$

13. $^{-}6 - {}^{-}9$ **14.** $^{-}10 - {}^{-}8$ **15.** $^{-}25 - {}^{-}14$ **16.** $^{-}47 - {}^{-}56$

★ Simplify.

17. $^{+}8 + {}^{-}3 + {}^{+}6 - {}^{-}9$ **18.** $^{+}3 - {}^{+}8 - {}^{-}4 - {}^{-}9$ **19.** $^{-}6 - {}^{-}3 + {}^{-}9 + {}^{+}4$

20. $^{-}1 + {}^{+}2 - {}^{-}3 + {}^{+}4$ **21.** $^{-}9 + {}^{+}7 + {}^{+}3 - {}^{-}6$ **22.** $^{+}8 + {}^{+}4 - {}^{-}2 - {}^{-}5$

Multiply. *(Use with page 290.)*

1. ${}^{+}3 \cdot {}^{+}6$ 2. ${}^{+}9 \cdot {}^{+}8$ 3. ${}^{+}5 \cdot {}^{+}6$ 4. ${}^{-}3 \cdot {}^{-}4$ 5. ${}^{-}6 \cdot {}^{-}2$

6. ${}^{-}7 \cdot {}^{-}8$ 7. ${}^{+}6 \cdot {}^{-}3$ 8. ${}^{+}2 \cdot {}^{-}4$ 9. ${}^{+}8 \cdot {}^{-}7$ 10. ${}^{-}9 \cdot {}^{+}4$

11. ${}^{-}8 \cdot {}^{+}3$ 12. ${}^{-}6 \cdot {}^{+}9$ 13. $0 \cdot {}^{+}4$ 14. ${}^{-}9 \cdot 0$ 15. ${}^{+}1 \cdot {}^{-}6$

16. ${}^{+}9 \cdot {}^{-}1$ 17. ${}^{-}9 \cdot {}^{-}13$ 18. ${}^{-}11 \cdot {}^{-}6$ 19. ${}^{-}13 \cdot {}^{+}18$ 20. ${}^{+}23 \cdot {}^{+}17$

★ 21. ${}^{+}5 \cdot {}^{-}6 \cdot {}^{+}4$ ★ 22. ${}^{-}4 \cdot {}^{+}6 \cdot {}^{-}5$ ★ 23. ${}^{-}3 \cdot {}^{-}6 \cdot {}^{-}4$

★ 24. ${}^{-}8 \cdot {}^{+}5 \cdot {}^{+}9$ ★ 25. ${}^{+}6 \cdot {}^{+}3 \cdot {}^{-}4$ ★ 26. ${}^{-}7 \cdot {}^{+}6 \cdot {}^{-}3$

Divide. *(Use with page 294.)*

1. ${}^{+}10 \div {}^{+}2$ 2. ${}^{-}16 \div {}^{-}8$ 3. ${}^{-}64 \div {}^{-}8$ 4. ${}^{+}48 \div {}^{-}8$

5. ${}^{+}32 \div {}^{-}4$ 6. ${}^{-}45 \div {}^{+}9$ 7. ${}^{-}72 \div {}^{+}9$ 8. $0 \div {}^{-}6$

9. $\frac{{}^{+}36}{{}^{+}6}$ 10. $\frac{{}^{-}40}{{}^{-}5}$ 11. $\frac{{}^{-}16}{{}^{-}4}$ 12. $\frac{{}^{+}56}{{}^{-}8}$ 13. $\frac{{}^{+}35}{{}^{-}7}$ 14. $\frac{{}^{-}64}{{}^{+}8}$

15. $\frac{{}^{-}54}{{}^{+}9}$ 16. $\frac{0}{{}^{+}5}$ 17. $\frac{{}^{-}15}{{}^{-}15}$ 18. $\frac{{}^{-}32}{{}^{-}1}$ 19. $\frac{{}^{+}70}{{}^{-}10}$ 20. $\frac{{}^{-}42}{{}^{+}21}$

★ 21. $({}^{+}81 \div {}^{-}9) \div {}^{+}3$ ★ 22. ${}^{+}92 \div ({}^{-}16 \div {}^{+}4)$

★ 23. $({}^{-}64 \div {}^{+}8) \div ({}^{-}12 \div {}^{-}6)$ ★ 24. $({}^{+}28 \div {}^{-}7) \div ({}^{-}24 \div {}^{-}12)$

Solve and check. *(Use with page 296.)*

1. $x + {}^{+}6 = {}^{+}8$ 2. $x + {}^{-}6 = {}^{-}4$ 3. $x + {}^{-}3 = {}^{+}9$ 4. $x - {}^{+}3 = {}^{+}5$

5. $x - {}^{-}5 = {}^{-}8$ 6. $x - {}^{-}9 = {}^{-}4$ 7. ${}^{+}3x + {}^{+}5 = {}^{+}14$ 8. ${}^{+}3x + {}^{-}7 = {}^{-}19$

9. ${}^{+}6x - {}^{+}4 = {}^{+}8$ 10. $\frac{x}{{}^{+}2} + {}^{-}2 = {}^{+}5$ 11. $\frac{x}{{}^{-}3} - {}^{+}4 = {}^{-}3$ 12. $\frac{x}{{}^{+}9} + {}^{-}3 = {}^{-}2$

13. ${}^{+}4x = {}^{+}28$ 14. ${}^{+}9x = {}^{-}72$ 15. ${}^{-}3x = {}^{-}27$ 16. ${}^{-}3x = {}^{+}12$ 17. ${}^{+}5x = {}^{-}25$

18. $\frac{x}{{}^{+}4} = {}^{-}3$ 19. $\frac{x}{{}^{-}3} = {}^{+}7$ 20. $\frac{x}{{}^{+}6} = {}^{+}6$ 21. $\frac{x}{{}^{-}4} = {}^{-}12$ 22. $\frac{x}{{}^{-}1} = {}^{+}1$

★ Solve. Replacements for x: ${}^{-}8, {}^{-}7, \ldots, {}^{+}7, {}^{+}8$

23. $x + {}^{+}2 > {}^{+}5$ 24. $x + {}^{-}5 > {}^{-}2$ 25. ${}^{+}2x > {}^{+}8$

26. ${}^{-}5x > {}^{-}26$ 27. ${}^{+}2x + {}^{+}3 > {}^{+}2$ 28. ${}^{+}7x + {}^{-}3 > {}^{+}2$

Add. *(Use with page 301.)*

1. $^{+}3 + {}^{+}9$ 2. $^{-}8 + {}^{-}6$ 3. $^{-}9 + {}^{+}4$ 4. $^{-}6 + {}^{+}8$

Subtract.

5. $^{+}6 - {}^{-}3$ 6. $^{+}7 - {}^{+}5$ 7. $^{-}7 - {}^{-}3$ 8. $^{-}4 - {}^{+}7$

Multiply.

9. $^{+}8 \cdot {}^{+}3$ 10. $^{-}9 \cdot {}^{-}5$ 11. $^{+}6 \cdot {}^{-}5$ 12. $^{-}3 \cdot {}^{+}6$

Divide.

13. $^{+}32 \div {}^{-}4$ 14. $^{+}64 \div {}^{+}8$ 15. $\frac{^{-}63}{^{-}7}$ 16. $\frac{^{-}20}{^{+}5}$

Solve.

17. $x - {}^{+}3 = {}^{-}7$ 18. $x + {}^{-}8 = {}^{-}4$ 19. $\frac{x}{^{-}2} = {}^{+}9$ 20. $^{+}3x + {}^{+}5 = {}^{+}14$

Write in the form $\frac{a}{b}$. *(Use with page 304.)*

1. 7 2. $^{-}6$ 3. 0 4. 12 5. 0.7 6. $^{-}0.3$

7. $^{-}6.93$ 8. 4.013 9. $^{-}4.9$ 10. $^{-}3.0001$ ★ 11. $\frac{\frac{1}{3}}{9}$ ★ 12. $\frac{\frac{1}{4}}{20}$

Compare. Replace ≣ with >, <, or =.

13. $^{-}7$ ≣ $2\frac{3}{4}$ 14. 5 ≣ $^{-}2.7$ 15. 3 ≣ $^{-}4.7$ 16. $^{-}1.8$ ≣ 2.4 17. $\frac{1}{6}$ ≣ 0

18. $\frac{^{-}1}{8}$ ≣ 0 19. $\frac{^{-}3}{4}$ ≣ $\frac{^{-}6}{8}$ 20. $\frac{3}{4}$ ≣ $\frac{^{-}1}{2}$ 21. $^{-}1$ ≣ $\frac{^{-}3}{4}$ 22. $^{-}1\frac{2}{5}$ ≣ $^{-}1\frac{3}{4}$

23. $^{-}1.4$ ≣ $^{-}8.0$ 24. $^{-}3\frac{1}{2}$ ≣ $^{-}1\frac{1}{4}$ ★ 25. $\frac{\frac{1}{2}}{5}$ ≣ $\frac{\frac{2}{3}}{8}$ ★ 26. $\frac{\frac{3}{4}}{5}$ ≣ $\frac{\frac{2}{5}}{7}$ ★ 27. $\frac{\frac{5}{6}}{3}$ ≣ $\frac{\frac{3}{4}}{2}$

Write terminating decimals. *(Use with page 306.)*

1. $\frac{4}{5}$ 2. $\frac{5}{8}$ 3. $\frac{^{-}9}{10}$ 4. $\frac{^{-}13}{25}$ 5. $\frac{9}{40}$ 6. $\frac{^{-}7}{50}$

7. $\frac{9}{4}$ 8. $\frac{^{-}15}{8}$ 9. $2\frac{3}{20}$ 10. $^{-}4\frac{7}{10}$ ★ 11. $\frac{^{-}3}{125}$ ★ 12. $\frac{119}{200}$

Write repeating decimals.

13. $\frac{7}{9}$ 14. $\frac{^{-}2}{7}$ 15. $\frac{5}{11}$ 16. $\frac{^{-}8}{9}$ 17. $^{-}2\frac{5}{6}$ 18. $4\frac{4}{11}$

19. $\frac{4}{3}$ 20. $\frac{11}{6}$ 21. $\frac{^{-}9}{7}$ ★ 22. $\frac{7}{33}$ ★ 23. $^{-}1\frac{1}{99}$ ★ 24. $^{-}2\frac{13}{45}$

Add and simplify. *(Use with page 308.)*

1. $\frac{1}{5} + \frac{2}{5}$　**2.** $^{-}\frac{7}{10} + {^{-}\frac{3}{10}}$　**3.** $^{-}\frac{5}{6} + {^{-}\frac{3}{6}}$　**4.** $\frac{3}{4} + {^{-}\frac{3}{4}}$

5. $\frac{5}{6} + \frac{3}{8}$　**6.** $^{-}\frac{3}{5} + {^{-}\frac{3}{4}}$　**7.** $^{-}\frac{2}{3} + \frac{1}{2}$　**8.** $^{-}\frac{3}{4} + \frac{5}{8}$

9. $^{-}\frac{7}{9} + \frac{1}{9}$　**10.** $\frac{5}{9} + {^{-}\frac{2}{3}}$　**11.** $^{-}\frac{3}{10} + {^{-}\frac{7}{10}}$　**12.** $^{-}\frac{1}{4} + \frac{7}{8}$

13. $0.8 + {^{-}0.4}$　**14.** $^{-}0.09 + {^{-}0.06}$　**15.** $7.3 + {^{-}8.1}$　**16.** $^{-}3.7 + 6.2$

★ **17.** $^{-}\frac{2}{3} + \frac{4}{5} + {^{-}\frac{6}{7}}$　★ **18.** $\frac{3}{4} + {^{-}\frac{1}{2}} + \frac{3}{5}$　★ **19.** $^{-}\frac{7}{9} + {^{-}\frac{5}{6}} + {^{-}\frac{1}{3}}$　★ **20.** $\frac{1}{4} + {^{-}\frac{3}{7}} + \frac{5}{14}$

Subtract and simplify. *(Use with page 310.)*

1. $\frac{3}{4} - \frac{1}{4}$　**2.** $\frac{5}{6} - {^{-}\frac{1}{6}}$　**3.** $^{-}\frac{5}{9} - \frac{1}{9}$　**4.** $^{-}\frac{5}{7} - {^{-}\frac{2}{7}}$

5. $^{-}\frac{3}{5} - \frac{1}{2}$　**6.** $\frac{1}{2} - {^{-}\frac{3}{4}}$　**7.** $\frac{5}{6} - \frac{3}{8}$　**8.** $^{-}\frac{7}{12} - {^{-}\frac{3}{4}}$

9. $\frac{7}{8} - {^{-}\frac{3}{8}}$　**10.** $^{-}\frac{7}{12} - \frac{5}{12}$　**11.** $^{-}\frac{7}{8} - 0$　**12.** $0 - {^{-}\frac{3}{5}}$

13. $0.9 - {^{-}0.5}$　**14.** $^{-}1.07 - {^{-}1.06}$　**15.** $3.4 - {^{-}1.7}$　**16.** $^{-}4.6 - 8.0$

★ **17.** $\left({^{-}\frac{2}{5}} - {^{-}\frac{4}{5}}\right) - \frac{1}{5}$　★ **18.** $\left({^{-}\frac{3}{4}} - \frac{1}{2}\right) - {^{-}\frac{5}{8}}$　★ **19.** $\frac{2}{3} - \left({^{-}\frac{7}{8}} - \frac{3}{4}\right)$　★ **20.** $^{-}\frac{3}{5} - \left(\frac{7}{9} - {^{-}\frac{2}{3}}\right)$

Multiply and simplify. *(Use with page 312.)*

1. $\frac{2}{3} \cdot \frac{3}{4}$　**2.** $^{-}\frac{5}{6} \cdot {^{-}\frac{1}{2}}$　**3.** $^{-}\frac{3}{4} \cdot \frac{2}{7}$　**4.** $\frac{5}{8} \cdot {^{-}\frac{1}{2}}$

5. $1\frac{3}{8} \cdot {^{-}\frac{8}{3}}$　**6.** $^{-}1\frac{1}{2} \cdot {^{-}\frac{3}{3}}$　**7.** $^{-}7.8 \cdot 0.4$　**8.** $0.6 \cdot {^{-}0.1}$

9. $^{-}1.6 \cdot {^{-}2.3}$　★ **10.** $^{-}\frac{3}{4} \cdot \frac{4}{5} \cdot {^{-}\frac{2}{3}}$　★ **11.** $8 \cdot {^{-}\frac{5}{6}} \cdot \frac{4}{5}$　★ **12.** $^{-}0.6 \cdot {^{-}0.4} \cdot 0.3$

Divide and simplify.

13. $0.16 \div {^{-}0.4}$　**14.** $^{-}0.32 \div {^{-}0.4}$　**15.** $\frac{5}{6} \div \frac{1}{2}$　**16.** $^{-}\frac{3}{4} \div \frac{2}{3}$

17. $\frac{1}{3} \div {^{-}\frac{2}{3}}$　**18.** $^{-}\frac{7}{8} \div {^{-}\frac{3}{4}}$　**19.** $8 \div {^{-}\frac{4}{7}}$　**20.** $^{-}1\frac{3}{4} \div {^{-}\frac{2}{5}}$

21. $^{-}1\frac{1}{2} \div 1\frac{5}{6}$　★ **22.** $\left({^{-}\frac{2}{3}} \div \frac{4}{9}\right) - {^{-}\frac{1}{8}}$　★ **23.** $\left(1\frac{3}{7} \div {^{-}\frac{3}{5}}\right) \div 1\frac{2}{3}$　★ **24.** $1\frac{3}{4} \div \left({^{-}\frac{5}{8}} \div {^{-}\frac{5}{16}}\right)$

Compute. *(Use with page 319.)*

1. 3^2 **2.** 11^2 **3.** $(^-1)^2$ **4.** $(^-17)^2$ **5.** $\left(\frac{1}{4}\right)^2$ **6.** $\left(\frac{^-5}{8}\right)^2$

7. $(0.9)^2$ **8.** $(1.6)^2$ **9.** $(^-2.3)^2$ ★**10.** $(1.05)^2$ ★**11.** $(^-0.003)^2$ ★**12.** $(0.0004)^2$

Give 2 numbers whose square is the given number.

13. 36 **14.** 64 **15.** 81 **16.** 144 ★**17.** 10,000 ★**18.** 625

Give 2 square roots. *(Use with page 320.)*

1. 121 **2.** 400 **3.** $\frac{9}{4}$ **4.** $\frac{16}{49}$ **5.** 0.81 **6.** 0.0004

Find square roots.

7. $\sqrt{25}$ **8.** $^-\sqrt{64}$ **9.** $\sqrt{0.25}$ **10.** $^-\sqrt{0.09}$ **11.** $^-\sqrt{0.0049}$ **12.** $\sqrt{8{,}100}$

13. $^-\sqrt{1{,}600}$ **14.** $^-\sqrt{\frac{1}{4}}$ **15.** $^-\sqrt{\frac{9}{64}}$ **16.** $\sqrt{\frac{49}{100}}$ ★**17.** $\sqrt{0.000009}$ ★**18.** $^-\sqrt{\frac{900}{10{,}000}}$

Estimate, then find the exact square root.

19. $\sqrt{324}$ **20.** $\sqrt{729}$ **21.** $\sqrt{1{,}156}$ **22.** $\sqrt{2{,}116}$ **23.** $\sqrt{5{,}184}$ **24.** $\sqrt{6{,}889}$

Estimate, then find the square root to the nearest tenth.

25. $\sqrt{3}$ **26.** $\sqrt{6}$ **27.** $\sqrt{17}$ **28.** $\sqrt{35}$ **29.** $\sqrt{68}$ **30.** $\sqrt{85}$

Solve. First use rounded numbers. *(Use with page 348.)*

1. A set of golf clubs sells for $297.75. During a sale it sold for $189.50. How much was saved during the sale?

2. Mr. Aarons bought 5 cans of tennis balls. He paid $14.90 for them. How much is one can of balls?

3. A baseball club bought 18 baseballs that cost $7.98 each. How much did they spend on all the balls?

4. A golf umbrella is marked $6.95 during a sale. This is $2.50 less than the regular price. What is the regular price?

5. Joanna bought a fishing rod for $31.98, fishing boots for $19.75 and a tackle box for $8.79. How much did she spend in all?

6. Jay paid $28.98 for a warm-up suit. Pete paid $36.89 for the same suit. How much more did Pete pay?

7. Ms. Sherman paid $5.96 for 4 pairs of tennis socks. Each pair was the same price. How much did each pair cost?

8. Mr. Edwards bought 8 rubber balls for his school. Each ball was $4.89. How much did he pay in all?

Table of Measures

Length

1 kilometer (km) = 1,000 meters
1 hectometer (hm) = 100 meters
1 dekameter (dam) = 10 meters
1 meter (m)
1 decimeter (dm) = 0.1 meter
1 centimeter (cm) = 0.01 meter
1 millimeter (mm) = 0.001 meter

1 foot (ft) = 12 inches (in.)
1 yard (yd) = { 3 feet; 36 inches }
1 mile (mi) = { 5,280 feet; 1,760 yards }

Mass/Weight

1 kilogram (kg) = 1,000 grams
1 hectogram (hg) = 100 grams
1 dekagram (dag) = 10 grams
1 gram (g)
1 decigram (dg) = 0.1 gram
1 centigram (cg) = 0.01 gram
1 milligram (mg) = 0.001 gram
1 metric ton (t) = 1,000 kilograms

1 pound (lb) = 16 ounces (oz)
1 ton (T) = 2,000 pounds

Capacity

1 kiloliter (kL) = 1,000 liters
1 hectoliter (hL) = 100 liters
1 dekaliter (daL) = 10 liters
1 liter (L)
1 deciliter (dL) = 0.1 liter
1 centiliter (cL) = 0.01 liter
1 milliliter (mL) = 0.001 liter

1 teaspoon = 5 milliliters
1 tablespoon = 12.5 milliliters

1 liter = 1,000 cubic centimeters (cm^3)
1 milliliter = 1 cubic centimeter

1 cup (c) = 8 fluid ounces (fl oz)
1 pint (pt) = 2 cups
1 quart (qt) = 2 pints
1 gallon (gal) = 4 quarts

Time

1 minute (min) = 60 seconds (s)
1 hour (h) = 60 minutes
1 day (d) = 24 hours
1 week = 7 days
1 year (y) = { 12 months; 365 days }
1 decade = 10 years
1 century = 100 years

GLOSSARY

This glossary contains an example, an illustration, or a brief description of important terms used in this book.

Absolute value of a number The number or its opposite, whichever is positive. (page 278)
Examples $|^+5| = {}^+5$
$|^-5| = {}^+5$

Acute angle An angle whose measure is less than 90°. (page 194)

Addition property for equations The same number may be added to each side of an equation to form an equivalent equation.
If $a = b$, then $a + c = b + c$. (page 58)

Alternate interior angles In the figure below, $\angle a$ and $\angle d$ are alternate interior angles, and so are $\angle$b and $\angle c$. (page 212)

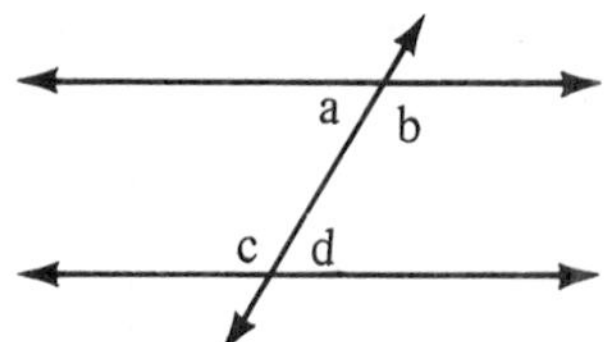

Associative property of addition For all numbers a, b, and c, $(a + b) + c = a + (b + c)$. (page 48)
Example $(3 + 4) + 5 = 3 + (4 + 5)$

Associative property of multiplication For all numbers a, b, and c, $(a \cdot b) \cdot c = a \cdot (b \cdot c)$. (page 48)
Example $(3 \cdot 2) \cdot 5 = 3 \cdot (2 \cdot 5)$

Bisect To divide into two congruent parts. (page 197)

Central angle An angle whose vertex is at the center of a circle. (page 390)

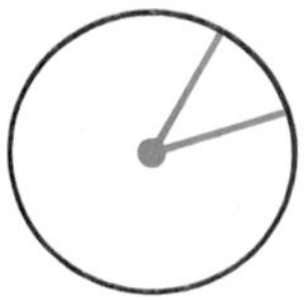

Circumference Distance around a circle. (page 208)

Common factor A factor of two or more numbers. (page 156)
Example 2 is a common factor of 8 and 10.

Common multiple A multiple of two or more numbers. (page 158)
Example 12 is a common multiple of 3 and 4.

Commutative property of addition For all numbers a and b, $a + b = b + a$. (page 48)
Example $6 + 4 = 4 + 6$

Commutative property of multiplication For all numbers a and b, $a \cdot b = b \cdot a$. (page 48)
Example $5 \cdot 3 = 3 \cdot 5$

Complementary angles Two angles, the sum of whose measures is 90°. (page 210)

Composite number A number that has more than two factors. (page 12)
Example 10 is a composite number.
Factors 1, 2, 5, 10

Congruent figures Figures that have the same size and shape. (page 332)

Coordinates Numbers matched with points on a line. Number pairs matched with points on a plane. (page 381)

Corresponding angles In the figure below, pairs of corresponding angles are $\angle a$ and $\angle e$, $\angle b$ and $\angle f$, $\angle c$ and $\angle g$, $\angle d$ and $\angle h$. (page 212)

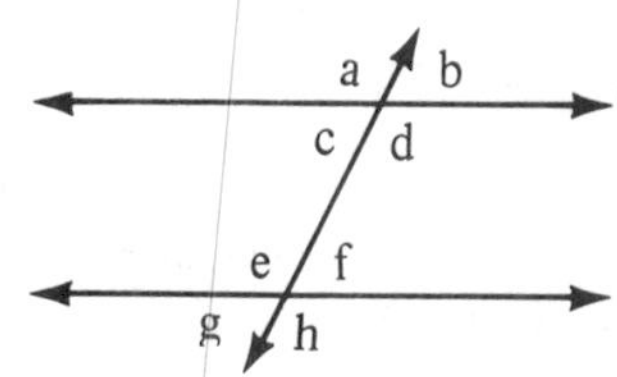

Cosine A trigonometric ratio. $\cos A = \frac{b}{c}$ (page 340)

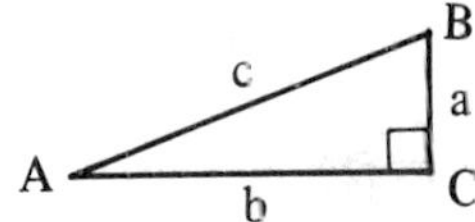

Decimal A number shown with a decimal point. (page 78)

Examples 0.84 $0.1\overline{212}$

Denominator In $\frac{5}{8}$, 8 is the denominator. (page 160)

Diagonal A line segment joining two nonconsecutive vertices of a polygon. $\overline{AC}$ is a diagonal. (page 200)

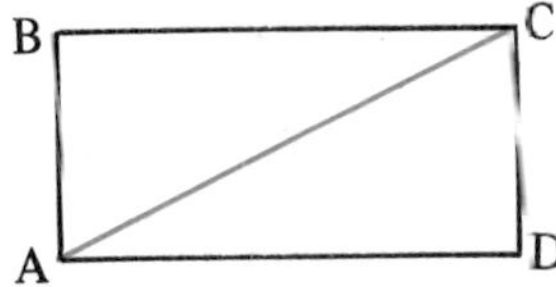

Discount Amount deducted from the marked price. (page 258)

Distributive property For all numbers a, b, and c, $a \cdot (b + c) = (a \cdot b) + (a \cdot c)$. (page 48)

Example $3 \cdot (2 + 4) = (3 \cdot 2) + (3 \cdot 4)$

Divisible If a number is divided by a second number and the remainder is zero, the number is divisible by the second number. (page 10)

Example 18 is divisible by 2, but not by 4.

Division property for equations Each side of an equation may be divided by the same number and an equivalent equation is formed.

If $a = b$, $\frac{a}{c} = \frac{b}{c}$, $c \neq 0$. (page 64)

Equilateral triangle A triangle with the three sides the same length. (page 195)

Equivalent equations Two equations with the same solution. (page 58)

Example $2x = 6$ $x = 3$

Equivalent fractions Fractional numerals for the same number. (page 160)

Example $\frac{1}{2} = \frac{4}{8}$

Exponent In 10^4, 4 is the exponent. It means that 10 is used as a factor 4 times: $10^4 = 10 \cdot 10 \cdot 10 \cdot 10$. (page 90)

Extremes In a proportion the first and fourth terms are the extremes. (page 240)

Example $\frac{1}{2} = \frac{5}{10}$

1 and 10 are the extremes.

Factor A number to be multiplied. (page 12)

Example $2 \times 4 = 8$ 2 and 4 are factors.

Graph of an equation A picture of all solutions to an equation. (page 370)

Greatest common factor The largest common factor of two or more numbers. (page 156)

Example For 9 and 15,

3 is the greatest common factor.

Greatest possible error One half the smallest unit of measurement used. (page 134)

Hypotenuse The longest side of a right triangle. The side opposite the right angle. $\overline{AB}$ is the hypotenuse. (page 324)

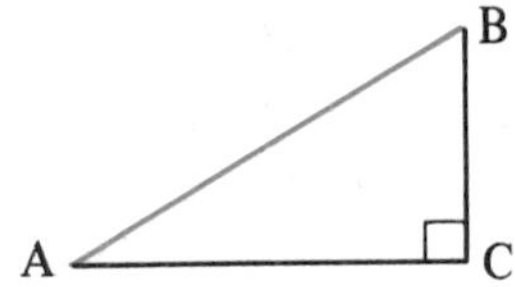

Infinite Continues without end; endless. (page 306)

Integer Any of these numbers:
$\ldots, {}^-2, {}^-1, 0, 1, 2, \ldots$ (page 270)

Interest Payment for use of money. (page 266)

Irrational number A number named by a nonrepeating and nonterminating decimal. (page 314)

Examples 0.123123312333... $\sqrt{28}$

Isosceles triangle A triangle with two or more sides the same length. (page 195)

Least common multiple The smallest common multiple of two or more numbers. (page 158)

Example For 6 and 9,

18 is the least common multiple.

Glossary

Mean, in a proportion The means are the second and the third terms of a proportion. (page 240)
Example $\frac{1}{2} = \frac{3}{6}$
2 and 3 are the means.

Mean, in statistics The average of a set of numbers. (page 384)
Example The mean for 13, 16, 26, 33 is 22.

Median When numbers are arranged in order, the middle number or the average of the middle two numbers. (page 385)
Examples The median for 17, 19, 23 is 19.
The median for 8, 11, 15, 19 is 13.

Mixed number A number such as $3\frac{1}{5}$ or $9\frac{2}{3}$ (page 166).

Mode The number occurring most often in a set of numbers. (page 384)

Multiple A number that is the product of the given number and another factor. (page 158)
Example A multiple of 2 is 12.

Multiplication property for equations If each side of an equation is multiplied by the same number, the result is an equivalent equation.
If $a = b$, $ac = bc$, $c \neq 0$. (page 64)

Numerator In $\frac{3}{4}$, 3 is the numerator. (page 160)

Obtuse angle An angle whose measure is more than 90° and less than 180°. (page 194)

Opposite The sum of a number and its opposite is zero. (page 278)
Example $^{-}12 + {}^{+}12 = 0$
$^{-}12$ is the opposite of $^{+}12$.
$^{+}12$ is the opposite of $^{-}12$.

Origin The point assigned to 0 on the number line or the point where the x- and y-axes intersect. (page 276)

Parallel lines Two or more lines in a plane that do not intersect. (page 212)

Parallelogram A quadrilateral with both pairs of opposite sides parallel. (page 198)

Percent Ratio of a number to 100, using the % sign. (page 248)
Example 8% means 8 out of 100.

Perfect square A number that can be named as the product of two equal factors. (page 319)
Example 16 is a perfect square because
$16 = 4 \cdot 4$.

Perimeter Sum of the lengths of the sides of a polygon. (page 202)

Periods in numerals The groups of three digits set off by a comma in a numeral. (page 2)

Perpendicular lines Two lines that intersect so that each angle they form measures 90°. (page 214)

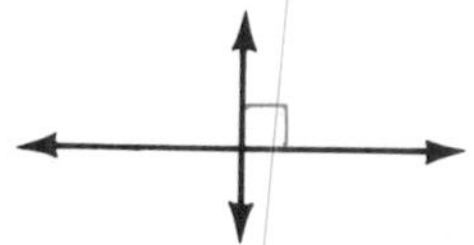

Polygon A simple closed curve made up of line segments. (page 198)

Precision The smaller the unit with which a measurement is made, the more precise the measurement. (page 134)

Prime factorization A factorization in which all factors are prime numbers. (page 156)
Example $30 = 2 \cdot 3 \cdot 5$

Prime number A natural number with exactly two factors, itself and one. (page 12)

Principal The amount of money on which interest is paid. (page 266)

Prism A solid with two parallel lines and congruent bases that are polygons. (page 356)

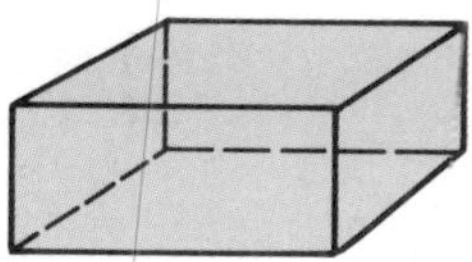

Probability The number of favorable outcomes divided by the number of all possible outcomes. A number from 0 to 1. (page 392)

Proportion A statement of equality for two ratios. (page 240)
Example $\frac{3}{6} = \frac{1}{2}$

Pyramid A solid figure with triangular regions for faces and a polygonal region for a base. (page 352)

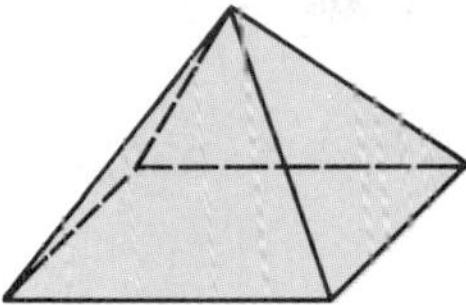

Pythagorean relationship A relationship between the measures of the sides of a right triangle: $a^2 + b^2 = c^2$. (page 324)

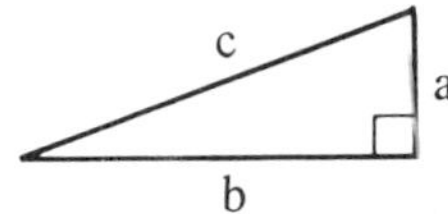

Quadrants The x-axis and the y-axis separate the plane into four parts called quadrants. (page 372)

Quadrilateral A polygon with 4 sides. (page 198)

Radius A line segment from a point on a circle to the center of the circle. (page 208)

Range The difference between the largest and the smallest number in a set of data. Sometimes, the range is given as an interval. (page 384)
Example The range for 3, 8, 11, and 15 is 3 to 15.

Ratio Comparison of two numbers by division. (page 239)

Rational number A number that can be expressed in the form $\frac{a}{b}$ where a and b are integers and $b \neq 0$. (page 304)

Real numbers The set of rational and irrational numbers. (page 326)

Reciprocals Two numbers whose product is 1. (page 181)
Example $\frac{3}{4}$ and $\frac{4}{3}$ are reciprocals of each other because $\frac{3}{4} \cdot \frac{4}{3} = 1$.

Regular polygon A polygon with all sides the same length and all angles the same size. (page 200)

Relatively prime Two numbers whose only common factor is 1. (page 157)
Example 3 and 8 are relatively prime.

Repeating decimal A decimal with one or more digits repeating endlessly. (page 306)
Examples $0.3\overline{3}$ $0.0\overline{909}$

Rhombus A parallelogram with all sides congruent. (page 198)

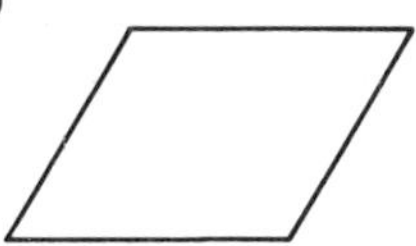

Right angle An angle of 90°. (page 194)

Sample space The set of possible outcomes of an experiment. (page 394)
Example If a die is tossed, the sample space is $\{1, 2, 3, 4, 5, 6\}$.

Scale drawing A drawing that has the same shape as an object, but that can be larger, the same size, or smaller than the object. (page 338)

Scalene triangle A triangle with no two sides the same length. (page 195)

Scientific notation Expressing a number as a product of two factors. One factor is a power of 10. The other factor is from 1 to 10. (page 92)
Example 2.3×10^4 is a scientific notation for 23,000.

Significant digits Those digits used to express the number of units of measurement in a measurement. (page 140)
Example In 0.061 meter, the unit of measurement is 0.001 meter, and there are 61 of the units. 6 and 1 are significant digits, but 0 is not.

Similar triangles Triangles with the same shape, but not necessarily the same size. (page 336)

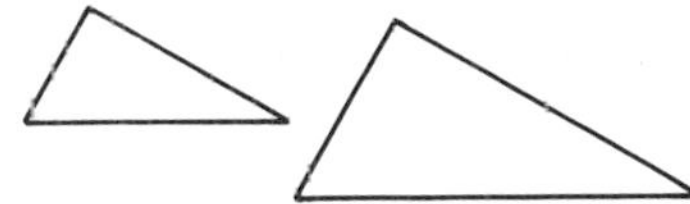

Glossary

Simplest form A fraction is in simplest form when its numerator and denominator are relatively prime. (page 162)

Examples $\frac{4}{5}$ $\frac{9}{11}$

Sine A trigonometric ratio. $\sin A = \frac{a}{c}$ (page 340)

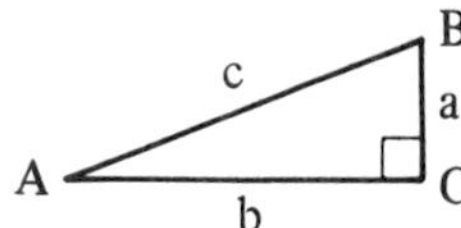

Solution(s) A replacement that makes a number sentence true. (page 54)

Examples $2x + 8 = 14$ 3 is a solution.
$x < 4$ 0, 1, 2, 3 are solutions.

Square root A number that when multiplied by itself gives the original number. (page 320)

Example 5 is the square root of 25.

Straight angle An angle whose measurement is 180°. (page 194)

Subtraction property for equations The same number may be subtracted from each side of an equation to form an equivalent equation.
If $a = b$, then $a - c = b - c$. (page 58)

Supplementary angles Two angles, the sum of whose measures is 180°. (page 210)

Surface area The total area of the surface of a solid. (page 352)

Symmetry The correspondence of parts on opposite sides of a point, line, or plane. (page 381)

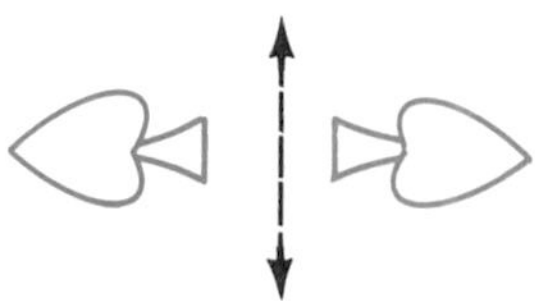

Tangent A trigonometric ratio. $\tan A = \frac{a}{b}$ (page 340)

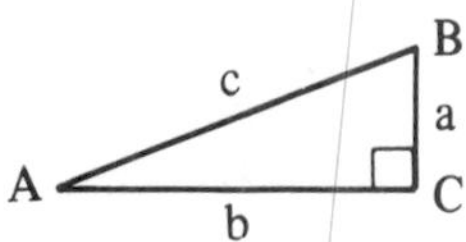

Terminating decimal A decimal that does not repeat. (page 306)

Example 0.75

Transversal A line intersecting two or more lines at a different point on each line. $\overleftrightarrow{AB}$ is a transversal. (page 212)

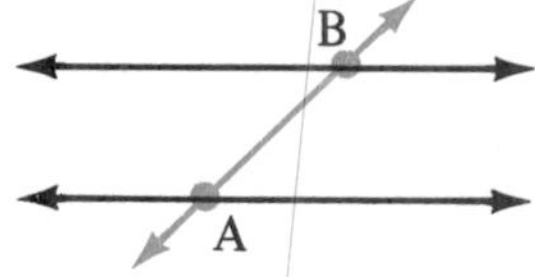

Trapezoid A quadrilateral with exactly one pair of parallel sides. (page 198)

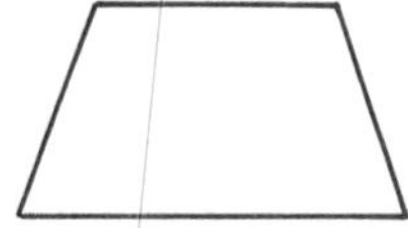

Variable A letter or other symbol that represents a number. (page 54)

Vertex A point common to two rays of an angle or two sides of a polygon. (page 192)

Vertical angles Angles formed by two intersecting lines. $\angle a$ and $\angle b$ form a pair of vertical angles. (page 212)

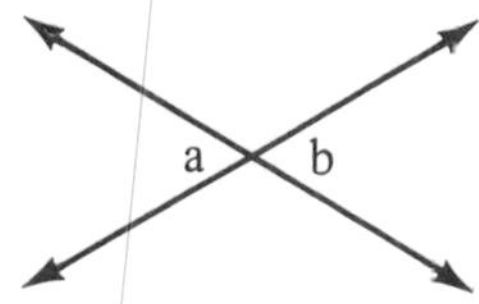

Whole number Any of these numbers: 0, 1, 2, 3, ... (page 2)

Glossary

SYMBOL LIST

		Page
$\doteq$	is approximately equal to	4
$<$	is less than	72
$>$	is greater than	72
10^5	ten to the fifth power	90
$\overline{AB}$	line segment *AB*	190
$\cong$	is congruent to	190
$\triangle ABC$	triangle *ABC*	190
$\overrightarrow{AB}$	ray *AB*	192
$\angle ABC$	angle *ABC*	192
$m \angle A$	measure of angle *A*	192
π	pi (about 3.14)	208
$\overleftrightarrow{AB}$	line *AB*	212
$\parallel$	is parallel to	212
$\perp$	is perpendicular to	214
3:4	three to four	239
10%	ten percent	248
$^-3$	negative three	276
$^+3$	positive three	276
$\lvert ^-2 \rvert$	absolute value of negative 2	278
$0.3\overline{3}$	repeating decimal	306
$\sqrt{}$	square root	320
$\sim$	is similar to	336

Glossary

INDEX

G *means the word is listed in the Glossary.*

A

Absolute values of integers, 278–279, 286, **G**
Accuracy and Speed Drill, *see* Race Time
Activity
angle construction, 196–197
congruent triangle construction, 334–335
Acute angle, 194, **G**
Acute triangle, 194
Addition
basic facts, 7; Race Time, 22
of consecutive whole numbers, 315
of decimals, 102–103
estimating in, 28–29, 106–107
of fractions, 168–169
of integers, 280–283, 286
mental, 23
of metric units, 136
of mixed numbers, 170–171
properties of: for integers, 292; for whole numbers, 48–49
of rational numbers, 308–309
and subtraction undoing each other in equations, 56–57
of whole numbers, 24–25
Addition property for equations, 58–59, 296, **G**
Aid to Memory, 131, 137
Algebraic expressions, 226–227
Alternate interior angles, 212–213, **G**
constructing parallel lines using, 216–217
Angles, 192–197
acute, 194, **G**
alternate interior, 212–213, **G**
angles and triangles classified by, 194
bisecting, 197
central, 390–391, **G**
complementary, 210–211, **G**
congruent, 192–193
consecutive, of a parallelogram, 210–211
construction of, 196–197
corresponding, *see* Corresponding angles
obtuse, 194, **G**
pairs of, 210–211
of polygons, 200–201
right, 194, **G**
sides of, 192
straight, 194, 200, **G**
supplementary, 210–211, **G**
vertical, 212–213, **G**
Areas
of circles, 346
in customary system, 350–351
in metric system, 342–346
of parallelograms, 344
of rectangles, 140–141, 344
surface, in metric system, 352–353
of trapezoids, 344–345
of triangles, 344
ASA (angle-side-angle) principle, 335
Associative properties of addition and multiplication
for integers, 292
for whole numbers, 48–49, **G**
Average of a set of data, 384–385
Axes, 372

B

Bar graphs, 316–317, 386–387
Base, 90–91
Basic Facts Review, 7
Basic Skills Check, 19, 53, 77, 99, 127, 155, 189, 223, 247, 275, 303, 331, 369, 401
Bisecting angles, 197, **G**
Borrowing money, 266–267
Brainteaser(s), 6, 15, 30, 42, 63, 73, 87, 93, 107, 133, 135, 143, 151, 171, 211, 215, 243, 261, 269, 287, 291, 311, 321, 343, 355, 380
Broken-line graphs, 68–69, 387

C

Calculator Activity, 13, 49, 59, 81, 172, 241, 253, 315
Capacity
customary units of, 148
metric units of, 128–129, 144, 358–359
Career
architects, 364
astronomers, 328
plumbers and pipefitters, 124
programmers, 186
research analysts, 398
wholesalers, 300
Cash, value of, 100–101
Celsius temperature, 149

Index

Central angle, 390–391, **G**
Chapter Review, 17, 51, 75, 97, 125, 153, 187, 219–220, 245, 273, 301, 329, 365–366, 399
Chapter Test, 18, 52, 76, 98, 126, 154, 188, 221–222, 246, 274, 302, 330, 367–368, 400
Charts, 100–101
Circle graphs, 288–289, 390–391
Circles, 208–209
  areas of, 346
Circumferences, 208–209, **G**
Classifying triangles
  by angles, 194
  by sides, 195
Coins, value of, 100–101
Commissions, 272
Common factors, 156, **G**
Common multiples, 158, **G**
Commutative properties of addition and multiplication
  for integers, 292
  for whole numbers, 48–49, **G**
Comparing
  decimals, 82–83
  fractions, 164–165
  integers, 276
Complementary angles, 210–211, **G**
Complex fractions, 181
Composite numbers, 12–13, **G**
Compound interest, 268–269
Compound probability, 396–397
Computation skills
  with decimals: addition, 102–103; division, 116–119; multiplication, 110–113; subtraction, 104–105
  with fractions: addition, 168–171; division, 182–183; multiplication, 178–180; subtraction, 173–175
  with integers: addition, 280–283, 286; division, 294–295; multiplication, 290–291; subtraction, 284–285
  with rational numbers: addition, 308–309; division, 312–313; multiplication, 312–313; subtraction, 310–311
  with whole numbers: addition, 24–25, 315; division, 38–42; 116–117; multiplication, 34–37; 110–111; subtraction, 26–27
Conclusions, 234–235, 241
Cones, volumes of, 361
Congruent angles, 192–193
Congruent triangles, 332–333, **G**
  constructing, 334–335
Consecutive numbers, 20–21
  product of, 59
Construction, *see* Geometric construction
Consumer applications and skills
  borrowing money, 266–267
  buying cars, 218
  determining better buys, 96
  estimating answers in metric system, 138–139
  figuring compound interest, 268–269
  finding commissions, 272
  finding regular prices, 258–259
  finding sales tax, 254–255
  getting paid in cash, 100–101
  reading telephone bills, 74
  reading train tables, 16
  solving word problems, 88–89
  using discounts and sales, 258–259, 264–265
  using rounding in shopping, 348–349
  using scale drawings, 338–339
  using tables, 152
Coordinates, 381, **G**
Corresponding angles, 212–213, 332, 336, **G**
  constructing parallel lines using, 216–217
Corresponding sides, 332, 336
Cosine, 340–341, 402, **G**
Cover-up technique with equations, 54–55
Customary system
  acre, 350–351
  area in, 350–351
  capacity in, 148
  cubic unit, 362
  cup, 148
  fluid ounce (fl oz), 148
  foot (ft), 146–147; cubic (ft^3), 362; square (ft^2), 350–351
  gallon (gal), 148
  inch (in.), 146–147; cubic ($in.^3$), 362; square ($in.^2$), 350–351
  length in, 146–147
  mile (mi), 146–147; square (mi^2), 350–351
  ounce (oz), 148
  pint (pt), 148
  pound (lb), 148
  quart (qt), 148
  square unit, 350–351
  tablespoon (tbs), 148
  ton, 148
  volume in, 362
  weight in, 148
  yard (yd), 146–147; cubic (yd^3), 362; square (yd^2), 350–351
Cylinders
  surface areas of, 352
  volumes of, 356–357

D

Data
graphing, 386–387
interpreting, 384–385
Date, time zones and, 150–151
Daylight Savings Time, 151
Decimal places in products, 112
Decimal points
lining up, 102. 104, 116
multiplication by "moving", 110
Decimals, G
addition of, 102–103
comparing, 82–83
division of: by decimals, 118–119; by whole numbers, 116–117
equations with, 122–123
estimating, 106–107, 121
fractions and, 184–185
Keeping Fit, 145, 159, 185, 204, 238, 260, 363, 375
multiplication of: by decimals, 112–113; by whole numbers, 110–111
negative exponents and, 298
non-terminating, 314
ordering, 82–83
percents and, 248, 252–253
place value for, 78–81
powers of 10 and, 90–91
rational numbers and, 304–307, 314
repeating, *see* Repeating decimals
rounding, 84–85
rounding quotients with, 120
subtraction of, 104–105
terminating, 306–307, 314, **G**
writing, 78–79
Denominator, 160, **G**
Diagnostic Review, *see* Basic Facts Review; Keeping Fit
Diagonal, 200–201, **G**
Diameter of a circle, 208–209
Differences
estimating, 28–29
estimating decimal, 106–107
Discounts, 258–259, 264–265, **G**
Distance formula, 236–237
Distributive property, 48–49, 292, **G**
Divisibility of whole numbers, 10–11, **G**
Division
basic facts, 7; Race Time, 31
of decimals: by decimals, 118–119; by whole numbers, 116–117
estimating in, 46–47, 121
in exponential notation, 90–91
of fractions, 182–183
of integers, 294–295
of mixed numbers, 182–183
and multiplication undoing each other in equations, 56–57
of rational numbers, 312–313
rounding quotients in, 120
shortcut in, 42
using scientific notation, 94–95
of whole numbers, 38–42
by zero, 294
zeros in, 44–45
by 1-digit numbers, 38–39
by 2- and 3-digit numbers, 40–41
Division property for equations, 64–67, 296, **G**

E

Equations
addition property for, 58–59, 296, **G**
cover-up technique with, 54–55
with decimals, 122–123
division property for, 64–67, 296, **G**
doing and undoing, 56–57
equivalent, 58–59, 64–65, **G**
in finding percents, 256–257
graphing, 370–371, 376–377
graphing integer pairs for, 374–375
inequalities, *see* Inequalities
with integers, 296–297
Keeping Fit, 86, 145, 185
making up word problems from, 232
multiplication property for, 64–67, 296, **G**
selecting, to solve word problems, 88–89
solving, 60–61
subtraction property for, 58–59, 296, **G**
using two equation properties, 70–71
word sentences translated into, 228–229
writing, 228–229; from word problems, 230–231
Equilateral triangles, 195, **G**
perimeters of, 202
Equivalent equations, 58–59, 64–65, **G**
Equivalent fractions, 160–161, 164, 239, **G**
Estimating
answers in metric system, 138–139
decimals, 106–107, 121
products and quotients, 46–47, 121
square roots, 320–321
sums and differences, 28–29; with decimals, 106–107
whole numbers, 28–29, 46–47

Index

Evaluating expressions, 224–225
Evaluation, *see* Chapter Test
Even numbers, 20–21
Expanded numerals, *see* Numerals, writing expanded
Exponents, 90–91, **G**
expanded numerals with, 299
negative, and decimals, 298
Expressions
algebraic, 226–227
evaluating, 224–225
open, 226–227
Extremes of a proportion, 240, 242, 244, **G**

F

Factorials, 59
Factors, 12–13, **G**
Find Out!
Aid to Memory, 131, 137
Brainteaser(s), 6, 15, 30, 42, 63, 73, 87, 93, 107, 133, 135, 143, 151, 171, 211, 215, 243, 261, 269, 287, 291, 311, 321, 343, 355, 380
Calculator Activity, 13, 49, 59, 81, 172, 241, 253, 295, 315
Flow chart, 380
Formulas
for areas: of circles, 346; of rectangles, parallelograms, trapezoids, and triangles, 344
for circumferences of circles, 208–209
distance, 236–237
for finding the sum of consecutive whole numbers, 315
lever, 242–243
for perimeters of equilateral triangles, rectangles, and squares, 202
for volumes: of cones and pyramids, 360–361; of prisms and cylinders, 356–357
Fractions
addition of, 168–169
comparing, 164–165
complex, 181
decimals and, 184–185
division of, 182–183
equivalent, 160–161, 164, 239, **G**
Keeping Fit, 204, 238, 260, 293, 363, 375
mixed numbers and, 166–167
multiplication of, 178–179
percent and, 248, 250–251
reciprocals, 181, 182, **G**
sequences of, 171, 243
simplifying, 162–163
subtraction of, 173
Frequency tables, 388–389

G

Geometric constructions
angles, 196–197
bisecting angles, 197
congruent triangles, 334–335
parallel lines, 216–217
perpendicular lines, 214–215
Geometry
angles, *see* Angles
areas, *see* Areas
circles, 208–209
circumferences, 208–209, **G**
cylinders, *see* Cylinders
diagonal, 200–201, **G**
diameters of circles, 208–209
hexagon, 198
isosceles triangle, 195, **G**
line segments, *see* Line segments
lines, 190–191
octagon, 198
parallelograms, *see* Parallelograms
pentagon, 198
point, 190
polygons, 198–199, **G**
prisms, 356–357, **G**
pyramids, *see* Pyramids
quadrilaterals, 198–199, 200, **G**
radius of a circle, 208–209, **G**
rays, 192
rectangle, 198
rectangular prisms, 356–357
rhombus, 198, **G**
solid, surface area of a, 352–353
square, 198
surface area in metric system, 352–353
trapezoid, 198, **G**
triangles, *see* Triangles
vertex, 192, **G**
Graphing
data, 386–387
equations, 370–371, 376–377, **G**
inequalities, 370–371, 378–379
integer pairs for equations, 374–375
integers on a number line, 370–371
Graphs
bar, 316–317, 386–387
broken-line 68–69, 387
circle, 288–289, 390–391
solving problems with, 382–383
Greatest common factor (GCF), 156–157, **G**
Greatest possible error, 134–135, **G**

H

Hexagon, 198
Histograms, 388–389
Horizontal number line, 372
Hypotenuse, 324–325, **G**

Index

I

Increase, percent, 270–271
Inequalities
graphing, 370–371, 378–379
solving, 72–73; replacements as integers, 72–73, 370–371
Integer pairs, graphing, for equations, 374–375
Integers, G
absolute values of, 278–279, 286
addition of, 280–283, 286
comparing, 276
division of, 294–295
equations with, 296–297
graphing, on a number line, 270–271
integer pairs, graphing, for equations, 374–375
Keeping Fit, 307
multiplication of, 290–291
on the number line, 276–283
opposites of, 278–279
ordered pairs, 372–377
properties of, 292
as rational numbers, 304–305
as replacements for inequalities, 370–371
subtraction of, 284–285
Interest, 266–269, **G**
compound, 268–269
International Date Line, 150–151
Interpreting data, 384–385
Inverse property of integers, 292
Irrational numbers, 314, **G**
on real number line, 326–327
square roots as, 323
Isosceles triangle, 195, **G**

K

Keeping Fit
decimals, 159, 185, 204, 238, 260, 363, 375
equations, 86, 145, 185
fractions, 238, 260, 293, 363, 375
integers, 307
number theory, 43, 108, 145, 185
numeration, 43, 108
whole numbers, 43, 62, 86, 108, 145, 185, 204, 363

L

Least common multiple (LCM), 158–159, 168, **G**
Length
customary units of, 146–147
metric units of, 128–136
Lever formula, 242–243
Line of symmetry, 381
Line segments, 190–191
measuring, 73
in polygons, 198–199
Lines, 190–191
parallel, *see* Parallel lines
perpendicular, 214–215

M

Maintenance, *see* Basic Skills Check; Keeping Fit
Mass, metric units of, 128–129, 142–143
Mean of a set of data, 384–385, **G**
Means of a proportion, 240, 242, 244, **G**
Measurement, *see also* Customary system; Metric system
greatest possible error, 134–135, **G**
measuring line segments, 73
precision, 134–135, **G**
Median of a set of data, 384–385, **G**
Mental addition, 23
Metric system
are (a), 342–343
area in, 342–346
capacity in, 128–129, 144, 358–359
Celsius temperature, 149
centigram (cg), 142
centimeter (cm), 130–136; cubic (cm^3), 354–361; square (cm^2), 342–343
cubic unit, 354–355, 358–359
decigram (dg), 142
decimeter (dm), 130–133
dekagram (dag), 142
dekameter (dam), 130, 132–133
estimating answers in, 138–139
gram (g), 128, 142–143
hectare (ha), 342–343
hectogram (hg), 142
hectometer (hm), 130–133
kilogram (kg), 128–129, 142–143
kilometer (km), 130–136
length in, 128–136
liter (L), 128–129, 144
mass in, 128–129, 142–143
meter (m), 128–136; cubic (m^3) 354–355; square (m^2), 342–343
milligram (mg), 142–143
milliliter (mL), 144
millimeter (mm), 130–136; cubic (mm^3), 354–355; square (mm^2), 342, 343
place value and the, 132–133
square unit, 140–141, 342–346, 352–353
surface area in, 352–353
ton (t), 142–143
volumes in, 354–355; of cones and pyramids, 360–361; of prisms and cylinders, 356–357

Mid-Chapter Review, 6, 30, 63, 87, 109, 137, 172, 205, 233, 261, 287, 315, 347, 380
Mixed numbers, G
addition of, 170–171
division of, 182–183
fractions and, 166–167
multiplication of, 180
sequences of, 243
subtraction of, 174–175
Mode of a set of data, 384–385, **G**
Money
borrowing, 266–267
value of, 100–101
Multiples, 158–159, **G**
Multiplication
basic facts, 7; Race Time, 31
of decimals, 112–113
and division undoing each other in equations, 56–57
estimating in, 46–47, 121
in exponential notation, 90–91
of fractions, 178–179
of integers, 290–291
of mixed numbers, 180
by "moving" the decimal point, 110
order of, 224–225
by powers of 10, 110; to get whole number divisors, 118
properties of: for integers, 292; for whole numbers, 48–49
of rational numbers, 312–313
special method for, 137
of two numbers in the 90's, 131
using scientific notation, 94–95
of whole numbers, 34–37; and decimals, 110–111
zeros in, 44–45
Multiplication property for equations, 64–67, 296, **G**

N

Negative exponents and decimals, 298
Negative integers, *see* Integers
Non-terminating decimals, 314
Number lines
graphing integers on, 370–371
integers on, 276–283
origins of, 276, 372
perpendicular, 372
rational numbers on, 304–305, 308
real, 326–327
Number theory
divisibility of whole numbers, 10–11
factors, 12–13, **G**
greatest common factor (GCF), 156–157, **G**
Keeping Fit, 43, 108, 145, 185
least common multiple (LCM), 158–159, 168, **G**
Numbers/Numeration
completing patterns, *see* Patterns
composite, 12–13, **G**
consecutive, *see* Consecutive numbers
irrational, *see* Irrational numbers
Keeping Fit, 43, 108
mixed, *see* Mixed numbers
place value, *see* Place value
prime, 12–13, **G**
rational, *see* Rational numbers
real, *see* Real numbers
relatively prime, 157, 162, **G**
whole, *see* Whole numbers
Numerals
standard: to scientific notation, 92–93; word names for, 2
writing expanded: for decimals, 80–81; with exponents, 299
writing standard, 2–3; for decimals, 80–81; with exponents, 299; for negative exponents, 298
Numerator, 160, **G**

O

Obtuse angle, 194, **G**
Obtuse triangle, 194
Octagon, 198
Odd numbers, consecutive, 20–21
One
multiplication property of: for integers, 292; for whole numbers, 48–49
probability of, 392
Open expressions, 226–227
Opposite property of integers, 292
Opposites
of integers, 278–279, **G**
of pictures, 261
of rational numbers, 308, 310
Order of operations, rules for the, 224–225
Ordered pairs, 372–377
Ordering
decimals, 82–83
whole numbers, 2–3
Origin of a number line, 276, 372, **G**

P

Parallel lines, 212–213, **G**
constructing, 216–217
Parallelograms, 198, **G**
areas of, 344
consecutive angles of, 210–211
Parentheses, operations within, 224–225
Pascal's Triangle, 15

Patterns
of multiples of 1,001, 13
in multiplication, 295; with 8, 81
Pascal's Triangle, 15
in sequences of whole numbers, 49
Pentagon, 198
Percent change, 270–271
Percents, G
decimals and, 248, 252–253
equations in finding, 256–257
finding, 256–257; of whole numbers, 254–255
finding the number, 258–259
fractions and, 248, 250–251
Keeping Fit, 323, 363, 395
meaning of, 248–249
Perfect squares, 319, **G**
Perimeters, G
of polygons, 202–203
of rectangles and squares, 202
Period names, 2
Perpendicular lines, 214–215, **G**
Place value
and the metric system, 132–133
for decimals, 78–81
for whole numbers, 2–3
Points, 190
plotting, 372–377
Polygons, 198–199, **G**
angles of, 200–201
perimeters of, 202–203
regular, 200–201, **G**
Positive integers, *see* Integers
Powers of 10, 90–91
multiplication by, 110; to get whole number divisors, 118
Precision in measurement, 134–135, **G**
Prime factorization, 156, **G**
Prime numbers, 12–13, **G**
Principal for interest, 266–269, **G**
Prisms, volumes of, 356–357, **G**
Probability, 392–397, **G**
compound, 396–397
defining, 392, 394, 396
finding, 392–397
predicting, 394–395
of zero and one, 392
Problem-Solving Applications
careers, 124, 186, 300, 328, 364, 398
determining the better buy, 96
distance formula, 236–237
finding commissions, 272
lever formula, 242
reading telephone bills, 74
reading train tables, 16
solving word problems, 50
using charts, 218
using proportions, 244
using tables, 152
Problem-Solving Skills
drawing diagrams, 32–33
estimating answers in metric system, 138–139
making up word problems from equations, 232
selecting equations to solve word problems, 88–89
solving word problems: with graphs, 382–383; with not enough information, 206–207; with too much information, 176–177
using bar graphs, 316–317
using broken-line graphs, 68–69
using circle graphs, 288–289
using the four-step problem-solving method, 8–9
using rounding in shopping, 348–349
writing equations from word problems, 230–231
Products
of consecutive numbers, 59
decimal places in, 112
estimating, 46–47, 121
Properties
for equations, *see under* Equations
for integers, 292
for whole numbers, 48–49
Proportion, 240–241, 244, **G**
in scale drawings, 338–339
Protractor, 192
Pyramids, G
surface areas of, 352
volumes of, 360–361
Pythagorean relationship for right triangles, 324–325, **G**

Q

Quadrants, 372, **G**
Quadrilaterals, 198–199, 200, **G**
Quotients
estimating, 46–47, 121
rounding, 120

R

Race Time, 22, 31
Radius of a circle, 208–209, **G**
Range of a set of data, 384–385, **G**
Rate per year for interest, 266–269
Rational numbers, G
addition of, 308–309
decimals and, 304–307, 314
division of, 312–313
multiplication of, 312–313
on a number line, 304–305, 308

Index

opposites of, 308, 310
on real number line, 326–327
reciprocals of, 312
repeating decimals as, 318
square roots as, 323
squares of, 319
subtraction of, 310–311
Ratios, 239, 240, **G**
trigonometric, *see* Trigonometric ratios
Rays, 192
Reading
decimals, 78–79
whole numbers, 2–3
Real numbers, G
real number line, 326–327
square roots, finding, 320–321
squares of, 319
Reasoning, 234–235, 291
Reciprocals
of fractions, 181, 182, **G**
of rational numbers, 312
Rectangles, 198
areas of, 140–141, 344
perimeters of, 202
Rectangular prisms, volumes of, 356–357
Regular polygons, 200–201, **G**
Relatively prime numbers, 157, 162, **G**
Repeating decimals, 306–307, **G**
as irrational numbers, 318
Reports, making and using, 1
Review, *see* Chapter Review; Mid-Chapter Review
Rhombus, 198, **G**
Right angle, 194, **G**
Right triangles, 194
Pythagorean relationship for, 324–325
Rounding, 28; *see also* Estimating
decimals, 84–85
quotients, 120
using, in shopping, 348–349
whole numbers, 4–5

S

Sales, 264–265
Sales tax, 254–255
Sample space, 394–395, **G**
SAS (side-angle-side) principle, 335
Scale drawings, 338–339, **G**
Scalene triangle, 195, **G**
Scientific notation, 92–95, **G**
computing with, 94–95
to standard numerals, 92–93
Sequences, 14–15
completing, 6, 143
of fractions, 171, 243
in multiplication, 241
Sides
of angles, 192
of polygons, finding, 199
of triangles: corresponding, 332, 336; triangles, classified by, 195
Significant digits, 140–141, **G**
Similar triangles, 336–337, **G**
Simplifying fractions, 162–163, **G**
Sine, 340–341, 402, **G**
Solid, surface area of a, 352–353
Special Topic
area in customary system, 350–351
compound interest, 268–269
compound probability, 396–397
computing with scientific notation, 94–95
constructing parallel lines, 216–217
coordinates, 381
customary units: of capacity and weight, 148; of length, 146–147
finding sums by multiplication, 20–21
frequency tables, 388–389
graphing inequalities, 378–379
histograms, 388–389
mental addition, 23
properties: of integers, 292; of whole numbers, 48–49
real number line, 326
reasoning, 234–235
repeating decimals as rational numbers, 318
shortcut in division, 42
symmetry, 381
trigonometric ratios, 340–341
using absolute value to add integers, 286
using significant digits, 140–141
volume in customary system, 362
volumes of cones and pyramids, 360–361
Speed and Accuracy Drill, *see* Race Time
Square, 198
area of a, 342–343
perimeter of a, 202
Square root table, 322–323
Square roots, finding, 320–321, **G**
Squares
perfect, of numbers, 319, **G**
of rational numbers, 319
SSS (side-side-side) principle, 334
Standard numerals, *see under* Numerals
Statistics, 384–385, 388–389
Straight angle, 194, 200, **G**
Subtraction
and addition undoing each other in equations, 56–57

Index

basic facts, 7; Race Time, 22
of decimals, 104–105
estimating in, 28–29, 106–107
of fractions, 173
of integers, 284–285
of metric units, 136
of mixed numbers, 174–175
order of, 224–225
of rational numbers, 310–311
of whole numbers, 26–27
Subtraction property for equations, 58–59, 296, **G**
Sums
estimating, 28–29
estimating decimal, 106–107
finding, by multiplication, 20–21
formula for finding the, of consecutive whole numbers, 315
Supplementary angles, 210–211, **G**
Surface area in metric system, 352–353, **G**
Symmetry, 381, **G**

T

Tangent, 340–341, 402, **G**
Temperature, Celsius, 149
Terminating decimals, 306–307, 314, **G**
Thermometer, 149
Time in years for interest, 266–269
Time zones, 150–151
Transversal, 212–213, **G**
Trapezoid, 198, **G**
area of a, 344–345
Triangles, 190–191, 194–195, 198
acute, 194
areas of, 344
classified: by angles, 194; by sides, 195
congruent, *see* Congruent triangles
corresponding sides of, 332, 336
equilateral, *see* Equilateral triangles
isosceles, 195, **G**
obtuse, 194
right, *see* Right triangles
scalene, 195, **G**
similar, 336–337, **G**
Trigonometric ratios, 340–341
table of, 402
Trigonometry, 340
True proportions, 240–241

V

Variable, 54, **G**
Vertex, 192, **G**
Vertical angles, 212–213, **G**
Vertical number line, 372
Volume
in customary system, 362
in metric system, 354–355
Volumes
of cones and pyramids, 360–361
of prisms and cylinders, 356–357

W

Weight, customary units of, 148
Whole numbers, G
addition of, 24–25; consecutive, 315
divisibility of, 10–11
division of, 38–42
division of decimals by, 116–117
estimating, 28–29, 46–47
estimating decimals to nearest, 121
factors of, 12–13
finding percents of, 254–255
Keeping Fit, 43, 62, 86, 108, 145, 185, 204, 363
multiplication of, 34–37; and decimals, 110–111
ordering, 2–3
patterns in sequences of, 49
percent and, 250–251
place value for, 2–3
properties for, 48–49
reading and writing, 2–3
rounding, 4–5
squares of, 319
subtraction of, 26–27
Word names, 2
Word problems, *see also* Problem-Solving Applications; Problem-Solving Skills
Writing
decimals, 78–79
equations, 228–231
whole number names, 2–3

X

***x*-axis,** 372
***x*-coordinate,** 372

Y

***y*-axis,** 372
***y*-coordinate,** 372

Z

Zero(s)
addition and multiplication properties of, 48–49
division by, 294
in division of decimals, 116
in multiplication of decimals, 112
in multiplication and division of whole numbers, 44–45
probability of, 392
Zero properties of integers, 292
Zones, time, 150–151

ANSWERS TO THE LEARNING STAGE

This section contains answers to the learning stage only.

CHAPTER 1

PAGE 2

A. **1.** eighty-seven thousand, nine hundred sixty-four
2. five hundred sixty-four thousand, one hundred ninety-two
3. three hundred fourteen million, sixteen thousand, nine hundred twelve
4. nine hundred seventy-four billion, one hundred eighty-four million, three hundred twelve thousand, one hundred forty-seven

B. **5.** 23,000 **6.** 4,167,000
7. 6,700,425 **8.** 45,600,024,000

C. **9.** 81,341,007; 81,341,070 81,341,700; 82,373,710

D. **10.** 14,500 **11.** 500,000
12. 23,500,000
13. 500,000,000

PAGE 4

A. **1.** 6,000 **2.** 38,000
3. 531,000 **4.** 1,790,000

B. **5.** 50,000 **6.** 630,000
7. 2,640,000 **8.** 7,000,000

C. **9.** 500,000 **10.** 800,000
11. 5,800,000 **12.** 555,600,000

D. **13.** 9,000,000 **14.** 35,000,000
15. 489,000,000

PAGE 8

A. **1.** How many hours were worked in all to prepare the scenery?
2. Twelve students; each worked 16 hours on the scenery.
3. Multiplication
4. $16 \times 12 = n$
5. 192 **6.** 12 **7.** 16
8. 192 hours **9.** yes

B. **10.** 14 rows

PAGE 10

A. **1.** yes **2.** no **3.** yes **4.** yes

B. **5.** 2, 5, 10 **6.** 2 **7.** 5
8. 2, 5, 10 **9.** 2 **10.** 5
11. 2 **12.** 2, 5, 10 **13.** 2 **14.** 5

C. **15.** neither **16.** 3 **17.** 3
18. 3, 9 **19.** 3, 9 **20.** neither
21. 3, 9 **22.** 3, 9
23. 3 **24.** 3, 9

D. **25.** 6 **26.** no **27.** no
28. 6 **29.** 6

PAGE 12

A. **1.** 1, 2, 3, 4, 6, 12
2. 1, 2, 4, 5, 10, 20
3. 1, 2, 3, 6, 9, 18
4. 1, 23
5. 1, 2, 3, 4, 6, 9, 12, 18, 36

B. **6.** 2, 3, 5, 7
7. 4, 6

C. **8.** no **9.** yes **10.** no
11. no **12.** yes **13.** yes

D. **14.** yes **15.** no **16.** yes
17. no **18.** yes **19.** yes

PAGE 14

A. **1.** Add 3 to each number.
2. Multiply each number by 3.

B. **3.** 243 **4.** 65

C. **5.** 21, 28, 36
6. 240, 1,440, 10,080

D. **7.** 22, 23, 28
8. 22, 23, 46

CHAPTER 2

PAGES 20–21

A. **1.** 9 **2.** 25

B. **3.** 12 **4.** 40

C. **5.** 35 **6.** 105

PAGE 24

A. **1.** 452 **2.** 3,643
3. 945 **4.** $73.14
5. 132,752

B. **6.** 2,920 **7.** $551.55

C. **8.** 15,360 **9.** $252.95
10. 59,330 **11.** 2,572,158
12. 16,844 **13.** 86,239

PAGE 26

A. 1. 516 2. 5,374
3. 25,819 4. $611,117

B. 5. 355 6. 2,229
7. 31,604 8. $828,889

C. 9. 363 10. 1,406
11. 1,864 12. 46,241

PAGE 28

A. 1. 1,100 2. 7,800
3. 560 4. 7,400
5. 72,400

B. 6. 400 7. 3,000
8. 560 9. 2,700
10. 14,400

C. 11. 1,600 12. 13,700
13. 7,900 14. 85,000
15. 12,060

PAGE 32

A. 1. $499.99 2. 720 m 3. 350 cm

B. 4. 3 km 5. 115 cm

PAGE 34

A. 1. 1,872 2. 9,184
3. 10,530 4. 112,648
5. $1,707.75

B. 6. 144 7. 720 8. 864

C. 9. 1,645 10. 30,958
11. 410,976 12. 583,398
13. $11,450.65

PAGE 36

A. 1. 158,912
2. 995,320
3. 15,897,867
4. 8,071,656
5. 30,135,571
6. 255,750,768

B. 7. 169,728
8. 991,420
9. 5,296,100
10. 58,201,500

PAGE 38

A. 1. 143 2. $474
3. 149 4. 408
5. 32 6. $86
7. 344 8. 432

B. 9. 806 10. 403
11. 1,707 12. 1,203
13. 54r2 14. 163r1
15. 78r2 16. 395r5

C. 17. 212 18. $432
19. 3,323 20. 2,034
21. 317 22. 952
23. 812r2 24. 3,020r1

PAGE 40

A. 1. 24 2. 54r2
3. $234 4. 43

B. 5. 181 6. 256
7. 63r3 8. 1,689r32
9. 47 10. 697
11. 144r583

PAGE 44

A. 1. 240 2. 350
3. 600 4. 4,500
5. 32,000
6. 72,000
7. 420,000
8. 150,000
9. 320,000
10. 3,200,000
11. 32,000,000
12. 45,000,000
13. 3,200
14. 18,000
15. 280,000
16. 2,800,000

B. 17. 4 18. 6 19. 2
20. 8 21. 40
22. 40 23. 60
24. 60 25. 20
26. 30 27. 300

PAGE 46

A. 1. 1,800 2. $1,200
3. 42,000 4. 4,000,000

B. 5. 4,000
6. $32,000
7. 280,000
8. $5,400,000

C. 9. 3 10. $20
11. 86 12. 233

D. 13. 2 14. 7
15. 300 16. 700

PAGE 48

A. 1. associative property of addition
2. property of zero for multiplication
3. distributive property
4. commutative property of addition
5. commutative property of multiplication
6. associative property of multiplication
7. property of zero for addition
8. property of one for multiplication

B. 9. $n = 7$ 10. $n = 8$
11. $n = 0$ 12. $n = 8$
13. $n = 4$ 14. $n = 42$
15. $n = 1$ 16. $n = 5$

CHAPTER 3

PAGES 54–55

A. **1.** 15 **2.** 150 **3.** 9
B. **4.** 4 **5.** 15 **6.** 16
C. **7.** 5 **8.** 3 **9.** 4

PAGE 56

A. **1.** $x + 5$
2. $x + 5 - 5$
3. x
B. **4.** 7 **5.** 4 **6.** $\frac{3}{4}$ **7.** 0.4
C. **8.** $x - 3$
9. $x - 3 + 3$
10. x
D. **11.** 2 **12.** 9 **13.** $\frac{1}{2}$ **14.** 0.4
E. **15.** divide by 3 **16.** divide by 4
17. multiply by 2 **18.** multiply by 5

PAGE 58

A. **1.** $x = 2; x + 3 = 2 + 3$
2. $y = 3; y + 4 = 7$
B. Answers may vary. Examples:
3. $x = 7; x + 4 = 7 + 4$
4. $b = 12; b + 1 = 12 + 1$
5. $c = 4; c + 9 = 4 + 9$
6. $d = 24; d + 3 = 24 + 3$
C. Answers may vary. Examples:
7. $x + 7 = 12; x = 5$
8. $d + 8 = 14; d = 6$
9. $n + 4 = 15; n = 11$
10. $r + 6 = 10; r = 4$
D. **11.** yes **12.** no

PAGE 60

A. **1.** 4 **2.** 5 **3.** 8
B. **4.** 3 **5.** 7 **6.** 7
C. **7.** 4 **8.** 5 **9.** 8
D. **10.** 11 **11.** 17 **12.** 23
E. **13.** 5 **14.** 9 **15.** 16
16. 14 **17.** 46 **18.** 39

PAGE 64

A. **1.** $x = 2; 3 \cdot x = 3 \cdot 2$
2. $n = 3; 4 \cdot n = 12; 2 \cdot n = 6$
B. Answers may vary. Examples:
3. $x = 4; 3x = 12$
4. $x = 6; 2 \cdot x = 2 \cdot 6$
5. $x = 8; 5x = 40$
6. $x = 0.7; 3x = 2.1$
C. Answers may vary. Examples:
7. $4x = 8; x = 2$
8. $6x = 30; x = 5$
9. $8x = 24; x = 3$
10. $9x = 18; x = 2$
D. **11.** yes **12.** yes

PAGE 66

A. **1.** divide by 3 **2.** multiply by 3
3. divide by 12
B. **4.** multiply by 4
5. $\frac{x}{4} \cdot 4 = 10 \cdot 4$
6. $x = 40$ **7.** 40
C. **8.** 16 **9.** 72
10. 13 **11.** 34
D. **12.** 28 **13.** 7
14. 6 **15.** 312

PAGE 68

A. **1.** about 230 **2.** 100 **3.** about 130
4. more people over 21 **5.** up
B. **6.** $1,250 **7.** 1, 2, 3, 5
8. about $400 **9.** generally up

PAGE 70

A. **1.** add 4 to both sides of equation
2. $\frac{n}{2} - 4 + 4 = 7 + 4$
3. $\frac{n}{2} = 11$ **4.** $n = 22$
5. 22 **6.** $\frac{22}{2} - 4 = 7$
B. **7.** 6 **8.** 23 **9.** 10
10. 16 **11.** 64 **12.** 42

PAGE 72

A. **1.** $x - 4 = 3$ **2.** 7 **3.** yes
4. no **5.** 8, 9, 10
B. **6.** $2x = 8$ **7.** 4 **8.** no
9. yes **10.** 5, 6, 7, 8, 9, 10
C. **11.** 3, 4, 5, 6, 7, 8, 9, 10
12. 0, 1, 2
13. 5, 6, 7, 8, 9, 10

CHAPTER 4

PAGE 78

A. **1.** tenths
2. thousandths
3. millionths
4. hundredths
B. **5.** four tenths
6. seventy-five hundredths
7. four hundred thirteen thousand one hundred twenty-eight millionths
8. six and nine thousand four hundred twelve ten-thousandths
C. **9.** 0.065
10. 0.0065
11. 2.300
12. 2.00003
13. 21.000005

PAGE 80

A. **1.** 960 **2.** 0.90468 **3.** 20.52

B. **4.** 10 **5.** 0.1
6. 0.01, 0.02
7. 0.001, 0.007

C. **8.** 3×0.1 **9.** 7×0.01 **10.** 9×0.001
11. 3×0.0001 **12.** 7×0.000001
13. 2×10 **14.** $8 \times 1{,}000$ **15.** $7 \times 10{,}000$

D. **16.** $(3 \times 1{,}000) + (8 \times 100) + (7 \times 10) + (6 \times 1)$
17. $(1 \times 100{,}000) + (4 \times 10{,}000) + (3 \times 1{,}000) + (7 \times 100) + (6 \times 10) + (2 \times 1)$
18. $(2 \times 0.1) \times (4 \times 0.01) + (1 \times 0.001)$
19. $(7 \times 0.1) \times (8 \times 0.01) + (6 \times 0.001) + (0 \times 0.0001) + (2 \times 0.00001)$

PAGE 82

A. **1.** 0.70 **2.** 0.60
3. 0.10 **4.** 3.00
5. 8.10

B. **6.** 0.500 **7.** 0.800
8. 0.320
9. 3.000
10. 4.000

C. **11.** $>$ **12.** $<$
13. $>$ **14.** $=$

D. **15.** $>$ **16.** $>$
17. $<$ **18.** $<$

E. **19.** $>$ **20.** $>$
21. $<$ **22.** $=$

F. **23.** $0.9 > 0.134 > 0.06$
24. $0.37 > 0.037 > 0.0037$
25. $0.201 > 0.13 > 0.07$
26. $0.4 > 0.104 > 0.03006$

PAGE 84

A. **1.** 0.435 **2.** 0.742
3. 2.315 **4.** 3.006
5. 0.169 **6.** 0.170
7. 6.099 **8.** 3.000

B. **9.** 0.05 **10.** 0.05
11. 0.01 **12.** 0.61
13. 6.42 **14.** 7.01
15. 9.00 **16.** 3.00

C. **17.** 9.7 **18.** 0.3
19. 1.1 **20.** 3.4
21. 2.5 **22.** 6.9
23. 2.9 **24.** 4.0

D. **25.** 6 **26.** 7
27. 3 **28.** 7
29. 1 **30.** 0
31. 1 **32.** 0

PAGE 88

A. **1.** c

PAGE 90

A. **1.** 10^7 **2.** 10^9 **3.** 10^8

B. **4.** 10^6 **5.** 10^6
6. 10^7 **7.** 10^5

C. **8.** 10^3 **9.** 10^2
10. 10^4 **11.** 10^5
12. 10^5 **13.** 10^1
14. 10^8 **15.** 10^7 **16.** 10^0

PAGE 92

A. **1.** yes **2.** no **3.** no
4. yes **5.** yes

B. **6.** 5×10^2 **7.** 4×10^4
8. 6×10^5 **9.** 7×10^6
10. 8×10^7

C. **11.** 7.4×10^3 **12.** 8.6×10^5
13. 3.8×10^6 **14.** 4.61×10^{11}

D. **15.** 31,000 **16.** 6,200,000
17. 600,000,000
18. 7,310,000,000

PAGE 94

A. **1.** 9.3×10^{13} **2.** 4.27×10^{16}

B. **3.** 6×10^{16} **4.** 9×10^{15}
5. 8×10^{13} **6.** 4×10^{16}

C. **7.** 2.8×10^{10} **8.** 1.8×10^{14}
9. 2.1×10^{13} **10.** 1.6×10^{19}

D. **11.** 2×10^6 **12.** 3.6×10^3

CHAPTER 5

PAGE 100

A. **1.** $89.35
2. eight $10 bills; one $5 bill; four $1 bills
3. $89
4. 1 quarter; 1 dime
5. $0.35

B. **6.** twenty-nine $10 bills; three $5 bills; eight $1 bills
7. 2 half dollars, 4 quarters, 1 dime, 1 nickel, 9 pennies
8. yes

PAGE 102

A. **1.** 1.8 **2.** 11.85
3. 8.930 **4.** 48.0573

B. **5.** 12.708 **6.** 1.556 **7.** 11.016

C. **8.** $33.34 **9.** $75.97
10. $2.54 **11.** $946.41

PAGE 104

A. 1. 0.17 2. 0.186
3. 0.7 4. 1.788
5. 6.1529

B. 6. 0.33 7. 0.084
8. 0.178 9. 2.21

C. 10. 2.9 11. 7.3
12. 54.53 13. 92.581

D. 14. $5.91 15. $2.86
16. $11.04 17. $34.59
18. $137.74

PAGE 106

A. 1. 6 2. 15
3. 3 4. 3

B. 5. 1.5 6. 16.2
7. 0.7 8. 2.4

C. 9. $31 10. $29
11. $4 12. $13

PAGE 110

A. 1. 0.6 2. 2.8
3. 12.8 4. 4.68
5. 1.56

B. 6. 13.86 7. 138.6
8. 1,386 9. 234

C. 10. 90 11. 900
12. 80 13. 3,100

PAGE 112

A. 1. 0.48 2. 0.936
3. 4.3491 4. 0.4182

B. 5. 0.0012 6. 0.00952
7. 0.000008 8. 0.016024
9. 1.206 10. 1.7572
11. 0.6042 12. 0.044356

PAGE 114

A. 1. $6.21
2. $3.36

PAGE 116

A. 1. 0.2 2. 0.3
3. 6.1 4. 1.9

B. 5. 0.03 6. 0.07
7. 0.21 8. 2.88
9. 0.003 10. 0.030
11. 0.100 12. 4.332
13. 4.8 14. 2.45
15. 0.023 16. 2.01
17. 0.507 18. 3.52
19. 0.451 20. 0.25

PAGE 118

A. 1. 4 2. 4 3. 5 4. 6

B. 5. 6 6. 4 7. 3 8. 21

C. 9. 0.12 10. 0.23
11. 4,000 12. 34

PAGE 120

A. 1. 1.7 2. 1.6
3. 1.8 4. 2.1

B. 5. 0.43 6. 2.98
7. 0.07 8. 0.43

PAGE 121

A. 1. 18 2. 24 3. 2.1

B. 4. 2 5. 0.6
6. 4 7. 60

PAGE 122

A. 1. 2.8 2. 2.2 3. 0.4
4. 2.6 5. 0.05 6. 6
7. 3.6 8. 0.04 9. 0.72

B. 10. 0.3, 0.3
11. 1.2
12. 2,2 13. 0.6

C. 14. 0.4 15. 0.5 16. 3
17. 5 18. 1.2 19. 0.16

CHAPTER 6

PAGE 130

A. 1. 7,000 2. 600
3. 500 4. 4
5. 2,000 6. 30,000

B. 7. 5 8. 0.7 9. 6
10. 2.5 11. 9 12. 0.8

PAGE 132

A. 1. 67.8 2. 0.000678
3. 678 4. 6.78

B. 5. 521 6. 3,200
7. 2,400 8. 2.4
9. 0.432 10. 0.037

PAGE 134

A. 1. $\overline{AB} = 3$ cm, $\overline{BC} = 5$ cm, $\overline{AC} = 5$ cm
2. $\overline{AB} = 32$ mm, $\overline{BC} = 54$ mm, $\overline{AC} = 49$ mm
3. Measurements to the nearest millimeter are more precise.

B. 4. 8 mm 5. neither 6. 7.4 mm
7. 0.3 cm 8. 9 in. 9. 0.04 mi

C. 10. 0.1 cm
11. 0.05 cm
12. 0.05 cm

D. 13. 0.05 cm 14. 0.5 m
15. 0.5 mm 16. 0.005 km

PAGE 136

A. 1. 15.2 cm 2. 16.14 m
3. 12.599 km 4. 1.941 m

B. 5. 3.7 cm 6. 5.76 m
7. 4.754 km 8. 46.505 km

PAGE 138

A. 1. 400 2. 80 3. 5 km/h

B. 4. 400 km 5. 300 km
6. 100 km 7. 800; 800 km

C. 8. $0.30 9. 80 L 10. $24.00; $24

PAGE 140

A. 1. 34; 2 2. 12; 2
3. 3; 1 4. 14; 2

B. 5. 17 m^2
6. 308 cm^2

PAGE 142

A. 1. 3,500 2. 42,000
3. 5,600 4. 25,000

B. 5. 0.125 6. 0.050
7. 0.225 8. 0.005

C. 9. 7,000 10. 4.5

PAGE 144

A. 1. 3,000 2. 8,000
3. 0.002 4. 0.015
5. 5,600 6. 12,800
7. 0.017 8. 0.384

PAGE 146

A. 1. 24 2. 72
3. 108 4. 9
5. 10,560 6. 5,280
7. 4 8. 6
9. 2 10. 2
11. 4 12. 3
13. 6 14. 12
15. 13,200 16. 40
17. 10 18. 5, 4
19. 1, 5

PAGE 148

A. 1. 48 2. 4,000
3. 1000 4. 4
5. 2 6. 5

B. 7. 6 8. 32 9. 6
10. 8 11. 3 12. 6

PAGE 149

A. 1. 100°C 2. 0°C 3. 100°

B. 4. cold 5. hot
6. comfortable

C. 7. about 30°C 8. about 10°C

PAGE 150

A. 1. 3, later
2. 2 pm 3. 2 pm

B. 4. 11:30 am
5. 12:30 am

C. 6. no
7. one day earlier
8. 12:00 noon, June 8th

CHAPTER 7

PAGES 156–157

A. 1. 1, 2, 4, 5, 10, 20
1, 2, 3, 5, 6, 10, 15, 30
2. 1, 2, 5, 10 3. 10
4. $2 \cdot 2 \cdot 5$; $2 \cdot 3 \cdot 5$
5. 10 6. 10

B. 7. 6 8. 18
9. 1 10. 6

C. 11. yes 12. no
13. yes 14. yes

PAGE 158

A. 1. 3, 6, 9, 12, 15
2. 8, 16, 24, 32, 40
3. 12, 24, 36, 48, 60

B. 4. 8, 16, 24, 32, 40, 48, 56, . . .
5. 12, 24, 36, 48, 60, 72, 84, . . .
6. 24

C. 7. 24 8. 20
9. 45 10. 12
11. 18 12. 24
13. 36 14. 24

PAGE 160

A. 1. $\frac{2}{6}, \frac{3}{9}, \frac{4}{12}$ 2. $\frac{4}{10}, \frac{6}{15}, \frac{8}{20}$

B. 3. 2 4. 12 5. 8 6. 15

PAGE 162

A. 1. yes 2. yes 3. no
4. no 5. no

B. 6. 4 7. $\frac{1}{3}$
8. yes; The numerator and denominator are relatively prime.

C. 9. $\frac{1}{2}$ 10. $\frac{3}{4}$ 11. $\frac{2}{5}$ 12. $\frac{2}{5}$
13. $\frac{2}{3}$ 14. $\frac{2}{3}$ 15. $\frac{1}{5}$ 16. $\frac{3}{4}$
17. $\frac{2}{5}$ 18. $\frac{3}{4}$

PAGE 164

A. 1. > 2. < 3. > 4. =

B. 5. 24 6. $\frac{9}{24}, \frac{4}{24}$
7. > 8. >

C. 9. > 10. < 11. = 12. <

PAGE 166

A. 1. $1\frac{1}{2}$ 2. $1\frac{1}{2}$ 3. $2\frac{1}{3}$
4. $1\frac{1}{2}$ 5. $2\frac{3}{5}$

B. 6. $\frac{19}{6}$ 7. $\frac{17}{3}$ 8. $\frac{37}{5}$
9. $\frac{11}{6}$ 10. $\frac{15}{4}$ 11. $\frac{13}{2}$

C. 12. $\frac{13}{4}$ 13. $\frac{47}{8}$
14. $\frac{25}{6}$ 15. $\frac{5}{2}$

PAGE 168

A. **1.** $\frac{5}{8}$ **2.** 1 **3.** $\frac{1}{3}$ **4.** $1\frac{3}{10}$
5. $1\frac{1}{3}$ **6.** $\frac{1}{2}$ **7.** $\frac{9}{10}$ **8.** $2\frac{1}{4}$

B. **9.** 10 **10.** 5 **11.** 4
12. $\frac{9}{10}$ **13.** $\frac{9}{10}$

C. **14.** $\frac{7}{8}$ **15.** $\frac{13}{24}$ **16.** $1\frac{1}{6}$
17. $1\frac{9}{20}$ **18.** $1\frac{1}{12}$

PAGE 170

A. **1.** $5\frac{7}{8}$ **2.** $3\frac{3}{4}$ **3.** $5\frac{3}{4}$
4. $6\frac{13}{24}$ **5.** $7\frac{2}{3}$

B. **6.** $4\frac{1}{4}$ **7.** $6\frac{1}{2}$ **8.** $8\frac{1}{8}$
9. $13\frac{7}{12}$ **10.** $11\frac{7}{8}$

C. **11.** $6\frac{1}{5}$ **12.** $8\frac{1}{4}$ **13.** $10\frac{1}{4}$

PAGE 173

A. **1.** $\frac{2}{3}$ **2.** $\frac{3}{5}$ **3.** $\frac{1}{2}$
4. $\frac{2}{5}$ **5.** $\frac{2}{3}$

B. **6.** $\frac{7}{20}$ **7.** $\frac{1}{2}$ **8.** $\frac{5}{24}$
9. $\frac{7}{15}$ **10.** $\frac{7}{12}$

PAGE 174

A. **1.** $1\frac{1}{2}$ **2.** $3\frac{1}{6}$ **3.** $3\frac{5}{24}$
4. $3\frac{1}{3}$ **5.** $2\frac{7}{12}$

B. **6.** $5\frac{3}{8}$ **7.** $5\frac{1}{6}$ **8.** $2\frac{1}{2}$
9. $1\frac{3}{8}$ **10** $4\frac{1}{5}$

C. **11.** $4\frac{4}{5}$ **12.** $3\frac{5}{8}$ **13.** $1\frac{11}{15}$
14. $4\frac{19}{24}$ **15.** $2\frac{11}{12}$

PAGE 176

A. **1.** the cost of 10 cans
2. The cost of 2 cans is $0.79.
3. the number of cans in a case (24)
4. The cost of 10 cans is $3.95.

B. **5.** the cost of a dozen large size bottles
6. the cost of one large size bottle
7. the cost of the next smaller size
8. The cost of a dozen bottles is $11.88.

PAGE 178

A. **1.** $\frac{2}{15}$ **2.** $\frac{3}{40}$ **3.** $\frac{1}{12}$ **4.** $\frac{1}{20}$

B. **5.** 6 **6.** 8 **7.** $1\frac{1}{5}$ **8.** $4\frac{1}{2}$

C. **9.** $\frac{5}{24}$ **10.** $\frac{21}{40}$ **11.** $\frac{3}{5}$

D. **12.** $\frac{5}{8}$ **13.** $\frac{2}{3}$ **14.** $\frac{4}{15}$ **15.** 4

PAGE 180

A. **1.** 28 **2.** $27\frac{1}{5}$
3. $26\frac{1}{4}$ **4.** [illegible]$\frac{2}{3}$
5. $1\frac{5}{8}$ **6.** 10
7. $4\frac{7}{12}$ **8.** $6\frac{3}{5}$

PAGE 181

A. **1.** 1 **2.** 1 **3.** 1 **4.** 1

B. **5.** $\frac{3}{2}$ **6.** $\frac{7}{5}$ **7.** $\frac{1}{6}$ **8.** $\frac{4}{13}$

C. **9.** $\frac{4}{3}$ **10.** $\frac{\frac{8}{21}}{1}$ **11.** $\frac{8}{21}$

D. **12.** $\frac{2}{3}$ **13.** $\frac{1}{2}$ **14.** $\frac{1}{6}$ **15.** $\frac{1}{6}$

PAGE 182

A. **1.** 6 **2.** $\frac{6}{1}$ **3.** 4 **4.** 4

B. **5.** 6 **6.** $\frac{3}{20}$ **7.** 6 **8.** $\frac{9}{10}$

C. **9.** $8\frac{5}{8}$ **10.** $\frac{5}{18}$ **11.** $1\frac{5}{6}$ **12.** $2\frac{3}{16}$

PAGES 184–185

A. **1.** 0.2 **2.** 0.4
3. 1.5 **4.** 1.2
5. 3.5

B. **6.** 0.25 **7.** 0.04
8. 0.04 **9.** 0.16
10. 1.25

C. **11.** 0.375 **12.** 0.625
13. 0.025 **14.** 0.075
15. 0.008

D. **16.** 2.5 **17.** 3.75
18. 4.2 **19.** 4.04
20. 3.125

CHAPTER 8

PAGE 192

A. **1.** E
2. $\overrightarrow{ED}$, $\overrightarrow{EC}$
3. $\angle CED$, $\angle DEC$, $\angle E$

C. **9.** 30° **10.** 60° **11.** 90°
12. 120° **13.** 30° **14.** 60°
15. 120° **16.** 90°

D. **17.** $\angle STU \cong \angle PQR$

PAGES 194–195

A. **1.** right **2.** obtuse
3. obtuse **4.** acute

B. **5.** acute **6.** right **7.** obtuse

C. **8.** isosceles **9.** scalene
10. equilateral **11.** scalene

PAGES 198–199

A. 1. quadrilateral
2. pentagon
3. octagon

B. 4. 1 5. 2 6. They are congruent.
7. It is a parallelogram with all four sides congruent.
8. It is a parallelogram with four right angles.
9. It is a rectangle with all four sides congruent.

C. 10. 7 mm 11. 60° 12. 5 cm

PAGES 200–201

A. 1. 180° 2. 122° 3. 58°

B. 4. A, B, C, D 5. $\overline{BD}$

C. 6. 180° 7. 360°

D. 8. 60° 9. 90° 10. 108°

PAGE 202

A. 1. 94 m 2. 18 ft 3. 145 mm

B. 4. 100 mm 5. 10.2 cm 6. 32 cm

C. 7. $p = 3s$ 8. 72 cm

PAGE 206

A. 1. the measure of $\angle T$
2. the measure of $\angle R$
3. no

B. 4. $m\angle U$ and $m\angle V$
5. $m\angle U$ and $m\angle V$
6. yes
7. $m\angle W = 60°$

C. 8. no
9. the length of the rectangle

PAGES 208–209

A. 1. 124 cm 2. 1 m
3. 4.2 cm 4. 19.2 in.

B. 5. 16 m 6. 3 cm
7. 7.5 mm 8. 1.9 in.

C. 9. 10π m 10. 3.5π cm
11. 8π mm 12. 10.8π m

D. 13. 34.54 cm 14. 65.94 mm
15. 56.52 mm 16. 9.42 in.

PAGE 210

A. 1. complementary
2. supplementary
3. supplementary
4. complementary

B. 5. 60° 6. 66° 7. 23°
8. 36° 9. 1°

C. 10. 150° 11. 60° 12. 126°
13. 63° 14. 1°

D. 15. 90° 16. 180° 17. 90°

E. 18. 63° 19. 48° 20. 50°

PAGE 212

A. 1. $\angle w$ and $\angle z$
2. $\angle a$ and $\angle w$, $\angle x$ and $\angle c$, $\angle z$ and $\angle d$

B. 4. They are congruent.
6. They are congruent.

C. 7. 50° 8. 130°
9. 120° 10. 60°

PAGE 214

A. 1. 90° 2. 90°

PAGE 216

A. 1. 1

CHAPTER 9

PAGE 225

A. 1. 18 2. 48 3. 24 4. 0

B. 5. 64 6. 17

PAGE 226

A. 1. $n - 4$ 2. $n + 3$ 3. $\frac{n}{3}$
4. $2n + 3$ 5. $\frac{1}{2}n$ 6. n^2

B. 7. 8 more than a number
8. 7 less than a number
9. 3 times a number
10. a number divided by 3
11. the square of a number
12. 3 more than twice a number
13. 4 less than 3 times a number
14. 3 more than $\frac{1}{2}$ of a number

PAGE 228

A. 1. $n + 6 = 47$
2. $n - 8 = 63$
3. $\frac{n}{8} = 18$
4. $3n = 129$

B. 5. $2n$
6. $2n - 4$
7. $2n - 4 = 18$

C. 8. $2x - 9 = 47$
9. $3x + 7 = 43$
10. $7x - 5 = 23$

PAGE 230

A. 1. How many hours did Abe work?
2. $4x$
3. $4x = 92$; $x = 23$; Abe worked 23 hours.

B. 4. What was the cost of each shirt?
5. $3n$
6. $3n - 5$
7. $3n - 5 = 43$; $n = 16$; Each shirt costs $16.

PAGE 234

A. **1.** yes **2.** yes **3.** no
B. **4.** no

PAGE 236

A. **1.** $d = rt$ **2.** $180 = r \cdot 4$
3. $r = 45$ mph
B. **4.** $d = rt$ **5.** $260 = 65 \cdot t$
6. $t = 4$ hours

PAGE 239

A. **1.** 9:3 or $\frac{9}{3}$ **2.** 9:12 or $\frac{9}{12}$
B. **3.** yes **4.** no **5.** yes

PAGE 240

A. **1.** no **2.** yes **3.** yes
B. **4.** 2 and 2 **5.** 3 and 2
6. 8 and 2 **7.** 5 and 40
C. **8.** 16 **9.** 16 **10.** yes
D. **11.** 20 **12.** 4 **13.** 9

PAGE 242

A. **1.** $w_1 \cdot d_1 = w_2 \cdot d_2$
2. $10 \cdot 6 = x \cdot 2$
3. $x = 30$;
The mass of the rock is 30 kg.
B. **4.** $w_1 \cdot d_1 = w_2 \cdot d_2$
5. $16 \cdot 5 = x \cdot 4$
6. $x = 20$ A mass of 20 kg will balance the 16 kg mass.

CHAPTER 10

PAGE 248

A. **1.** 4% **2.** 7% **3.** 13%
4. 34% **5.** 68%
B. **6.** $\frac{9}{100}$ **7.** $\frac{12}{100}$ **8.** $\frac{25}{100}$
9. $\frac{63}{100}$ **10.** $\frac{99}{100}$
C. **11.** 5% **12.** 7% **13.** 13%
14. 29% **15.** 69%
D. **16.** 0.04 **17.** 0.07 **18.** 0.12
19. 0.39 **20.** 0.86

PAGE 250

A. **1.** $\frac{1}{10}$ **2.** $\frac{1}{4}$ **3.** $\frac{2}{5}$
4. 1 **5.** 2
B. **6.** $\frac{1}{8}$ **7.** $\frac{1}{6}$ **8.** $\frac{9}{200}$
9. $\frac{1}{400}$ **10.** $\frac{1}{200}$
C. **11.** 75%
D. **12.** 50% **13.** $12\frac{1}{2}\%$ **14.** $\frac{1}{2}\%$
15. 300% **16.** 175%

PAGE 252

A. **1.** 0.07 **2.** 0.81
3. 1.30 **4.** 0.004
5. 0.026
B. **6.** 0.63 **7.** 1.50
8. 0.005 **9.** 0.023
10. 0.0304
C. **11.** 0.0025 **12.** 0.002
13. 0.0075 **14.** 0.025
15. 0.0525
D. **16.** 78% **17.** 50% **18.** 100%
19. 240% **20.** 7.5%

PAGE 254

A. **1.** 5.2 **2.** 18 **3.** 18
B. **4.** $140\% \times 65 = n$
5. $1.40 \times 65 = n$
6. $n = 91$
7. 91
C. **8.** 2 **9.** 4 **10.** 15.75
D. **11.** 30 **12.** 9 **13.** 8

PAGE 256

A. **1.** $n \cdot 30 = 12$
2. $n = 0.40$
3. 40%
B. **4.** 12% **5.** $62\frac{1}{2}\%$
C. **6.** 300% **7.** 525%
D. **8.** $n \cdot 10 = 0.05$
9. $n = 0.005$
10. 0.5%
E. **11.** $2\frac{1}{2}\%$ **12.** 0.25%

PAGE 258

A. **1.** $48 = 40\% \cdot n$
2. 0.40
3. $n = 120$
4. $48 = 0.40 \times 120$
B. **5.** 24 **6.** 27
7. 42 **8.** 54
C. **9.** 4 **10.** 4
11. 800 **12.** 2,000

PAGE 262

A. **1.** Hammer cost $5.95
How much money was returned?
$2.20
B. **2.** Mini-problem 1
Second chair cost $149.50
First chair cost $125.00
Additional cost? $24.50
Mini-problem 2
Gave $50.00
Additional cost $24.50
Change? $25.50

PAGE 264

A. **1.** \$12, \$36
2. \$7.75, \$23.25
3. \$4.45, \$13.35
B. **4.** \$14.40 **5.** \$16.80 **6.** \$19.20
C. **7.** \$4 **8.** $\$4 = n \cdot 16$
9. $n = 0.25$ **10.** 25%

PAGE 266

A. **1.** \$1,008 **2.** \$330
B. **3.** \$3,815 **4.** \$4,936.75
5. \$1,380 **6.** \$517.50
7. \$6,695 **8.** \$2,463

PAGE 268

A. **1.** \$70 **2.** \$1,070 **3.** \$74.90
4. \$1,144.90 **5.** \$1,225.04
B. **6.** \$848.72 **7.** \$265.34

PAGE 270

A. **1.** 4 **2.** $4 = r \cdot 32$
3. $r = \frac{1}{8}$ **4.** 12.5%
B. **5.** 20% **6.** 25%

CHAPTER 11

PAGE 276

A. **1.** positive four
2. negative four
3. positive one
4. negative thirteen
5. positive twenty-eight
B. **6.** $^{-}7$ **7.** $^{-}5$ **8.** $^{-}4$
9. $^{+}5$ **10.** $^{+}7$
C. **11.** $>$ **12.** $<$ **13.** $>$ **14.** $<$

PAGE 278

A. **3.** on $+1$
4. on -4
B. **5.** $^{-}6$ **6.** $^{+}7$ **7.** $^{-}15$
8. $^{+}11$ **9.** $^{+}43$ **10.** $^{-}73$
C. **11.** $^{+}5$ **12.** $^{+}5$
D. **13.** $^{+}9$ **14.** $^{+}7$ **15.** $^{+}21$
16. $^{+}16$ **17.** $^{+}37$ **18.** $^{+}86$
E. **19.** $<$ **20.** $>$ **21.** $=$

PAGE 280

A. **1.** $^{+}4$ **2.** $^{+}7$
3. $^{+}3$ **4.** $^{+}6$
B. **5.** $^{+}87$ **6.** $^{+}41$
7. $^{+}72$ **8.** $^{+}31$
C. **9.** $^{-}4$ **10.** $^{-}6$
11. $^{-}4$ **12.** $^{-}6$
D. **13.** $^{-}29$ **14.** $^{+}82$
15. $^{-}56$ **16.** $^{+}73$
17. $^{+}24$ **18.** $^{+}44$ **19.** $^{-}79$

PAGES 282–283

A. **4.** $^{-}3$
B. **5.** $^{+}1$ **6.** $^{-}3$ **7.** $^{+}2$
C. **8.** positive **9.** 8 **10.** $^{+}8$
D. **11.** $^{+}4$ **12.** $^{-}3$ **13.** $^{-}15$ **14.** $^{-}6$
E. **15.** 0 **16.** 0 **17.** 0 **18.** 0

PAGE 284

A. **1.** $^{-}6$ **2.** $^{+}14$ **3.** $^{+}3$
B. **4.** $^{-}3$ **5.** $^{-}3$ **6.** $^{+}4$ **7.** $^{+}4$
8. $^{+}8$ **9.** $^{-}5$ **10.** $^{-}8$ **11.** $^{+}7$
C. **12.** $^{+}2$ **13.** $^{+}2$
14. $^{+}11$ **15.** $^{+}11$
16. $^{+}11$ **17.** $^{-}4$
18. $^{+}7$ **19.** $^{-}15$

PAGE 286

A. **1.** $^{+}11$ **2.** $^{+}13$
3. $^{-}13$ **4.** $^{-}10$
B. **5.** $^{+}8$ **6.** $^{-}3$
7. $^{+}4$ **8.** $^{-}7$

PAGE 288

A. **1.** Program C **2.** 25%
3. 15 **4.** 18 **5.** 27
B. **6.** 100% **7.** non-union
8. 138 **9.** 262%

PAGE 290

A. **1.** $^{+}56$ **2.** $^{+}6$ **3.** $^{+}63$ **4.** $^{+}35$
B. **5.** $^{-}6$ **6.** $^{-}12$
7. 0 **8.** $^{-}18$
9. $^{-}28$ **10.** $^{-}54$
C. **11.** $^{-}18$ **12.** $^{-}20$
13. $^{-}8$ **14.** $^{-}8$
15. $^{-}42$ **16.** $^{-}54$
D. **17.** $^{+}5$ **18.** $^{+}10$
19. $^{+}27$ **20.** $^{+}32$
21. $^{+}63$ **22.** $^{+}56$

PAGE 292

A. **1.** yes **2.** yes **3.** yes
4. yes **5.** yes **6.** yes
7. yes **8.** yes **9.** yes

PAGE 294

A. **1.** $^{+}4$ **2.** $^{+}4$ **3.** $^{+}3$
4. $^{+}8$ **5.** $^{+}8$ **6.** $^{+}2$
7. $^{-}6$ **8.** $^{-}6$ **9.** $^{-}6$
10. $^{-}3$ **11.** $^{-}17$ **12.** $^{-}6$
B. **13.** 0 **14.** 0
15. no answer possible
16. no answer possible
C. **17.** 0 **18.** $^{-}1$
19. no answer possible **20.** 0

PAGE 296

A. **1.** $^{-}7$ **2.** $^{+}11$ **3.** $^{-}12$
B. **4.** $^{+}8$ **5.** $^{+}8$ **6.** $^{-}5$
C. **7.** $^{-}21$ **8.** $^{+}32$ **9.** $^{-}54$
D. **10.** $^{+}4$ **11.** $^{-}4$ **12.** $^{+}3$

PAGE 298

A. **1.** $^{-}1$ **2.** $^{-}2$
3. $^{-}4$ **4.** 10
5. 100 **6.** 100,000
B. **7.** 100 **8.** 0.01
9. 10 **10.** 0.1
11. 1,000,000 **12.** 0.000001
C. **13.** 10^1 **14.** 10^{-1} **15.** 10^3
16. 10^{-3} **17.** 10^2 **18.** 10^{-2}

PAGE 299

A. **1.** 2 **2.** $^{-}1$ **3.** $^{-}3$ **4.** $^{-}5$
B. **5.** $(3 \times 10^0) + (4 \times 10^{-1}) + (6 \times 10^{-2}) + (7 \times 10^{-3})$
6. $(2 \times 10^1) + (8 \times 10^0) + (5 \times 10^{-1}) + (1 \times 10^{-2}) + (0 \times 10^{-3}) + (6 \times 10^{-4})$
7. $(3 \times 10^2) + (7 \times 10^1) + (4 \times 10^0) + (6 \times 10^{-1}) + (9 \times 10^{-2}) + (1 \times 10^{-3}) + (8 \times 10^{-4}) + (0 \times 10^{-5}) + (2 \times 10^{-6})$
C. **8.** 346.878 **9.** 4,200.634

CHAPTER 12

PAGE 304

A. **1.** $\frac{+8}{+1}$ **2.** $\frac{-8}{+1}$ **3.** $\frac{-5}{+1}$
4. $\frac{+5}{+1}$ **5.** $\frac{0}{+1}$
B. **6.** $\frac{6}{10}$ **7.** $\frac{33}{10}$ **8.** $^{-}\frac{1}{10}$
9. $^{-}\frac{628}{100}$ **10.** $^{-}\frac{782}{100}$
C. **11.** $<$ **12.** $<$ **13.** $<$ **14.** $>$

PAGE 306

A. **1.** $^{-}0.5$ **2.** 0.12
3. $^{-}0.125$ **4.** 0.4
5. 1.4 **6.** $^{-}3.5$
7. $^{-}4.3$ **8.** 2.625
B. **9.** 0.1818 **10.** 18 **11.** $0.\overline{18}$
C. **12.** $0.\overline{66}$ **13.** $0.\overline{1}$
14. $^{-}1.\overline{3}$ **15.** $^{-}3.\overline{142857}$
16. $0.\overline{4}$
D. **17.** terminating **18.** repeating
19. repeating **20.** terminating
21. terminating

PAGE 308

A. **1.** $^{-}\frac{4}{7}$ **2.** $\frac{2}{5}$
3. $^{-}1\frac{1}{4}$ **4.** $^{-}5.8$
B. **5.** $^{-}\frac{1}{3}$ **6.** $^{-}\frac{1}{2}$
7. $^{-}\frac{1}{2}$ **8.** 1.4
9. $\frac{1}{4}$ **10.** $\frac{1}{2}$
11. $^{-}\frac{1}{12}$ **12.** $^{-}2.5$
C. **13.** $\frac{1}{2}$ **14.** $^{-}\frac{3}{4}$
15. $\frac{5}{6}$ **16.** $^{-}1.2$
D. **17.** 0 **18.** 0 **19.** 0 **20.** 0

PAGE 310

A. **1.** $\frac{3}{8}$ **2.** $\frac{1}{2}$
B. **3.** $^{-}1$ **4.** $^{-}\frac{3}{5}$ **5.** $^{-}0.4$ **6.** 5.7
C. **7.** 2 **8.** $\frac{3}{4}$ **9.** $1\frac{1}{4}$
D. **10.** $1\frac{5}{8}$ **11.** $^{-}1\frac{5}{12}$ **12.** $^{-}\frac{11}{24}$ **13.** $^{-}9\frac{1}{6}$
E. **14.** $^{-}\frac{1}{2}$ **15.** $\frac{2}{3}$ **16.** $^{-}\frac{1}{3}$ **17.** $^{-}0.4$
18. 0 **19.** 0 **20.** 0 **21.** 0

PAGE 312

A. **1.** $^{-}\frac{2}{5}$ **2.** $\frac{3}{8}$ **3.** $^{-}2$ **4.** $^{-}3.22$
B. **5.** $\frac{1}{2}$ **6.** $^{-}\frac{7}{30}$ **7.** $^{-}\frac{2}{3}$ **8.** $1\frac{1}{4}$
C. **9.** $^{-}\frac{4}{3}$ **10.** $^{-}\frac{8}{5}$ **11.** $\frac{4}{3}$ **12.** $^{-}\frac{2}{3}$
D. **13.** $\frac{15}{16}$ **14.** $^{-}4$ **15.** $^{-}\frac{1}{4}$ **16.** 2

PAGE 314

A. **1.** rational **2.** irrational
3. rational **4.** irrational

PAGE 316

A. **1.** 35
2. 55
3. October
4. November
5. 20
B. **6.** 15 fiction, 20 biographies
7. October
8. November

PAGE 318

A. **1.** $\frac{1}{9}$ **2.** $\frac{8}{9}$ **3.** $\frac{2}{3}$
B. **4.** $\frac{2}{11}$ **5.** $\frac{1}{11}$ **6.** $\frac{6}{11}$

PAGE 319

A. **1.** 16 **2.** 64 **3.** 9
4. $\frac{4}{9}$ **5.** $\frac{4}{9}$ **6.** 0.16
7. 5.29 **8.** 3.61
9. 9.61 **10.** 17.64
B. **11.** $^{-}5$ **12.** 10, $^{-}10$
C. **13.** no **14.** yes **15.** yes
16. yes **17.** no

Answers to the Learning Stage

PAGE 320

A. **1.** 5, $^-5$ **2.** 10, $^-10$ **3.** $\frac{2}{3}$, $\frac{^-2}{3}$
4. 0.3, $^-0.3$ **5.** 0.8, $^-0.8$
B. **6.** 6 **7.** 9 **8.** $\frac{1}{6}$
9. $^-0.4$ **10.** $^-20$
C. **11.** 17
D. **12.** 15 **13.** 23 **14.** 31
15. 53 **16.** 92
E. **17.** 2.2
F. **18.** 2.6 **19.** 3.3 **20.** 4.9
21. 8.5 **22.** 9.7

PAGES 322–323

A. **1.** 2.646 **2.** 3.162
3. 5.385 **4.** 6.403
B. **5.** rational **6.** irrational
7. irrational **8.** rational

PAGE 324

A. **1.** 13 **2.** 15
B. **3.** 9 **4.** 8

PAGES 326–327

A. **1.** $\sqrt{5}$ **2.** $\sqrt{13}$
B. **7.** $\sqrt{2}$
C. **9.** $^-2$, $^-1.6\overline{6}$, $^-1$, $\frac{^-1}{2}$, 0, 0.3$\overline{3}$, 0.764, 1, 2
10. $^-\sqrt{3}$, $^-0.909009\ldots$, $\sqrt{2}$, 1.5678 . . .

CHAPTER 13

PAGE 332

A. **1.** $\overline{LM} \cong \overline{PQ}$; $\overline{MN} \cong \overline{QR}$; $\overline{NL} \cong \overline{RP}$
2. $\angle L \cong \angle P$; $\angle N \cong \angle R$; $\angle M \cong \angle Q$
B. **3.** $x = 11$ cm
4. $x = 60°$

PAGES 334–335

A. **6.** yes
B. **12.** yes
C. **17.** yes

PAGE 336

A. **1.** yes **2.** yes **3.** yes
B. **4.** *PR* **5.** 6 **6.** 12 **7.** $x = 3$
C. **8.** $x = 50$

PAGE 338

A. **1.** 3 cm
2. $0.5x = 3$; $x = 6$ m
3. 6 m
B. **4.** 4 cm
5. $\frac{1}{800} = \frac{4 \text{ cm}}{x}$
6. $x = 3{,}200$ cm
7. 32 m
C. **8.** 2 m
9. $2x = 4.8$; $x = 2.4$ cm
10. 3.3 cm
11. 2.4 cm × 3.3 cm

PAGES 340–341

A. **1.** 5 **2.** 3 **3.** 4
B. **4.** $\frac{3}{4}$ **5.** $\frac{3}{5}$ **6.** $\frac{4}{5}$ **7.** $\frac{4}{3}$
C. **8.** 0.616
9. 0.934
10. 3.487
11. adjacent
12. opposite
13. tangent
14. 72.7
15. 72.7 m

PAGES 342–343

A. **1.** 12 m^2 **2.** 132 cm^2
3. 60 mm^2 **4.** 6 m^2
B. **5.** 16 cm^2 **6.** 121 m^2
C. **9.** parallelogram
10. 8
11. 16 square units
12. The area of a trapezoid is one half the area of a parallelogram.
13. 8 square units
D. **14.** 66 mm^2
15. 24 cm^2

PAGES 344–345

A. **1.** 100 **2.** 1,000,000
3. 20,000 **4.** 400
5. 3,000,000 **6.** 1,000,000
B. **7.** 0.01 **8.** 0.000001
9. 0.000001 **10.** 0.0025
11. 0.0005 **12.** 4
C. **13.** 20,000 **14.** 4 **15.** 400
D. **16.** km^2 **17.** m^2 **18.** ha
19. cm^2 **20.** mm^2 **21.** m^2

PAGE 346

A. **1.** 314 cm^2 **2.** 50.2 m^2
3. 78.5 cm^2 **4.** 254.3 cm^2
B. **5.** 452.16 cm^2
6. 113.04 cm^2
8. 339.12 cm^2

PAGE 348

1. $2.00 **2.** 20 **3.** multiplication
4. $40.00 **5.** $47.76 **6.** yes

PAGE 350

A. **1.** 432 **2.** 36
3. 8 **4.** 2
B. **5.** 12 yd^2 **6.** 12 yd^2
C. **7.** 87,120 **8.** 1,280

PAGE 352

A. **1.** 528 cm^2 **2.** 864 cm^2

B. **3.** circle **4.** 12.56 cm^2

5. 25.12 cm^2 **6.** rectangle

7. 10 cm **8.** 12.56 cm

9. 125.6 cm^2 **10.** 150.72 cm^2

C. **11.** 64 cm^2

12. 48 cm^2

13. 192 cm^2

14. 256 cm^2

PAGE 354

A. **1.** 4,000,000

2. 7,000

3. 1,000,000,000

B. **4.** 0.000008

5. 0.0005

6. 0.009

7. 5

8. 0.007

PAGE 356

A. **1.** 240 m^3

2. 27 cm^3

B. **3.** triangle

4. 30 cm^2

5. 540 cm^3

C. **6.** circle

7. 314 cm^2

8. 9,420 cm^3

D. **9.** 48,000 mm^3

10. 100,048 cm^3

PAGE 358

A. **1.** 5 **2.** 2.5

3. 10 **4.** 0.65

B. **5.** 8,000 **6.** 7,300

7. 3,000 **8.** 2,500

C. **9.** 3 **10.** 400

11. 240 **12.** 7.4

D. **13.** 7 g **14.** 34.1 g

15. 2,300 g **16.** 3,400 g

E. **17.** 3,000 cm^3 **18.** 8 cm^3

19. 341.7 cm^3 **20.** 4,600 cm^3

PAGES 360–361

A. **5.** $\frac{1}{3}$ full **6.** $\frac{1}{3}$

B. **7.** 70 m^3 **8.** 192 cm^3

C. **9.** $\frac{1}{3}$ **10.** $\frac{1}{3}$

D. **11.** 50.24 cm^3 **12.** 628 cm^3

PAGE 362

A. **1.** 54 **2.** 270

3. 5,184 **4.** 17,280

5. 2 **6.** 5

CHAPTER 14

PAGE 370

A. **1.–3.**

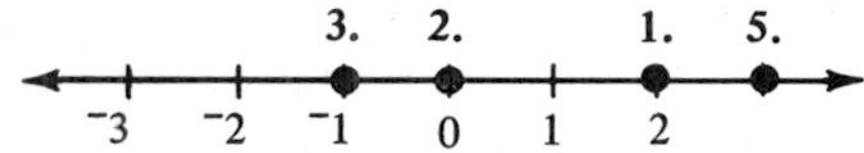

4. $x = 3$

5. See graph above.

C. **6.–11.**

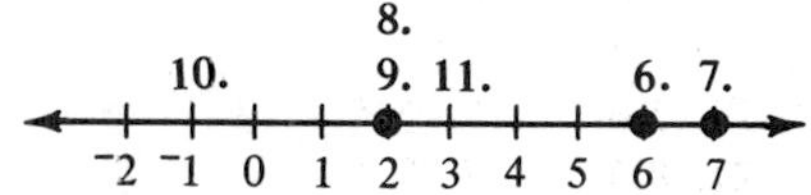

PAGE 372

A. **1.** (3, 2) **2.** (2, 3) **3.** $(^{-}2, 2)$

4. $(^{-}3, ^{-}1)$ **5.** $(1, ^{-}2)$ **6.** $(^{-}2, ^{-}3)$

7. $(^{-}3, 1)$ **8.** $(4, ^{-}2)$ **9.** (1, 0)

B. **10.–14.**

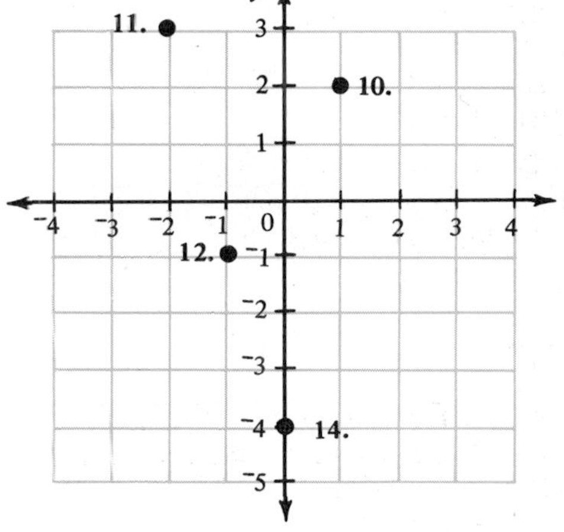

C. **15.** first **16.** fourth

17. second **18.** third

PAGE 374

A. **1.** $y = 4$ **2.** $y = 6$

B. **3.** (0, 4) **4.** (1, 5)

5. (2, 6) **6.** (3, 7)

7.

x	y
$^{-}2$	$^{-}3$
$^{-}1$	$^{-}1$
0	1
1	3

Continued on page 456

PAGE 374 (continued)

C. **8.** (⁻2, ⁻3); (⁻1, ⁻1); (0, 1); (1, 3)

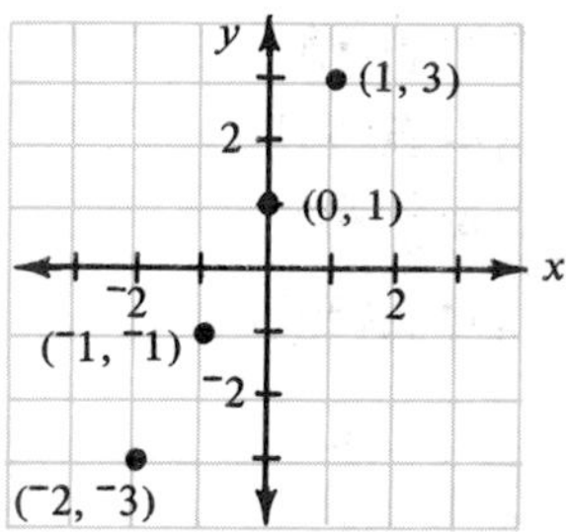

PAGE 376

A. **1.** yes **2.** no

x	⁻2	⁻1	0	1	2
y	⁻4	⁻2	0	2	4

4. (⁻2, ⁻4); (⁻1, ⁻2); (0, 0); (1, 2); (2, 4)

5.–6.

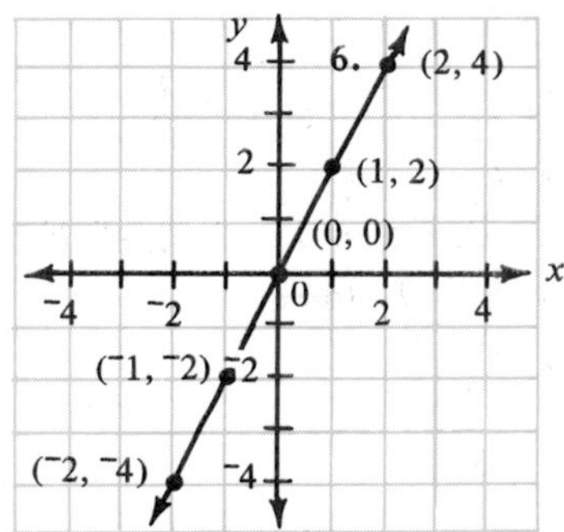

C. **7.** (2, 3) (1, 1) (0, ⁻1) (⁻1, ⁻3) (⁻2, ⁻5)

8. (2, 1) (0, 0) (⁻2, ⁻1) (⁻4, ⁻2) (⁻6, ⁻3)

9. (2, ⁻3) (1, ⁻1) (0, 1) (⁻1, 3) (⁻2, 5)

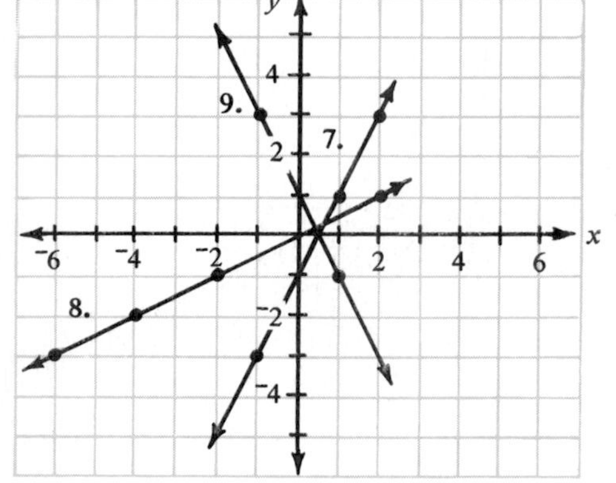

PAGE 378

A. **1.**

x	y
⁻2	⁻5
⁻1	⁻3
0	⁻1
1	1
2	3

2.

3. no **4.** yes **5.** See graph above.

B. **6.–7.**

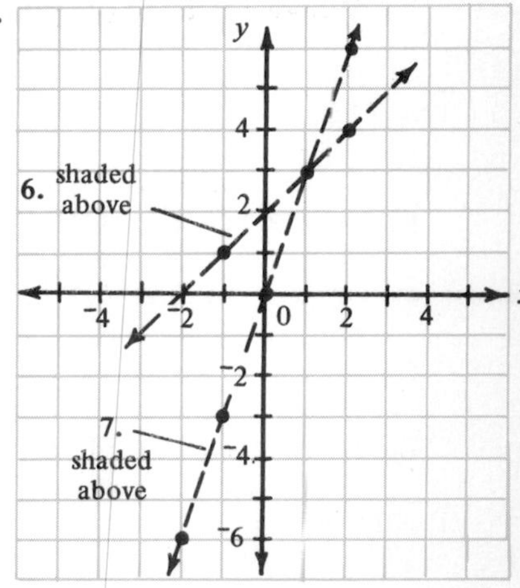

8.–9.

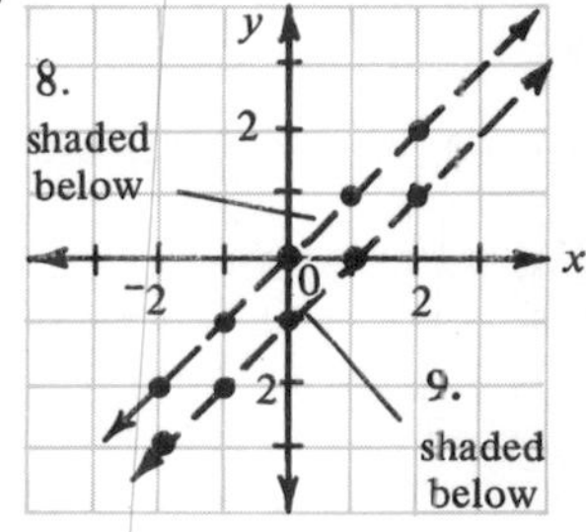

PAGE 382

A. **4.** The lines intersect at noon.

5. The son will overtake his father at noon.

B. **6.** In twelve weeks both José and Susan will have 48 records.

PAGE 384

A. **1.** 100, 95, 90, 85, 85, 85, 80, 75, 70

2. 70 to 100

3. 85

4. 85

5. 85

B. **6.** 108

7. 784

C. **8.** 6 salaries; $246, $182, $156, $105, $98, $75

9. no

10. $156 and $105

11. $130.50

PAGE 389

A. **1.** 82 **2.** yes

B. **3.** 100 × 3 (300); 95; 91 × 2 (182); 90; 89; 87 × 2 (174); 85 × 2 (170); 83 × 2 (166); 82 × 4 (328); 81; 77 × 2 (154); 76; 73; 72; 70 × 3 (210); 66; 64; 50

4. 2,440 **5.** $81\frac{1}{3}$

PAGE 390

A. **1.** 4 **2.** 360°

B. **3.** $\frac{4}{30}$ or $\frac{2}{15}$; 48°

4. $\frac{8}{30}$ or $\frac{4}{15}$; 96°

5. $\frac{5}{30}$ or $\frac{1}{6}$; 60°

6. $\frac{3}{30}$ or $\frac{1}{10}$; 36°

PAGE 392

A. **1.** 4 **2.** 8

3. $\frac{4}{8}$ **4.** $\frac{1}{2}$

B. **5.** $\frac{1}{5}$ **6.** $\frac{4}{5}$

C. **7.** $\frac{4}{4}$ or 1 **8.** $\frac{0}{4}$ or 0

PAGE 394

A. **1.** $\frac{1}{6}$ **2.** $\frac{1}{2}$ **3.** $\frac{1}{2}$

B. **4.** (H, T) **5.** (T, T) **6.** (T, H)

C. **7.** $\frac{1}{4}$ **8.** 25

PAGE 396

A. **1.** $\frac{7}{12}$ **2.** $\frac{1}{12}$ **3.** $\frac{2}{3}$

B. **4.** $\frac{1}{2}$ **5.** $\frac{1}{2}$

6. (H, H); (H, T); (T, T); (T, H)

7. $\frac{1}{4}$ **8.** true

C. **9.** $\frac{15}{56}$

PHOTO CREDITS

All HRW Photos by Jay Good except the following:

Chapter 1: p. 1—J. Wilson/FPG; p. 10—HRW Photo by Ken Lax; p. 12—Copyright by The California Institute of Technology and Carnegie Institution of Washington. Reproduced by permission from The Hale Observatories.

Chapter 2: pp. 20–21—HRW Photo by Steve Langerman; p. 23—HRW Photo by Russell Dian; p. 25—Sam Morales, courtesy of AMF; p. 27—HRW Photo by Bill Hubbell.

Chapter 3: p. 67—HRW Photo by Steve Langerman; p. 74—courtesy of AT&T.

Chapter 4: pp. 82–83—HRW Photo by Ken Karp.

Chapter 5: pp. 100–101—Courtesy of Clay Crafts Coummunity; p. 111—Reflejo; p. 122—HRW Photo by Ken Karp; p. 124—HRW Photo by Russell Dian.

Chapter 6: p. 128—*top* Leo de Wys, Inc.; *bottom* Uniphoto; p. 129—Jay Maisel/Image Bank; p. 152—Cal Herbert/DPI.

Chapter 7: p. 158—HRW Photo by Bill Hubbell; pp. 162–163
p. 186—HRW Photo by Russell Dian.

Chapter 8: p. 191—HRW Photo by Bill Hubbell; p. 207—HRW Photo by Russell Dian; p. 217—Barrie Rokeach; p. 218—Dan McCoy/Rainbow.

Chapter 9: p. 230—middle HRW Photo by Danny Quat; p. 231—HRW Photo by Bill Hubbell; p. 236—Courtesy of Boeing Airlines; p. 234—Metropolitan Museum of Art; gift of Thomas Ryan, 1910; p. 244—HRW Photo by Steve Langerman.

Chapter 10: p. 250—Courtesy of Tech Hi Fi; p. 264—*top* HRW Photo by Ken Lax; p. 266—HRW Photo by Christina Thompson; p. 269—HRW Photo by Russell Dian; p. 272—HRW Photo by Russell Dian.

Chapter 11: p. 281—Owen Franken/Stock Boston; p. 282—HRW Photo by Ken Karp, courtesy of Bache, Halsey, Stuart, Shields, Inc.; p. 283—Jim Collen/Uniphoto; p. 288—HRW Photo by Russell Dian; p. 291—HRW Photo by Russell Dian; p. 294—Taurus Photos; p. 295—Takehide Kazam; Peter Arnold; p. 300—HRW Photo by Russell Dian.

Chapter 12: p. 304—Sefton/DPI: p. 305—Steve Thompson/Uniphoto; p. 308—Courtesy of American Bank Note; p. 316—HRW Photo by Steve Langerman; p. 328—HRW Photo by Russell Dian.

Chapter 13: pp. 332–333—Shostal Associates; p. 364—HRW Photo by Russell Dian.

Chapter 14: p. 383—Arthur d'Arazian/Image Bank; p. 394—HRW Photo by Steve Langerman; p. 398—HRW Photo by Russell Dian.

Title page, Race Time and Keeping Fit Photos: All HRW Photos by William Hubbell except p. 86 and p. 238—HRW Photos by Russell Dian.

ART CREDITS

llustrated by Stan Skardinski and William Harmuth, represented by Evelyne Johnson, Associates

1 2 3 4 5 6 7 8 9 10 11 12 13 14 15 16 17 18 19 20 21 22

1 2 3 4 5 6 7 8 9 10 11 12 13 14 15 16 17 18 19 20 21 22